LATINO U.S.A. : A CARTOON HISTORY

ALSO BY ILAN STAVANS

FICTION THE DISAPPEARANCE • THE ONE-HANDED PIANIST AND OTHER STORIES

NONFICTION THE RIDDLE OF CANTINFLAS • DICTIONARY DAYS • ON BORROWED WORDS • SPANGLISH • THE HISPANIC CONDITION • ART AND ANGER • RESURRECTING HEBREW • A CRITIC'S JOURNEY • THE INVETERATE DREAMER • OCTAVIO PAZ: A MEDITATION • IMAGINING COLUMBUS • BANDIDO • ¡LOTERIA! (WITH TERESA VILLEGAS) • JOSE VASCONCELOS: THE PROPHET OF RACE • RETURN TO CENTRO HISTÓRICO

CONVERSATIONS KNOWLEDGE AND CENSORSHIP (WITH VERÓNICA ALBIN) • WHAT IS LA HISPANIDAD? (WITH IVÁN JAKSIĆ) • ILAN STAVANS: EIGHT CONVERSATIONS (WITH NEAL SOKOL) • WITH ALL THINE HEART (WITH MORDECAI DRACHE) • CONVERSATIONS WITH ILAN STAVANS • LOVE AND LANGUAGE (WITH VERÓNICA ALBIN)

ANTHOLOGIES THE NORTON ANTHOLOGY OF LATINO LITERATURE • TROPICAL SYNAGOGUES • THE OXFORD BOOK OF LATIN AMERICAN ESSAYS • THE SCHOCKEN BOOK OF MODERN SEPHARDIC LITERATURE • LENGUA FRESCA (WITH HAROLD AUGENBRAUM) • WÁCHALE! • THE SCROLL AND THE CROSS • THE OXFORD BOOK OF JEWISH STORIES MUTUAL IMPRESSIONS • GROWING UP LATINO (WITH HAROLD AUGENBRAUM) • THE FSG BOOKS OF 20th CENTURY LATIN AMERICAN POETRY

COMICS MR. SPIC GOES TO WASHINGTON (WITH ROBERTO WEIL) • ONCE@9:53 (WITH MARCELO BRODSKY)

TRANSLATION SENTIMENTAL SONGS, BY FELIPE ALFAU • THE PLAIN IN FLAMES, BY JUAN RULFO (WITH HAROLD AUGENBRAUM)

EDITIONS CÉSAR VALLEJO: SPAIN, TAKE THIS CHALICE FROM ME • THE POETRY OF PABLO NERUDA • ENCYCLOPEDIA LATINA (4 VOLUMES) • I EXPLAIN A FEW THINGS • THE COLLECTED STORIES OF CALVERT CASEY • ISAAC BASHEVIS SINGER: COLLECTED STORIES (3 VOLUMES) • CESAR CHAVEZ: AN ORGANIZER' TALE • RUBÉN DARÍO: SELECTED WRITINGS

GENERAL THE ESSENTIAL ILAN STAVANS

ALSO BY LALO ALCARAZ

MIGRA MOUSE: POLITICAL CARTOONS ON IMMIGRATION •
• LA CUCARACHA: THE FIRST COLLECTION FROM THE DAILY COMIC STRIP BY LALO ALCARAZ •
CARTOONISTA! POLITICAL CARTOONS BY LALO ALCARAZ •
• POCHO.COM: NEWS Y SATIRE

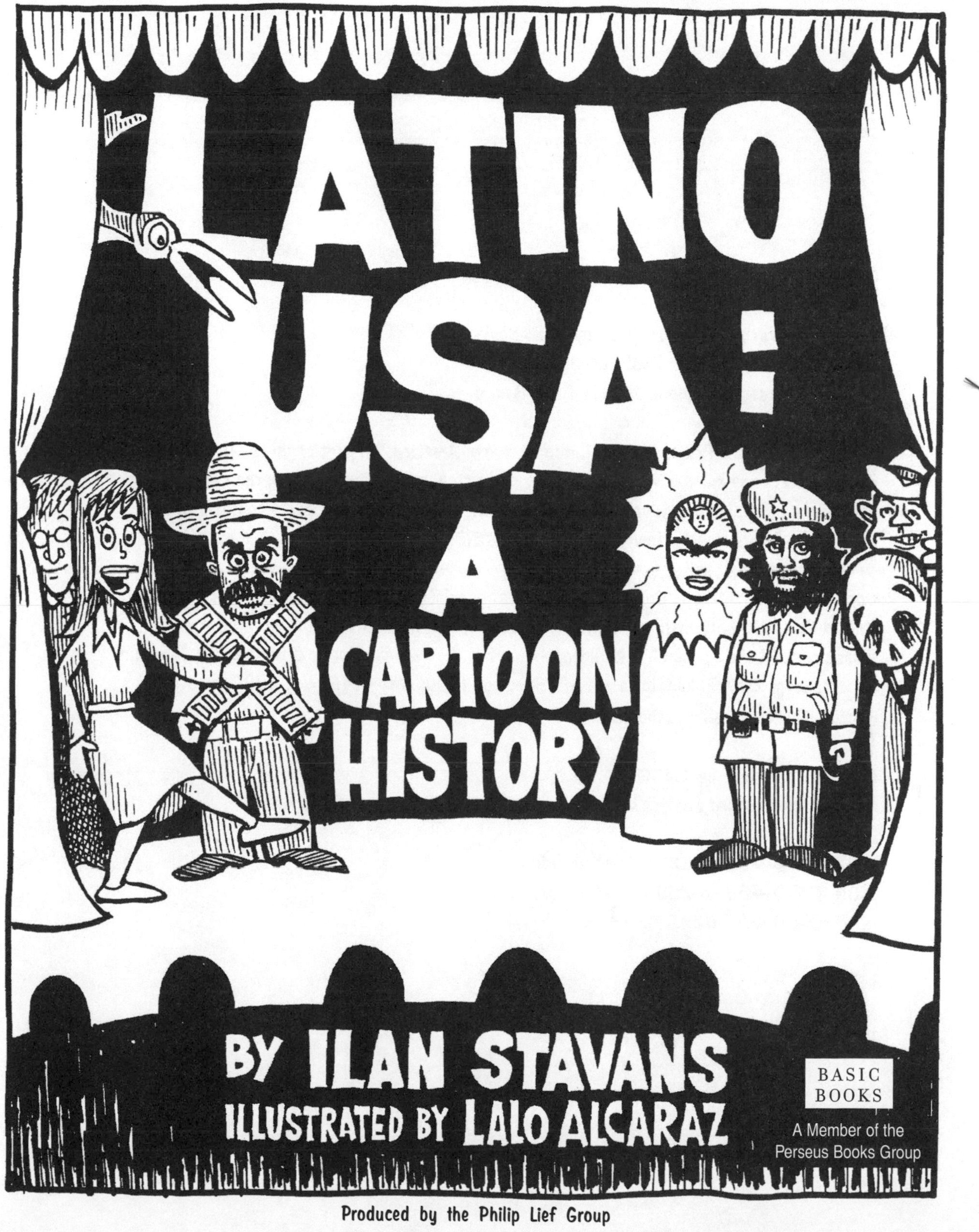
LATINO U.S.A.:
A CARTOON HISTORY
BY ILAN STAVANS
ILLUSTRATED BY LALO ALCARAZ
BASIC BOOKS
A Member of the Perseus Books Group

Produced by the Philip Lief Group

Copyright © 2000 by The Philip Lief Group, Inc. and Ilan Stavans

Hardcover first published in 2000 by Basic Books,
A Member of the Perseus Books Group
Paperback first published in 2012 by Basic Books

Books published by Basic Books are available at special discounts for bulk purchases in the United States by corporations, institutions, and other organizations. For more information, please contact the Special Markets Department at the Perseus Books Group, 2300 Chestnut Street, Suite 200, Philadelphia, PA 19103, or call (800) 810-4145, ext. 5000, or e-mail special.markets@perseusbooks.com.

Produced by the Philip Lief Group, Inc.
A CIP catalog record for this book is available from the Library of Congress.

ISBN 978-0-465-08221-6 (hardcover)
ISBN 978-0-465-08250-6 (paperback)
ISBN 978-0-465-02953-2 (e-book)

LSC-C

10 9 8 7 6

TO MY STUDENTS AT AMHERST COLLEGE

CONTENTS

NOTE TO THE FIFTEENTH ANNIVERSARY EDITION

It isn't really fifteen years, more like twelve. But time feels longer when news is baaaaaaaad. While Latinos are the country's largest (more than fifty million), its move to the middle class now appears to go at turtle-speed.

Supreme Court Justice Sonia Sotomayor is in the Supreme Court. But is she a token? If demography sets the tone, shouldn't there be a Mexican, a Cuban, or a Dominican? Why are so many of us poor, in jail, or being deported? Is the United States truly a democracy? This new edition adds an entirely new Part 5 into the contents in which major historical events such as 9/11 and the "war on terror" are discussed, as are the immigration debate and the Dream Act, Arizona's racial-profiling law and its dismantling of Ethnic Studies, the economic recession that started in 2008, and other unwelcome news.

Should Latino USA be updated every decade and a half? Why not!!!! As long as Latinos remain mere cartoons in the nation's mosaic, the narrators in this retelling—Calavera, the Teacher, Toucán, Cantinflas, and the Author—should find something to complain about. And to ridicule. Laughter is an antidote to pain.

FOREWORD

¡¡¡Splash!!! ¡¡¡Kaboom!!! Ay diosito, y ahora, ¿quién nos salvará?
-Kalimán: El hombre increíble

Pop art, the highbrows say, is junk. It results, so the argument goes, from the masses wanting to satisfy their spiritual thirst without any sense of refinement. Pure art is the result of an artist's finding an aesthetic way to channel his purposeful alienation from society into an original and authentic creation. But pop art—in German, *kitsch*— is art by imitation: second-rate, derivative, a hand-me-down. It does not come about out of inspiration but is assembled, manufactured, and thus, has no soul to speak of.

The problem with this view, of course, is that it is utterly false, to say nothing of snobbish and supercilious. If everything popular is by definition unworthy and inadequate, then all modernity, from beginning to end, is counterfeit, particularly in the vast regions of the globe where Europe was for endless years the sole provider of so-called legitimate art.

I came of age in Mexico, in the 1970s, surrounded by fast food, American TV sitcoms, cartoons, and Muzak. "Is there a true national art?" asked the intellectuals, distressed by the prevailing "colonial" mentality. The United States is nothing but artificial, they claimed, looking instead to Mexico's rich past. Why, then, I might have retorted, does the country need so much trash to survive? Why is *Star Wars* so popular? Furthermore, why is pop art in Mexico—soaps, comic strips, rock music—so deceptive? They would point at muralists Diego Rivera and Frida Kahlo, musicians Carlos Chávez and Silvestre Revueltas, litteratteurs Ramón López Velarde, and Alfonso Reyes as models to emulate.

I was overexposed to this "illiteracy," this bastard nature of pop art, which supposedly underlined the abysmal ignorance of the masses. All kitsch is pernicious, but Mexican kitsch is twice as bad, for it is derived from an already derivative product—a Xerox of a Xerox. Nothing in this argument made sense to me. I loved Indiana Jones, ate burritos at Taco Bell, watched episode after episode of *Simplemente María*, listened to Juan Gabriel, and voraciously read the strips El Payo, Kalimán, and *Los supermachos*. My feeling, had I been asked, was that the authenticity of it all was found precisely in its beautiful unoriginality. Pop culture, my instinct told me, was much closer to the nation's collective psyche than anything by Kahlo and Reyes.

Comic strips and cartoons were my favorite pastime. They were known invariably as *los monitos, los comics, las tiras.* I dreamed, from early on, of becoming first a graphic artist and then a filmmaker. I was held spellbound by the union of word and image. A baroque kiosk just a few blocks from my house festively displayed all sorts of comic books. I found in them, and my friends did too, a much-needed dose of adventure, laughter, and satire. Poetic language, Aristotelian unity, intellectual sophistication, these were alien terms to me. What I wanted most was salvation through escape to become a superhero—*a la mexicana*—part mariachi and part Spiderman, to ridicule the ruling political elite, to travel to the Chiapas rainforest by horse with a flamboyant maid by my side. A cheap imagination? Well, perhaps, but vivid nonetheless. TV and comics were not noxious. I found them electrifying.

Mine was not an escapist middle-class mentality, as I have often heard it described. Mexico's population in its entirety, men and women, children and adults, rich and poor, rulers and the populace, also visited the kiosk, delivering the rigorous 3.50 pesos without any misgivings whatsoever. Paul Theroux, in his 1979 travelogue *The Old Patagonian Express*, writes that, arriving in San Luis Potosí, "I went to the plaza and bought a Mexican newspaper... the rest of the [train] passengers bought comic books." The division between haves and have-nots is clear, Theroux being among the latter. I can hardly invoke, as I look back, a more egalitarian pastime, one as democratic in its mission. And things have hardly changed since I grew up and since Theroux visited Mexico. Just ask any street vendor to describe who the audience for comics really is: *todo el mundo*, he will automatically say, just about everybody. A few comics were imports badly translated into Spanish, but most of the ones I read were not. They proudly displayed the logo *Hecho en México*, certifying not only that they were written, designed, and produced by nationals, but that nationals, too, consumed them en masse.

I am aware of the argument, defended most prominently by Irene Herner, and by Ariel Dorfman with Armand Mattelart in their book *How to Read Donald Duck*, that, in the so-called Third World, the comics industry is linked to American imperialism. Walt Disney's characters, so the litany goes, are hardly about innocence. Their tainted message is designed "to colonize the minds of children all over Latin America." Nonsense, I say, *puras tonterías*. Our global culture is not about exclusion and isolation, but about cosmopolitanism, which, etymologically, derives from the Greek terms *cosmos* and *polis*, a planetary city.

My strip heroes were definitely locals. Kalimán, among them, an immensely handsome, intellectually portentous macho, defied stereotypes. Raised by Tibetan monks, his mission is to ensure the security of the earth, not just Mexico, through his astonishing breadth of knowledge and enviable bodily strength. Who ever said Mexicans are dumb and without role models? Blue-eyed, uncorrupted, generous, he was much like Borges's Funes the Memorious: he spoke all human languages, was a walking encyclopedia, and even communicated with animals. These attributes were sustained by daily yoga exercises, meditation, and physical relaxation. Batman and Superman, Kalimán's role models, in my eyes seemed to pale when compared to him.

Equally compelling were other superheroes of more indigenous breeds, such as El Zorro and El Payo, the former a mestizo in nineteenth-century New Mexico, the latter a charro with an admirable sense of righteousness. Or El Santo, a masked wrestler. Or Chanoc himself, a Mayan ace raised in Ixtac, on the southern coast of Mexico, whose portentous swimming habits and expertise with knives allow him to kill one gigantic animal after another. Or some more prosaic quadruped, like Paquín and El Chamaco, Rocambole, Memín and Detective Fisgón, Adelita and Condorito. Sure, they are all manipulative, repetitive, and predictable. But they were a source of national pride, too. How many enjoyable school-bus rides did we spend together? How often did I hide them inside a history textbook, trusting they could offer a better lesson in civics?

Unlike elitist art, comics, although not quite anonymous, pay little attention to ownership. An author's name, with very few exceptions, is invisible. One of the exceptions is Eduardo del Río, aka Rius, probably the most prolific, versatile, and personal of Mexico's cartoonists. Born in 1935 in Zamora, Michoacán, he went to school in the nation's capital and, before becoming a national figure, he worked in a bar, a bottling plant, a funeral parlor, and as a delivery boy in a firm that distributed Walt Disney's comics. He began working as a cartoonist for various newspapers until, switching to comic strips, he produced *Los supermachos*, a political satire that, in the late 1960s, attacked President Gustavo Díaz Ordaz. It was adapted to theater and made into a film, *Calzonsin Inspector*, by Alfonso Arau, famous as the director of *Like Water for Chocolate*. Rius ran into trouble with the government for his strong Marxist views. He was fired and rehired elsewhere. Eventually he managed to build his own one-man company, which produced another landmark film, *Los agachados*.

Ideology, obviously, is at the core of his art. His characters are social types, archetypes, and stereotypes. His style, displayed in some 2,000 original fouilletons and booklets, most notably *Cuba Libre* and *El amor en los tiempos del Sida*, is not quite what strip readers are used to. Instead of developing a plot, he often explores national and international issues by dropping capsules of commentary that mix information with humor. He pioneered this didactic approach in *Marx for Beginners* and *The Myth of the Virgin of Guadalupe*, which are available in English, too.

(I stopped reading Rius one specific day, when a most anti-Semitic installment of *Los agachados*, endorsing Hitler, reached my hand. I have kept the strip with me, a testament to my disillusion.)

I came to learn that there are more comic strip publishers in Mexico than in any other Latin American country by far and I had also witnessed the boom of Mexican comics. Individual weekly issues had print runs varying between 300,000 and almost 9 million copies, by all accounts an astronomical number, particularly when compared to the Lilliputian number of books sold by literary figures. For example, books by authors of the stature of Carlos Fuentes often sold fewer than 10,000 copies per title in half a decade. And this huge number of comics didn't include exports to Central or South America and especially to areas of the United States highly populated with Latin Americans: East Los Angeles, Chicago's Pilsen and La Villita, and San Francisco's Mission District. ¡Jijole!, El Chamaco would say.

The true roots of the strips, these "filthy artifacts," as arrogant intellectuals called them, are much contested in the artistic and academic communities. Some attribute the inspiration to Egyptian hieroglyphics and perhaps to illuminated Medieval manuscripts. Some even claim Aztec codices, ancient writings, and other pre-Columbian images as the true sources of Mexican comics. While I agree some inspiration may have been drawn from the Aztecs and other pre-Columbian societies, I believe that the strips have the exact same inspiration that nurtured the highbrow yet populist art of Rivera and Kahlo—the *retablos*, anonymous paintings that include a written prayer, which were offered by Catholic believers to Jesus Christ and the Virgin de Guadalupe as a token of appreciation for a miracle performed. I also believe the cartoonists drew inspiration from the engravings and pennydreadfuls (sensationalist writings of crime or violent adventure) of lampoonist José Guadalupe Posada. Posada invented the *calavera*, a skeleton poking fun at death and destiny that, with time, has come to represent for Mexico what Uncle Sam does for the United States.

I remember studying many a calavera with scrupulous eyes. What did I see? Myself? The histrionics of those around me? A perfect mask, no doubt. Masks, indeed, are what Mexican pop culture are all about: faces hidden behind faces. The Mexican shuts himself from the world, wrote Octavio Paz. "In his harsh solitude, which is both barbed and courteous, everything serves him as a defense: silence and words, politeness and disdain, irony and resignation." What Posada did so well, and modern strips continue doing, is to exploit, effortlessly, the smile behind those masks.

This passion for graphic art, for using images as vehicles of communication, is not accidental. It is inherent to Mexican culture, whereas the written word is, in many ways, an imported property. The way the Mexicans have turned words into a communication tool, both in conjunction with graphic images and alone, however, is astonishing.

As I matured, I came to realize the whole Hispanic world was home to millions of comic strips. My cadre of idols grew dramatically. From Posada and Rius, I graduated to Abel Quezada, whose endearing work was featured in *The New Yorker* in the 1980s. I then found my all-time favorite, Quino, the nom de plume of Joaquín Lavado, the Argentinean artist responsible for creating the character of Mafalda, a little girl whose sharpness and wisdom make her readers realize how convoluted our modern times are. ("Please stop the world!" she screams in a strip, "I want to get off!") I soon appreciated the deftness and flair with which

Fernando Botero, the master Colombian painter, turned cartoons into highbrow art. This led me to realize how fragile the line is between avant-garde and "junk." By the time I settled in the United States, graffiti and the Chicano cartoons and murals in California by Frank Romero and Ester Hernández had become a magnet, for what is street art if not the attempt to return iconography to the masses?

As Hispanics—a large majority of them Mexicans—cross the Rio Grande to become Latinos, they might switch languages, but their joie de vivre remains intact. I myself have always been fascinated by the challenges of capturing the joys, nuances, and multiple dimensions of Latino culture within the context of the English language. Hence, when a phone call from Sheila Friedling, an old friend and editor of an early book of mine, came with the invitation to do a cartoon history of Latinos, I was enthralled. Long-dormant adolescent memories surfaced, and Rius's art flashed into my mind. I also thought of a favorite experimental book I once read, *Fantomas contra los vampiros multinacionales* by Julio Cortázar, and fruitlessly looked for my old copy. Cortázar appropriated the character of the legendary French thief Fantomas, a Robin Hood of sorts, to ruminate, through cartoons, against U.S. imperialism. It surely was not the most inspired performance by the author of *Hopscotch*, but it was unquestionably an endearing tryout. And I reread *Cosmicomics* too, a fin-de-siècle novel by Italo Calvino, inspired by comics inspired by novels. I even asked myself: When did I really become a writer? Was it by reading one too many installments of *Los supermachos* or when I finished *Don Quixote*, fully hypnotized by its magic? The opportunity had arrived to become, finally, a manufacturer of kitsch, while paying tribute to a core aspect of my upbringing that I had cast aside when I focused my professional career on the muses of literature and academia.

In developing the manuscript for *Latino U.S.A.: A Cartoon History*, I consciously sought to combine the solemnity of so-called serious literature and history with the inherently theatrical and humorous nature of the comics. The experience was liberating: as an essayist, I am handcuffed by the abstraction of words, by the merciless need to make a cohesive, persuasive argument with words only. Cartoons and comics present the perfect stage to blend words and images, and engage the reader with their freshness, imagination, caricatures, and fantastical and delightfully irreverent overtones. Naturally thespian in their format, with characters spouting lines against an ever-changing backdrop of realistic and exaggerated settings, cartoons and comics can be more anarchic than a typical drama. My models from the theatrical world were Cervantes and Rius, Pirandello, and Chanoc... as imagined by Mafalda.

My objective was to represent Hispanic civilization as a fiesta of types, archetypes, and stereotypes. As soon as I began sketching the layout, Posada's calaveras took control of me, as did other cliche figurines: a toucan, displayed regularly in books by Gabriel García Márquez, Isabel Allende, and the like; a beautiful señorita, addressing the exuberant sexuality I grew up with; Cantinflas, a beloved comedian known, paradoxically, as "the Hispanic Charlie Chaplin" (even after Chaplin described himself as "second best to Cantinflas"); a masked wrestler; and so on. By featuring these strips as the narrators and counternarrators of their own history and as actors on an imaginary stage, I avoided using, as much as possible, an official, impartial tone, embracing instead the rhythms of carnival. My "unofficialness" translated itself into what I think is a less Europeanized, more democratic viewpoint. History, of course, is a kaleidoscope where nothing is absolute. The human past and present are far more malleable than the future. This, in short, is my own account, a pastiche of angles I have made my own.

Matching with cartoonist Lalo López Alcaraz was the key relationship that shaped the vision, humor, and form of the book. Ever since I came across his cartoon La Cucaracha in *LA Weekly* and read *Pocho*, his satirical Chicano magazine, I realized I had found my artistic soulmate. I was born in Distrito Federal, he in San Diego: between the two of us, I trust, we are able to capture the perspectives of both south and north of the Rio Grande; also, both of us are fluent in Spanish and English with a fascination with Spanglish, the new integration of these two languages. His strips are about mischief and caprice, poking fun at human nature without compromising historical integrity. I trust his strips and my ideas are complementary echoes, echooooooes. . . Everything in them is purposeful imitation.

—Ilan Stavans

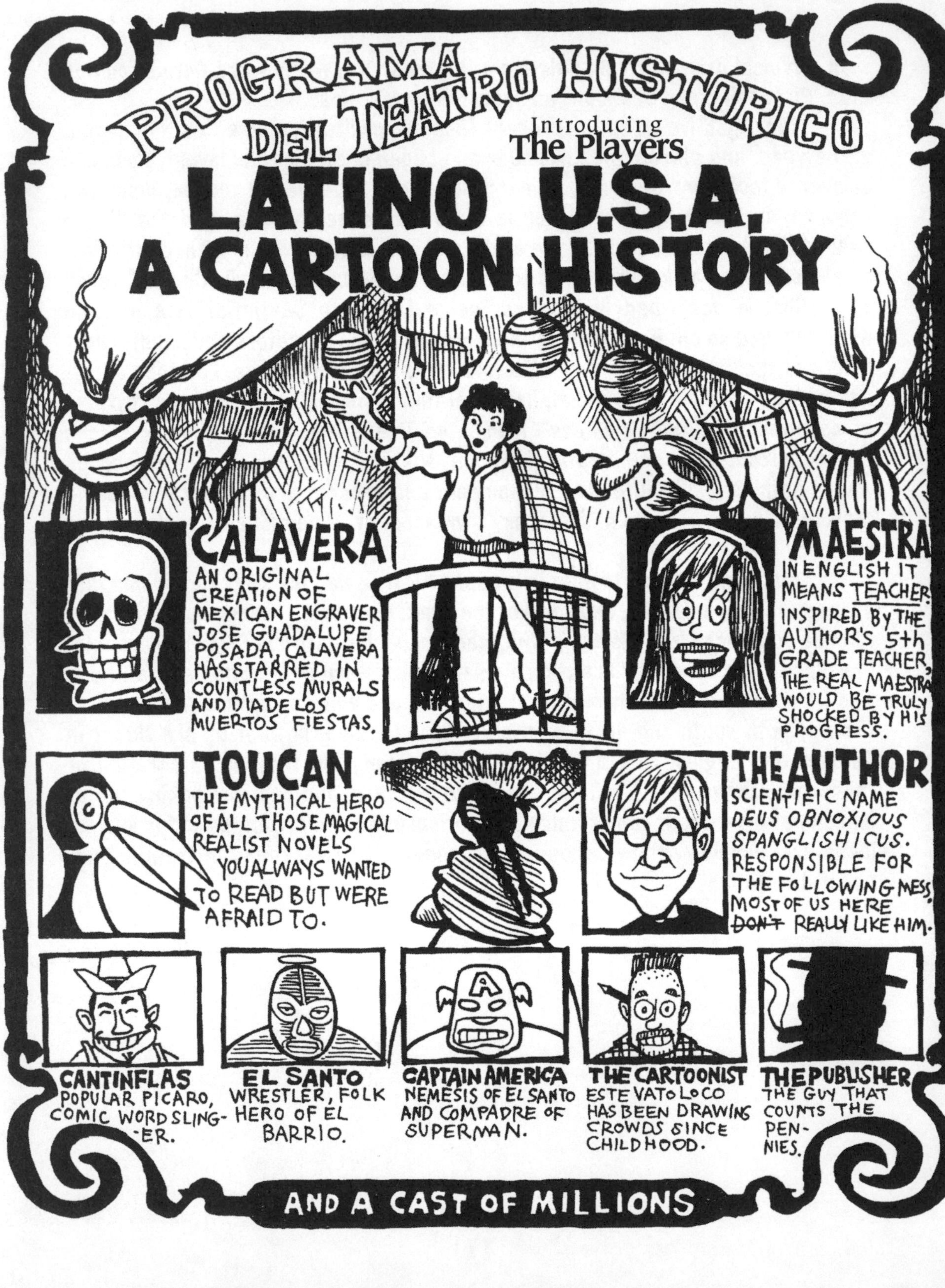
PROGRAMA DEL TEATRO HISTÓRICO
Introducing The Players
LATINO U.S.A. A CARTOON HISTORY
CALAVERA
AN ORIGINAL CREATION OF MEXICAN ENGRAVER JOSE GUADALUPE POSADA, CALAVERA HAS STARRED IN COUNTLESS MURALS AND DIA DE LOS MUERTOS FIESTAS.
MAESTRA
IN ENGLISH IT MEANS TEACHER. INSPIRED BY THE AUTHOR'S 5th GRADE TEACHER, THE REAL MAESTRA WOULD BE TRULY SHOCKED BY HIS PROGRESS.
TOUCAN
THE MYTHICAL HERO OF ALL THOSE MAGICAL REALIST NOVELS YOU ALWAYS WANTED TO READ BUT WERE AFRAID TO.
THE AUTHOR
SCIENTIFIC NAME DEUS OBNOXIOUS SPANGLISHICUS. RESPONSIBLE FOR THE FOLLOWING MESS. MOST OF US HERE ~~DON'T~~ REALLY LIKE HIM.
CANTINFLAS
POPULAR PICARO, COMIC WORD SLING--ER.
EL SANTO
WRESTLER, FOLK HERO OF EL BARRIO.
CAPTAIN AMERICA
NEMESIS OF EL SANTO AND COMPADRE OF SUPERMAN.
THE CARTOONIST
ESTE VATO LOCO HAS BEEN DRAWING CROWDS SINCE CHILDHOOD.
THE PUBLISHER
THE GUY THAT COUNTS THE PEN-NIES.
AND A CAST OF MILLIONS

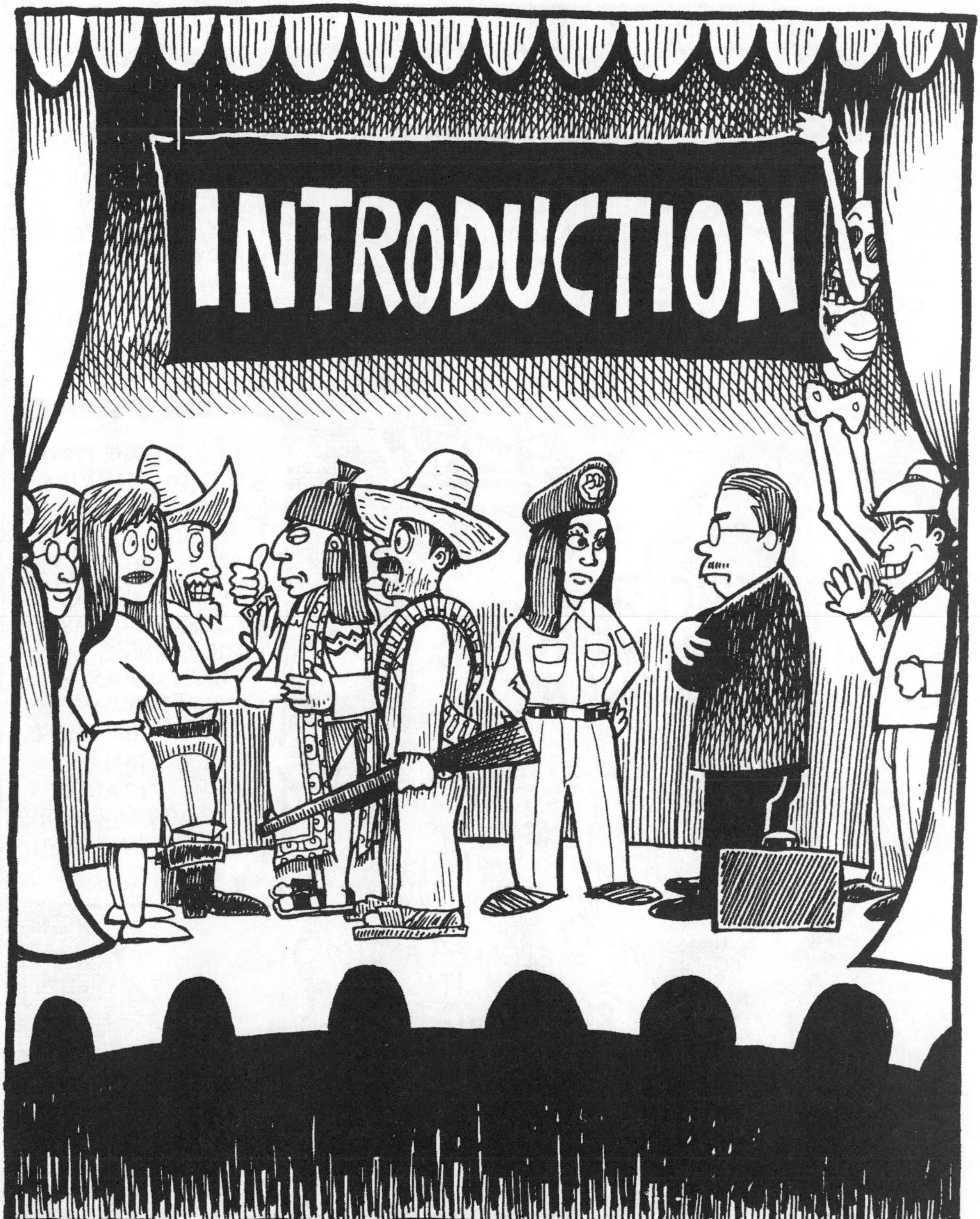
INTRODUCTION

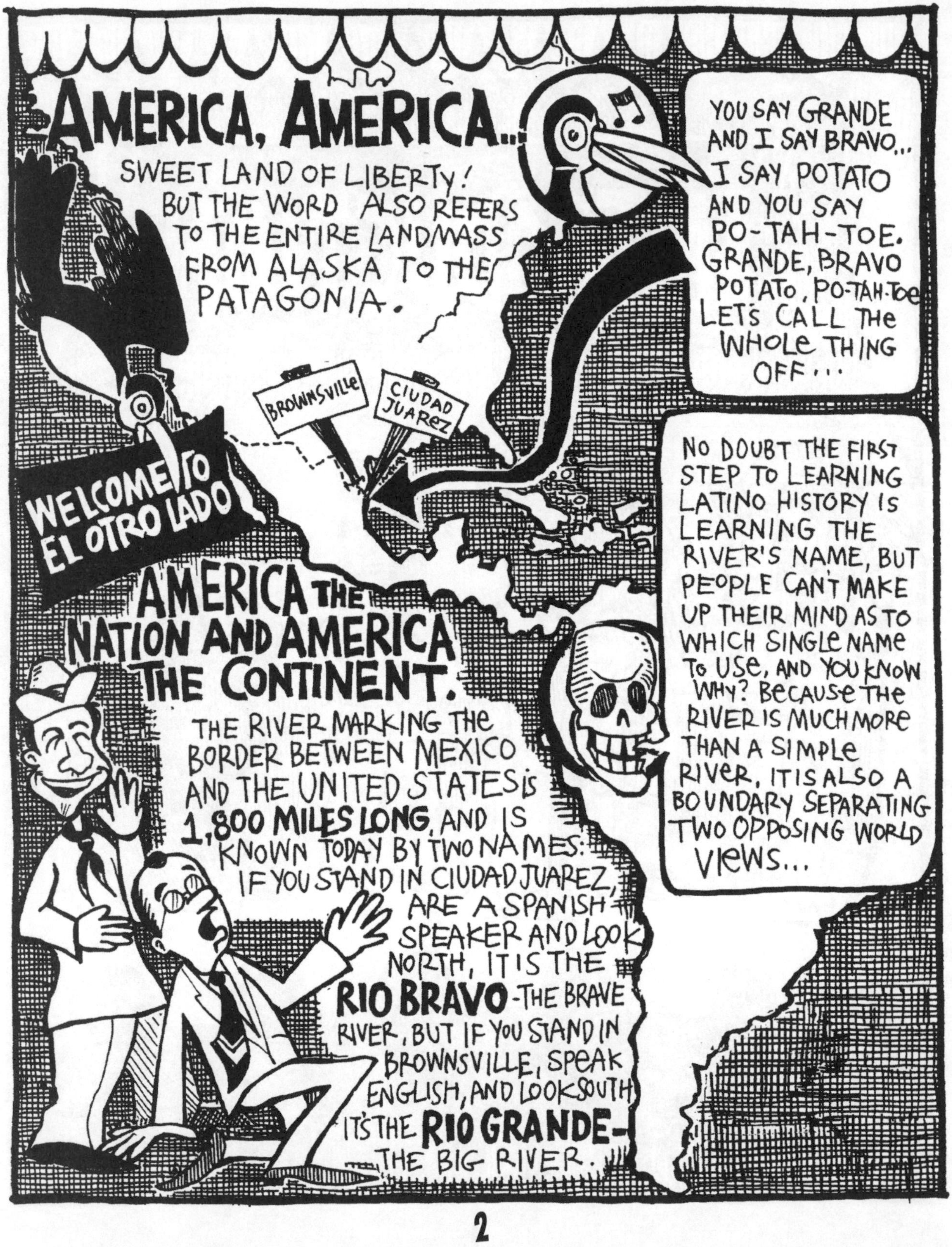
AMERICA, AMERICA...
SWEET LAND OF LIBERTY! BUT THE WORD ALSO REFERS TO THE ENTIRE LANDMASS FROM ALASKA TO THE PATAGONIA.
YOU SAY GRANDE AND I SAY BRAVO... I SAY POTATO AND YOU SAY PO-TAH-TOE. GRANDE, BRAVO POTATO, PO-TAH-TOE LET'S CALL THE WHOLE THING OFF...
BROWNSVILLE
CIUDAD JUAREZ
WELCOME TO EL OTRO LADO
NO DOUBT THE FIRST STEP TO LEARNING LATINO HISTORY IS LEARNING THE RIVER'S NAME, BUT PEOPLE CAN'T MAKE UP THEIR MIND AS TO WHICH SINGLE NAME TO USE, AND YOU KNOW WHY? BECAUSE THE RIVER IS MUCH MORE THAN A SIMPLE RIVER. IT IS ALSO A BOUNDARY SEPARATING TWO OPPOSING WORLD VIEWS...
AMERICA THE NATION AND AMERICA THE CONTINENT.
THE RIVER MARKING THE BORDER BETWEEN MEXICO AND THE UNITED STATES IS 1,800 MILES LONG, AND IS KNOWN TODAY BY TWO NAMES: IF YOU STAND IN CIUDAD JUAREZ, ARE A SPANISH SPEAKER AND LOOK NORTH, IT IS THE RIO BRAVO-THE BRAVE RIVER. BUT IF YOU STAND IN BROWNSVILLE, SPEAK ENGLISH, AND LOOK SOUTH IT'S THE RIO GRANDE-THE BIG RIVER.

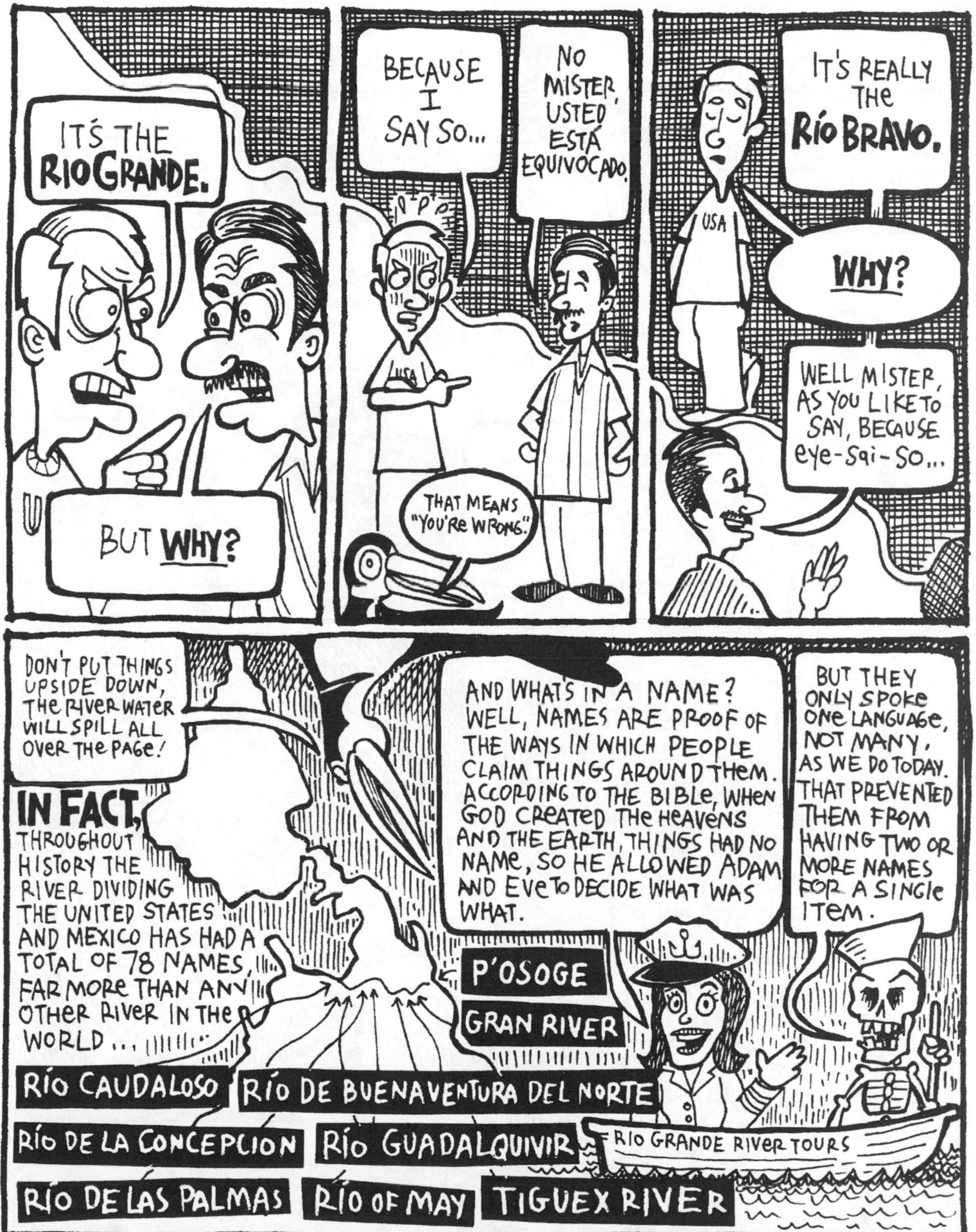

IT'S THE RIO GRANDE.
BUT WHY?
BECAUSE I SAY SO...
NO MISTER, USTED ESTÁ EQUIVOCADO.
THAT MEANS "YOU'RE WRONG."
IT'S REALLY THE RÍO BRAVO.
WHY?
WELL MISTER, AS YOU LIKE TO SAY, BECAUSE eye-sai-so...
DON'T PUT THINGS UPSIDE DOWN, THE RIVER WATER WILL SPILL ALL OVER THE PAGE!
IN FACT, THROUGHOUT HISTORY THE RIVER DIVIDING THE UNITED STATES AND MEXICO HAS HAD A TOTAL OF 78 NAMES, FAR MORE THAN ANY OTHER RIVER IN THE WORLD...
AND WHAT'S IN A NAME? WELL, NAMES ARE PROOF OF THE WAYS IN WHICH PEOPLE CLAIM THINGS AROUND THEM. ACCORDING TO THE BIBLE, WHEN GOD CREATED THE HEAVENS AND THE EARTH, THINGS HAD NO NAME, SO HE ALLOWED ADAM AND EVE TO DECIDE WHAT WAS WHAT.
BUT THEY ONLY SPOKE ONE LANGUAGE, NOT MANY, AS WE DO TODAY. THAT PREVENTED THEM FROM HAVING TWO OR MORE NAMES FOR A SINGLE ITEM.
P'OSOGE
GRAN RIVER
RÍO CAUDALOSO
RÍO DE BUENAVENTURA DEL NORTE
RÍO DE LA CONCEPCION
RÍO GUADALQUIVIR
RÍO DE LAS PALMAS
RÍO OF MAY
TIGUEX RIVER
RIO GRANDE RIVER TOURS
USA

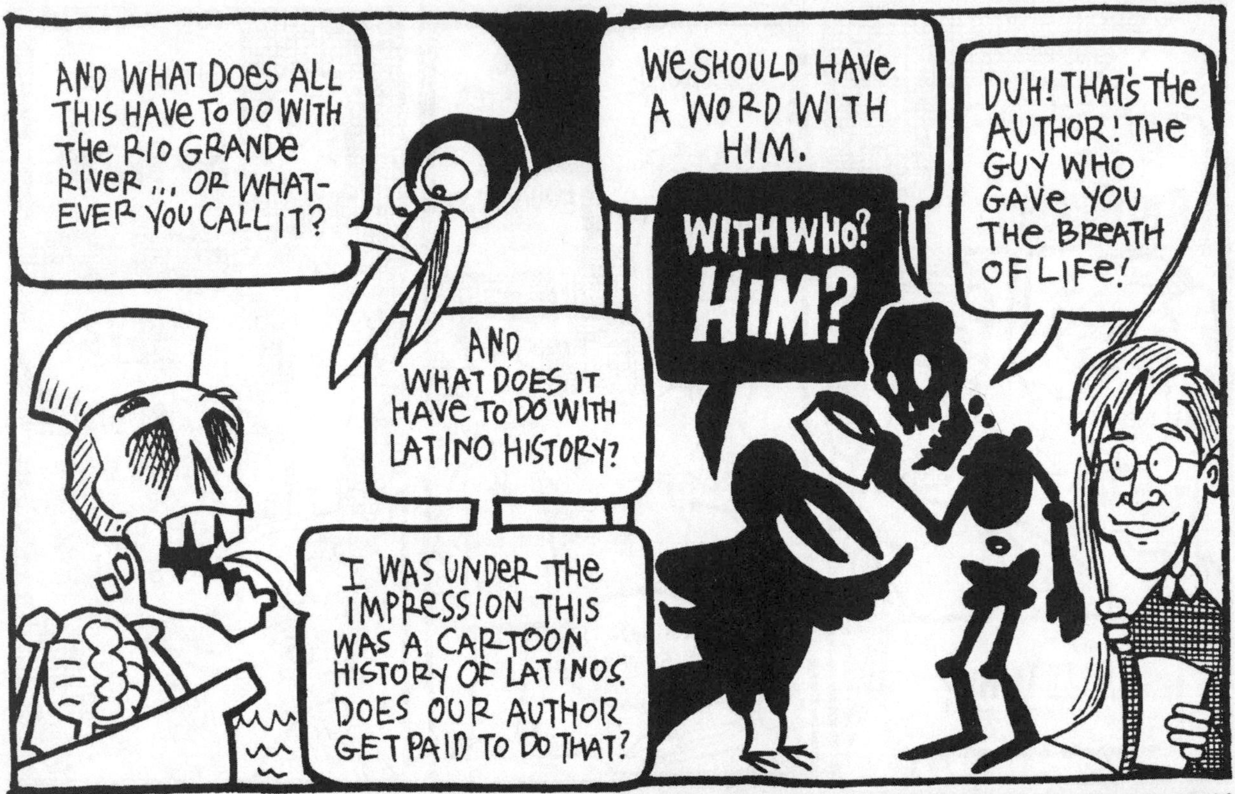
AND WHAT DOES ALL THIS HAVE TO DO WITH THE RIO GRANDE RIVER ... OR WHATEVER YOU CALL IT?
WE SHOULD HAVE A WORD WITH HIM.
DUH! THAT'S THE AUTHOR! THE GUY WHO GAVE YOU THE BREATH OF LIFE!
AND WHAT DOES IT HAVE TO DO WITH LATINO HISTORY?
WITH WHO? HIM?
I WAS UNDER THE IMPRESSION THIS WAS A CARTOON HISTORY OF LATINOS. DOES OUR AUTHOR GET PAID TO DO THAT?

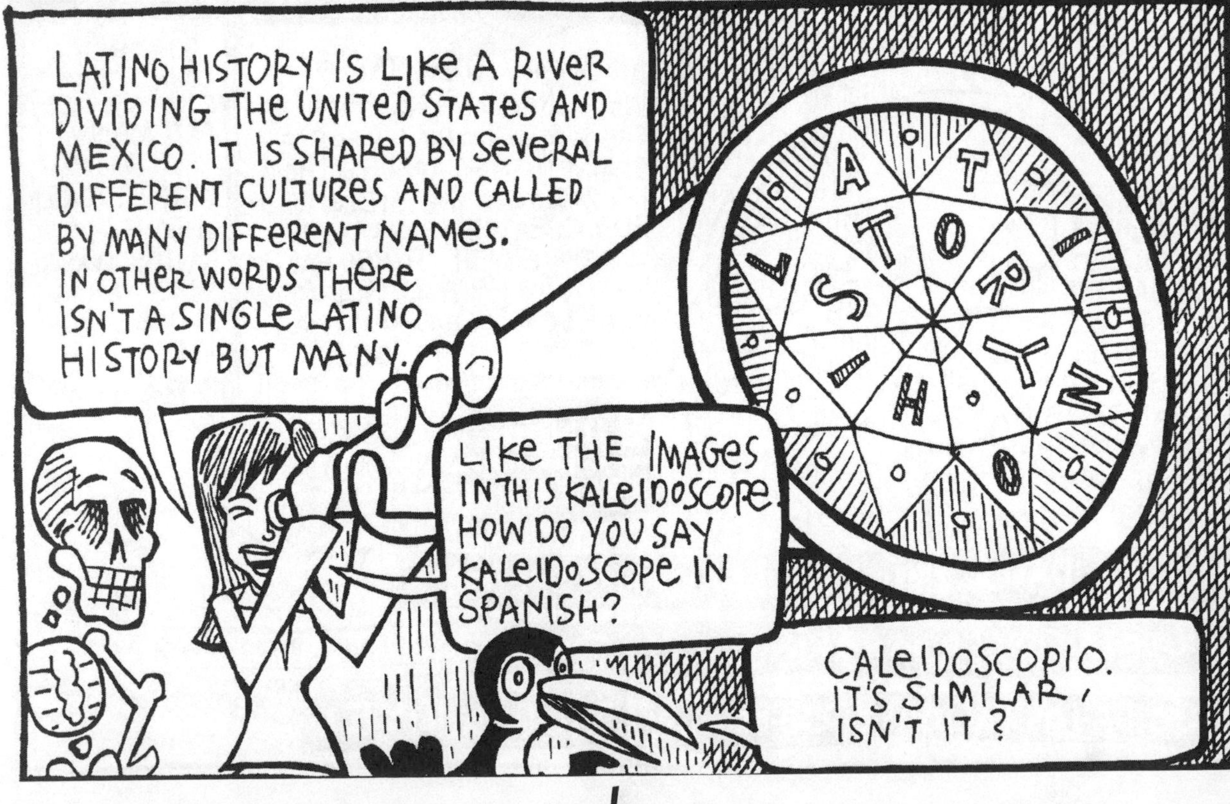
LATINO HISTORY IS LIKE A RIVER DIVIDING THE UNITED STATES AND MEXICO. IT IS SHARED BY SEVERAL DIFFERENT CULTURES AND CALLED BY MANY DIFFERENT NAMES. IN OTHER WORDS THERE ISN'T A SINGLE LATINO HISTORY BUT MANY.
LIKE THE IMAGES IN THIS KALEIDOSCOPE. HOW DO YOU SAY KALEIDOSCOPE IN SPANISH?
CALEIDOSCOPIO. IT'S SIMILAR, ISN'T IT?

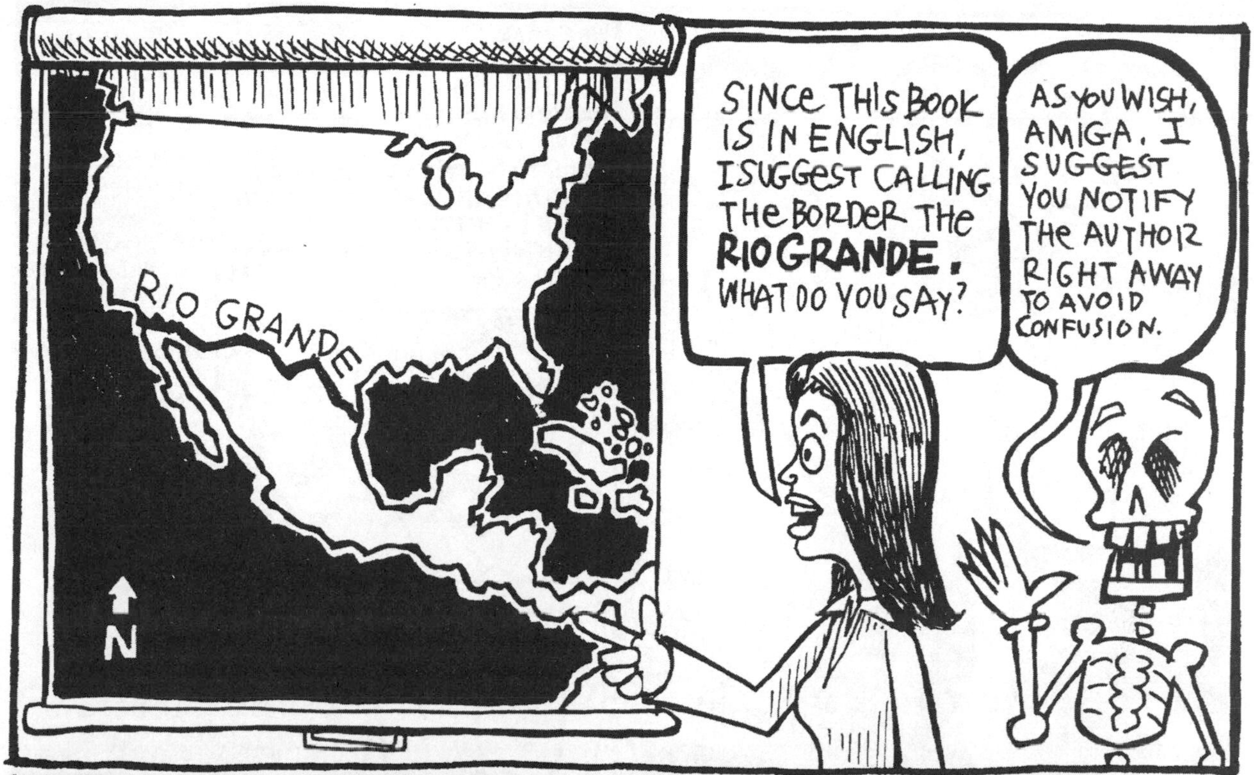
RIO GRANDE
N
SINCE THIS BOOK IS IN ENGLISH, I SUGGEST CALLING THE BORDER THE **RIO GRANDE.** WHAT DO YOU SAY?
AS YOU WISH, AMIGA. I SUGGEST YOU NOTIFY THE AUTHOR RIGHT AWAY TO AVOID CONFUSION.

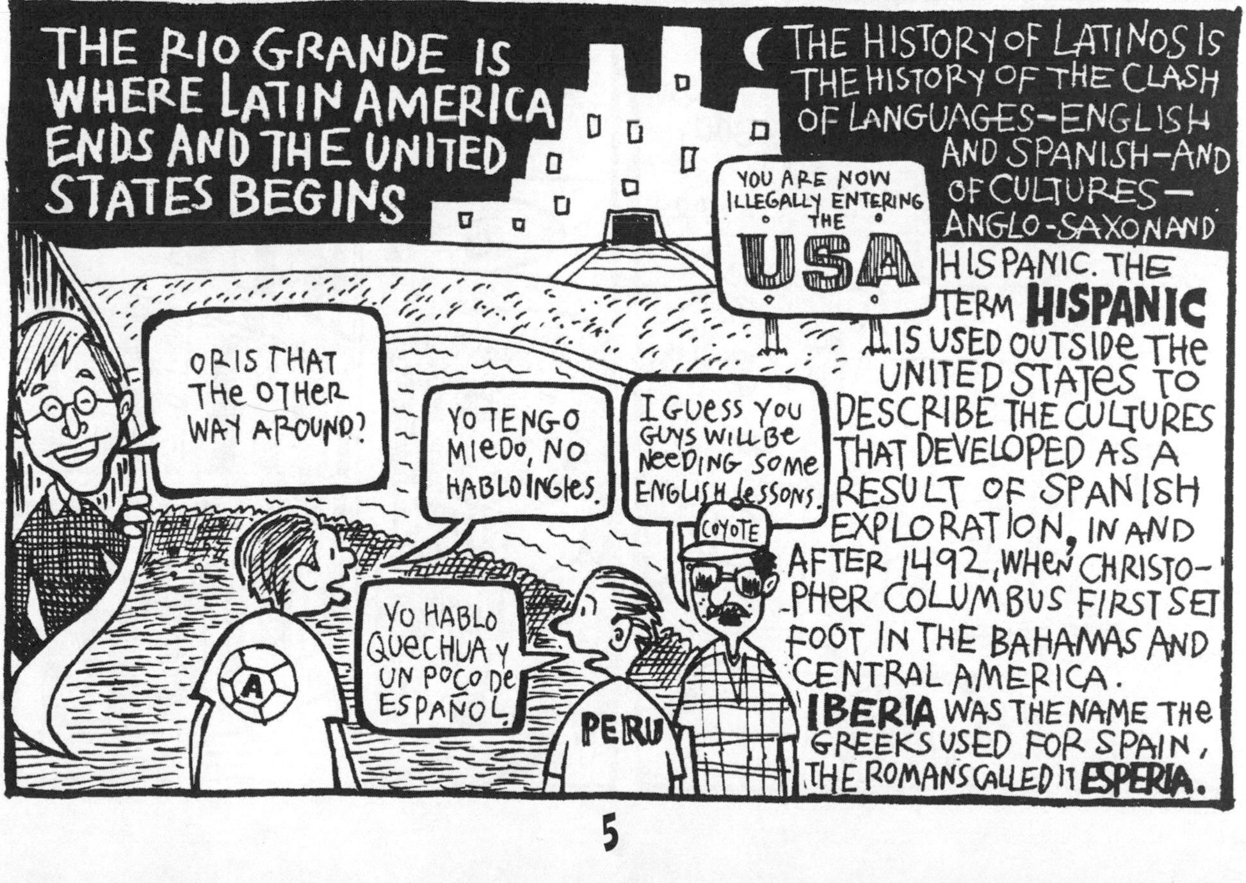
THE RIO GRANDE IS WHERE LATIN AMERICA ENDS AND THE UNITED STATES BEGINS
THE HISTORY OF LATINOS IS THE HISTORY OF THE CLASH OF LANGUAGES—ENGLISH AND SPANISH—AND OF CULTURES—ANGLO-SAXON AND HISPANIC. THE TERM **HISPANIC** IS USED OUTSIDE THE UNITED STATES TO DESCRIBE THE CULTURES THAT DEVELOPED AS A RESULT OF SPANISH EXPLORATION, IN AND AFTER 1492, WHEN CHRISTOPHER COLUMBUS FIRST SET FOOT IN THE BAHAMAS AND CENTRAL AMERICA. **IBERIA** WAS THE NAME THE GREEKS USED FOR SPAIN, THE ROMANS CALLED IT **ESPERIA.**
YOU ARE NOW ILLEGALLY ENTERING THE USA
OR IS THAT THE OTHER WAY AROUND?
YO TENGO MIEDO, NO HABLO INGLES.
I GUESS YOU GUYS WILL BE NEEDING SOME ENGLISH LESSONS.
COYOTE
YO HABLO QUECHUA Y UN POCO DE ESPAÑOL.
A
PERU

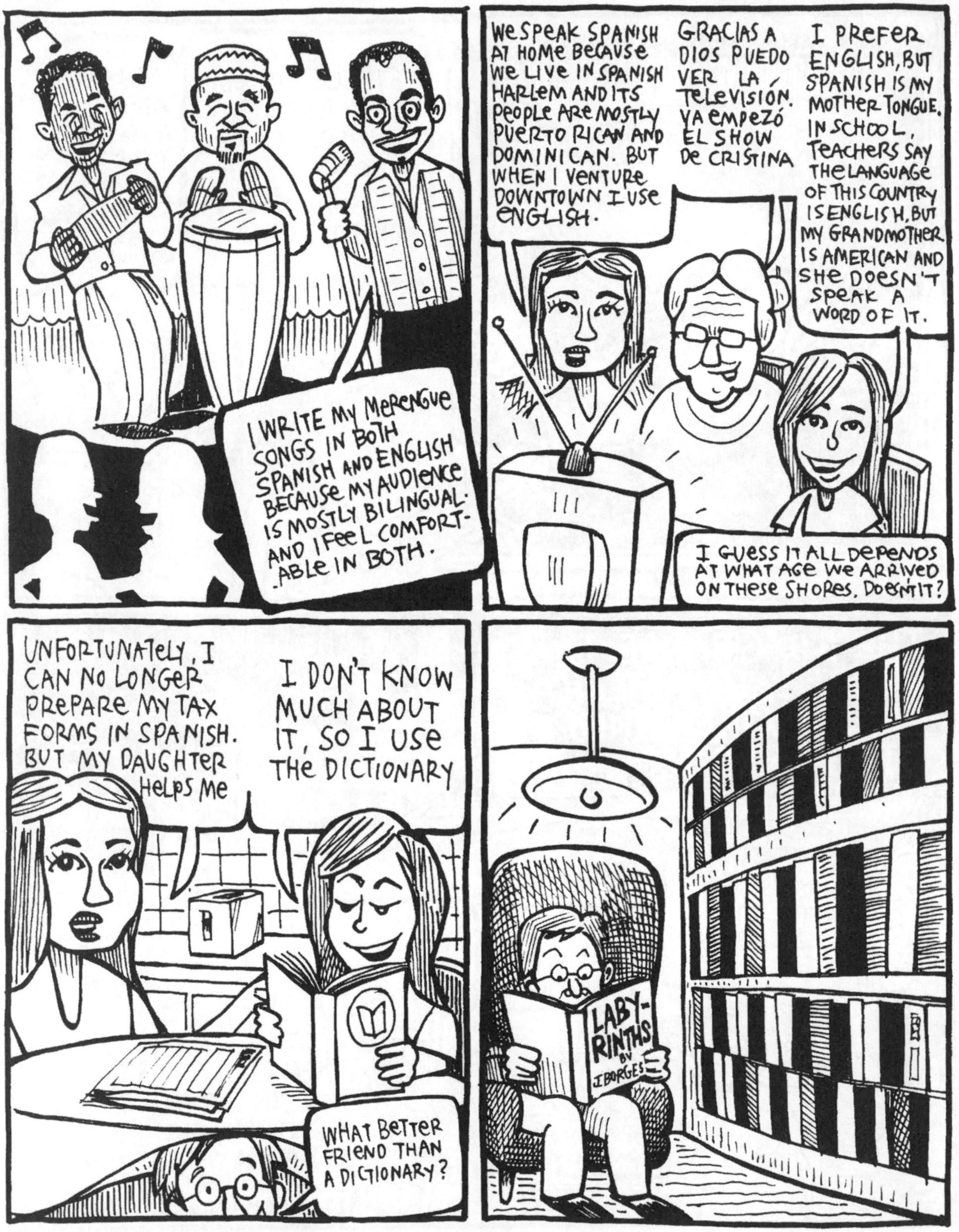
I WRITE MY MERENGUE SONGS IN BOTH SPANISH AND ENGLISH BECAUSE MY AUDIENCE IS MOSTLY BILINGUAL. AND I FEEL COMFORT-ABLE IN BOTH.
WE SPEAK SPANISH AT HOME BECAUSE WE LIVE IN SPANISH HARLEM AND ITS PEOPLE ARE MOSTLY PUERTO RICAN AND DOMINICAN. BUT WHEN I VENTURE DOWNTOWN I USE ENGLISH.
GRACIAS A DIOS PUEDO VER LA TELEVISIÓN. YA EMPEZÓ EL SHOW DE CRISTINA
I PREFER ENGLISH, BUT SPANISH IS MY MOTHER TONGUE. IN SCHOOL, TEACHERS SAY THE LANGUAGE OF THIS COUNTRY IS ENGLISH, BUT MY GRANDMOTHER IS AMERICAN AND SHE DOESN'T SPEAK A WORD OF IT.
I GUESS IT ALL DEPENDS AT WHAT AGE WE ARRIVED ON THESE SHORES, DOESN'T IT?
UNFORTUNATELY, I CAN NO LONGER PREPARE MY TAX FORMS IN SPANISH. BUT MY DAUGHTER HELPS ME
I DON'T KNOW MUCH ABOUT IT, SO I USE THE DICTIONARY
WHAT BETTER FRIEND THAN A DICTIONARY?
LABY-RINTHS BY J. BORGES

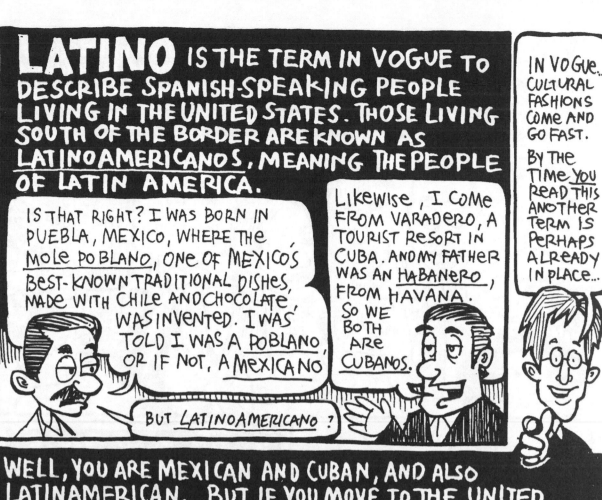

LATINO IS THE TERM IN VOGUE TO DESCRIBE SPANISH-SPEAKING PEOPLE LIVING IN THE UNITED STATES. THOSE LIVING SOUTH OF THE BORDER ARE KNOWN AS LATINOAMERICANOS, MEANING THE PEOPLE OF LATIN AMERICA.

IN VOGUE... CULTURAL FASHIONS COME AND GO FAST.

BY THE TIME _YOU_ READ THIS ANOTHER TERM IS PERHAPS ALREADY IN PLACE...

IS THAT RIGHT? I WAS BORN IN PUEBLA, MEXICO, WHERE THE MOLE POBLANO, ONE OF MEXICO'S BEST-KNOWN TRADITIONAL DISHES, MADE WITH CHILE AND CHOCOLATE, WAS INVENTED. I WAS TOLD I WAS A POBLANO, OR IF NOT, A MEXICANO.

BUT LATINOAMERICANO?

LIKEWISE, I COME FROM VARADERO, A TOURIST RESORT IN CUBA. AND MY FATHER WAS AN HABANERO, FROM HAVANA. SO WE BOTH ARE CUBANOS.

WELL, YOU ARE MEXICAN AND CUBAN, AND ALSO LATINAMERICAN. BUT IF YOU MOVE TO THE UNITED STATES, YOU WILL CALL YOURSELVES LATINOS, NOT LATINOAMERICANOS

¡SÍ SEÑOR! THAT'S THE TRUTH, LA PURITITA VERDAD!

AND YOU KNOW WHAT? IN THE PAST OTHER TERMS WERE ALSO USED INCLUDING **HISPANICS** AND **THE SPANISH PEOPLE.**

I LIKE "HISPANIC" THE BEST...

"HISPANIC" MAKES ME PANIC!

LATINOS ARE A GROUP MADE OF MANY SUBGROUPS. THE U.S. CENSUS BUREAU HAS ESTABLISHED THAT THERE ARE AROUND 70 DIFFERENT VARIATIONS OF LATINOS DEPENDING ON THEIR RACE, GENDER, LANGUAGE, COUNTRY OF ORIGIN, etc. THE 1990 CENSUS COUNTED A TOTAL OF 25 MILLION, BUT THAT IS WITHOUT THE <u>INDOCUMENTADOS</u>.

THAT IS, ALIENS WITHOUT LEGAL DOCUMENTS.

"ALIEN," I HATE THE WORD. WHAT ARE LATINOS, EXTRA-TERRESTRIAL?

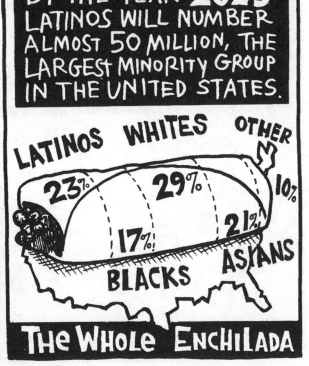

BY THE YEAR **2025** LATINOS WILL NUMBER ALMOST 50 MILLION, THE LARGEST MINORITY GROUP IN THE UNITED STATES.

LATINOS WHITES OTHER
23% 29% 10%
17% 21%
BLACKS ASIANS
THE WHOLE ENCHILADA

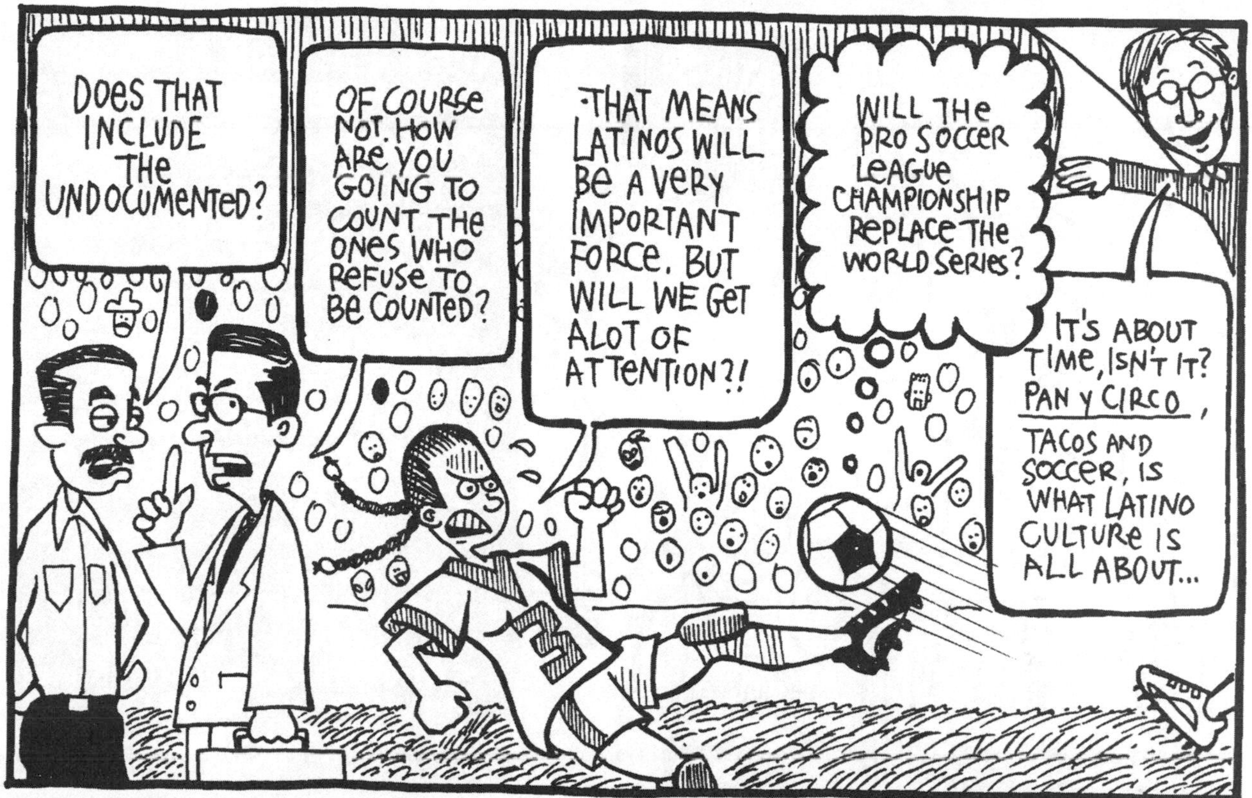
DOES THAT INCLUDE THE UNDOCUMENTED?
OF COURSE NOT. HOW ARE YOU GOING TO COUNT THE ONES WHO REFUSE TO BE COUNTED?
THAT MEANS LATINOS WILL BE A VERY IMPORTANT FORCE. BUT WILL WE GET ALOT OF ATTENTION?!
WILL THE PRO SOCCER LEAGUE CHAMPIONSHIP REPLACE THE WORLD SERIES?
IT'S ABOUT TIME, ISN'T IT? PAN Y CIRCO, TACOS AND SOCCER, IS WHAT LATINO CULTURE IS ALL ABOUT...
3

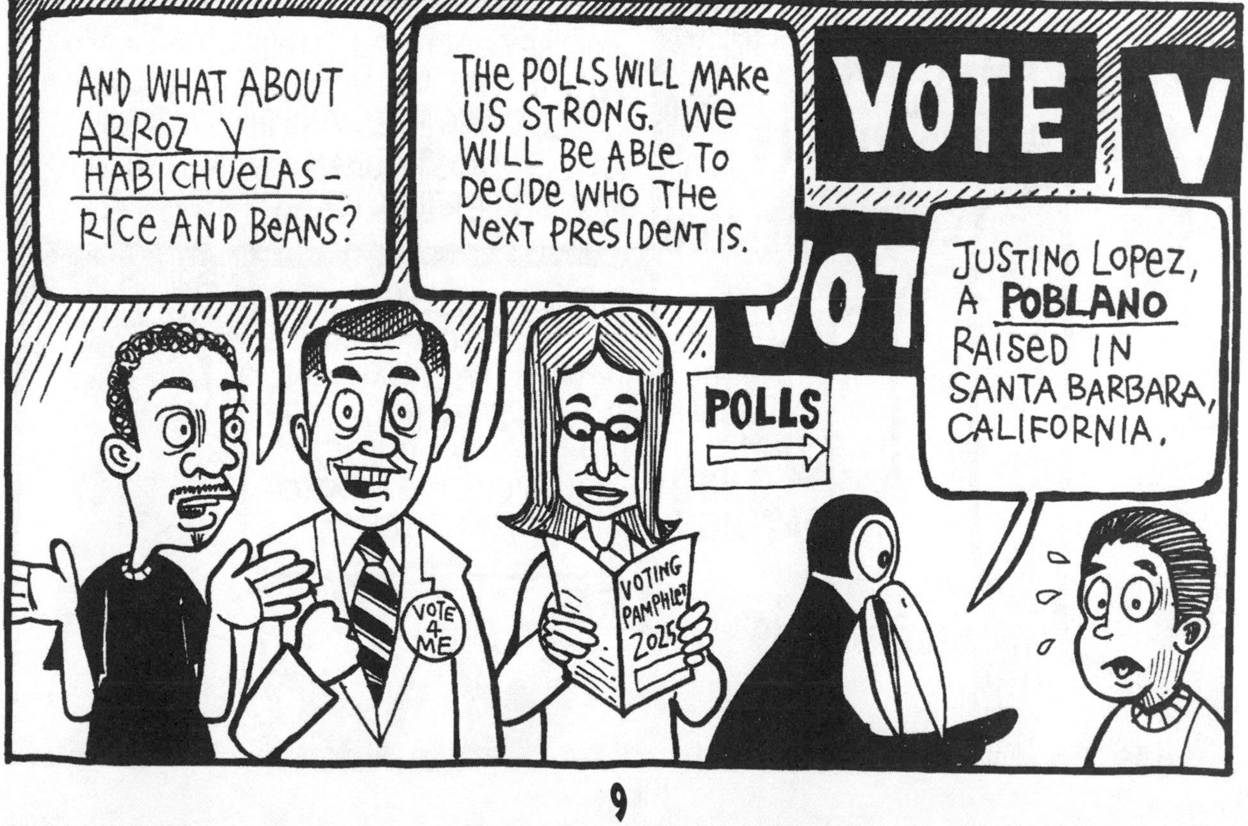
AND WHAT ABOUT ARROZ Y HABICHUELAS - RICE AND BEANS?
THE POLLS WILL MAKE US STRONG. WE WILL BE ABLE TO DECIDE WHO THE NEXT PRESIDENT IS.
VOTE
V
VOT
POLLS
JUSTINO LOPEZ, A POBLANO RAISED IN SANTA BARBARA, CALIFORNIA.
VOTE 4 ME
VOTING PAMPHLET 2025

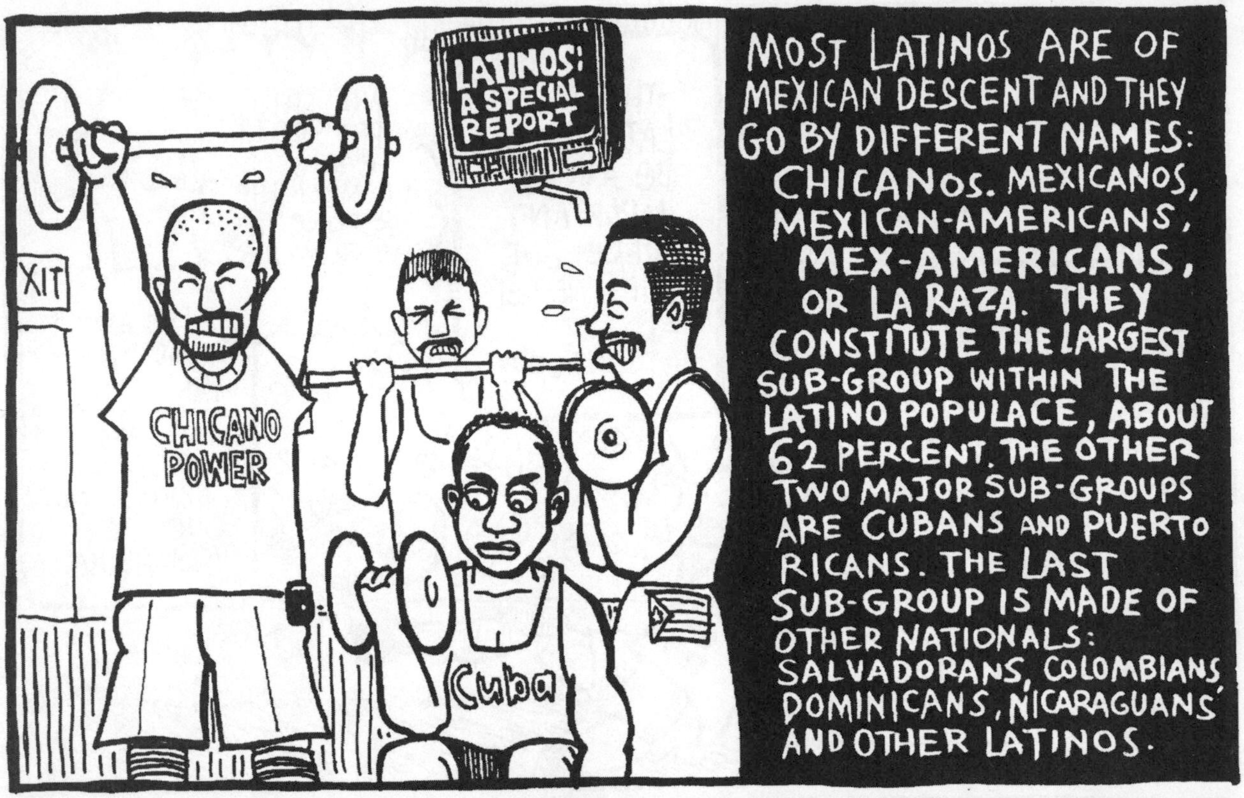
LATINOS: A SPECIAL REPORT
XIT
CHICANO POWER
Cuba
MOST LATINOS ARE OF MEXICAN DESCENT AND THEY GO BY DIFFERENT NAMES: CHICANOS. MEXICANOS, MEXICAN-AMERICANS, MEX-AMERICANS, OR LA RAZA. THEY CONSTITUTE THE LARGEST SUB-GROUP WITHIN THE LATINO POPULACE, ABOUT 62 PERCENT. THE OTHER TWO MAJOR SUB-GROUPS ARE CUBANS AND PUERTO RICANS. THE LAST SUB-GROUP IS MADE OF OTHER NATIONALS: SALVADORANS, COLOMBIANS DOMINICANS, NICARAGUANS' AND OTHER LATINOS.

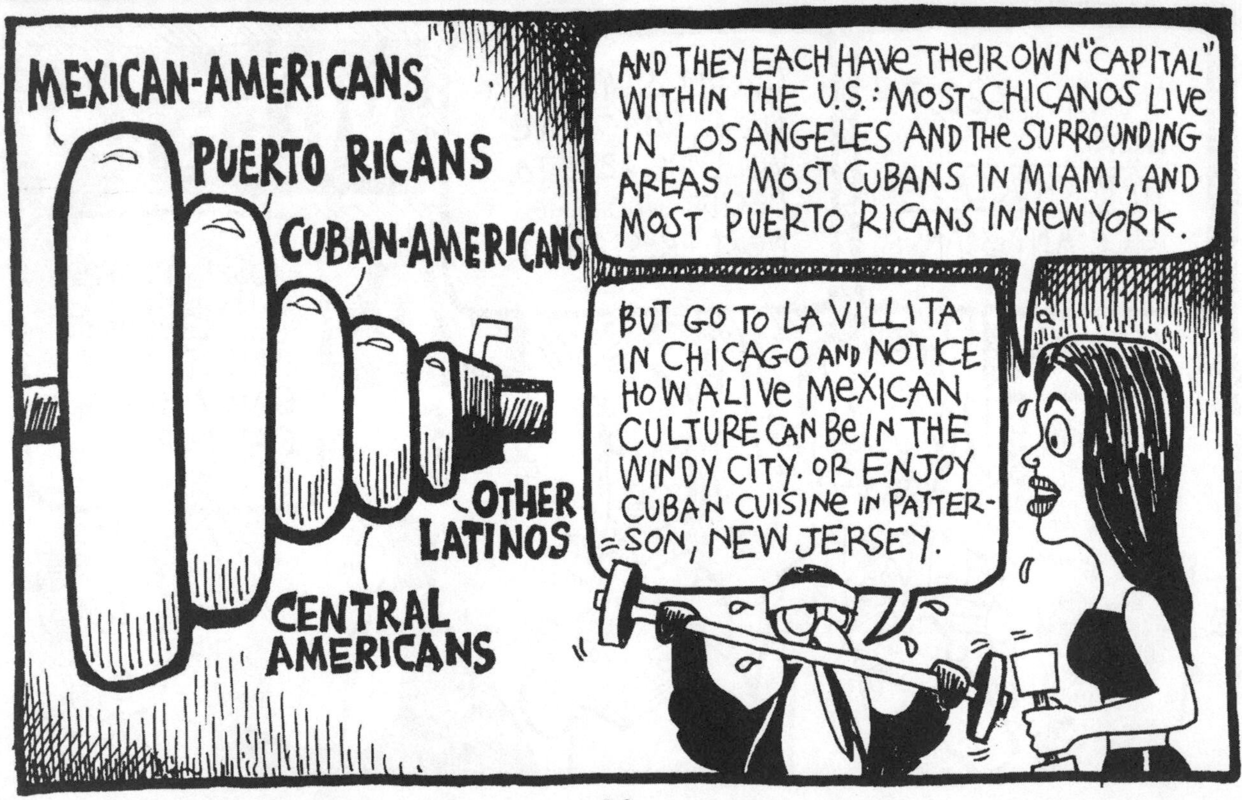
MEXICAN-AMERICANS
PUERTO RICANS
CUBAN-AMERICANS
OTHER LATINOS
CENTRAL AMERICANS
AND THEY EACH HAVE THEIR OWN "CAPITAL" WITHIN THE U.S.: MOST CHICANOS LIVE IN LOS ANGELES AND THE SURROUNDING AREAS, MOST CUBANS IN MIAMI, AND MOST PUERTO RICANS IN NEW YORK.
BUT GO TO LA VILLITA IN CHICAGO AND NOTICE HOW ALIVE MEXICAN CULTURE CAN BE IN THE WINDY CITY. OR ENJOY CUBAN CUISINE IN PATTERSON, NEW JERSEY.

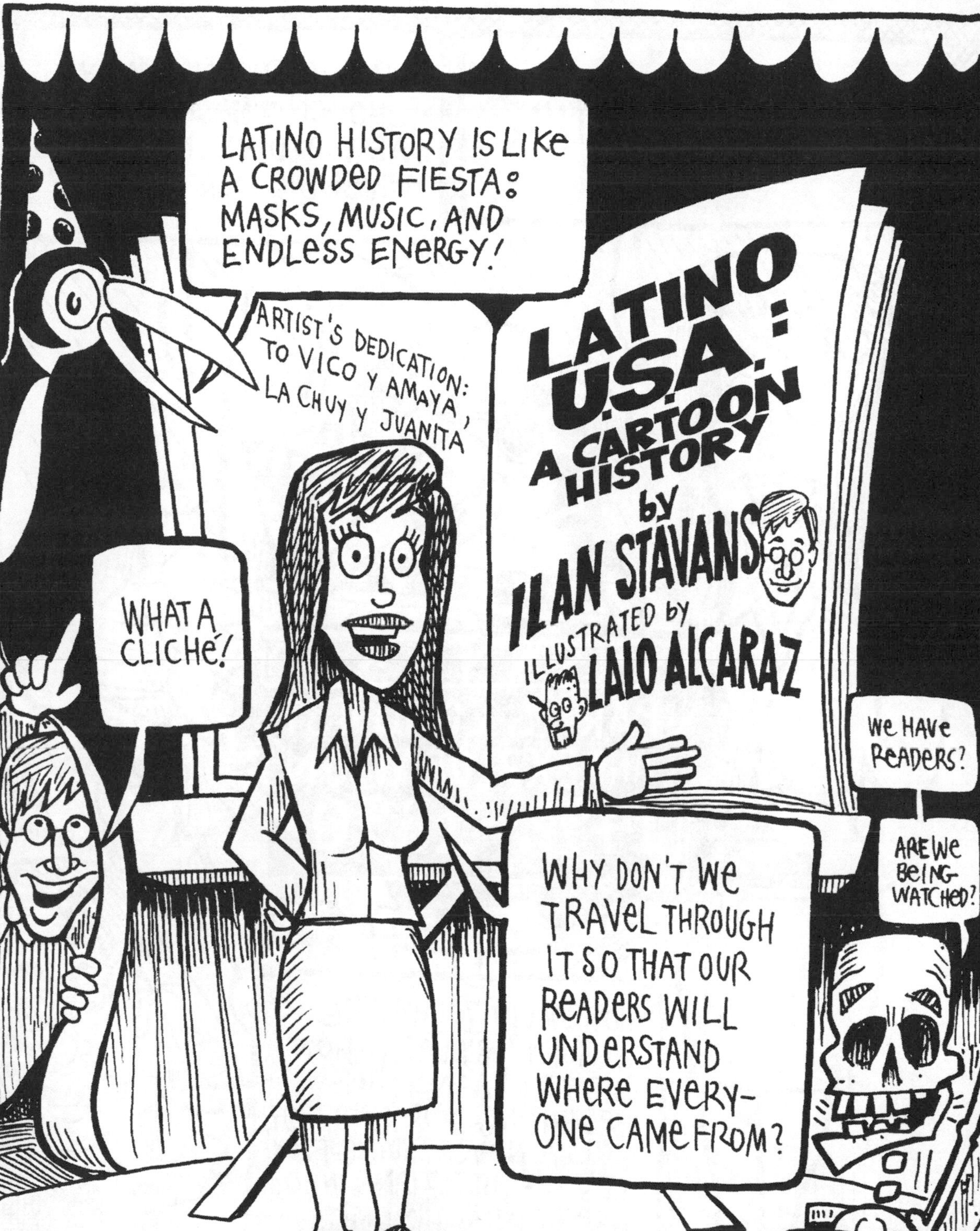
LATINO HISTORY IS LIKE A CROWDED FIESTA: MASKS, MUSIC, AND ENDLESS ENERGY!
ARTIST'S DEDICATION: TO VICO Y AMAYA, LA CHUY Y JUANITA
LATINO U.S.A.: A CARTOON HISTORY
by ILAN STAVANS
ILLUSTRATED by LALO ALCARAZ
WHAT A CLICHÉ!
WE HAVE READERS?
ARE WE BEING WATCHED?
WHY DON'T WE TRAVEL THROUGH IT SO THAT OUR READERS WILL UNDERSTAND WHERE EVERYONE CAME FROM?

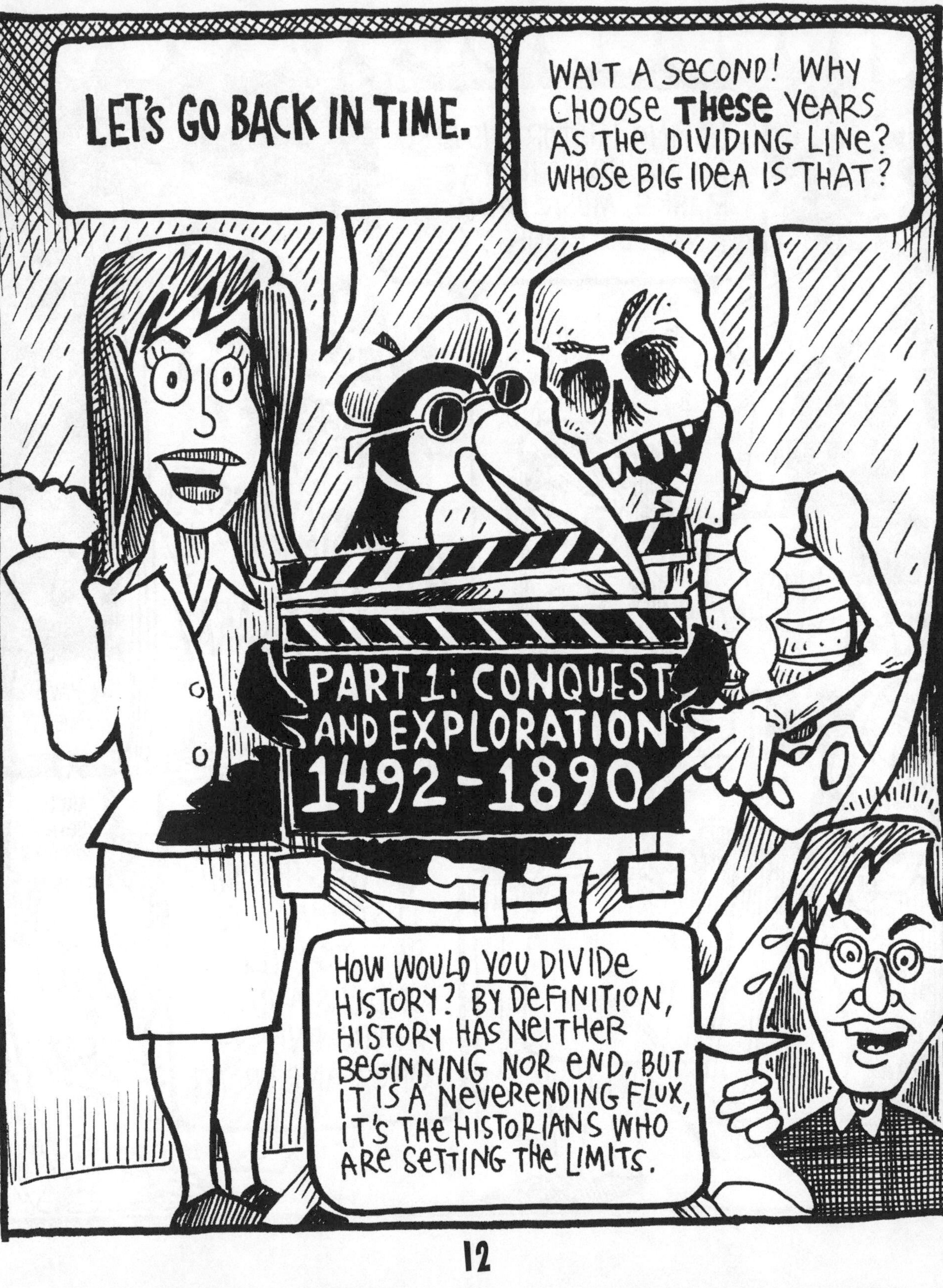
LET'S GO BACK IN TIME.
WAIT A SECOND! WHY CHOOSE THESE YEARS AS THE DIVIDING LINE? WHOSE BIG IDEA IS THAT?
PART 1: CONQUEST AND EXPLORATION 1492-1890
HOW WOULD YOU DIVIDE HISTORY? BY DEFINITION, HISTORY HAS NEITHER BEGINNING NOR END, BUT IT IS A NEVERENDING FLUX, IT'S THE HISTORIANS WHO ARE SETTING THE LIMITS.

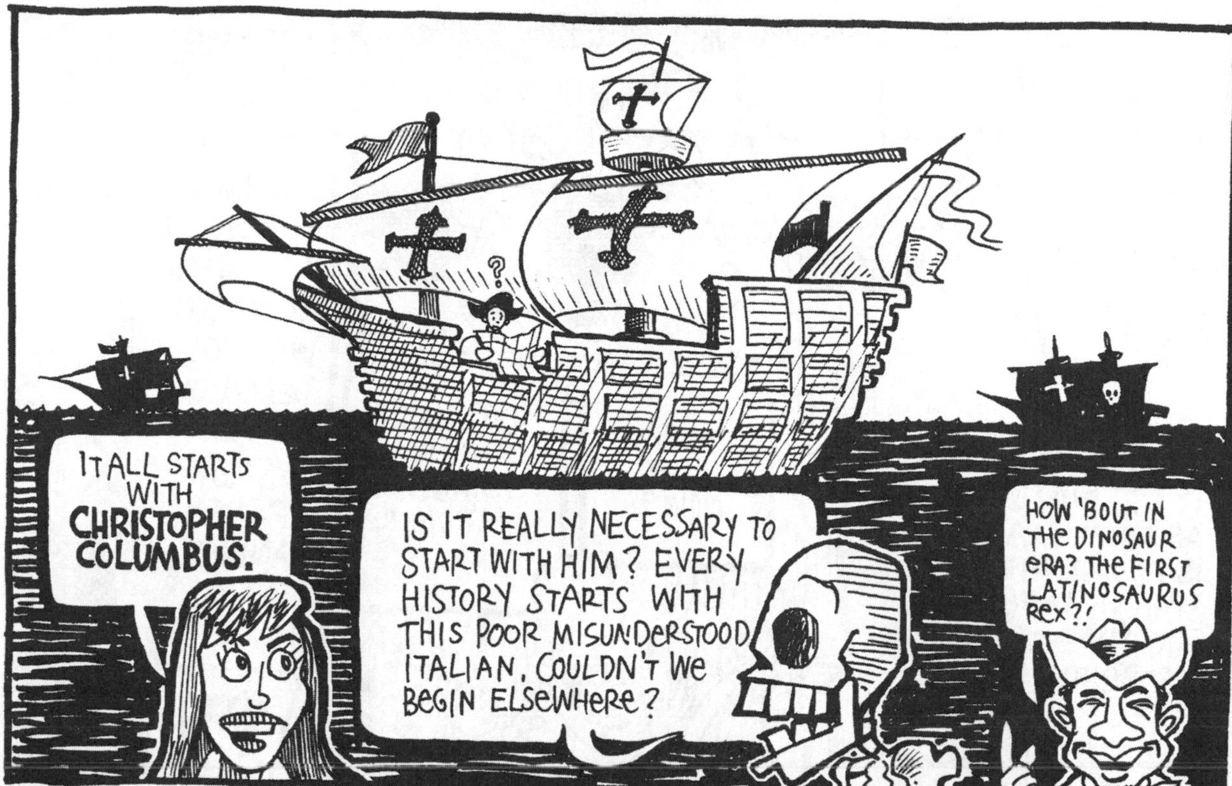
IT ALL STARTS WITH CHRISTOPHER COLUMBUS.
IS IT REALLY NECESSARY TO START WITH HIM? EVERY HISTORY STARTS WITH THIS POOR MISUNDERSTOOD ITALIAN. COULDN'T WE BEGIN ELSEWHERE?
HOW 'BOUT IN THE DINOSAUR ERA? THE FIRST LATINOSAURUS REX?!

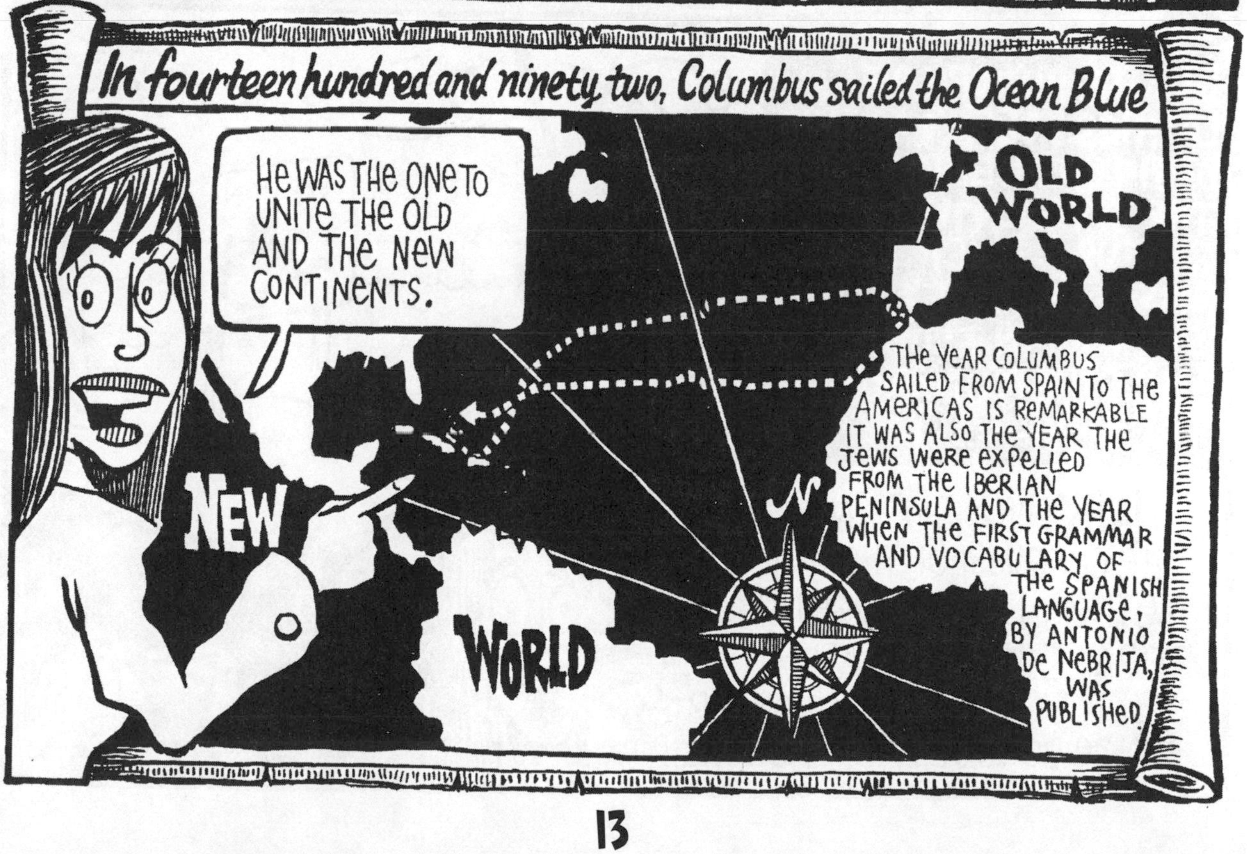
In fourteen hundred and ninety two, Columbus sailed the Ocean Blue
HE WAS THE ONE TO UNITE THE OLD AND THE NEW CONTINENTS.
OLD WORLD
NEW WORLD
THE YEAR COLUMBUS SAILED FROM SPAIN TO THE AMERICAS IS REMARKABLE. IT WAS ALSO THE YEAR THE JEWS WERE EXPELLED FROM THE IBERIAN PENINSULA AND THE YEAR WHEN THE FIRST GRAMMAR AND VOCABULARY OF THE SPANISH LANGUAGE, BY ANTONIO DE NEBRIJA, WAS PUBLISHED.

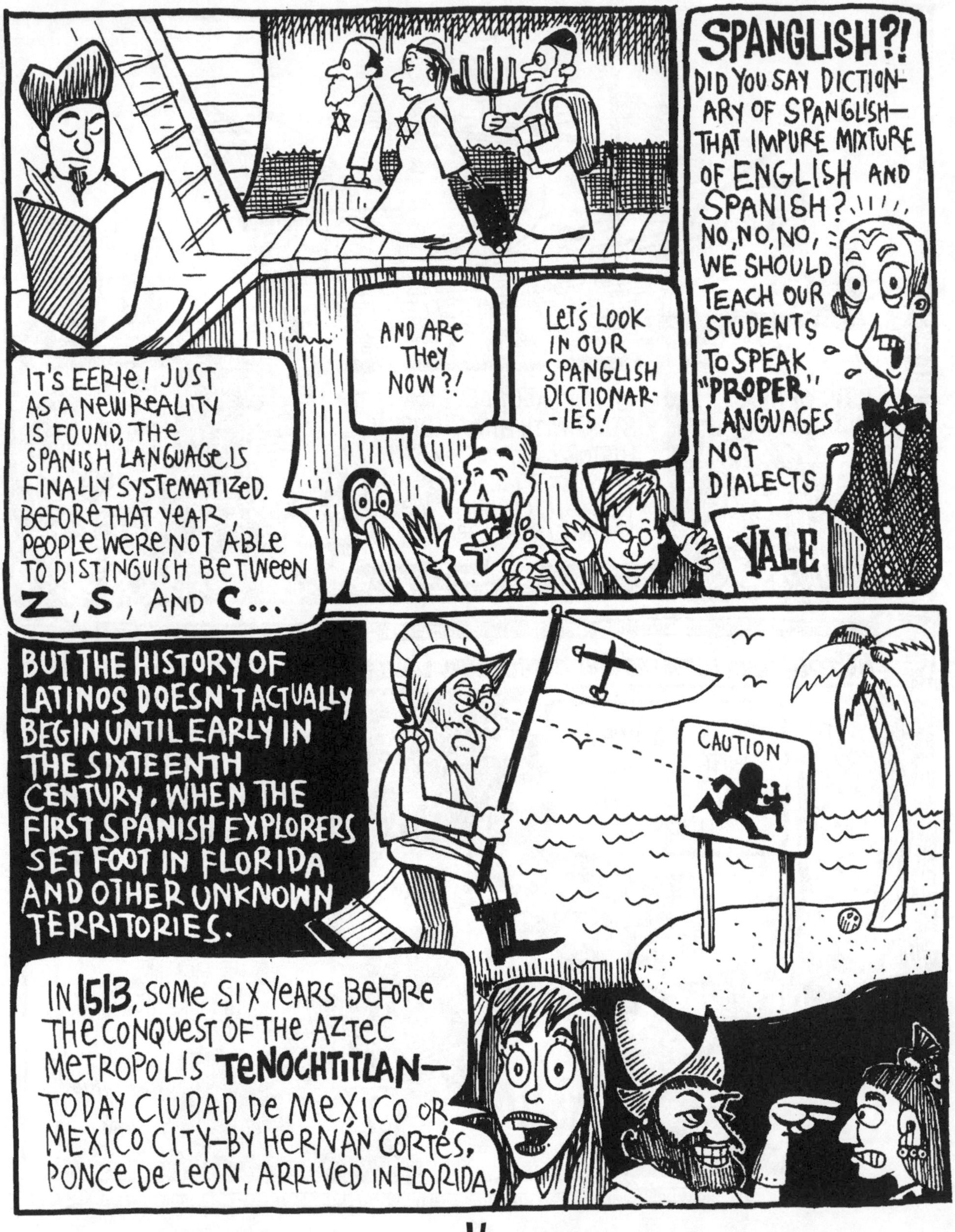
IT'S EERIE! JUST AS A NEW REALITY IS FOUND, THE SPANISH LANGUAGE IS FINALLY SYSTEMATIZED. BEFORE THAT YEAR, PEOPLE WERE NOT ABLE TO DISTINGUISH BETWEEN Z, S, AND C...
AND ARE THEY NOW?!
LET'S LOOK IN OUR SPANGLISH DICTIONAR-IES!
SPANGLISH?! DID YOU SAY DICTION-ARY OF SPANGLISH— THAT IMPURE MIXTURE OF ENGLISH AND SPANISH? NO, NO, NO, WE SHOULD TEACH OUR STUDENTS TO SPEAK "PROPER" LANGUAGES NOT DIALECTS
YALE
BUT THE HISTORY OF LATINOS DOESN'T ACTUALLY BEGIN UNTIL EARLY IN THE SIXTEENTH CENTURY, WHEN THE FIRST SPANISH EXPLORERS SET FOOT IN FLORIDA AND OTHER UNKNOWN TERRITORIES.
CAUTION
IN 1513, SOME SIX YEARS BEFORE THE CONQUEST OF THE AZTEC METROPOLIS TENOCHTITLAN— TODAY CIUDAD DE MEXICO OR MEXICO CITY—BY HERNÁN CORTÉS, PONCE DE LEON, ARRIVED IN FLORIDA.

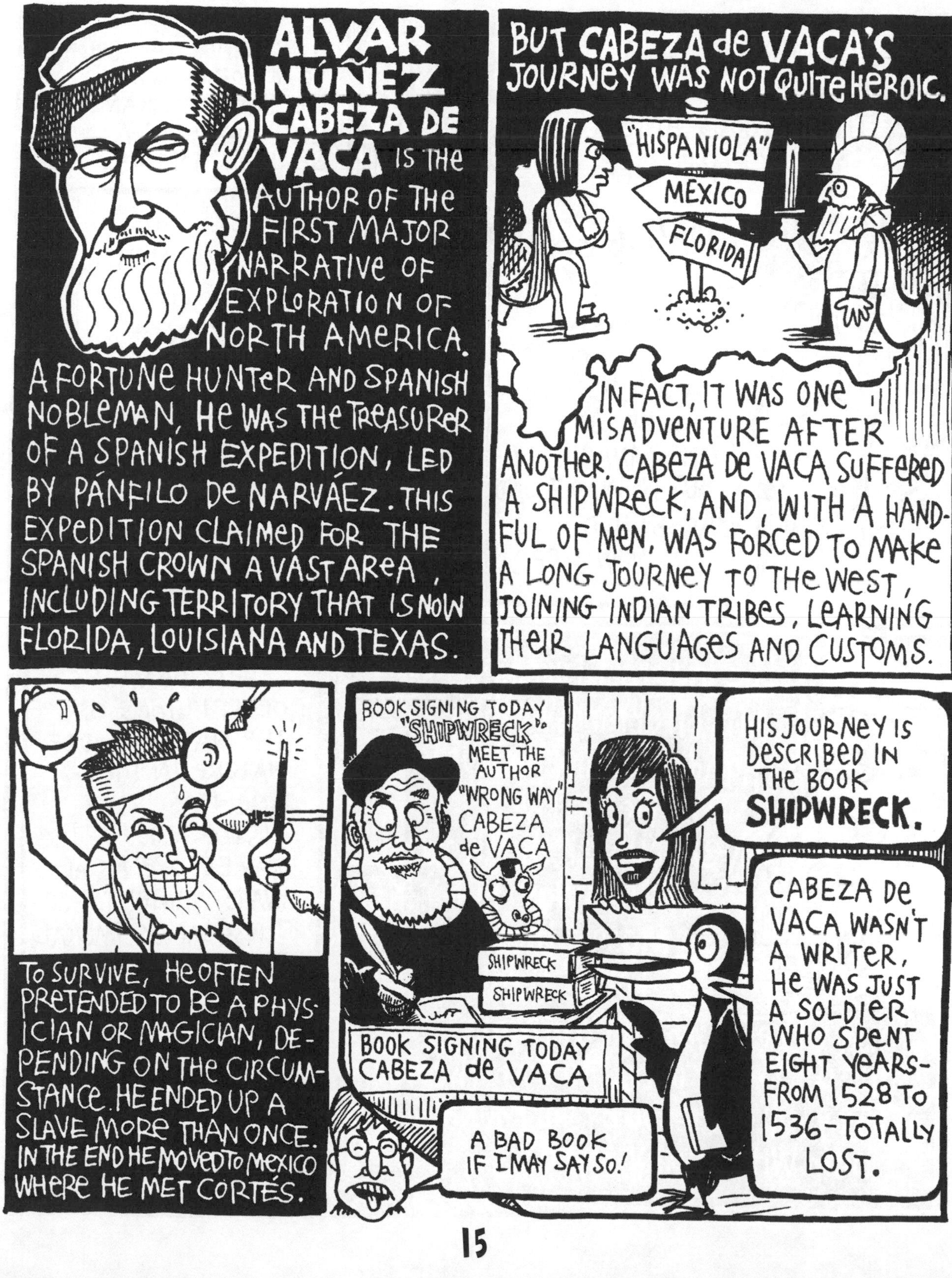

ALVAR NÚÑEZ CABEZA DE VACA IS THE AUTHOR OF THE FIRST MAJOR NARRATIVE OF EXPLORATION OF NORTH AMERICA.
A FORTUNE HUNTER AND SPANISH NOBLEMAN, HE WAS THE TREASURER OF A SPANISH EXPEDITION, LED BY PÁNFILO DE NARVÁEZ. THIS EXPEDITION CLAIMED FOR THE SPANISH CROWN A VAST AREA , INCLUDING TERRITORY THAT IS NOW FLORIDA, LOUISIANA AND TEXAS.
BUT CABEZA de VACA'S JOURNEY WAS NOT QUITE HEROIC.
"HISPANIOLA"
MEXICO
FLORIDA
IN FACT, IT WAS ONE MISADVENTURE AFTER ANOTHER. CABEZA DE VACA SUFFERED A SHIPWRECK, AND, WITH A HANDFUL OF MEN, WAS FORCED TO MAKE A LONG JOURNEY TO THE WEST, JOINING INDIAN TRIBES, LEARNING THEIR LANGUAGES AND CUSTOMS.
TO SURVIVE, HE OFTEN PRETENDED TO BE A PHYSICIAN OR MAGICIAN, DEPENDING ON THE CIRCUMSTANCE. HE ENDED UP A SLAVE MORE THAN ONCE. IN THE END HE MOVED TO MEXICO WHERE HE MET CORTÉS.
BOOK SIGNING TODAY "SHIPWRECK" MEET THE AUTHOR "WRONG WAY" CABEZA de VACA
SHIPWRECK
SHIPWRECK
BOOK SIGNING TODAY CABEZA de VACA
HIS JOURNEY IS DESCRIBED IN THE BOOK SHIPWRECK.
CABEZA DE VACA WASN'T A WRITER, HE WAS JUST A SOLDIER WHO SPENT EIGHT YEARS- FROM 1528 TO 1536-TOTALLY LOST.
A BAD BOOK IF I MAY SAY SO!

YES, HE WAS THE FIRST LATINO TO BE LOST... THIS REMINDS ME OF THE FAMOUS AMERICAN SPIRITUAL:

AMAZING GRACE
HOW SWEET THE SOUND
THAT SAVED A WRETCH LIKE ME
I ONCE WAS LOST BUT NOW AM FOUND
WAS BLIND BUT NOW I SEE

A SPIRITUAL THAT BELONGS TO ALL OF US. AMONG MEXICAN-AMERICANS, A CORRIDO TELLS A SIMILAR THEME.

QUE TRISTE SE ENCUENTRA EL HOMBRE
CUANDO ANDA AUSENTE
CUANDO ANDA AUSENTE
ALLA LEJOS DE SU PATRIA.
PIORMENTE SI SE ACUERDA DE SUS PADRES Y SU CHATA
¡AY QUE DESTINO!
PARA SENTARME A LLORAR.

TO BE LOST... AH, WHAT AN UNFORTUNATE AND ALL TOO COMMON OCCURRENCE.

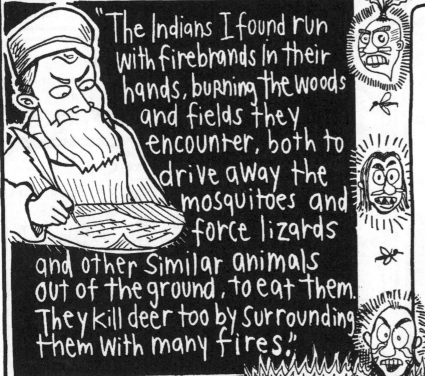

"The Indians I found run with firebrands in their hands, burning the woods and fields they encounter, both to drive away the mosquitoes and force lizards and other similar animals out of the ground, to eat them. They kill deer too by surrounding them with many fires."

CABEZA DE VACA'S DESCRIPTIONS OF THE NATIVES AND OF NATURE IN THE AMERICAS IS SO DISTORTED. IT'S THE WAY EUROPEANS ALWAYS WANTED TO SEE THESE LANDS- MAGICAL, EXOTIC, FILLED WITH PRIMITIVE UNCIVILIZED PEOPLE. IT WOULD TAKE CENTURIES TO OVERCOME THESE MISCONCEPTIONS.

16

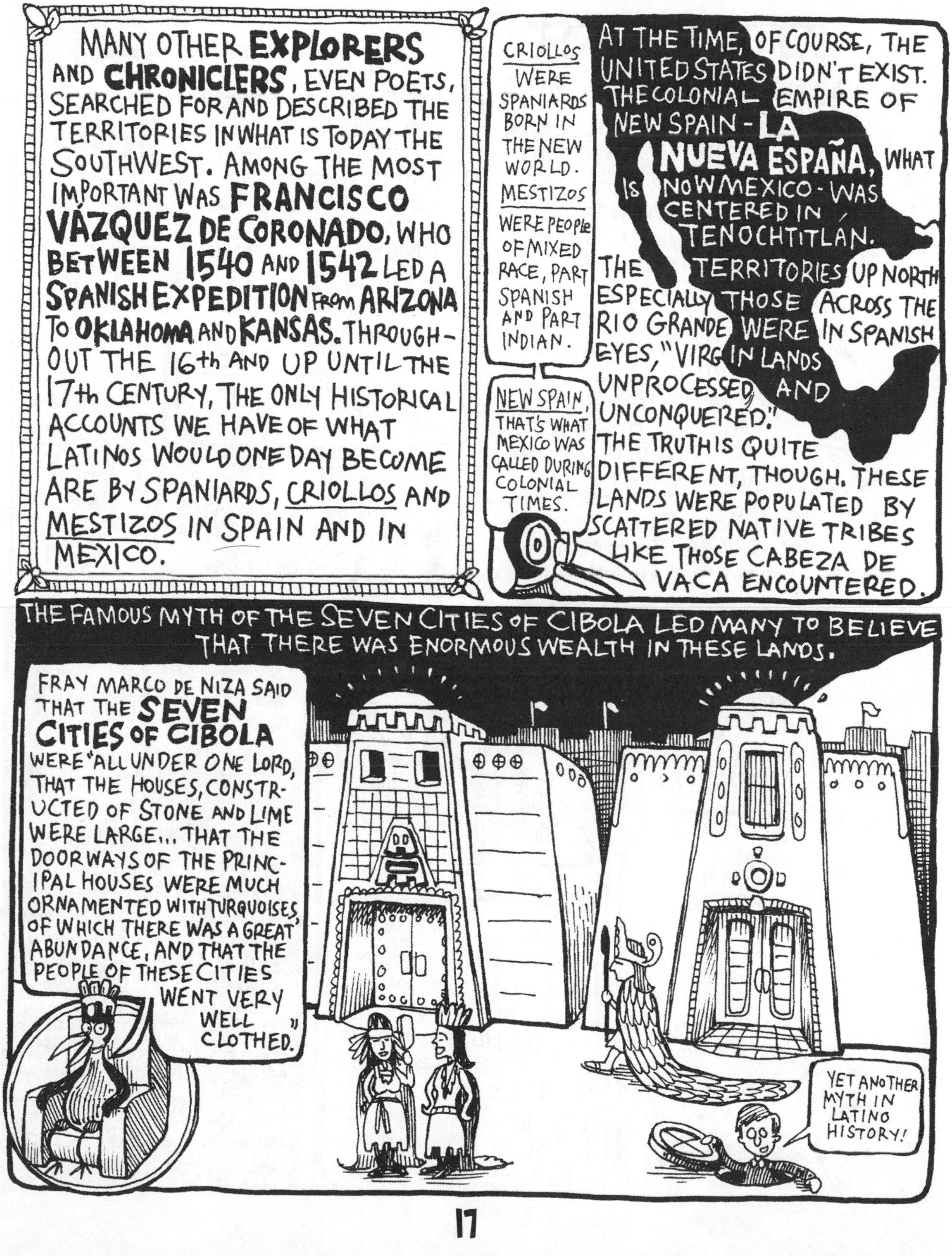
MANY OTHER EXPLORERS AND CHRONICLERS, EVEN POETS, SEARCHED FOR AND DESCRIBED THE TERRITORIES IN WHAT IS TODAY THE SOUTHWEST. AMONG THE MOST IMPORTANT WAS FRANCISCO VÁZQUEZ DE CORONADO, WHO BETWEEN 1540 AND 1542 LED A SPANISH EXPEDITION FROM ARIZONA TO OKLAHOMA AND KANSAS. THROUGHOUT THE 16th AND UP UNTIL THE 17th CENTURY, THE ONLY HISTORICAL ACCOUNTS WE HAVE OF WHAT LATINOS WOULD ONE DAY BECOME ARE BY SPANIARDS, CRIOLLOS AND MESTIZOS IN SPAIN AND IN MEXICO.
CRIOLLOS WERE SPANIARDS BORN IN THE NEW WORLD. MESTIZOS WERE PEOPLE OF MIXED RACE, PART SPANISH AND PART INDIAN.
NEW SPAIN, THAT'S WHAT MEXICO WAS CALLED DURING COLONIAL TIMES.
AT THE TIME, OF COURSE, THE UNITED STATES DIDN'T EXIST. THE COLONIAL EMPIRE OF NEW SPAIN - LA NUEVA ESPAÑA, WHAT IS NOW MEXICO - WAS CENTERED IN TENOCHTITLAN.
THE TERRITORIES UP NORTH ESPECIALLY THOSE ACROSS THE RIO GRANDE WERE IN SPANISH EYES, "VIRGIN LANDS UNPROCESSED AND UNCONQUERED." THE TRUTH IS QUITE DIFFERENT, THOUGH. THESE LANDS WERE POPULATED BY SCATTERED NATIVE TRIBES LIKE THOSE CABEZA DE VACA ENCOUNTERED.
THE FAMOUS MYTH OF THE SEVEN CITIES OF CIBOLA LED MANY TO BELIEVE THAT THERE WAS ENORMOUS WEALTH IN THESE LANDS.
FRAY MARCO DE NIZA SAID THAT THE SEVEN CITIES OF CIBOLA WERE "ALL UNDER ONE LORD, THAT THE HOUSES, CONSTRUCTED OF STONE AND LIME WERE LARGE... THAT THE DOORWAYS OF THE PRINCIPAL HOUSES WERE MUCH ORNAMENTED WITH TURQUOISES, OF WHICH THERE WAS A GREAT ABUNDANCE, AND THAT THE PEOPLE OF THESE CITIES WENT VERY WELL CLOTHED."
YET ANOTHER MYTH IN LATINO HISTORY!

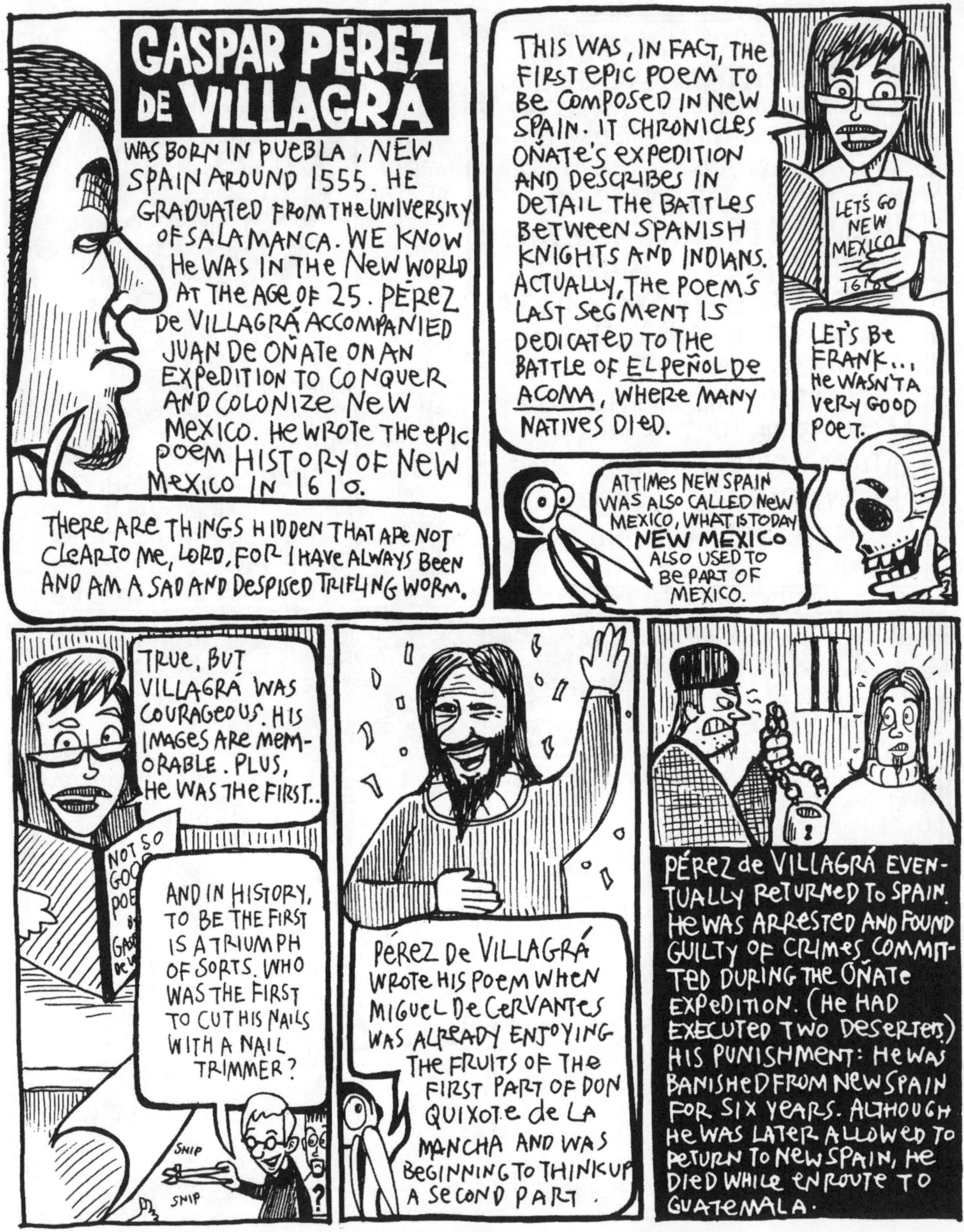

GASPAR PÉREZ DE VILLAGRÁ
WAS BORN IN PUEBLA, NEW SPAIN AROUND 1555. HE GRADUATED FROM THE UNIVERSITY OF SALAMANCA. WE KNOW HE WAS IN THE NEW WORLD AT THE AGE OF 25. PÉREZ DE VILLAGRÁ ACCOMPANIED JUAN DE OÑATE ON AN EXPEDITION TO CONQUER AND COLONIZE NEW MEXICO. HE WROTE THE EPIC POEM HISTORY OF NEW MEXICO IN 1610.
THERE ARE THINGS HIDDEN THAT ARE NOT CLEAR TO ME, LORD, FOR I HAVE ALWAYS BEEN AND AM A SAD AND DESPISED TRIFLING WORM.
THIS WAS, IN FACT, THE FIRST EPIC POEM TO BE COMPOSED IN NEW SPAIN. IT CHRONICLES OÑATE'S EXPEDITION AND DESCRIBES IN DETAIL THE BATTLES BETWEEN SPANISH KNIGHTS AND INDIANS. ACTUALLY, THE POEM'S LAST SEGMENT IS DEDICATED TO THE BATTLE OF EL PEÑOL DE ACOMA, WHERE MANY NATIVES DIED.
LET'S GO NEW MEXICO 1610
LET'S BE FRANK... HE WASN'T A VERY GOOD POET.
AT TIMES NEW SPAIN WAS ALSO CALLED NEW MEXICO, WHAT IS TODAY NEW MEXICO ALSO USED TO BE PART OF MEXICO.
TRUE, BUT VILLAGRÁ WAS COURAGEOUS. HIS IMAGES ARE MEMORABLE. PLUS, HE WAS THE FIRST...
NOT SO GOO POE
AND IN HISTORY, TO BE THE FIRST IS A TRIUMPH OF SORTS. WHO WAS THE FIRST TO CUT HIS NAILS WITH A NAIL TRIMMER?
SNIP
SNIP
?
PÉREZ DE VILLAGRÁ WROTE HIS POEM WHEN MIGUEL DE CERVANTES WAS ALREADY ENJOYING THE FRUITS OF THE FIRST PART OF DON QUIXOTE DE LA MANCHA AND WAS BEGINNING TO THINK UP A SECOND PART.
PÉREZ DE VILLAGRÁ EVENTUALLY RETURNED TO SPAIN. HE WAS ARRESTED AND FOUND GUILTY OF CRIMES COMMITTED DURING THE OÑATE EXPEDITION. (HE HAD EXECUTED TWO DESERTERS) HIS PUNISHMENT: HE WAS BANISHED FROM NEW SPAIN FOR SIX YEARS. ALTHOUGH HE WAS LATER ALLOWED TO RETURN TO NEW SPAIN, HE DIED WHILE EN ROUTE TO GUATEMALA.

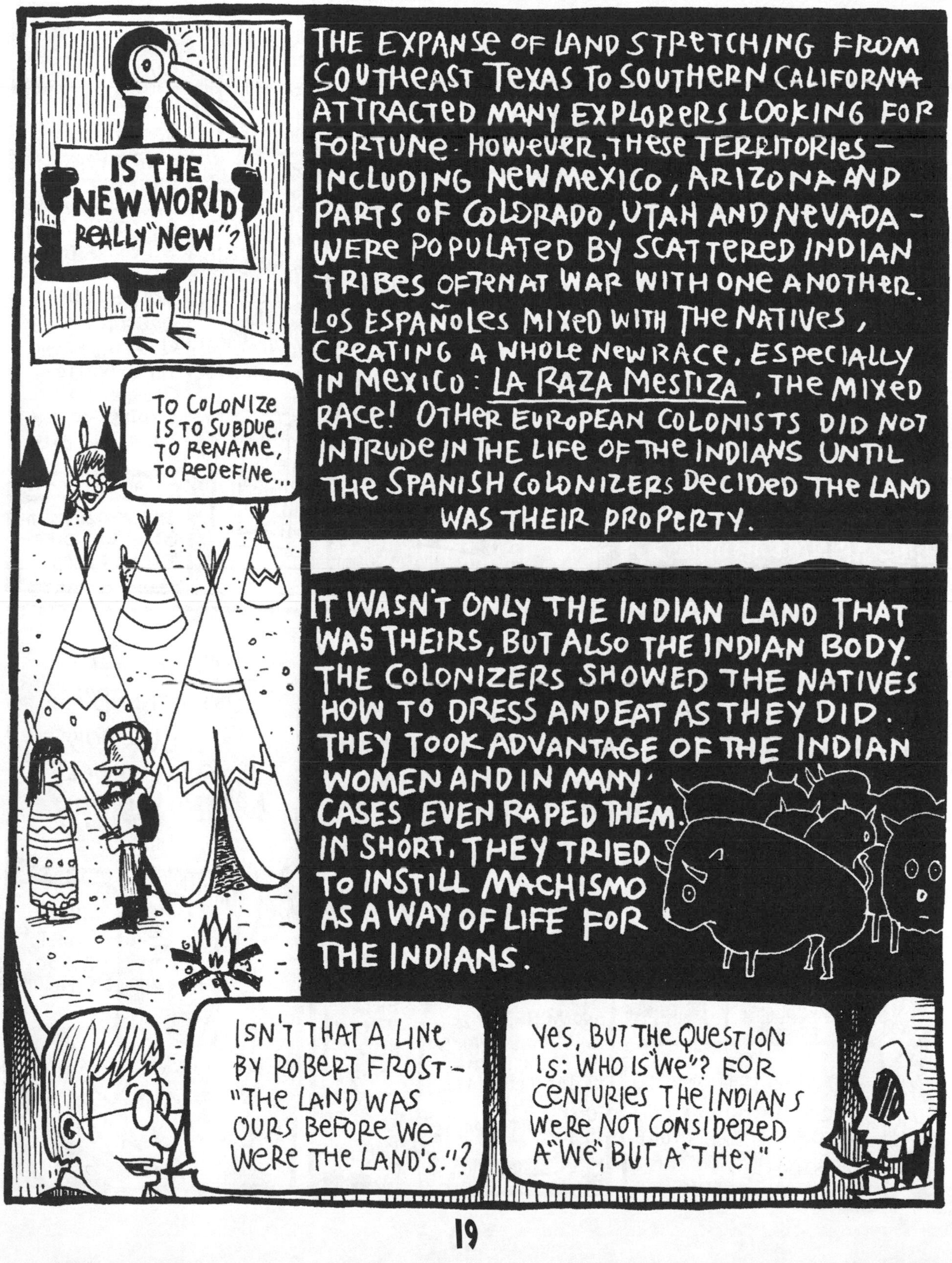

IS THE NEW WORLD REALLY "NEW"?

THE EXPANSE OF LAND STRETCHING FROM SOUTHEAST TEXAS TO SOUTHERN CALIFORNIA ATTRACTED MANY EXPLORERS LOOKING FOR FORTUNE. HOWEVER, THESE TERRITORIES — INCLUDING NEW MEXICO, ARIZONA AND PARTS OF COLORADO, UTAH AND NEVADA — WERE POPULATED BY SCATTERED INDIAN TRIBES OFTEN AT WAR WITH ONE ANOTHER. LOS ESPAÑOLES MIXED WITH THE NATIVES, CREATING A WHOLE NEW RACE, ESPECIALLY IN MEXICO: LA RAZA MESTIZA, THE MIXED RACE! OTHER EUROPEAN COLONISTS DID NOT INTRUDE IN THE LIFE OF THE INDIANS UNTIL THE SPANISH COLONIZERS DECIDED THE LAND WAS THEIR PROPERTY.

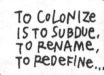

TO COLONIZE IS TO SUBDUE, TO RENAME, TO REDEFINE...

IT WASN'T ONLY THE INDIAN LAND THAT WAS THEIRS, BUT ALSO THE INDIAN BODY. THE COLONIZERS SHOWED THE NATIVES HOW TO DRESS AND EAT AS THEY DID. THEY TOOK ADVANTAGE OF THE INDIAN WOMEN AND IN MANY CASES, EVEN RAPED THEM. IN SHORT, THEY TRIED TO INSTILL MACHISMO AS A WAY OF LIFE FOR THE INDIANS.

ISN'T THAT A LINE BY ROBERT FROST — "THE LAND WAS OURS BEFORE WE WERE THE LAND'S"?

YES, BUT THE QUESTION IS: WHO IS "WE"? FOR CENTURIES THE INDIANS WERE NOT CONSIDERED A "WE", BUT A "THEY"

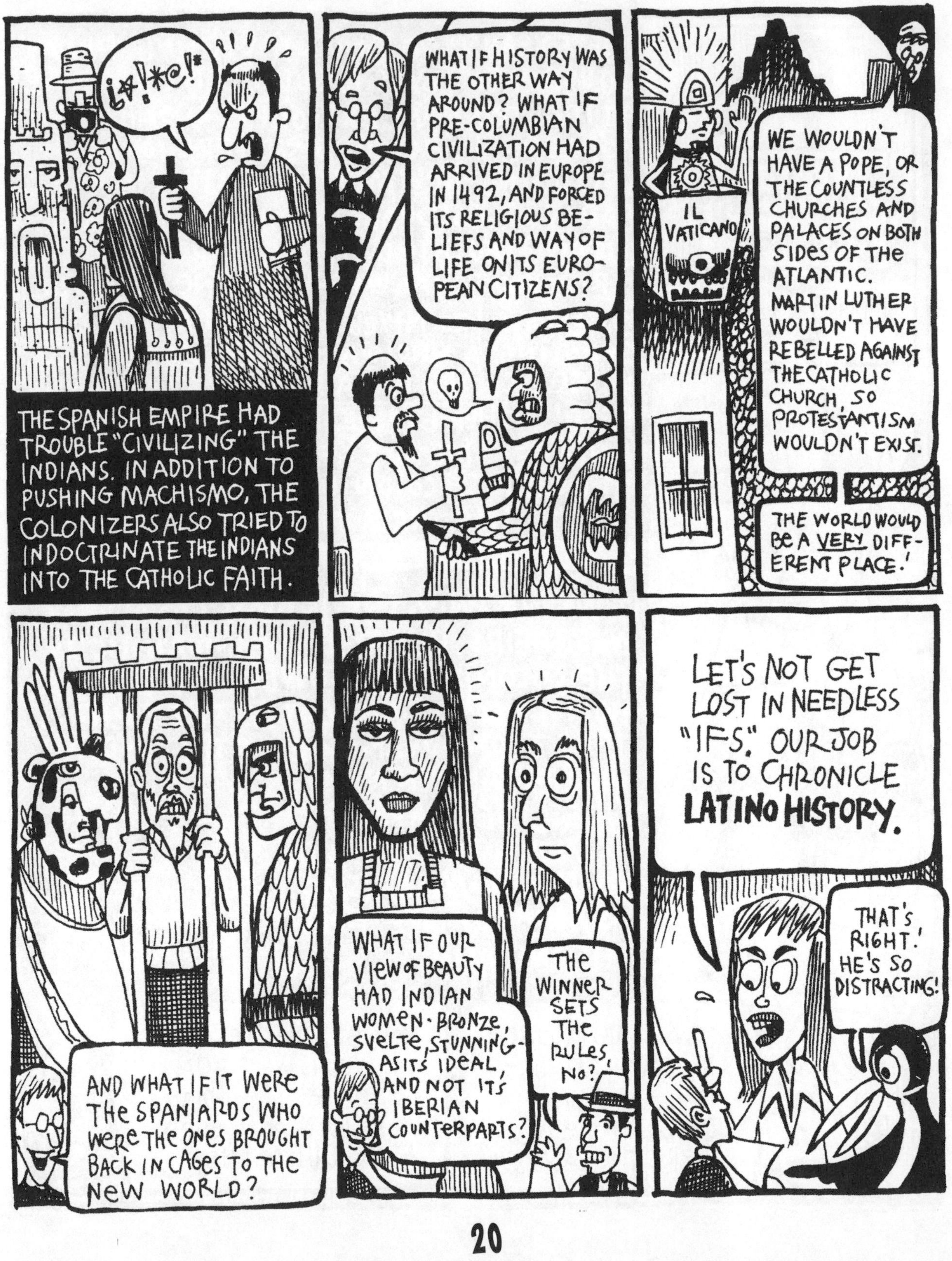
THE SPANISH EMPIRE HAD TROUBLE "CIVILIZING" THE INDIANS. IN ADDITION TO PUSHING MACHISMO, THE COLONIZERS ALSO TRIED TO INDOCTRINATE THE INDIANS INTO THE CATHOLIC FAITH.
WHAT IF HISTORY WAS THE OTHER WAY AROUND? WHAT IF PRE-COLUMBIAN CIVILIZATION HAD ARRIVED IN EUROPE IN 1492, AND FORCED ITS RELIGIOUS BELIEFS AND WAY OF LIFE ON ITS EUROPEAN CITIZENS?
IL VATICANO
WE WOULDN'T HAVE A POPE, OR THE COUNTLESS CHURCHES AND PALACES ON BOTH SIDES OF THE ATLANTIC. MARTIN LUTHER WOULDN'T HAVE REBELLED AGAINST THE CATHOLIC CHURCH, SO PROTESTANTISM WOULDN'T EXIST.
THE WORLD WOULD BE A VERY DIFFERENT PLACE!
AND WHAT IF IT WERE THE SPANIARDS WHO WERE THE ONES BROUGHT BACK IN CAGES TO THE NEW WORLD?
WHAT IF OUR VIEW OF BEAUTY HAD INDIAN WOMEN - BRONZE, SVELTE, STUNNING - AS ITS IDEAL, AND NOT ITS IBERIAN COUNTERPARTS?
THE WINNER SETS THE RULES, NO?
LET'S NOT GET LOST IN NEEDLESS "IFS." OUR JOB IS TO CHRONICLE LATINO HISTORY.
THAT'S RIGHT! HE'S SO DISTRACTING!

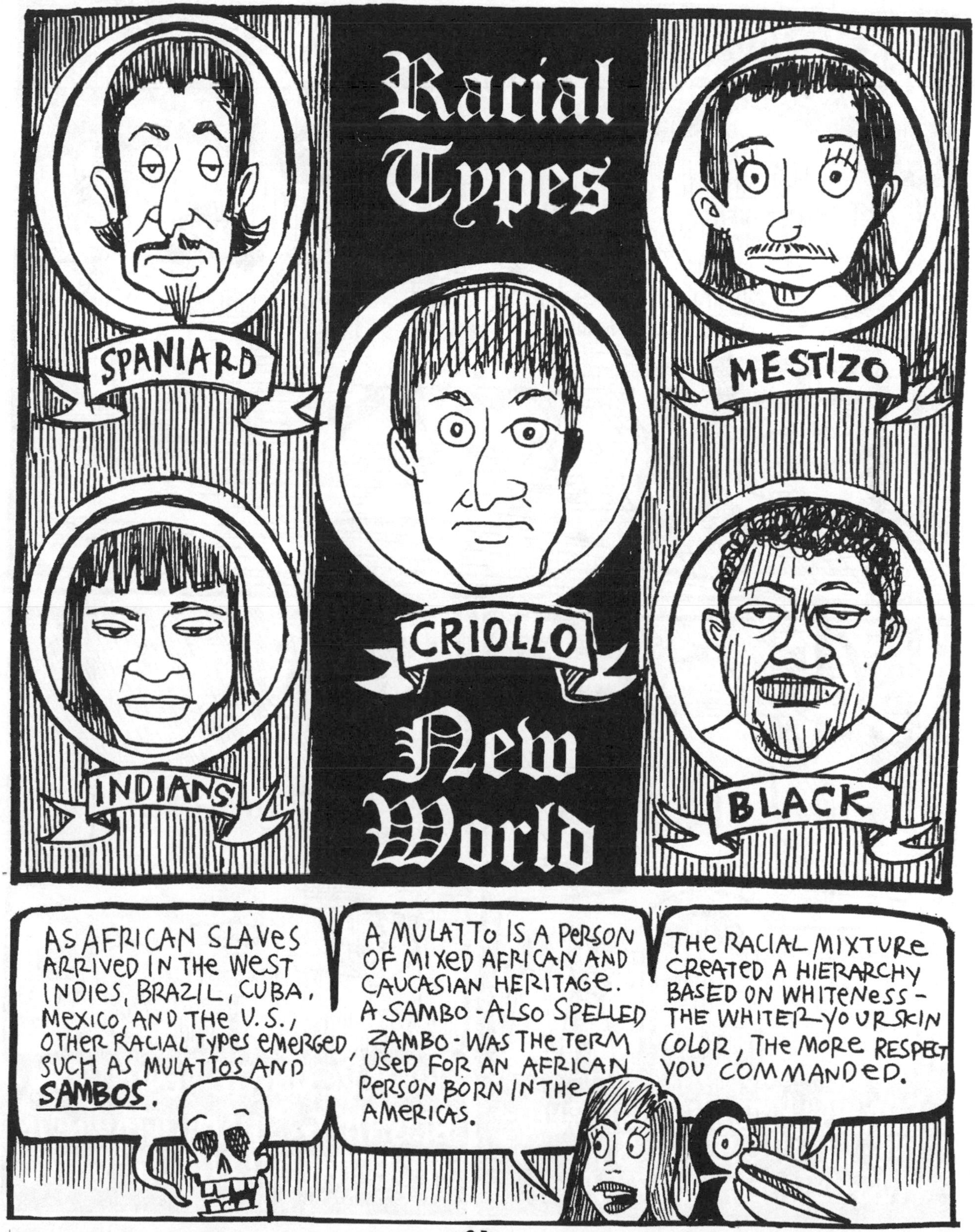
Racial Types
SPANIARD
MESTIZO
CRIOLLO
INDIANS
BLACK
New World
AS AFRICAN SLAVES ARRIVED IN THE WEST INDIES, BRAZIL, CUBA, MEXICO, AND THE U.S., OTHER RACIAL TYPES EMERGED, SUCH AS MULATTOS AND SAMBOS.
A MULATTO IS A PERSON OF MIXED AFRICAN AND CAUCASIAN HERITAGE. A SAMBO - ALSO SPELLED ZAMBO - WAS THE TERM USED FOR AN AFRICAN PERSON BORN IN THE AMERICAS.
THE RACIAL MIXTURE CREATED A HIERARCHY BASED ON WHITENESS - THE WHITER YOUR SKIN COLOR, THE MORE RESPECT YOU COMMANDED.

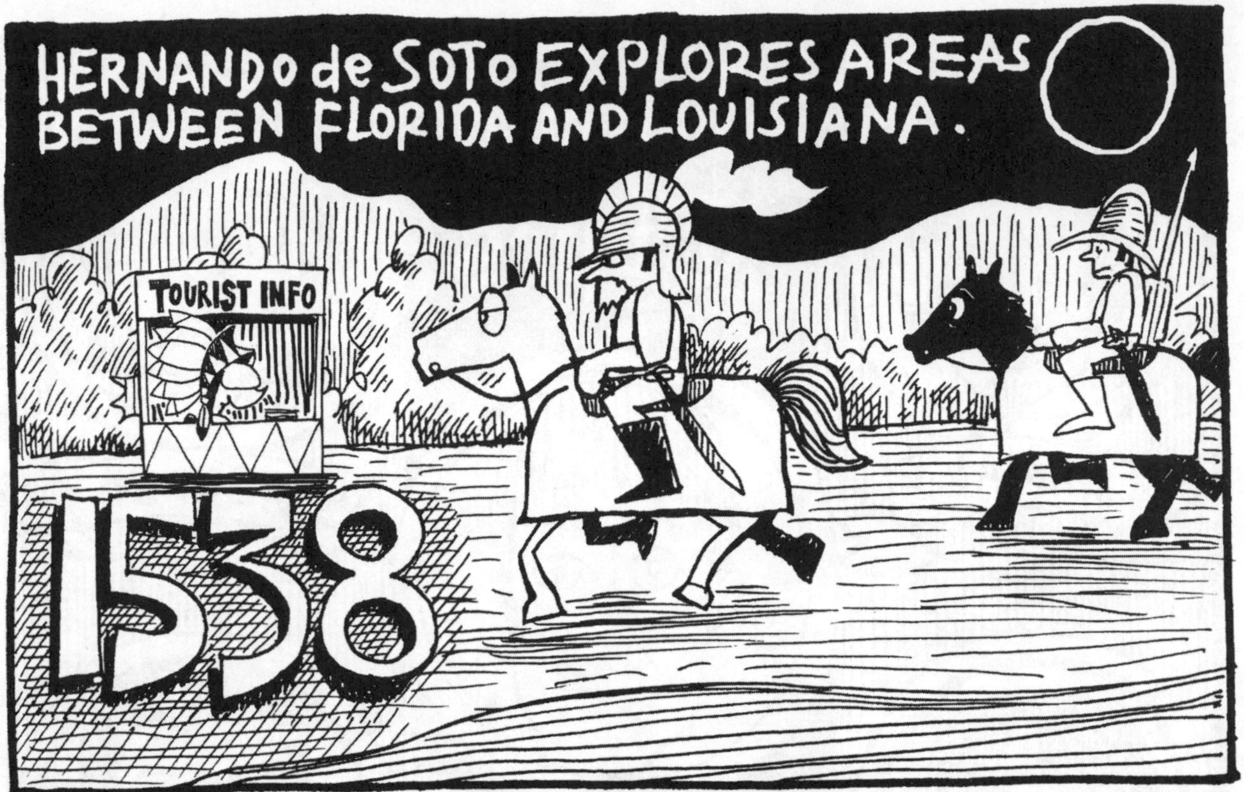
HERNANDO de SOTO EXPLORES AREAS BETWEEN FLORIDA AND LOUISIANA.
TOURIST INFO
1538

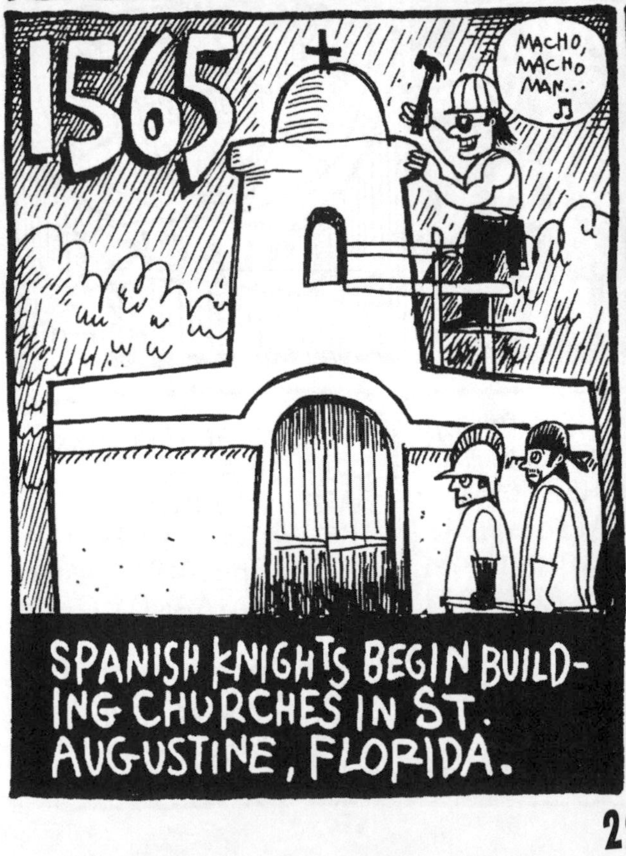
1565
MACHO, MACHO MAN... ♫
SPANISH KNIGHTS BEGIN BUILDING CHURCHES IN ST. AUGUSTINE, FLORIDA.

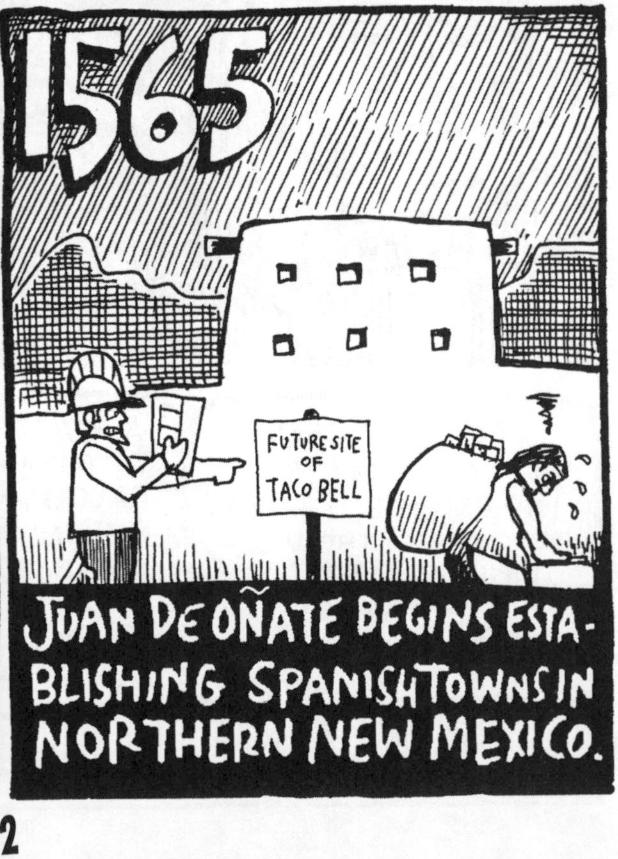
1565
FUTURE SITE OF TACO BELL
JUAN DE OÑATE BEGINS ESTABLISHING SPANISH TOWNS IN NORTHERN NEW MEXICO.

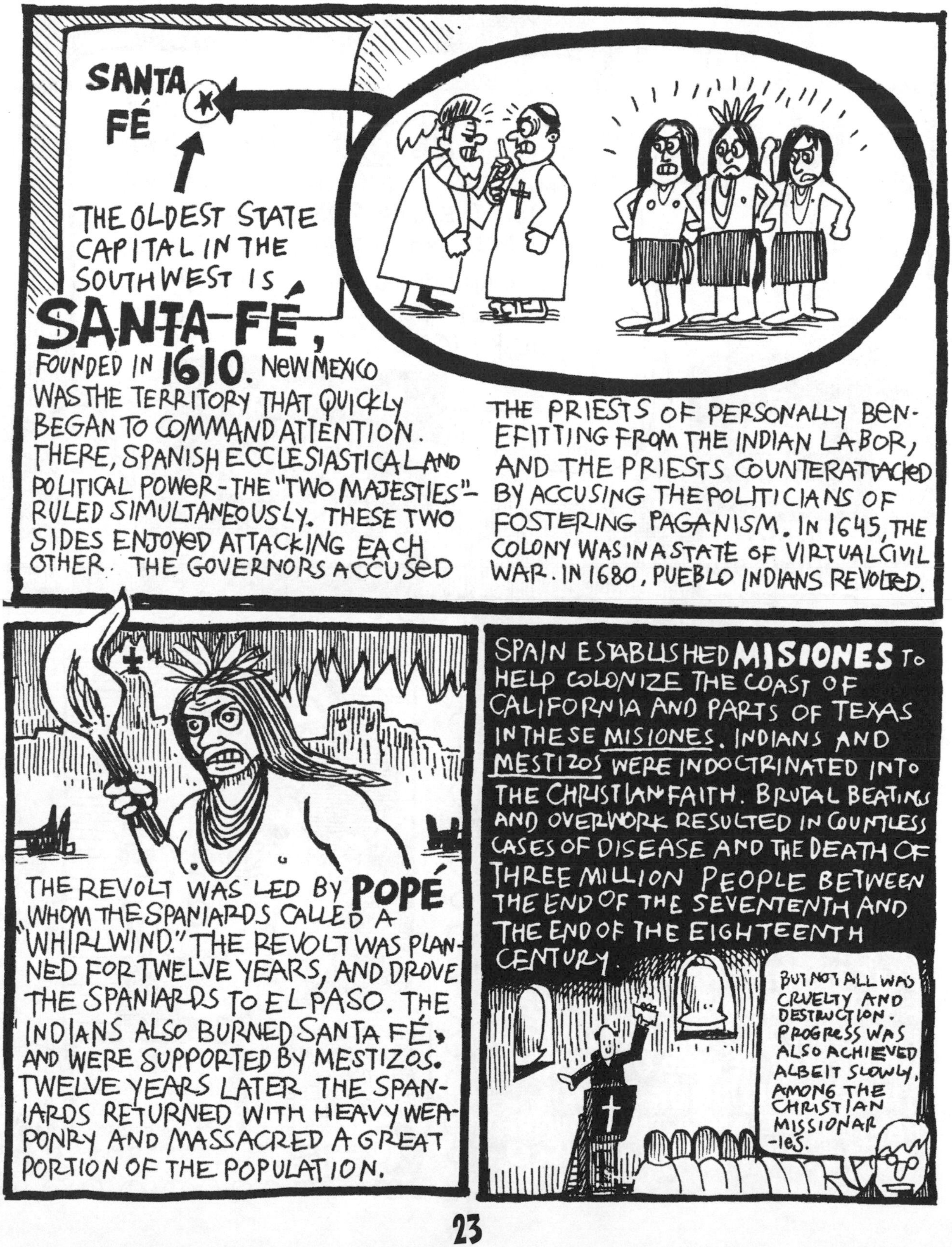
SANTA FÉ
THE OLDEST STATE CAPITAL IN THE SOUTHWEST IS SANTA FÉ, FOUNDED IN 1610. NEW MEXICO WAS THE TERRITORY THAT QUICKLY BEGAN TO COMMAND ATTENTION. THERE, SPANISH ECCLESIASTICAL AND POLITICAL POWER - THE "TWO MAJESTIES" - RULED SIMULTANEOUSLY. THESE TWO SIDES ENJOYED ATTACKING EACH OTHER. THE GOVERNORS ACCUSED THE PRIESTS OF PERSONALLY BENEFITTING FROM THE INDIAN LABOR, AND THE PRIESTS COUNTERATTACKED BY ACCUSING THE POLITICIANS OF FOSTERING PAGANISM. IN 1645, THE COLONY WAS IN A STATE OF VIRTUAL CIVIL WAR. IN 1680, PUEBLO INDIANS REVOLTED.
THE REVOLT WAS LED BY POPÉ WHOM THE SPANIARDS CALLED A "WHIRLWIND." THE REVOLT WAS PLANNED FOR TWELVE YEARS, AND DROVE THE SPANIARDS TO EL PASO. THE INDIANS ALSO BURNED SANTA FÉ, AND WERE SUPPORTED BY MESTIZOS. TWELVE YEARS LATER THE SPANIARDS RETURNED WITH HEAVY WEAPONRY AND MASSACRED A GREAT PORTION OF THE POPULATION.
SPAIN ESTABLISHED MISIONES TO HELP COLONIZE THE COAST OF CALIFORNIA AND PARTS OF TEXAS. IN THESE MISIONES, INDIANS AND MESTIZOS WERE INDOCTRINATED INTO THE CHRISTIAN FAITH. BRUTAL BEATINGS AND OVERWORK RESULTED IN COUNTLESS CASES OF DISEASE AND THE DEATH OF THREE MILLION PEOPLE BETWEEN THE END OF THE SEVENTEENTH AND THE END OF THE EIGHTEENTH CENTURY.
BUT NOT ALL WAS CRUELTY AND DESTRUCTION. PROGRESS WAS ALSO ACHIEVED ALBEIT SLOWLY, AMONG THE CHRISTIAN MISSIONARIES.

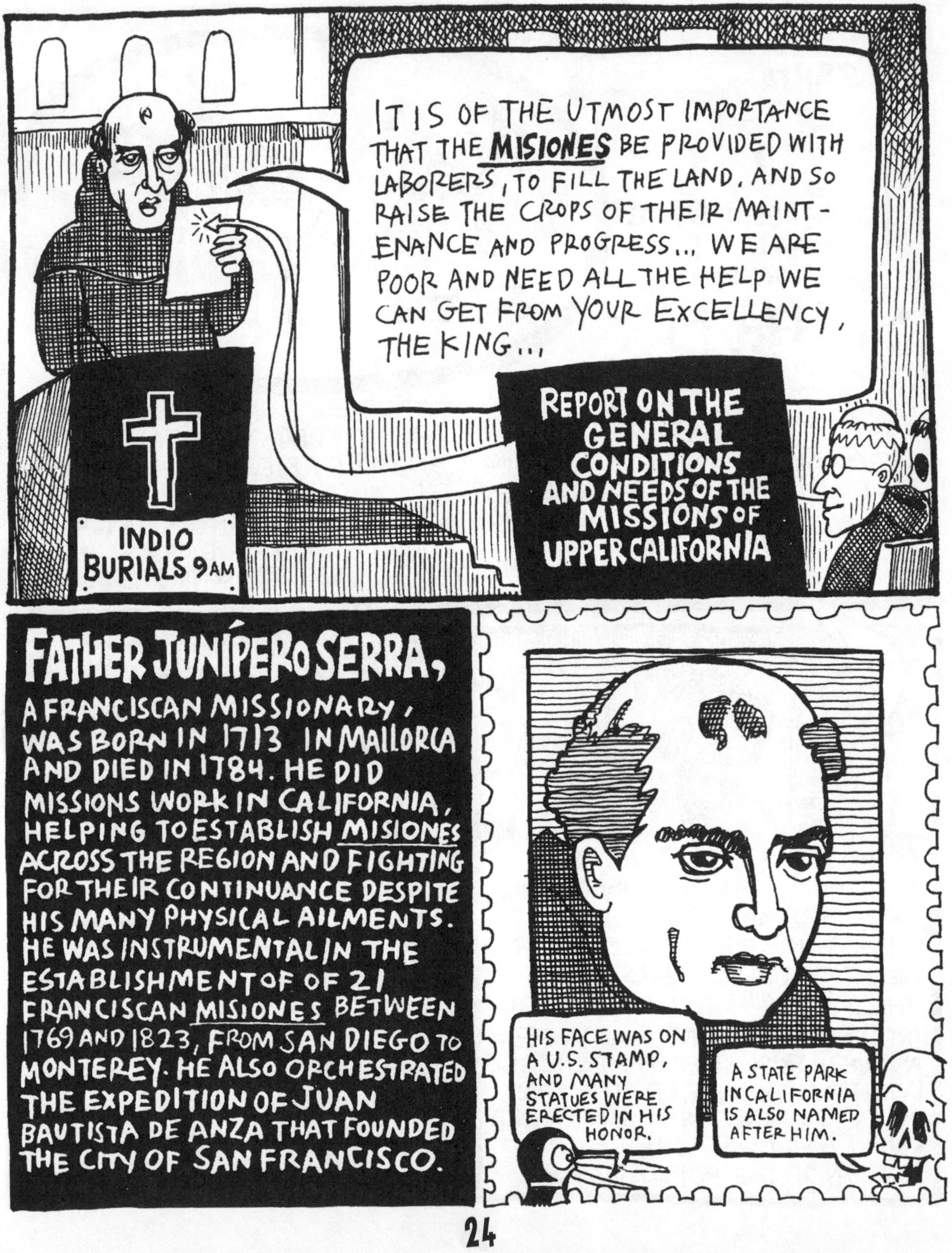
IT IS OF THE UTMOST IMPORTANCE THAT THE MISIONES BE PROVIDED WITH LABORERS, TO FILL THE LAND, AND SO RAISE THE CROPS OF THEIR MAINT- ENANCE AND PROGRESS... WE ARE POOR AND NEED ALL THE HELP WE CAN GET FROM YOUR EXCELLENCY, THE KING...
REPORT ON THE GENERAL CONDITIONS AND NEEDS OF THE MISSIONS OF UPPER CALIFORNIA
INDIO BURIALS 9AM
FATHER JUNÍPERO SERRA,
A FRANCISCAN MISSIONARY, WAS BORN IN 1713 IN MALLORCA AND DIED IN 1784. HE DID MISSIONS WORK IN CALIFORNIA, HELPING TO ESTABLISH MISIONES ACROSS THE REGION AND FIGHTING FOR THEIR CONTINUANCE DESPITE HIS MANY PHYSICAL AILMENTS. HE WAS INSTRUMENTAL IN THE ESTABLISHMENT OF OF 21 FRANCISCAN MISIONES BETWEEN 1769 AND 1823, FROM SAN DIEGO TO MONTEREY. HE ALSO ORCHESTRATED THE EXPEDITION OF JUAN BAUTISTA DE ANZA THAT FOUNDED THE CITY OF SAN FRANCISCO.
HIS FACE WAS ON A U.S. STAMP, AND MANY STATUES WERE ERECTED IN HIS HONOR.
A STATE PARK IN CALIFORNIA IS ALSO NAMED AFTER HIM.

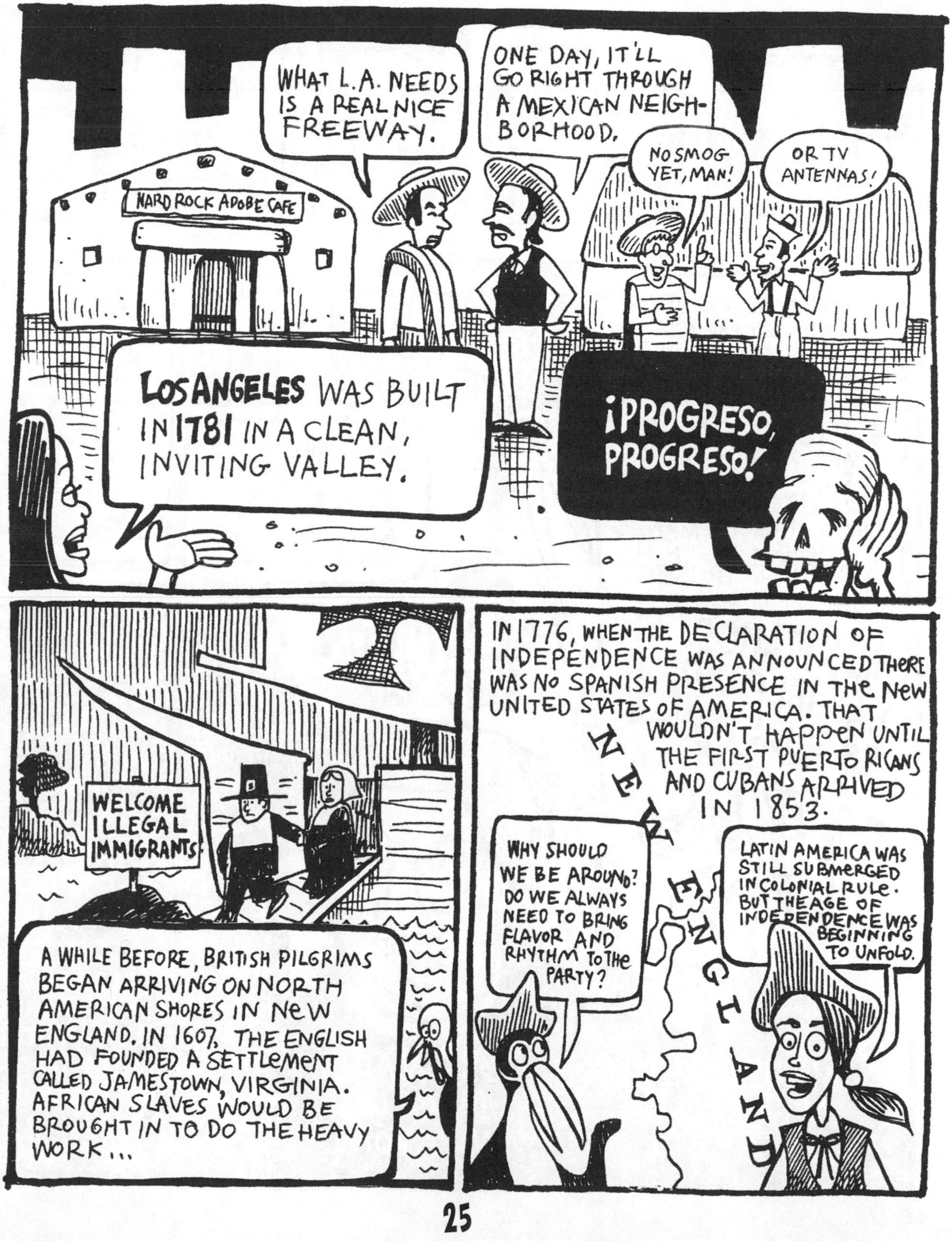

WHAT L.A. NEEDS IS A REAL NICE FREEWAY.
ONE DAY, IT'LL GO RIGHT THROUGH A MEXICAN NEIGH-BORHOOD.
HARD ROCK ADOBE CAFE
NO SMOG YET, MAN!
OR TV ANTENNAS!
LOS ANGELES WAS BUILT IN 1781 IN A CLEAN, INVITING VALLEY.
¡PROGRESO, PROGRESO!
WELCOME ILLEGAL IMMIGRANTS
A WHILE BEFORE, BRITISH PILGRIMS BEGAN ARRIVING ON NORTH AMERICAN SHORES IN NEW ENGLAND. IN 1607, THE ENGLISH HAD FOUNDED A SETTLEMENT CALLED JAMESTOWN, VIRGINIA. AFRICAN SLAVES WOULD BE BROUGHT IN TO DO THE HEAVY WORK...
IN 1776, WHEN THE DECLARATION OF INDEPENDENCE WAS ANNOUNCED THERE WAS NO SPANISH PRESENCE IN THE NEW UNITED STATES OF AMERICA. THAT WOULDN'T HAPPEN UNTIL THE FIRST PUERTO RICANS AND CUBANS ARRIVED IN 1853.
NEW ENGLAND
WHY SHOULD WE BE AROUND? DO WE ALWAYS NEED TO BRING FLAVOR AND RHYTHM TO THE PARTY?
LATIN AMERICA WAS STILL SUBMERGED IN COLONIAL RULE. BUT THE AGE OF INDEPENDENCE WAS BEGINNING TO UNFOLD.

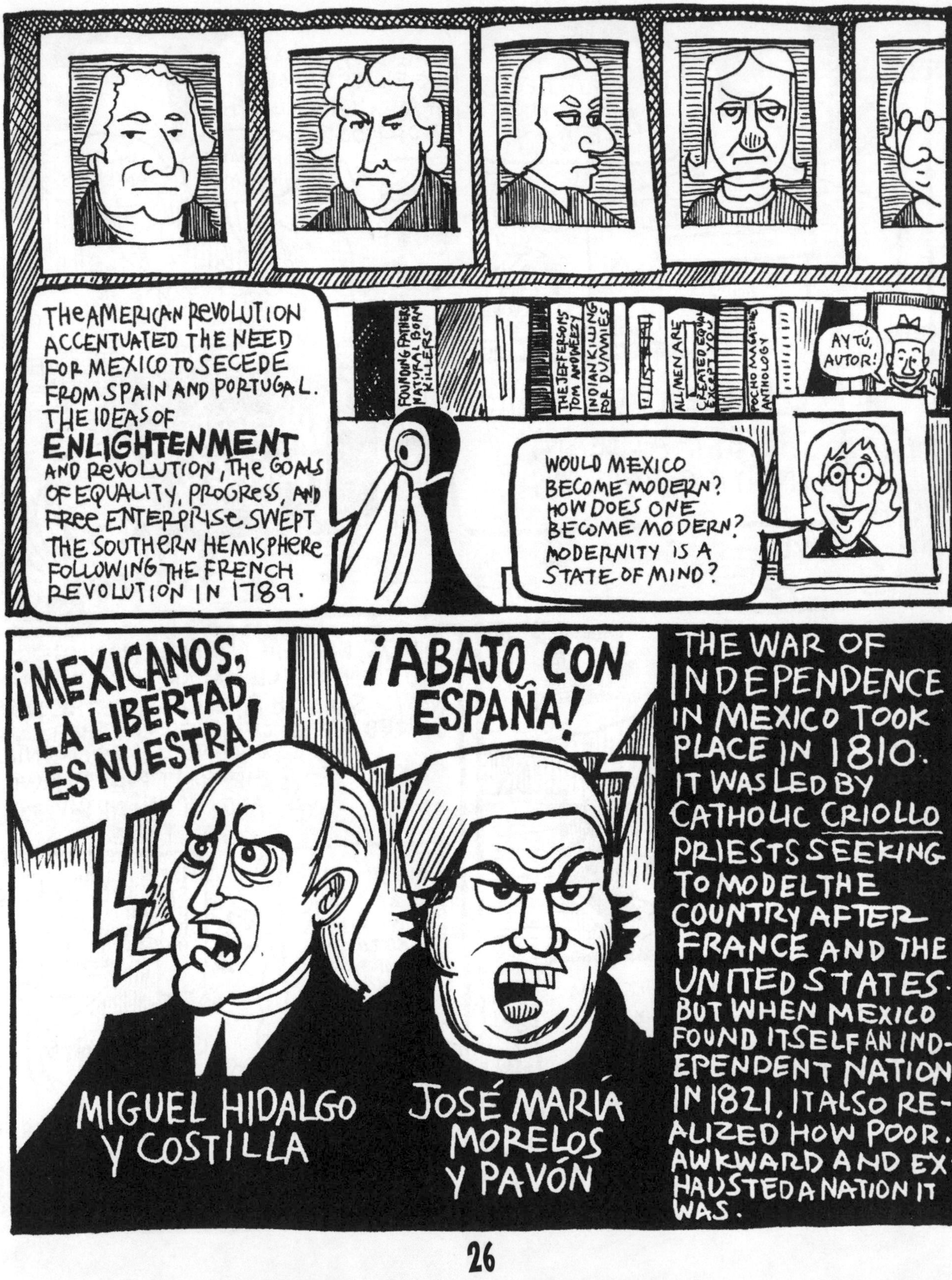
THE AMERICAN REVOLUTION ACCENTUATED THE NEED FOR MEXICO TO SECEDE FROM SPAIN AND PORTUGAL. THE IDEAS OF **ENLIGHTENMENT** AND REVOLUTION, THE GOALS OF EQUALITY, PROGRESS, AND FREE ENTERPRISE SWEPT THE SOUTHERN HEMISPHERE FOLLOWING THE FRENCH REVOLUTION IN 1789.
FOUNDING FATHERS NATURAL BORN KILLERS
THE JEFFERSONS TOM AND WEEZY
INDIAN KILLING FOR DUMMIES
ALL MEN ARE CREATED EQUAL EXCEPT YOU
POCHO MAGAZINE ANTHOLOGY
AY TÚ, AUTOR!
WOULD MEXICO BECOME MODERN? HOW DOES ONE BECOME MODERN? MODERNITY IS A STATE OF MIND?
¡MEXICANOS, LA LIBERTAD ES NUESTRA!
¡ABAJO CON ESPAÑA!
THE WAR OF INDEPENDENCE IN MEXICO TOOK PLACE IN 1810. IT WAS LED BY CATHOLIC CRIOLLO PRIESTS SEEKING TO MODEL THE COUNTRY AFTER FRANCE AND THE UNITED STATES. BUT WHEN MEXICO FOUND ITSELF AN INDEPENDENT NATION IN 1821, IT ALSO REALIZED HOW POOR, AWKWARD AND EXHAUSTED A NATION IT WAS.
MIGUEL HIDALGO Y COSTILLA
JOSÉ MARÍA MORELOS Y PAVÓN

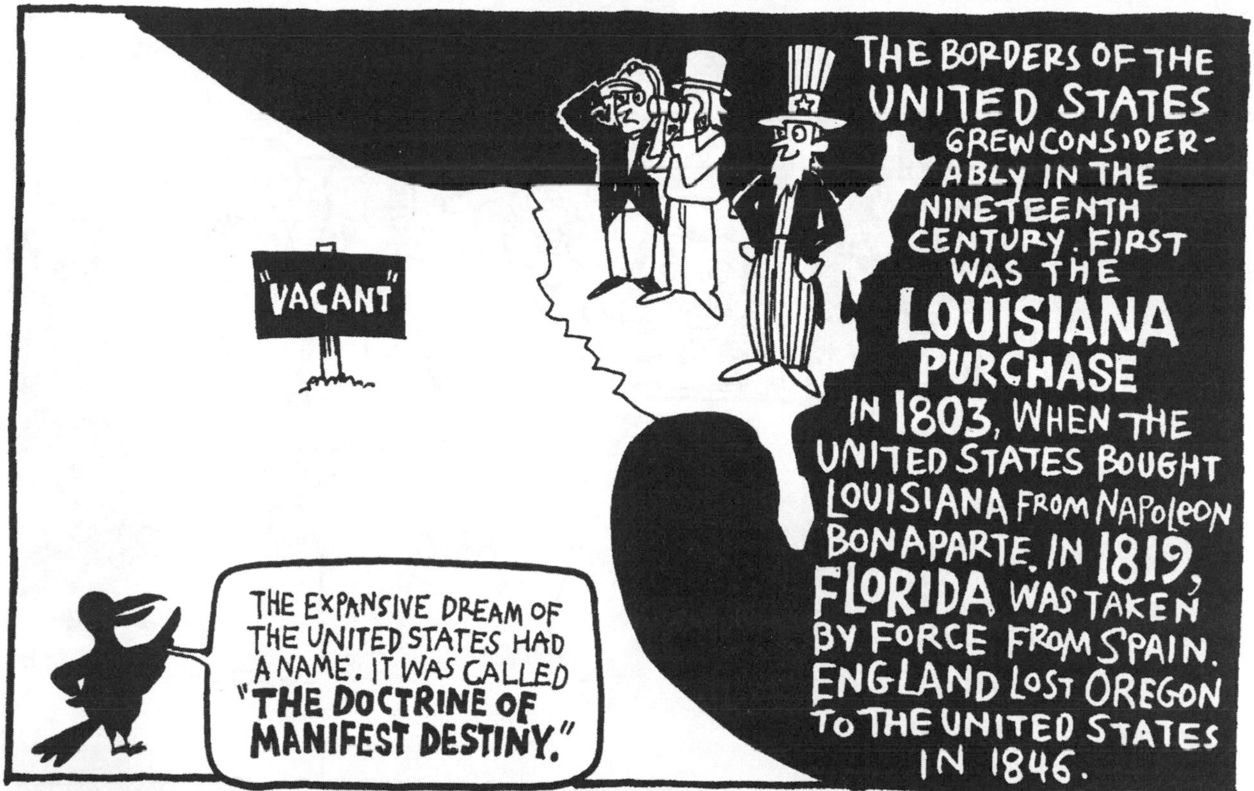
"VACANT"
THE BORDERS OF THE UNITED STATES GREW CONSIDERABLY IN THE NINETEENTH CENTURY. FIRST WAS THE LOUISIANA PURCHASE IN 1803, WHEN THE UNITED STATES BOUGHT LOUISIANA FROM NAPOLEON BONAPARTE. IN 1819, FLORIDA WAS TAKEN BY FORCE FROM SPAIN. ENGLAND LOST OREGON TO THE UNITED STATES IN 1846.
THE EXPANSIVE DREAM OF THE UNITED STATES HAD A NAME. IT WAS CALLED "THE DOCTRINE OF MANIFEST DESTINY."

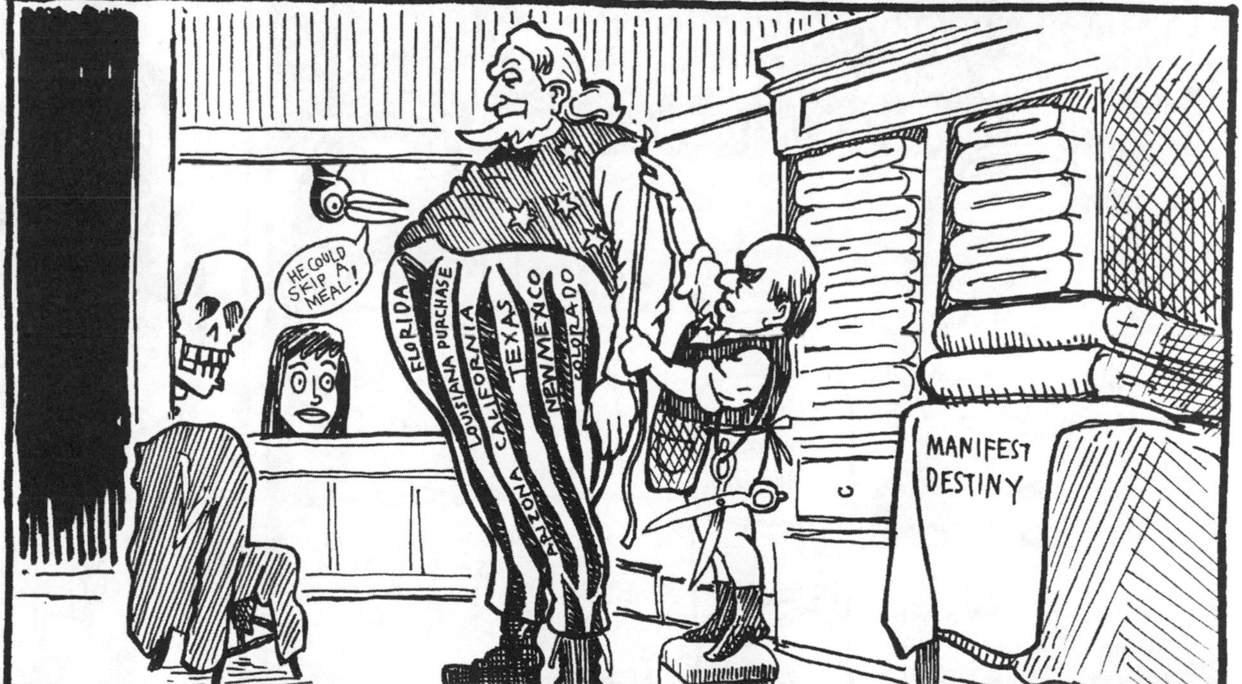
HE COULD SKIP A MEAL!
FLORIDA
LOUISIANA PURCHASE
LOUISIANA
CALIFORNIA
TEXAS
ARIZONA
NEW MEXICO
COLORADO
MANIFEST DESTINY

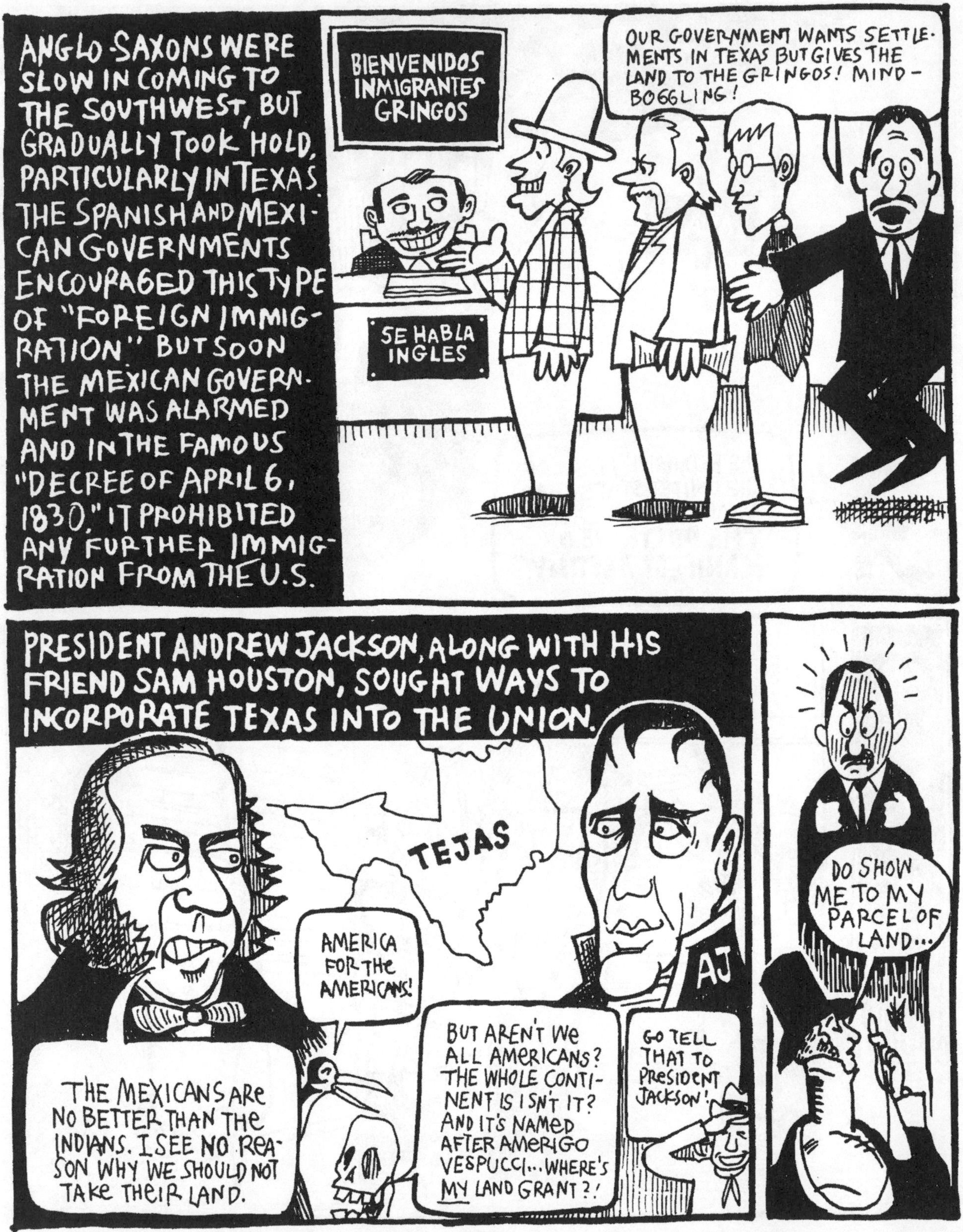
ANGLO-SAXONS WERE SLOW IN COMING TO THE SOUTHWEST, BUT GRADUALLY TOOK HOLD, PARTICULARLY IN TEXAS. THE SPANISH AND MEXICAN GOVERNMENTS ENCOURAGED THIS TYPE OF "FOREIGN IMMIGRATION" BUT SOON THE MEXICAN GOVERNMENT WAS ALARMED AND IN THE FAMOUS "DECREE OF APRIL 6, 1830," IT PROHIBITED ANY FURTHER IMMIGRATION FROM THE U.S.
BIENVENIDOS INMIGRANTES GRINGOS
SE HABLA INGLES
OUR GOVERNMENT WANTS SETTLEMENTS IN TEXAS BUT GIVES THE LAND TO THE GRINGOS! MIND-BOGGLING!
PRESIDENT ANDREW JACKSON, ALONG WITH HIS FRIEND SAM HOUSTON, SOUGHT WAYS TO INCORPORATE TEXAS INTO THE UNION.
TEJAS
THE MEXICANS ARE NO BETTER THAN THE INDIANS. I SEE NO REASON WHY WE SHOULD NOT TAKE THEIR LAND.
AMERICA FOR THE AMERICANS!
BUT AREN'T WE ALL AMERICANS? THE WHOLE CONTINENT IS ISN'T IT? AND IT'S NAMED AFTER AMERIGO VESPUCCI... WHERE'S MY LAND GRANT?!
AJ
GO TELL THAT TO PRESIDENT JACKSON!
DO SHOW ME TO MY PARCEL OF LAND...

AH, REMEMBER THE ALAMO! BUT, ¿QUIÉN SE ACUERDA DEL ALAMO?

HISTORY BOOKS TELL US ONLY HALF THE STORY ABOUT THE FAMOUS 12 DAY **BATTLE OF THE ALAMO** IN **1836**. ENGLISH-SPEAKING TEXTS GLORIFY THE AMERICANS, EVEN THOUGH THEY LOST, AND CELEBRATE SAM HOUSTON AS THE FIRST PRESIDENT OF THE "REPUBLIC OF TEXAS." THE MEXICANS ARE CONDEMN-ED AS TRAITORS AND RUFFIANS.

BUT THE STORY IS MORE COMPLEX! FOR INSTANCE, MEXICO HAD RECENTLY ANN-OUNCED IT WOULD FREE ALL SLAVES IN TEXAS, WHICH SHOCKED THE ANGLO-SAXONS. TEXAS HAD MANY GRIEVANCES AGAINST MEXICO.

JAMES BOWIE

WILLIAM TRAVIS

DAVEY CROCKETT

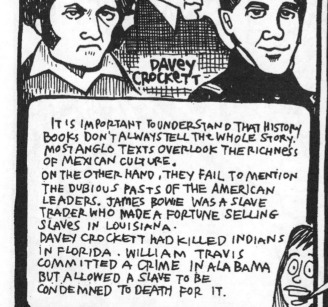

IT IS IMPORTANT TO UNDERSTAND THAT HISTORY BOOKS DON'T ALWAYS TELL THE WHOLE STORY. MOST ANGLO TEXTS OVERLOOK THE RICHNESS OF MEXICAN CULTURE. ON THE OTHER HAND, THEY FAIL TO MENTION THE DUBIOUS PASTS OF THE AMERICAN LEADERS. JAMES BOWIE WAS A SLAVE TRADER WHO MADE A FORTUNE SELLING SLAVES IN LOUISIANA. DAVEY CROCKETT HAD KILLED INDIANS IN FLORIDA. WILLIAM TRAVIS COMMITTED A CRIME IN ALABAMA BUT ALLOWED A SLAVE TO BE CONDEMNED TO DEATH FOR IT.

THE MEXICAN ARMY, WITH MORE THAN 6,000 MEN, SHOWED UP IN SAN ANTONIO ON FEBRUARY 23, 1863, AND LAID SIEGE TO THE ALAMO, A MISSION THAT HAD BEEN CONVERTED INTO A FORTRESS. ONLY 187 TEXANS DEFENDED THE PLACE. ON MARCH 6, THE MEXICANS ASSAULTED THE FORT-RESS, CAPTURING IT, AND KILLING THE DEFENDERS. THE ONLY SURVIVOR—SO THE LEGEND GOES—WAS A SERVANT WHO CRIED "REMEMBER THE ALAMO"!

NO ONE WAS TRULY VICTORIOUS. MEXICO MIGHT HAVE WON THE BATTLE, BUT MANY MEXICANS WERE KILLED. AND THE TEXANS SUFFERED A TERRIBLE DEFEAT.

29

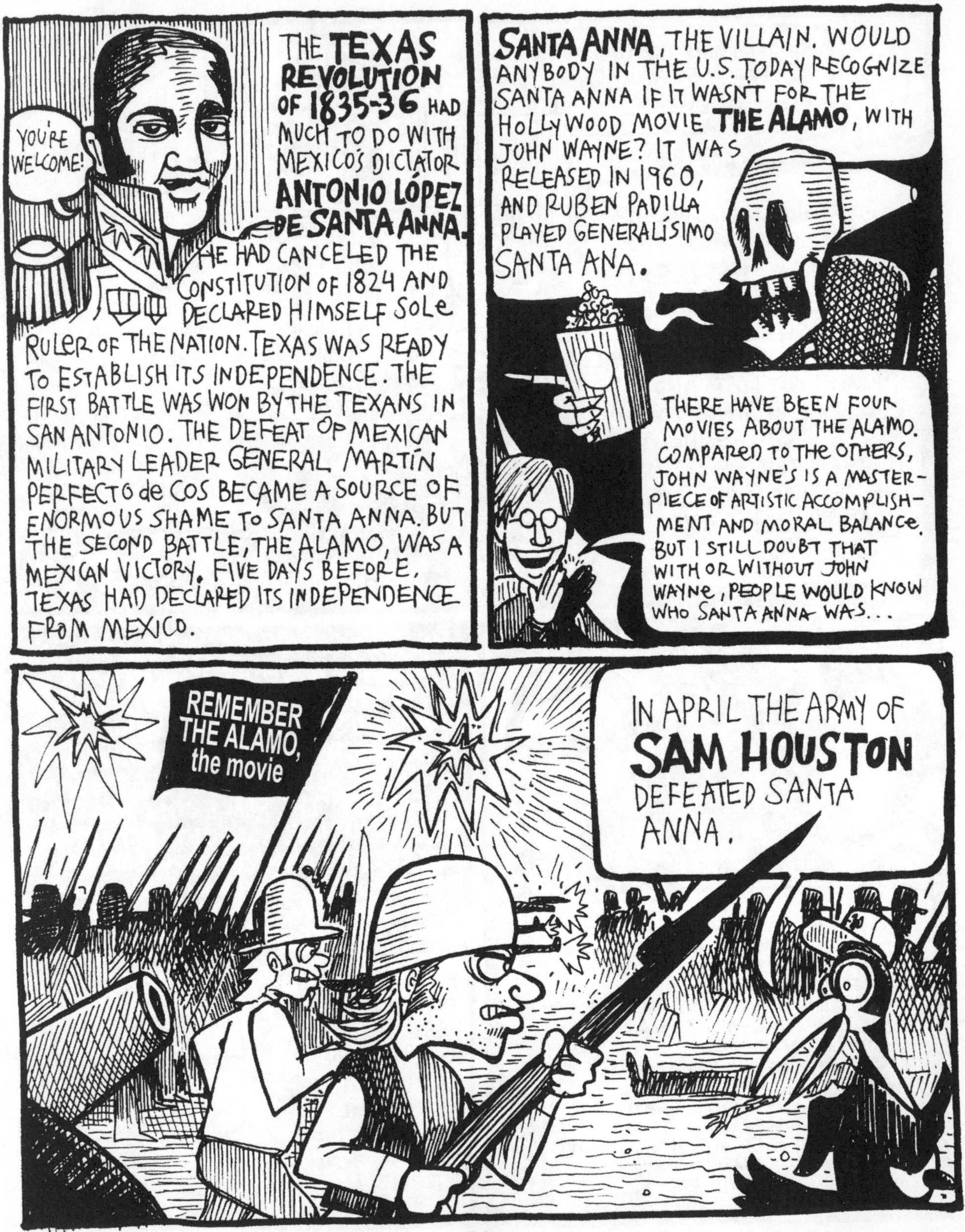
THE TEXAS REVOLUTION OF 1835-36 HAD MUCH TO DO WITH MEXICO'S DICTATOR ANTONIO LÓPEZ DE SANTA ANNA.
YOU'RE WELCOME!
HE HAD CANCELED THE CONSTITUTION OF 1824 AND DECLARED HIMSELF SOLE RULER OF THE NATION. TEXAS WAS READY TO ESTABLISH ITS INDEPENDENCE. THE FIRST BATTLE WAS WON BY THE TEXANS IN SAN ANTONIO. THE DEFEAT OF MEXICAN MILITARY LEADER GENERAL MARTÍN PERFECTO de COS BECAME A SOURCE OF ENORMOUS SHAME TO SANTA ANNA. BUT THE SECOND BATTLE, THE ALAMO, WAS A MEXICAN VICTORY. FIVE DAYS BEFORE, TEXAS HAD DECLARED ITS INDEPENDENCE FROM MEXICO.
SANTA ANNA, THE VILLAIN. WOULD ANYBODY IN THE U.S. TODAY RECOGNIZE SANTA ANNA IF IT WASN'T FOR THE HOLLYWOOD MOVIE THE ALAMO, WITH JOHN WAYNE? IT WAS RELEASED IN 1960, AND RUBEN PADILLA PLAYED GENERALÍSIMO SANTA ANA.
THERE HAVE BEEN FOUR MOVIES ABOUT THE ALAMO. COMPARED TO THE OTHERS, JOHN WAYNE'S IS A MASTERPIECE OF ARTISTIC ACCOMPLISHMENT AND MORAL BALANCE. BUT I STILL DOUBT THAT WITH OR WITHOUT JOHN WAYNE, PEOPLE WOULD KNOW WHO SANTA ANNA WAS...
REMEMBER THE ALAMO, the movie
IN APRIL THE ARMY OF SAM HOUSTON DEFEATED SANTA ANNA.

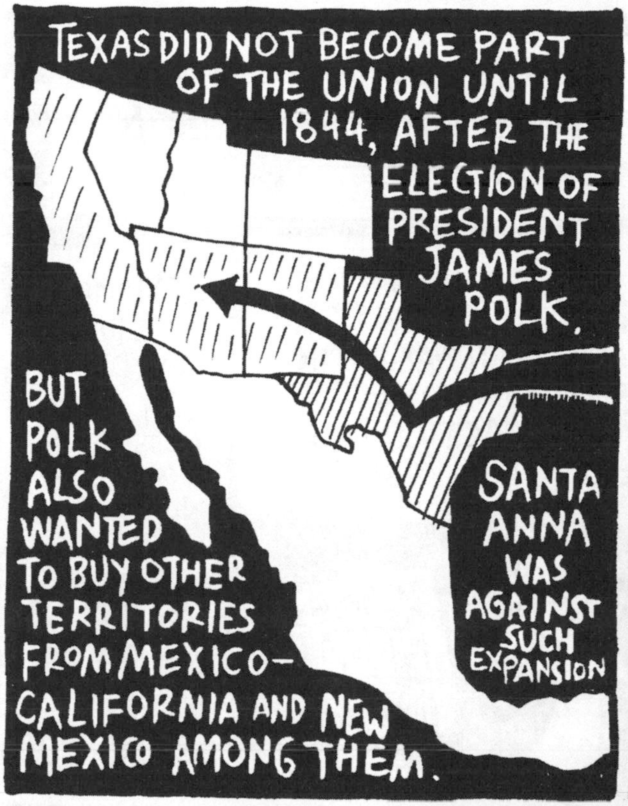
TEXAS DID NOT BECOME PART OF THE UNION UNTIL 1844, AFTER THE ELECTION OF PRESIDENT JAMES POLK.
BUT POLK ALSO WANTED TO BUY OTHER TERRITORIES FROM MEXICO-CALIFORNIA AND NEW MEXICO AMONG THEM.
SANTA ANNA WAS AGAINST SUCH EXPANSION

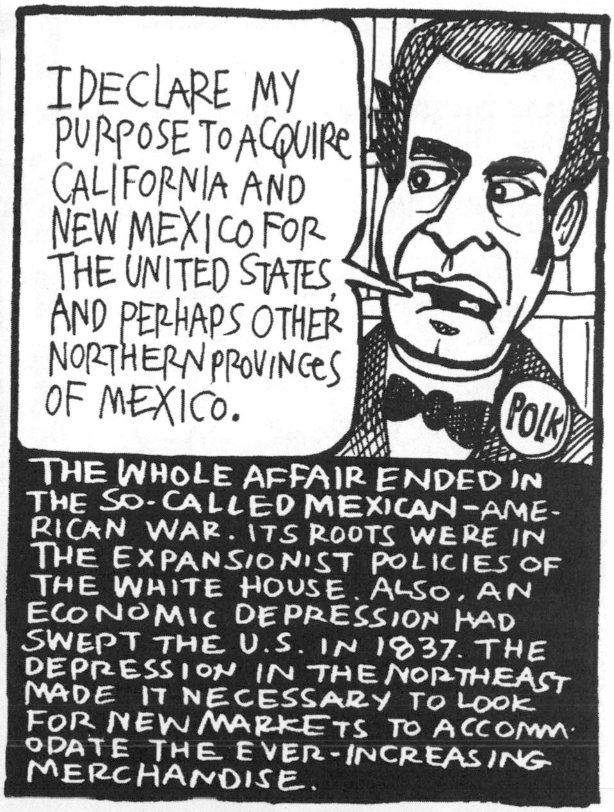
I DECLARE MY PURPOSE TO ACQUIRE CALIFORNIA AND NEW MEXICO FOR THE UNITED STATES, AND PERHAPS OTHER NORTHERN PROVINCES OF MEXICO.
POLK
THE WHOLE AFFAIR ENDED IN THE SO-CALLED MEXICAN-AMERICAN WAR. ITS ROOTS WERE IN THE EXPANSIONIST POLICIES OF THE WHITE HOUSE. ALSO, AN ECONOMIC DEPRESSION HAD SWEPT THE U.S. IN 1837. THE DEPRESSION IN THE NORTHEAST MADE IT NECESSARY TO LOOK FOR NEW MARKETS TO ACCOMMODATE THE EVER-INCREASING MERCHANDISE.

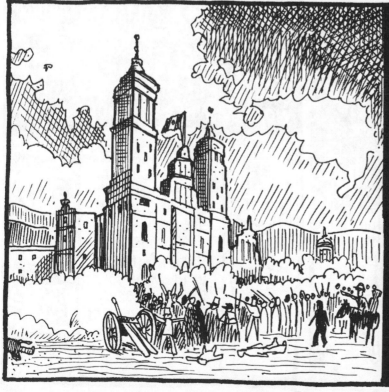

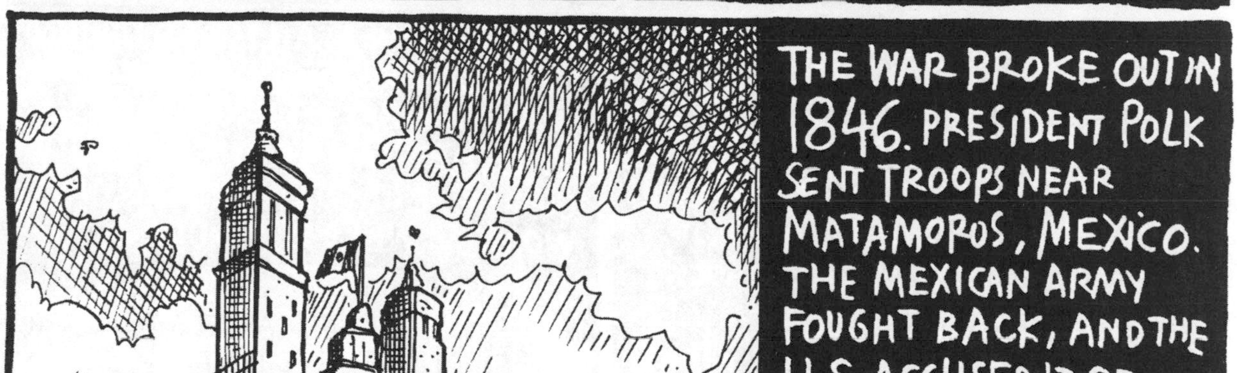
THE WAR BROKE OUT IN 1846. PRESIDENT POLK SENT TROOPS NEAR MATAMOROS, MEXICO. THE MEXICAN ARMY FOUGHT BACK, AND THE U.S. ACCUSED IT OF "INVADING AMERICAN TERRITORY." SO THE U.S. MILITARY ATTACKED THE CITY OF MONTERREY, MEXICO (THE CAPITAL OF THE STATE OF NUEVO LEÓN) AND MARCHED INTO SANTA FÉ AND TAOS.

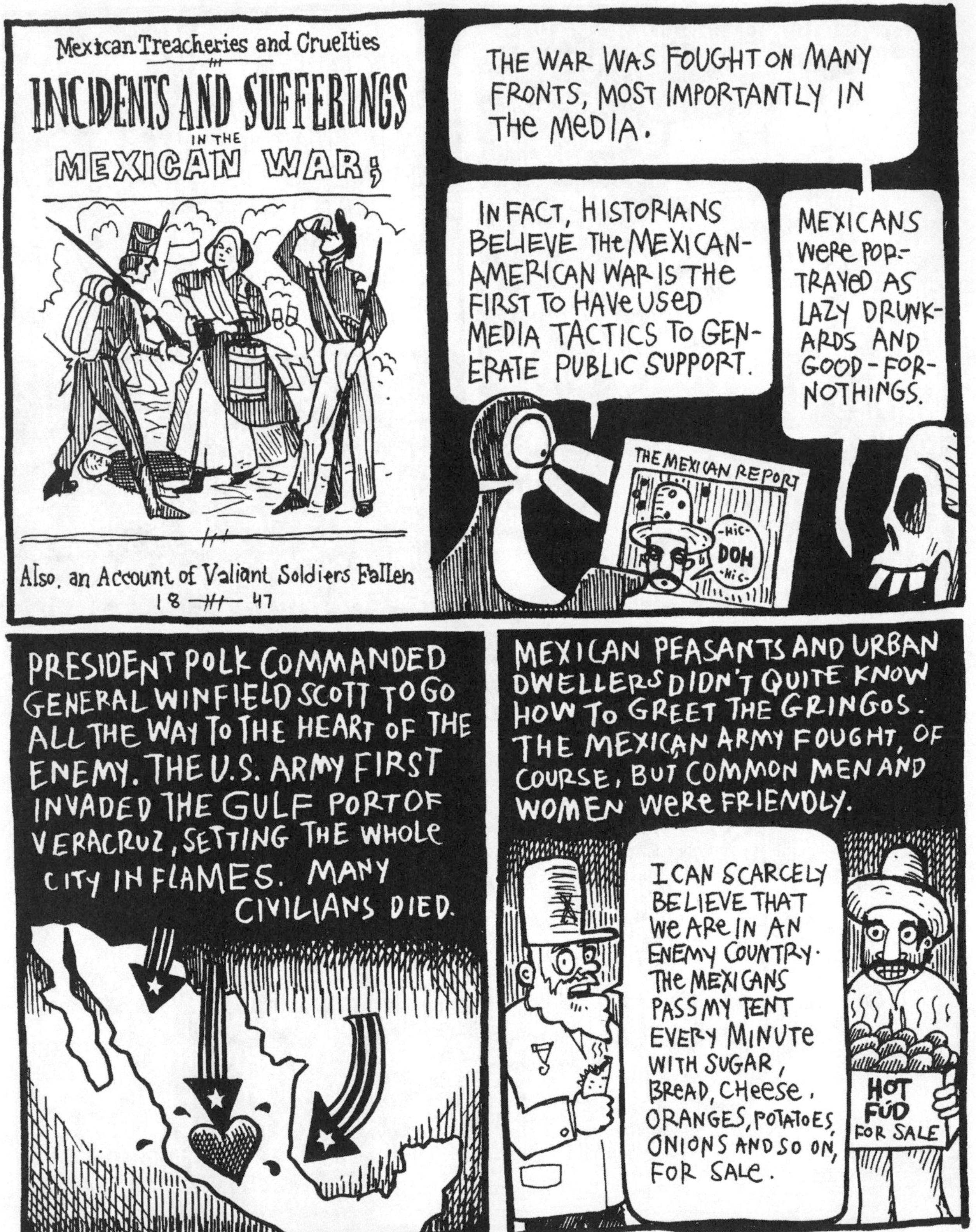
Mexican Treacheries and Cruelties
INCIDENTS AND SUFFERINGS IN THE MEXICAN WAR;
Also, an Account of Valiant Soldiers Fallen
1847
THE WAR WAS FOUGHT ON MANY FRONTS, MOST IMPORTANTLY IN THE MEDIA.
IN FACT, HISTORIANS BELIEVE THE MEXICAN-AMERICAN WAR IS THE FIRST TO HAVE USED MEDIA TACTICS TO GENERATE PUBLIC SUPPORT.
MEXICANS WERE PORTRAYED AS LAZY DRUNKARDS AND GOOD-FOR-NOTHINGS.
THE MEXICAN REPORT
-HIC-
DOH
-HIC-
PRESIDENT POLK COMMANDED GENERAL WINFIELD SCOTT TO GO ALL THE WAY TO THE HEART OF THE ENEMY. THE U.S. ARMY FIRST INVADED THE GULF PORT OF VERACRUZ, SETTING THE WHOLE CITY IN FLAMES. MANY CIVILIANS DIED.
MEXICAN PEASANTS AND URBAN DWELLERS DIDN'T QUITE KNOW HOW TO GREET THE GRINGOS. THE MEXICAN ARMY FOUGHT, OF COURSE, BUT COMMON MEN AND WOMEN WERE FRIENDLY.
I CAN SCARCELY BELIEVE THAT WE ARE IN AN ENEMY COUNTRY. THE MEXICANS PASS MY TENT EVERY MINUTE WITH SUGAR, BREAD, CHEESE, ORANGES, POTATOES, ONIONS AND SO ON, FOR SALE.
HOT FÚD FOR SALE

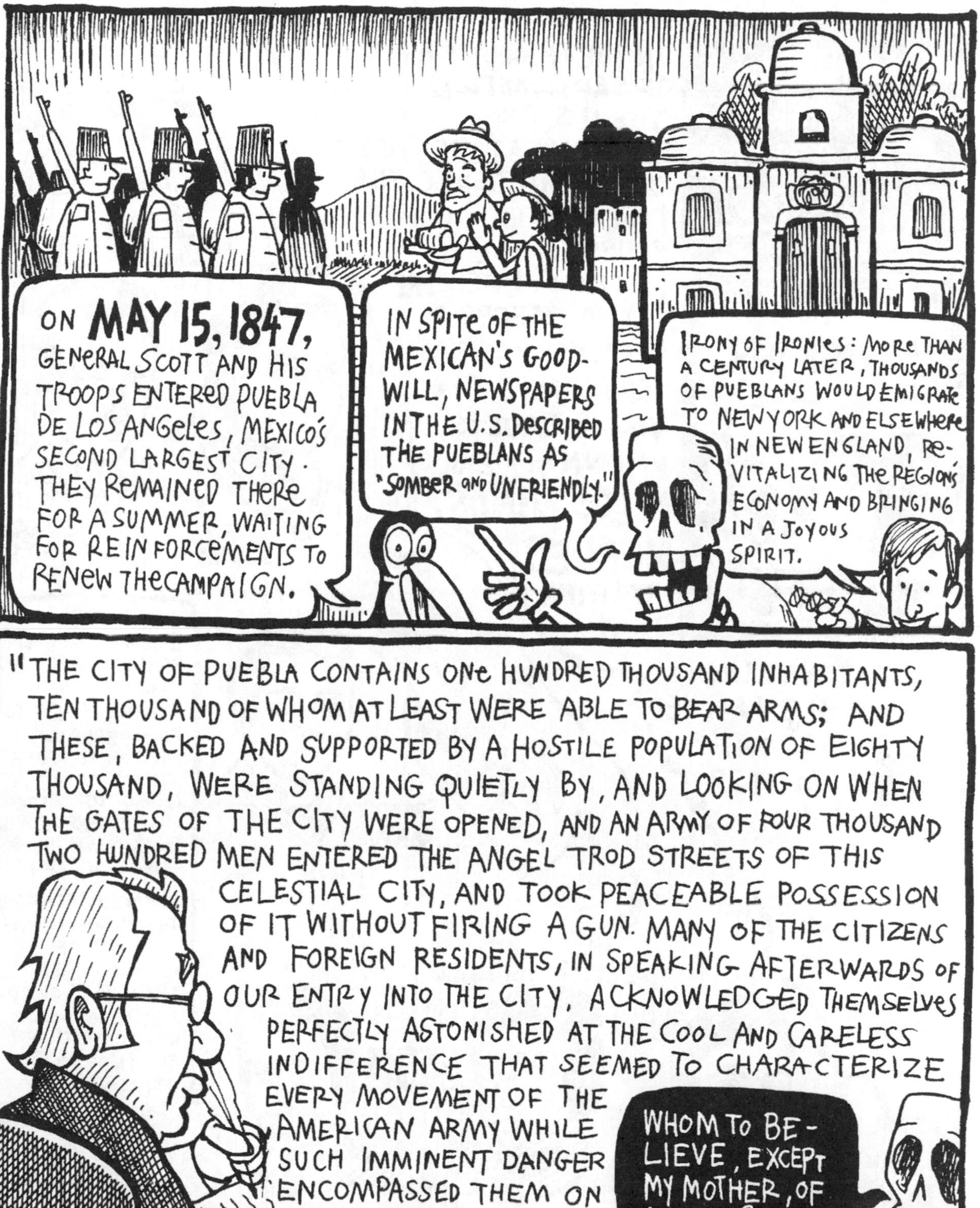
ON MAY 15, 1847, GENERAL SCOTT AND HIS TROOPS ENTERED PUEBLA DE LOS ANGELES, MEXICO'S SECOND LARGEST CITY. THEY REMAINED THERE FOR A SUMMER, WAITING FOR REINFORCEMENTS TO RENEW THE CAMPAIGN.
IN SPITE OF THE MEXICAN'S GOODWILL, NEWSPAPERS IN THE U.S. DESCRIBED THE PUEBLANS AS "SOMBER AND UNFRIENDLY."
IRONY OF IRONIES: MORE THAN A CENTURY LATER, THOUSANDS OF PUEBLANS WOULD EMIGRATE TO NEW YORK AND ELSEWHERE IN NEW ENGLAND, REVITALIZING THE REGION'S ECONOMY AND BRINGING IN A JOYOUS SPIRIT.
"THE CITY OF PUEBLA CONTAINS ONE HUNDRED THOUSAND INHABITANTS, TEN THOUSAND OF WHOM AT LEAST WERE ABLE TO BEAR ARMS; AND THESE, BACKED AND SUPPORTED BY A HOSTILE POPULATION OF EIGHTY THOUSAND, WERE STANDING QUIETLY BY, AND LOOKING ON WHEN THE GATES OF THE CITY WERE OPENED, AND AN ARMY OF FOUR THOUSAND TWO HUNDRED MEN ENTERED THE ANGEL TROD STREETS OF THIS CELESTIAL CITY, AND TOOK PEACEABLE POSSESSION OF IT WITHOUT FIRING A GUN. MANY OF THE CITIZENS AND FOREIGN RESIDENTS, IN SPEAKING AFTERWARDS OF OUR ENTRY INTO THE CITY, ACKNOWLEDGED THEMSELVES PERFECTLY ASTONISHED AT THE COOL AND CARELESS INDIFFERENCE THAT SEEMED TO CHARACTERIZE EVERY MOVEMENT OF THE AMERICAN ARMY WHILE SUCH IMMINENT DANGER ENCOMPASSED THEM ON ALL SIDES."
WHOM TO BELIEVE, EXCEPT MY MOTHER, OF COURSE?

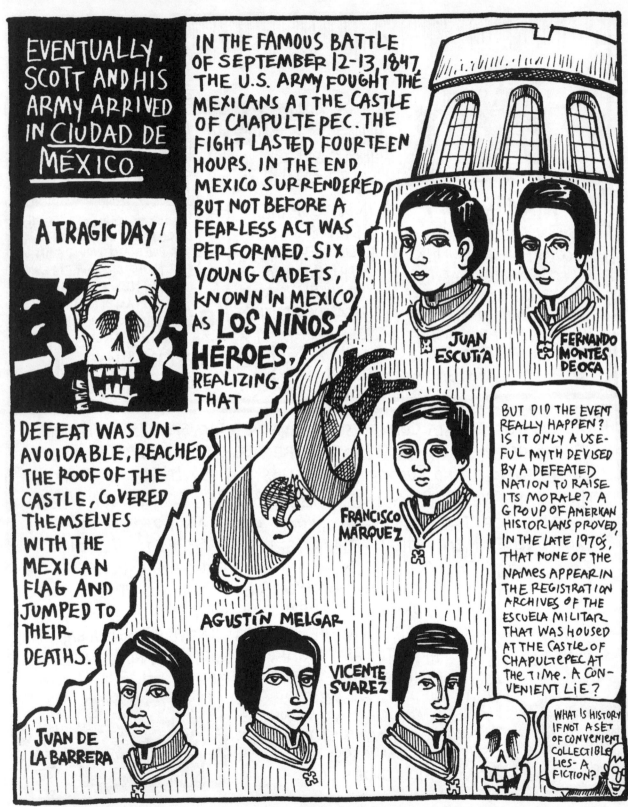

EVENTUALLY, SCOTT AND HIS ARMY ARRIVED IN <u>CIUDAD DE MÉXICO</u>.

A TRAGIC DAY!

IN THE FAMOUS BATTLE OF SEPTEMBER 12-13, 1847, THE U.S. ARMY FOUGHT THE MEXICANS AT THE CASTLE OF CHAPULTEPEC. THE FIGHT LASTED FOURTEEN HOURS. IN THE END MEXICO SURRENDERED BUT NOT BEFORE A FEARLESS ACT WAS PERFORMED. SIX YOUNG CADETS, KNOWN IN MEXICO AS **LOS NIÑOS HÉROES**, REALIZING THAT DEFEAT WAS UNAVOIDABLE, REACHED THE ROOF OF THE CASTLE, COVERED THEMSELVES WITH THE MEXICAN FLAG AND JUMPED TO THEIR DEATHS.

JUAN ESCUTÍA

FERNANDO MONTES DE OCA

FRANCISCO MÁRQUEZ

AGUSTÍN MELGAR

VICENTE SUÁREZ

JUAN DE LA BARRERA

BUT DID THE EVENT REALLY HAPPEN? IS IT ONLY A USEFUL MYTH DEVISED BY A DEFEATED NATION TO RAISE ITS MORALE? A GROUP OF AMERICAN HISTORIANS PROVED, IN THE LATE 1970's, THAT NONE OF THE NAMES APPEAR IN THE REGISTRATION ARCHIVES OF THE ESCUELA MILITAR THAT WAS HOUSED AT THE CASTLE OF CHAPULTEPEC AT THE TIME. A CONVENIENT LIE?

WHAT IS HISTORY IF NOT A SET OF CONVENIENT COLLECTIBLE LIES- A FICTION?

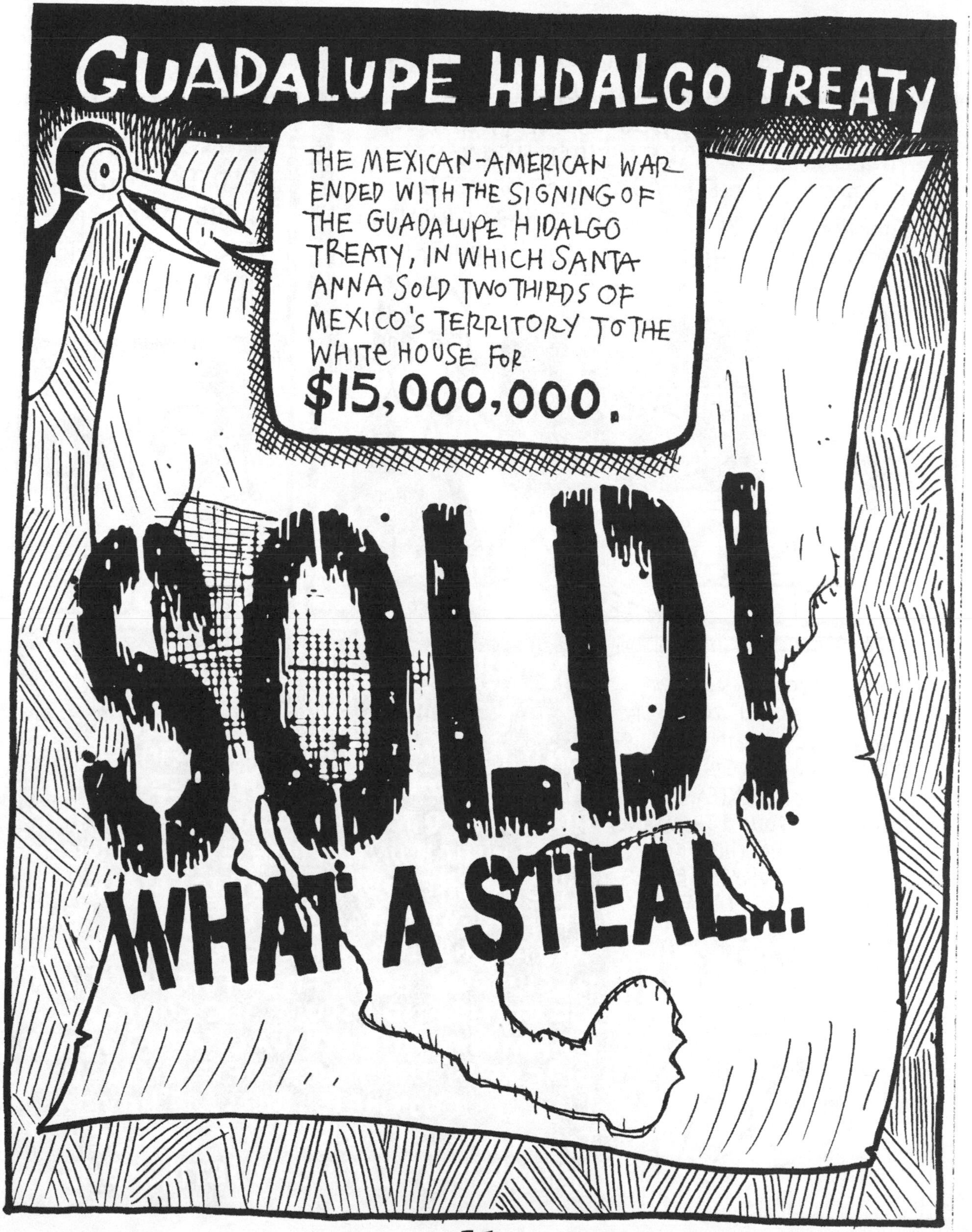
GUADALUPE HIDALGO TREATY
THE MEXICAN-AMERICAN WAR ENDED WITH THE SIGNING OF THE GUADALUPE HIDALGO TREATY, IN WHICH SANTA ANNA SOLD TWO THIRDS OF MEXICO'S TERRITORY TO THE WHITE HOUSE FOR $15,000,000.
SOLD!
WHAT A STEAL..

IN MEXICO, A FAMOUSLY CRUEL JOKE CLAIMS THAT THE COUNTRY HAD BEEN IN SUCH A TERRIBLE STATE BECAUSE OF TWO MAJOR HISTORICAL MISTAKES. FIRST, HERNÁN CORTÉS DIDN'T FULLY DESTROY THE AZTEC EMPIRE, HE ONLY SUBDUED IT. HAD HE REALLY "DESTROYED" IT, HISTORY WOULD HAVE BEEN TOTALLY DIFFERENT.

AND SECOND?

THE SECOND MISTAKE WAS SANTA ANNA'S. HE ONLY SOLD TWO-THIRDS OF THE MEXICAN TERRITORY, NOT THE WHOLE THING.

!!

SOME HISTORIANS ARGUE THAT LATINO HISTORY PER SE REALLY BEGINS AT THIS POINT, WHEN A CONSIDERABLE NUMBER OF MEXICANS SUDDENLY FOUND THEMSELVES LIVING WITHIN THE GEOGRAPHICAL BOUNDARIES OF THE UNITED STATES.

TREATY

!!

IN THE NAME OF ALMIGHTY GOD: THE UNITED STATES OF AMERICA, AND THE UNITED MEXICAN STATES, ANIMATED BY A SINCERE DESIRE TO PUT AN END TO THE CALAMITIES OF THE WAR WHICH UNHAPPILY EXISTS BETWEEN THE TWO REPUBLICS, AND TO ESTABLISH UPON A SOLID BASIS RELATIONS OF PEACE AND FRIENDSHIP, WHICH SHALL CONFER RECIPROCAL BENEFITS UPON THE CITIZENS OF BOTH, AND ASSURE THE CONCORD, HARMONY AND MUTUAL CONFIDENCE WHEREIN THE TWO PEOPLE SHOULD LIVE, AS GOOD NEIGHBORS ... [HAVE SIGNED THIS] TREATY OF PEACE, FRIENDSHIPS, LIMITS AND SETTLEMENTS ...

Article VIII

Mexicans now established in territories previously belonging to Mexico, and which remain for the future within the limits of the United States, as defined by the present treaty, shall be free to continue where they now reside, or to return at any time to the Mexican Republic, retaining the property which they posses in the said territiories, or disposing thereof, and removing the proceeds wherever they please; without their being subjected, on this account, to any contribution, tax or change whatever.

Article IX

The Mexicans who, in the territories aforementioned, shall not preserve the character of citizens of the Mexican republic, comfortably with what is stipulated in the preceding article, shall be incorporated into the Union of the United States and be admitted, at the proper time (to be judged of by the Congress of the United States) to the enjoyment of all the rights of citizens...

THIS MEANS MEXICANS COULD DECIDE TO BECOME U.S. CITIZENS OR PACK THEIR BAGS AND LEAVE FOR MEXICO. A DIFFICULT CHOICE, DON'T YOU THINK? WHAT WOULD YOU DO? REMAIN IN ENEMY LAND?

IT WASN'T THAT SIMPLE! MOST MEXICAN FRONTIER DWELLERS IN NEW MEXICO, CALIFORNIA, AND ARIZONA HAD AMBIVALENT FEELINGS TOWARD THE CORRUPT GOVERNMENT IN CIUDAD DE MEXICO, AND ESPECIALLY TOWARD SANTA ANNA

AND WHAT ABOUT THE SPANISH LANGUAGE? WAS IT DECLARED ILLEGAL? WAS THE ENGLISH LANGUAGE FORCED ON THOSE IN THE NEWLY ACQUIRED TERRITORIES?

THE ISSUE OF LANGUAGE WAS COMPLICATED. ENGLISH WAS QUICKLY INSTALLED AS THE BUSINESS TONGUE, FORCING SPANISH INTO THE PRIVATE DOMESTIC REALM.

〈ESPAÑOL〉

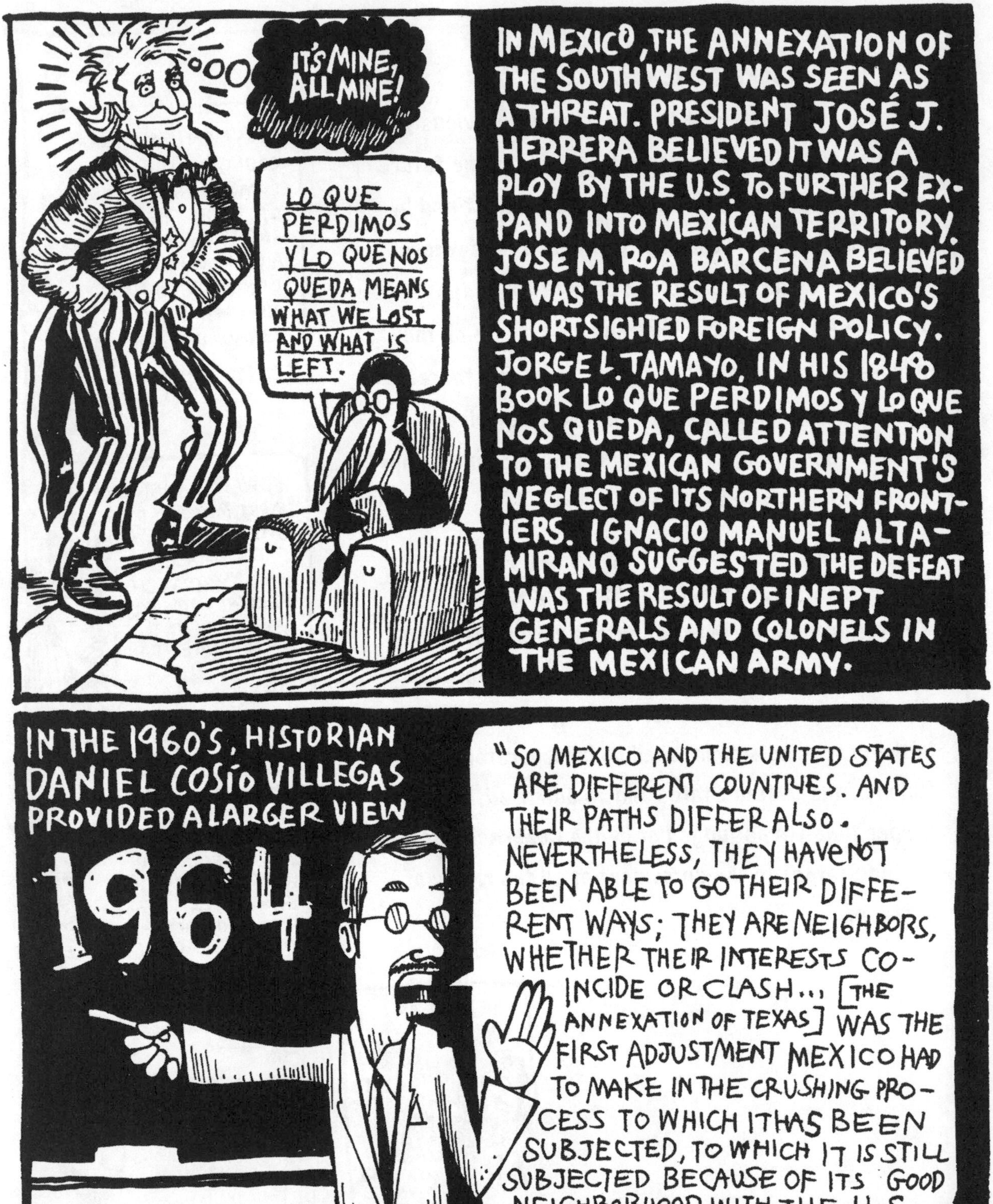
IT'S MINE, ALL MINE!
LO QUE PERDIMOS Y LO QUE NOS QUEDA MEANS WHAT WE LOST AND WHAT IS LEFT.
IN MEXICO, THE ANNEXATION OF THE SOUTHWEST WAS SEEN AS A THREAT. PRESIDENT JOSÉ J. HERRERA BELIEVED IT WAS A PLOY BY THE U.S. TO FURTHER EXPAND INTO MEXICAN TERRITORY. JOSE M. ROA BÁRCENA BELIEVED IT WAS THE RESULT OF MEXICO'S SHORTSIGHTED FOREIGN POLICY. JORGE L. TAMAYO, IN HIS 1848 BOOK LO QUE PERDIMOS Y LO QUE NOS QUEDA, CALLED ATTENTION TO THE MEXICAN GOVERNMENT'S NEGLECT OF ITS NORTHERN FRONTIERS. IGNACIO MANUEL ALTAMIRANO SUGGESTED THE DEFEAT WAS THE RESULT OF INEPT GENERALS AND COLONELS IN THE MEXICAN ARMY.
IN THE 1960'S, HISTORIAN DANIEL COSÍO VILLEGAS PROVIDED A LARGER VIEW
1964
"SO MEXICO AND THE UNITED STATES ARE DIFFERENT COUNTRIES. AND THEIR PATHS DIFFER ALSO. NEVERTHELESS, THEY HAVE NOT BEEN ABLE TO GO THEIR DIFFERENT WAYS; THEY ARE NEIGHBORS, WHETHER THEIR INTERESTS COINCIDE OR CLASH... [THE ANNEXATION OF TEXAS] WAS THE FIRST ADJUSTMENT MEXICO HAD TO MAKE IN THE CRUSHING PROCESS TO WHICH IT HAS BEEN SUBJECTED, TO WHICH IT IS STILL SUBJECTED BECAUSE OF ITS GOOD NEIGHBORHOOD WITH THE U.S.

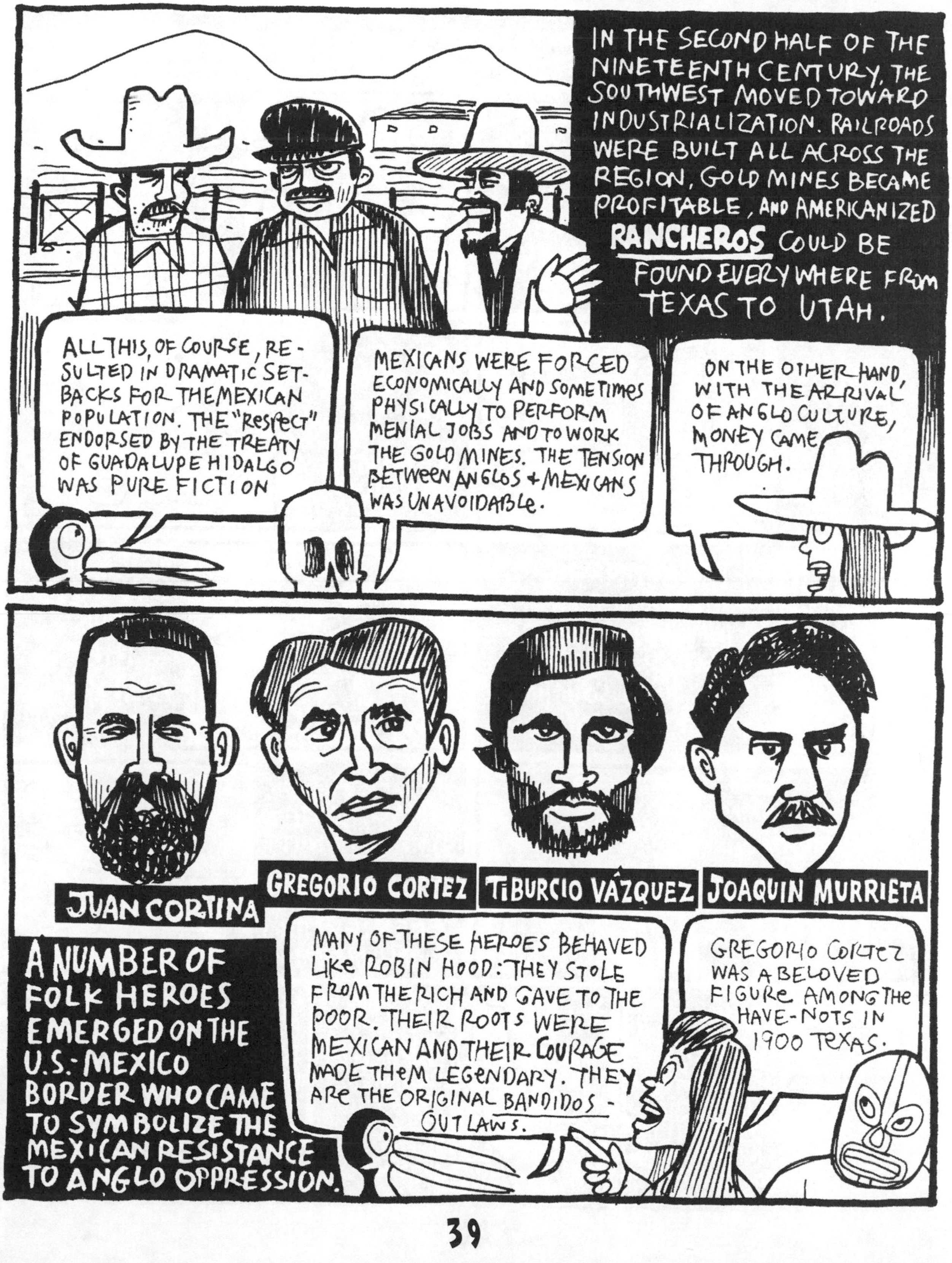
IN THE SECOND HALF OF THE NINETEENTH CENTURY, THE SOUTHWEST MOVED TOWARD INDUSTRIALIZATION. RAILROADS WERE BUILT ALL ACROSS THE REGION, GOLD MINES BECAME PROFITABLE, AND AMERICANIZED RANCHEROS COULD BE FOUND EVERYWHERE FROM TEXAS TO UTAH.
ALL THIS, OF COURSE, RESULTED IN DRAMATIC SETBACKS FOR THE MEXICAN POPULATION. THE "RESPECT" ENDORSED BY THE TREATY OF GUADALUPE HIDALGO WAS PURE FICTION
MEXICANS WERE FORCED ECONOMICALLY AND SOMETIMES PHYSICALLY TO PERFORM MENIAL JOBS AND TO WORK THE GOLD MINES. THE TENSION BETWEEN ANGLOS + MEXICANS WAS UNAVOIDABLE.
ON THE OTHER HAND, WITH THE ARRIVAL OF ANGLO CULTURE, MONEY CAME THROUGH.
JUAN CORTINA
GREGORIO CORTEZ
TIBURCIO VÁZQUEZ
JOAQUIN MURRIETA
A NUMBER OF FOLK HEROES EMERGED ON THE U.S.-MEXICO BORDER WHO CAME TO SYMBOLIZE THE MEXICAN RESISTANCE TO ANGLO OPPRESSION.
MANY OF THESE HEROES BEHAVED LIKE ROBIN HOOD: THEY STOLE FROM THE RICH AND GAVE TO THE POOR. THEIR ROOTS WERE MEXICAN AND THEIR COURAGE MADE THEM LEGENDARY. THEY ARE THE ORIGINAL BANDIDOS - OUTLAWS.
GREGORIO CORTEZ WAS A BELOVED FIGURE AMONG THE HAVE-NOTS IN 1900 TEXAS.

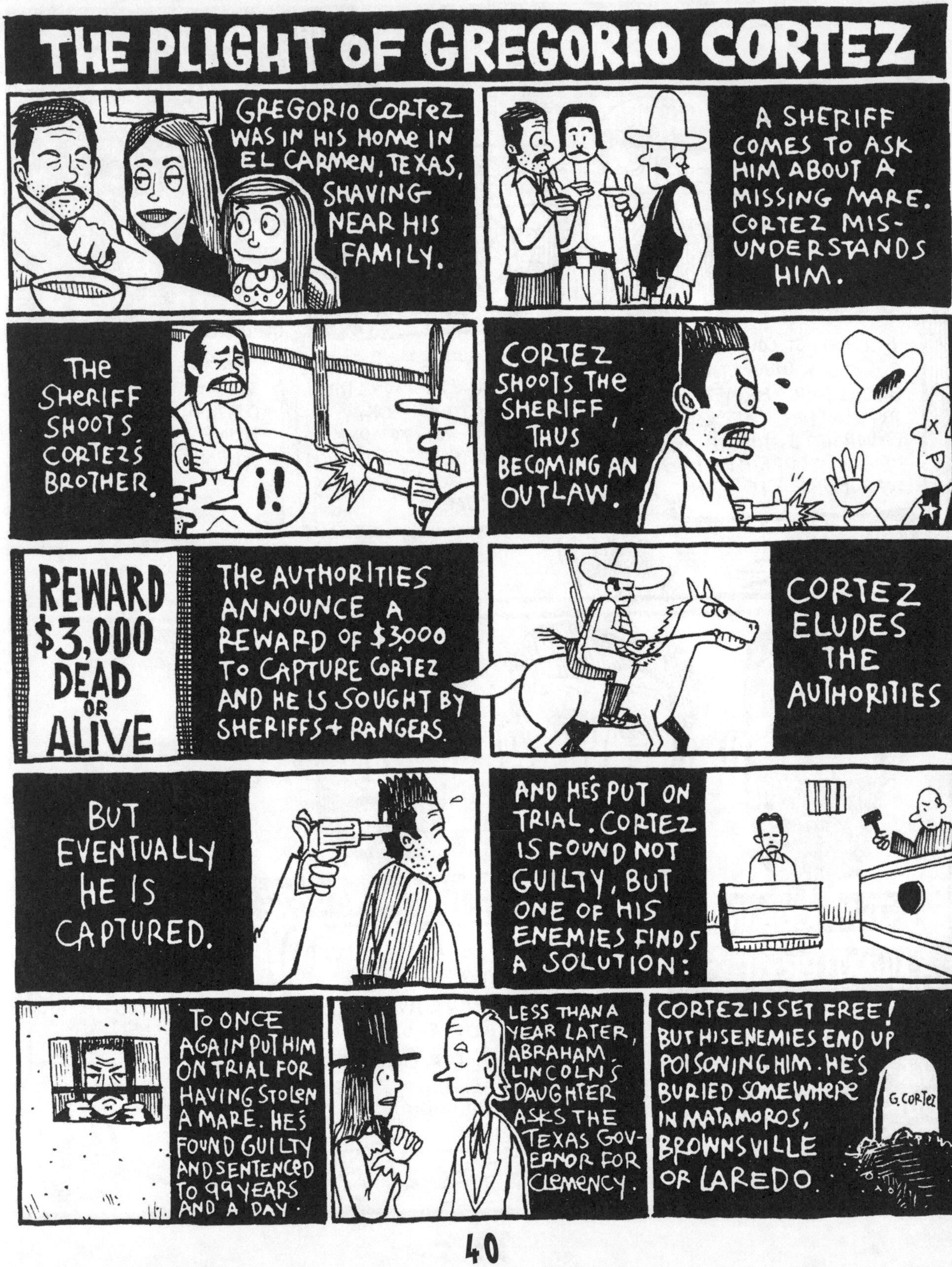
THE PLIGHT OF GREGORIO CORTEZ
GREGORIO CORTEZ WAS IN HIS HOME IN EL CARMEN, TEXAS, SHAVING NEAR HIS FAMILY.
A SHERIFF COMES TO ASK HIM ABOUT A MISSING MARE. CORTEZ MIS-UNDERSTANDS HIM.
THE SHERIFF SHOOTS CORTEZ'S BROTHER.
¡!
CORTEZ SHOOTS THE SHERIFF, THUS BECOMING AN OUTLAW.
REWARD $3,000 DEAD OR ALIVE
THE AUTHORITIES ANNOUNCE A REWARD OF $3,000 TO CAPTURE CORTEZ AND HE IS SOUGHT BY SHERIFFS + RANGERS.
CORTEZ ELUDES THE AUTHORITIES
BUT EVENTUALLY HE IS CAPTURED.
AND HE'S PUT ON TRIAL. CORTEZ IS FOUND NOT GUILTY, BUT ONE OF HIS ENEMIES FINDS A SOLUTION:
TO ONCE AGAIN PUT HIM ON TRIAL FOR HAVING STOLEN A MARE. HE'S FOUND GUILTY AND SENTENCED TO 99 YEARS AND A DAY.
LESS THAN A YEAR LATER, ABRAHAM LINCOLN'S DAUGHTER ASKS THE TEXAS GOVERNOR FOR CLEMENCY.
CORTEZ IS SET FREE! BUT HIS ENEMIES END UP POISONING HIM. HE'S BURIED SOMEWHERE IN MATAMOROS, BROWNSVILLE OR LAREDO.
G. CORTEZ

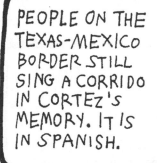

PEOPLE ON THE TEXAS-MEXICO BORDER STILL SING A CORRIDO IN CORTEZ'S MEMORY. IT IS IN SPANISH.

A CORRIDO IS A BORDER SONG — A BALLAD — CELEBRATING THE LIFE AND ACHIEVEMENTS OF A FOLK HERO.

THIS IS HOW PARTS OF IT WOULD GO IN ENGLISH. IT'S BEAUTY IS LOST IN THE TRANSLATION.

YO NO SOY AMERICANO
PERO COMPRENDO EL INGLÉS
YO LO APRENDÍ CON MI HERMANO
AL DERECHO Y AL REVÉS

A CUALQUIER AMERICANO
LO HAGO
TEMBLAR A MIS PIES

"The Ballad of Gregorio Cortez"

In the county of El Carmen
Look what has happened;
The Major Sheriff died,
Leaving Román badly wounded.

The next day, in the morning,
When people arrived,
They said to one another,
"It is known who killed him."

They went around asking questions,
About three hours afterward;
They found the wrongdoer
Has been Gregorio Cortez.

Now they have outlawed Cortez
Throughout the whole state;
Let him be taken, dead or alive;
He has killed several men.

Then said Gregorio Cortez,
with his pistol in his hand,
"I don't regret that I killed him;
I regret my brother's death."

The Americans were coming;
They seemed to fly through the air;
Because they were going to get
Three thousand dollars they offered.

He struck out for Gonzales;
Several sheriffs saw him;
They decided not to follow
Because they were
    afraid of him.

GREGORIO CORTEZ
T-SHIRTS XL
ONLY

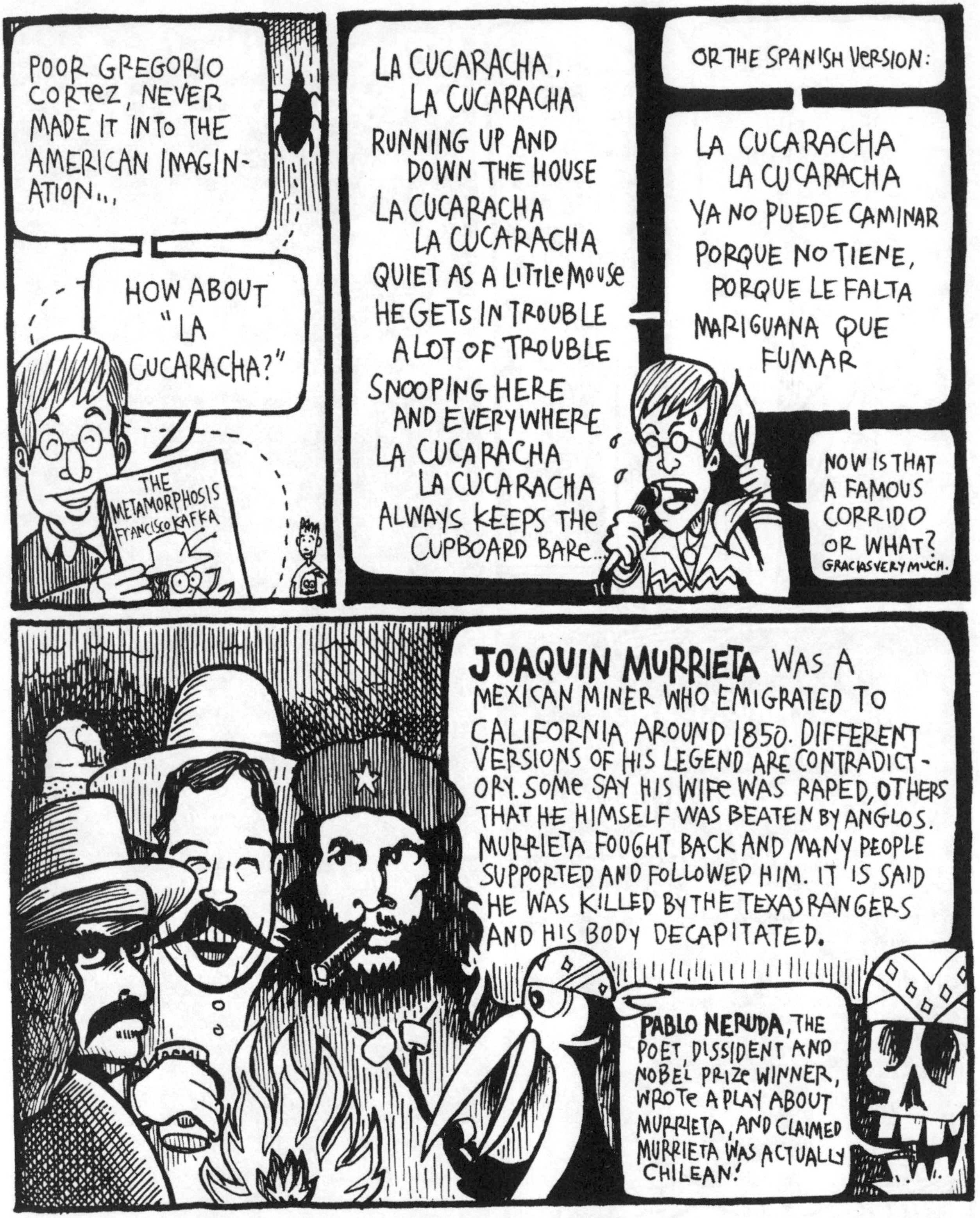
POOR GREGORIO CORTEZ, NEVER MADE IT INTO THE AMERICAN IMAGINATION...
HOW ABOUT "LA CUCARACHA?"
THE METAMORPHOSIS FRANCISCO KAFKA
LA CUCARACHA, LA CUCARACHA RUNNING UP AND DOWN THE HOUSE LA CUCARACHA LA CUCARACHA QUIET AS A LITTLE MOUSE HE GETS IN TROUBLE A LOT OF TROUBLE SNOOPING HERE AND EVERYWHERE LA CUCARACHA LA CUCARACHA ALWAYS KEEPS THE CUPBOARD BARE...
OR THE SPANISH VERSION:
LA CUCARACHA LA CUCARACHA YA NO PUEDE CAMINAR PORQUE NO TIENE, PORQUE LE FALTA MARIGUANA QUE FUMAR
NOW IS THAT A FAMOUS CORRIDO OR WHAT? GRACIAS VERY MUCH.
JOAQUIN MURRIETA WAS A MEXICAN MINER WHO EMIGRATED TO CALIFORNIA AROUND 1850. DIFFERENT VERSIONS OF HIS LEGEND ARE CONTRADICTORY. SOME SAY HIS WIFE WAS RAPED, OTHERS THAT HE HIMSELF WAS BEATEN BY ANGLOS. MURRIETA FOUGHT BACK AND MANY PEOPLE SUPPORTED AND FOLLOWED HIM. IT IS SAID HE WAS KILLED BY THE TEXAS RANGERS AND HIS BODY DECAPITATED.
PABLO NERUDA, THE POET, DISSIDENT AND NOBEL PRIZE WINNER, WROTE A PLAY ABOUT MURRIETA, AND CLAIMED MURRIETA WAS ACTUALLY CHILEAN!

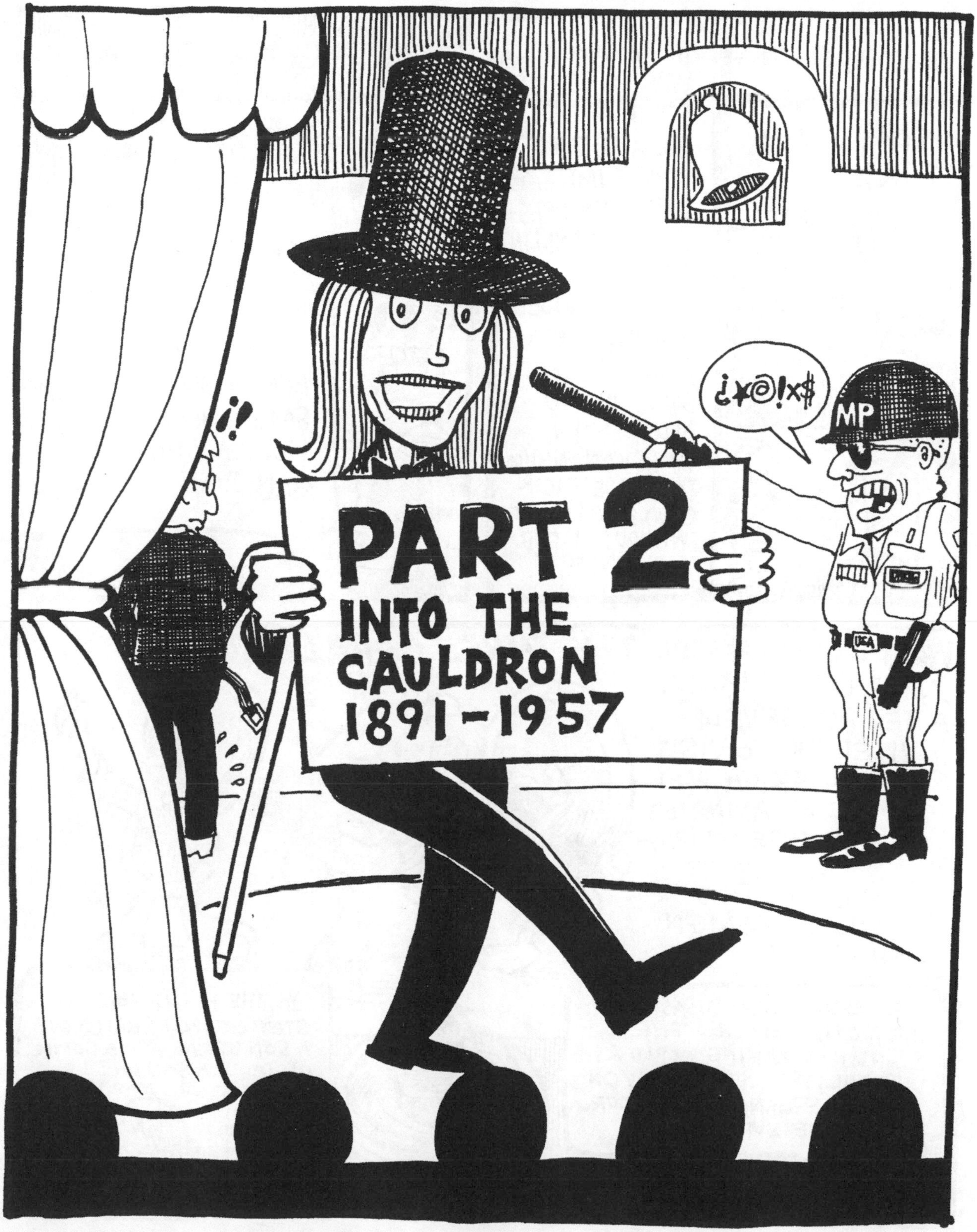
¡!
PART 2
INTO THE
CAULDRON
1891-1957
¿¥@!x$
MP

WHAT DID THE **GOOD NEIGHBOR POLICY** STAND FOR?

IN SPANISH IT WAS CALLED "LA POLITICA DEL BUEN VECINO." IT WAS IMPLEMENTED BY PRESIDENT FRANKLIN DELANO ROOSEVELT. IT WAS DEVISED SO THAT THE ALMIGHTY UNITED STATES WOULD ALLOW LATIN AMERICAN NATIONS TO CHOOSE THEIR OWN GOVERNMENT WITHOUT INTERFERENCE.

LESSON #14 — FDR

1935 FDR

BUT IT WAS SELDOM IMPLEMENTED.

IN FACT, IT ONLY SERVED TO STRESS THE DIVISION BETWEEN THE HAVES AND THE HAVE-NOTS, SAY BETWEEN FLORIDA AND SAN JUAN.

FDR

TODAY

WALT DISNEY CREATED ***THE THREE CABALLEROS*** IN THE LATE THIRTIES AFTER ROOSEVELT INVITED HIM TO VISIT SOUTH AMERICA AND PRODUCE AN ANIMATED MOTION PICTURE PORTRAYING THE NEIGHBORS SOUTH OF THE RIO GRANDE AS BENIGN SIMPÁTICOS.

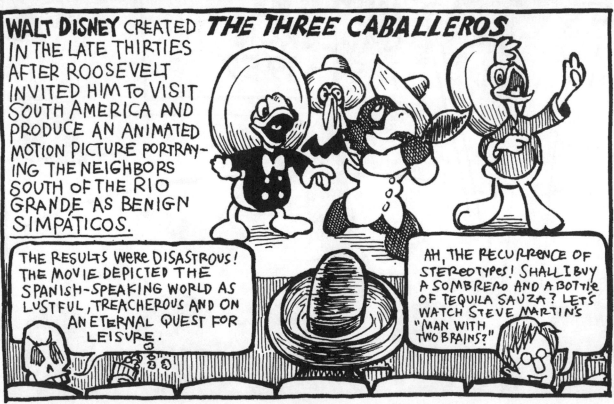

THE RESULTS WERE DISASTROUS! THE MOVIE DEPICTED THE SPANISH-SPEAKING WORLD AS LUSTFUL, TREACHEROUS AND ON AN ETERNAL QUEST FOR LEISURE.

AH, THE RECURRENCE OF STEREOTYPES! SHALL I BUY A SOMBRERO AND A BOTTLE OF TEQUILA SAUZA? LET'S WATCH STEVE MARTIN'S "MAN WITH TWO BRAINS?"

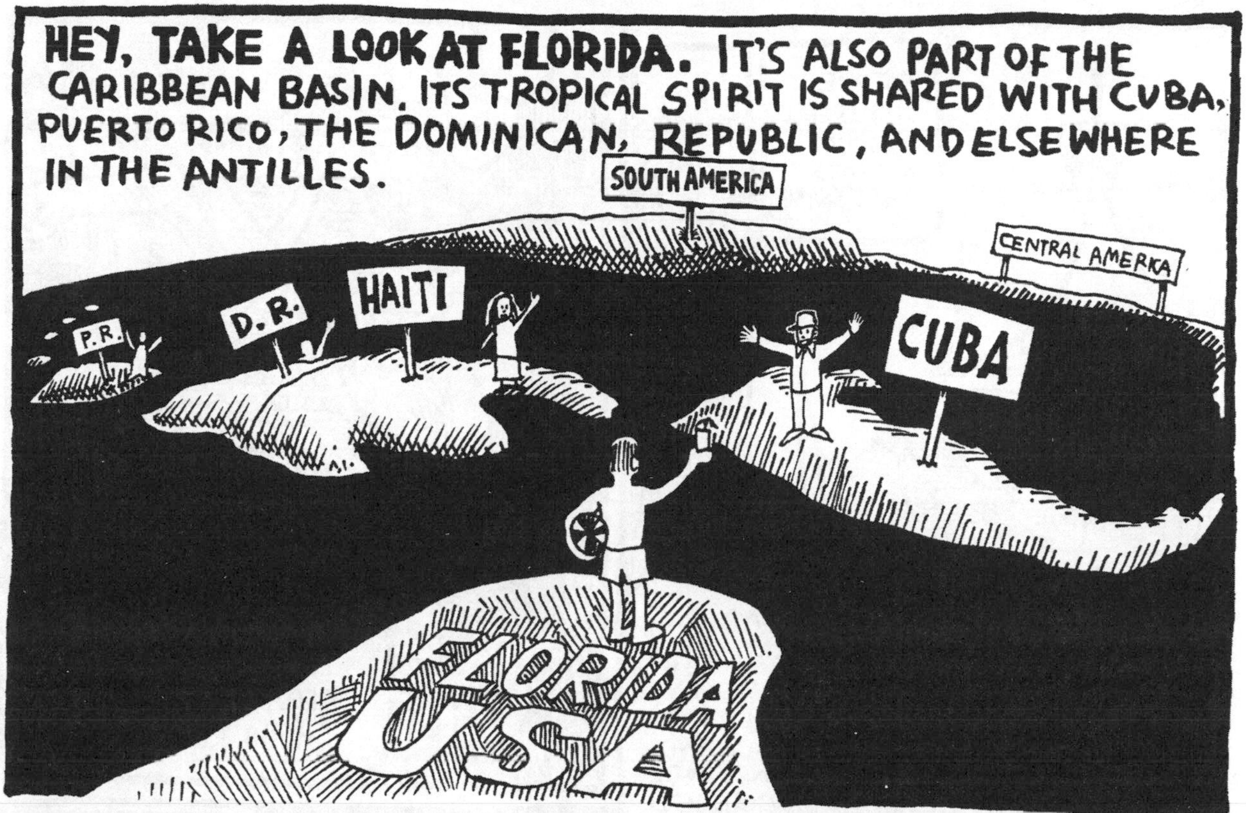
HEY, TAKE A LOOK AT FLORIDA. IT'S ALSO PART OF THE CARIBBEAN BASIN. ITS TROPICAL SPIRIT IS SHARED WITH CUBA, PUERTO RICO, THE DOMINICAN REPUBLIC, AND ELSEWHERE IN THE ANTILLES.
SOUTH AMERICA
CENTRAL AMERICA
P.R.
D.R.
HAITI
CUBA
FLORIDA
USA

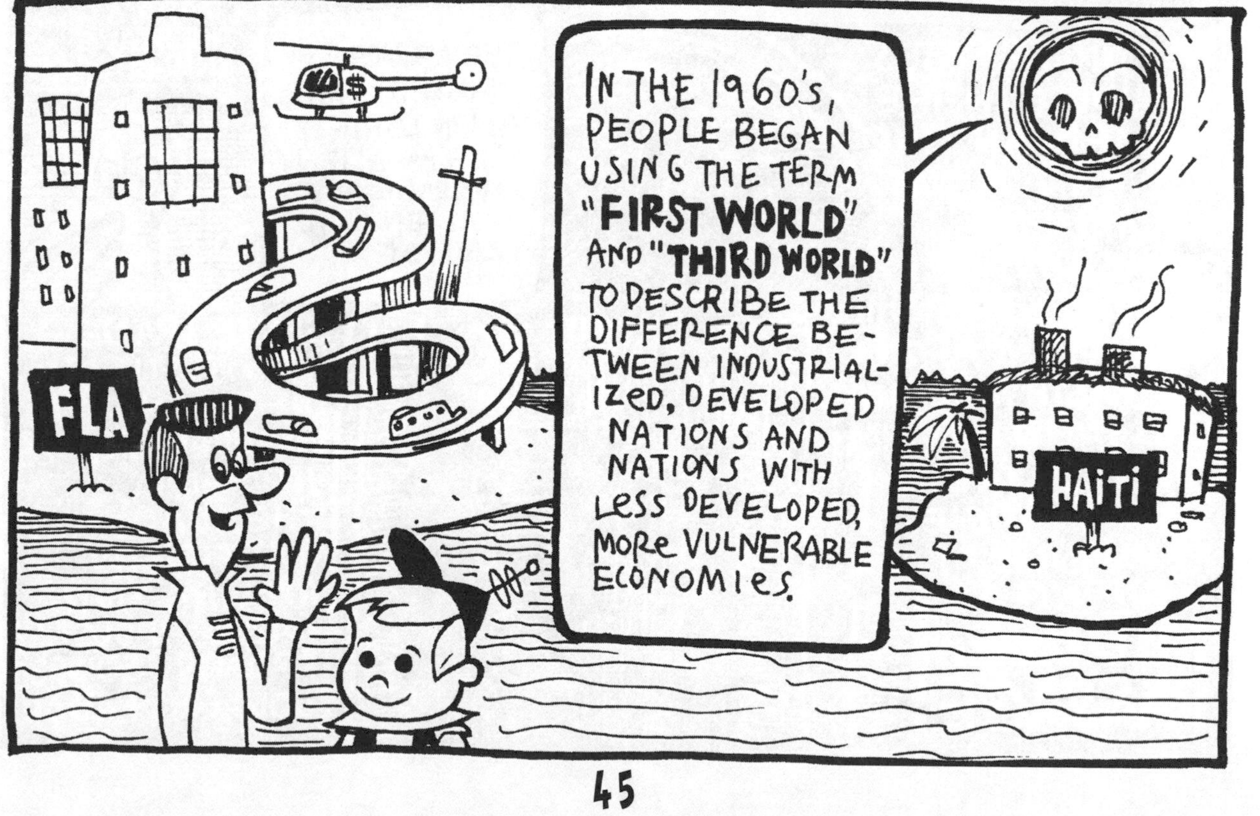
IN THE 1960'S, PEOPLE BEGAN USING THE TERM "FIRST WORLD" AND "THIRD WORLD" TO DESCRIBE THE DIFFERENCE BETWEEN INDUSTRIALIZED, DEVELOPED NATIONS AND NATIONS WITH LESS DEVELOPED, MORE VULNERABLE ECONOMIES.
FLA
HAITI

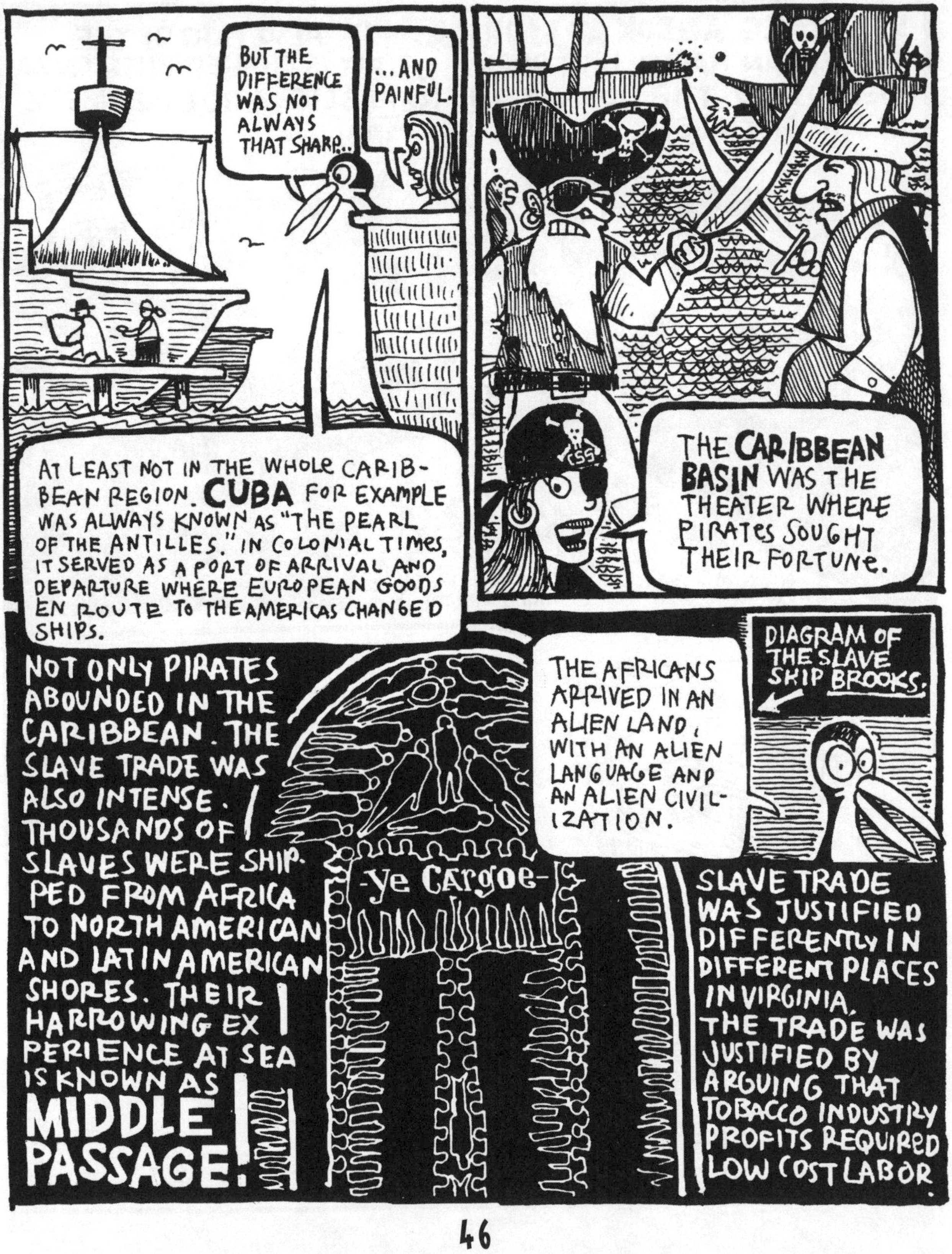
BUT THE DIFFERENCE WAS NOT ALWAYS THAT SHARP...
...AND PAINFUL.
AT LEAST NOT IN THE WHOLE CARIBBEAN REGION. CUBA FOR EXAMPLE WAS ALWAYS KNOWN AS "THE PEARL OF THE ANTILLES." IN COLONIAL TIMES, IT SERVED AS A PORT OF ARRIVAL AND DEPARTURE WHERE EUROPEAN GOODS EN ROUTE TO THE AMERICAS CHANGED SHIPS.
CSS
THE CARIBBEAN BASIN WAS THE THEATER WHERE PIRATES SOUGHT THEIR FORTUNE.
NOT ONLY PIRATES ABOUNDED IN THE CARIBBEAN. THE SLAVE TRADE WAS ALSO INTENSE. THOUSANDS OF SLAVES WERE SHIPPED FROM AFRICA TO NORTH AMERICAN AND LATIN AMERICAN SHORES. THEIR HARROWING EXPERIENCE AT SEA IS KNOWN AS MIDDLE PASSAGE!
-Ye Cargoe-
THE AFRICANS ARRIVED IN AN ALIEN LAND, WITH AN ALIEN LANGUAGE AND AN ALIEN CIVILIZATION.
DIAGRAM OF THE SLAVE SHIP BROOKS.
SLAVE TRADE WAS JUSTIFIED DIFFERENTLY IN DIFFERENT PLACES IN VIRGINIA, THE TRADE WAS JUSTIFIED BY ARGUING THAT TOBACCO INDUSTRY PROFITS REQUIRED LOW COST LABOR.

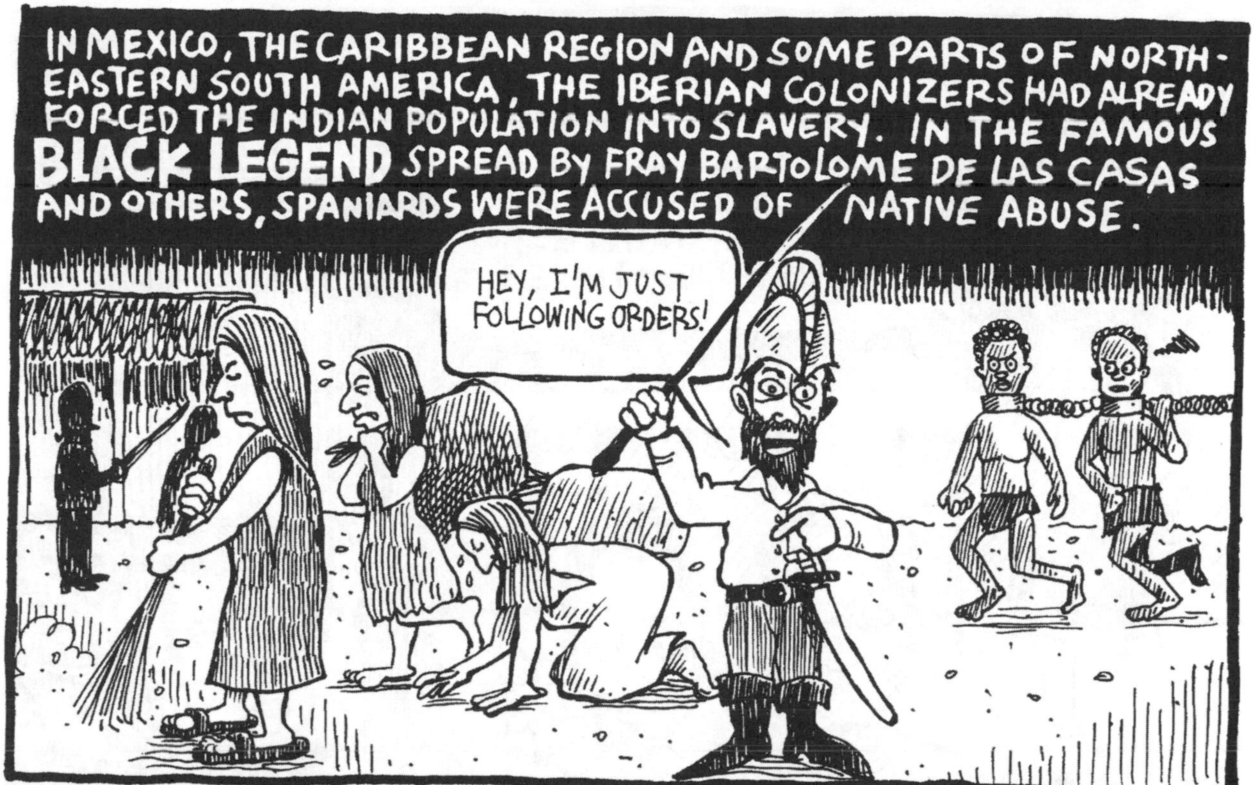
IN MEXICO, THE CARIBBEAN REGION AND SOME PARTS OF NORTH-EASTERN SOUTH AMERICA, THE IBERIAN COLONIZERS HAD ALREADY FORCED THE INDIAN POPULATION INTO SLAVERY. IN THE FAMOUS BLACK LEGEND SPREAD BY FRAY BARTOLOME DE LAS CASAS AND OTHERS, SPANIARDS WERE ACCUSED OF NATIVE ABUSE.
HEY, I'M JUST FOLLOWING ORDERS!

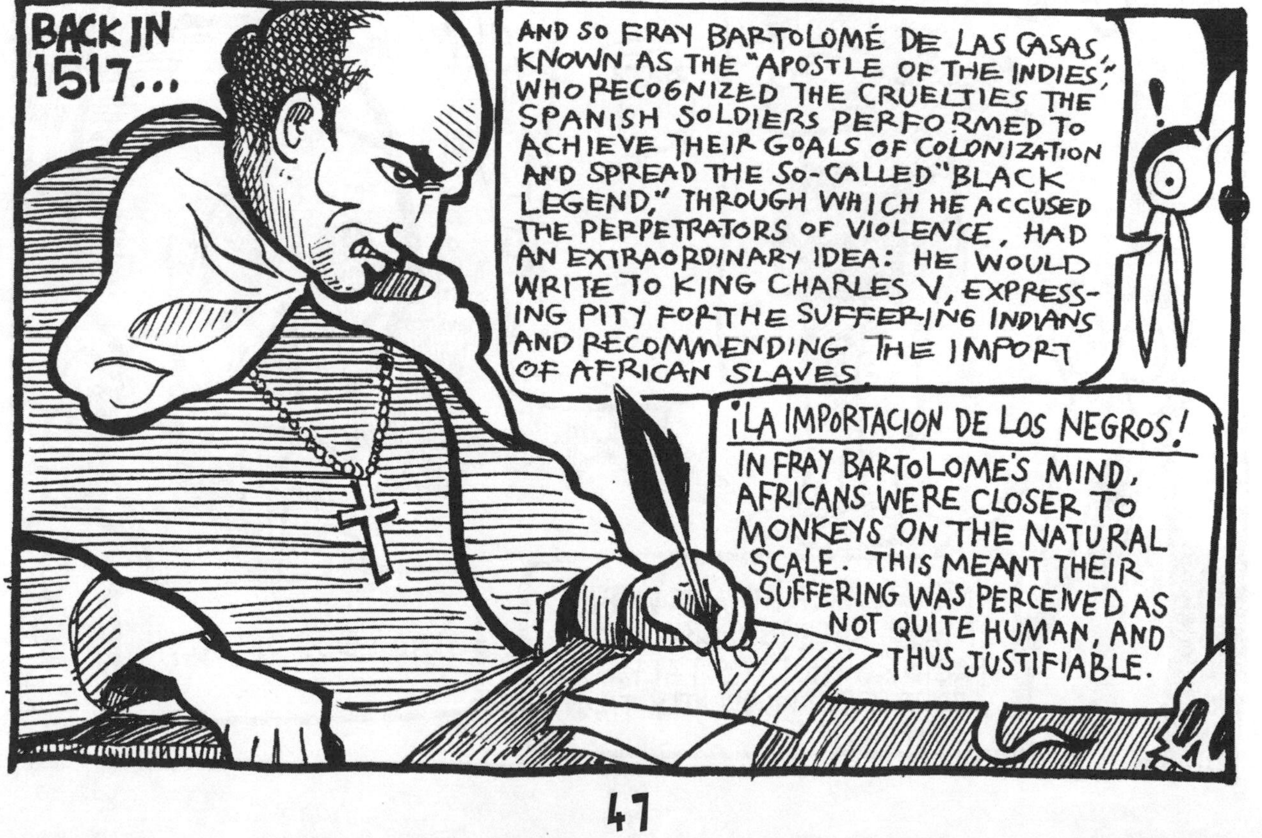
BACK IN 1517...
AND SO FRAY BARTOLOMÉ DE LAS CASAS, KNOWN AS THE "APOSTLE OF THE INDIES," WHO RECOGNIZED THE CRUELTIES THE SPANISH SOLDIERS PERFORMED TO ACHIEVE THEIR GOALS OF COLONIZATION AND SPREAD THE SO-CALLED "BLACK LEGEND," THROUGH WHICH HE ACCUSED THE PERPETRATORS OF VIOLENCE, HAD AN EXTRAORDINARY IDEA: HE WOULD WRITE TO KING CHARLES V, EXPRESSING PITY FOR THE SUFFERING INDIANS AND RECOMMENDING THE IMPORT OF AFRICAN SLAVES.
!
¡LA IMPORTACION DE LOS NEGROS!
IN FRAY BARTOLOME'S MIND, AFRICANS WERE CLOSER TO MONKEYS ON THE NATURAL SCALE. THIS MEANT THEIR SUFFERING WAS PERCEIVED AS NOT QUITE HUMAN, AND THUS JUSTIFIABLE.

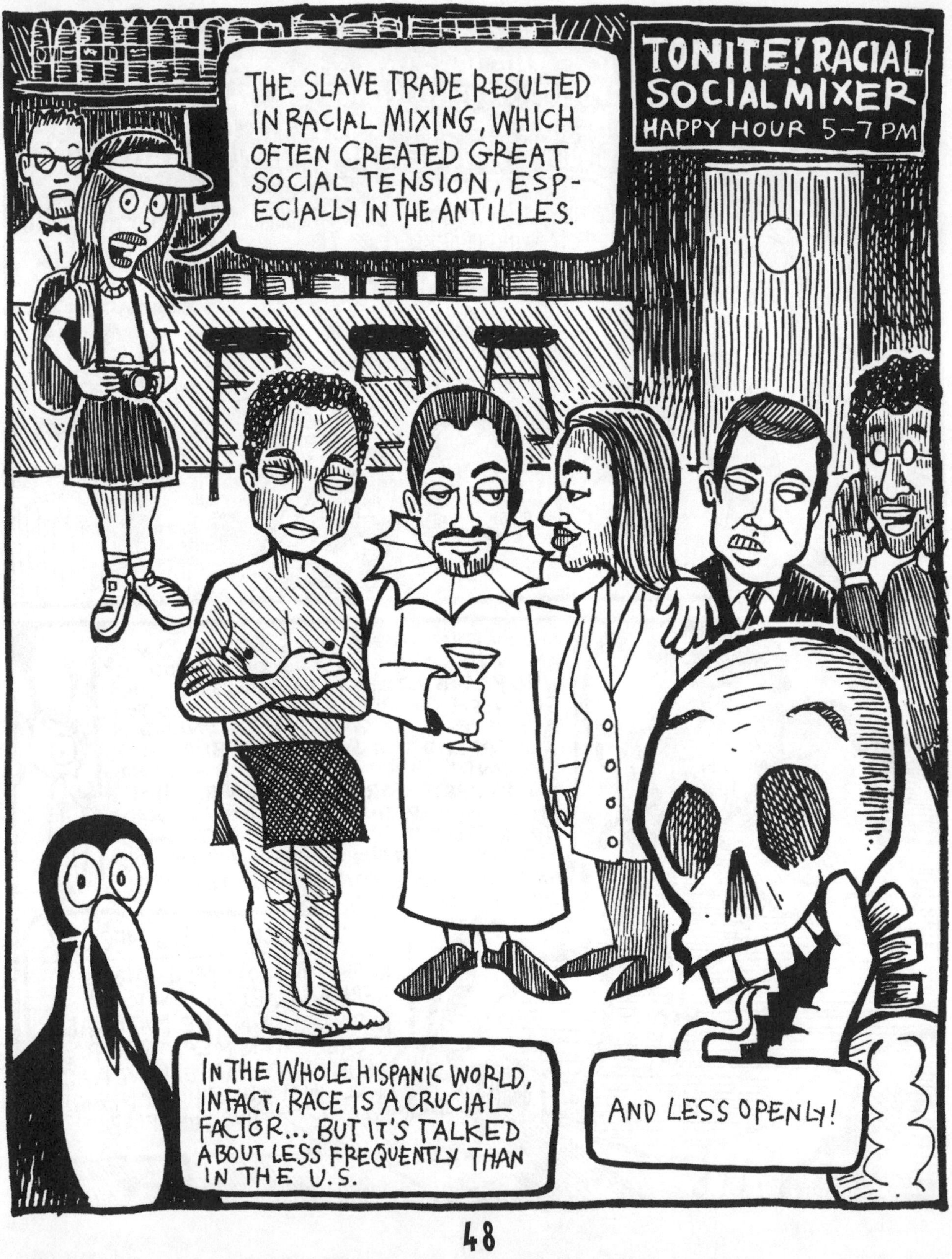
THE SLAVE TRADE RESULTED IN RACIAL MIXING, WHICH OFTEN CREATED GREAT SOCIAL TENSION, ESPECIALLY IN THE ANTILLES.
TONITE! RACIAL SOCIAL MIXER
HAPPY HOUR 5-7 PM
IN THE WHOLE HISPANIC WORLD, IN FACT, RACE IS A CRUCIAL FACTOR... BUT IT'S TALKED ABOUT LESS FREQUENTLY THAN IN THE U.S.
AND LESS OPENLY!

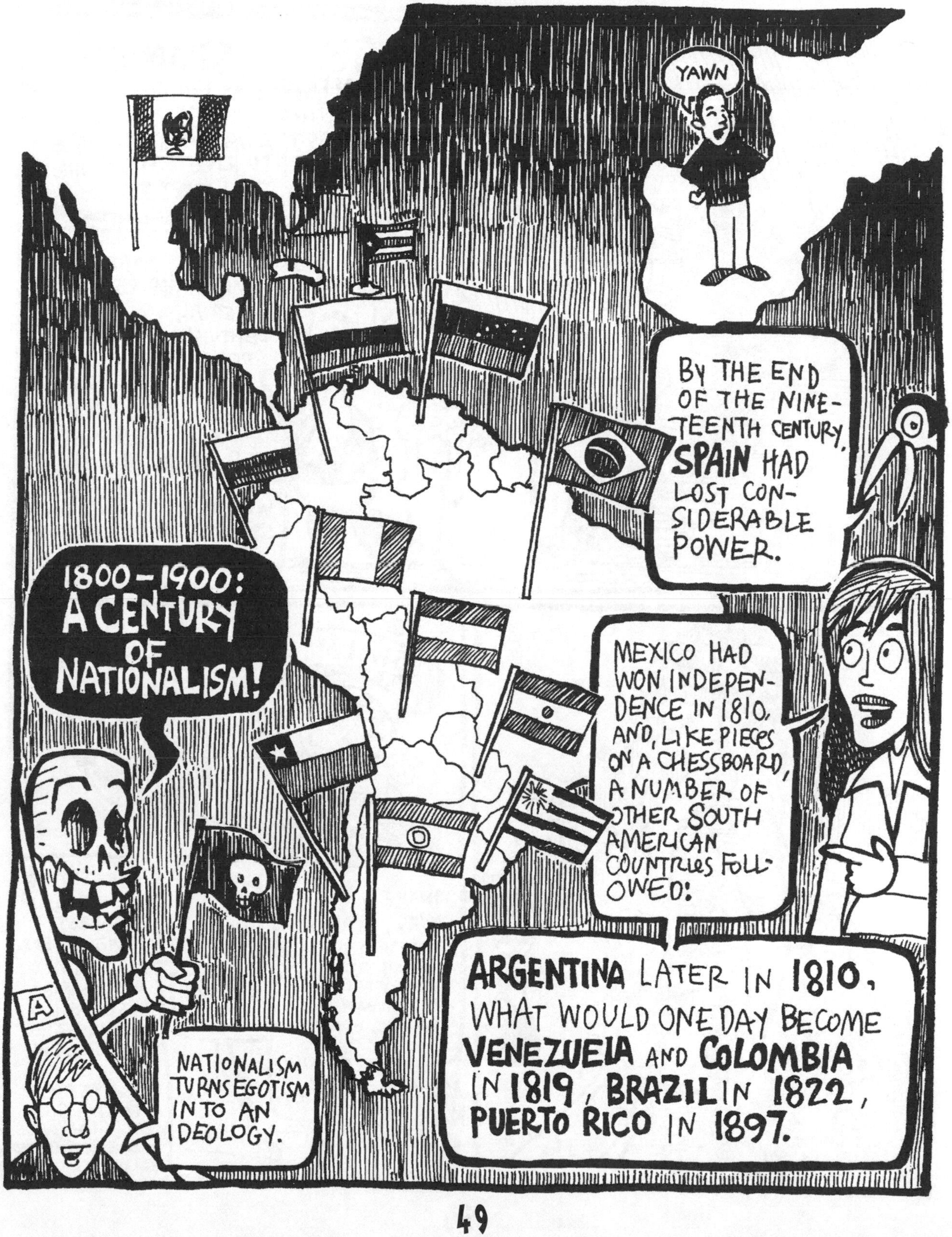

YAWN
1800-1900: A CENTURY OF NATIONALISM!
BY THE END OF THE NINETEENTH CENTURY, SPAIN HAD LOST CONSIDERABLE POWER.
MEXICO HAD WON INDEPENDENCE IN 1810, AND, LIKE PIECES ON A CHESSBOARD, A NUMBER OF OTHER SOUTH AMERICAN COUNTRIES FOLLOWED:
A
NATIONALISM TURNS EGOTISM INTO AN IDEOLOGY.
ARGENTINA LATER IN 1810, WHAT WOULD ONE DAY BECOME VENEZUELA AND COLOMBIA IN 1819, BRAZIL IN 1822, PUERTO RICO IN 1897.

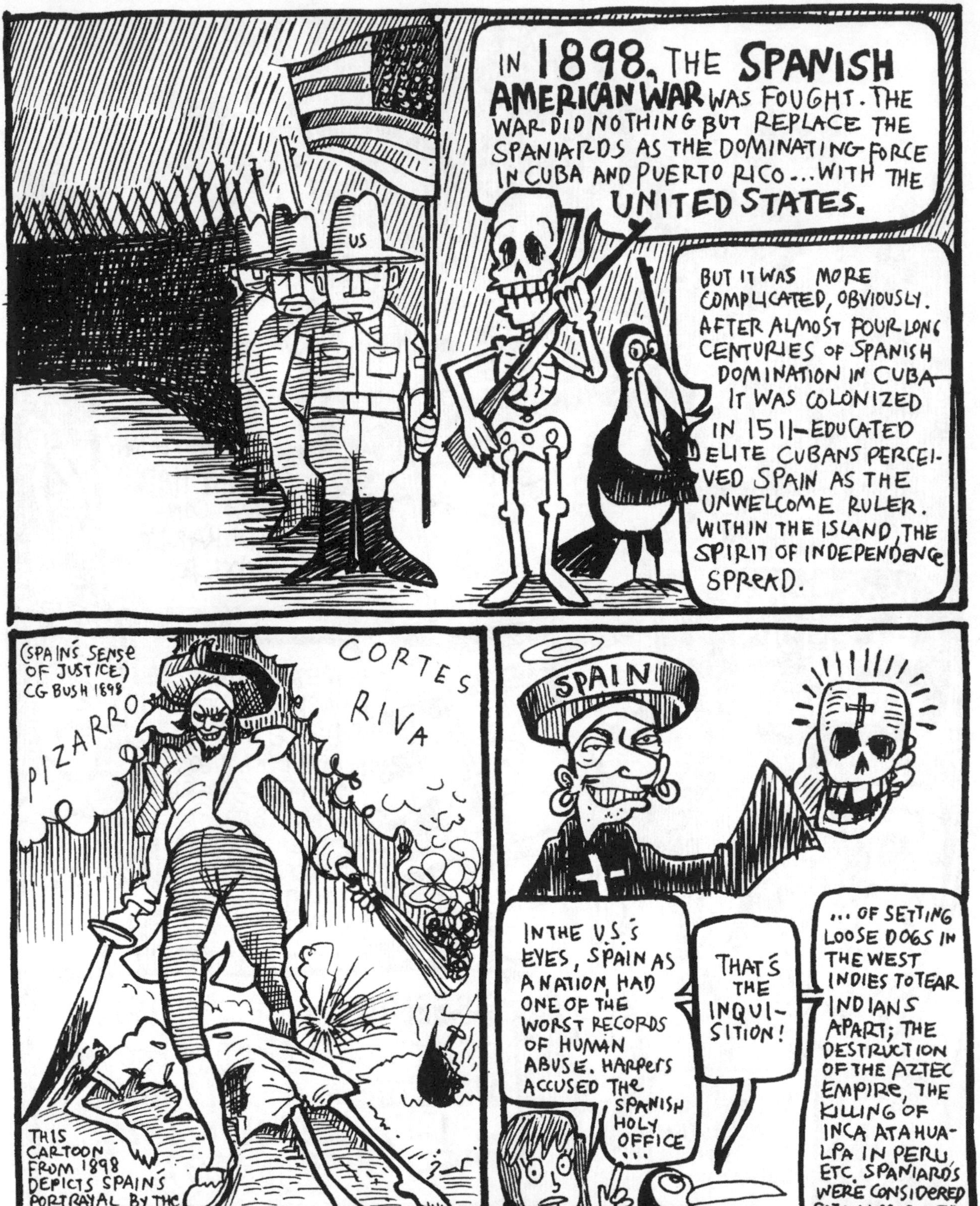
IN 1898, THE SPANISH AMERICAN WAR WAS FOUGHT. THE WAR DID NOTHING BUT REPLACE THE SPANIARDS AS THE DOMINATING FORCE IN CUBA AND PUERTO RICO...WITH THE UNITED STATES.
US
BUT IT WAS MORE COMPLICATED, OBVIOUSLY. AFTER ALMOST FOUR LONG CENTURIES OF SPANISH DOMINATION IN CUBA—IT WAS COLONIZED IN 1511—EDUCATED ELITE CUBANS PERCEIVED SPAIN AS THE UNWELCOME RULER. WITHIN THE ISLAND, THE SPIRIT OF INDEPENDENCE SPREAD.
(SPAIN'S SENSE OF JUSTICE) CG BUSH 1898
CORTES
RIVA
PIZARRO
THIS CARTOON FROM 1898 DEPICTS SPAIN'S PORTRAYAL BY THE U.S. AT THE TIME.
SPAIN
IN THE U.S.'S EYES, SPAIN AS A NATION, HAD ONE OF THE WORST RECORDS OF HUMAN ABUSE. HARPERS ACCUSED THE SPANISH HOLY OFFICE...
THAT'S THE INQUISITION!
... OF SETTING LOOSE DOGS IN THE WEST INDIES TO TEAR INDIANS APART; THE DESTRUCTION OF THE AZTEC EMPIRE, THE KILLING OF INCA ATAHUALPA IN PERU, ETC. SPANIARDS WERE CONSIDERED SATAN INCARNATE.

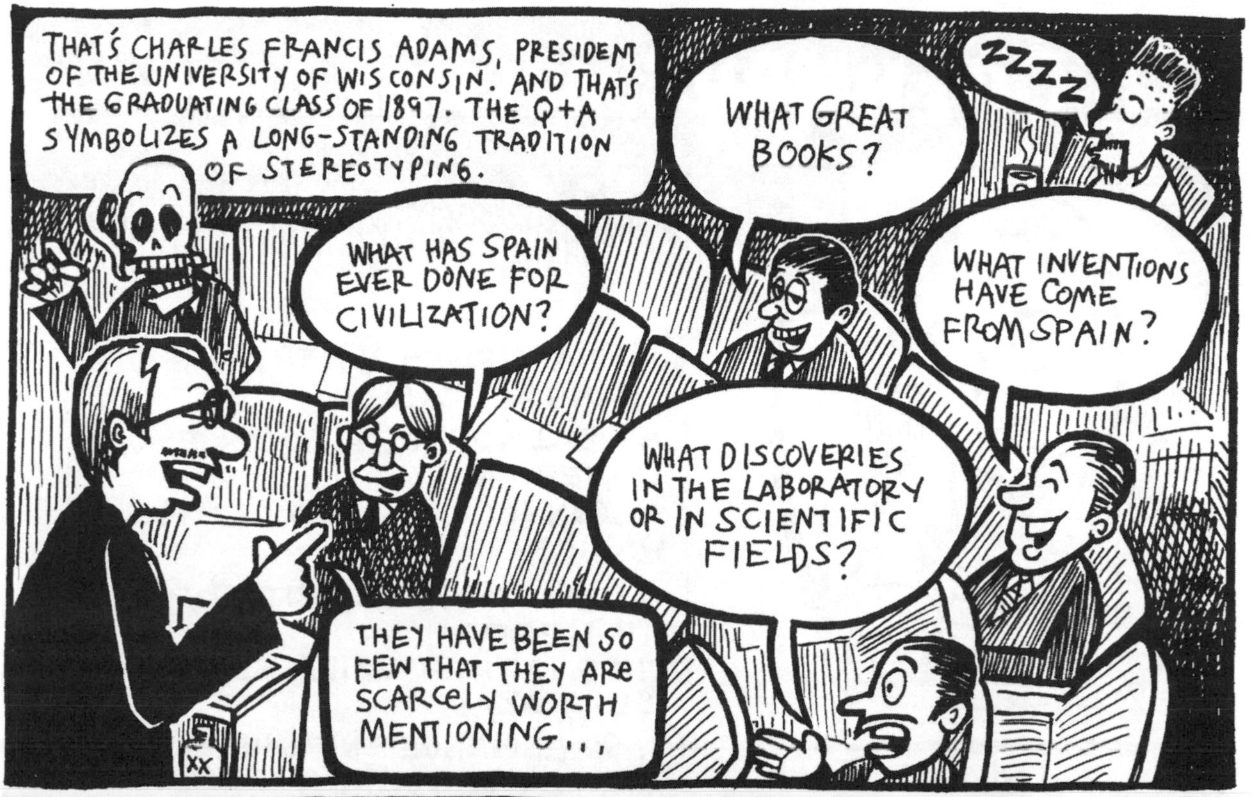
THAT'S CHARLES FRANCIS ADAMS, PRESIDENT OF THE UNIVERSITY OF WISCONSIN. AND THAT'S THE GRADUATING CLASS OF 1897. THE Q+A SYMBOLIZES A LONG-STANDING TRADITION OF STEREOTYPING.
WHAT GREAT BOOKS?
ZZZZ
WHAT HAS SPAIN EVER DONE FOR CIVILIZATION?
WHAT INVENTIONS HAVE COME FROM SPAIN?
WHAT DISCOVERIES IN THE LABORATORY OR IN SCIENTIFIC FIELDS?
THEY HAVE BEEN SO FEW THAT THEY ARE SCARCELY WORTH MENTIONING...
XX

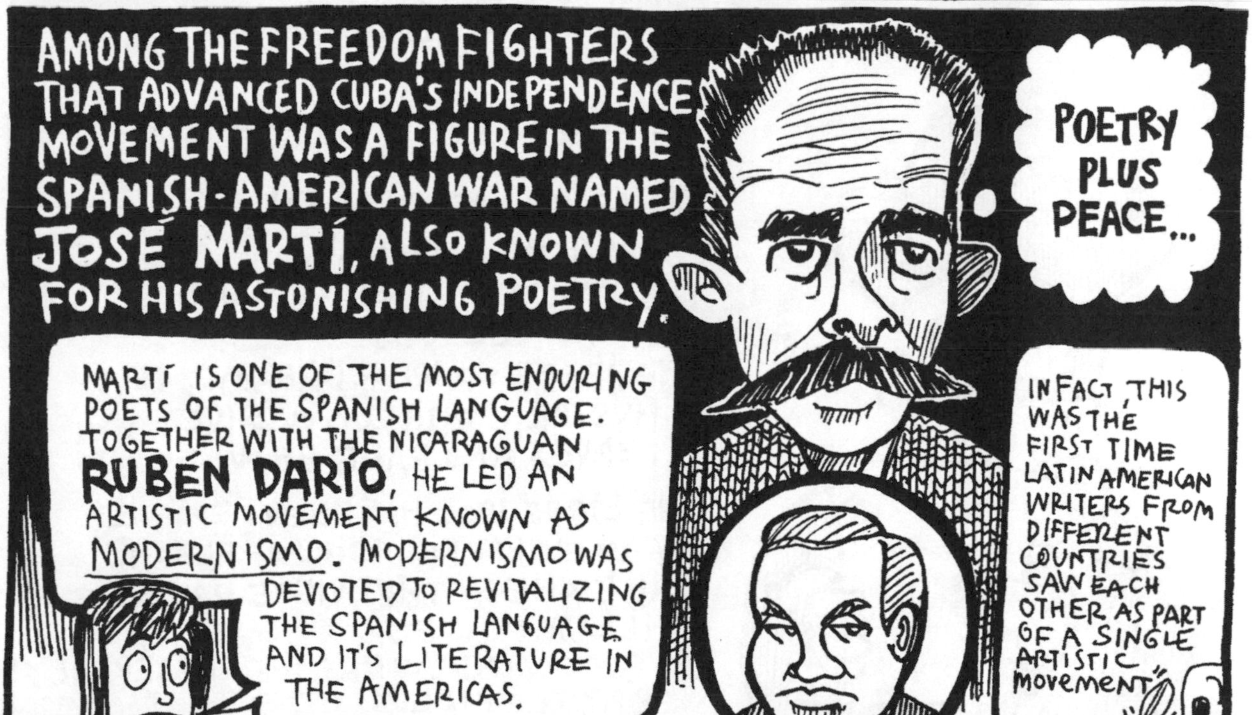
AMONG THE FREEDOM FIGHTERS THAT ADVANCED CUBA'S INDEPENDENCE MOVEMENT WAS A FIGURE IN THE SPANISH-AMERICAN WAR NAMED JOSÉ MARTÍ, ALSO KNOWN FOR HIS ASTONISHING POETRY.
POETRY PLUS PEACE...
MARTÍ IS ONE OF THE MOST ENDURING POETS OF THE SPANISH LANGUAGE. TOGETHER WITH THE NICARAGUAN RUBÉN DARÍO, HE LED AN ARTISTIC MOVEMENT KNOWN AS MODERNISMO. MODERNISMO WAS DEVOTED TO REVITALIZING THE SPANISH LANGUAGE AND IT'S LITERATURE IN THE AMERICAS.
IN FACT, THIS WAS THE FIRST TIME LATIN AMERICAN WRITERS FROM DIFFERENT COUNTRIES SAW EACH OTHER AS PART OF A SINGLE ARTISTIC MOVEMENT.

TO COLUMBUS, BY RUBÉN DARÍO AN EXCERPT

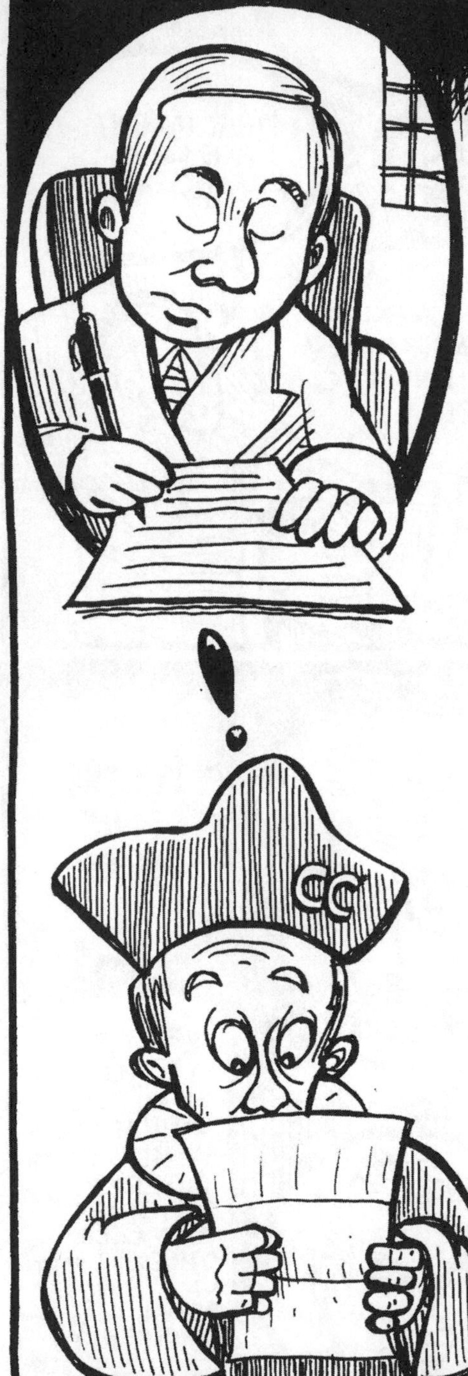
CC

TU INDIA VIRGEN Y HERMOSA DE
SANGRE CÁLIDA
LA PERLA DE TUS SUEÑOS, ES UNA
HISTERICA
CON CONVULSIVOS NERVIOS Y FRENTE
PÁLIDA
UN DESASTROSO ESPÍRITU POSEE
TU TIERRA:
DONDE LA TRIBU UNIDA BLANDIÓ
SUS MAZAS
HOY SE ENCIENDE ENTRE HERMANOS
PERPETUA GUERRA,
SE HIEREN Y DESTROZAN LAS
MISMAS RAZAS.

--------X--------

MISFORTUNATE ADMIRAL!
YOUR POOR AMERICA,
THE BEAUTIFUL INDIAN VIRGIN
OF HOT BLOOD,
THE PEARL OF YOUR DREAMS, IS A
HYSTERIC WITH CONVULSIVE
NERVES AND PALE BROW.
THE STONE IDOL HAS BEEN REPLACED
BY AN ENTHRONED IDOL OF FLESH,
AND EACH DAY THE WHITE DAWN
ILLUMINATES
ON BLOOD AND ASHES THE FRATERNAL
BATTLEFIELDS

A RESTLESS, CREATIVE, AND COMMITTED MAN, MARTÍ WAS BORN IN HAVANA IN 1853. HE WAS OFTEN DEPORTED, IMPRISONED, AND FORCED TO HARD LABOR BECAUSE OF HIS POLITICAL IDEAS. HE LIVED IN SPAIN, NEW YORK AND FLORIDA IN THE UNITED STATES AND TRAVELED TO MEXICO, CENTRAL AMERICA, THE DOMINICAN REPUBLIC AND JAMAICA. FOR MANY YEARS HE WORKED AS A CORRESPONDENT FOR VARIOUS NEWSPAPERS LIKE LA NACIÓN IN BUENOS AIRES, AND THE NEW YORK SUN. AS A JOURNALIST, HE REPORTED NATURAL DISASTERS, BUT ALSO POLITICAL AND SOCIAL EVENTS, AND HIS REPORTS WERE FILLED WITH COMPASSION. HE DIED IN BATTLE IN 1895

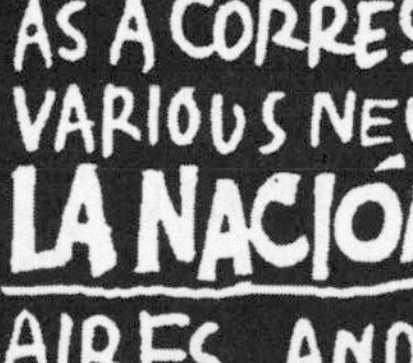

IN 1882, MARTÍ SETTLED IN NEW YORK AND FOUND THE FREEDOM TO WRITE HE HAD ALWAYS LONGED FOR IN HIS HOMELAND. MARTÍ WAS A PROLIFIC WRITER: HIS COMPLETE WORKS FILL 32 VOLUMES.

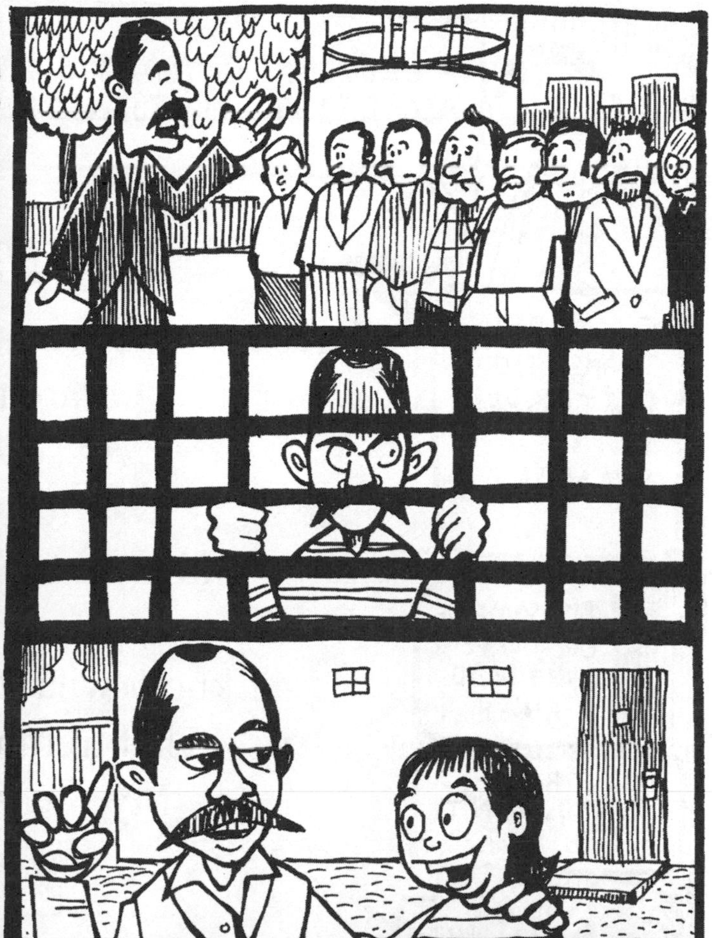

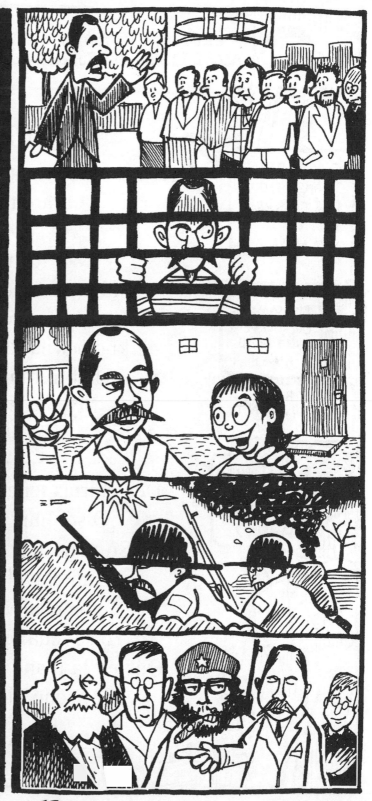

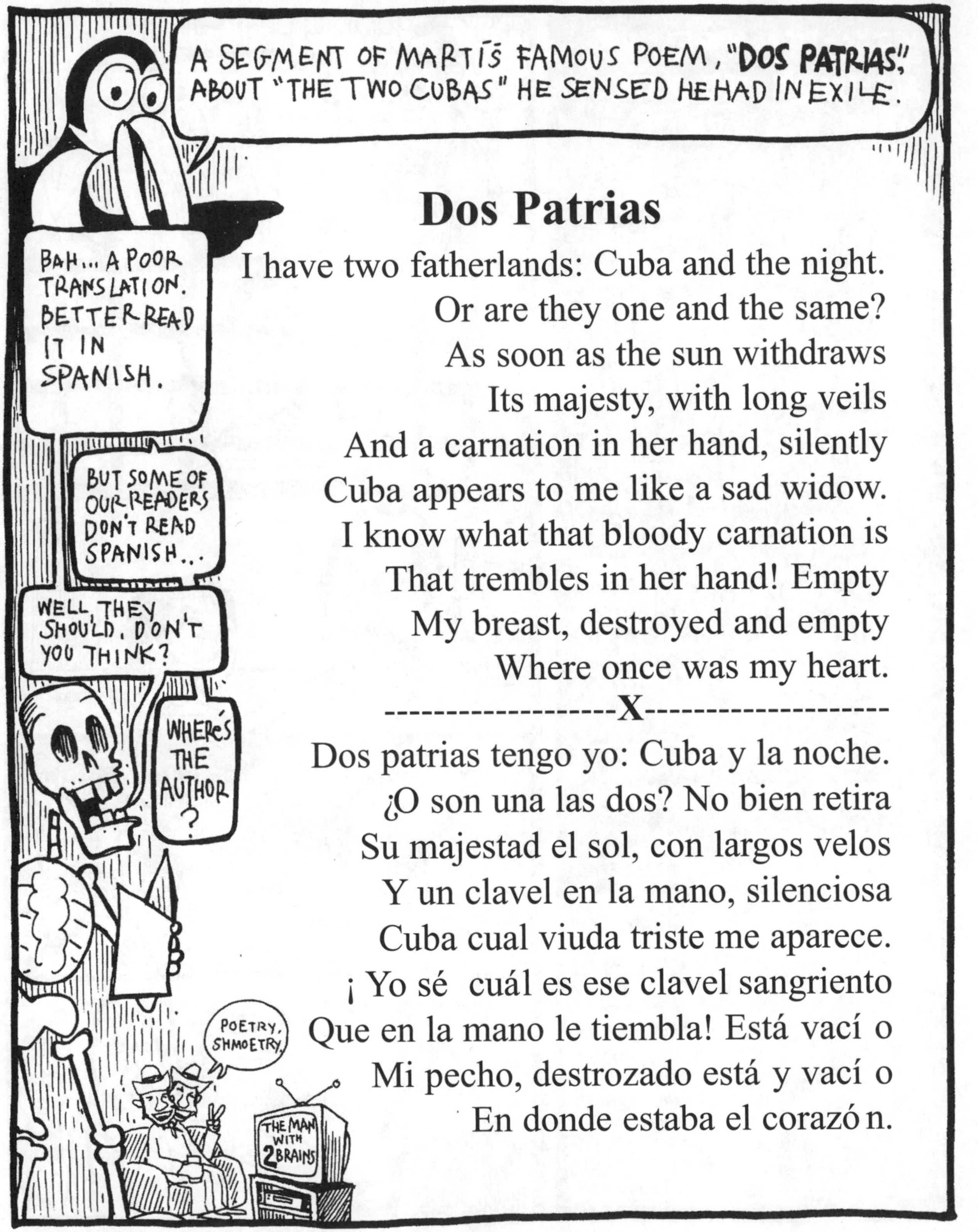
A SEGMENT OF MARTÍ'S FAMOUS POEM, "**DOS PATRIAS**," ABOUT "THE TWO CUBAS" HE SENSED HE HAD IN EXILE.
BAH... A POOR TRANSLATION. BETTER READ IT IN SPANISH.
BUT SOME OF OUR READERS DON'T READ SPANISH...
WELL THEY SHOULD. DON'T YOU THINK?
WHERE'S THE AUTHOR?
POETRY, SHMOETRY.
THE MAN WITH 2 BRAINS

Dos Patrias

I have two fatherlands: Cuba and the night.
Or are they one and the same?
As soon as the sun withdraws
Its majesty, with long veils
And a carnation in her hand, silently
Cuba appears to me like a sad widow.
I know what that bloody carnation is
That trembles in her hand! Empty
My breast, destroyed and empty
Where once was my heart.

-------------------**X**-------------------

Dos patrias tengo yo: Cuba y la noche.
¿O son una las dos? No bien retira
Su majestad el sol, con largos velos
Y un clavel en la mano, silenciosa
Cuba cual viuda triste me aparece.
¡ Yo sé cuál es ese clavel sangriento
Que en la mano le tiembla! Está vací o
Mi pecho, destrozado está y vací o
En donde estaba el corazó n.

REPORTS OF THE WAR WERE FREQUENT IN THE AMERICAN PRESS. AT FIRST, THE PERCEPTION OF CUBA IN POLITICAL CIRCLES AND THE MEDIA IN THE UNITED STATES WAS POSITIVE.

THE CLYDE OHIO ENTERPRISE
—— MAY 10, 1895 ——
CUBAN REBELS RAPIDLY BECOMING DISCOURAGED

MAY 14, 1896
MANY INSURGENTS KILLED

JAN 21 1897   25¢
THEY ARE PROUD OF IT
SPANIARDS TALK ABOUT A
"GREAT VICTORY" NEAR HAVANA
A BRUTAL SLAUGHTER

IT WAS YELLOW JOURNALISM, OF COURSE.

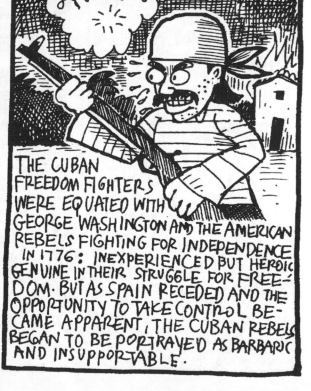

THE CUBAN FREEDOM FIGHTERS WERE EQUATED WITH GEORGE WASHINGTON AND THE AMERICAN REBELS FIGHTING FOR INDEPENDENCE IN 1776: INEXPERIENCED BUT HEROIC GENUINE IN THEIR STRUGGLE FOR FREEDOM. BUT AS SPAIN RECEDED AND THE OPPORTUNITY TO TAKE CONTROL BECAME APPARENT, THE CUBAN REBELS BEGAN TO BE PORTRAYED AS BARBARIC AND INSUPPORTABLE.

55

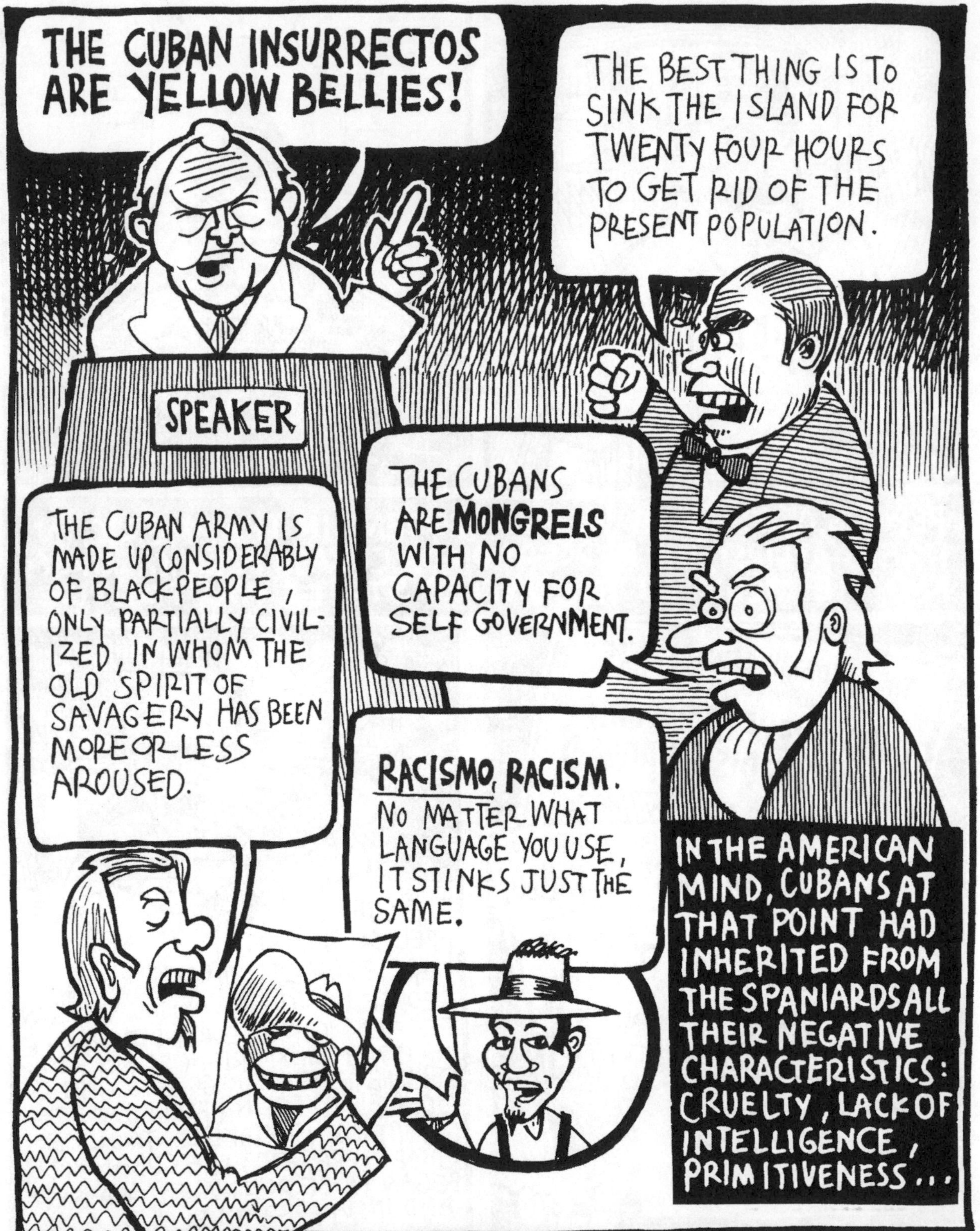
THE CUBAN INSURRECTOS ARE YELLOW BELLIES!
SPEAKER
THE BEST THING IS TO SINK THE ISLAND FOR TWENTY FOUR HOURS TO GET RID OF THE PRESENT POPULATION.
THE CUBAN ARMY IS MADE UP CONSIDERABLY OF BLACK PEOPLE, ONLY PARTIALLY CIVILIZED, IN WHOM THE OLD SPIRIT OF SAVAGERY HAS BEEN MORE OR LESS AROUSED.
THE CUBANS ARE MONGRELS WITH NO CAPACITY FOR SELF GOVERNMENT.
RACISMO, RACISM. NO MATTER WHAT LANGUAGE YOU USE, IT STINKS JUST THE SAME.
IN THE AMERICAN MIND, CUBANS AT THAT POINT HAD INHERITED FROM THE SPANIARDS ALL THEIR NEGATIVE CHARACTERISTICS: CRUELTY, LACK OF INTELLIGENCE, PRIMITIVENESS...

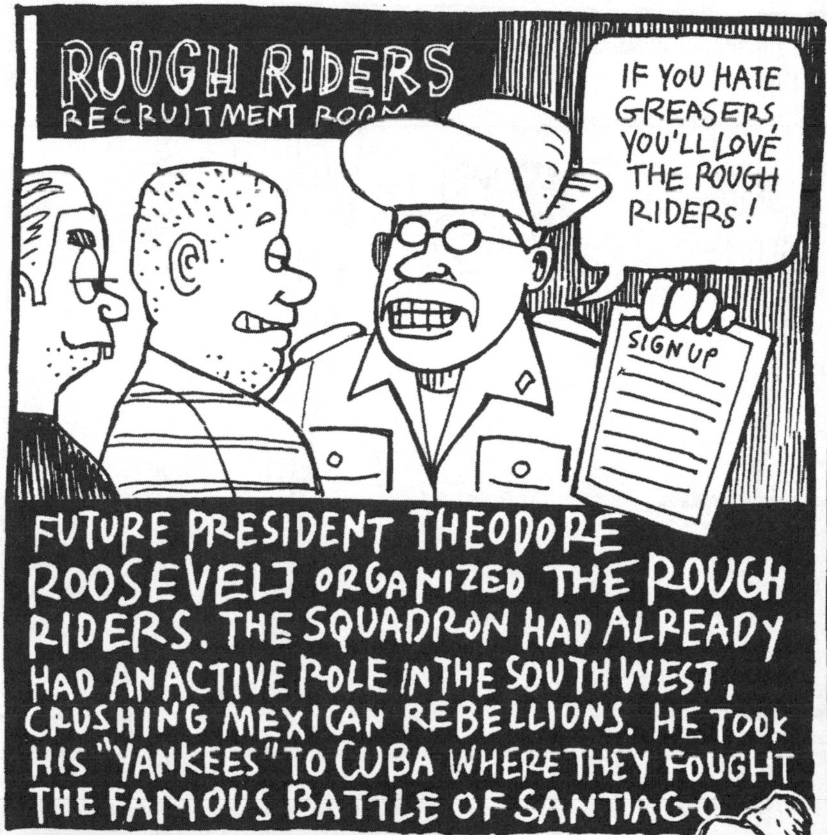
ROUGH RIDERS
RECRUITMENT ROOM
IF YOU HATE GREASERS, YOU'LL LOVE THE ROUGH RIDERS!
SIGN UP
FUTURE PRESIDENT THEODORE ROOSEVELT ORGANIZED THE ROUGH RIDERS. THE SQUADRON HAD ALREADY HAD AN ACTIVE ROLE IN THE SOUTH WEST, CRUSHING MEXICAN REBELLIONS. HE TOOK HIS "YANKEES" TO CUBA WHERE THEY FOUGHT THE FAMOUS BATTLE OF SANTIAGO.

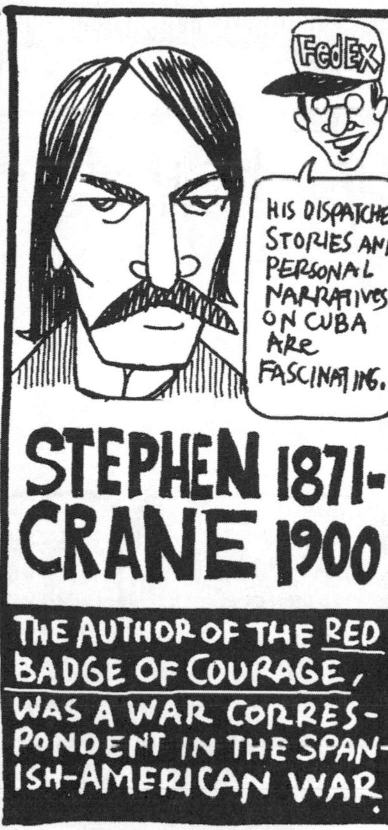
FedEx
HIS DISPATCHES, STORIES AND PERSONAL NARRATIVES ON CUBA ARE FASCINATING.
STEPHEN CRANE 1871-1900
THE AUTHOR OF THE RED BADGE OF COURAGE, WAS A WAR CORRESPONDENT IN THE SPANISH-AMERICAN WAR.

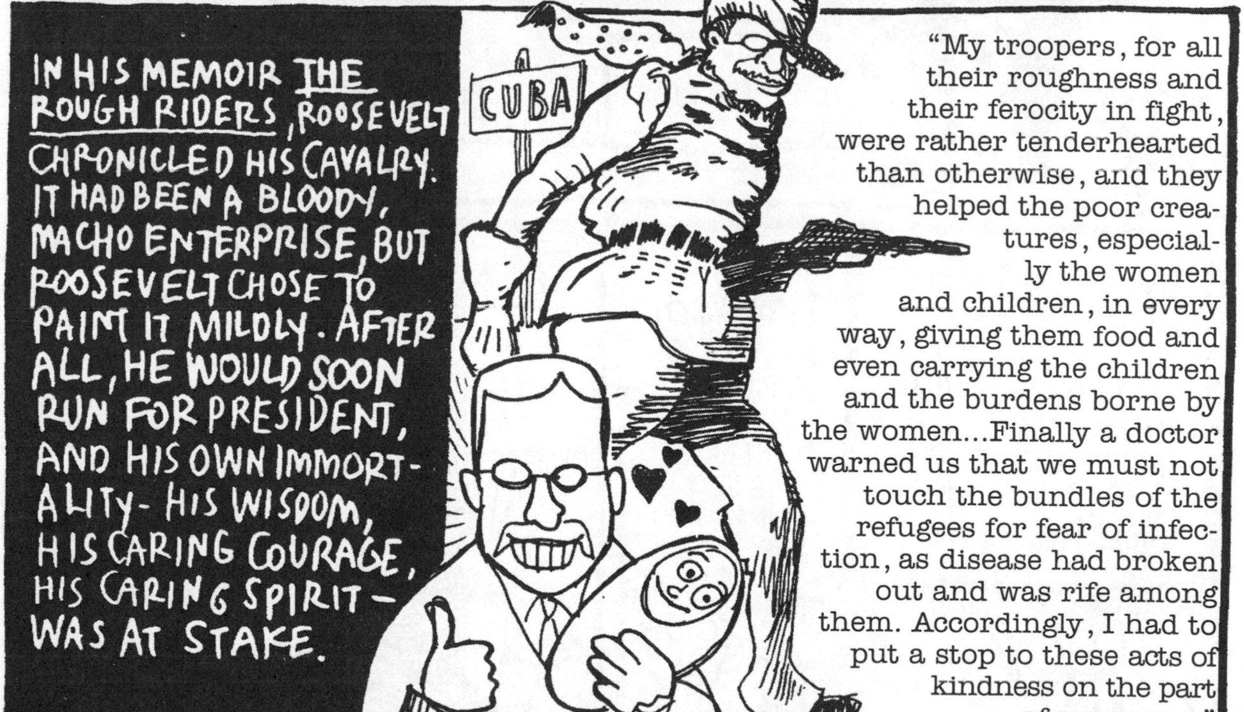
IN HIS MEMOIR THE ROUGH RIDERS, ROOSEVELT CHRONICLED HIS CAVALRY. IT HAD BEEN A BLOODY, MACHO ENTERPRISE, BUT ROOSEVELT CHOSE TO PAINT IT MILDLY. AFTER ALL, HE WOULD SOON RUN FOR PRESIDENT, AND HIS OWN IMMORTALITY- HIS WISDOM, HIS CARING COURAGE, HIS CARING SPIRIT- WAS AT STAKE.
CUBA
"My troopers, for all their roughness and their ferocity in fight, were rather tenderhearted than otherwise, and they helped the poor creatures, especially the women and children, in every way, giving them food and even carrying the children and the burdens borne by the women...Finally a doctor warned us that we must not touch the bundles of the refugees for fear of infection, as disease had broken out and was rife among them. Accordingly, I had to put a stop to these acts of kindness on the part of my men..."

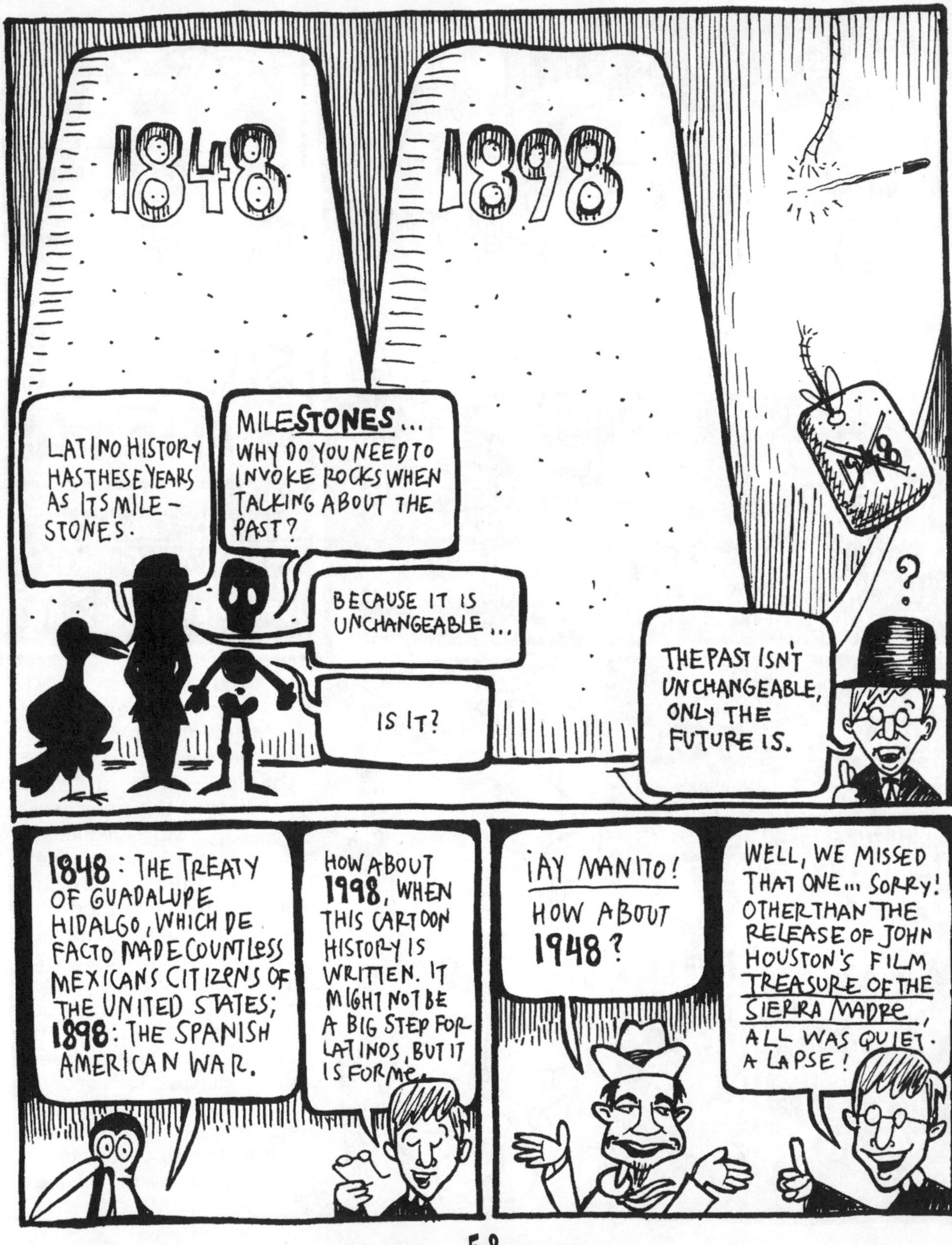
1848
1898
LATINO HISTORY HAS THESE YEARS AS ITS MILE-STONES.
MILESTONES... WHY DO YOU NEED TO INVOKE ROCKS WHEN TALKING ABOUT THE PAST?
BECAUSE IT IS UNCHANGEABLE...
IS IT?
?
THE PAST ISN'T UNCHANGEABLE, ONLY THE FUTURE IS.
1848: THE TREATY OF GUADALUPE HIDALGO, WHICH DE FACTO MADE COUNTLESS MEXICANS CITIZENS OF THE UNITED STATES; 1898: THE SPANISH AMERICAN WAR.
HOW ABOUT 1998, WHEN THIS CARTOON HISTORY IS WRITTEN. IT MIGHT NOT BE A BIG STEP FOR LATINOS, BUT IT IS FOR ME.
¡AY MANITO!
HOW ABOUT 1948?
WELL, WE MISSED THAT ONE... SORRY! OTHER THAN THE RELEASE OF JOHN HOUSTON'S FILM TREASURE OF THE SIERRA MADRE, ALL WAS QUIET. A LAPSE!

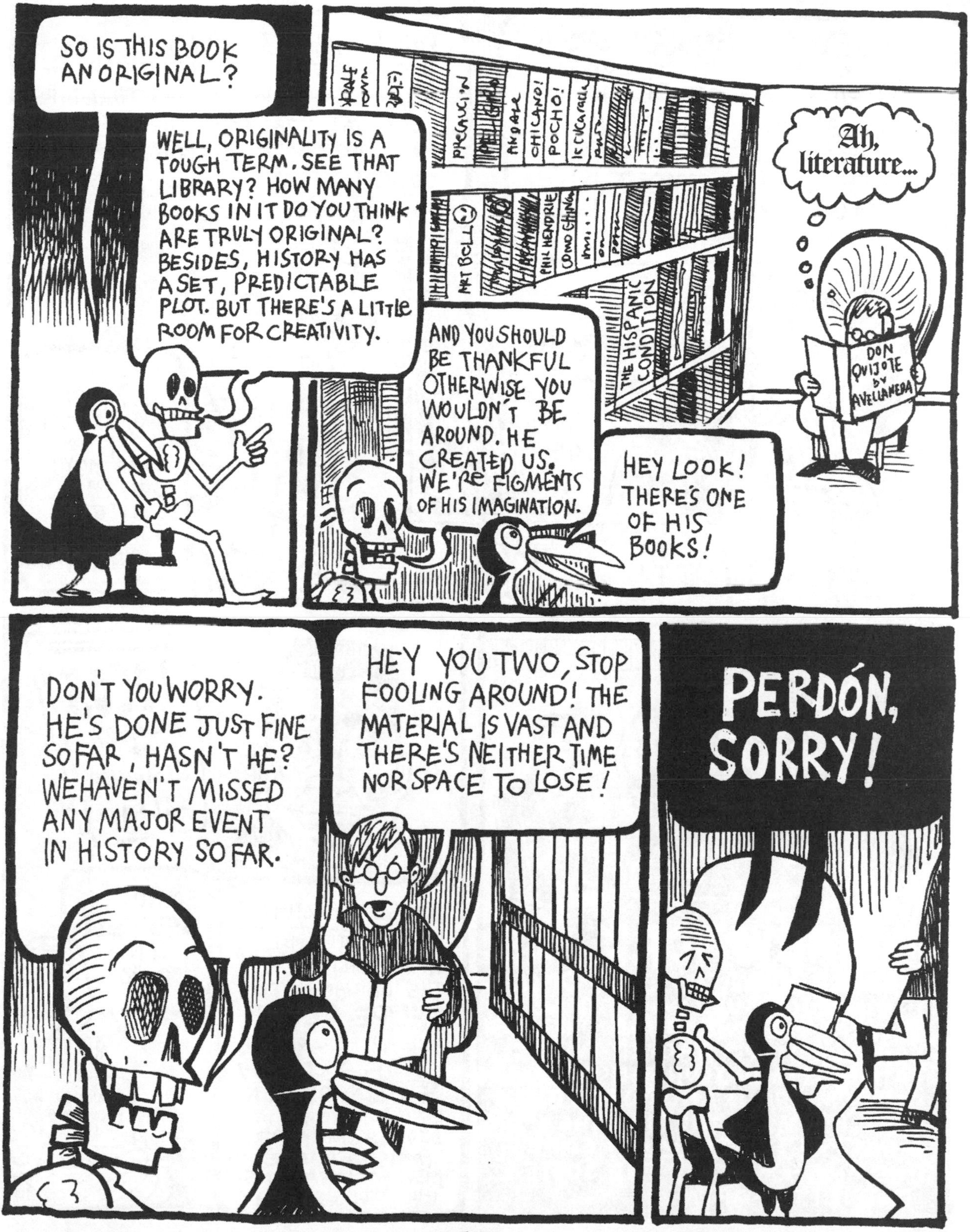
SO IS THIS BOOK AN ORIGINAL?
WELL, ORIGINALITY IS A TOUGH TERM. SEE THAT LIBRARY? HOW MANY BOOKS IN IT DO YOU THINK ARE TRULY ORIGINAL? BESIDES, HISTORY HAS A SET, PREDICTABLE PLOT. BUT THERE'S A LITTLE ROOM FOR CREATIVITY.
ANDALE
CHICANO!
POCHO!
PHIL HENDRIE
THE HISPANIC CONDITION
AND YOU SHOULD BE THANKFUL OTHERWISE YOU WOULDN'T BE AROUND. HE CREATED US. WE'RE FIGMENTS OF HIS IMAGINATION.
HEY LOOK! THERE'S ONE OF HIS BOOKS!
Ah, literature...
DON QUIJOTE by AVELLANEDA
DON'T YOU WORRY. HE'S DONE JUST FINE SO FAR, HASN'T HE? WE HAVEN'T MISSED ANY MAJOR EVENT IN HISTORY SO FAR.
HEY YOU TWO, STOP FOOLING AROUND! THE MATERIAL IS VAST AND THERE'S NEITHER TIME NOR SPACE TO LOSE!
PERDÓN, SORRY!

The **SPANISH-AMERICAN WAR** IS CRUCIAL IN THE HISTORY OF THE UNITED STATES. FOR THE FIRST TIME, AMERICA WAS PERCEIVED THE WORLD OVER AS A MILITARY POWER READY TO COMPETE WITH STRONG EUROPEAN NATIONS FOR GLOBAL DOMINATION.

FOR HISPANICS SOUTH OF THE RIO GRANDE AND IN THE CARIBBEAN SEA, IT WAS CLEAR THAT THE COLOSSAL NORTHERN NEIGHBOR HAD SOUTHBOUND DREAMS OF COLONIALISM.

ENGLAND'S JOHN BULL

WESTERN HEMISPHERE

UNCLE SAM

IN OTHER WORDS, JUST AS SPAIN WAS MOVING OUT, THE UNITED STATES WAS MOVING IN...

NEW YORK

WAS ALREADY A CENTER OF DISSENTING INTELLECTUAL AND POLITICAL DEBATE AT THE END OF THE NINETEENTH CENTURY. IT ATTRACTED POETS, PAINTERS, AND JOURNALISTS, MAINLY FROM SPAIN AND CUBA, BUT ALSO FROM PUERTO RICO. THEY'D MEET FOR <u>TERTULIAS</u> IN CAFES. THE MOST FAMOUS WAS THE **SOCIEDAD LITERARIA.**

LOCOS A COMEDY OF GESTURES —ALFAU—

THESE TERTULIAS WOULD LATER BE IMMORTALIZED BY THE IBERIAN NOVELIST **FELIPE ALFAU,** THE AUTHOR OF <u>LOCOS: A COMEDY OF GESTURES.</u> AN EXTRAORDINARY NOVEL ABOUT A GROUP OF SPANISH EMIGRES IN NEW YORK TALKING THEIR LIVES AWAY.

SOUNDS LIKE "SEINFELD" EN ESPAÑOL!

I HIGHLY RECOMMEND THIS NOVEL!

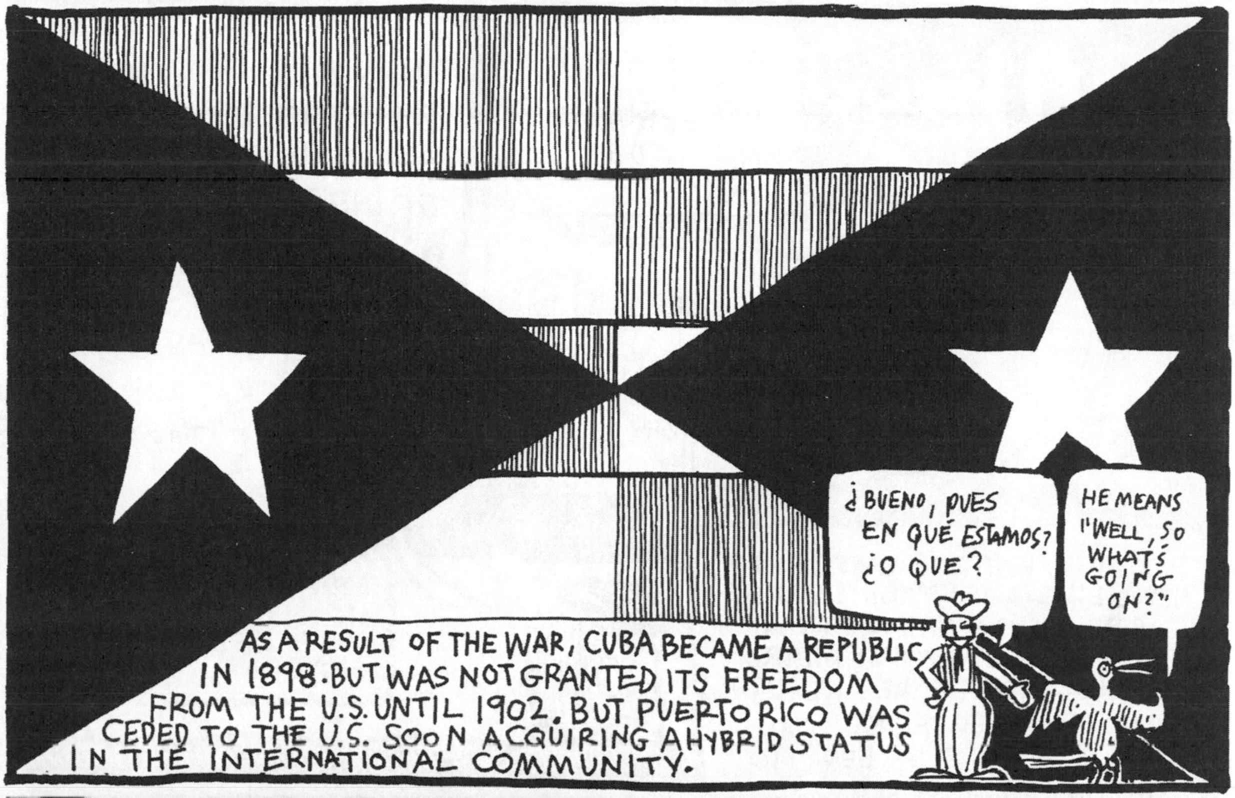
¿BUENO, PUES EN QUÉ ESTAMOS? ¿O QUE?
HE MEANS "WELL, SO WHAT'S GOING ON?"
AS A RESULT OF THE WAR, CUBA BECAME A REPUBLIC IN 1898. BUT WAS NOT GRANTED ITS FREEDOM FROM THE U.S. UNTIL 1902. BUT PUERTO RICO WAS CEDED TO THE U.S. SOON ACQUIRING A HYBRID STATUS IN THE INTERNATIONAL COMMUNITY.

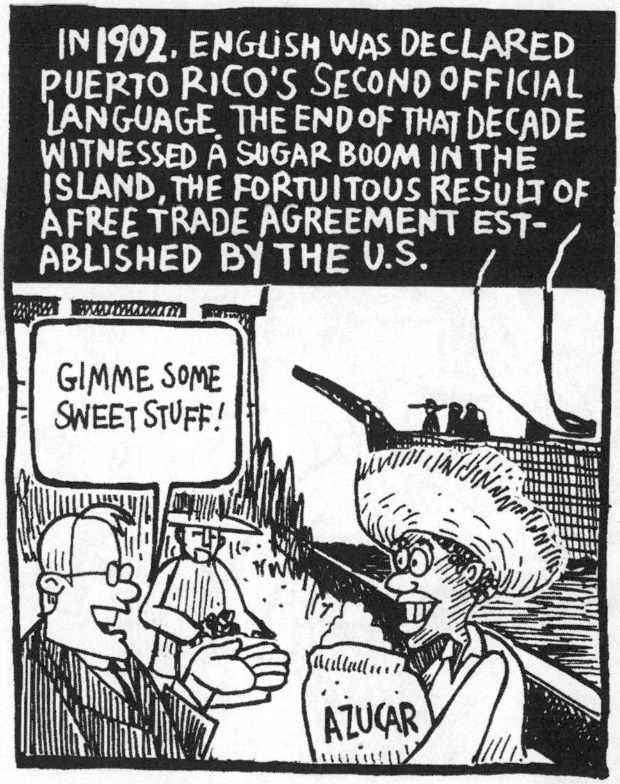
IN 1902, ENGLISH WAS DECLARED PUERTO RICO'S SECOND OFFICIAL LANGUAGE. THE END OF THAT DECADE WITNESSED A SUGAR BOOM IN THE ISLAND, THE FORTUITOUS RESULT OF A FREE TRADE AGREEMENT ESTABLISHED BY THE U.S.
GIMME SOME SWEET STUFF!
AZUCAR

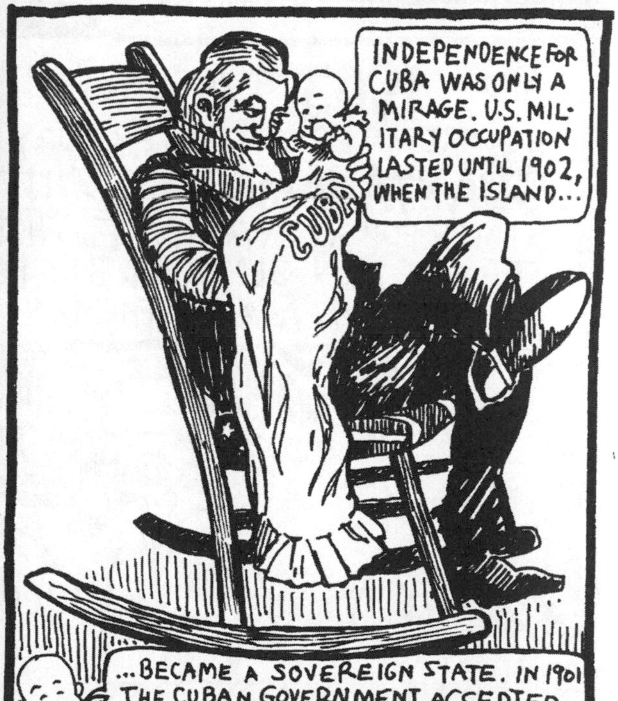
INDEPENDENCE FOR CUBA WAS ONLY A MIRAGE. U.S. MILITARY OCCUPATION LASTED UNTIL 1902, WHEN THE ISLAND...
CUBA
...BECAME A SOVEREIGN STATE. IN 1901 THE CUBAN GOVERNMENT ACCEPTED THE PLATT AMENDMENT, GRANTING WASHINGTON THE RIGHT OF INTERVENTION.

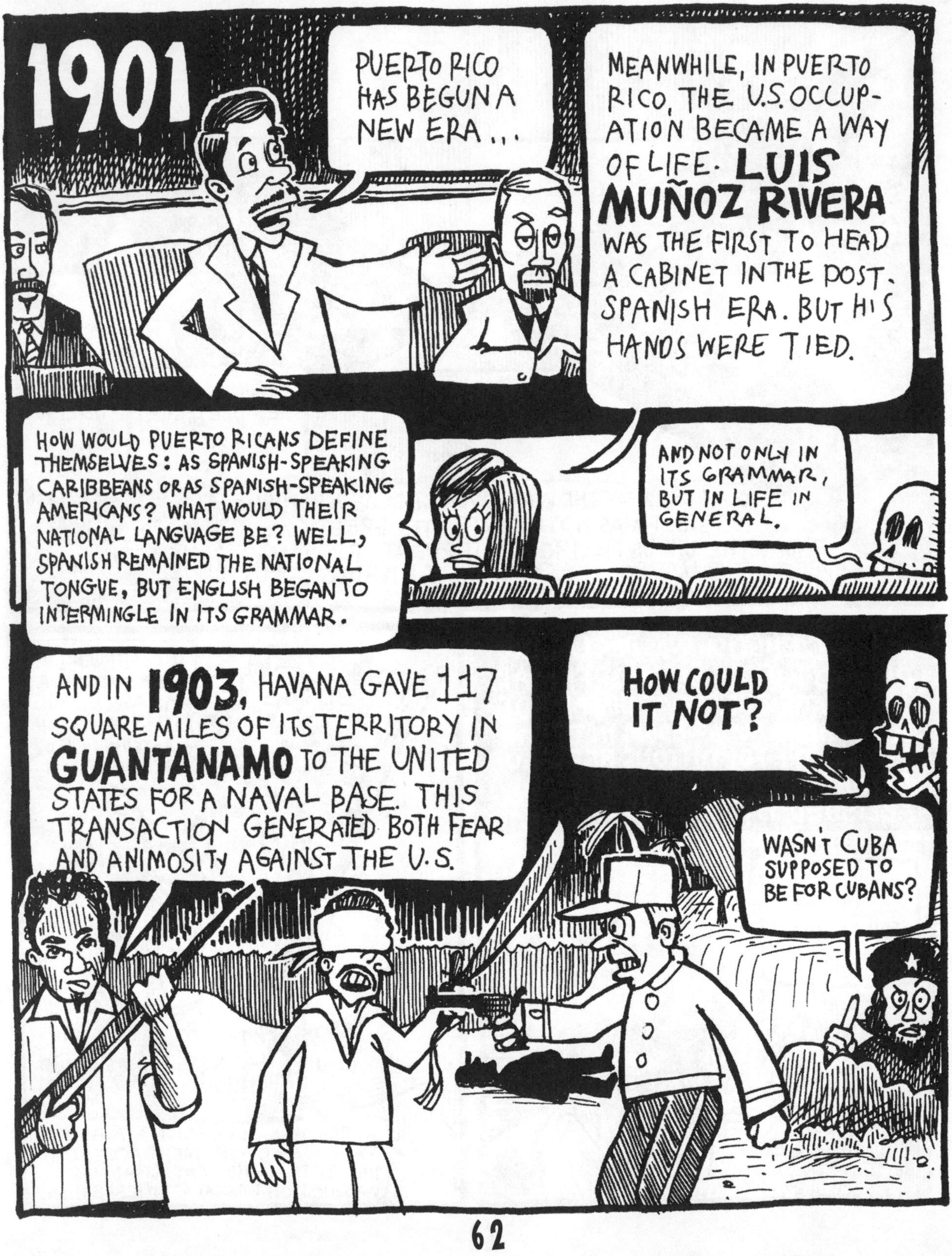
1901
PUERTO RICO HAS BEGUN A NEW ERA...
MEANWHILE, IN PUERTO RICO, THE U.S. OCCUPATION BECAME A WAY OF LIFE. LUIS MUÑOZ RIVERA WAS THE FIRST TO HEAD A CABINET IN THE POST-SPANISH ERA. BUT HIS HANDS WERE TIED.
HOW WOULD PUERTO RICANS DEFINE THEMSELVES: AS SPANISH-SPEAKING CARIBBEANS OR AS SPANISH-SPEAKING AMERICANS? WHAT WOULD THEIR NATIONAL LANGUAGE BE? WELL, SPANISH REMAINED THE NATIONAL TONGUE, BUT ENGLISH BEGAN TO INTERMINGLE IN ITS GRAMMAR.
AND NOT ONLY IN ITS GRAMMAR, BUT IN LIFE IN GENERAL.
AND IN 1903, HAVANA GAVE 117 SQUARE MILES OF ITS TERRITORY IN GUANTANAMO TO THE UNITED STATES FOR A NAVAL BASE. THIS TRANSACTION GENERATED BOTH FEAR AND ANIMOSITY AGAINST THE U.S.
HOW COULD IT NOT?
WASN'T CUBA SUPPOSED TO BE FOR CUBANS?

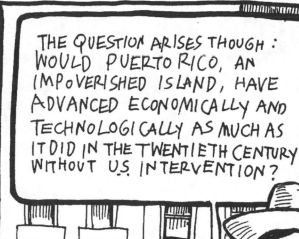

THE QUESTION ARISES THOUGH: WOULD PUERTO RICO, AN IMPOVERISHED ISLAND, HAVE ADVANCED ECONOMICALLY AND TECHNOLOGICALLY AS MUCH AS IT DID IN THE TWENTIETH CENTURY WITHOUT U.S. INTERVENTION?

A RHETORICAL QUESTION, TOUCAN! WHAT WOULD THE U.S. BE IF THE PILGRIMS HAD DECIDED TO SETTLE IN NEW ZEALAND AND NOT IN NORTH AMERICA? OR ARE YOU IN FAVOR OF INTERVENTION? SHOULD THE STRONG ALWAYS "ASSIST" THE WEAK?

BURRO PARKING

TO LATINOS, IMMIGRATION BEGAN TO LOOK LIKE AN ATTRACTIVE OPTION TO ESCAPE POVERTY, REPRESSION AND POLITICAL CORRUPTION.

CAN'T LIVE WITH YOU, CAN'T LIVE WITHOUT YOU!

KEY WEST

LANCHEROS

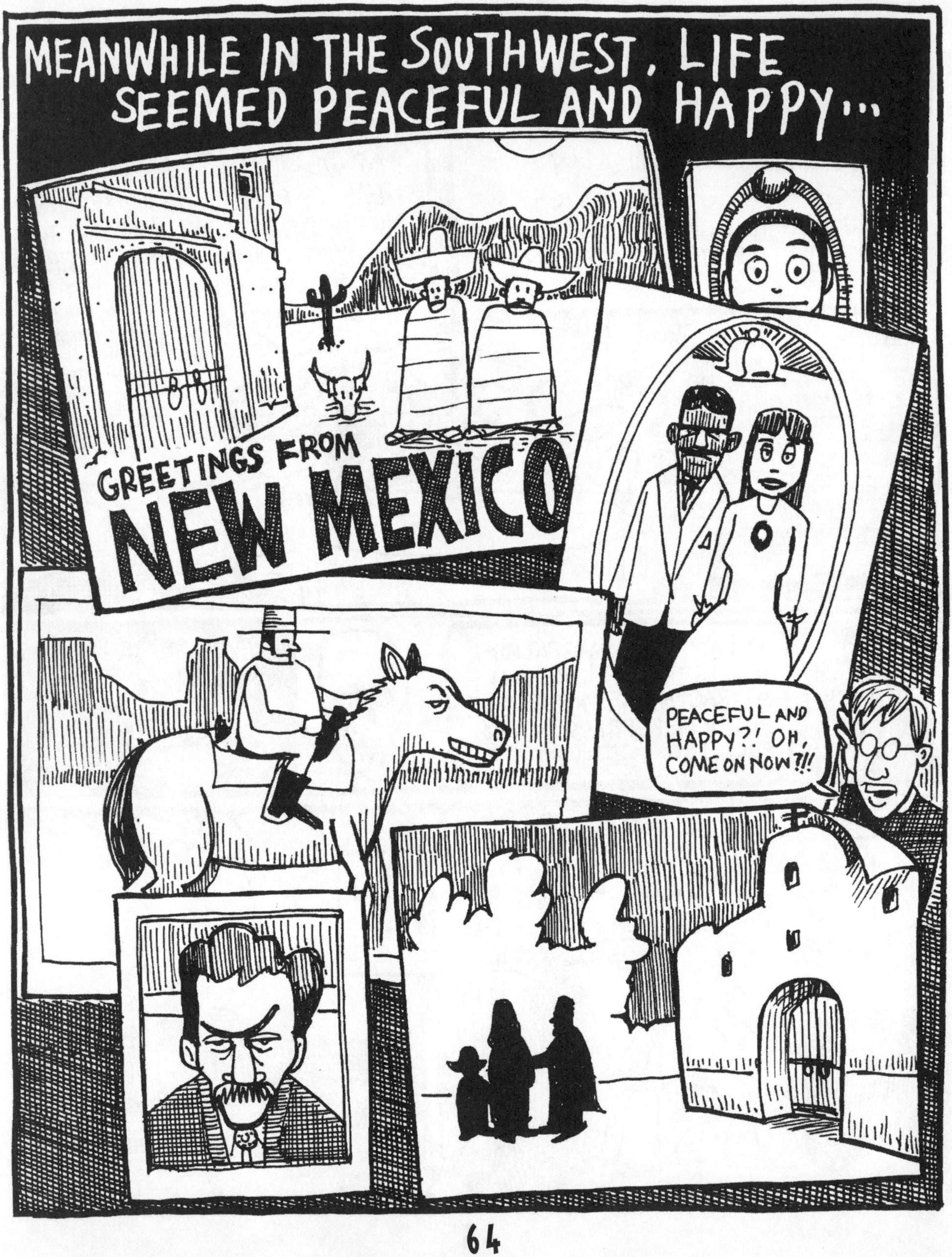
MEANWHILE IN THE SOUTHWEST, LIFE SEEMED PEACEFUL AND HAPPY...
GREETINGS FROM NEW MEXICO
PEACEFUL AND HAPPY?! OH, COME ON NOW?!!

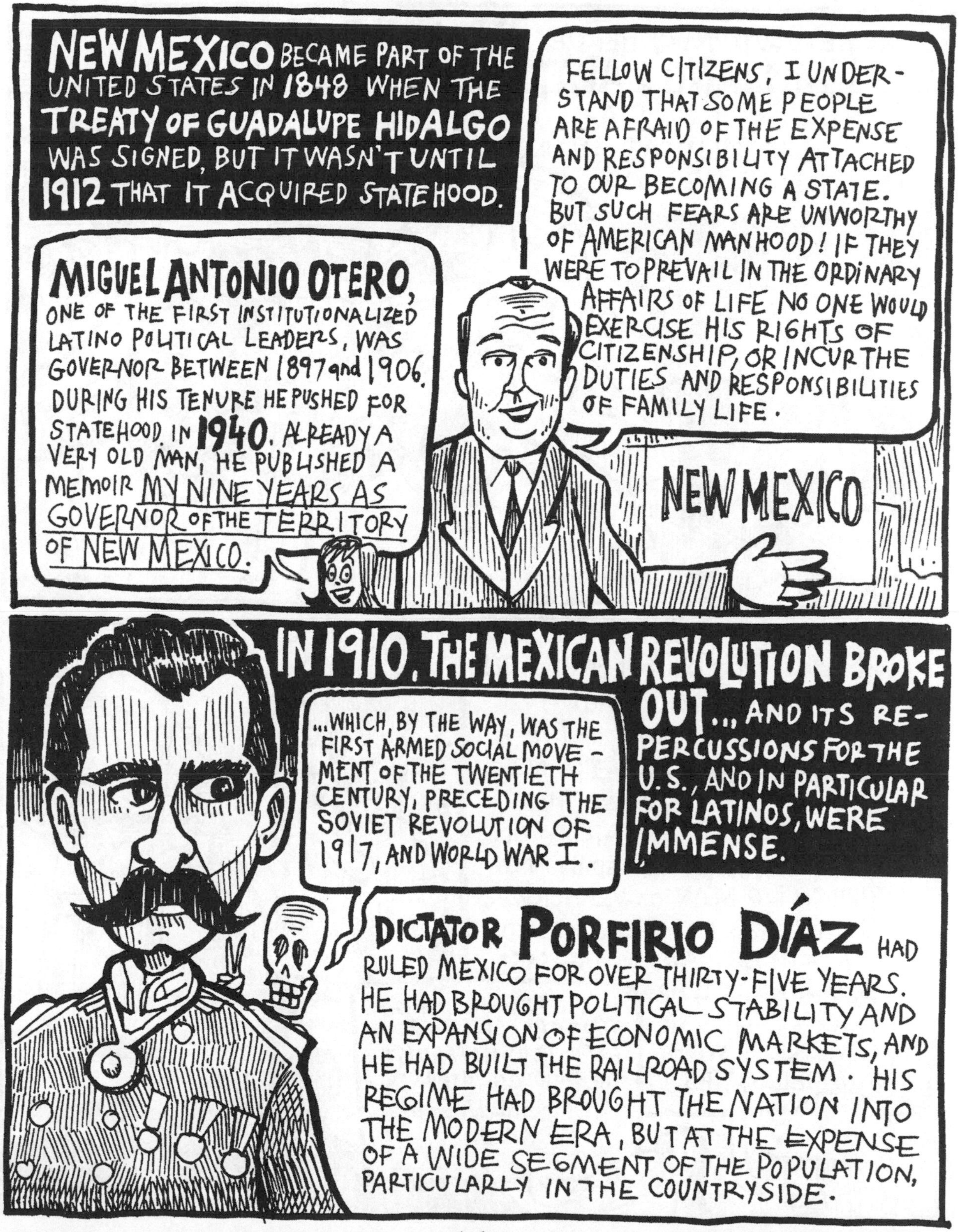
NEW MEXICO BECAME PART OF THE UNITED STATES IN 1848 WHEN THE TREATY OF GUADALUPE HIDALGO WAS SIGNED, BUT IT WASN'T UNTIL 1912 THAT IT ACQUIRED STATEHOOD.
FELLOW CITIZENS, I UNDERSTAND THAT SOME PEOPLE ARE AFRAID OF THE EXPENSE AND RESPONSIBILITY ATTACHED TO OUR BECOMING A STATE. BUT SUCH FEARS ARE UNWORTHY OF AMERICAN MANHOOD! IF THEY WERE TO PREVAIL IN THE ORDINARY AFFAIRS OF LIFE NO ONE WOULD EXERCISE HIS RIGHTS OF CITIZENSHIP, OR INCUR THE DUTIES AND RESPONSIBILITIES OF FAMILY LIFE.
MIGUEL ANTONIO OTERO, ONE OF THE FIRST INSTITUTIONALIZED LATINO POLITICAL LEADERS, WAS GOVERNOR BETWEEN 1897 and 1906. DURING HIS TENURE HE PUSHED FOR STATEHOOD. IN 1940, ALREADY A VERY OLD MAN, HE PUBLISHED A MEMOIR MY NINE YEARS AS GOVERNOR OF THE TERRITORY OF NEW MEXICO.
NEW MEXICO
IN 1910, THE MEXICAN REVOLUTION BROKE OUT..., AND ITS REPERCUSSIONS FOR THE U.S., AND IN PARTICULAR FOR LATINOS, WERE IMMENSE.
...WHICH, BY THE WAY, WAS THE FIRST ARMED SOCIAL MOVEMENT OF THE TWENTIETH CENTURY, PRECEDING THE SOVIET REVOLUTION OF 1917, AND WORLD WAR I.
DICTATOR PORFIRIO DÍAZ HAD RULED MEXICO FOR OVER THIRTY-FIVE YEARS. HE HAD BROUGHT POLITICAL STABILITY AND AN EXPANSION OF ECONOMIC MARKETS, AND HE HAD BUILT THE RAILROAD SYSTEM. HIS REGIME HAD BROUGHT THE NATION INTO THE MODERN ERA, BUT AT THE EXPENSE OF A WIDE SEGMENT OF THE POPULATION, PARTICULARLY IN THE COUNTRYSIDE.

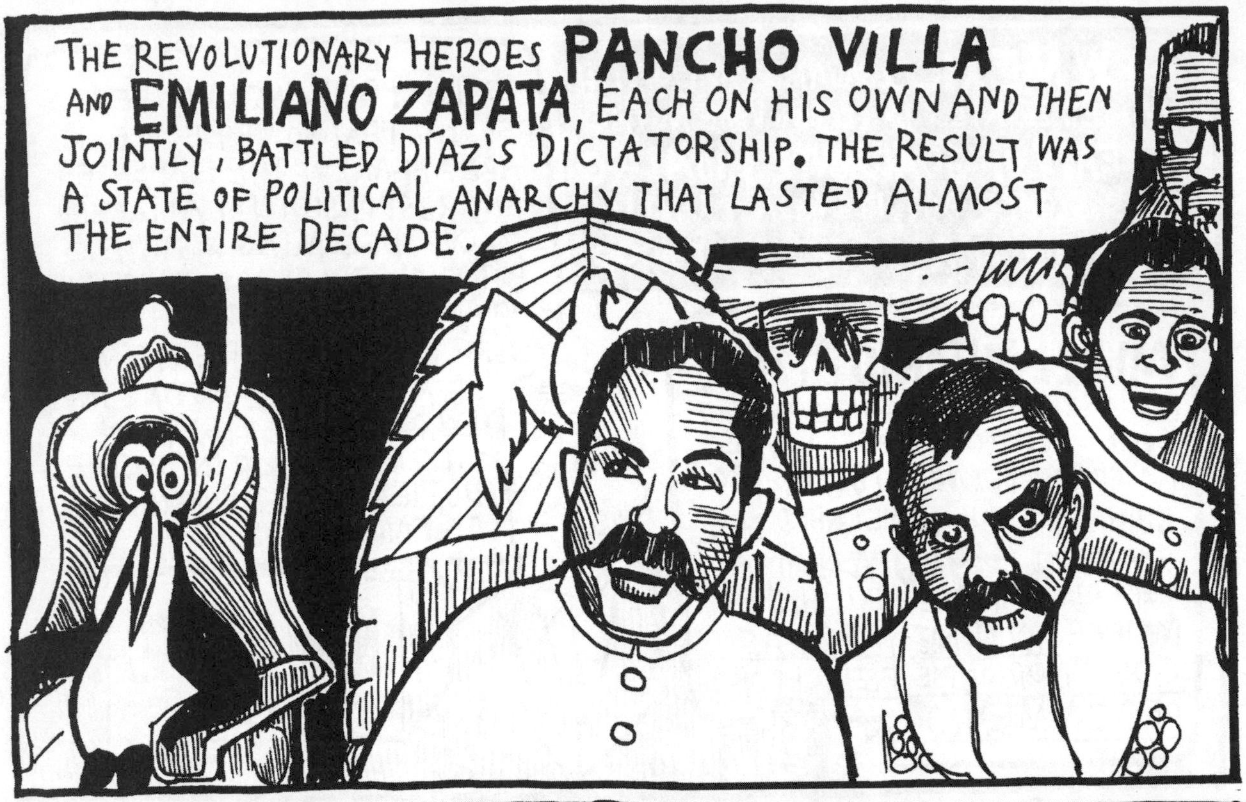
THE REVOLUTIONARY HEROES **PANCHO VILLA** AND **EMILIANO ZAPATA**, EACH ON HIS OWN AND THEN JOINTLY, BATTLED DÍAZ'S DICTATORSHIP. THE RESULT WAS A STATE OF POLITICAL ANARCHY THAT LASTED ALMOST THE ENTIRE DECADE.

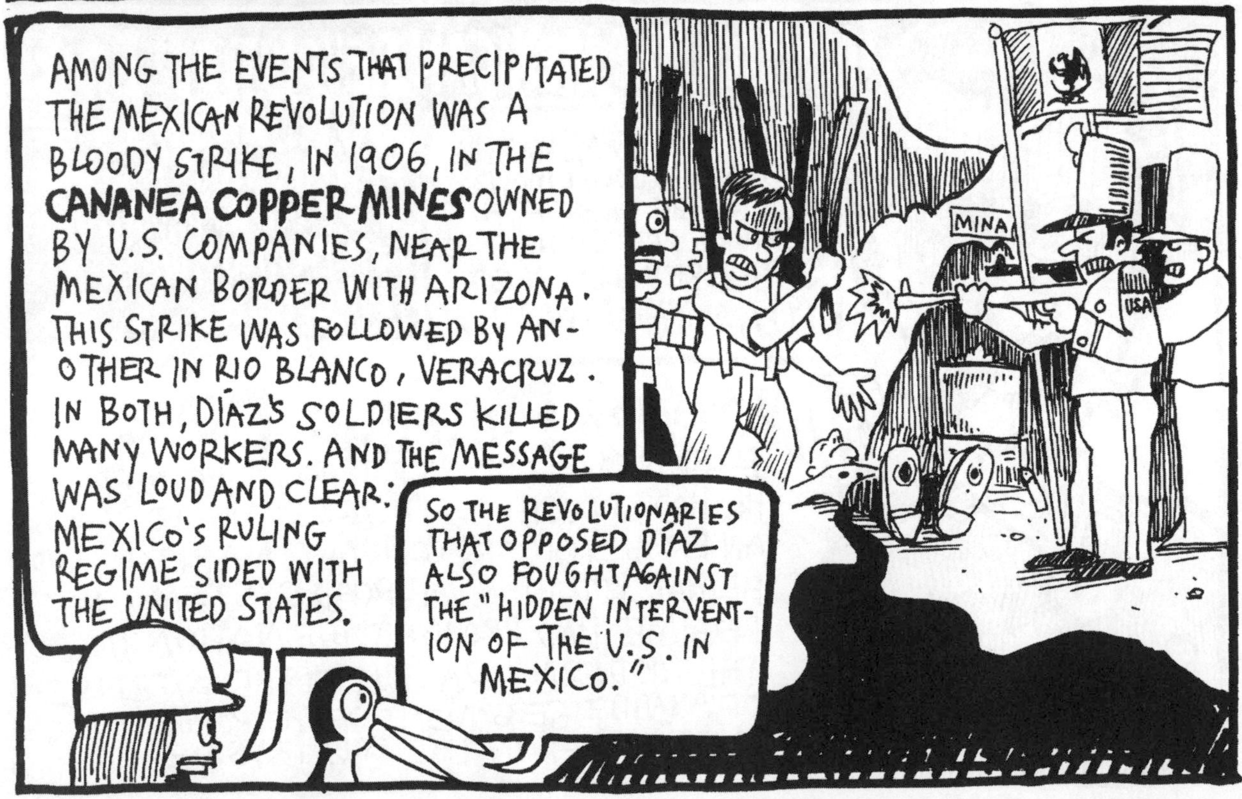
AMONG THE EVENTS THAT PRECIPITATED THE MEXICAN REVOLUTION WAS A BLOODY STRIKE, IN 1906, IN THE **CANANEA COPPER MINES** OWNED BY U.S. COMPANIES, NEAR THE MEXICAN BORDER WITH ARIZONA. THIS STRIKE WAS FOLLOWED BY ANOTHER IN RIO BLANCO, VERACRUZ. IN BOTH, DÍAZ'S SOLDIERS KILLED MANY WORKERS. AND THE MESSAGE WAS LOUD AND CLEAR: MEXICO'S RULING REGIME SIDED WITH THE UNITED STATES.
MINA
USA
SO THE REVOLUTIONARIES THAT OPPOSED DÍAZ ALSO FOUGHT AGAINST THE "HIDDEN INTERVENTION OF THE U.S. IN MEXICO."

ABOUT A FOURTH OF THE U.S. ARMY WAS "ON CALL" AT THE BORDER MEXICAN REBELS, LIKE VILLA, OCCASIONALLY WENT NORTHBOUND AND FOUGHT ON THE AMERICAN SIDE OF THE BORDER, AS IN THE FAMOUS BATTLE OF COLUMBUS, NEW MEXICO.

MILLIONS OF WOMEN JOINED THE ARMY ON THE BATTLEFIELD. THEY WERE KNOWN AS LAS SOLDADERAS - FEMALE CADETS. THEIR EFFORTS EVEN INSPIRED SONGS, SUCH AS "LA ADELITA."

La Güera y su gente improvisa sus trincheras; aunque es mujer tiene el grado de coronel; y sus trenzas no han impedido que ostente con orgullo sus estrellas.	The blondie and her people improvise a makeshift trench; even though she is a woman her rank is colonel; and her braids don't get in the way of her insignias.

67

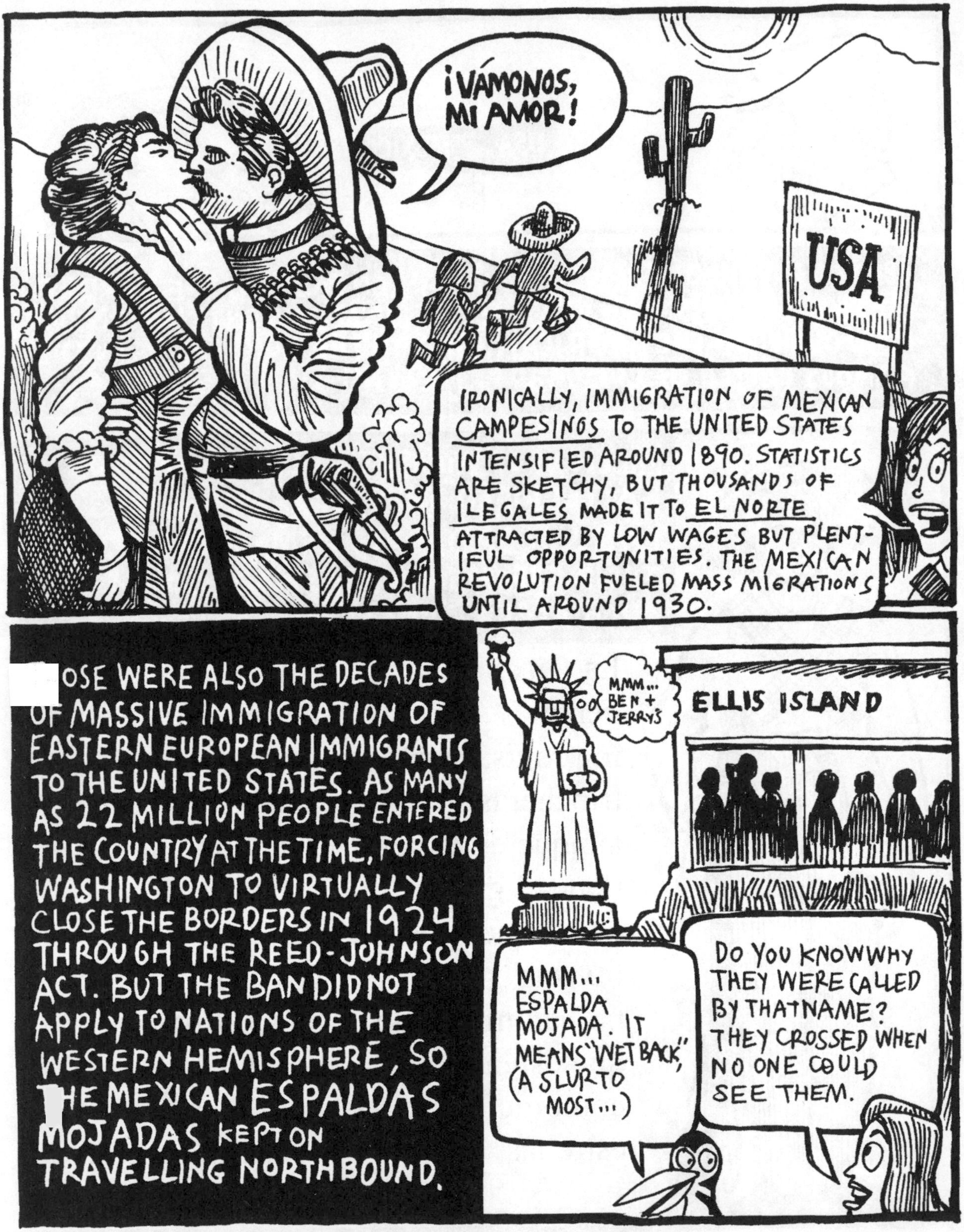
¡VÁMONOS, MI AMOR!
USA
IRONICALLY, IMMIGRATION OF MEXICAN CAMPESINOS TO THE UNITED STATES INTENSIFIED AROUND 1890. STATISTICS ARE SKETCHY, BUT THOUSANDS OF ILEGALES MADE IT TO EL NORTE ATTRACTED BY LOW WAGES BUT PLENTIFUL OPPORTUNITIES. THE MEXICAN REVOLUTION FUELED MASS MIGRATIONS UNTIL AROUND 1930.
OSE WERE ALSO THE DECADES OF MASSIVE IMMIGRATION OF EASTERN EUROPEAN IMMIGRANTS TO THE UNITED STATES. AS MANY AS 22 MILLION PEOPLE ENTERED THE COUNTRY AT THE TIME, FORCING WASHINGTON TO VIRTUALLY CLOSE THE BORDERS IN 1924 THROUGH THE REED-JOHNSON ACT. BUT THE BAN DID NOT APPLY TO NATIONS OF THE WESTERN HEMISPHERE, SO HE MEXICAN ESPALDAS MOJADAS KEPT ON TRAVELLING NORTHBOUND.
MMM... BEN + JERRY'S
ELLIS ISLAND
MMM... ESPALDA MOJADA. IT MEANS "WETBACK," (A SLUR TO MOST...)
DO YOU KNOW WHY THEY WERE CALLED BY THAT NAME? THEY CROSSED WHEN NO ONE COULD SEE THEM.

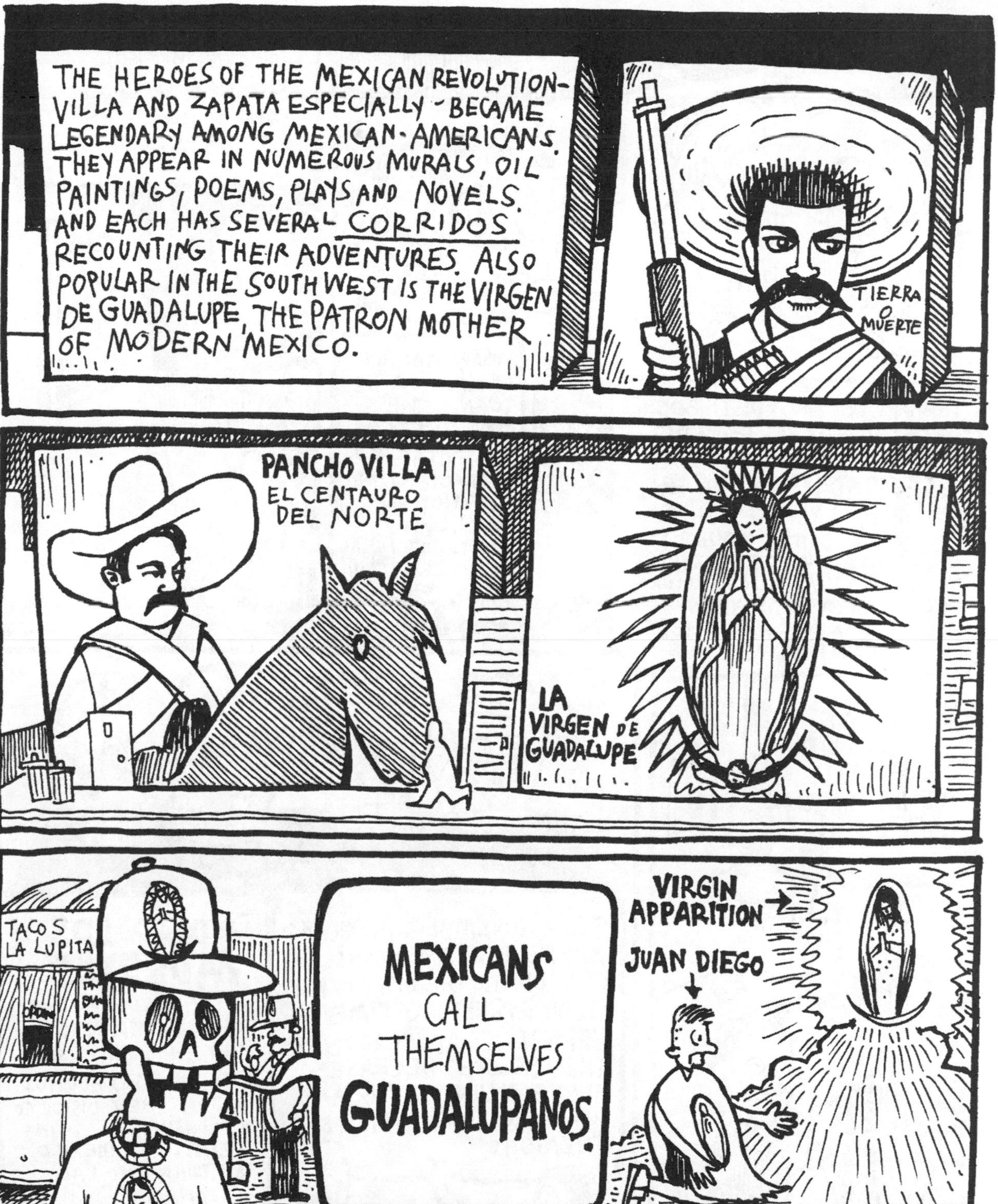
THE HEROES OF THE MEXICAN REVOLUTION- VILLA AND ZAPATA ESPECIALLY - BECAME LEGENDARY AMONG MEXICAN-AMERICANS. THEY APPEAR IN NUMEROUS MURALS, OIL PAINTINGS, POEMS, PLAYS AND NOVELS. AND EACH HAS SEVERAL CORRIDOS RECOUNTING THEIR ADVENTURES. ALSO POPULAR IN THE SOUTHWEST IS THE VIRGEN DE GUADALUPE, THE PATRON MOTHER OF MODERN MEXICO.
TIERRA O MUERTE
PANCHO VILLA
EL CENTAURO DEL NORTE
LA VIRGEN DE GUADALUPE
TACOS LA LUPITA
MEXICANS CALL THEMSELVES GUADALUPANOS.
VIRGIN APPARITION
JUAN DIEGO

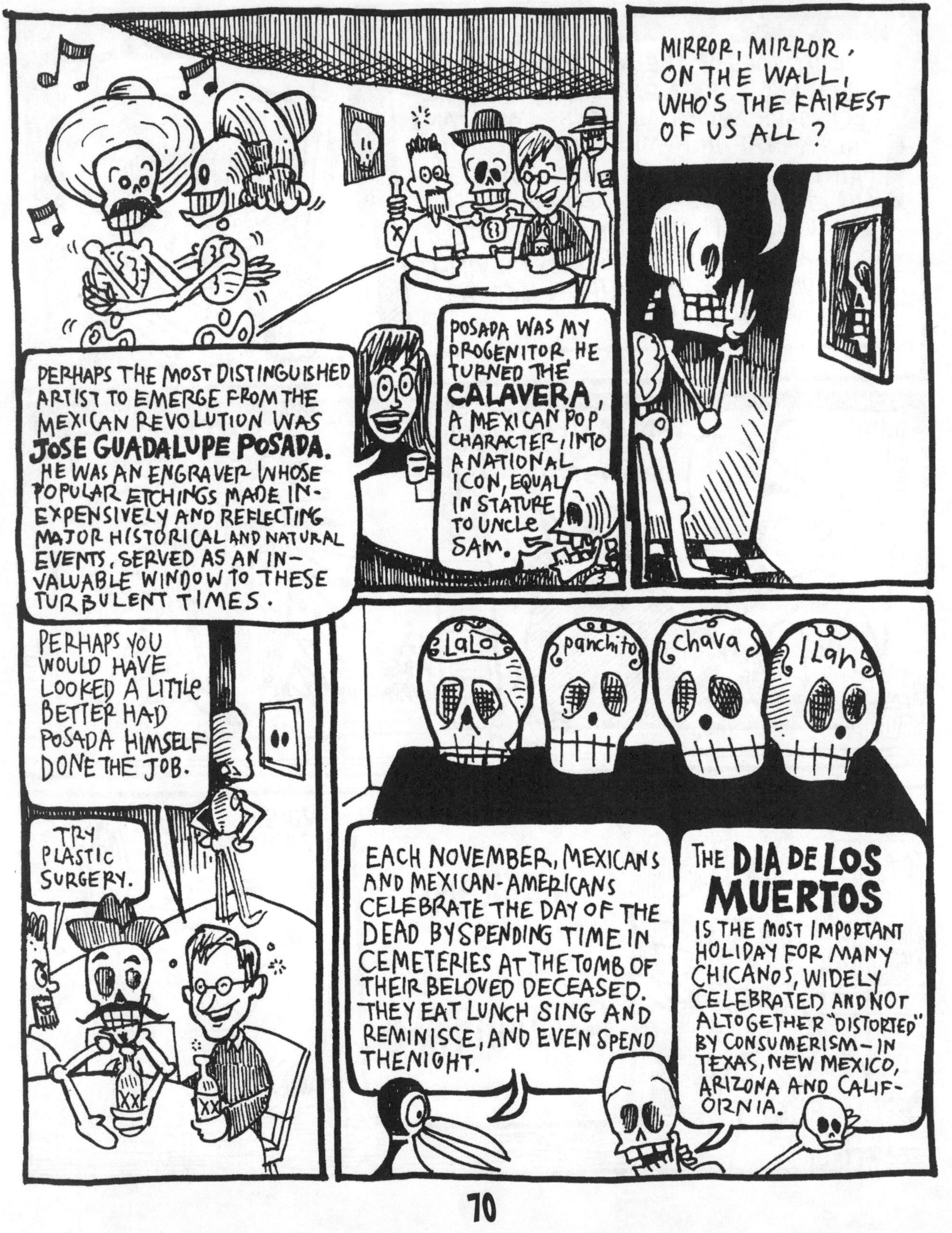
PERHAPS THE MOST DISTINGUISHED ARTIST TO EMERGE FROM THE MEXICAN REVOLUTION WAS **JOSE GUADALUPE POSADA.** HE WAS AN ENGRAVER WHOSE POPULAR ETCHINGS MADE IN-EXPENSIVELY AND REFLECTING MAJOR HISTORICAL AND NATURAL EVENTS, SERVED AS AN IN-VALUABLE WINDOW TO THESE TURBULENT TIMES.
POSADA WAS MY PROGENITOR. HE TURNED THE **CALAVERA**, A MEXICAN POP CHARACTER, INTO A NATIONAL ICON, EQUAL IN STATURE TO UNCLE SAM.
MIRROR, MIRROR, ON THE WALL, WHO'S THE FAIREST OF US ALL?
PERHAPS YOU WOULD HAVE LOOKED A LITTLE BETTER HAD POSADA HIMSELF DONE THE JOB.
TRY PLASTIC SURGERY.
XX
XX
LaLo
panchito
Chava
ILan
EACH NOVEMBER, MEXICANS AND MEXICAN-AMERICANS CELEBRATE THE DAY OF THE DEAD BY SPENDING TIME IN CEMETERIES AT THE TOMB OF THEIR BELOVED DECEASED. THEY EAT LUNCH SING AND REMINISCE, AND EVEN SPEND THE NIGHT.
THE **DIA DE LOS MUERTOS** IS THE MOST IMPORTANT HOLIDAY FOR MANY CHICANOS, WIDELY CELEBRATED AND NOT ALTOGETHER "DISTORTED" BY CONSUMERISM—IN TEXAS, NEW MEXICO, ARIZONA AND CALIF-ORNIA.

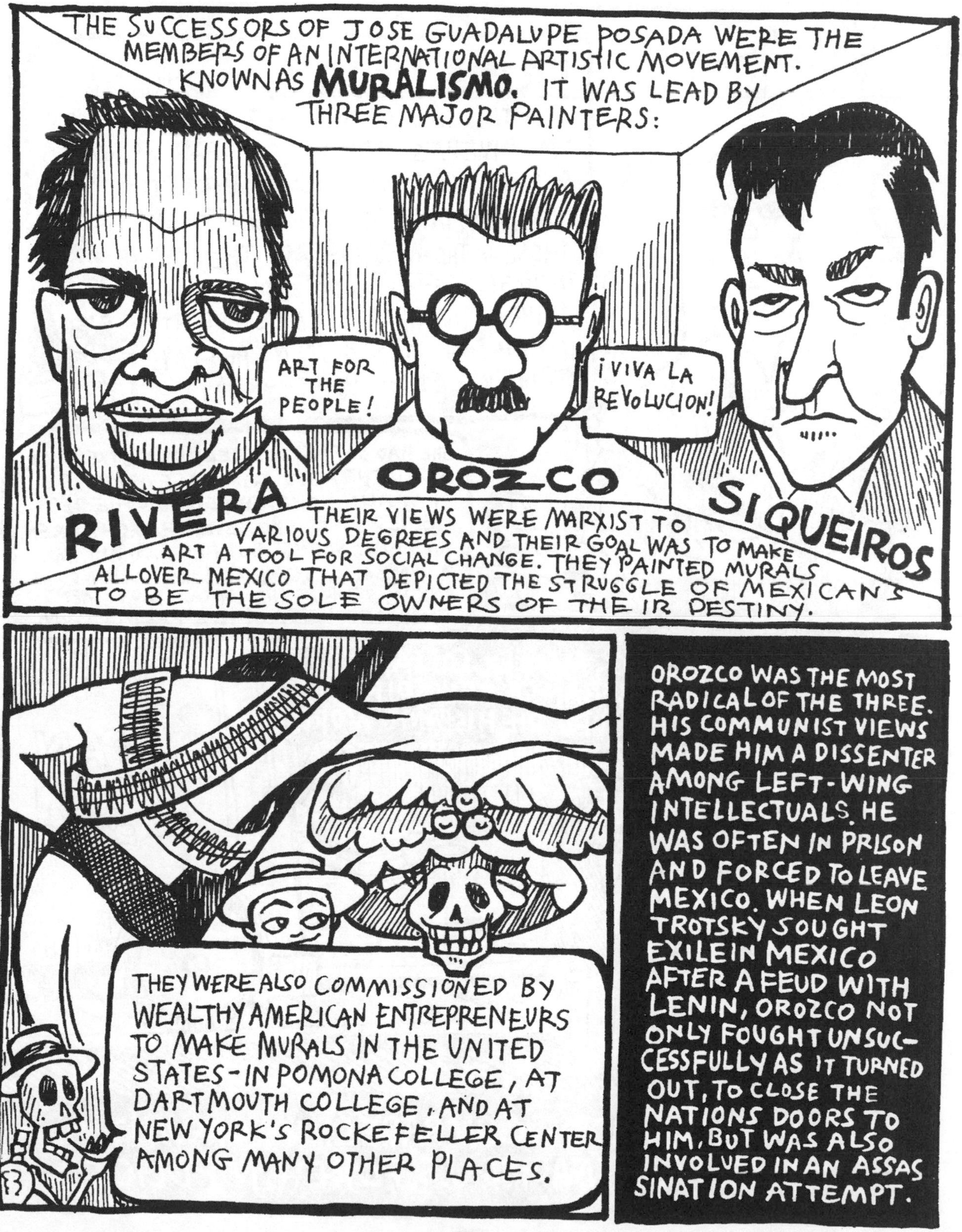
THE SUCCESSORS OF JOSE GUADALUPE POSADA WERE THE MEMBERS OF AN INTERNATIONAL ARTISTIC MOVEMENT. KNOWN AS **MURALISMO.** IT WAS LEAD BY THREE MAJOR PAINTERS:
ART FOR THE PEOPLE!
¡VIVA LA REVOLUCION!
RIVERA
OROZCO
SIQUEIROS
THEIR VIEWS WERE MARXIST TO VARIOUS DEGREES AND THEIR GOAL WAS TO MAKE ART A TOOL FOR SOCIAL CHANGE. THEY PAINTED MURALS ALL OVER MEXICO THAT DEPICTED THE STRUGGLE OF MEXICANS TO BE THE SOLE OWNERS OF THEIR DESTINY.
THEY WERE ALSO COMMISSIONED BY WEALTHY AMERICAN ENTREPRENEURS TO MAKE MURALS IN THE UNITED STATES - IN POMONA COLLEGE, AT DARTMOUTH COLLEGE, AND AT NEW YORK'S ROCKEFELLER CENTER AMONG MANY OTHER PLACES.
OROZCO WAS THE MOST RADICAL OF THE THREE. HIS COMMUNIST VIEWS MADE HIM A DISSENTER AMONG LEFT-WING INTELLECTUALS. HE WAS OFTEN IN PRISON AND FORCED TO LEAVE MEXICO. WHEN LEON TROTSKY SOUGHT EXILE IN MEXICO AFTER A FEUD WITH LENIN, OROZCO NOT ONLY FOUGHT UNSUCCESSFULLY AS IT TURNED OUT, TO CLOSE THE NATIONS DOORS TO HIM, BUT WAS ALSO INVOLVED IN AN ASSASSINATION ATTEMPT.

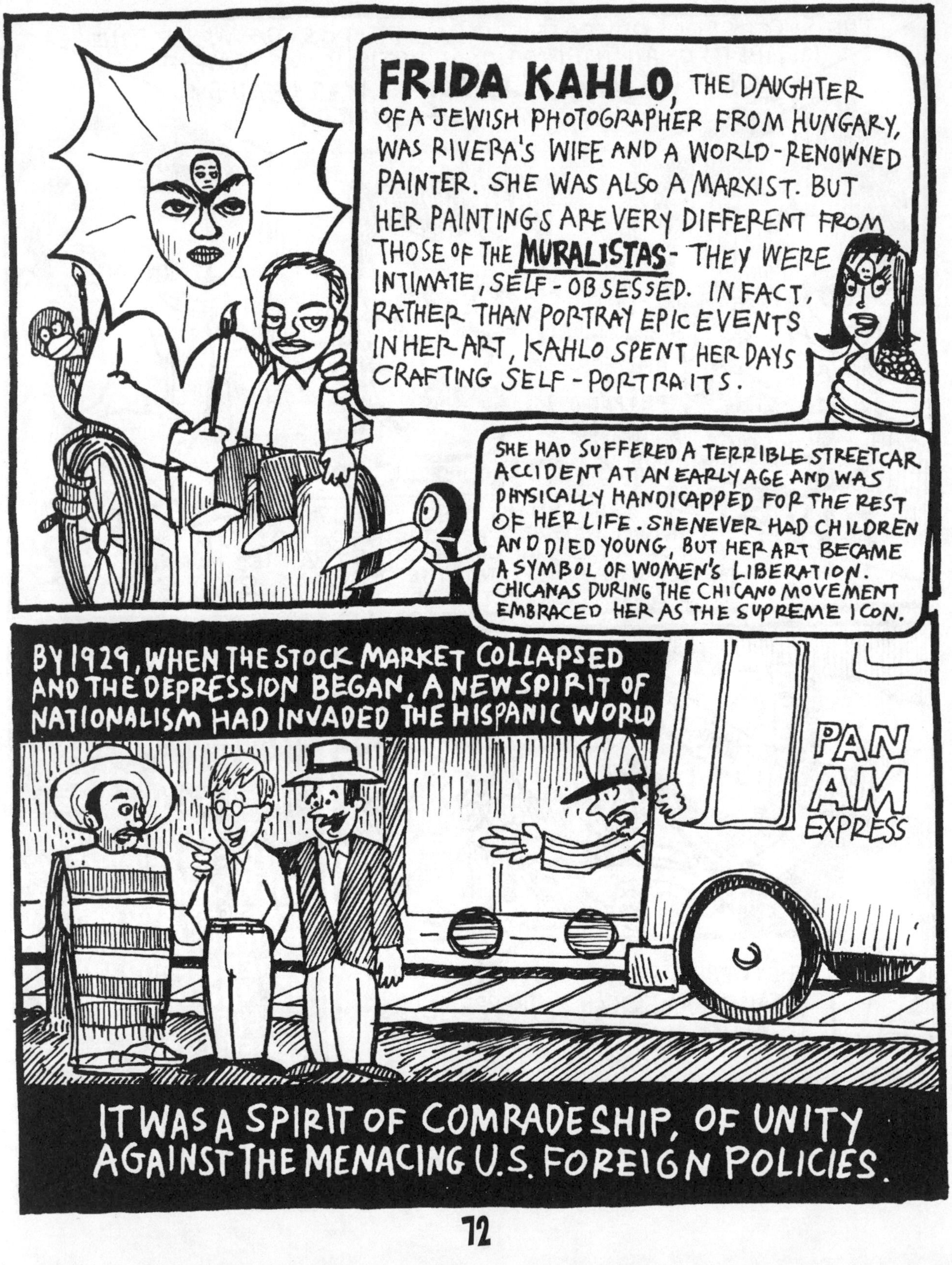
FRIDA KAHLO, THE DAUGHTER OF A JEWISH PHOTOGRAPHER FROM HUNGARY, WAS RIVERA'S WIFE AND A WORLD-RENOWNED PAINTER. SHE WAS ALSO A MARXIST. BUT HER PAINTINGS ARE VERY DIFFERENT FROM THOSE OF THE MURALISTAS- THEY WERE INTIMATE, SELF-OBSESSED. IN FACT, RATHER THAN PORTRAY EPIC EVENTS IN HER ART, KAHLO SPENT HER DAYS CRAFTING SELF-PORTRAITS.
SHE HAD SUFFERED A TERRIBLE STREETCAR ACCIDENT AT AN EARLY AGE AND WAS PHYSICALLY HANDICAPPED FOR THE REST OF HER LIFE. SHE NEVER HAD CHILDREN AND DIED YOUNG, BUT HER ART BECAME A SYMBOL OF WOMEN'S LIBERATION. CHICANAS DURING THE CHICANO MOVEMENT EMBRACED HER AS THE SUPREME ICON.
BY 1929, WHEN THE STOCK MARKET COLLAPSED AND THE DEPRESSION BEGAN, A NEW SPIRIT OF NATIONALISM HAD INVADED THE HISPANIC WORLD
PAN AM EXPRESS
IT WAS A SPIRIT OF COMRADESHIP, OF UNITY AGAINST THE MENACING U.S. FOREIGN POLICIES.

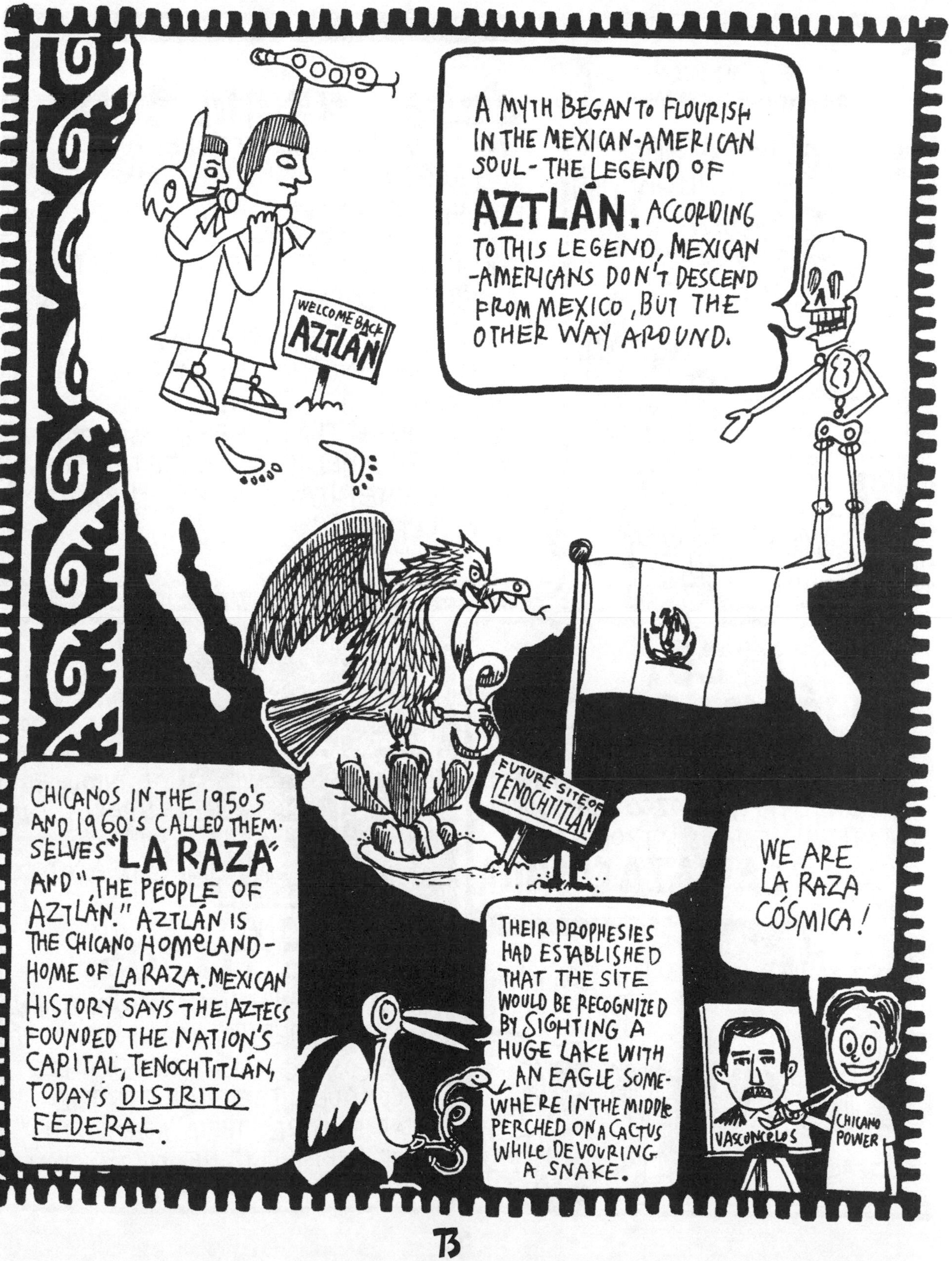
A MYTH BEGAN TO FLOURISH IN THE MEXICAN-AMERICAN SOUL - THE LEGEND OF AZTLÁN. ACCORDING TO THIS LEGEND, MEXICAN-AMERICANS DON'T DESCEND FROM MEXICO, BUT THE OTHER WAY AROUND.
WELCOME BACK AZTLÁN
CHICANOS IN THE 1950'S AND 1960'S CALLED THEMSELVES "LA RAZA" AND "THE PEOPLE OF AZTLÁN." AZTLÁN IS THE CHICANO HOMELAND - HOME OF LA RAZA. MEXICAN HISTORY SAYS THE AZTECS FOUNDED THE NATION'S CAPITAL, TENOCHTITLÁN, TODAYS DISTRITO FEDERAL.
FUTURE SITE OF TENOCHTITLÁN
THEIR PROPHESIES HAD ESTABLISHED THAT THE SITE WOULD BE RECOGNIZED BY SIGHTING A HUGE LAKE WITH AN EAGLE SOMEWHERE IN THE MIDDLE PERCHED ON A CACTUS WHILE DEVOURING A SNAKE.
WE ARE LA RAZA CÓSMICA!
VASCONCELOS
CHICANO POWER

WE IN THE AMERICAS ARE BY NATURE DREAMERS.

NOTHING WRONG WITH THAT!

JOSE ENRIQUE RODÓ

WAS AN URUGUAYAN INTELLECTUAL. IN 1900 HE PUBLISHED A BOOK TITLED **ARIEL.** IN IT HE ARGUES THAT THE YOUTH IN LATIN AMERICA NEEDED TO FIND THEIR OWN CHARACTER, THEIR OWN ROAD TO SUCCESS, AND NOT TO IMITATE THE UNITED STATES BLINDLY. RODÓ ALSO WROTE THAT WHEN COMPARED TO NORTH AMERICA'S MATERIALISM, LATIN AMERICA WAS MUCH MORE "SPIRITUAL."

THEN IN **1925, JOSÉ VASCONCELOS** MEXICO'S MINISTER OF EDUCATION AND A PROMOTER OF THE MURALIST ART OF RIVERA, OROZCO AND SIQUEIROS, WROTE HIS FAMOUS INTRODUCTORY ESSAY TO **LA RAZA CÓSMICA.**

THE COSMIC RACE.

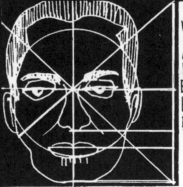

VASCONCELOS' ARGUMENT PROVED TO BE EXTRAORDINARILY INFLUENTIAL, ESPECIALLY AMONG CHICANOS.

HE CLAIMED THAT **MESTIZOS** A MIXTURE OF IBERIANS AND ABORIGINALS IN MESO AMERICA, WHICH HE CALLED "THE COSMIC RACE," WERE CALLED TO CONQUER THE GLOBE IN THE NEAR FUTURE. THEIR "ADAPTABILITY," THEIR HYBRIDITY, HE WROTE, WAS A FORMULA FOR SUCCESS.

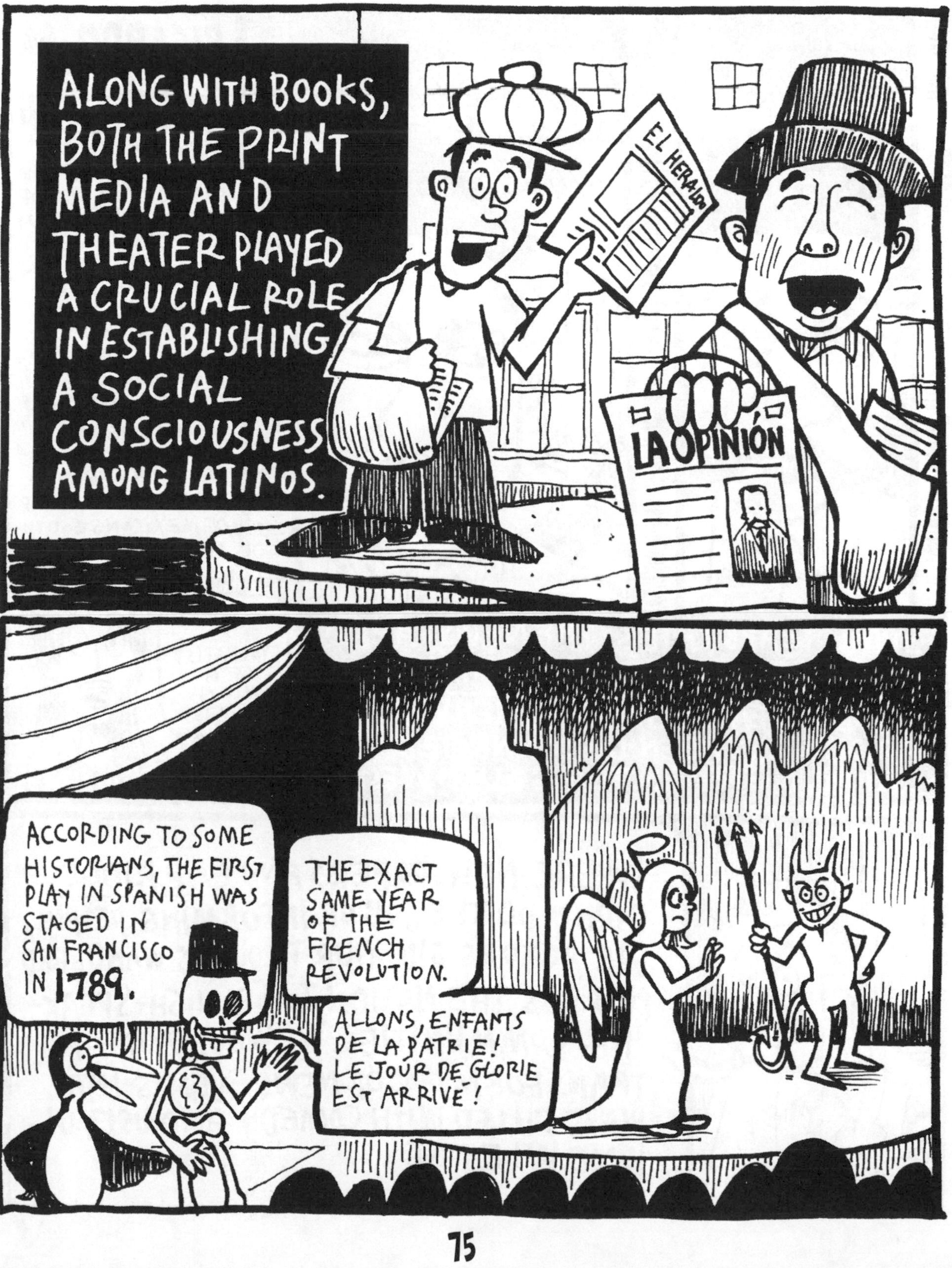
ALONG WITH BOOKS, BOTH THE PRINT MEDIA AND THEATER PLAYED A CRUCIAL ROLE IN ESTABLISHING A SOCIAL CONSCIOUSNESS AMONG LATINOS.
EL HERALDO
LA OPINIÓN
ACCORDING TO SOME HISTORIANS, THE FIRST PLAY IN SPANISH WAS STAGED IN SAN FRANCISCO IN 1789.
THE EXACT SAME YEAR OF THE FRENCH REVOLUTION.
ALLONS, ENFANTS DE LA PATRIE! LE JOUR DE GLOIRE EST ARRIVÉ!

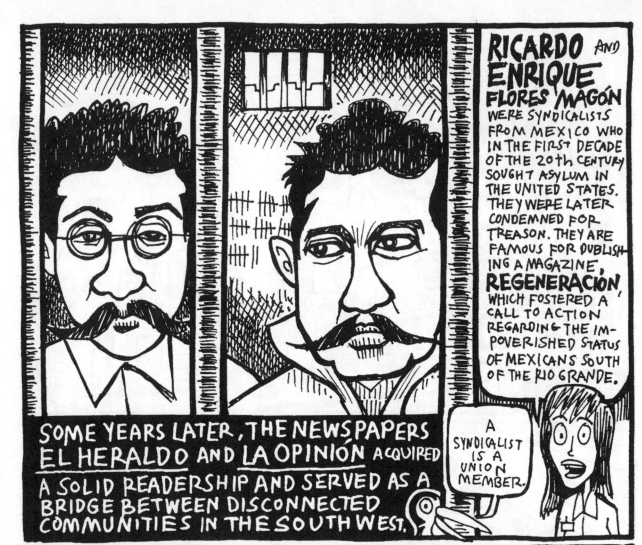

RICARDO AND ENRIQUE FLORES MAGÓN WERE SYNDICALISTS FROM MEXICO WHO IN THE FIRST DECADE OF THE 20th CENTURY SOUGHT ASYLUM IN THE UNITED STATES. THEY WERE LATER CONDEMNED FOR TREASON. THEY ARE FAMOUS FOR PUBLISHING A MAGAZINE, **REGENERACIÓN,** WHICH FOSTERED A CALL TO ACTION REGARDING THE IMPOVERISHED STATUS OF MEXICANS SOUTH OF THE RIO GRANDE.

SOME YEARS LATER, THE NEWSPAPERS EL HERALDO AND LA OPINIÓN ACQUIRED A SOLID READERSHIP AND SERVED AS A BRIDGE BETWEEN DISCONNECTED COMMUNITIES IN THE SOUTHWEST.

A SYNDICALIST IS A UNION MEMBER.

WHERE NEWSPAPERS AND <u>CORRIDOS</u> DIDN'T DO THE JOB OF INFORMING PEOPLE, WE ACTORS DID. OUR TROUPES WANDERED ACROSS THE NATION TO SPANISH-SPEAKING COMMUNITIES. WE WOULD OFTEN TRANSFORM MAJOR NEWS EVENTS INTO PLAYS FILLED WITH COMEDY AND USEFUL KNOWLEDGE.

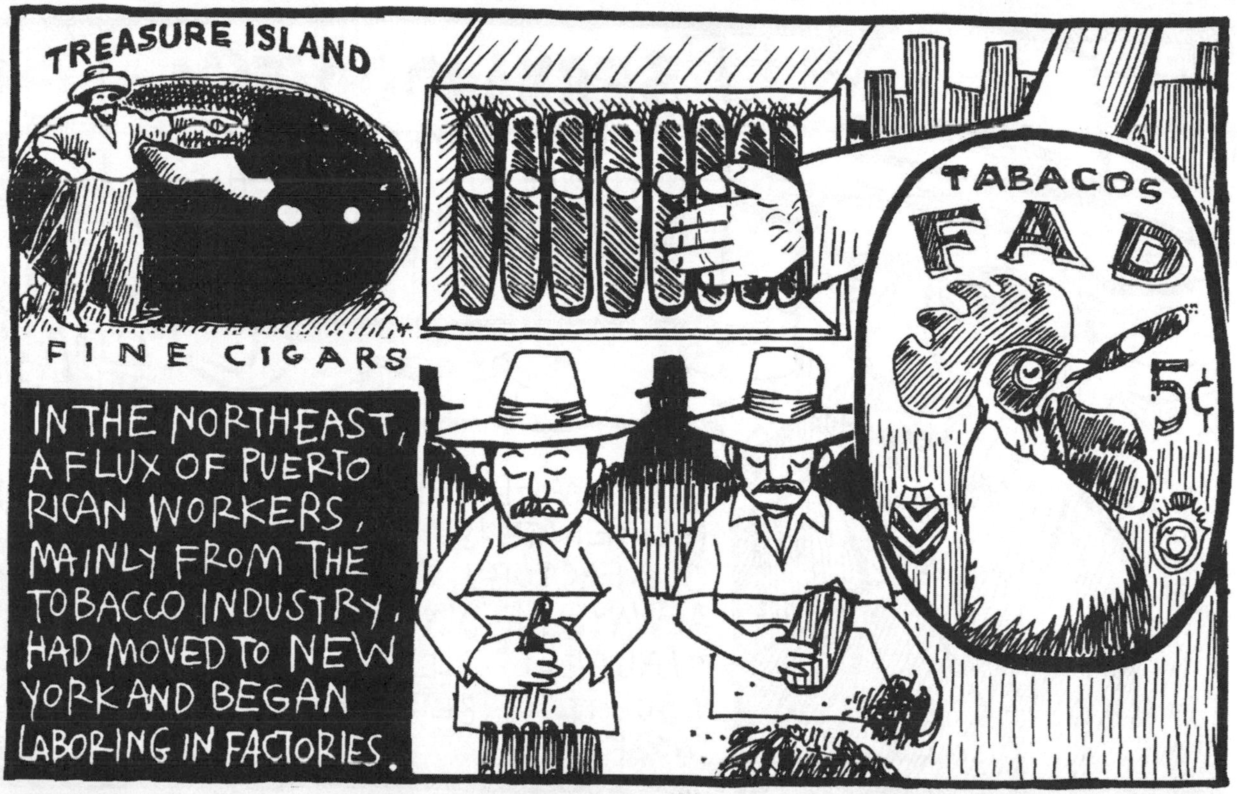
TREASURE ISLAND
FINE CIGARS
IN THE NORTHEAST, A FLUX OF PUERTO RICAN WORKERS, MAINLY FROM THE TOBACCO INDUSTRY, HAD MOVED TO NEW YORK AND BEGAN LABORING IN FACTORIES.
TABACOS
FAD
5¢

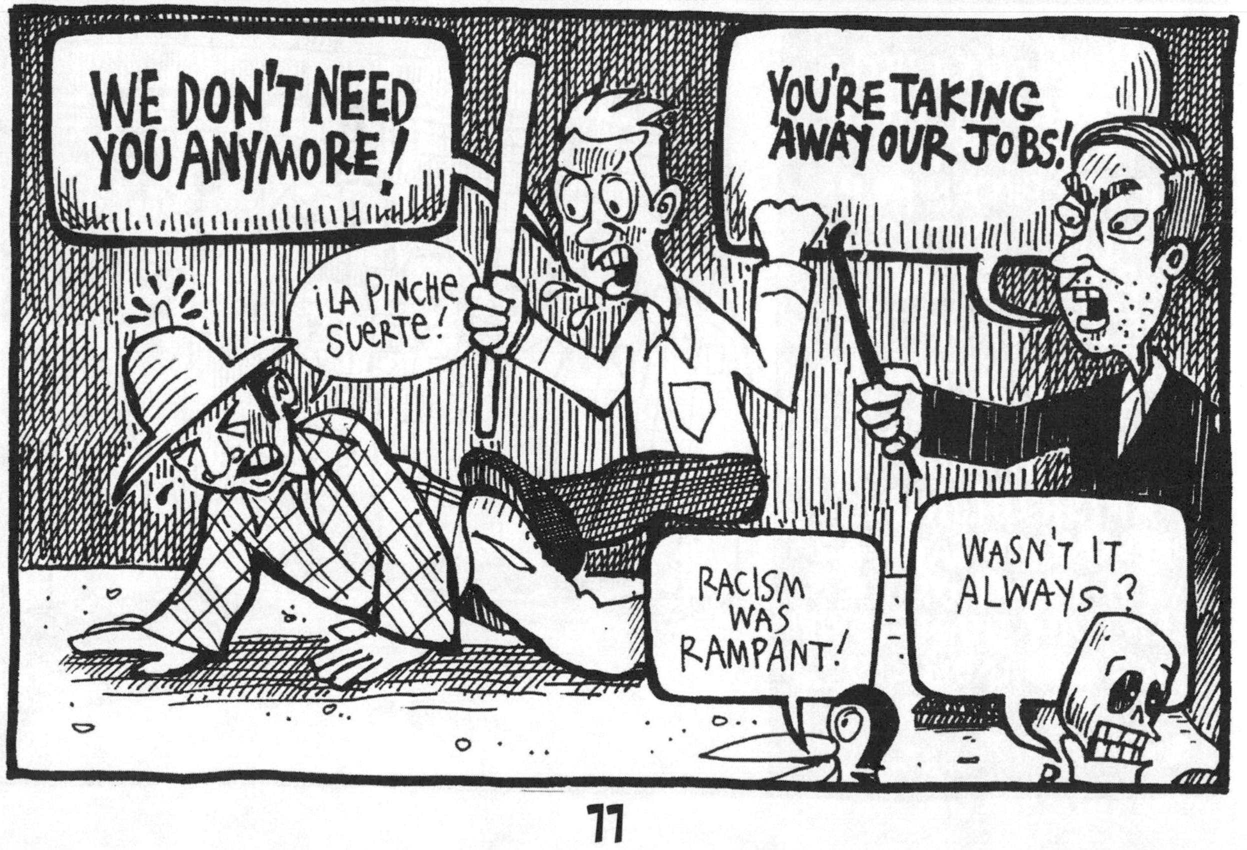
WE DON'T NEED YOU ANYMORE!
¡LA PINCHE SUERTE!
YOU'RE TAKING AWAY OUR JOBS!
RACISM WAS RAMPANT!
WASN'T IT ALWAYS?

BERNARDO VEGA, A TOBACCO WORKER, ARRIVED IN NEW YORK CITY IN 1916. IN HIS **MEMOIRS**, HE CHRONICLED THE PLIGHT OF PUERTO RICANS.

THE IMAGE OF PUERTO RICANS AS ILLITERATE IS AN ABERRATION. IN OUR FACTORY, PUERTO RICANS WERE ALWAYS READING: ZOLA, DUMAS, FLAUBERT, JULES VERNE... WE ALSO FOUGHT FOR BETTER CONDITIONS FOR ALL WORKERS.

THE VICIOUS CIRCLE OF POVERTY THAT ENTRAPPED THE PUERTO RICAN POPULATION IN THE NORTHEAST WAS THE RESULT OF THE POLITICAL SITUATION IN PUERTO RICO. NO SOONER DID THE SPANISH COLONIAL PRESENCE DISAPPEAR AT THE TURN OF THE CENTURY THAN PUERTO RICO WAS QUICKLY OVERWHELMED BY THE U.S.

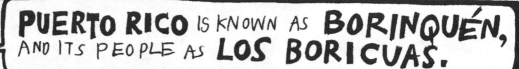

PUERTO RICO IS KNOWN AS BORINQUÉN, AND ITS PEOPLE AS LOS BORICUAS.

PUERTO RICO

BORINQUÉN MEANS "LAND OF THE BRAVE LORD." THIS WAS WHAT THE ARAWAK INDIANS CALLED THEIR ISLAND BEFORE THE SPANIARDS ARRIVED.

AZUCAR

IN 1932, THE SUGAR BOOM COLLAPSED AND MASSIVE WAVES OF PUERTO RICAN IMMIGRANTS BEGAN TO MOVE TO NEW YORK. THIS TREND WOULD PEAK IN 1945.

LIBERTAD BORINQUEÑA

USA

U$ BUSINESS

THE ISLAND BECAME A COMMONWEALTH OF THE UNITED STATES IN 1917. THAT YEAR, THE JONES ACT GAVE PUERTO RICANS U.S. CITIZENSHIP AND OBLIGATED U.S. ARMY SERVICE.

PUERTO RICO'S STATUS AS A NO MAN'S LAND, NEITHER FULLY CARIBBEAN NOR FULLY AMERICAN, BEGAN...

MANY PUERTO RICANS LEFT. THE MAJORITY WERE POOR JÍBAROS, PEASANTS FROM THE COUNTRYSIDE LOOKING FOR BETTER JOB OPPORTUNITIES, BUT MIDDLE- AND UPPER-MIDDLE CLASS PEOPLE ALSO CROSSED THE CHANNEL.

IN SPITE OF THE JONES ACT AND THE STATUS OF PUERTO RICO, THE DRIVE FOR ITS INDEPENDENCE HAS REMAINED UNABATED SINCE THE TIMES OF **JOSÉ DE DIEGO**, A NINETEENTH CENTURY PUERTO RICAN POET.

DE DIEGO WROTE THE POEM "TO THE PERSECUTED" TO EXPRESS HIS INDEPENDISTA SPIRIT.

RESURGE, BREATHE, SHOUT, WALK, FIGHT,
VIBRATE, GLIDE, THUNDER, SHINE FORTH...

DO AS THE RIVER RICH WITH NEW RAINWATER:

GROW.

OR LIKE THE SEA APPROACHING A ROCKY SHORE:

STRIKE.

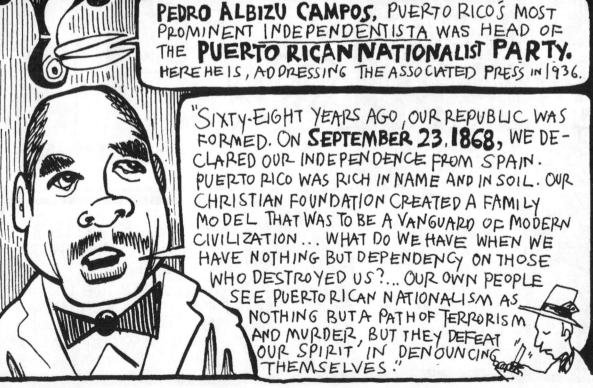

PEDRO ALBIZU CAMPOS, PUERTO RICO'S MOST PROMINENT **INDEPENDENTISTA** WAS HEAD OF THE **PUERTO RICAN NATIONALIST PARTY.** HERE HE IS, ADDRESSING THE ASSOCIATED PRESS IN 1936.

"SIXTY-EIGHT YEARS AGO, OUR REPUBLIC WAS FORMED. ON **SEPTEMBER 23, 1868**, WE DECLARED OUR INDEPENDENCE FROM SPAIN. PUERTO RICO WAS RICH IN NAME AND IN SOIL. OUR CHRISTIAN FOUNDATION CREATED A FAMILY MODEL THAT WAS TO BE A VANGUARD OF MODERN CIVILIZATION... WHAT DO WE HAVE WHEN WE HAVE NOTHING BUT DEPENDENCY ON THOSE WHO DESTROYED US?... OUR OWN PEOPLE SEE PUERTO RICAN NATIONALISM AS NOTHING BUT A PATH OF TERRORISM AND MURDER, BUT THEY DEFEAT OUR SPIRIT' IN DENOUNCING THEMSELVES."

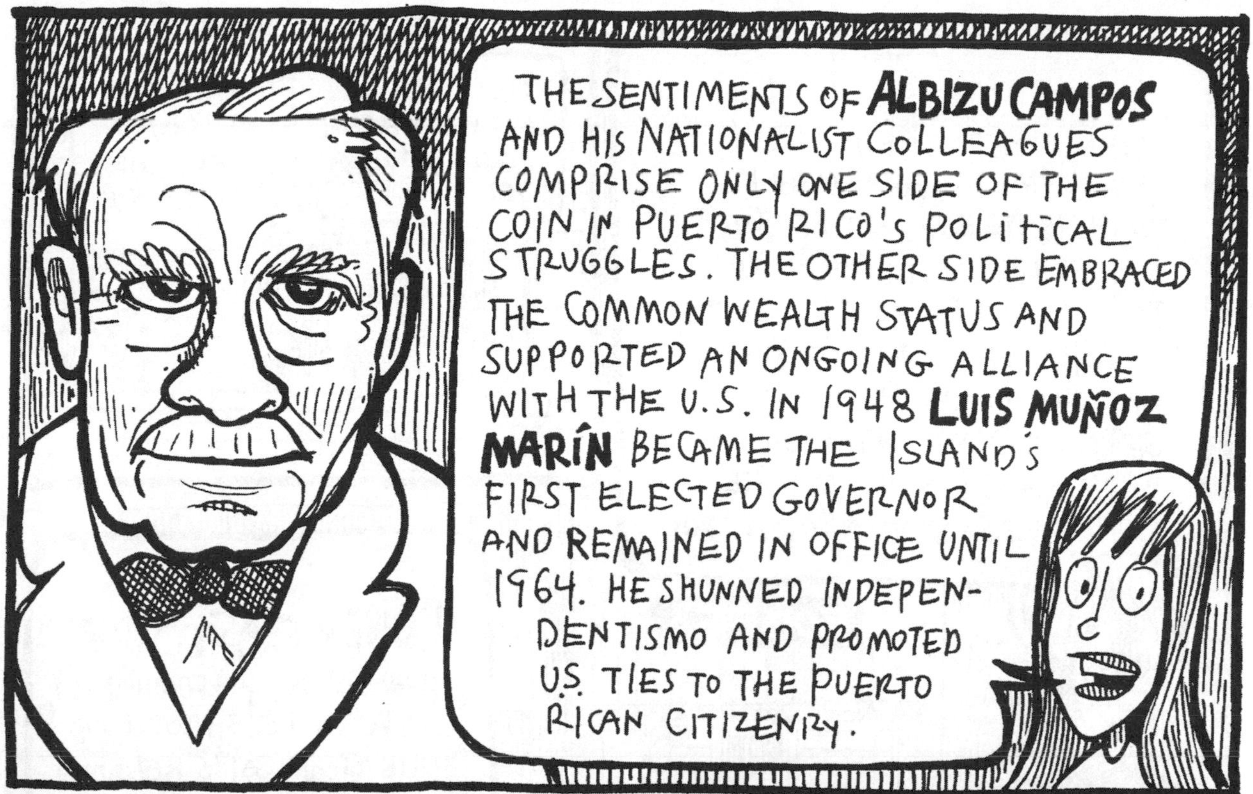
THE SENTIMENTS OF ALBIZU CAMPOS AND HIS NATIONALIST COLLEAGUES COMPRISE ONLY ONE SIDE OF THE COIN IN PUERTO RICO'S POLITICAL STRUGGLES. THE OTHER SIDE EMBRACED THE COMMONWEALTH STATUS AND SUPPORTED AN ONGOING ALLIANCE WITH THE U.S. IN 1948 LUIS MUÑOZ MARÍN BECAME THE ISLAND'S FIRST ELECTED GOVERNOR AND REMAINED IN OFFICE UNTIL 1964. HE SHUNNED INDEPENDENTISMO AND PROMOTED U.S. TIES TO THE PUERTO RICAN CITIZENRY.

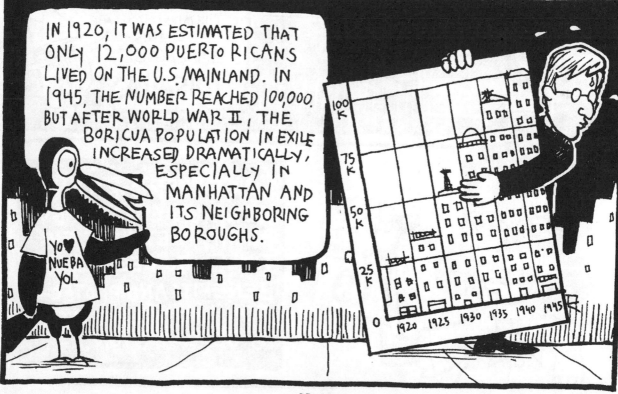

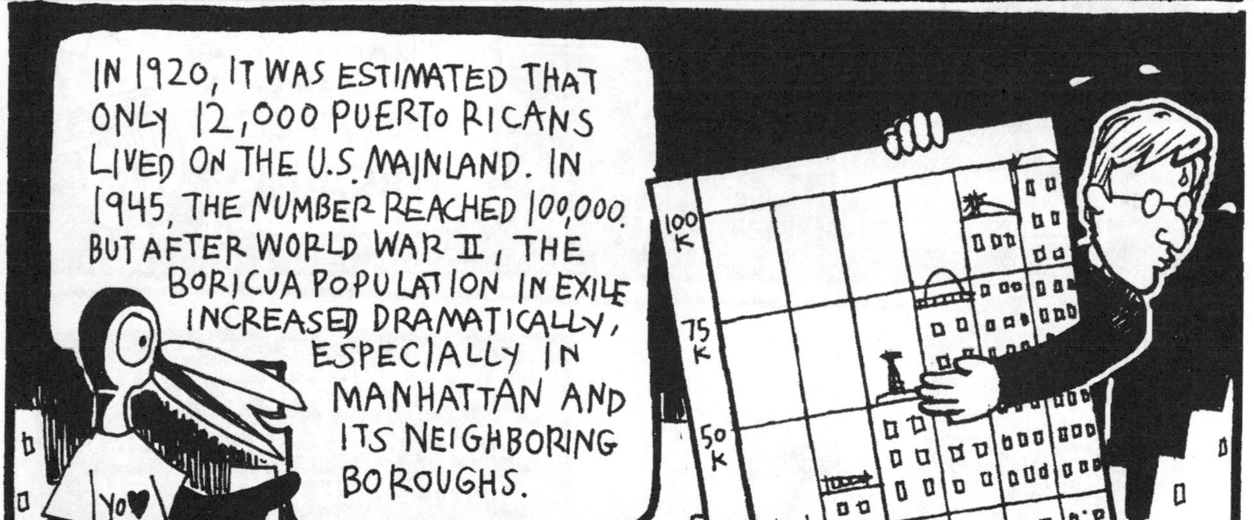
IN 1920, IT WAS ESTIMATED THAT ONLY 12,000 PUERTO RICANS LIVED ON THE U.S. MAINLAND. IN 1945, THE NUMBER REACHED 100,000. BUT AFTER WORLD WAR II, THE BORICUA POPULATION IN EXILE INCREASED DRAMATICALLY, ESPECIALLY IN MANHATTAN AND ITS NEIGHBORING BOROUGHS.
100 K
75 K
50 K
25 K
0
1920
1925
1930
1935
1940
1945
YO ♥ NUEBA YOL

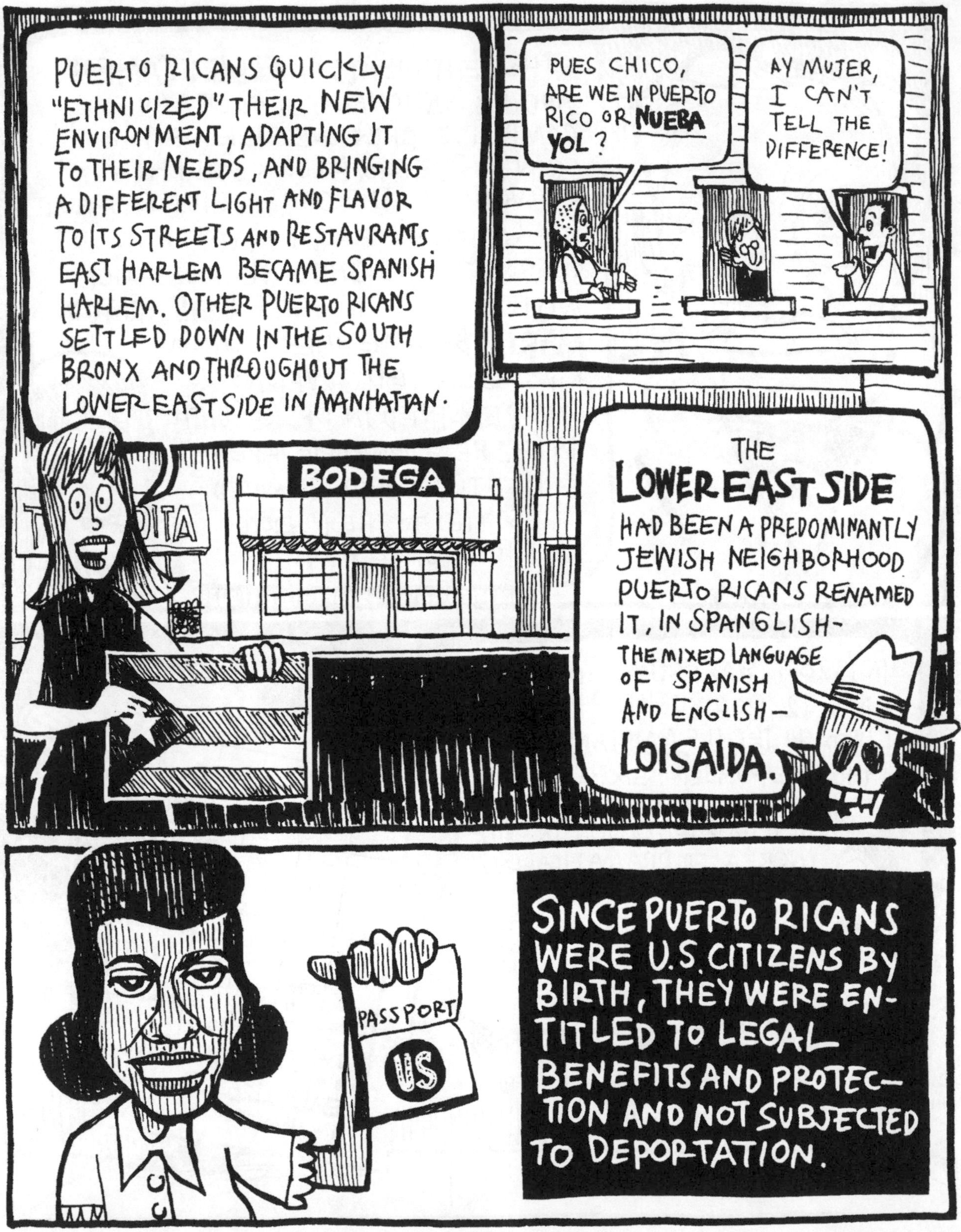
PUERTO RICANS QUICKLY "ETHNICIZED" THEIR NEW ENVIRONMENT, ADAPTING IT TO THEIR NEEDS, AND BRINGING A DIFFERENT LIGHT AND FLAVOR TO ITS STREETS AND RESTAURANTS. EAST HARLEM BECAME SPANISH HARLEM. OTHER PUERTO RICANS SETTLED DOWN IN THE SOUTH BRONX AND THROUGHOUT THE LOWER EAST SIDE IN MANHATTAN.
PUES CHICO, ARE WE IN PUERTO RICO OR NUEBA YOL?
AY MUJER, I CAN'T TELL THE DIFFERENCE!
BODEGA
THE LOWER EAST SIDE HAD BEEN A PREDOMINANTLY JEWISH NEIGHBORHOOD. PUERTO RICANS RENAMED IT, IN SPANGLISH— THE MIXED LANGUAGE OF SPANISH AND ENGLISH— LOISAIDA.
PASSPORT
US
SINCE PUERTO RICANS WERE U.S. CITIZENS BY BIRTH, THEY WERE ENTITLED TO LEGAL BENEFITS AND PROTECTION AND NOT SUBJECTED TO DEPORTATION.

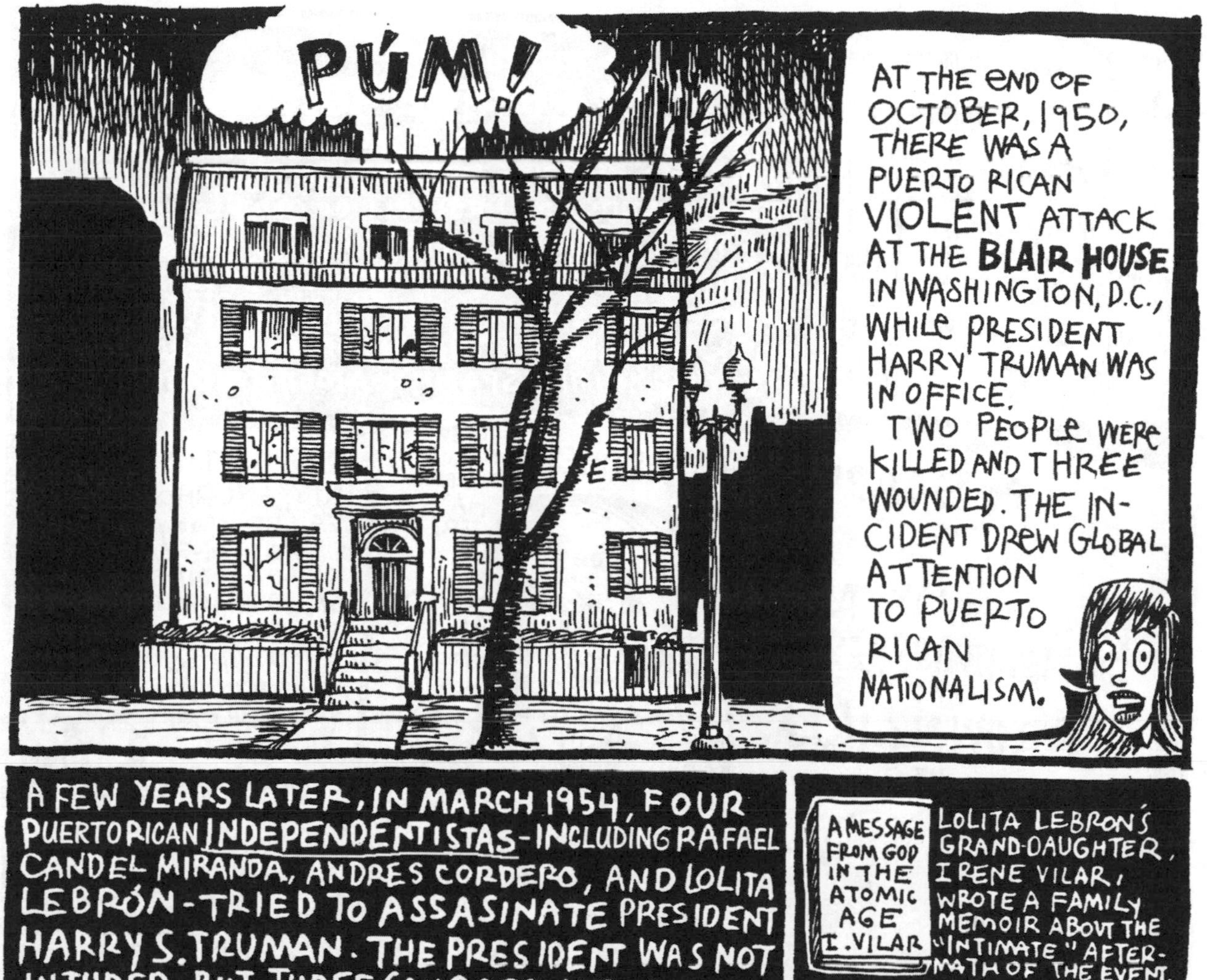
PÚM!
AT THE END OF OCTOBER, 1950, THERE WAS A PUERTO RICAN VIOLENT ATTACK AT THE **BLAIR HOUSE** IN WASHINGTON, D.C., WHILE PRESIDENT HARRY TRUMAN WAS IN OFFICE.
TWO PEOPLE WERE KILLED AND THREE WOUNDED. THE INCIDENT DREW GLOBAL ATTENTION TO PUERTO RICAN NATIONALISM.
A FEW YEARS LATER, IN MARCH 1954, FOUR PUERTORICAN INDEPENDENTISTAS - INCLUDING RAFAEL CANDEL MIRANDA, ANDRES CORDERO, AND LOLITA LEBRÓN - TRIED TO ASSASINATE PRESIDENT HARRY S. TRUMAN. THE PRESIDENT WAS NOT INJURED, BUT THREE CONGRESSMEN WERE. THE "TERRORISTS" WERE CAPTURED, SENT TO PRISON, AND NOT RELEASED UNTIL 1979.
eeek
DID THEY SAY "VIVA MEXICO?!"!
A MESSAGE FROM GOD IN THE ATOMIC AGE I. VILAR
LOLITA LEBRON'S GRAND-DAUGHTER, IRENE VILAR, WROTE A FAMILY MEMOIR ABOUT THE "INTIMATE" AFTERMATH OF THE EVENT.
"THE PEOPLE OF PUERTO RICO ARE PROFOUNDLY INDIGNANT AT THE ATTEMPT MADE AT BLAIR HOUSE, IN WHICH TWO PUERTORICAN NATIONALISTS WERE INVOLVED. WE WOULD FEEL ASHAMED OF CALLING OURSELVES PUERTO RICANS, IF IT WERE NOT FOR THE FACT THAT THE NATIONALIST GANGSTERS ARE LESS THAN 500 IN NUMBER, AMONG THE MORE THAN 2 MILLION DECENT, DEMOCRACY-LOVING AMERICAN CITIZENS THAT MAKE UP OUR COMMUNITY."
GOVERNOR LUIS MUÑOZ MARIN'S TELEVISED SPEECH

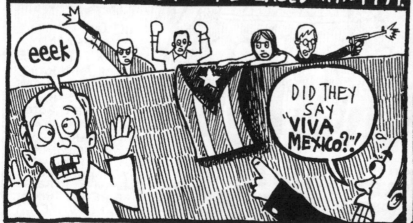

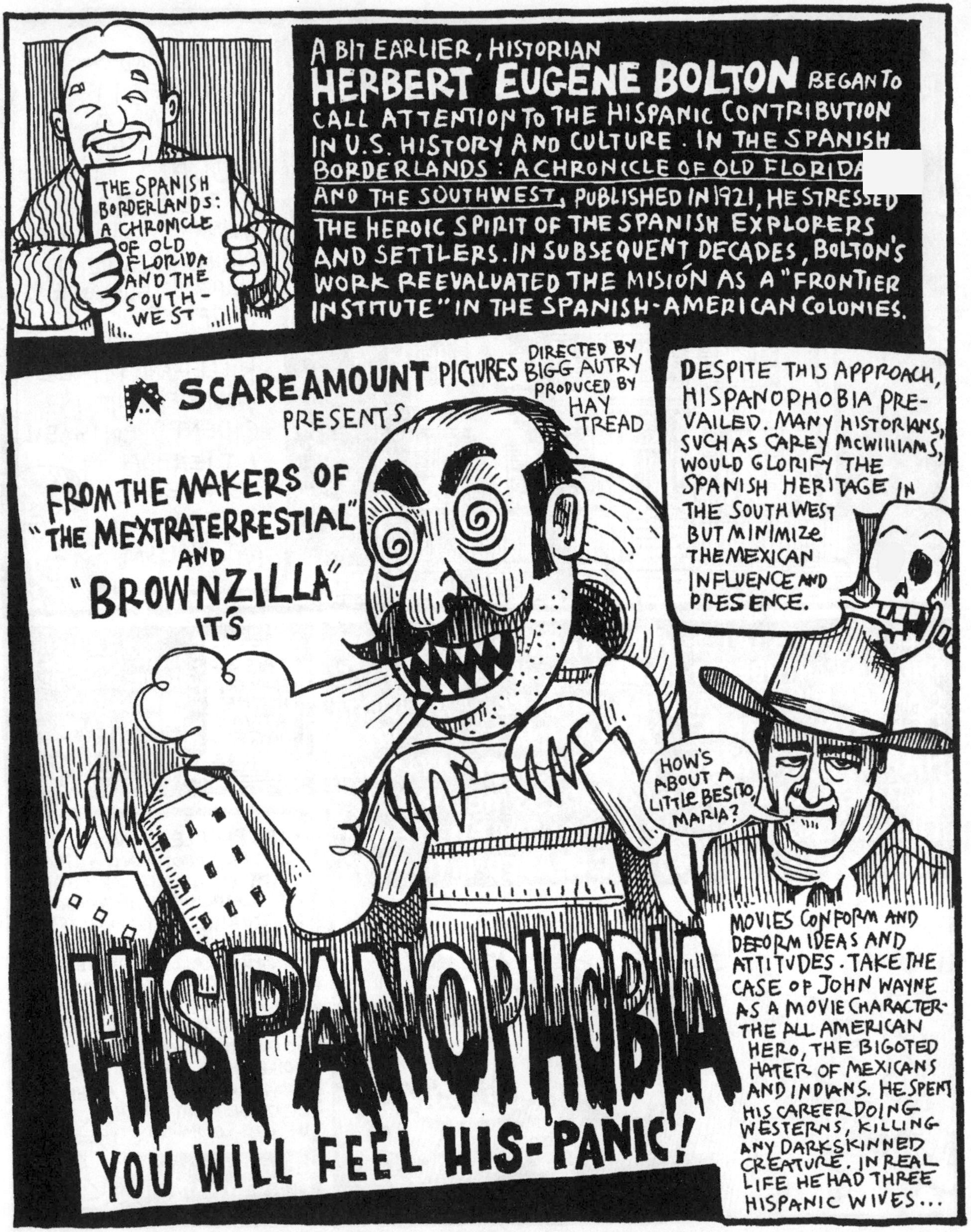
THE SPANISH BORDERLANDS: A CHRONICLE OF OLD FLORIDA AND THE SOUTH-WEST
A BIT EARLIER, HISTORIAN HERBERT EUGENE BOLTON BEGAN TO CALL ATTENTION TO THE HISPANIC CONTRIBUTION IN U.S. HISTORY AND CULTURE. IN THE SPANISH BORDERLANDS: A CHRONICLE OF OLD FLORIDA AND THE SOUTHWEST, PUBLISHED IN 1921, HE STRESSED THE HEROIC SPIRIT OF THE SPANISH EXPLORERS AND SETTLERS. IN SUBSEQUENT DECADES, BOLTON'S WORK REEVALUATED THE MISIÓN AS A "FRONTIER INSTITUTE" IN THE SPANISH-AMERICAN COLONIES.
SCAREAMOUNT PICTURES PRESENTS
DIRECTED BY BIGG AUTRY PRODUCED BY HAY TREAD
FROM THE MAKERS OF "THE MEXTRATERRESTIAL" AND "BROWNZILLA" IT'S
HISPANOPHOBIA
YOU WILL FEEL HIS-PANIC!
DESPITE THIS APPROACH, HISPANOPHOBIA PREVAILED. MANY HISTORIANS, SUCH AS CAREY McWILLIAMS, WOULD GLORIFY THE SPANISH HERITAGE IN THE SOUTHWEST BUT MINIMIZE THE MEXICAN INFLUENCE AND PRESENCE.
HOW'S ABOUT A LITTLE BESITO, MARIA?
MOVIES CONFORM AND DEFORM IDEAS AND ATTITUDES. TAKE THE CASE OF JOHN WAYNE AS A MOVIE CHARACTER-THE ALL AMERICAN HERO, THE BIGOTED HATER OF MEXICANS AND INDIANS. HE SPENT HIS CAREER DOING WESTERNS, KILLING ANY DARKSKINNED CREATURE. IN REAL LIFE HE HAD THREE HISPANIC WIVES...

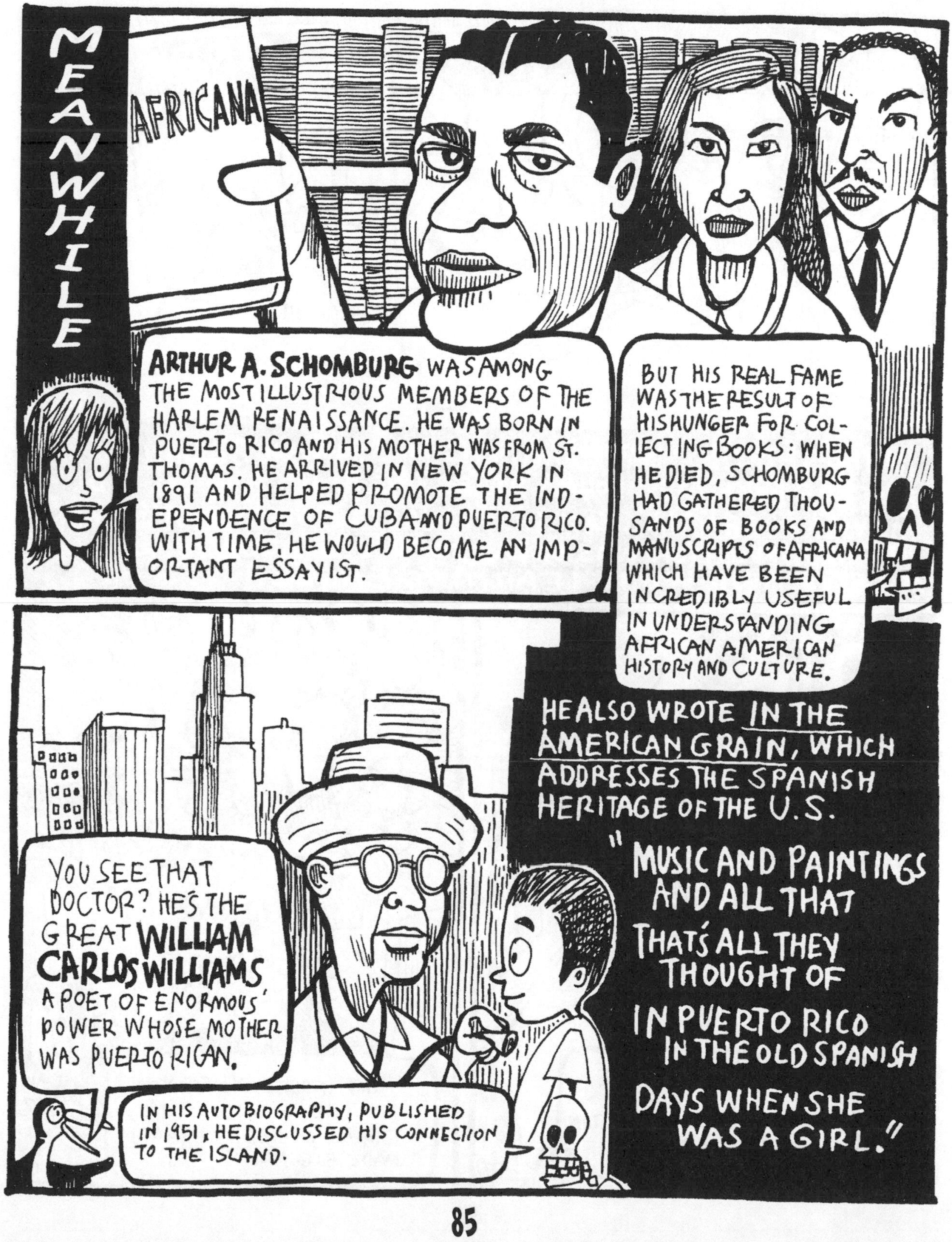
MEANWHILE
AFRICANA
ARTHUR A. SCHOMBURG WAS AMONG THE MOST ILLUSTRIOUS MEMBERS OF THE HARLEM RENAISSANCE. HE WAS BORN IN PUERTO RICO AND HIS MOTHER WAS FROM ST. THOMAS. HE ARRIVED IN NEW YORK IN 1891 AND HELPED PROMOTE THE INDEPENDENCE OF CUBA AND PUERTO RICO. WITH TIME, HE WOULD BECOME AN IMPORTANT ESSAYIST.
BUT HIS REAL FAME WAS THE RESULT OF HIS HUNGER FOR COLLECTING BOOKS: WHEN HE DIED, SCHOMBURG HAD GATHERED THOUSANDS OF BOOKS AND MANUSCRIPTS OF AFRICANA WHICH HAVE BEEN INCREDIBLY USEFUL IN UNDERSTANDING AFRICAN AMERICAN HISTORY AND CULTURE.
YOU SEE THAT DOCTOR? HE'S THE GREAT WILLIAM CARLOS WILLIAMS, A POET OF ENORMOUS POWER WHOSE MOTHER WAS PUERTO RICAN.
IN HIS AUTOBIOGRAPHY, PUBLISHED IN 1951, HE DISCUSSED HIS CONNECTION TO THE ISLAND.
HE ALSO WROTE IN THE AMERICAN GRAIN, WHICH ADDRESSES THE SPANISH HERITAGE OF THE U.S.
"MUSIC AND PAINTINGS AND ALL THAT THAT'S ALL THEY THOUGHT OF IN PUERTO RICO IN THE OLD SPANISH DAYS WHEN SHE WAS A GIRL."

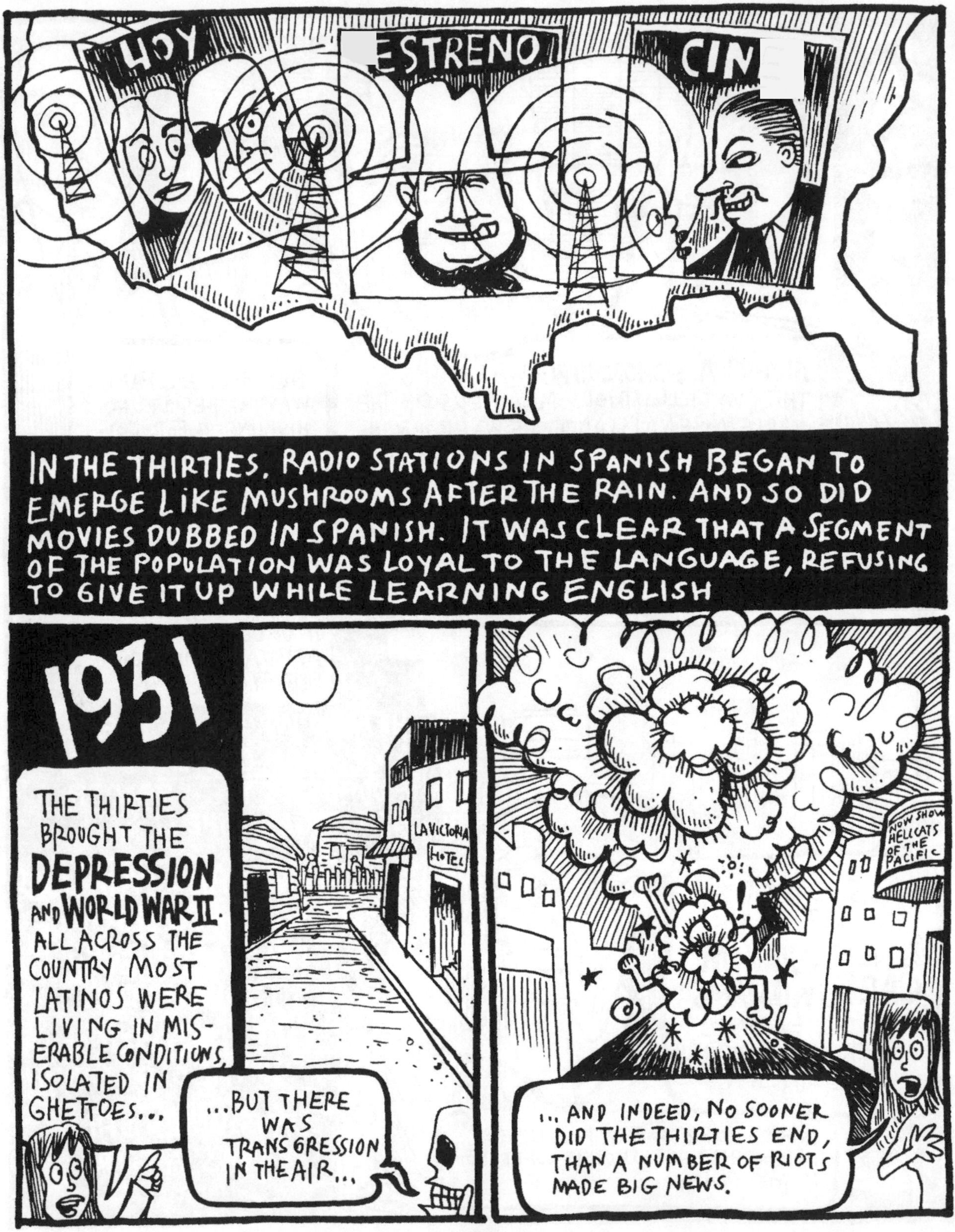
HOY
ESTRENO
CIN
IN THE THIRTIES, RADIO STATIONS IN SPANISH BEGAN TO EMERGE LIKE MUSHROOMS AFTER THE RAIN. AND SO DID MOVIES DUBBED IN SPANISH. IT WAS CLEAR THAT A SEGMENT OF THE POPULATION WAS LOYAL TO THE LANGUAGE, REFUSING TO GIVE IT UP WHILE LEARNING ENGLISH
1931
THE THIRTIES BROUGHT THE **DEPRESSION** AND **WORLD WAR II**. ALL ACROSS THE COUNTRY MOST LATINOS WERE LIVING IN MISERABLE CONDITIONS, ISOLATED IN GHETTOES...
LA VICTORIA
HOTEL
...BUT THERE WAS TRANSGRESSION IN THE AIR...
NOW SHOW HELLCATS OF THE PACIFIC
... AND INDEED, NO SOONER DID THE THIRTIES END, THAN A NUMBER OF RIOTS MADE BIG NEWS.

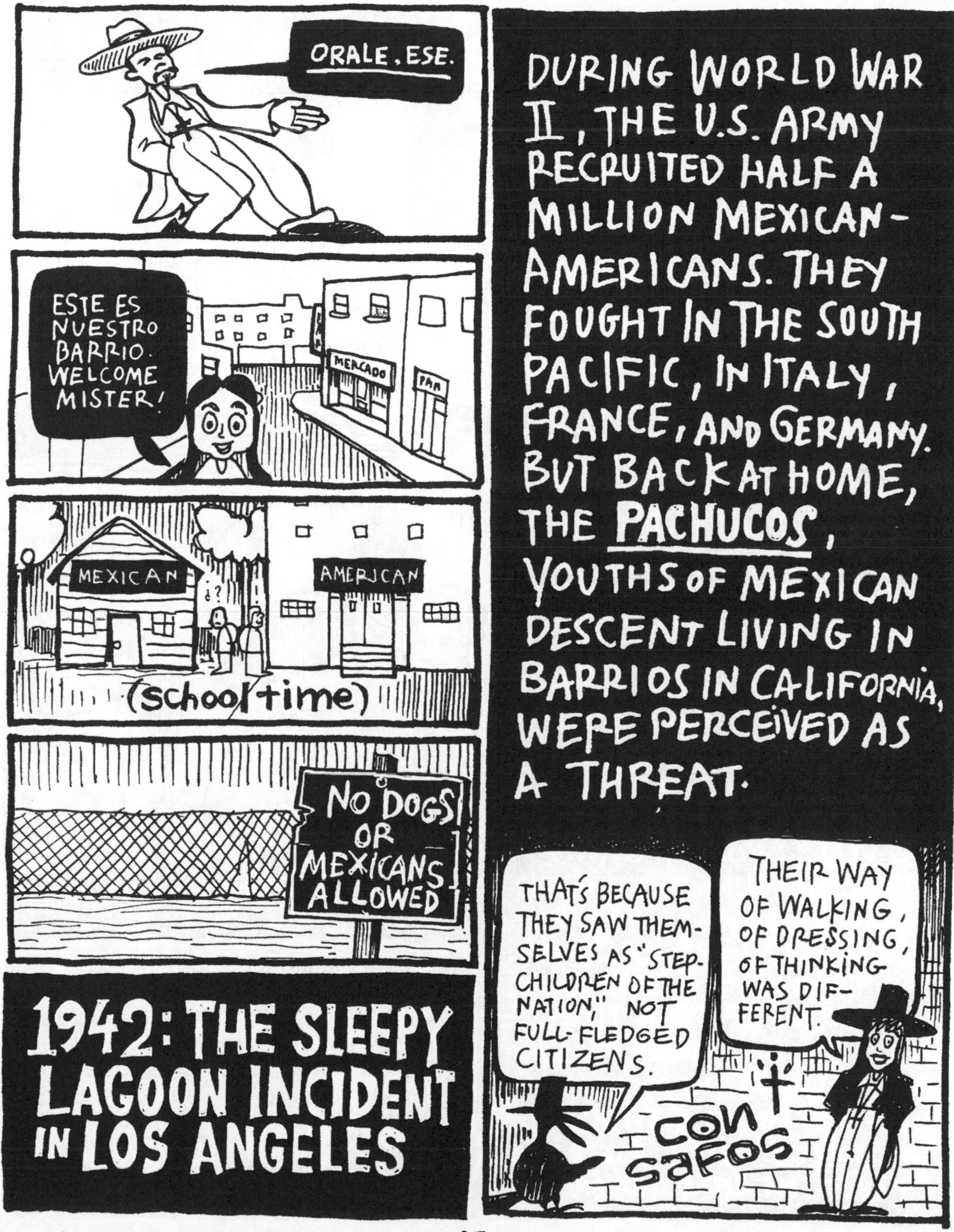
ORALE, ESE.
ESTE ES NUESTRO BARRIO. WELCOME MISTER!
MERCADO
BAR
MEXICAN
¿?
AMERICAN
(school time)
NO DOGS OR MEXICANS ALLOWED
1942: THE SLEEPY LAGOON INCIDENT IN LOS ANGELES
DURING WORLD WAR II, THE U.S. ARMY RECRUITED HALF A MILLION MEXICAN-AMERICANS. THEY FOUGHT IN THE SOUTH PACIFIC, IN ITALY, FRANCE, AND GERMANY. BUT BACK AT HOME, THE PACHUCOS, YOUTHS OF MEXICAN DESCENT LIVING IN BARRIOS IN CALIFORNIA, WERE PERCEIVED AS A THREAT.
THAT'S BECAUSE THEY SAW THEMSELVES AS "STEP-CHILDREN OF THE NATION," NOT FULL-FLEDGED CITIZENS.
THEIR WAY OF WALKING, OF DRESSING, OF THINKING WAS DIFFERENT.
CON SAFOS

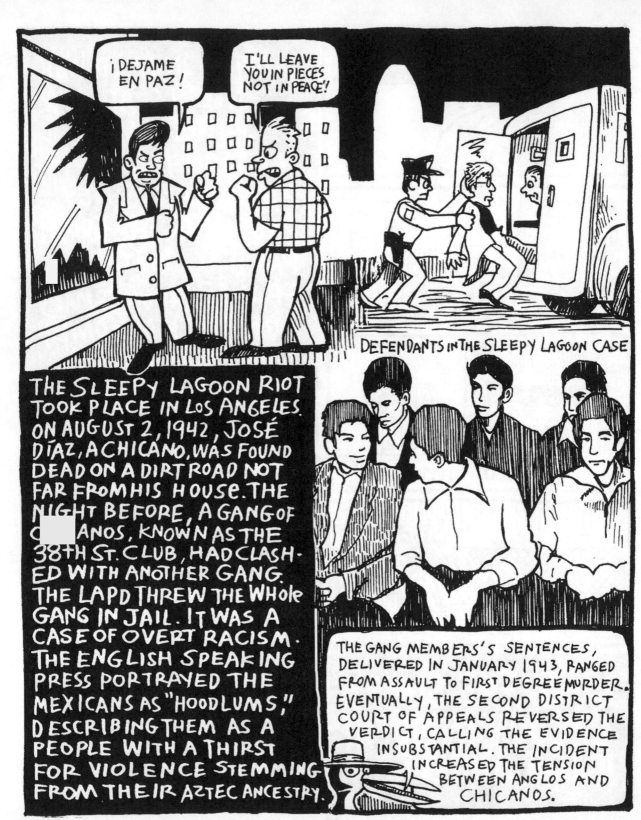

¡DEJAME EN PAZ!

I'LL LEAVE YOU IN PIECES NOT IN PEACE!

DEFENDANTS IN THE SLEEPY LAGOON CASE

THE SLEEPY LAGOON RIOT TOOK PLACE IN LOS ANGELES. ON AUGUST 2, 1942, JOSÉ DÍAZ, A CHICANO, WAS FOUND DEAD ON A DIRT ROAD NOT FAR FROM HIS HOUSE. THE NIGHT BEFORE, A GANG OF CHICANOS, KNOWN AS THE 38TH ST. CLUB, HAD CLASHED WITH ANOTHER GANG. THE LAPD THREW THE WHOLE GANG IN JAIL. IT WAS A CASE OF OVERT RACISM. THE ENGLISH SPEAKING PRESS PORTRAYED THE MEXICANS AS "HOODLUMS," DESCRIBING THEM AS A PEOPLE WITH A THIRST FOR VIOLENCE STEMMING FROM THEIR AZTEC ANCESTRY.

THE GANG MEMBERS'S SENTENCES, DELIVERED IN JANUARY 1943, RANGED FROM ASSAULT TO FIRST DEGREE MURDER. EVENTUALLY, THE SECOND DISTRICT COURT OF APPEALS REVERSED THE VERDICT, CALLING THE EVIDENCE INSUBSTANTIAL. THE INCIDENT INCREASED THE TENSION BETWEEN ANGLOS AND CHICANOS.

88

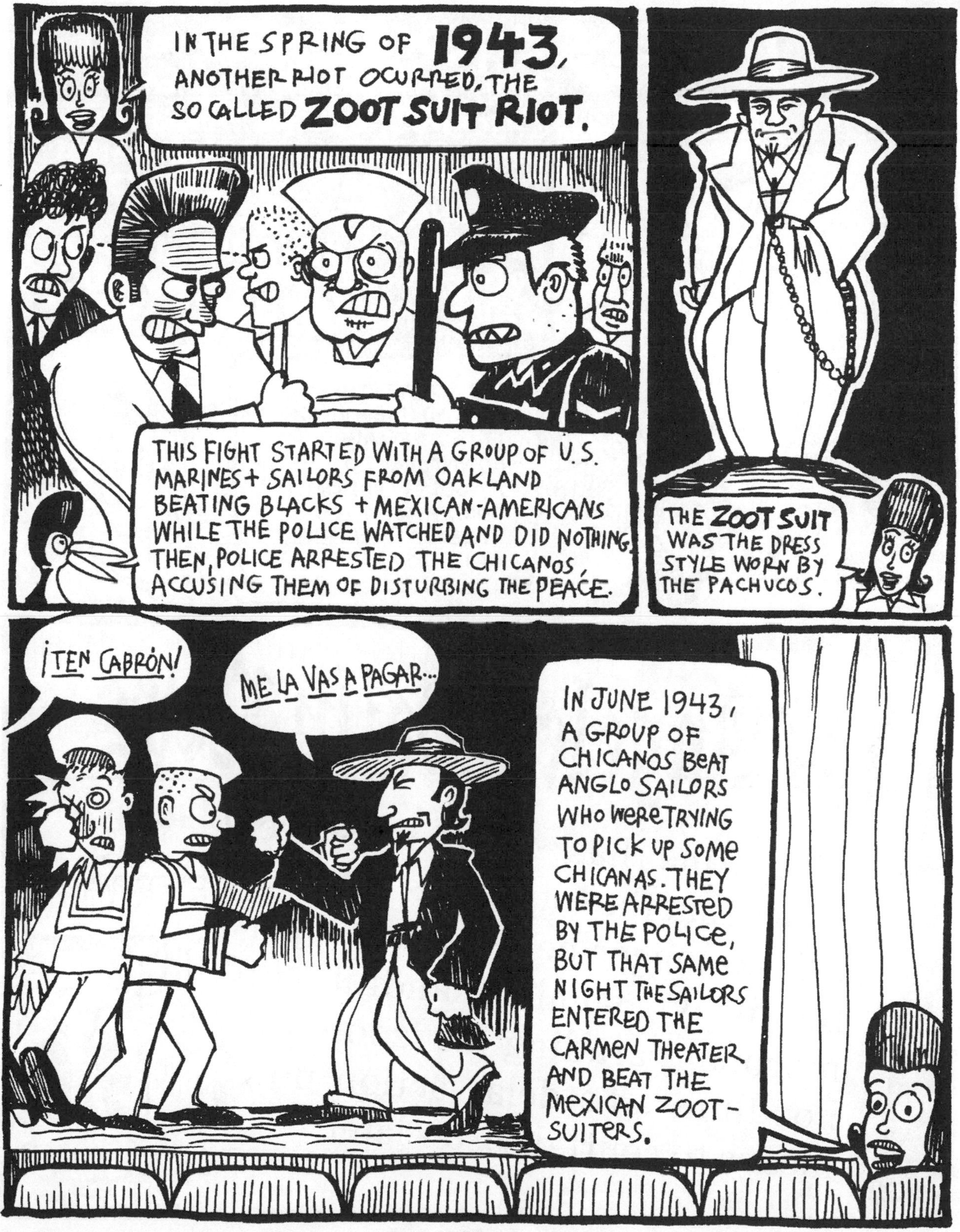
IN THE SPRING OF 1943, ANOTHER RIOT OCURRED, THE SO CALLED ZOOT SUIT RIOT.
THIS FIGHT STARTED WITH A GROUP OF U.S. MARINES + SAILORS FROM OAKLAND BEATING BLACKS + MEXICAN-AMERICANS WHILE THE POLICE WATCHED AND DID NOTHING. THEN, POLICE ARRESTED THE CHICANOS, ACCUSING THEM OF DISTURBING THE PEACE.
THE ZOOT SUIT WAS THE DRESS STYLE WORN BY THE PACHUCOS.
¡TEN CABRÓN!
ME LA VAS A PAGAR...
IN JUNE 1943, A GROUP OF CHICANOS BEAT ANGLO SAILORS WHO WERE TRYING TO PICK UP SOME CHICANAS. THEY WERE ARRESTED BY THE POLICE, BUT THAT SAME NIGHT THE SAILORS ENTERED THE CARMEN THEATER AND BEAT THE MEXICAN ZOOT-SUITERS.

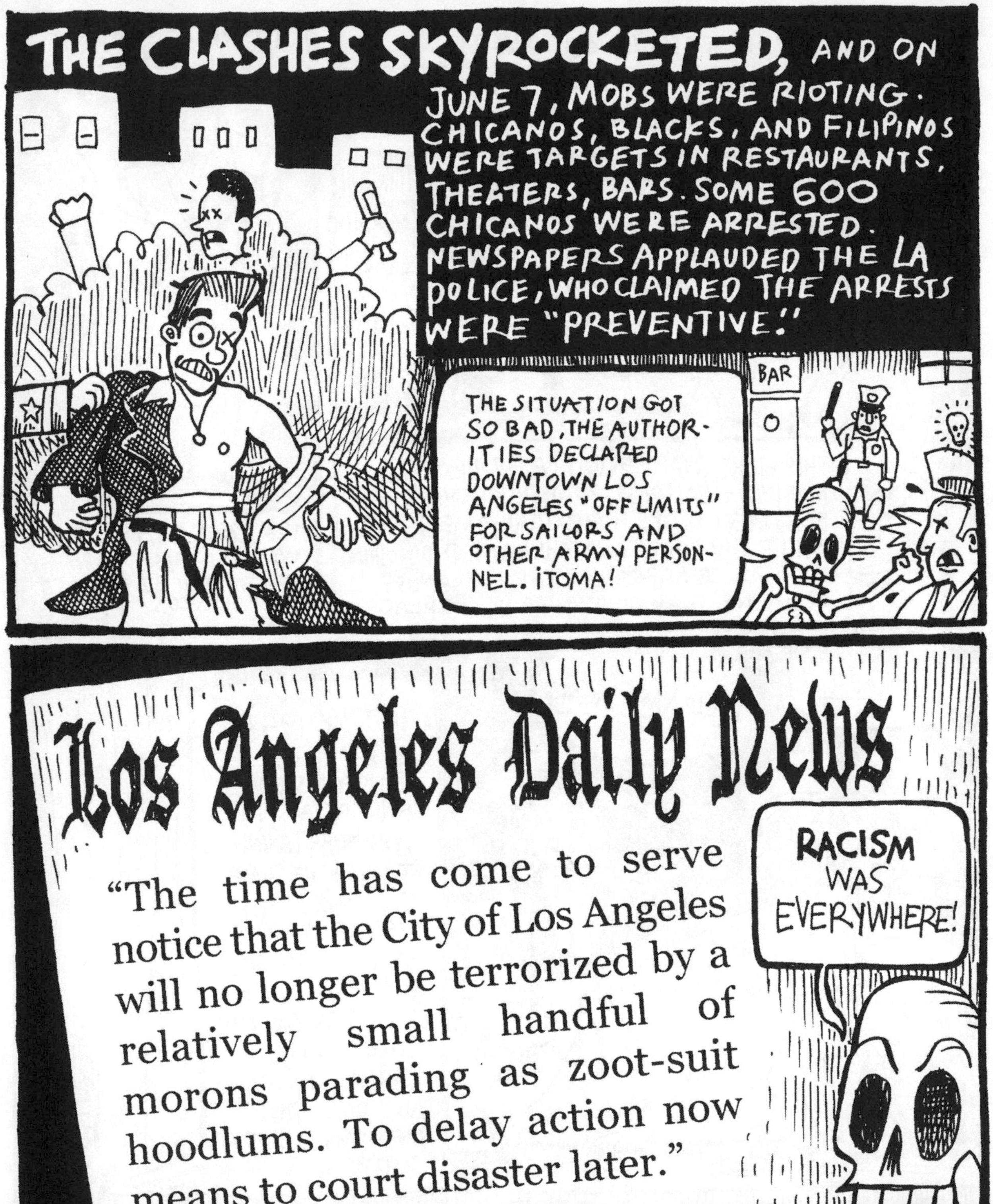
THE CLASHES SKYROCKETED, AND ON JUNE 7, MOBS WERE RIOTING. CHICANOS, BLACKS, AND FILIPINOS WERE TARGETS IN RESTAURANTS, THEATERS, BARS. SOME 600 CHICANOS WERE ARRESTED. NEWSPAPERS APPLAUDED THE LA POLICE, WHO CLAIMED THE ARRESTS WERE "PREVENTIVE."
BAR
THE SITUATION GOT SO BAD, THE AUTHORITIES DECLARED DOWNTOWN LOS ANGELES "OFF LIMITS" FOR SAILORS AND OTHER ARMY PERSONNEL. ¡TOMA!
Los Angeles Daily News
"The time has come to serve notice that the City of Los Angeles will no longer be terrorized by a relatively small handful of morons parading as zoot-suit hoodlums. To delay action now means to court disaster later."
RACISM WAS EVERYWHERE!

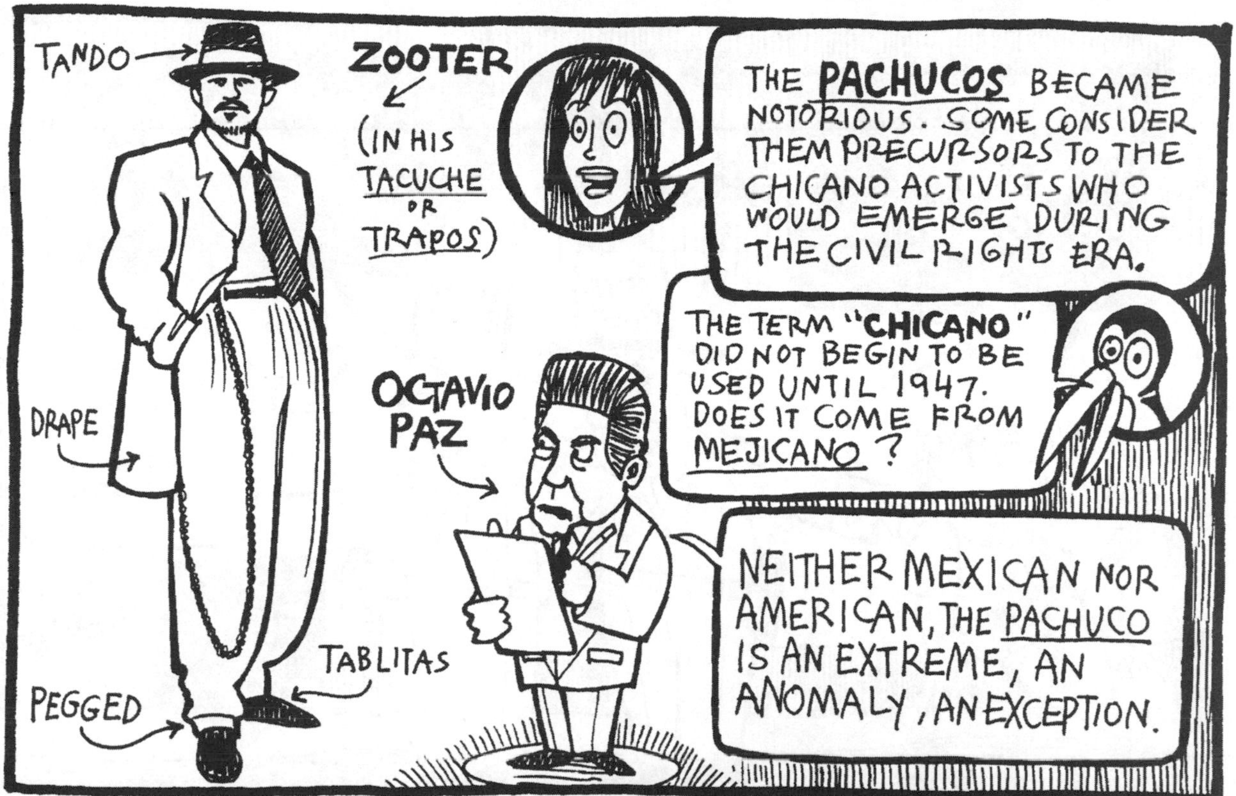
TANDO
ZOOTER
(IN HIS TACUCHE OR TRAPOS)
THE PACHUCOS BECAME NOTORIOUS. SOME CONSIDER THEM PRECURSORS TO THE CHICANO ACTIVISTS WHO WOULD EMERGE DURING THE CIVIL RIGHTS ERA.
THE TERM "CHICANO" DID NOT BEGIN TO BE USED UNTIL 1947. DOES IT COME FROM MEJICANO?
DRAPE
OCTAVIO PAZ
NEITHER MEXICAN NOR AMERICAN, THE PACHUCO IS AN EXTREME, AN ANOMALY, AN EXCEPTION.
TABLITAS
PEGGED

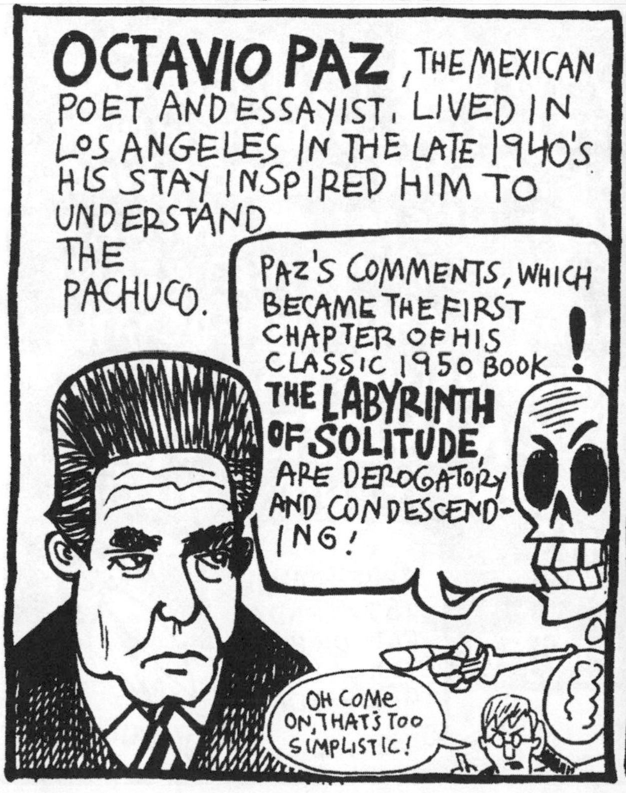
OCTAVIO PAZ, THE MEXICAN POET AND ESSAYIST, LIVED IN LOS ANGELES IN THE LATE 1940'S. HIS STAY INSPIRED HIM TO UNDERSTAND THE PACHUCO.
PAZ'S COMMENTS, WHICH BECAME THE FIRST CHAPTER OF HIS CLASSIC 1950 BOOK THE LABYRINTH OF SOLITUDE, ARE DEROGATORY AND CONDESCENDING!
!
OH COME ON, THAT'S TOO SIMPLISTIC!

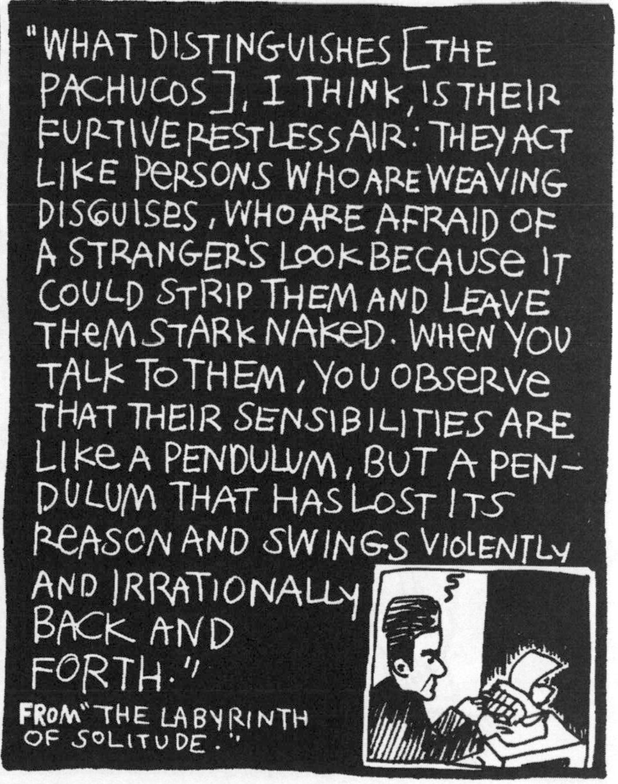
"WHAT DISTINGUISHES [THE PACHUCOS], I THINK, IS THEIR FURTIVE RESTLESS AIR: THEY ACT LIKE PERSONS WHO ARE WEAVING DISGUISES, WHO ARE AFRAID OF A STRANGER'S LOOK BECAUSE IT COULD STRIP THEM AND LEAVE THEM STARK NAKED. WHEN YOU TALK TO THEM, YOU OBSERVE THAT THEIR SENSIBILITIES ARE LIKE A PENDULUM, BUT A PENDULUM THAT HAS LOST ITS REASON AND SWINGS VIOLENTLY AND IRRATIONALLY BACK AND FORTH."
FROM "THE LABYRINTH OF SOLITUDE."

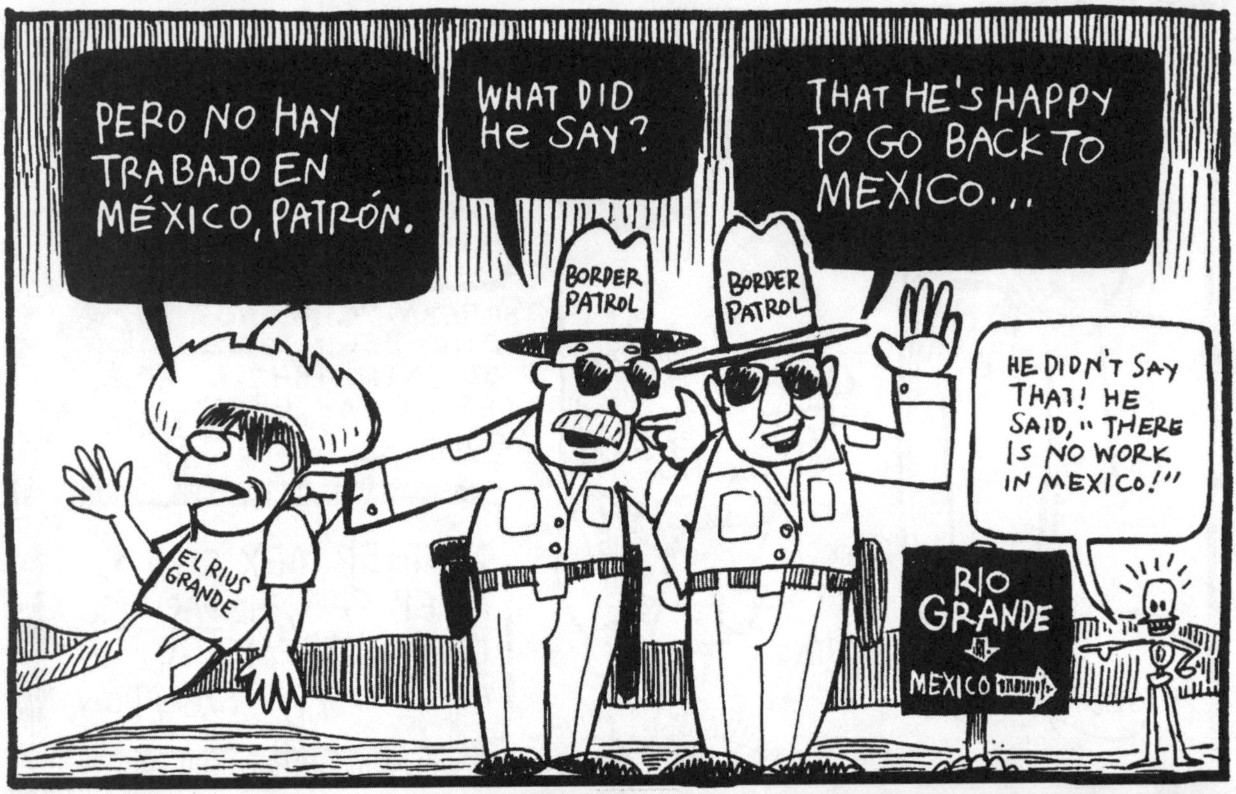
PERO NO HAY TRABAJO EN MÉXICO, PATRÓN.
WHAT DID He SAY?
THAT HE'S HAPPY TO GO BACK TO MEXICO...
BORDER PATROL
BORDER PATROL
HE DIDN'T SAY THAT! HE SAID, "THERE IS NO WORK IN MEXICO!"
EL RIUS GRANDE
RIO GRANDE
MEXICO

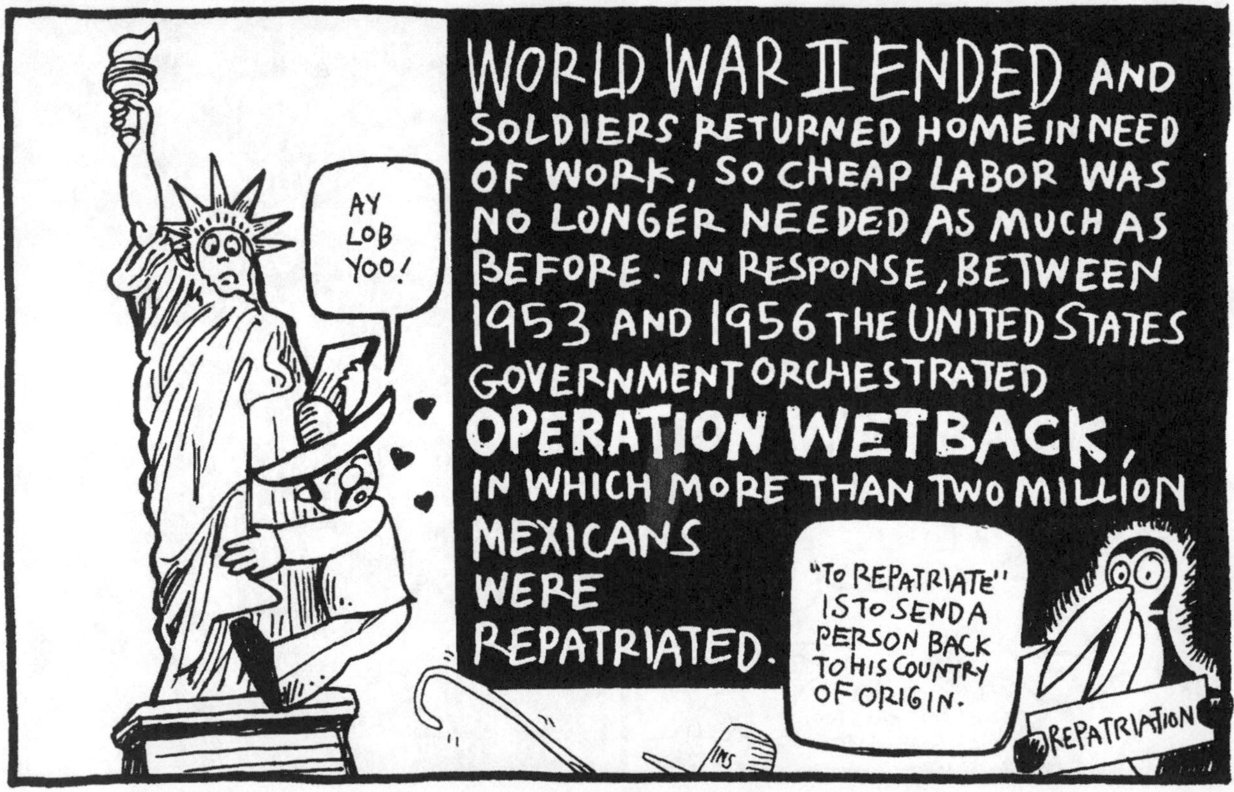
AY LOB YOO!
WORLD WAR II ENDED AND SOLDIERS RETURNED HOME IN NEED OF WORK, SO CHEAP LABOR WAS NO LONGER NEEDED AS MUCH AS BEFORE. IN RESPONSE, BETWEEN 1953 AND 1956 THE UNITED STATES GOVERNMENT ORCHESTRATED OPERATION WETBACK, IN WHICH MORE THAN TWO MILLION MEXICANS WERE REPATRIATED.
"TO REPATRIATE" IS TO SEND A PERSON BACK TO HIS COUNTRY OF ORIGIN.
INS
REPATRIATION

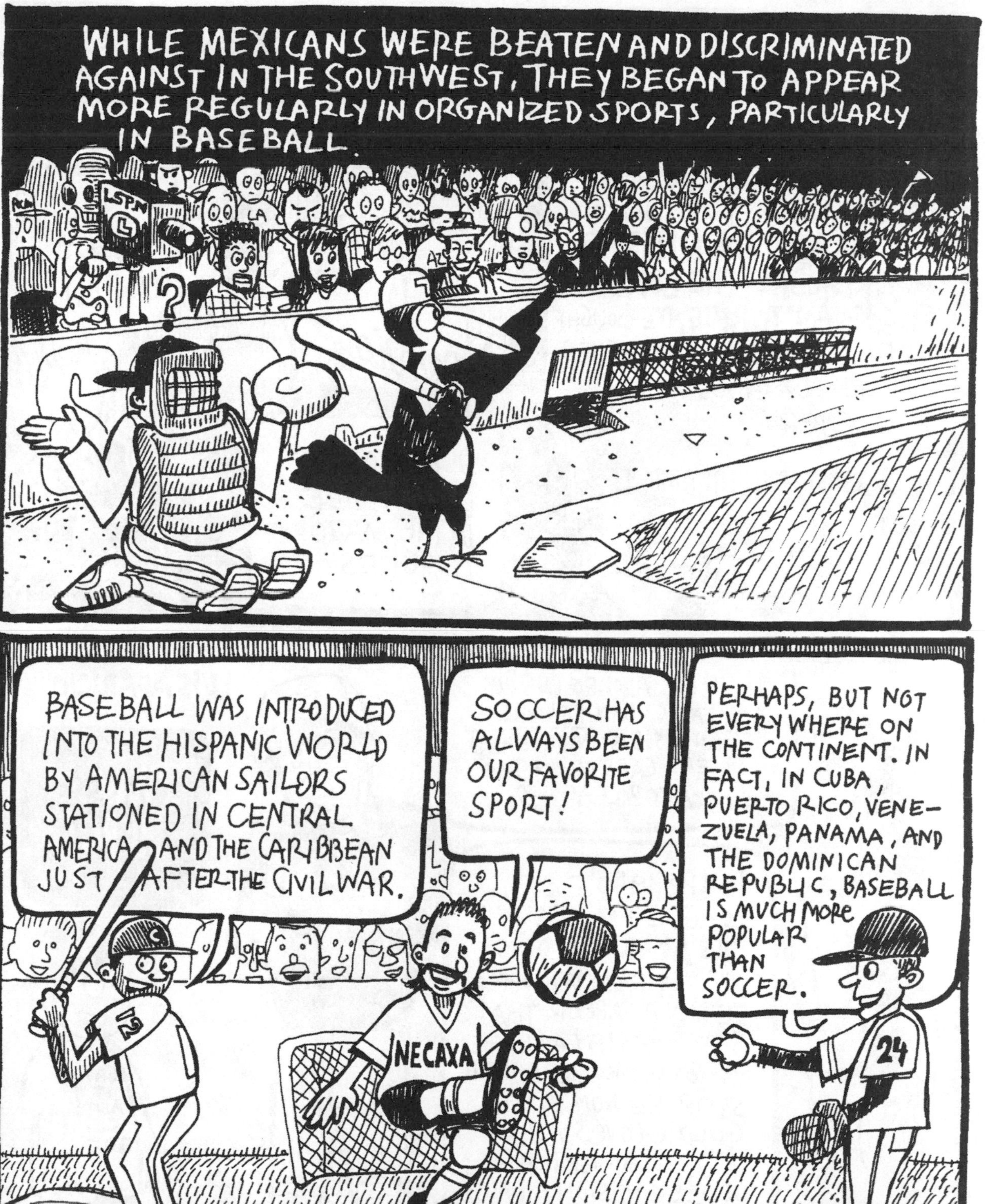

WHILE MEXICANS WERE BEATEN AND DISCRIMINATED AGAINST IN THE SOUTHWEST, THEY BEGAN TO APPEAR MORE REGULARLY IN ORGANIZED SPORTS, PARTICULARLY IN BASEBALL.
LSPN
?
BASEBALL WAS INTRODUCED INTO THE HISPANIC WORLD BY AMERICAN SAILORS STATIONED IN CENTRAL AMERICA AND THE CARIBBEAN JUST AFTER THE CIVIL WAR.
SOCCER HAS ALWAYS BEEN OUR FAVORITE SPORT!
PERHAPS, BUT NOT EVERYWHERE ON THE CONTINENT. IN FACT, IN CUBA, PUERTO RICO, VENE-ZUELA, PANAMA, AND THE DOMINICAN REPUBLIC, BASEBALL IS MUCH MORE POPULAR THAN SOCCER.
12
NECAXA
24

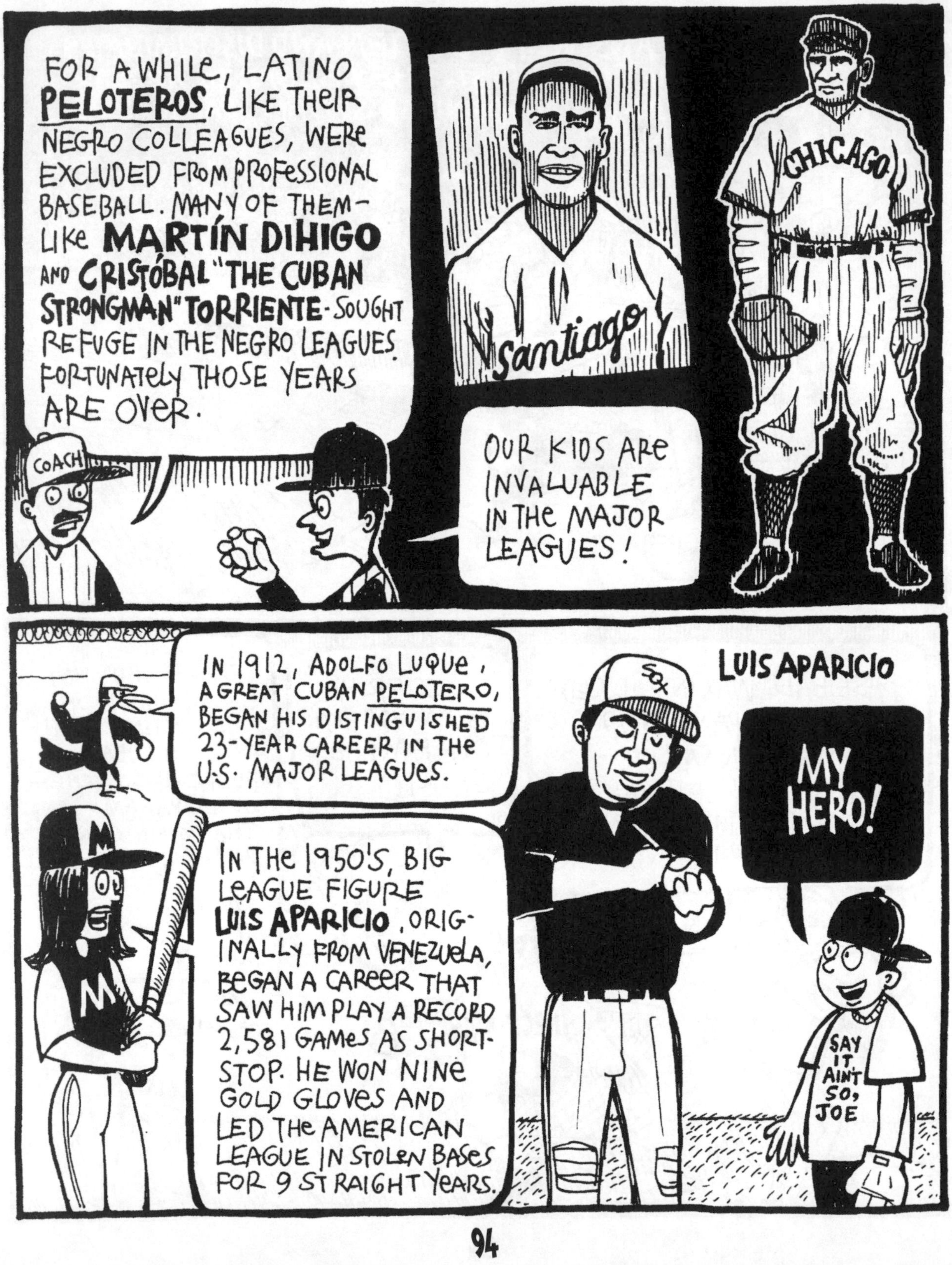
FOR A WHILE, LATINO PELOTEROS, LIKE THEIR NEGRO COLLEAGUES, WERE EXCLUDED FROM PROFESSIONAL BASEBALL. MANY OF THEM—LIKE MARTÍN DIHIGO AND CRISTÓBAL "THE CUBAN STRONGMAN" TORRIENTE—SOUGHT REFUGE IN THE NEGRO LEAGUES. FORTUNATELY THOSE YEARS ARE OVER.
COACH
Santiago
CHICAGO
OUR KIDS ARE INVALUABLE IN THE MAJOR LEAGUES!
IN 1912, ADOLFO LUQUE, A GREAT CUBAN PELOTERO, BEGAN HIS DISTINGUISHED 23-YEAR CAREER IN THE U.S. MAJOR LEAGUES.
IN THE 1950'S, BIG LEAGUE FIGURE LUIS APARICIO, ORIGINALLY FROM VENEZUELA, BEGAN A CAREER THAT SAW HIM PLAY A RECORD 2,581 GAMES AS SHORTSTOP. HE WON NINE GOLD GLOVES AND LED THE AMERICAN LEAGUE IN STOLEN BASES FOR 9 STRAIGHT YEARS.
SOX
LUIS APARICIO
MY HERO!
SAY IT AIN'T SO, JOE

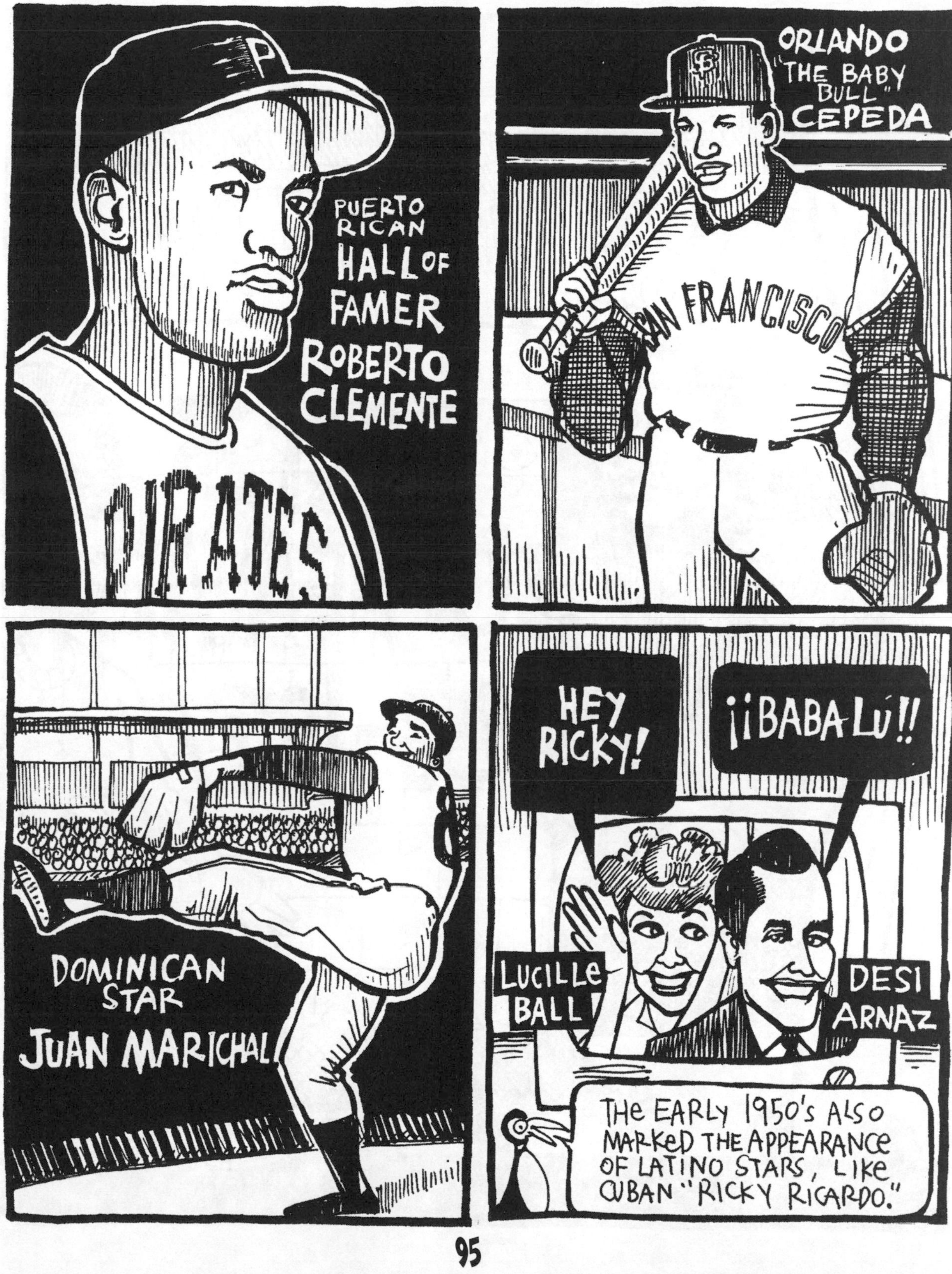
PUERTO RICAN HALL OF FAMER ROBERTO CLEMENTE
PIRATES
ORLANDO "THE BABY BULL" CEPEDA
SAN FRANCISCO
DOMINICAN STAR JUAN MARICHAL
HEY RICKY!
¡¡BABA-LÚ!!
LUCILLE BALL
DESI ARNAZ
THE EARLY 1950's ALSO MARKED THE APPEARANCE OF LATINO STARS, LIKE CUBAN "RICKY RICARDO."

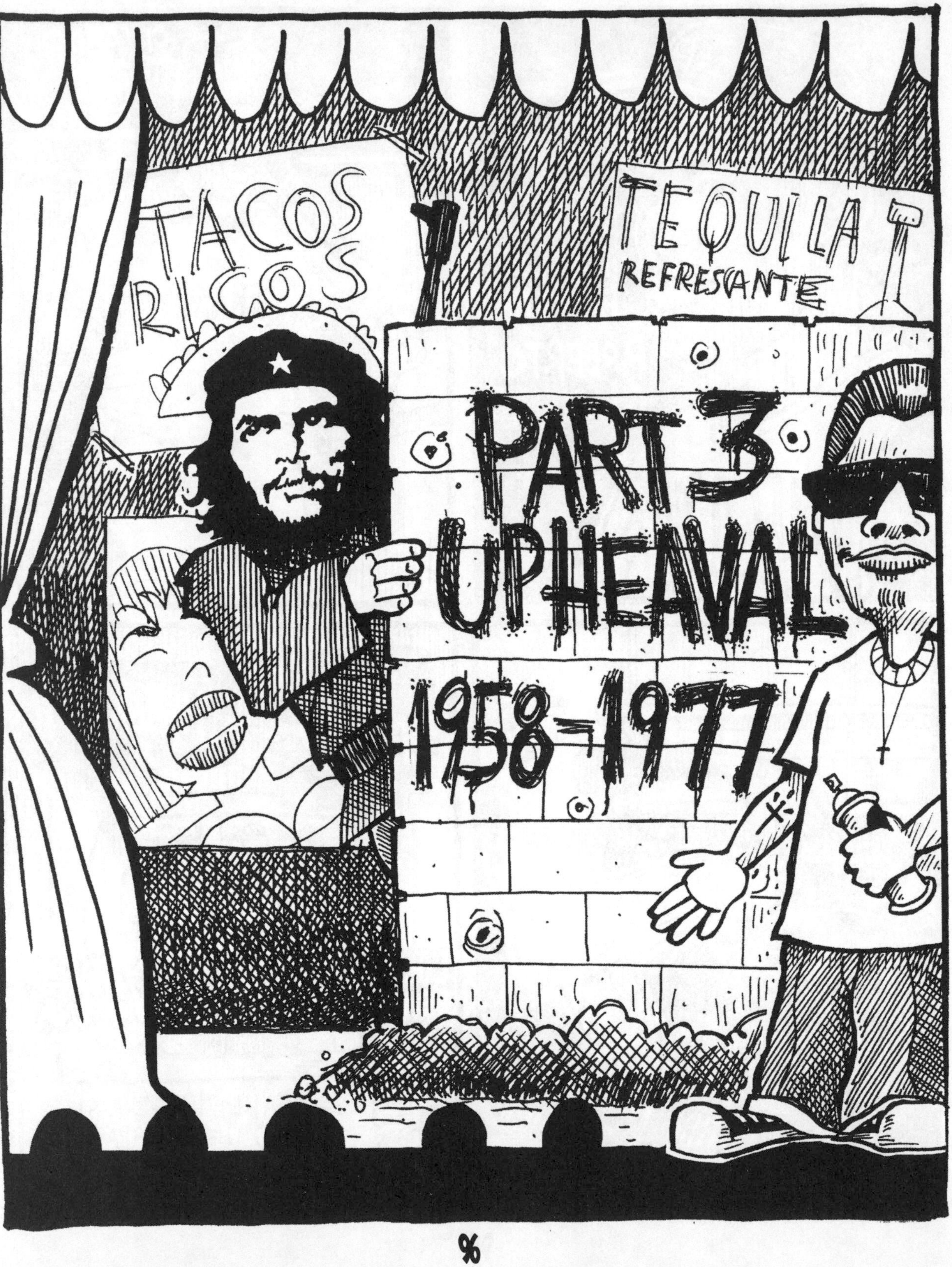
TACOS RICOS
TEQUILA
REFRESANTE
PART 3
UPHEAVAL
1958–1977

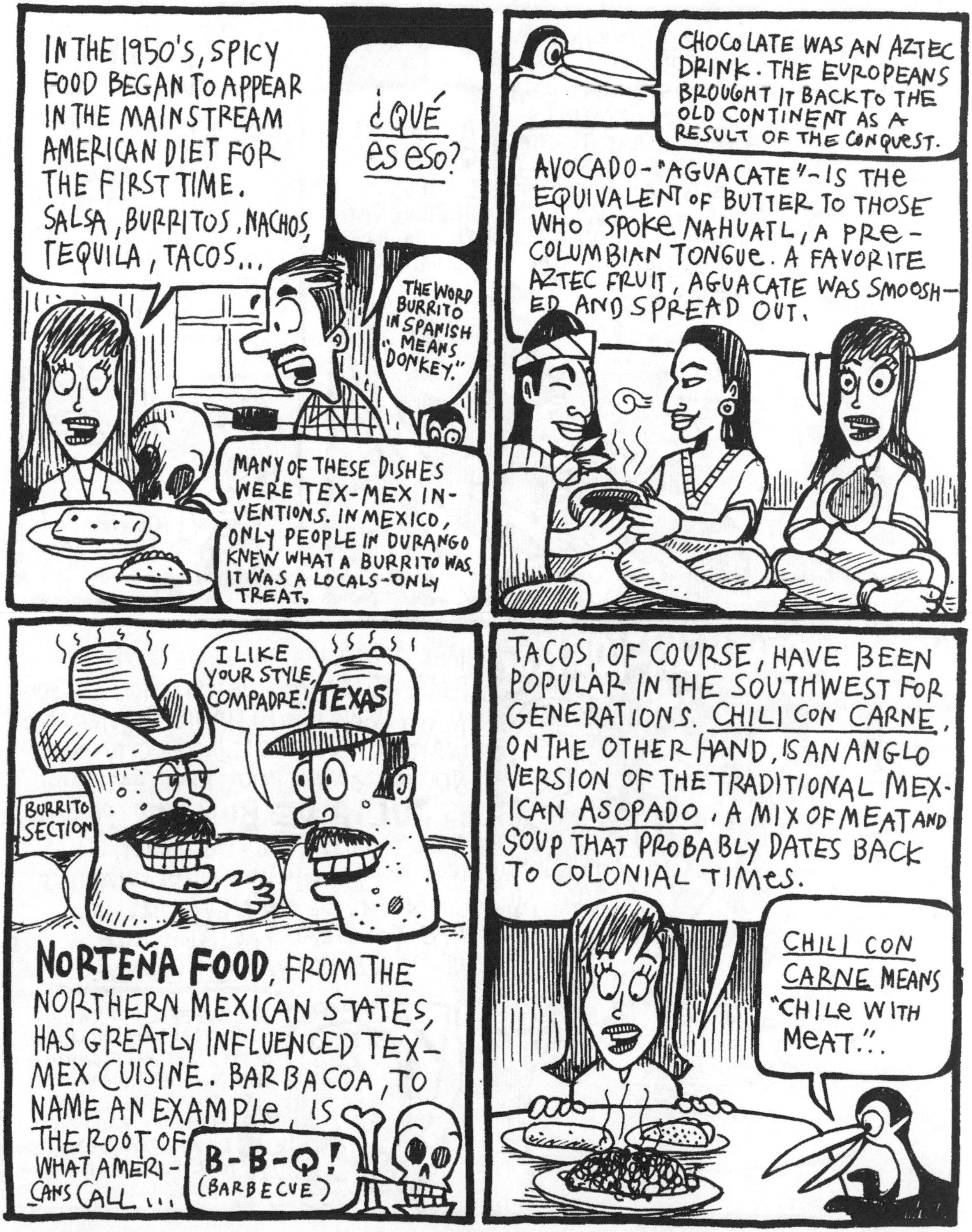
IN THE 1950'S, SPICY FOOD BEGAN TO APPEAR IN THE MAINSTREAM AMERICAN DIET FOR THE FIRST TIME. SALSA, BURRITOS, NACHOS, TEQUILA, TACOS...
¿QUÉ ES ESO?
THE WORD BURRITO IN SPANISH MEANS "DONKEY."
MANY OF THESE DISHES WERE TEX-MEX INVENTIONS. IN MEXICO, ONLY PEOPLE IN DURANGO KNEW WHAT A BURRITO WAS. IT WAS A LOCALS-ONLY TREAT.
CHOCOLATE WAS AN AZTEC DRINK. THE EUROPEANS BROUGHT IT BACK TO THE OLD CONTINENT AS A RESULT OF THE CONQUEST.
AVOCADO-"AGUACATE"-IS THE EQUIVALENT OF BUTTER TO THOSE WHO SPOKE NAHUATL, A PRE-COLUMBIAN TONGUE. A FAVORITE AZTEC FRUIT, AGUACATE WAS SMOOSHED AND SPREAD OUT.
I LIKE YOUR STYLE, COMPADRE!
TEXAS
BURRITO SECTION
NORTEÑA FOOD, FROM THE NORTHERN MEXICAN STATES, HAS GREATLY INFLUENCED TEX-MEX CUISINE. BARBACOA, TO NAME AN EXAMPLE, IS THE ROOT OF WHAT AMERICANS CALL...
B-B-Q! (BARBECUE)
TACOS, OF COURSE, HAVE BEEN POPULAR IN THE SOUTHWEST FOR GENERATIONS. CHILI CON CARNE, ON THE OTHER HAND, IS AN ANGLO VERSION OF THE TRADITIONAL MEXICAN ASOPADO, A MIX OF MEAT AND SOUP THAT PROBABLY DATES BACK TO COLONIAL TIMES.
CHILI CON CARNE MEANS "CHILE WITH MEAT."

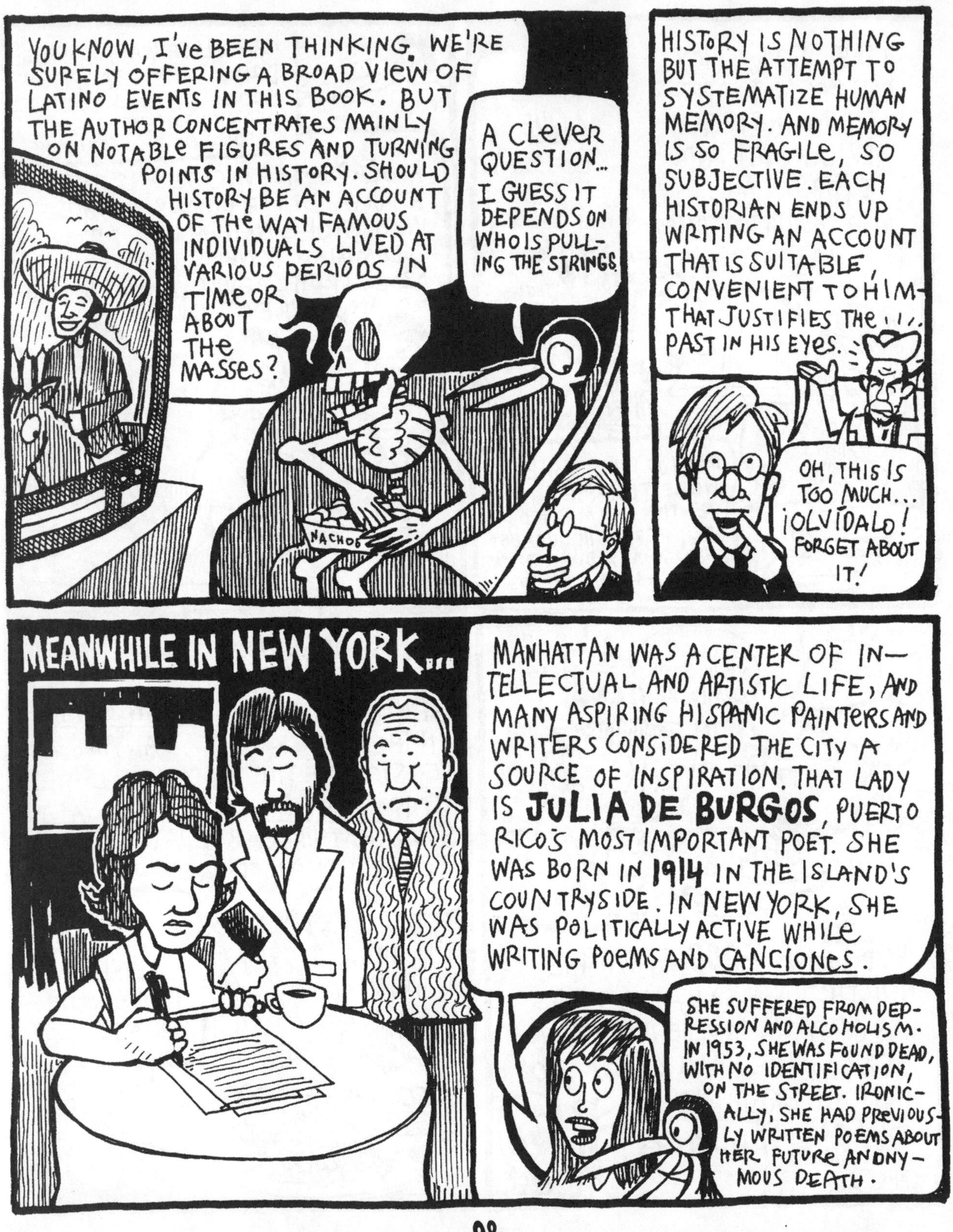
YOU KNOW, I'VE BEEN THINKING. WE'RE SURELY OFFERING A BROAD VIEW OF LATINO EVENTS IN THIS BOOK. BUT THE AUTHOR CONCENTRATES MAINLY ON NOTABLE FIGURES AND TURNING POINTS IN HISTORY. SHOULD HISTORY BE AN ACCOUNT OF THE WAY FAMOUS INDIVIDUALS LIVED AT VARIOUS PERIODS IN TIME OR ABOUT THE MASSES?
A CLEVER QUESTION... I GUESS IT DEPENDS ON WHO IS PULLING THE STRINGS.
NACHOS
HISTORY IS NOTHING BUT THE ATTEMPT TO SYSTEMATIZE HUMAN MEMORY. AND MEMORY IS SO FRAGILE, SO SUBJECTIVE. EACH HISTORIAN ENDS UP WRITING AN ACCOUNT THAT IS SUITABLE, CONVENIENT TO HIM-THAT JUSTIFIES THE PAST IN HIS EYES.
OH, THIS IS TOO MUCH... ¡OLVÍDALO! FORGET ABOUT IT!
MEANWHILE IN NEW YORK...
MANHATTAN WAS A CENTER OF INTELLECTUAL AND ARTISTIC LIFE, AND MANY ASPIRING HISPANIC PAINTERS AND WRITERS CONSIDERED THE CITY A SOURCE OF INSPIRATION. THAT LADY IS JULIA DE BURGOS, PUERTO RICO'S MOST IMPORTANT POET. SHE WAS BORN IN 1914 IN THE ISLAND'S COUNTRYSIDE. IN NEW YORK, SHE WAS POLITICALLY ACTIVE WHILE WRITING POEMS AND CANCIONES.
SHE SUFFERED FROM DEPRESSION AND ALCOHOLISM. IN 1953, SHE WAS FOUND DEAD, WITH NO IDENTIFICATION, ON THE STREET. IRONICALLY, SHE HAD PREVIOUSLY WRITTEN POEMS ABOUT HER FUTURE ANONYMOUS DEATH.

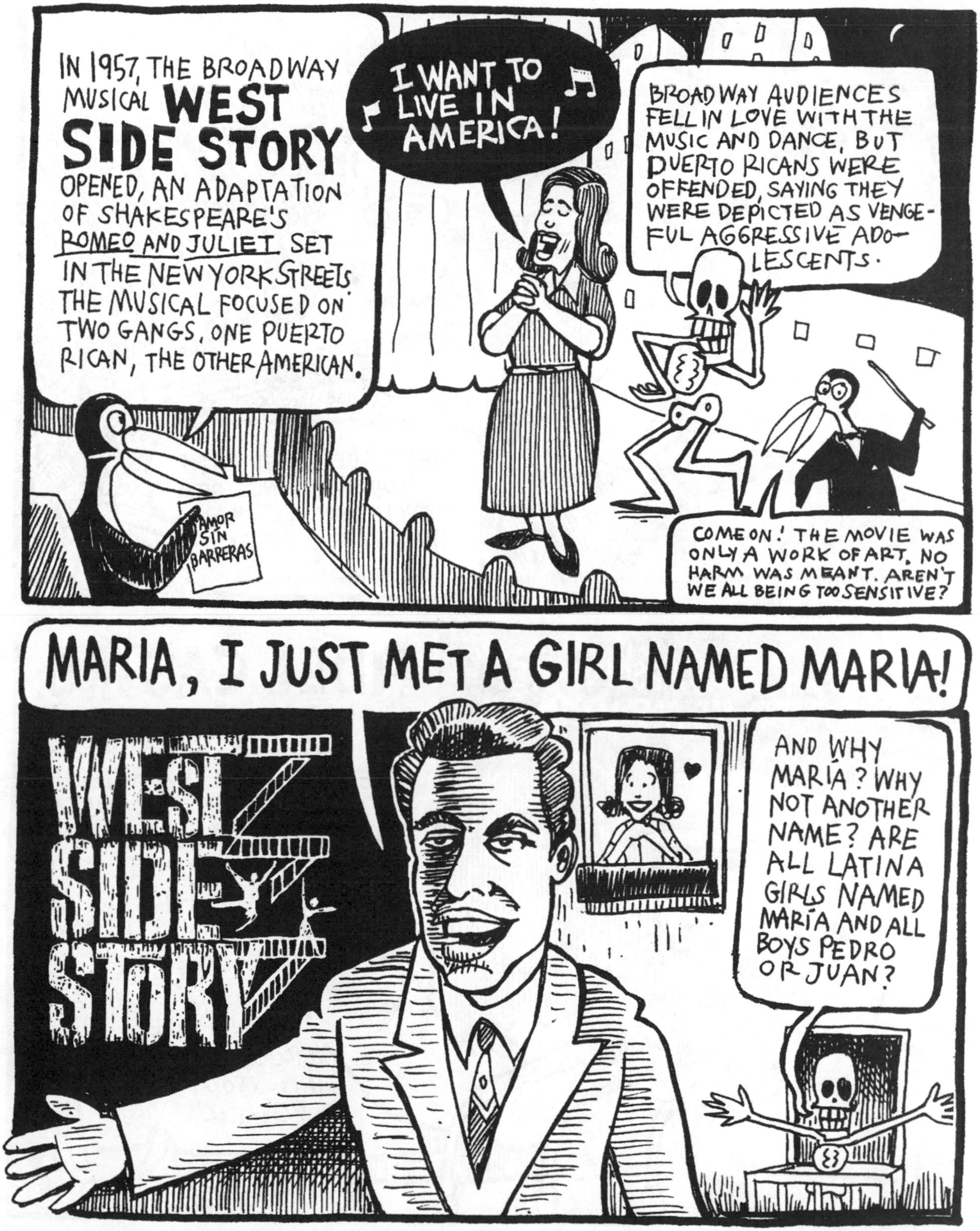
IN 1957, THE BROADWAY MUSICAL WEST SIDE STORY OPENED, AN ADAPTATION OF SHAKESPEARE'S ROMEO AND JULIET SET IN THE NEW YORK STREETS. THE MUSICAL FOCUSED ON TWO GANGS, ONE PUERTO RICAN, THE OTHER AMERICAN.
I WANT TO LIVE IN AMERICA!
BROADWAY AUDIENCES FELL IN LOVE WITH THE MUSIC AND DANCE, BUT PUERTO RICANS WERE OFFENDED, SAYING THEY WERE DEPICTED AS VENGEFUL AGGRESSIVE ADOLESCENTS.
AMOR SIN BARRERAS
COME ON! THE MOVIE WAS ONLY A WORK OF ART. NO HARM WAS MEANT. AREN'T WE ALL BEING TOO SENSITIVE?
MARIA, I JUST MET A GIRL NAMED MARIA!
WEST SIDE STORY
AND WHY MARIA? WHY NOT ANOTHER NAME? ARE ALL LATINA GIRLS NAMED MARIA AND ALL BOYS PEDRO OR JUAN?

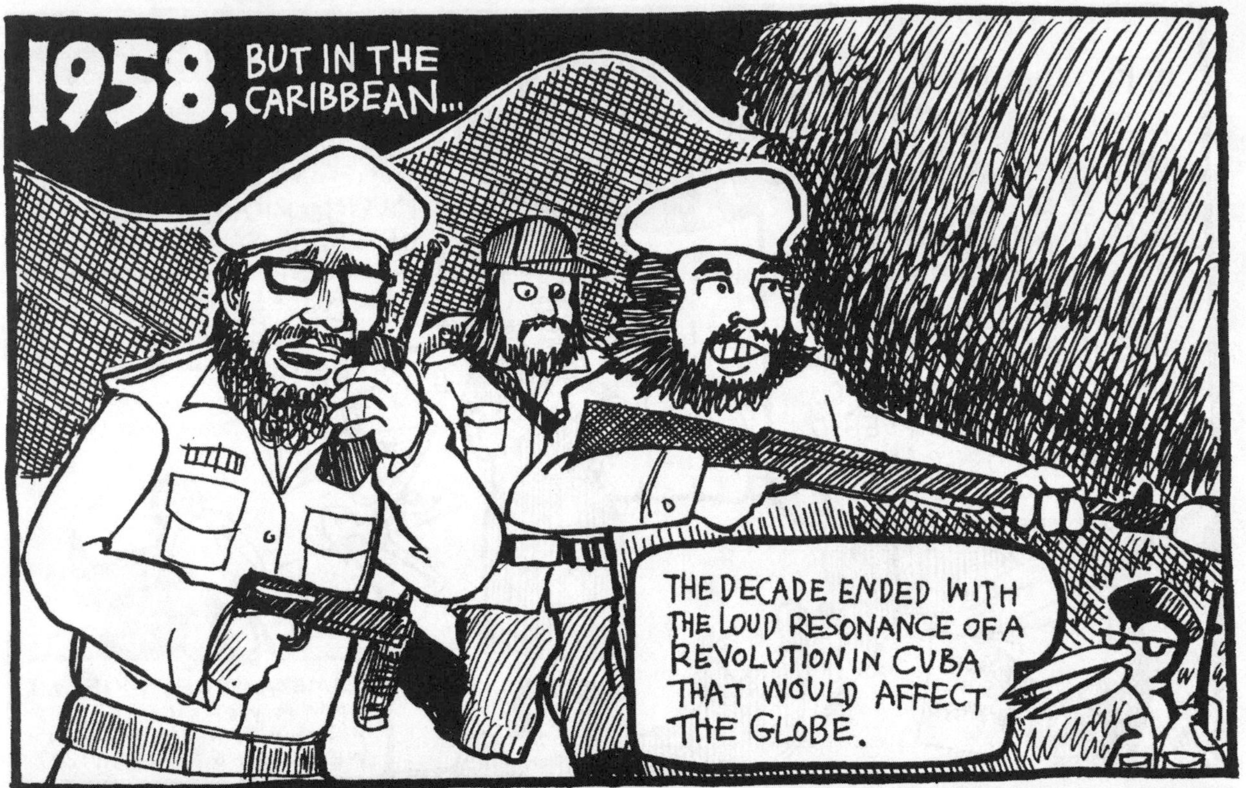
1958, BUT IN THE CARIBBEAN...
THE DECADE ENDED WITH THE LOUD RESONANCE OF A REVOLUTION IN CUBA THAT WOULD AFFECT THE GLOBE.

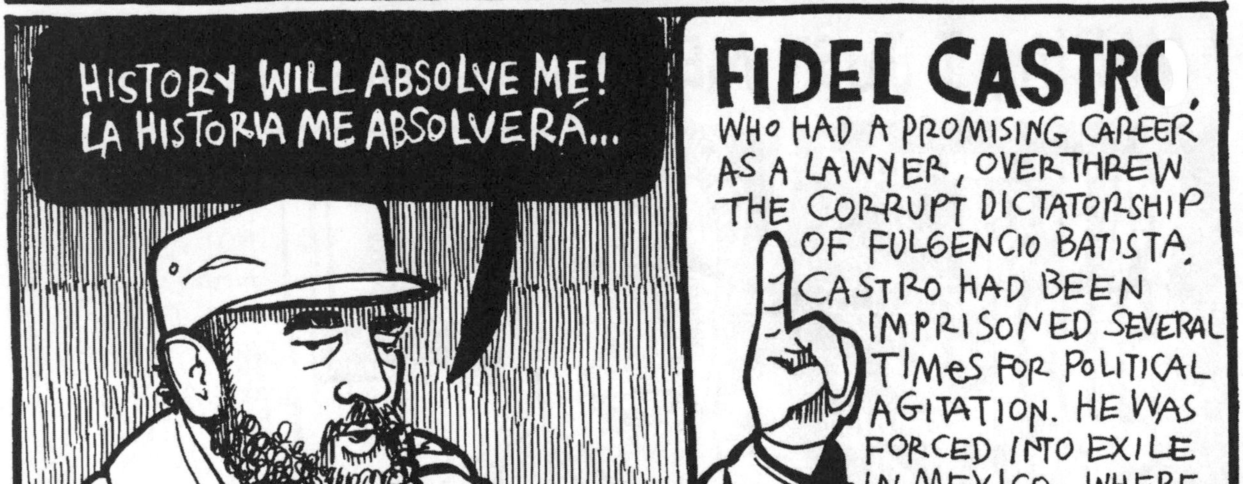
HISTORY WILL ABSOLVE ME! LA HISTORIA ME ABSOLVERÁ...
FIDEL CASTRO, WHO HAD A PROMISING CAREER AS A LAWYER, OVERTHREW THE CORRUPT DICTATORSHIP OF FULGENCIO BATISTA. CASTRO HAD BEEN IMPRISONED SEVERAL TIMES FOR POLITICAL AGITATION. HE WAS FORCED INTO EXILE IN MEXICO, WHERE HE PREPARED HIS TROOPS FOR THEIR FINAL JOURNEY TO POWER.

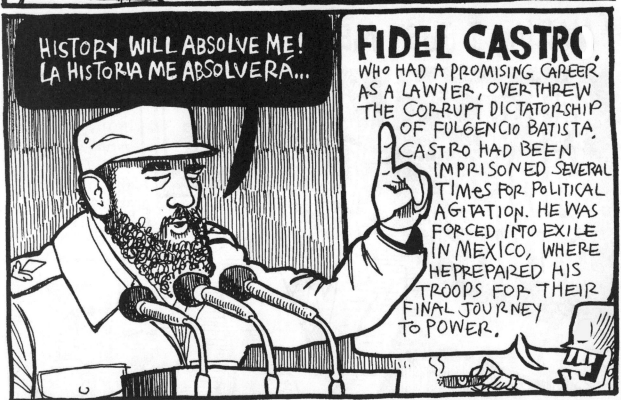

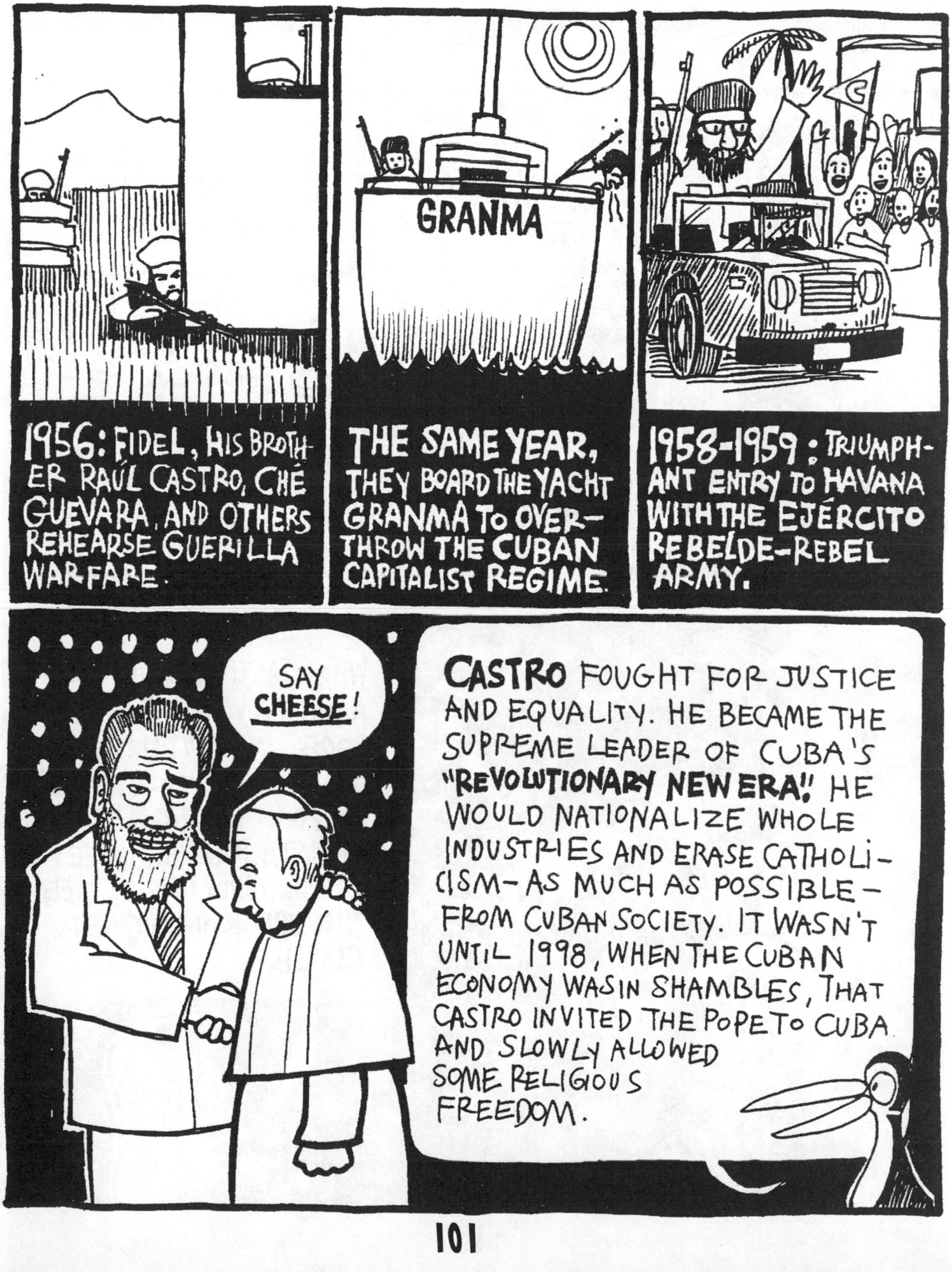
1956: FIDEL, HIS BROTHER RAÚL CASTRO, CHÉ GUEVARA, AND OTHERS REHEARSE GUERILLA WARFARE.
GRANMA
THE SAME YEAR, THEY BOARD THE YACHT GRANMA TO OVERTHROW THE CUBAN CAPITALIST REGIME.
1958-1959: TRIUMPHANT ENTRY TO HAVANA WITH THE EJÉRCITO REBELDE-REBEL ARMY.
SAY CHEESE!
CASTRO FOUGHT FOR JUSTICE AND EQUALITY. HE BECAME THE SUPREME LEADER OF CUBA'S "REVOLUTIONARY NEW ERA." HE WOULD NATIONALIZE WHOLE INDUSTRIES AND ERASE CATHOLICISM—AS MUCH AS POSSIBLE—FROM CUBAN SOCIETY. IT WASN'T UNTIL 1998, WHEN THE CUBAN ECONOMY WAS IN SHAMBLES, THAT CASTRO INVITED THE POPE TO CUBA AND SLOWLY ALLOWED SOME RELIGIOUS FREEDOM.

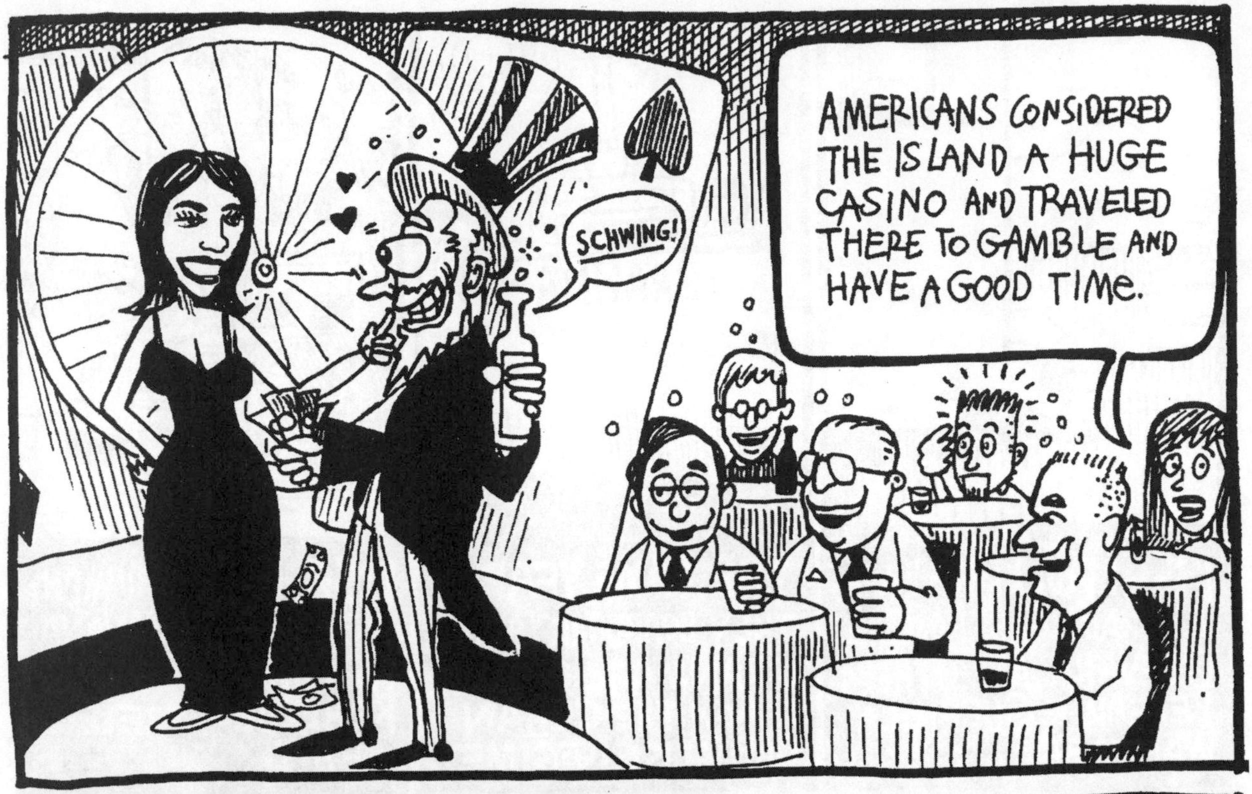
AMERICANS CONSIDERED THE ISLAND A HUGE CASINO AND TRAVELED THERE TO GAMBLE AND HAVE A GOOD TIME.
SCHWING!

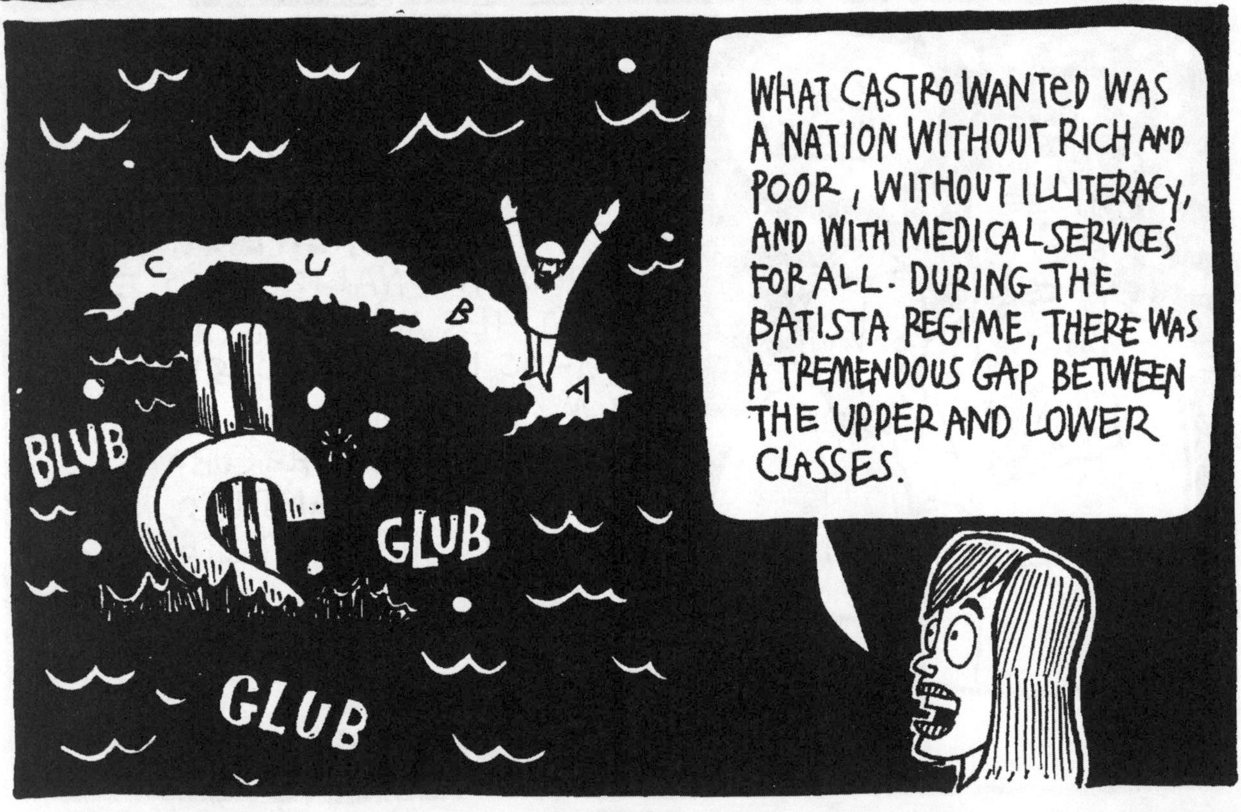
WHAT CASTRO WANTED WAS A NATION WITHOUT RICH AND POOR, WITHOUT ILLITERACY, AND WITH MEDICAL SERVICES FOR ALL. DURING THE BATISTA REGIME, THERE WAS A TREMENDOUS GAP BETWEEN THE UPPER AND LOWER CLASSES.
CUBA
BLUB
GLUB
GLUB

CASTRO ABOLISHED PRIVATE PROPERTY AND ESTABLISHED A PLAN FOR THE EQUAL DISTRIBUTION OF WEALTH. HE ALSO SENT DOCTORS AND TEACHERS TO POOR RURAL AREAS, SPREADING HIS MESSAGE.

SS EXILE

LOS POBRES

THE UNITED STATES TRIED TO STOP CASTRO BUT COULDN'T. AMERICAN LEADERS BEGAN TO FEAR THAT THE GHOST OF COMMUNISM WOULD SPREAD ALL OVER THE AMERICAS.

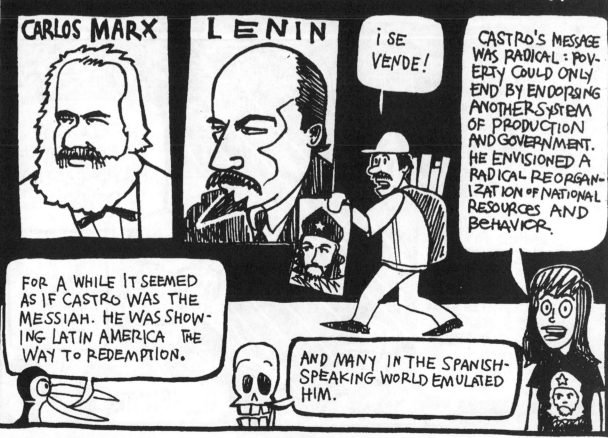

CARLOS MARX

LENIN

¡SE VENDE!

CASTRO'S MESSAGE WAS RADICAL: POVERTY COULD ONLY END BY ENDORSING ANOTHER SYSTEM OF PRODUCTION AND GOVERNMENT. HE ENVISIONED A RADICAL REORGANIZATION OF NATIONAL RESOURCES AND BEHAVIOR.

FOR A WHILE IT SEEMED AS IF CASTRO WAS THE MESSIAH. HE WAS SHOWING LATIN AMERICA THE WAY TO REDEMPTION.

AND MANY IN THE SPANISH-SPEAKING WORLD EMULATED HIM.

103

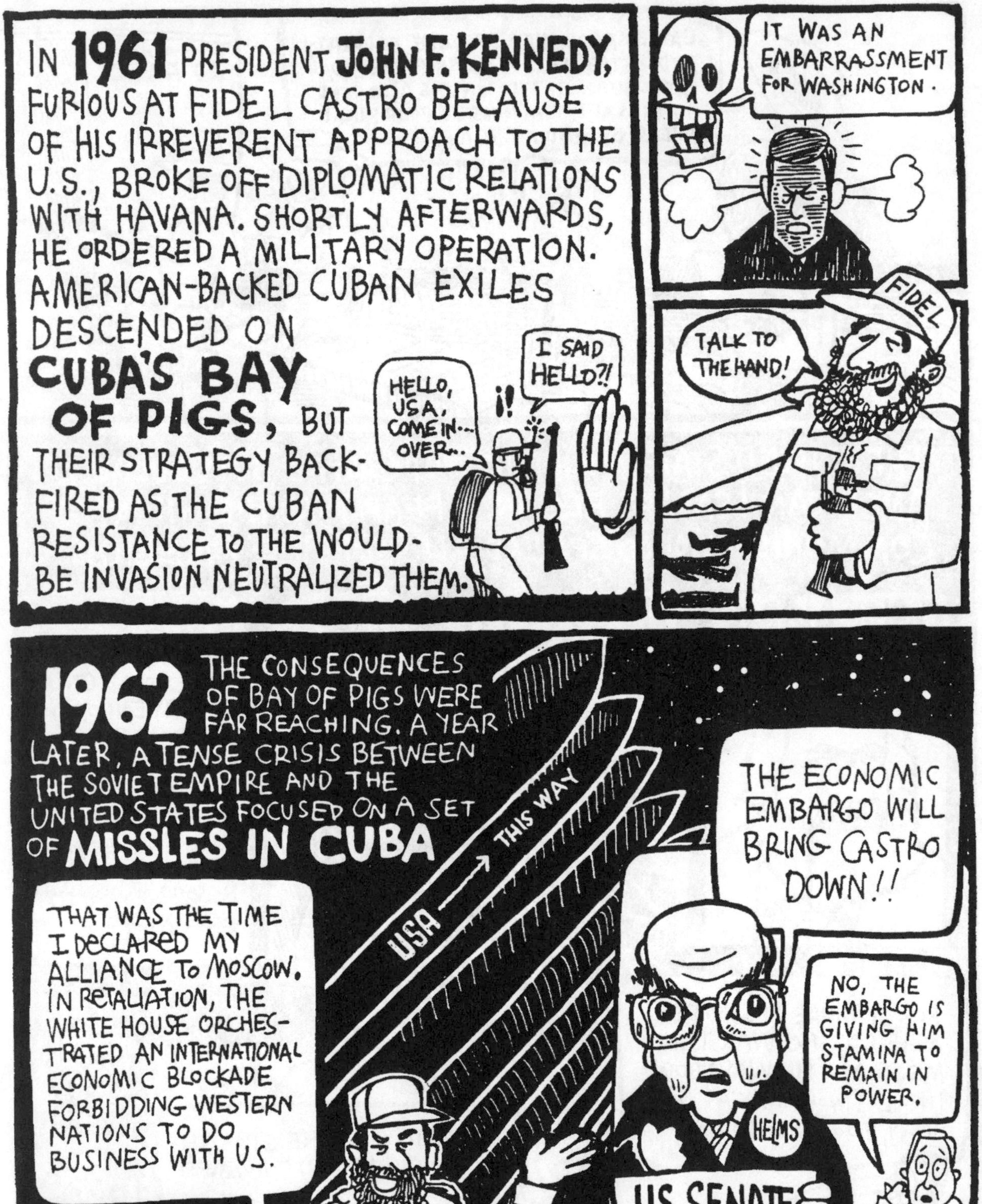

IN 1961 PRESIDENT JOHN F. KENNEDY, FURIOUS AT FIDEL CASTRO BECAUSE OF HIS IRREVERENT APPROACH TO THE U.S., BROKE OFF DIPLOMATIC RELATIONS WITH HAVANA. SHORTLY AFTERWARDS, HE ORDERED A MILITARY OPERATION. AMERICAN-BACKED CUBAN EXILES DESCENDED ON CUBA'S BAY OF PIGS, BUT THEIR STRATEGY BACKFIRED AS THE CUBAN RESISTANCE TO THE WOULD-BE INVASION NEUTRALIZED THEM.
HELLO, USA, COME IN... OVER...
¡!
I SAID HELLO?!
IT WAS AN EMBARRASSMENT FOR WASHINGTON.
FIDEL
TALK TO THE HAND!
1962 THE CONSEQUENCES OF BAY OF PIGS WERE FAR REACHING. A YEAR LATER, A TENSE CRISIS BETWEEN THE SOVIET EMPIRE AND THE UNITED STATES FOCUSED ON A SET OF MISSLES IN CUBA
USA → THIS WAY
THAT WAS THE TIME I DECLARED MY ALLIANCE TO MOSCOW. IN RETALIATION, THE WHITE HOUSE ORCHESTRATED AN INTERNATIONAL ECONOMIC BLOCKADE FORBIDDING WESTERN NATIONS TO DO BUSINESS WITH US.
THE ECONOMIC EMBARGO WILL BRING CASTRO DOWN!!
NO, THE EMBARGO IS GIVING HIM STAMINA TO REMAIN IN POWER.
HELMS
U.S. SENATE

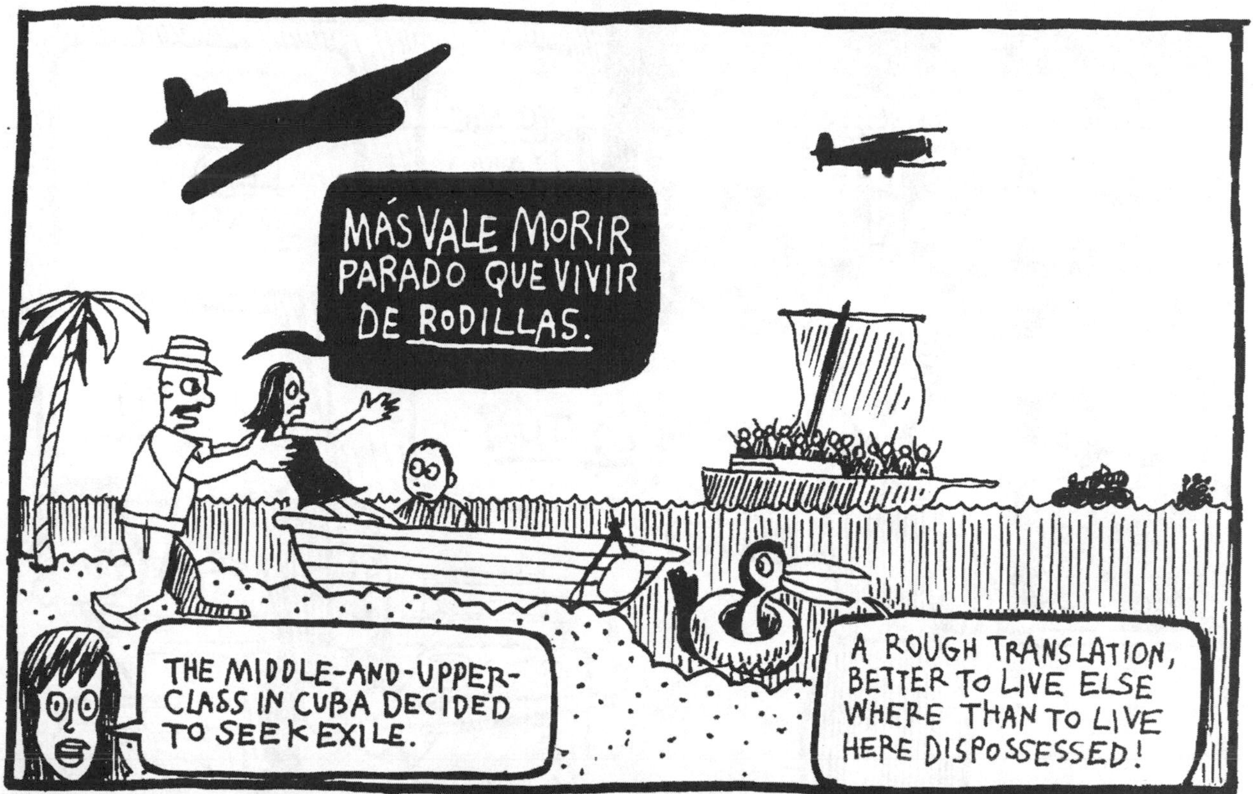
MÁS VALE MORIR PARADO QUE VIVIR DE RODILLAS.
THE MIDDLE-AND-UPPER-CLASS IN CUBA DECIDED TO SEEK EXILE.
A ROUGH TRANSLATION, BETTER TO LIVE ELSEWHERE THAN TO LIVE HERE DISPOSSESSED!

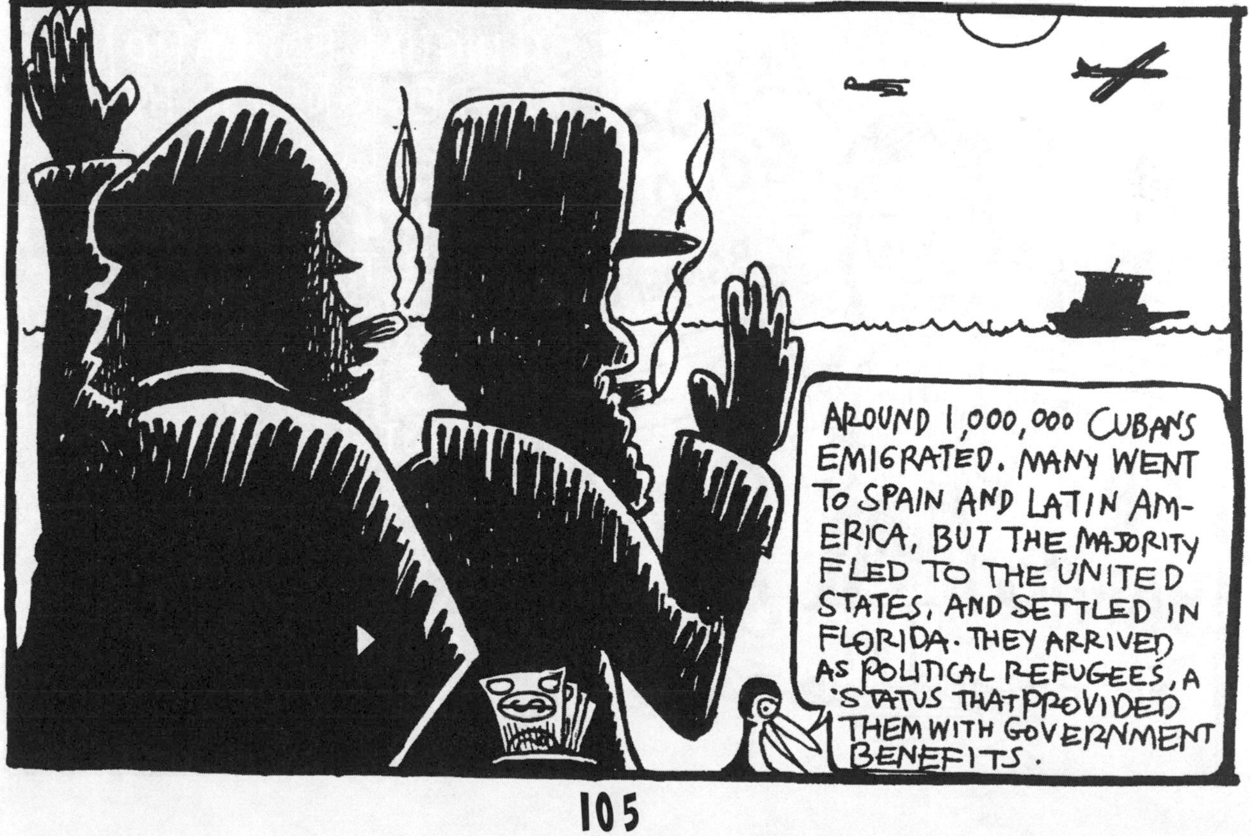
AROUND 1,000,000 CUBANS EMIGRATED. MANY WENT TO SPAIN AND LATIN AMERICA, BUT THE MAJORITY FLED TO THE UNITED STATES, AND SETTLED IN FLORIDA. THEY ARRIVED AS POLITICAL REFUGEES, A STATUS THAT PROVIDED THEM WITH GOVERNMENT BENEFITS.

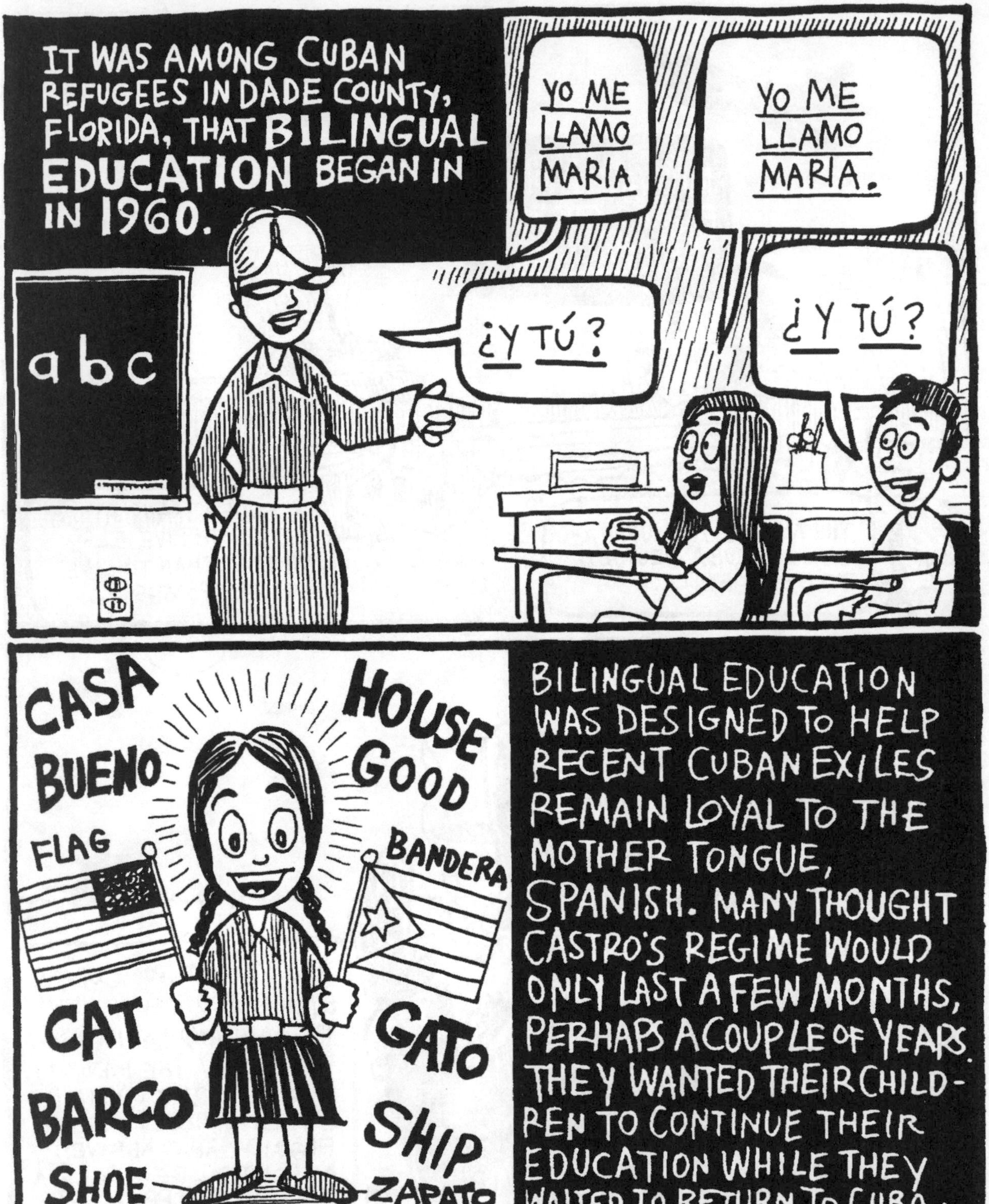
IT WAS AMONG CUBAN REFUGEES IN DADE COUNTY, FLORIDA, THAT BILINGUAL EDUCATION BEGAN IN IN 1960.
abc
YO ME LLAMO MARIA
YO ME LLAMO MARIA.
¿Y TÚ?
¿Y TÚ?
CASA
HOUSE
BUENO
GOOD
FLAG
BANDERA
CAT
GATO
BARCO
SHIP
SHOE
ZAPATO
BILINGUAL EDUCATION WAS DESIGNED TO HELP RECENT CUBAN EXILES REMAIN LOYAL TO THE MOTHER TONGUE, SPANISH. MANY THOUGHT CASTRO'S REGIME WOULD ONLY LAST A FEW MONTHS, PERHAPS A COUPLE OF YEARS. THEY WANTED THEIR CHILDREN TO CONTINUE THEIR EDUCATION WHILE THEY WAITED TO RETURN TO CUBA.

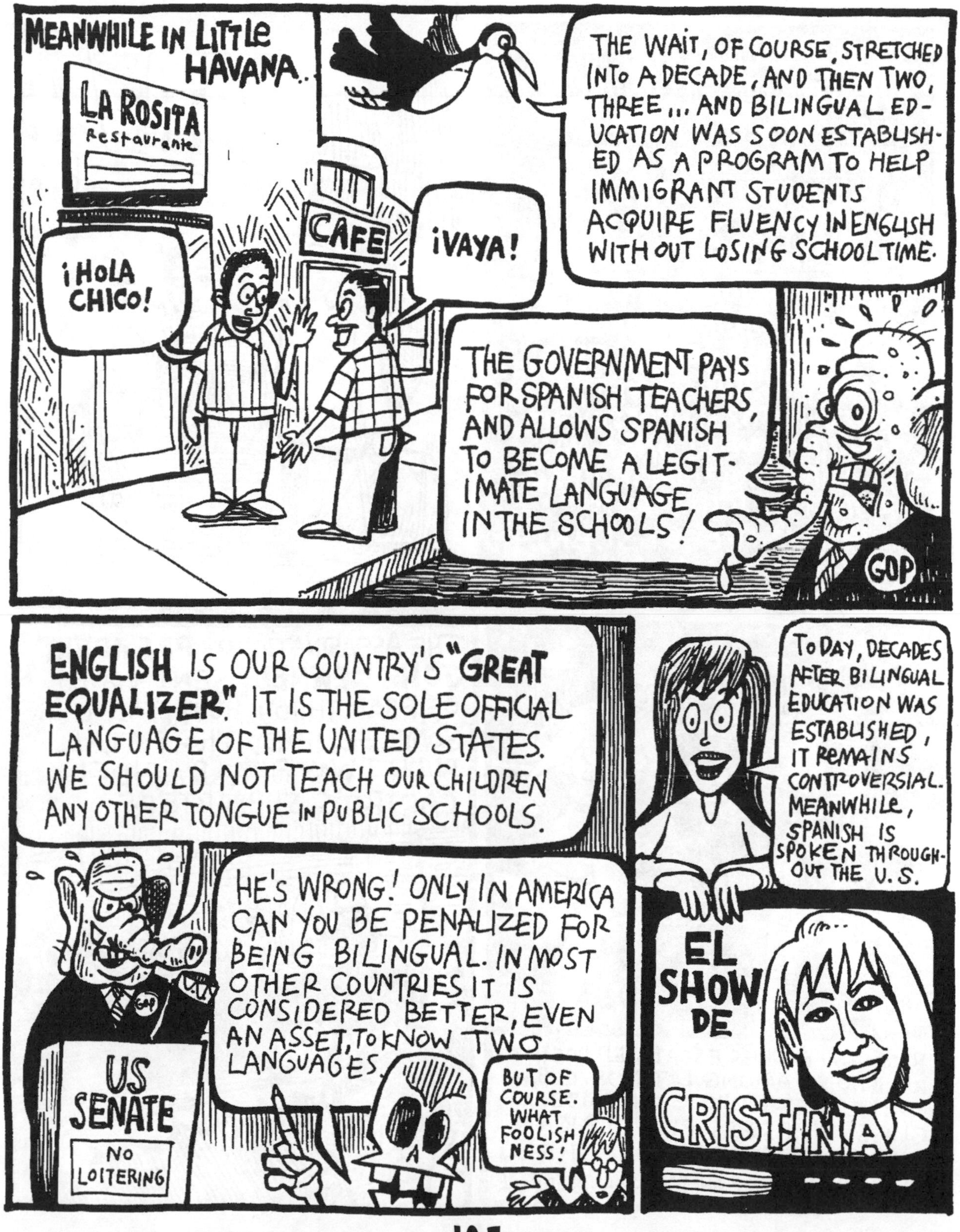
MEANWHILE IN LITTLE HAVANA..
LA ROSITA Restaurante
CAFE
¡HOLA CHICO!
¡VAYA!
THE WAIT, OF COURSE, STRETCHED INTO A DECADE, AND THEN TWO, THREE... AND BILINGUAL EDUCATION WAS SOON ESTABLISHED AS A PROGRAM TO HELP IMMIGRANT STUDENTS ACQUIRE FLUENCY IN ENGLISH WITHOUT LOSING SCHOOL TIME.
THE GOVERNMENT PAYS FOR SPANISH TEACHERS, AND ALLOWS SPANISH TO BECOME A LEGITIMATE LANGUAGE IN THE SCHOOLS!
GOP
ENGLISH IS OUR COUNTRY'S "GREAT EQUALIZER." IT IS THE SOLE OFFICIAL LANGUAGE OF THE UNITED STATES. WE SHOULD NOT TEACH OUR CHILDREN ANY OTHER TONGUE IN PUBLIC SCHOOLS.
US SENATE
NO LOITERING
HE'S WRONG! ONLY IN AMERICA CAN YOU BE PENALIZED FOR BEING BILINGUAL. IN MOST OTHER COUNTRIES IT IS CONSIDERED BETTER, EVEN AN ASSET, TO KNOW TWO LANGUAGES.
BUT OF COURSE. WHAT FOOLISHNESS!
TODAY, DECADES AFTER BILINGUAL EDUCATION WAS ESTABLISHED, IT REMAINS CONTROVERSIAL. MEANWHILE, SPANISH IS SPOKEN THROUGHOUT THE U.S.
EL SHOW DE CRISTINA

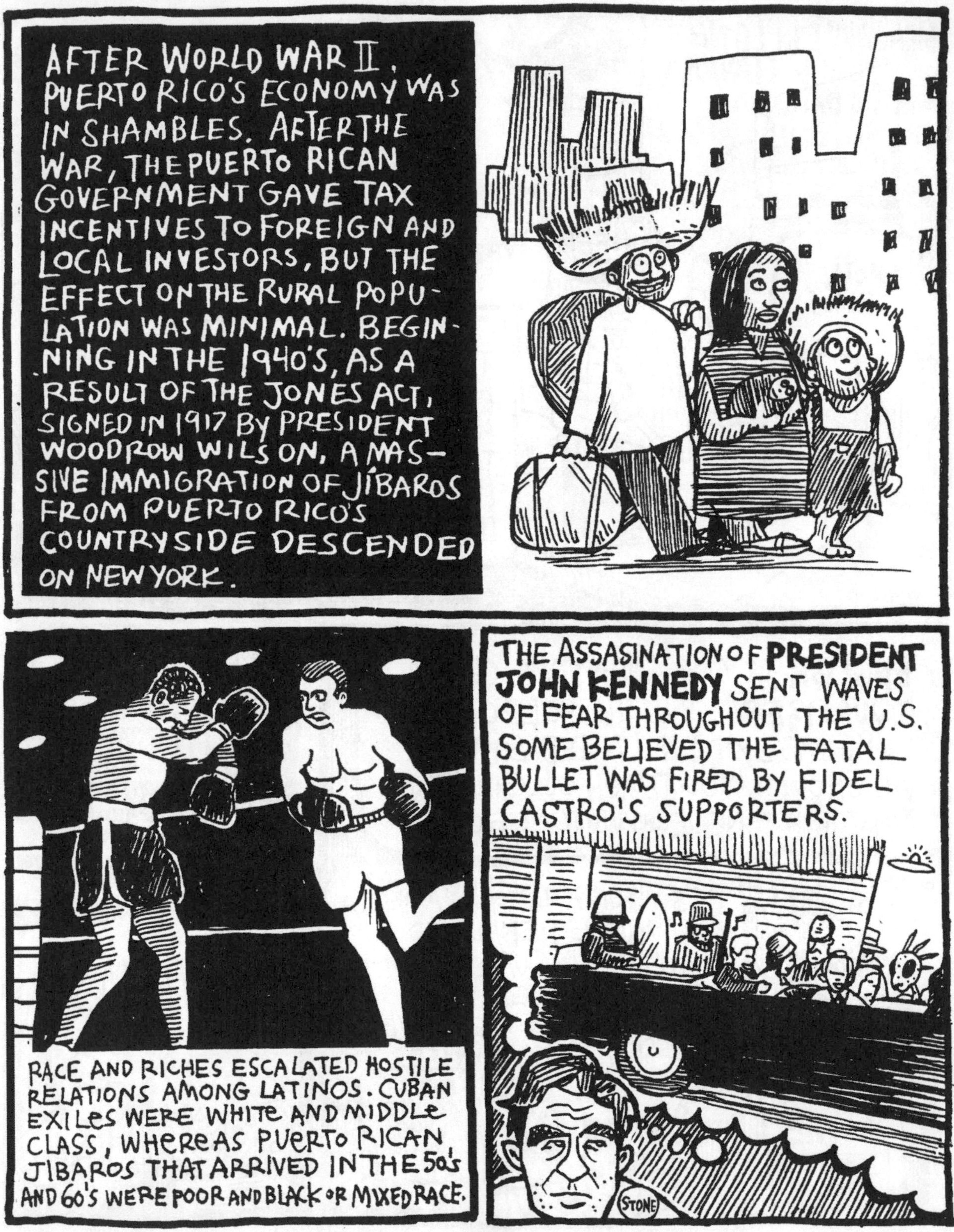
AFTER WORLD WAR II, PUERTO RICO'S ECONOMY WAS IN SHAMBLES. AFTER THE WAR, THE PUERTO RICAN GOVERNMENT GAVE TAX INCENTIVES TO FOREIGN AND LOCAL INVESTORS, BUT THE EFFECT ON THE RURAL POPULATION WAS MINIMAL. BEGINNING IN THE 1940'S, AS A RESULT OF THE JONES ACT, SIGNED IN 1917 BY PRESIDENT WOODROW WILSON, A MASSIVE IMMIGRATION OF JÍBAROS FROM PUERTO RICO'S COUNTRYSIDE DESCENDED ON NEW YORK.
RACE AND RICHES ESCALATED HOSTILE RELATIONS AMONG LATINOS. CUBAN EXILES WERE WHITE AND MIDDLE CLASS, WHEREAS PUERTO RICAN JIBAROS THAT ARRIVED IN THE 50'S AND 60'S WERE POOR AND BLACK OR MIXED RACE.
THE ASSASINATION OF **PRESIDENT JOHN KENNEDY** SENT WAVES OF FEAR THROUGHOUT THE U.S. SOME BELIEVED THE FATAL BULLET WAS FIRED BY FIDEL CASTRO'S SUPPORTERS.
STONE

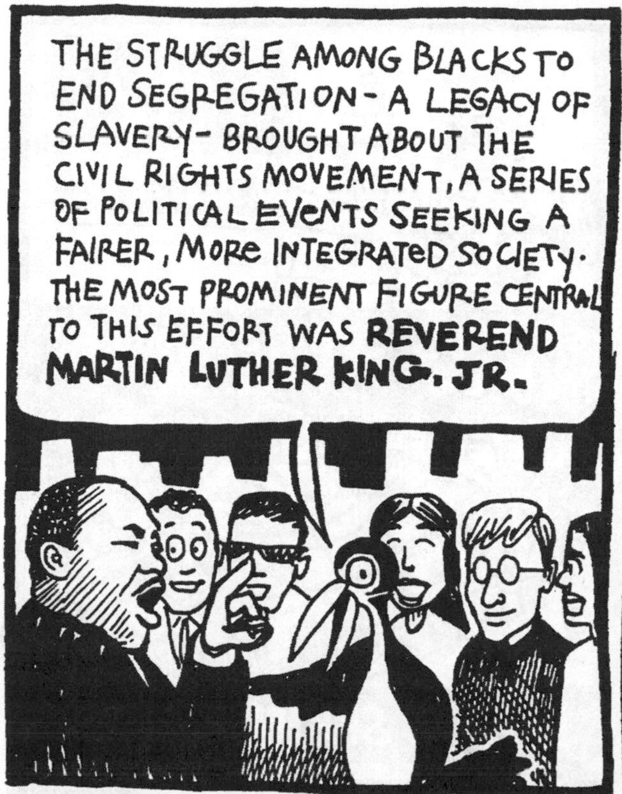
THE STRUGGLE AMONG BLACKS TO END SEGREGATION - A LEGACY OF SLAVERY - BROUGHT ABOUT THE CIVIL RIGHTS MOVEMENT, A SERIES OF POLITICAL EVENTS SEEKING A FAIRER, MORE INTEGRATED SOCIETY. THE MOST PROMINENT FIGURE CENTRAL TO THIS EFFORT WAS REVEREND MARTIN LUTHER KING, JR.

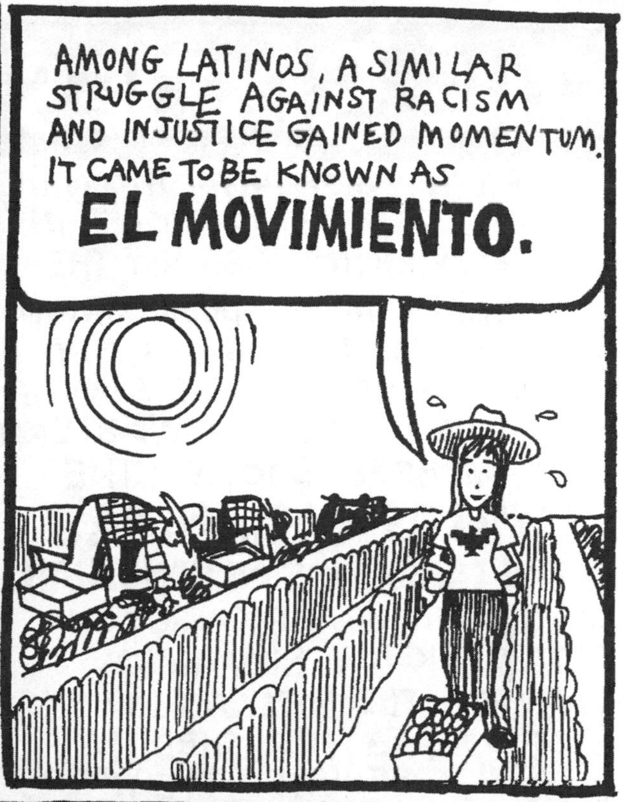
AMONG LATINOS, A SIMILAR STRUGGLE AGAINST RACISM AND INJUSTICE GAINED MOMENTUM. IT CAME TO BE KNOWN AS
EL MOVIMIENTO.

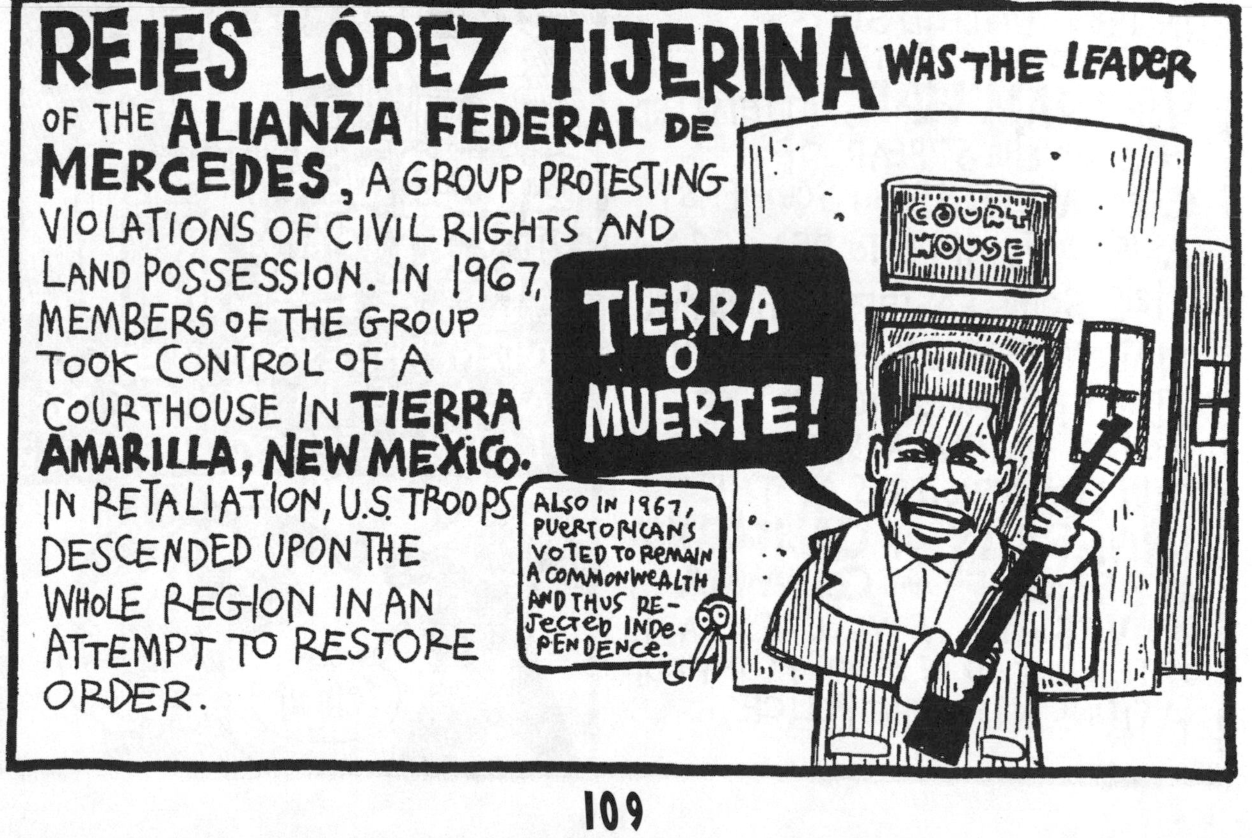
REIES LÓPEZ TIJERINA WAS THE LEADER OF THE ALIANZA FEDERAL DE MERCEDES, A GROUP PROTESTING VIOLATIONS OF CIVIL RIGHTS AND LAND POSSESSION. IN 1967, MEMBERS OF THE GROUP TOOK CONTROL OF A COURTHOUSE IN TIERRA AMARILLA, NEW MEXICO. IN RETALIATION, U.S. TROOPS DESCENDED UPON THE WHOLE REGION IN AN ATTEMPT TO RESTORE ORDER.
COURT HOUSE
TIERRA Ó MUERTE!
ALSO IN 1967, PUERTO RICANS VOTED TO REMAIN A COMMONWEALTH AND THUS REJECTED INDEPENDENCE.

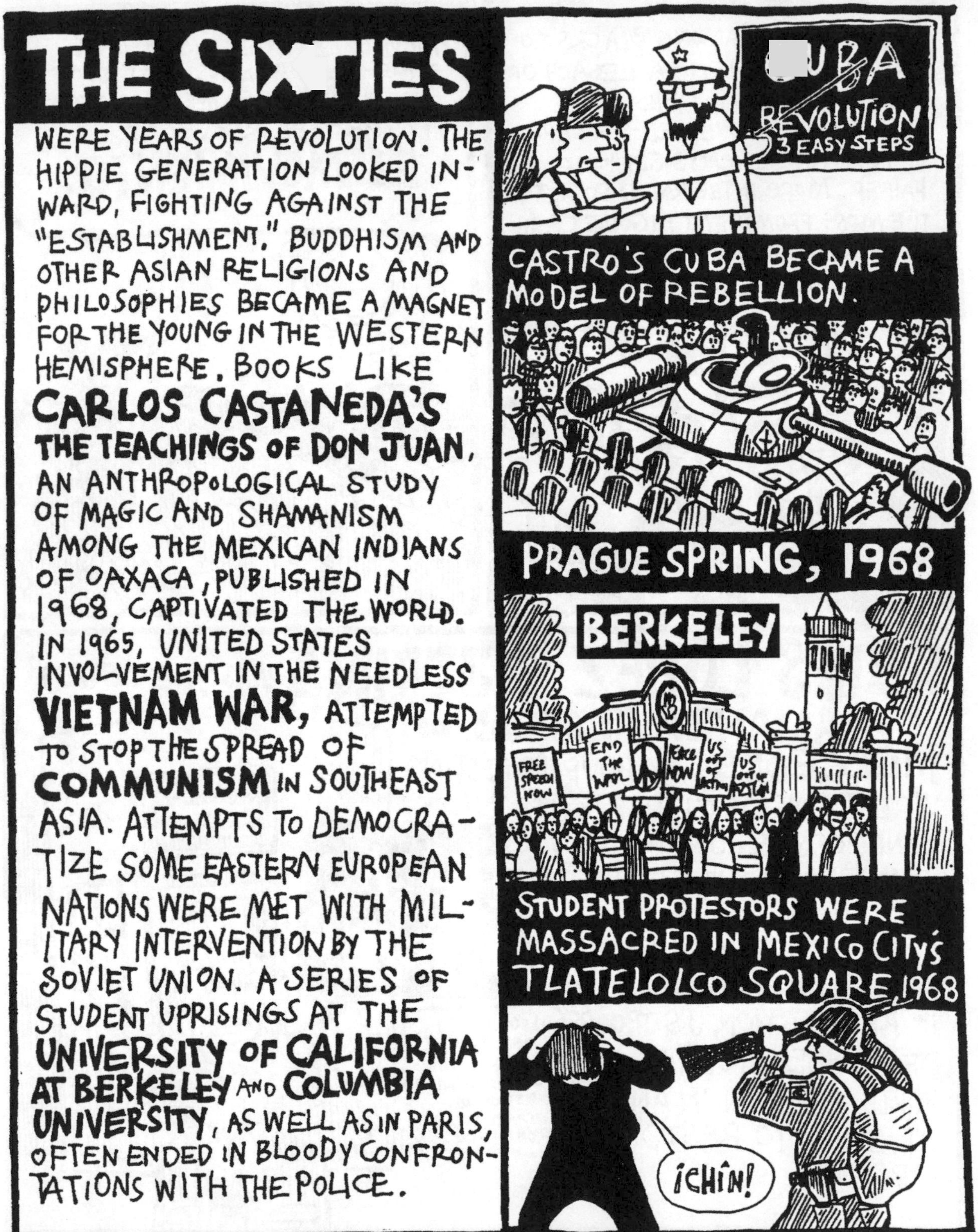
THE SIXTIES
WERE YEARS OF REVOLUTION. THE HIPPIE GENERATION LOOKED INWARD, FIGHTING AGAINST THE "ESTABLISHMENT." BUDDHISM AND OTHER ASIAN RELIGIONS AND PHILOSOPHIES BECAME A MAGNET FOR THE YOUNG IN THE WESTERN HEMISPHERE. BOOKS LIKE CARLOS CASTANEDA'S THE TEACHINGS OF DON JUAN, AN ANTHROPOLOGICAL STUDY OF MAGIC AND SHAMANISM AMONG THE MEXICAN INDIANS OF OAXACA, PUBLISHED IN 1968, CAPTIVATED THE WORLD. IN 1965, UNITED STATES INVOLVEMENT IN THE NEEDLESS VIETNAM WAR, ATTEMPTED TO STOP THE SPREAD OF COMMUNISM IN SOUTHEAST ASIA. ATTEMPTS TO DEMOCRATIZE SOME EASTERN EUROPEAN NATIONS WERE MET WITH MILITARY INTERVENTION BY THE SOVIET UNION. A SERIES OF STUDENT UPRISINGS AT THE UNIVERSITY OF CALIFORNIA AT BERKELEY AND COLUMBIA UNIVERSITY, AS WELL AS IN PARIS, OFTEN ENDED IN BLOODY CONFRONTATIONS WITH THE POLICE.
UBA
REVOLUTION
3 EASY STEPS
CASTRO'S CUBA BECAME A MODEL OF REBELLION.
PRAGUE SPRING, 1968
BERKELEY
FREE SPEECH NOW
END THE WAR
PEACE NOW
US OUT OF
US OUT OF AZTLAN
STUDENT PROTESTORS WERE MASSACRED IN MEXICO CITY'S TLATELOLCO SQUARE, 1968
¡CHÍN!

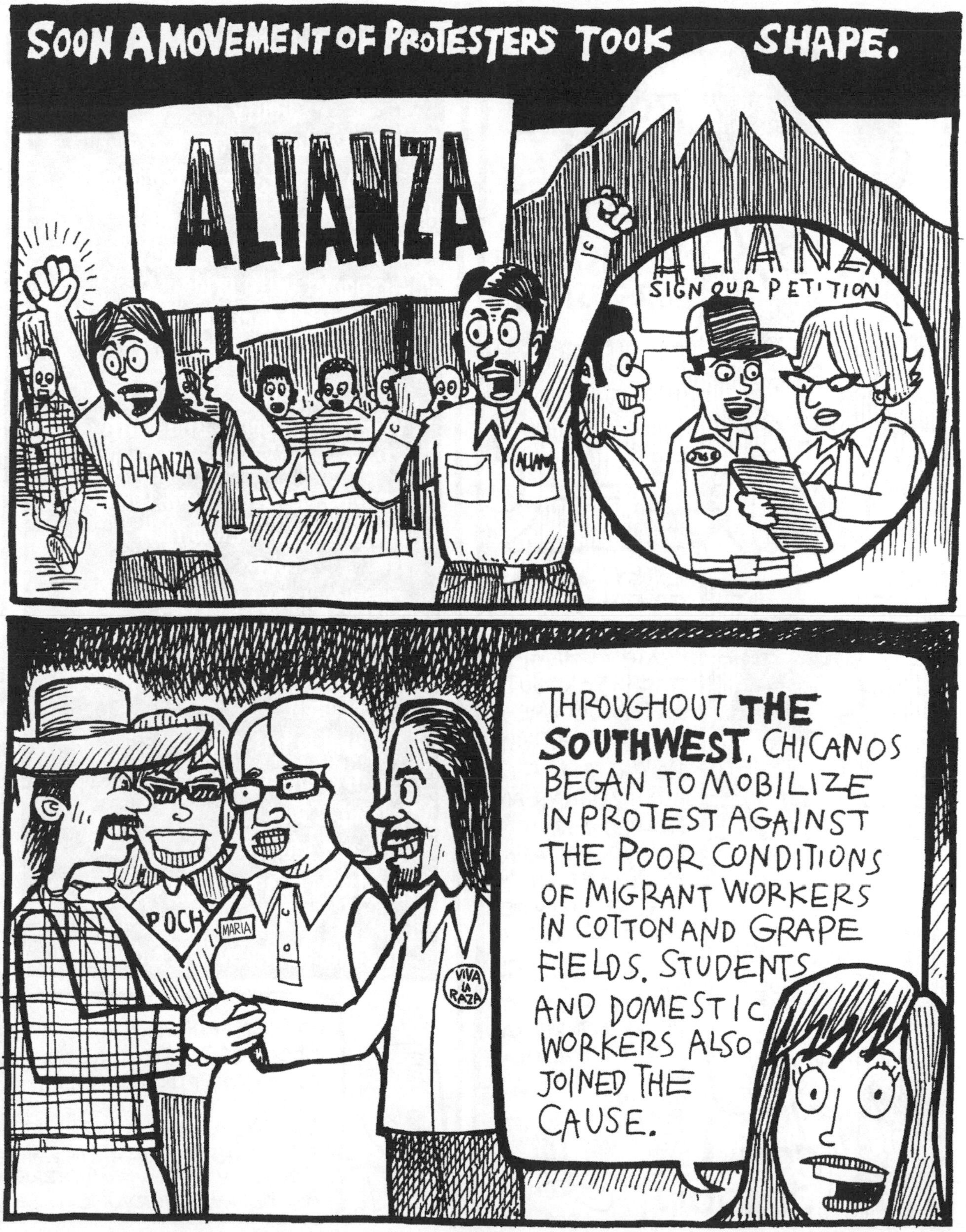
SOON A MOVEMENT OF PROTESTERS TOOK SHAPE.
ALIANZA
ALIANZA
SIGN OUR PETITION
MARIA
VIVA LA RAZA
THROUGHOUT **THE SOUTHWEST**, CHICANOS BEGAN TO MOBILIZE IN PROTEST AGAINST THE POOR CONDITIONS OF MIGRANT WORKERS IN COTTON AND GRAPE FIELDS. STUDENTS AND DOMESTIC WORKERS ALSO JOINED THE CAUSE.

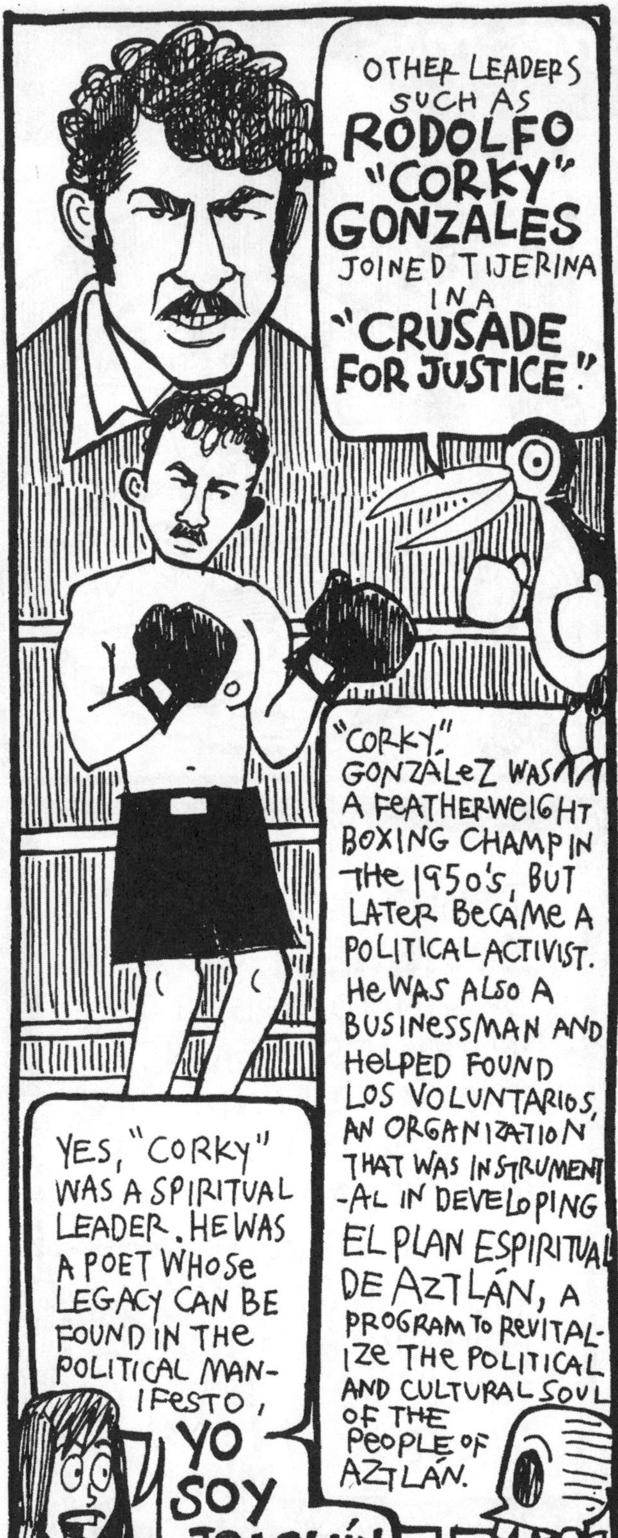
OTHER LEADERS SUCH AS RODOLFO "CORKY" GONZALES JOINED TIJERINA IN A "CRUSADE FOR JUSTICE."
"CORKY" GONZÁLEZ WAS A FEATHERWEIGHT BOXING CHAMP IN THE 1950'S, BUT LATER BECAME A POLITICAL ACTIVIST. HE WAS ALSO A BUSINESSMAN AND HELPED FOUND LOS VOLUNTARIOS, AN ORGANIZATION THAT WAS INSTRUMENT-AL IN DEVELOPING EL PLAN ESPIRITUAL DE AZTLÁN, A PROGRAM TO REVITAL-IZE THE POLITICAL AND CULTURAL SOUL OF THE PEOPLE OF AZTLÁN.
YES, "CORKY" WAS A SPIRITUAL LEADER. HE WAS A POET WHOSE LEGACY CAN BE FOUND IN THE POLITICAL MAN-IFESTO, YO SOY JOAQUÍN.

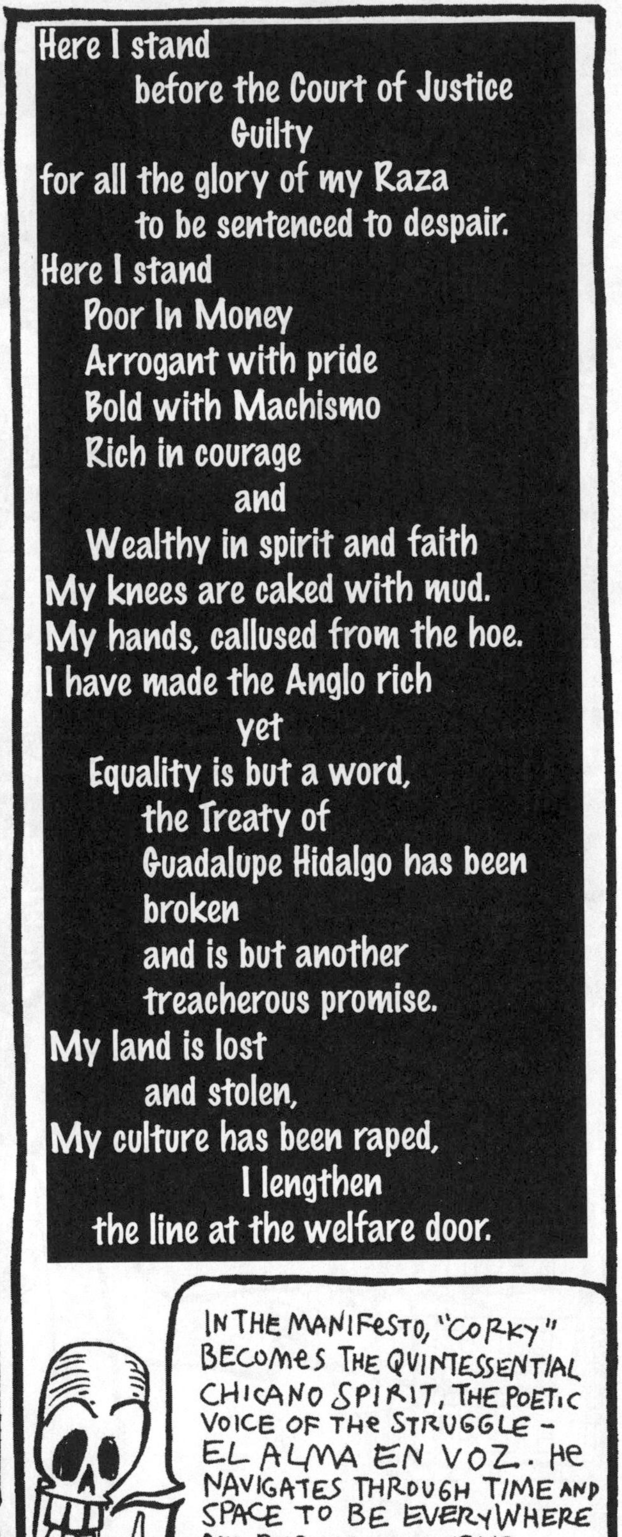
Here I stand
before the Court of Justice
Guilty
for all the glory of my Raza
to be sentenced to despair.
Here I stand
Poor In Money
Arrogant with pride
Bold with Machismo
Rich in courage
and
Wealthy in spirit and faith
My knees are caked with mud.
My hands, callused from the hoe.
I have made the Anglo rich
yet
Equality is but a word,
the Treaty of
Guadalupe Hidalgo has been
broken
and is but another
treacherous promise.
My land is lost
and stolen,
My culture has been raped,
I lengthen
the line at the welfare door.
IN THE MANIFESTO, "CORKY" BECOMES THE QUINTESSENTIAL CHICANO SPIRIT, THE POETIC VOICE OF THE STRUGGLE – EL ALMA EN VOZ. HE NAVIGATES THROUGH TIME AND SPACE TO BE EVERYWHERE AND BECOME EVERYONE.

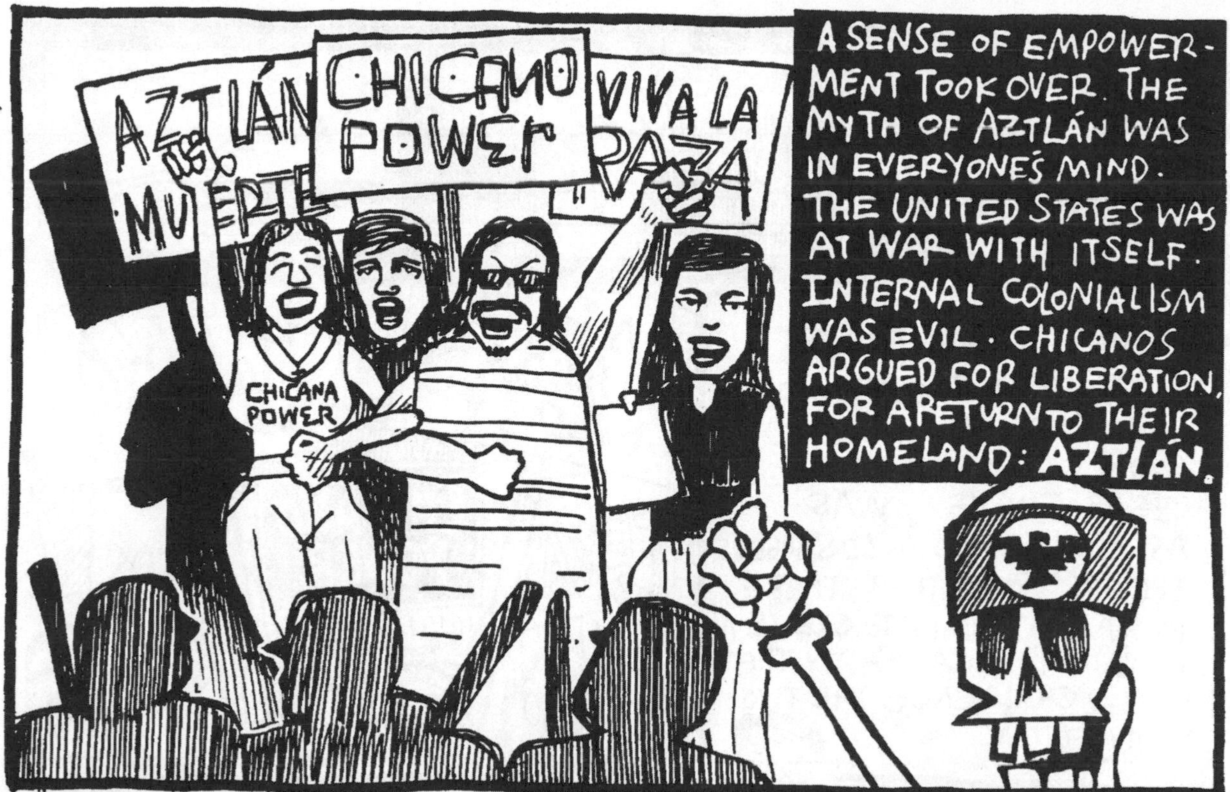
AZTLÁN
MUERTE
CHICANO POWER
VIVA LA RAZA
CHICANA POWER
A SENSE OF EMPOWERMENT TOOK OVER. THE MYTH OF AZTLÁN WAS IN EVERYONE'S MIND. THE UNITED STATES WAS AT WAR WITH ITSELF. INTERNAL COLONIALISM WAS EVIL. CHICANOS ARGUED FOR LIBERATION, FOR A RETURN TO THEIR HOMELAND: AZTLÁN.

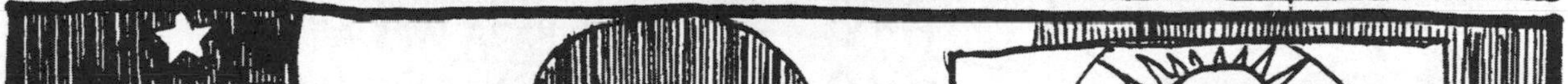
TEJAS
UFW
HUELGA
COLORADO
BROWN BERETS
MECHA

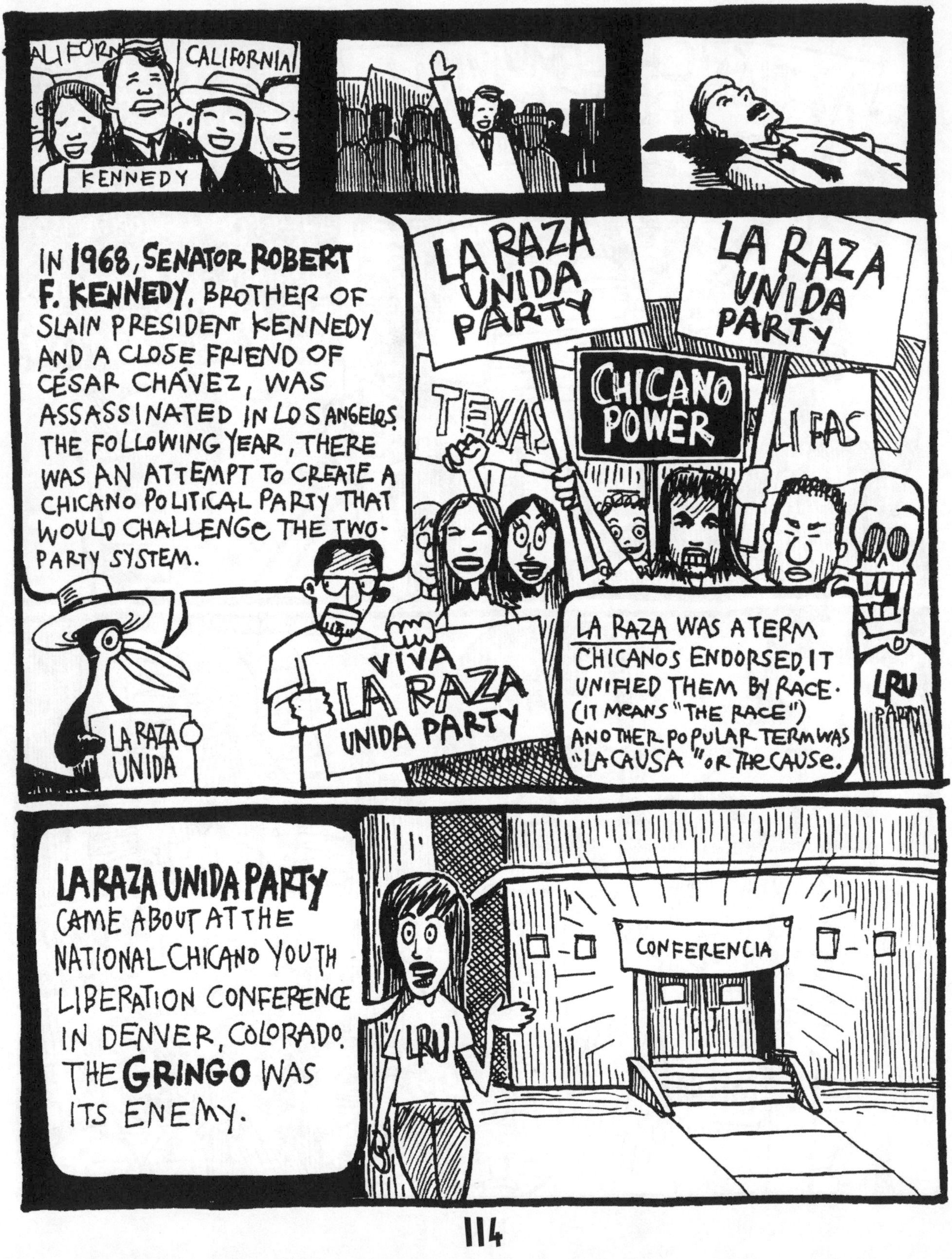

CALIFORNIA
KENNEDY
IN 1968, SENATOR ROBERT F. KENNEDY, BROTHER OF SLAIN PRESIDENT KENNEDY AND A CLOSE FRIEND OF CÉSAR CHÁVEZ, WAS ASSASSINATED IN LOS ANGELES. THE FOLLOWING YEAR, THERE WAS AN ATTEMPT TO CREATE A CHICANO POLITICAL PARTY THAT WOULD CHALLENGE THE TWO-PARTY SYSTEM.
LA RAZA UNIDA PARTY
LA RAZA UNIDA PARTY
TEXAS
CHICANO POWER
LA RAZA UNIDA
VIVA LA RAZA UNIDA PARTY
LA RAZA WAS A TERM CHICANOS ENDORSED, IT UNIFIED THEM BY RACE. (IT MEANS "THE RACE") ANOTHER POPULAR TERM WAS "LA CAUSA" OR THE CAUSE.
LRU PARTY
LA RAZA UNIDA PARTY CAME ABOUT AT THE NATIONAL CHICANO YOUTH LIBERATION CONFERENCE IN DENVER, COLORADO. THE GRINGO WAS ITS ENEMY.
CONFERENCIA
LRU

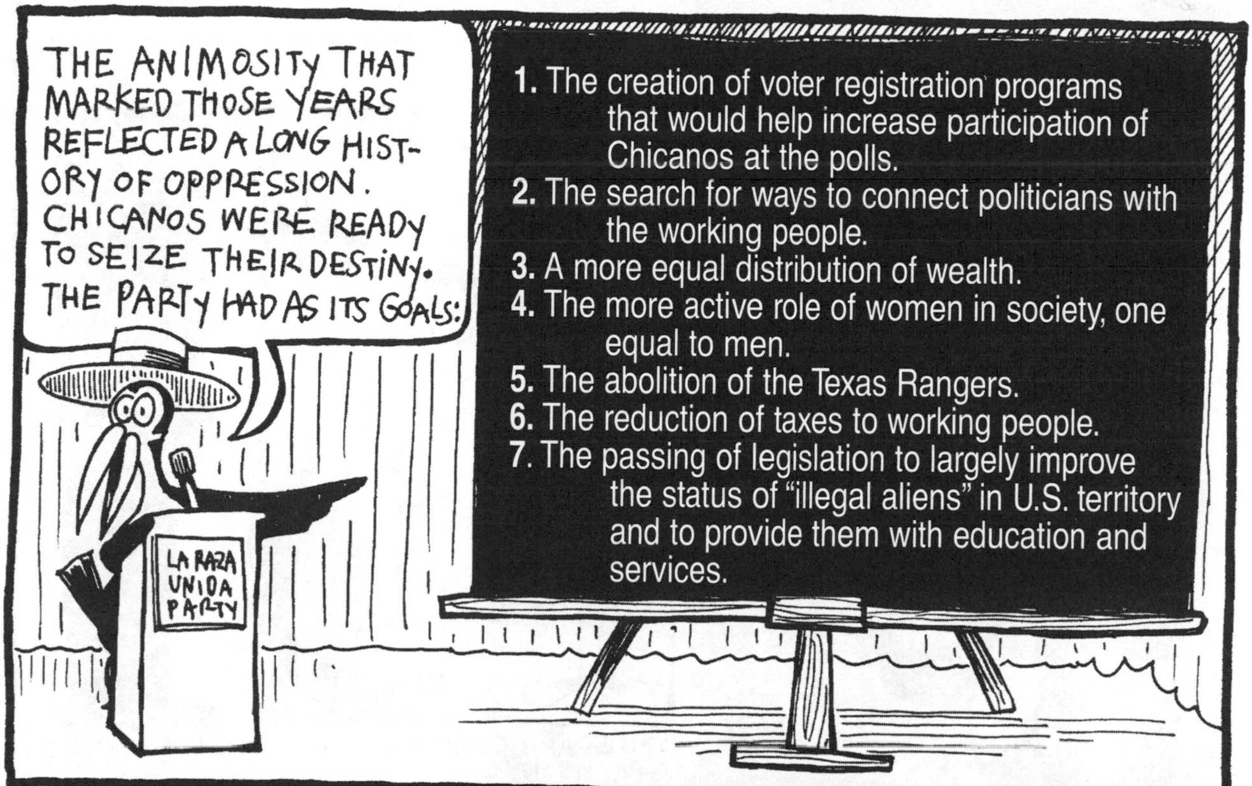
THE ANIMOSITY THAT MARKED THOSE YEARS REFLECTED A LONG HISTORY OF OPPRESSION. CHICANOS WERE READY TO SEIZE THEIR DESTINY. THE PARTY HAD AS ITS GOALS:
1. The creation of voter registration programs that would help increase participation of Chicanos at the polls.
2. The search for ways to connect politicians with the working people.
3. A more equal distribution of wealth.
4. The more active role of women in society, one equal to men.
5. The abolition of the Texas Rangers.
6. The reduction of taxes to working people.
7. The passing of legislation to largely improve the status of "illegal aliens" in U.S. territory and to provide them with education and services.
LA RAZA UNIDA PARTY

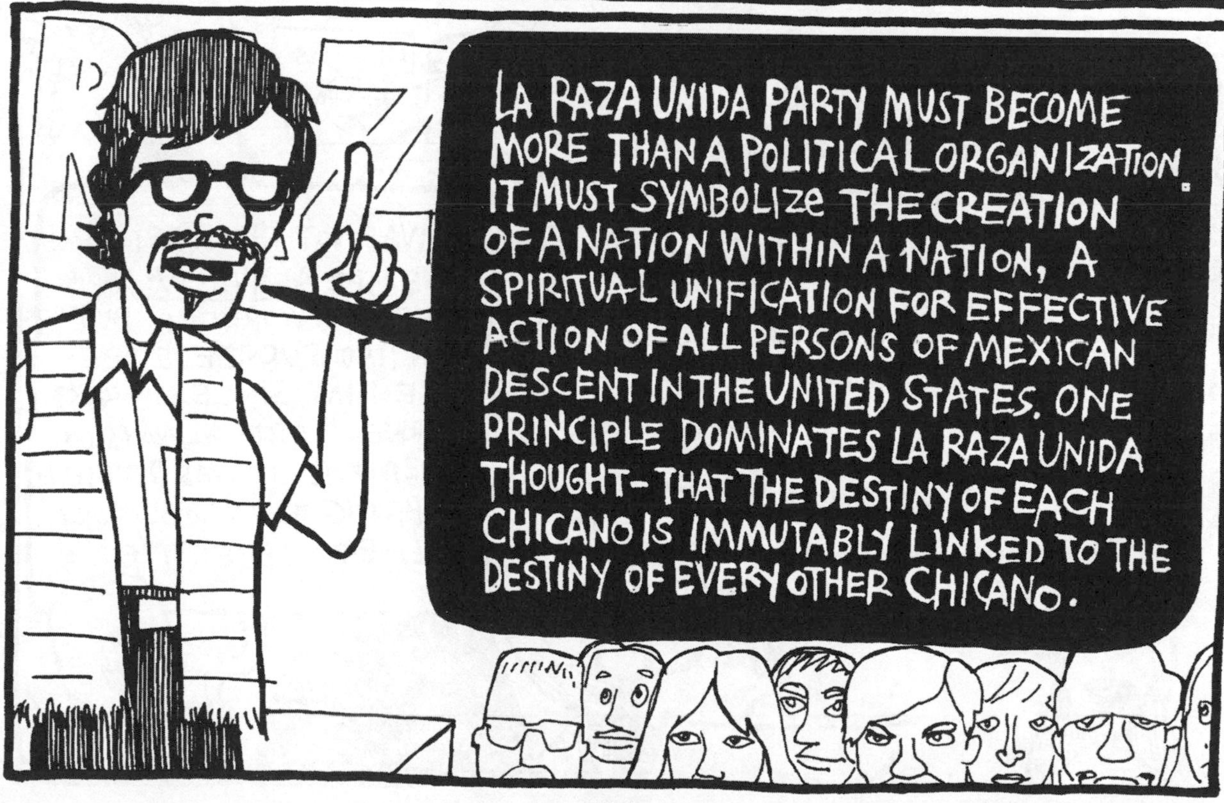
LA RAZA UNIDA PARTY MUST BECOME MORE THAN A POLITICAL ORGANIZATION. IT MUST SYMBOLIZE THE CREATION OF A NATION WITHIN A NATION, A SPIRITUAL UNIFICATION FOR EFFECTIVE ACTION OF ALL PERSONS OF MEXICAN DESCENT IN THE UNITED STATES. ONE PRINCIPLE DOMINATES LA RAZA UNIDA THOUGHT- THAT THE DESTINY OF EACH CHICANO IS IMMUTABLY LINKED TO THE DESTINY OF EVERY OTHER CHICANO.

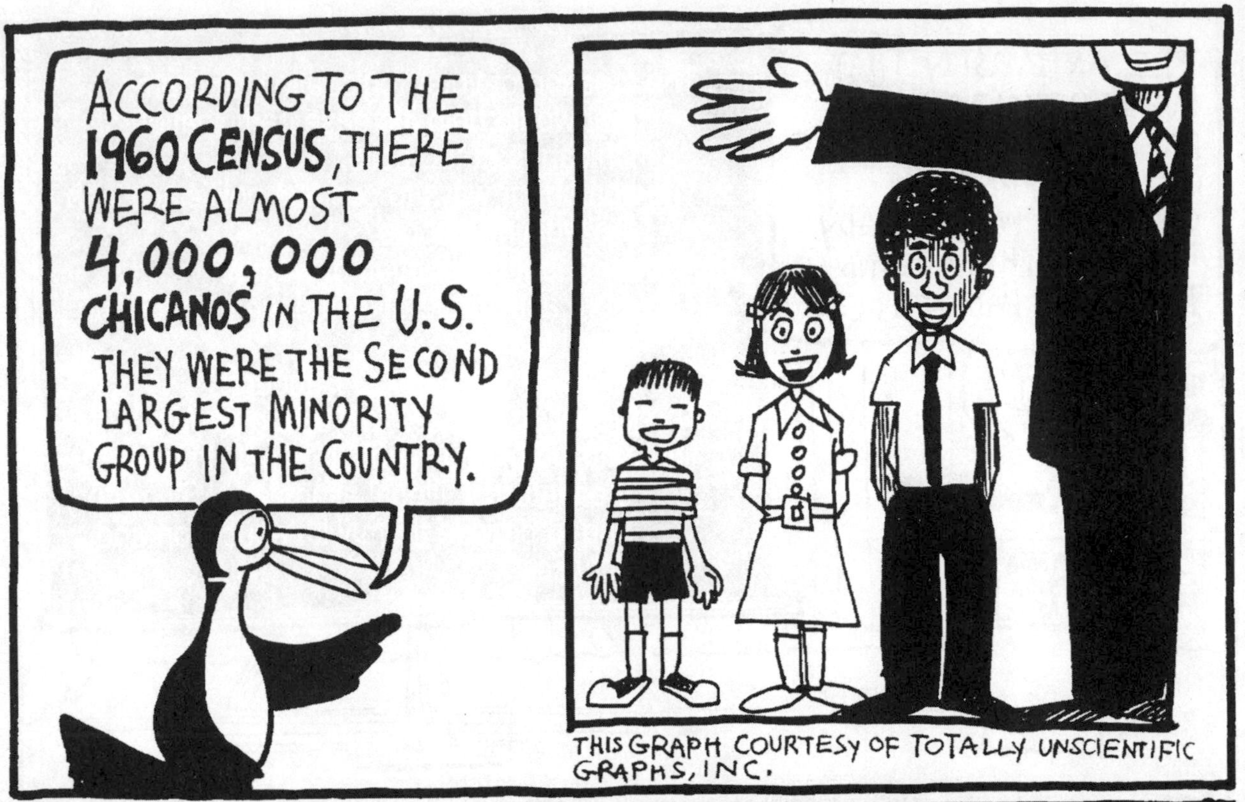
ACCORDING TO THE **1960 CENSUS**, THERE WERE ALMOST **4,000,000 CHICANOS** IN THE U.S. THEY WERE THE SECOND LARGEST MINORITY GROUP IN THE COUNTRY.
THIS GRAPH COURTESY OF TOTALLY UNSCIENTIFIC GRAPHS, INC.

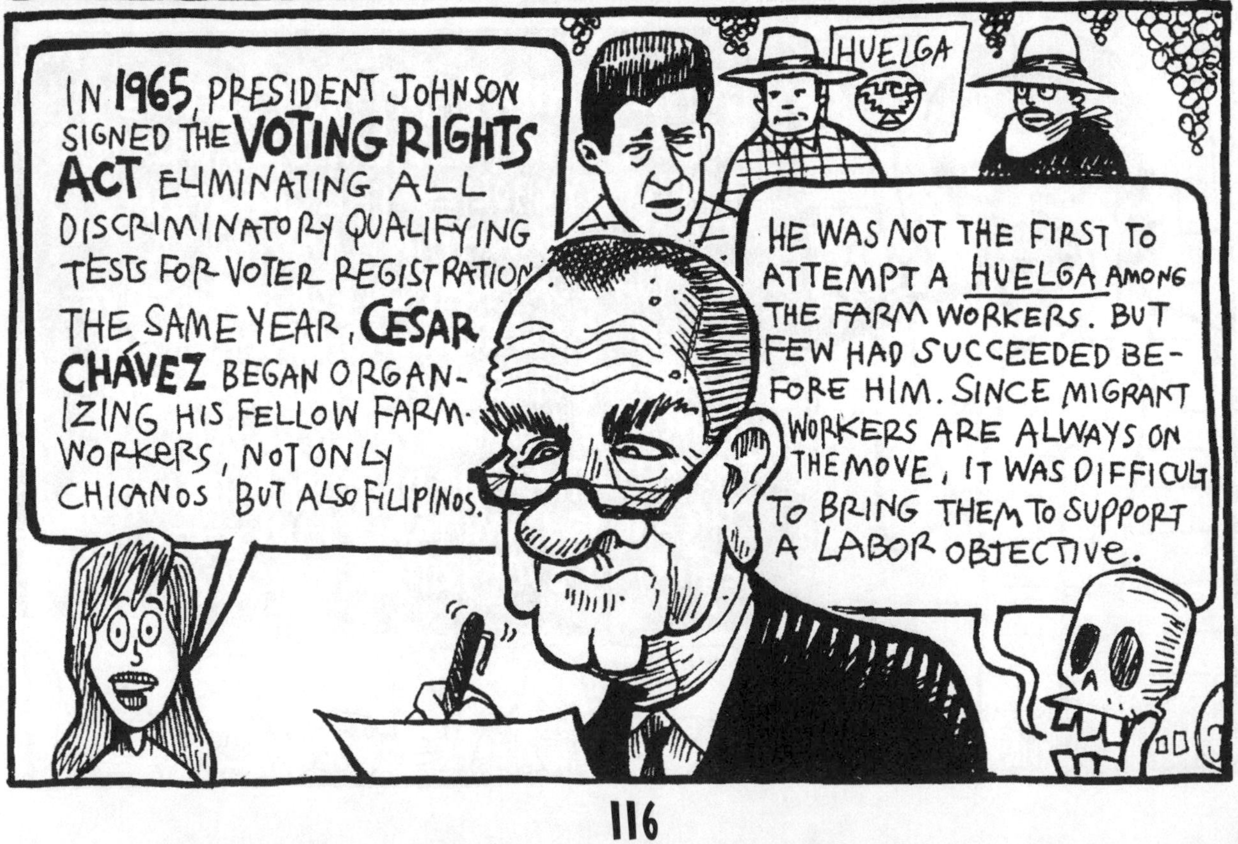
IN **1965**, PRESIDENT JOHNSON SIGNED THE **VOTING RIGHTS ACT** ELIMINATING ALL DISCRIMINATORY QUALIFYING TESTS FOR VOTER REGISTRATION.
THE SAME YEAR, **CÉSAR CHÁVEZ** BEGAN ORGANIZING HIS FELLOW FARMWORKERS, NOT ONLY CHICANOS BUT ALSO FILIPINOS.
HUELGA
HE WAS NOT THE FIRST TO ATTEMPT A HUELGA AMONG THE FARM WORKERS. BUT FEW HAD SUCCEEDED BEFORE HIM. SINCE MIGRANT WORKERS ARE ALWAYS ON THE MOVE, IT WAS DIFFICULT TO BRING THEM TO SUPPORT A LABOR OBJECTIVE.

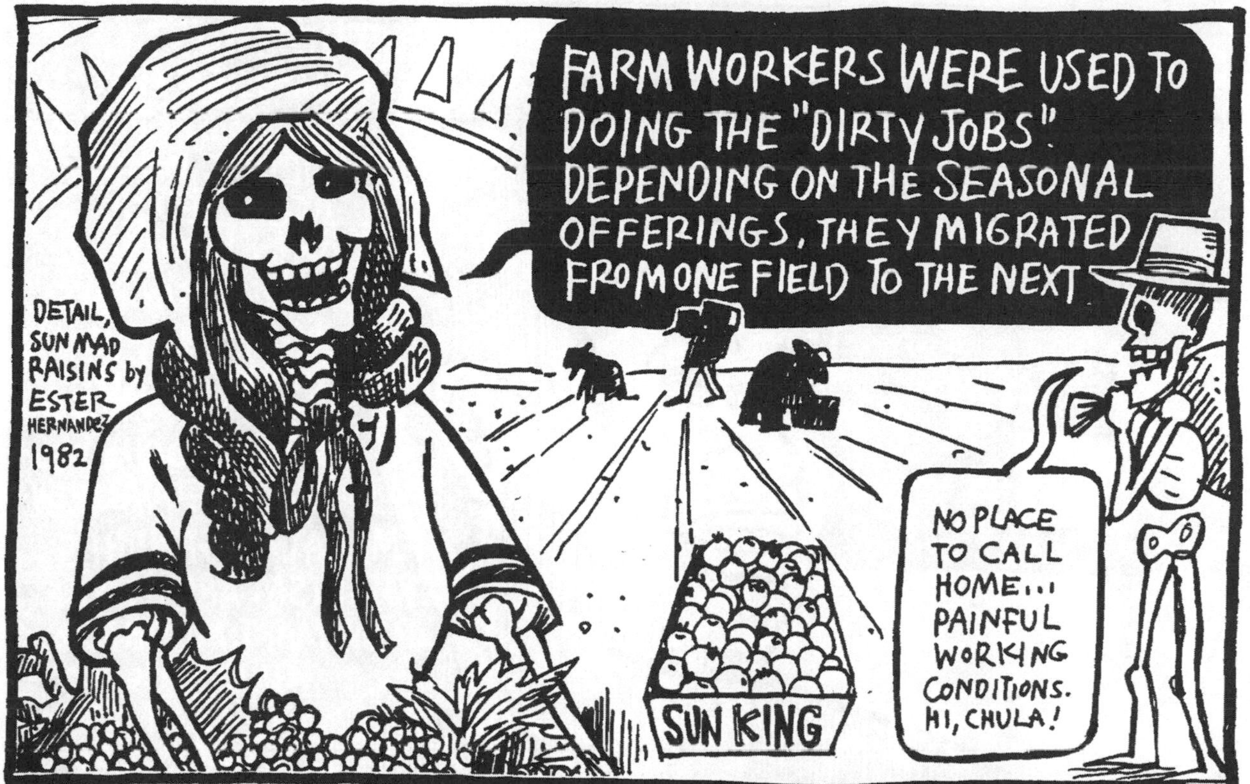
FARM WORKERS WERE USED TO DOING THE "DIRTY JOBS". DEPENDING ON THE SEASONAL OFFERINGS, THEY MIGRATED FROM ONE FIELD TO THE NEXT
DETAIL, SUN MAD RAISINS by ESTER HERNANDEZ 1982
SUN KING
NO PLACE TO CALL HOME... PAINFUL WORKING CONDITIONS. HI, CHULA!

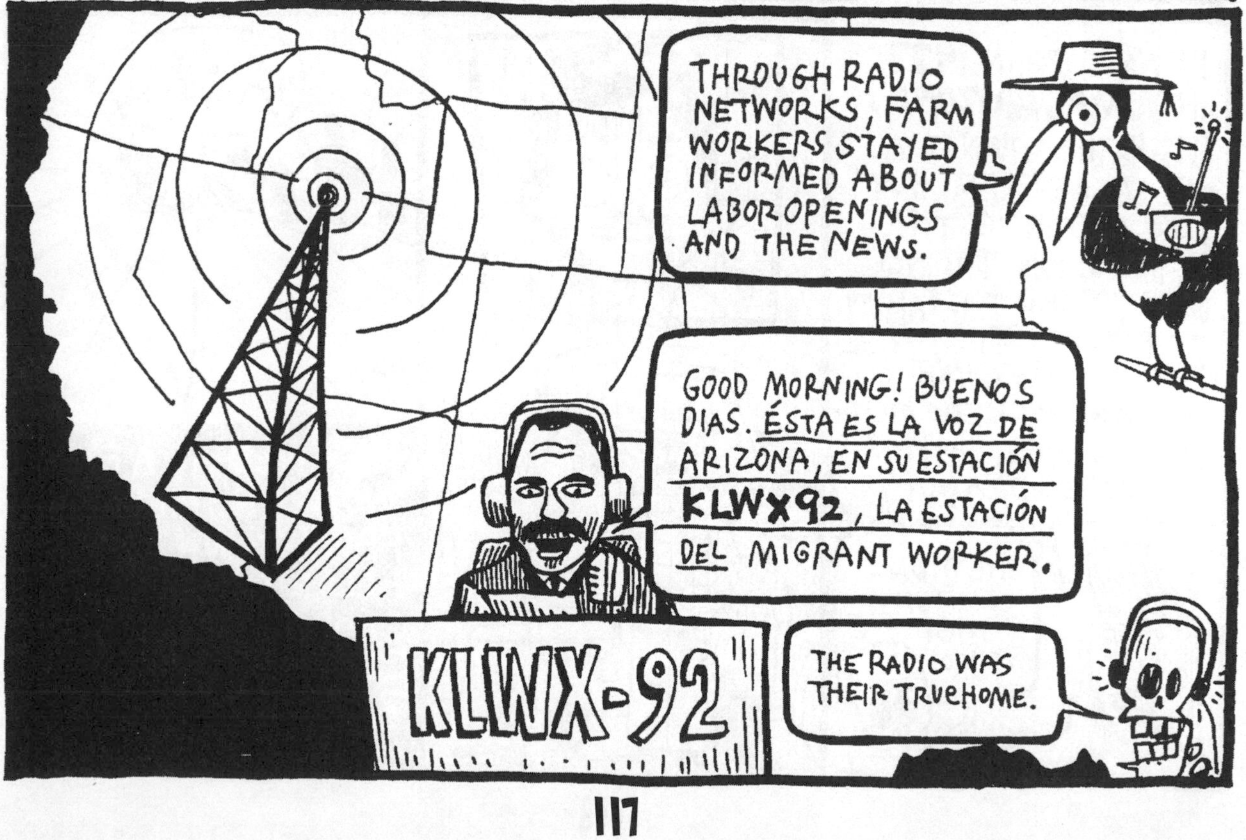
THROUGH RADIO NETWORKS, FARM WORKERS STAYED INFORMED ABOUT LABOR OPENINGS AND THE NEWS.
GOOD MORNING! BUENOS DIAS. ÉSTA ES LA VOZ DE ARIZONA, EN SU ESTACIÓN KLWX92, LA ESTACIÓN DEL MIGRANT WORKER.
KLWX-92
THE RADIO WAS THEIR TRUE HOME.

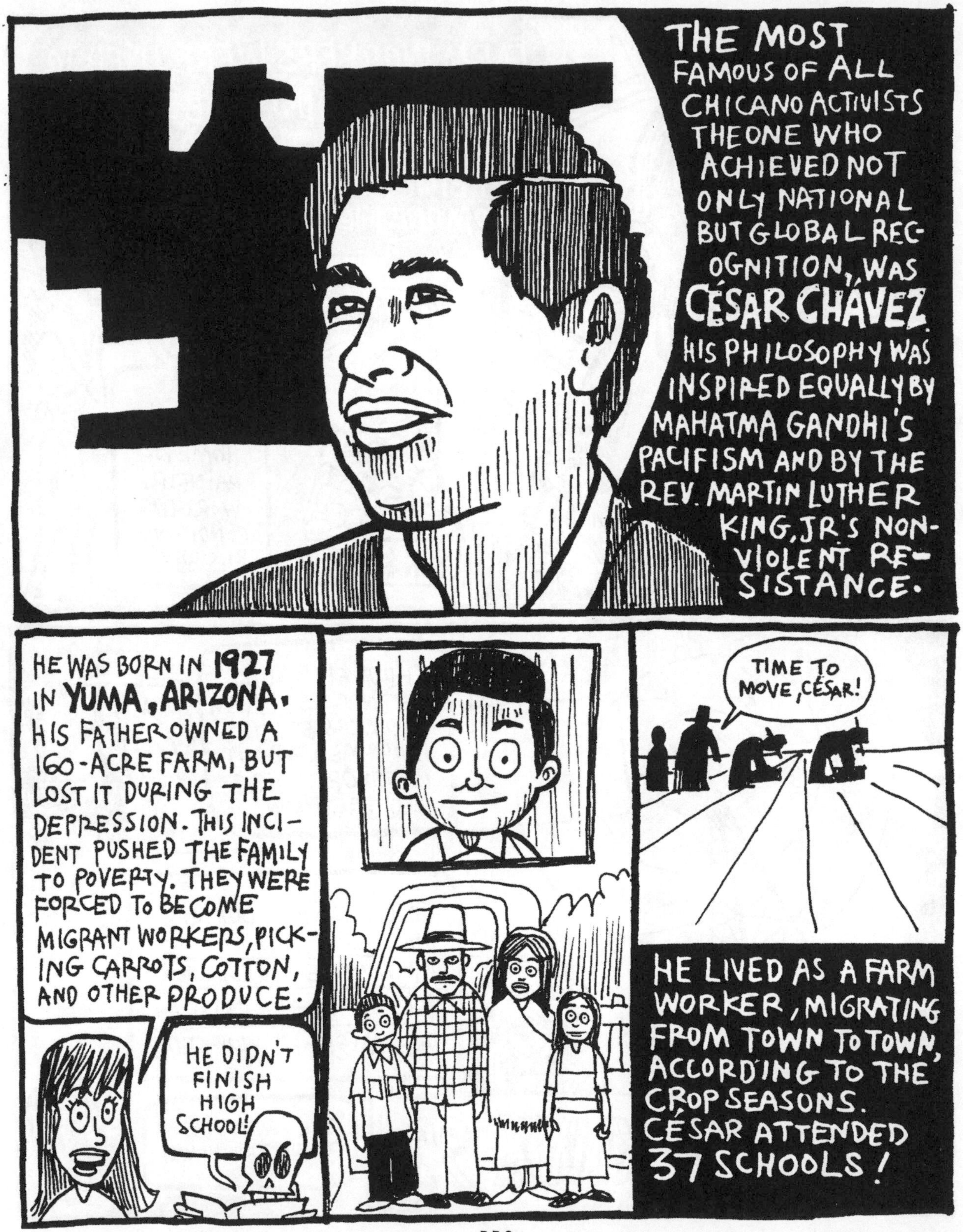
THE MOST FAMOUS OF ALL CHICANO ACTIVISTS THE ONE WHO ACHIEVED NOT ONLY NATIONAL BUT GLOBAL RECOGNITION, WAS CÉSAR CHÁVEZ. HIS PHILOSOPHY WAS INSPIRED EQUALLY BY MAHATMA GANDHI'S PACIFISM AND BY THE REV. MARTIN LUTHER KING, JR'S NONVIOLENT RESISTANCE.
HE WAS BORN IN 1927 IN YUMA, ARIZONA. HIS FATHER OWNED A 160-ACRE FARM, BUT LOST IT DURING THE DEPRESSION. THIS INCIDENT PUSHED THE FAMILY TO POVERTY. THEY WERE FORCED TO BECOME MIGRANT WORKERS, PICKING CARROTS, COTTON, AND OTHER PRODUCE.
HE DIDN'T FINISH HIGH SCHOOL!
TIME TO MOVE, CÉSAR!
HE LIVED AS A FARM WORKER, MIGRATING FROM TOWN TO TOWN, ACCORDING TO THE CROP SEASONS. CÉSAR ATTENDED 37 SCHOOLS!

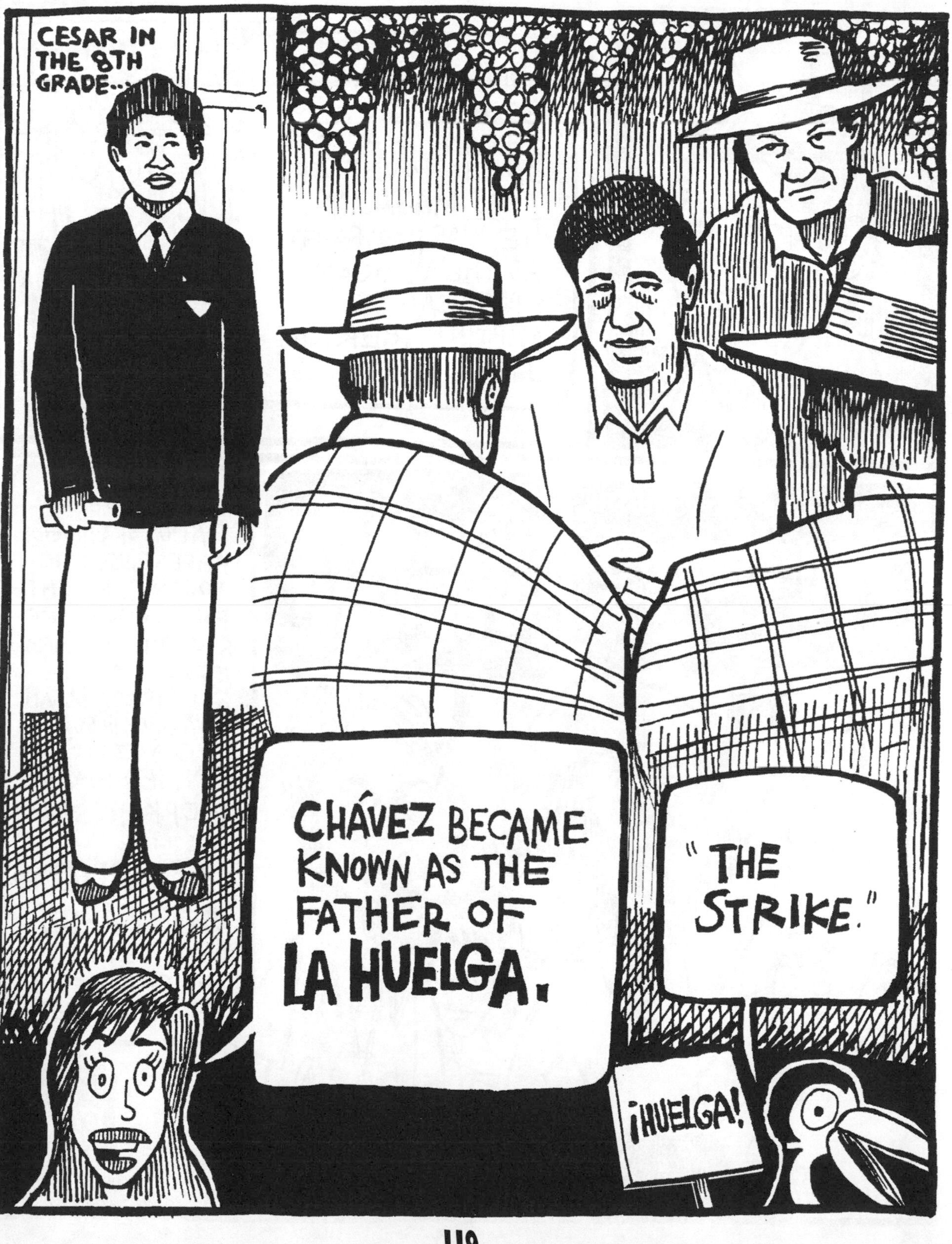
CESAR IN THE 8TH GRADE...
CHÁVEZ BECAME KNOWN AS THE FATHER OF LA HUELGA.
"THE STRIKE."
¡HUELGA!

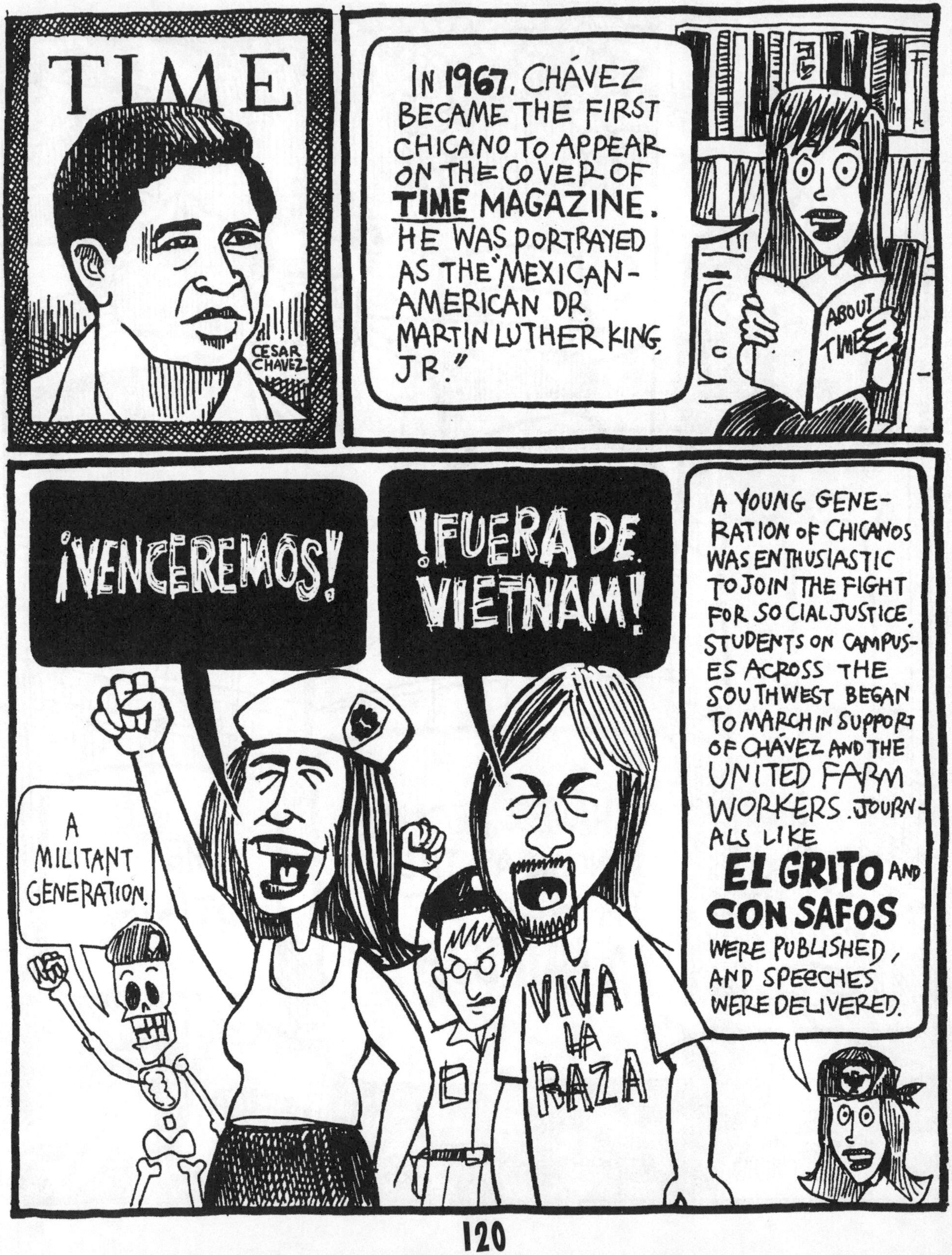
TIME
CESAR CHAVEZ
IN 1967, CHÁVEZ BECAME THE FIRST CHICANO TO APPEAR ON THE COVER OF TIME MAGAZINE. HE WAS PORTRAYED AS THE "MEXICAN-AMERICAN DR. MARTIN LUTHER KING, JR."
ABOUT TIME
¡VENCEREMOS!
!FUERA DE VIETNAM!
A YOUNG GENERATION OF CHICANOS WAS ENTHUSIASTIC TO JOIN THE FIGHT FOR SOCIAL JUSTICE. STUDENTS ON CAMPUSES ACROSS THE SOUTHWEST BEGAN TO MARCH IN SUPPORT OF CHÁVEZ AND THE UNITED FARM WORKERS. JOURNALS LIKE EL GRITO AND CON SAFOS WERE PUBLISHED, AND SPEECHES WERE DELIVERED.
A MILITANT GENERATION.
VIVA LA RAZA

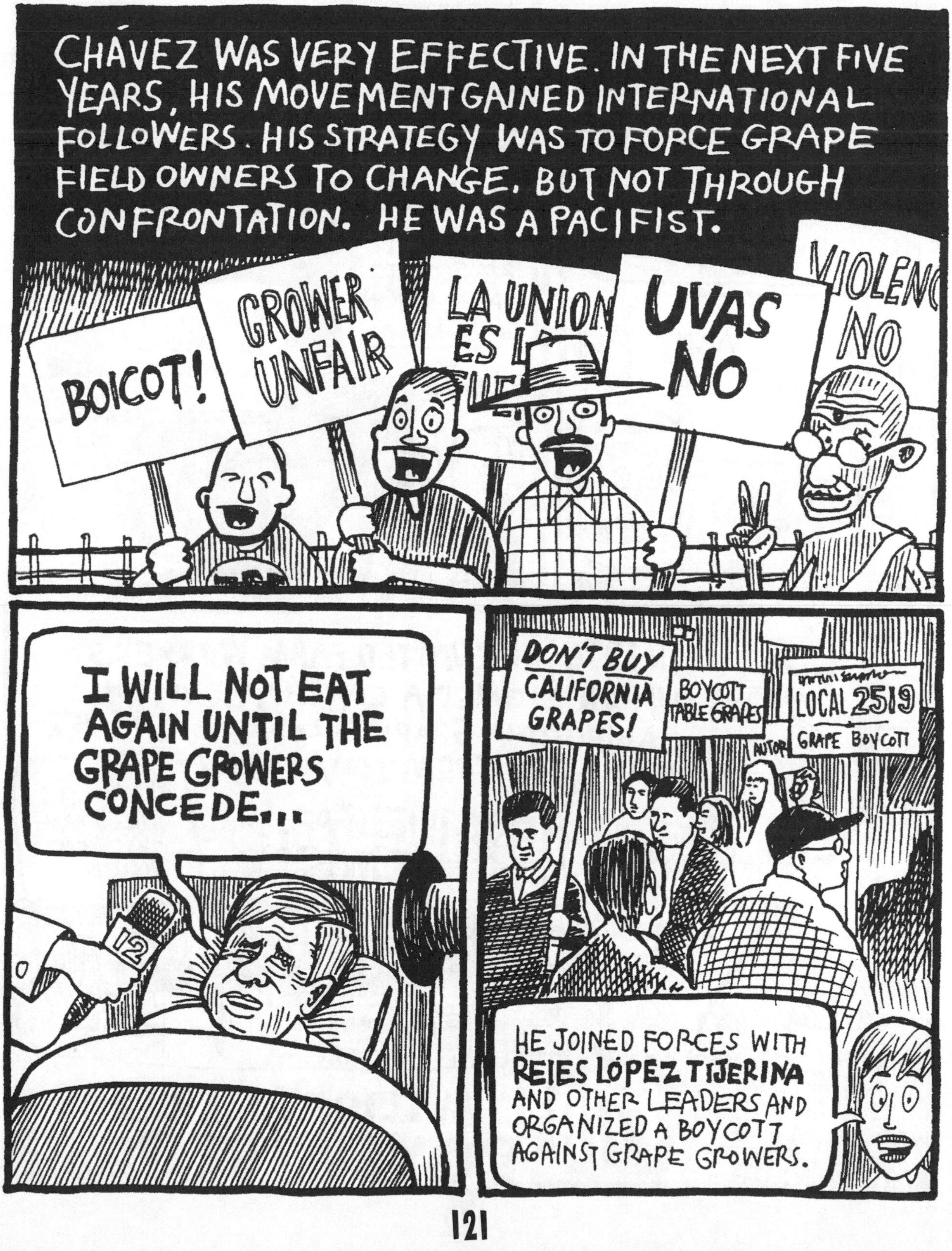
CHÁVEZ WAS VERY EFFECTIVE. IN THE NEXT FIVE YEARS, HIS MOVEMENT GAINED INTERNATIONAL FOLLOWERS. HIS STRATEGY WAS TO FORCE GRAPE FIELD OWNERS TO CHANGE, BUT NOT THROUGH CONFRONTATION. HE WAS A PACIFIST.
BOICOT!
GROWER UNFAIR
LA UNION
UVAS NO
VIOLENC NO
I WILL NOT EAT AGAIN UNTIL THE GRAPE GROWERS CONCEDE...
12
DON'T BUY CALIFORNIA GRAPES!
BOYCOTT TABLE GRAPES
LOCAL 2519 GRAPE BOYCOTT
HE JOINED FORCES WITH **REIES LÓPEZ TIJERINA** AND OTHER LEADERS AND ORGANIZED A BOYCOTT AGAINST GRAPE GROWERS.

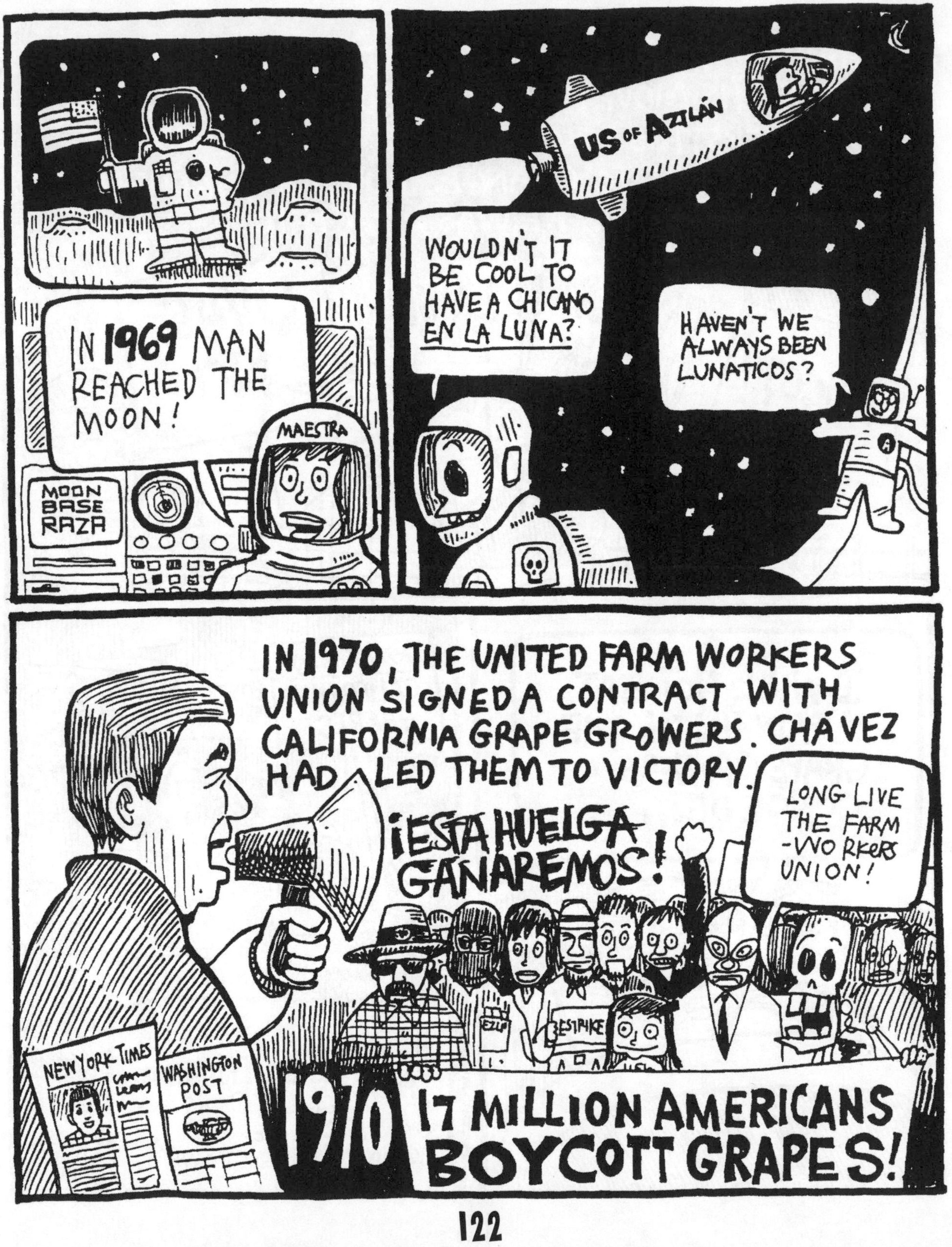
IN 1969 MAN REACHED THE MOON!
MAESTRA
MOON BASE RAZA
US OF AZTLÁN
WOULDN'T IT BE COOL TO HAVE A CHICANO EN LA LUNA?
HAVEN'T WE ALWAYS BEEN LUNATICOS?
IN 1970, THE UNITED FARM WORKERS UNION SIGNED A CONTRACT WITH CALIFORNIA GRAPE GROWERS. CHÁVEZ HAD LED THEM TO VICTORY.
¡ESTA HUELGA GANAREMOS!
LONG LIVE THE FARM-WORKERS UNION!
NEW YORK TIMES
WASHINGTON POST
1970 17 MILLION AMERICANS BOYCOTT GRAPES!

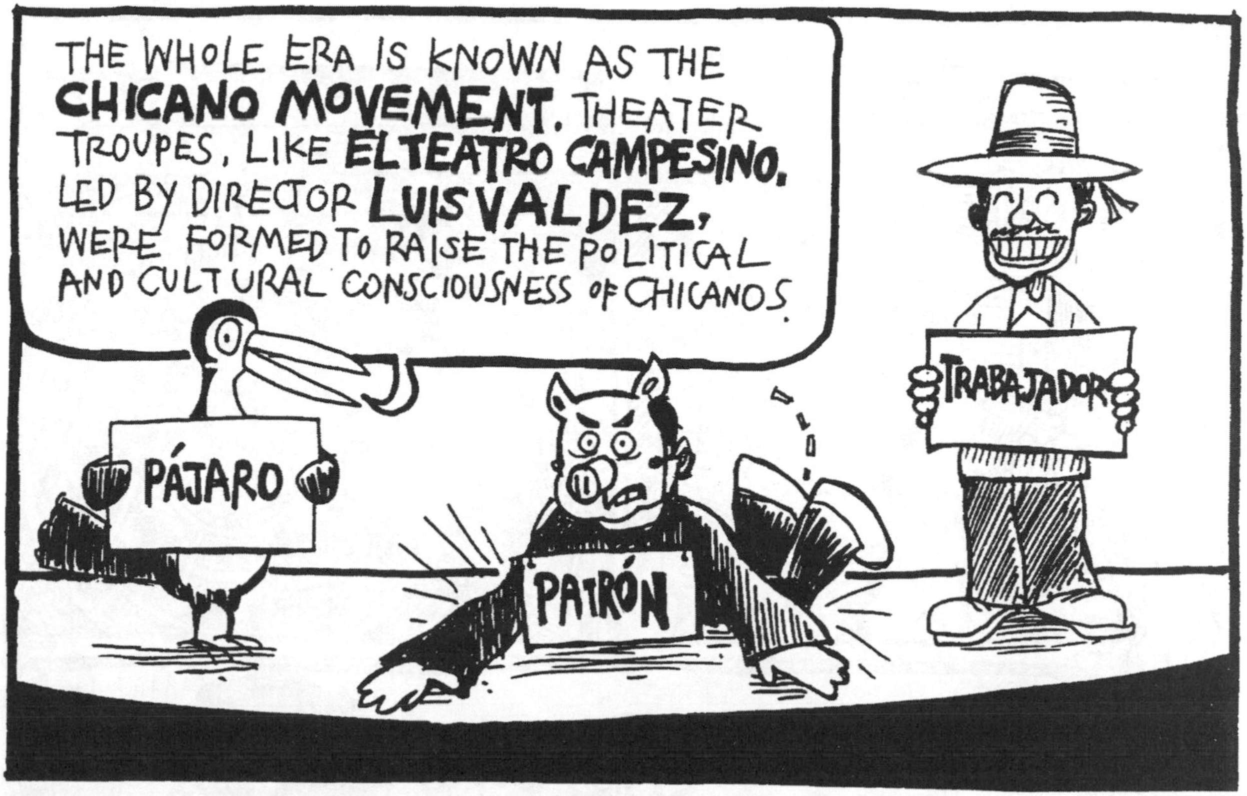
THE WHOLE ERA IS KNOWN AS THE CHICANO MOVEMENT. THEATER TROUPES, LIKE EL TEATRO CAMPESINO, LED BY DIRECTOR LUIS VALDEZ, WERE FORMED TO RAISE THE POLITICAL AND CULTURAL CONSCIOUSNESS OF CHICANOS.
PÁJARO
PATRÓN
TRABAJADOR

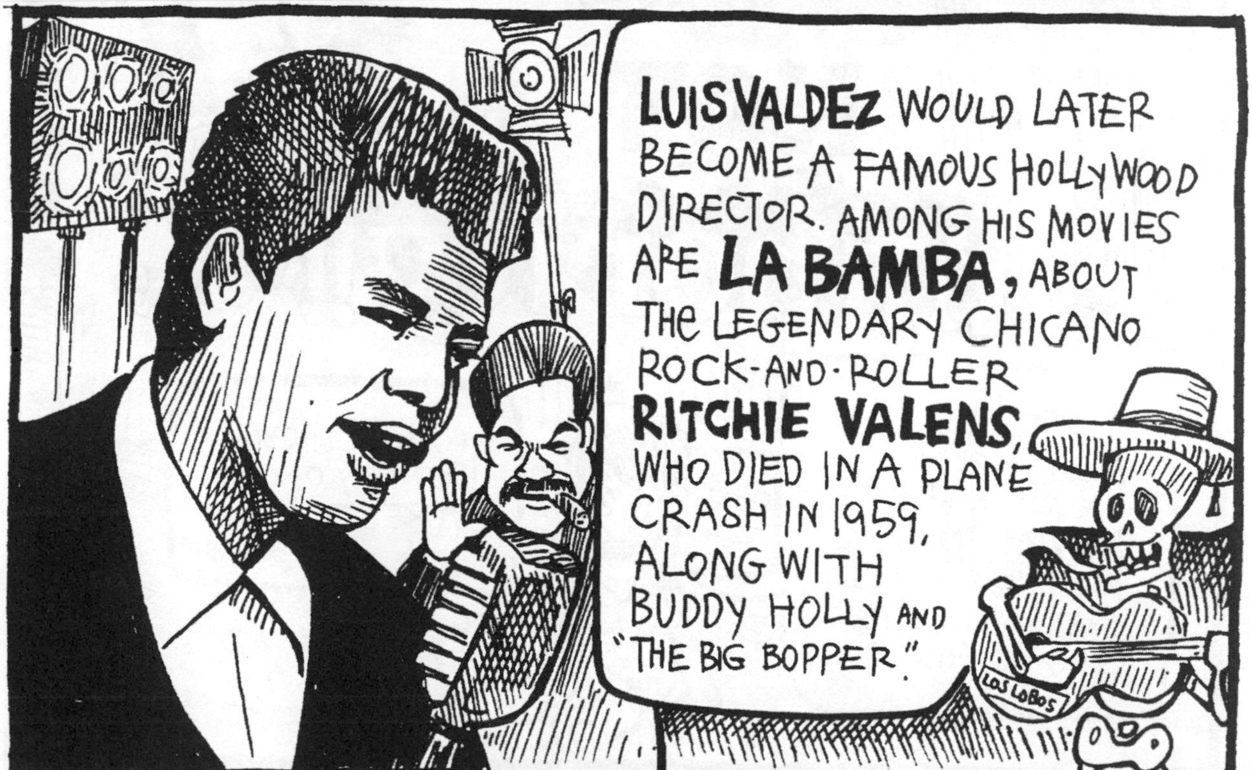
LUIS VALDEZ WOULD LATER BECOME A FAMOUS HOLLYWOOD DIRECTOR. AMONG HIS MOVIES ARE LA BAMBA, ABOUT THE LEGENDARY CHICANO ROCK-AND-ROLLER RITCHIE VALENS, WHO DIED IN A PLANE CRASH IN 1959, ALONG WITH BUDDY HOLLY AND "THE BIG BOPPER."
LOS LOBOS

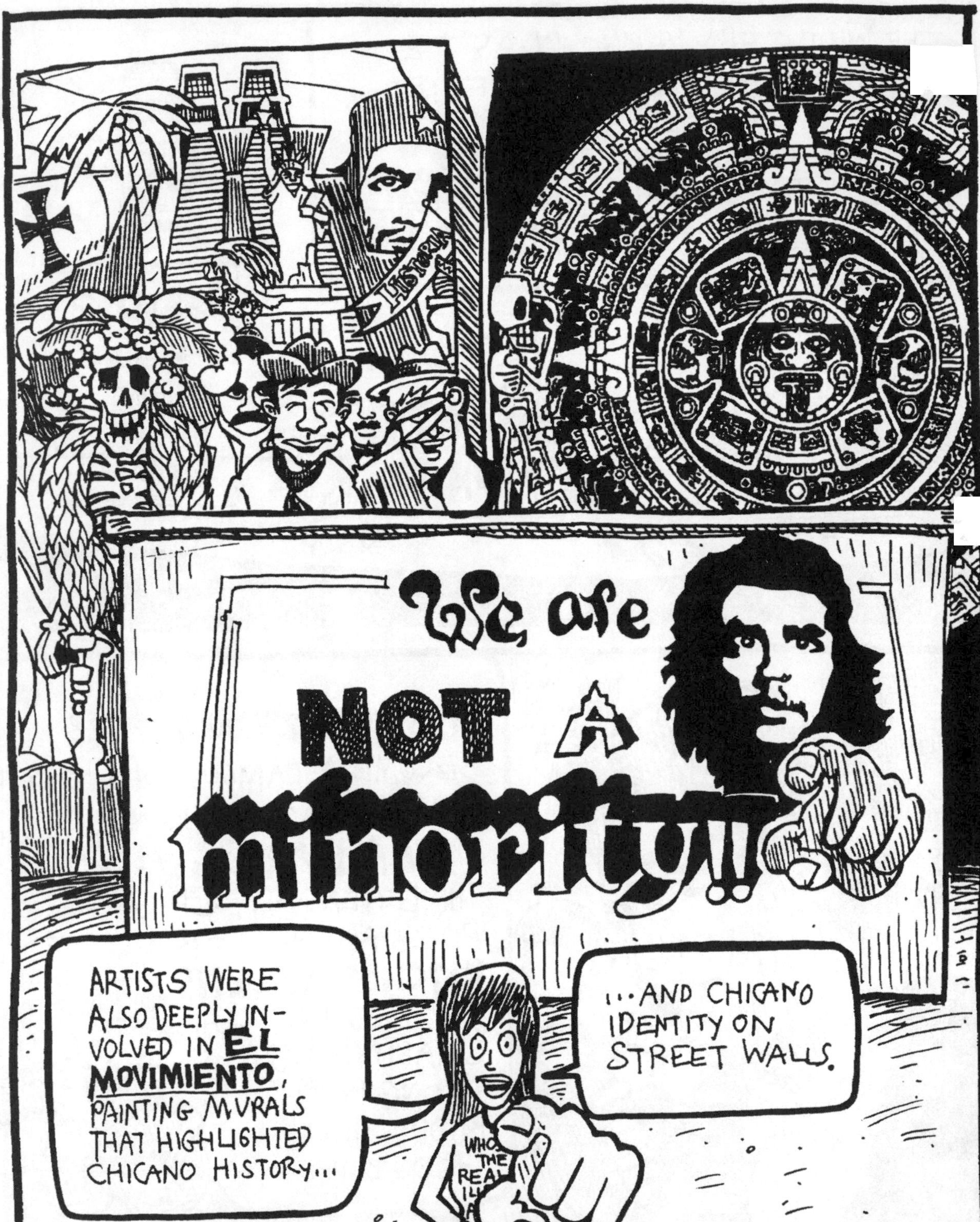
HISTORIA
We are NOT A minority!!
ARTISTS WERE ALSO DEEPLY IN-VOLVED IN **EL MOVIMIENTO**, PAINTING MURALS THAT HIGHLIGHTED CHICANO HISTORY...
...AND CHICANO IDENTITY ON STREET WALLS.

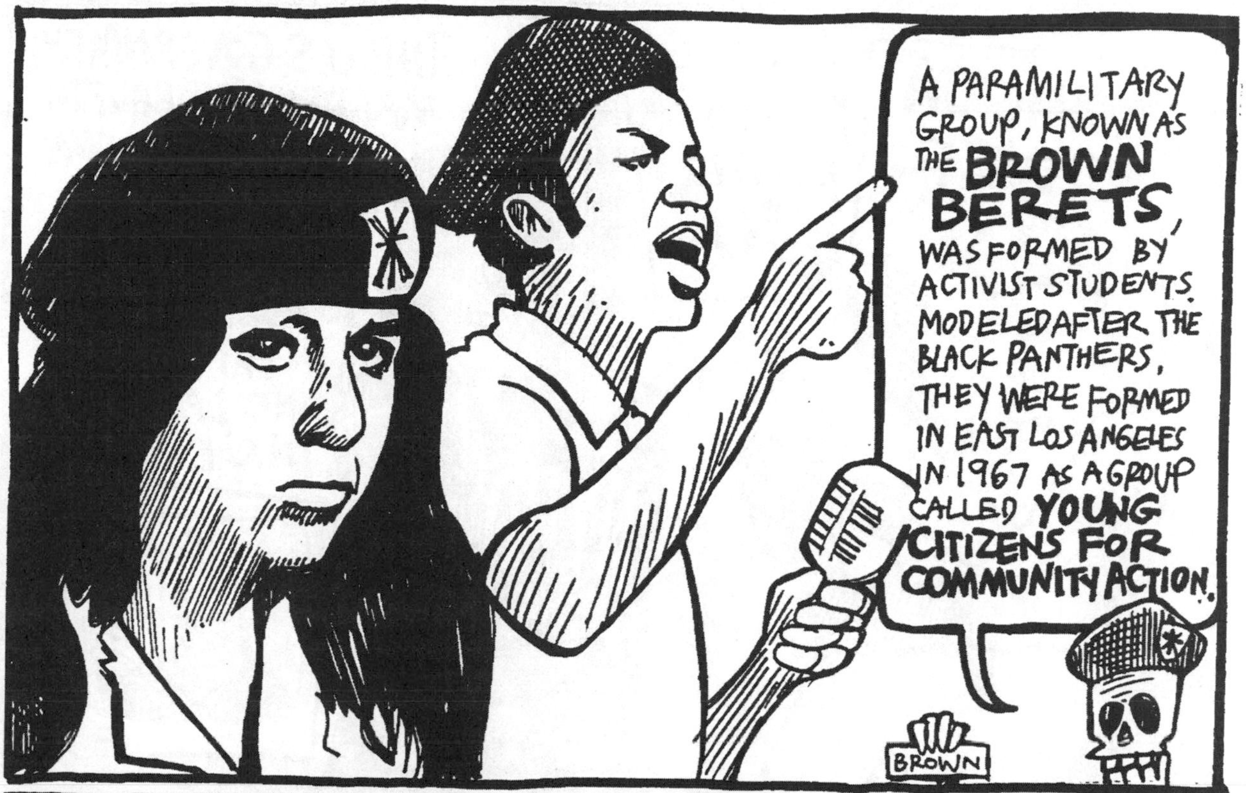
A PARAMILITARY GROUP, KNOWN AS THE **BROWN BERETS**, WAS FORMED BY ACTIVIST STUDENTS. MODELED AFTER THE BLACK PANTHERS, THEY WERE FORMED IN EAST LOS ANGELES IN 1967 AS A GROUP CALLED **YOUNG CITIZENS FOR COMMUNITY ACTION**.
BROWN

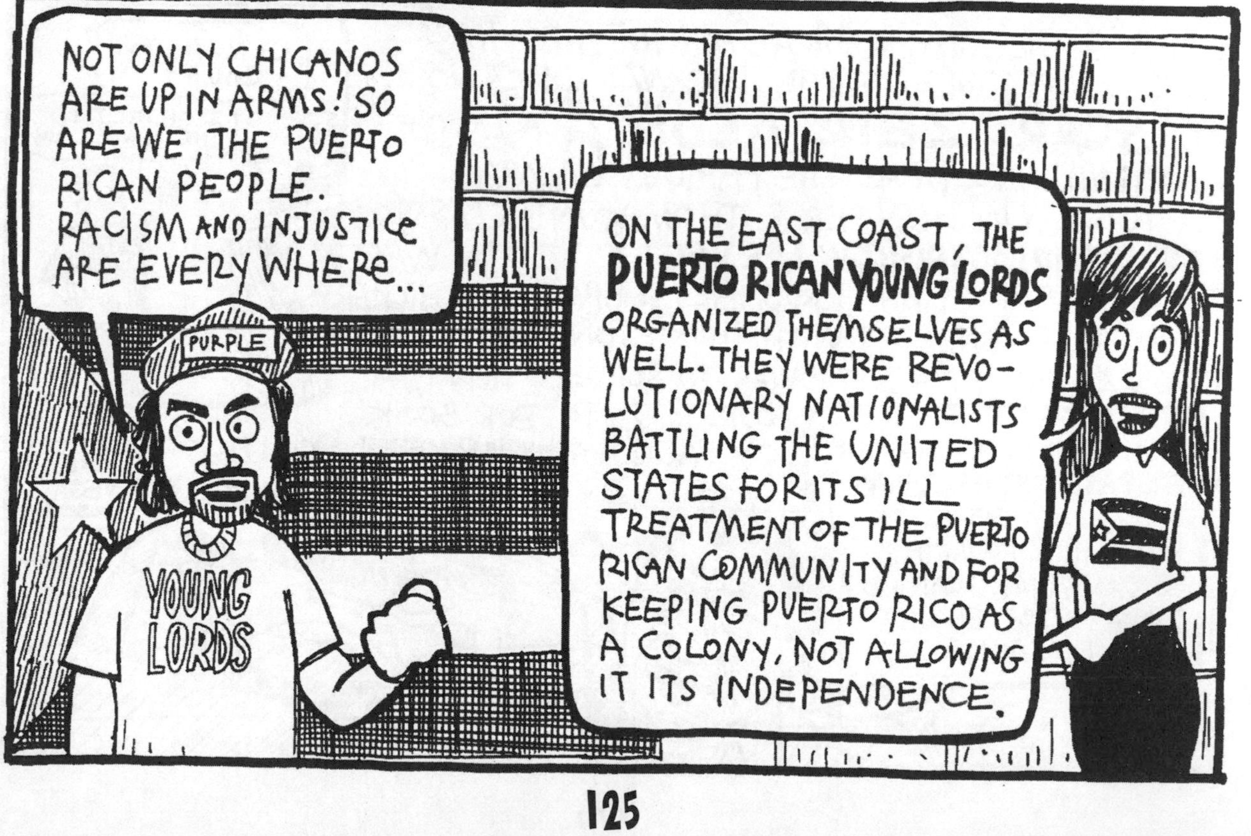
NOT ONLY CHICANOS ARE UP IN ARMS! SO ARE WE, THE PUERTO RICAN PEOPLE. RACISM AND INJUSTICE ARE EVERY WHERE...
PURPLE
YOUNG LORDS
ON THE EAST COAST, THE **PUERTO RICAN YOUNG LORDS** ORGANIZED THEMSELVES AS WELL. THEY WERE REVOLUTIONARY NATIONALISTS BATTLING THE UNITED STATES FOR ITS ILL TREATMENT OF THE PUERTO RICAN COMMUNITY AND FOR KEEPING PUERTO RICO AS A COLONY, NOT ALLOWING IT ITS INDEPENDENCE.

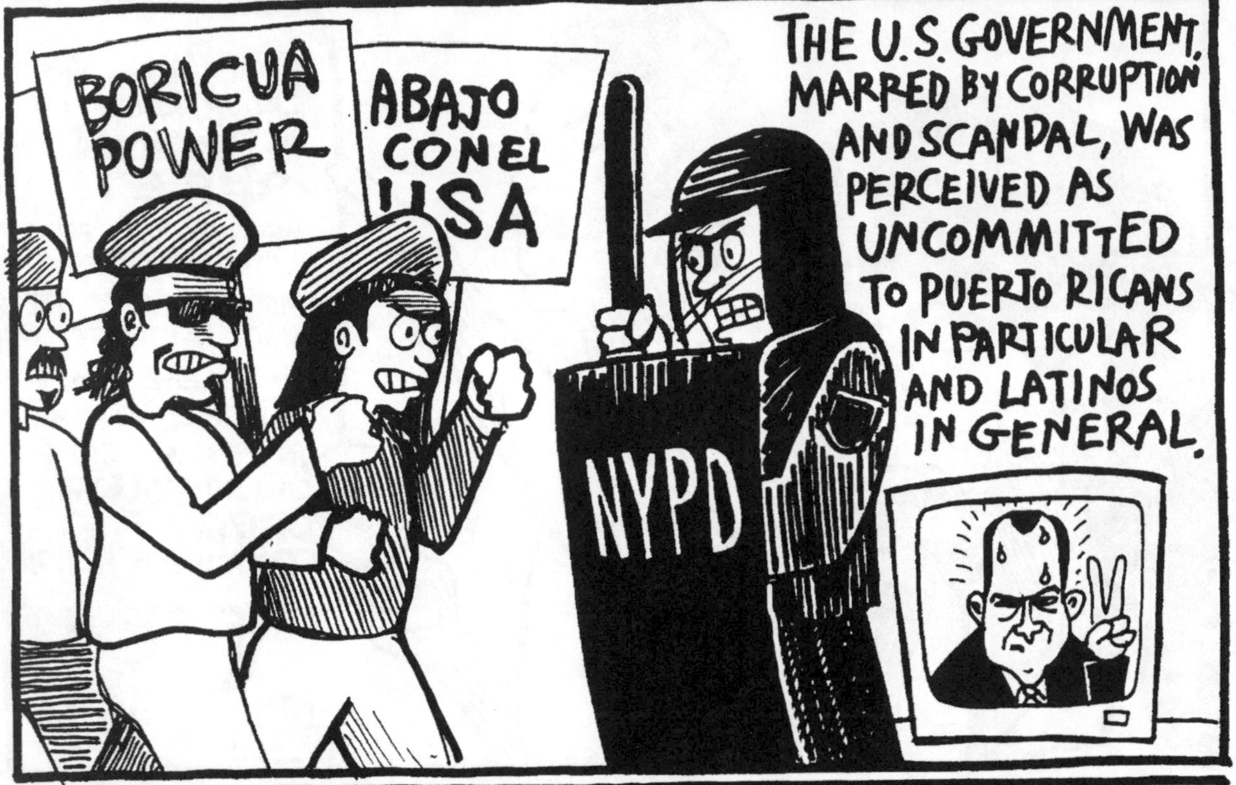
BORICUA POWER
ABAJO CON EL USA
THE U.S. GOVERNMENT, MARRED BY CORRUPTION AND SCANDAL, WAS PERCEIVED AS UNCOMMITTED TO PUERTO RICANS IN PARTICULAR AND LATINOS IN GENERAL.
NYPD

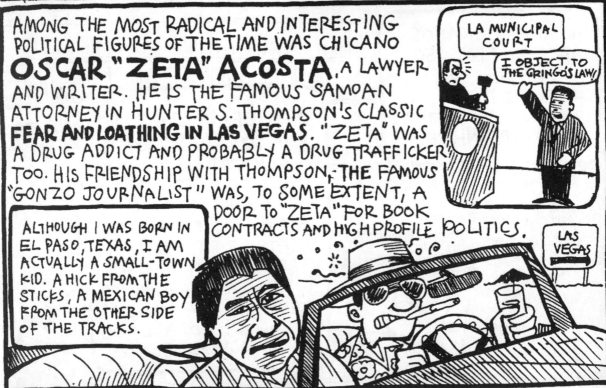

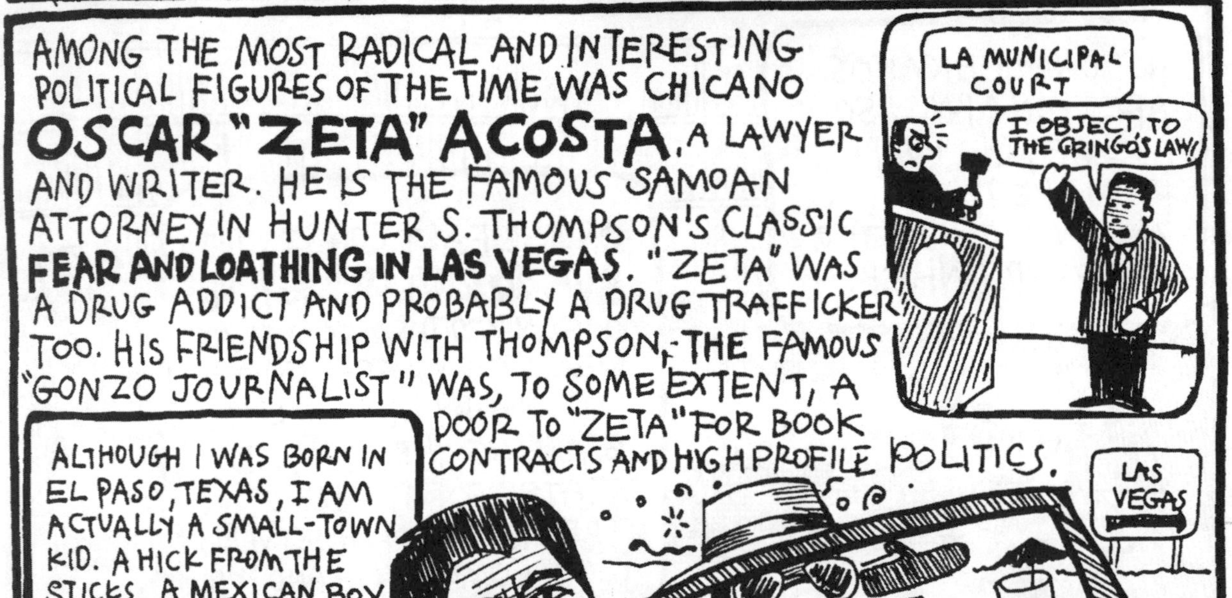
AMONG THE MOST RADICAL AND INTERESTING POLITICAL FIGURES OF THE TIME WAS CHICANO **OSCAR "ZETA" ACOSTA**, A LAWYER AND WRITER. HE IS THE FAMOUS SAMOAN ATTORNEY IN HUNTER S. THOMPSON'S CLASSIC **FEAR AND LOATHING IN LAS VEGAS**. "ZETA" WAS A DRUG ADDICT AND PROBABLY A DRUG TRAFFICKER TOO. HIS FRIENDSHIP WITH THOMPSON, THE FAMOUS "GONZO JOURNALIST" WAS, TO SOME EXTENT, A DOOR TO "ZETA" FOR BOOK CONTRACTS AND HIGH PROFILE POLITICS.
LA MUNICIPAL COURT
I OBJECT, TO THE GRINGO'S LAW!
ALTHOUGH I WAS BORN IN EL PASO, TEXAS, I AM ACTUALLY A SMALL-TOWN KID. A HICK FROM THE STICKS, A MEXICAN BOY FROM THE OTHER SIDE OF THE TRACKS.
LAS VEGAS

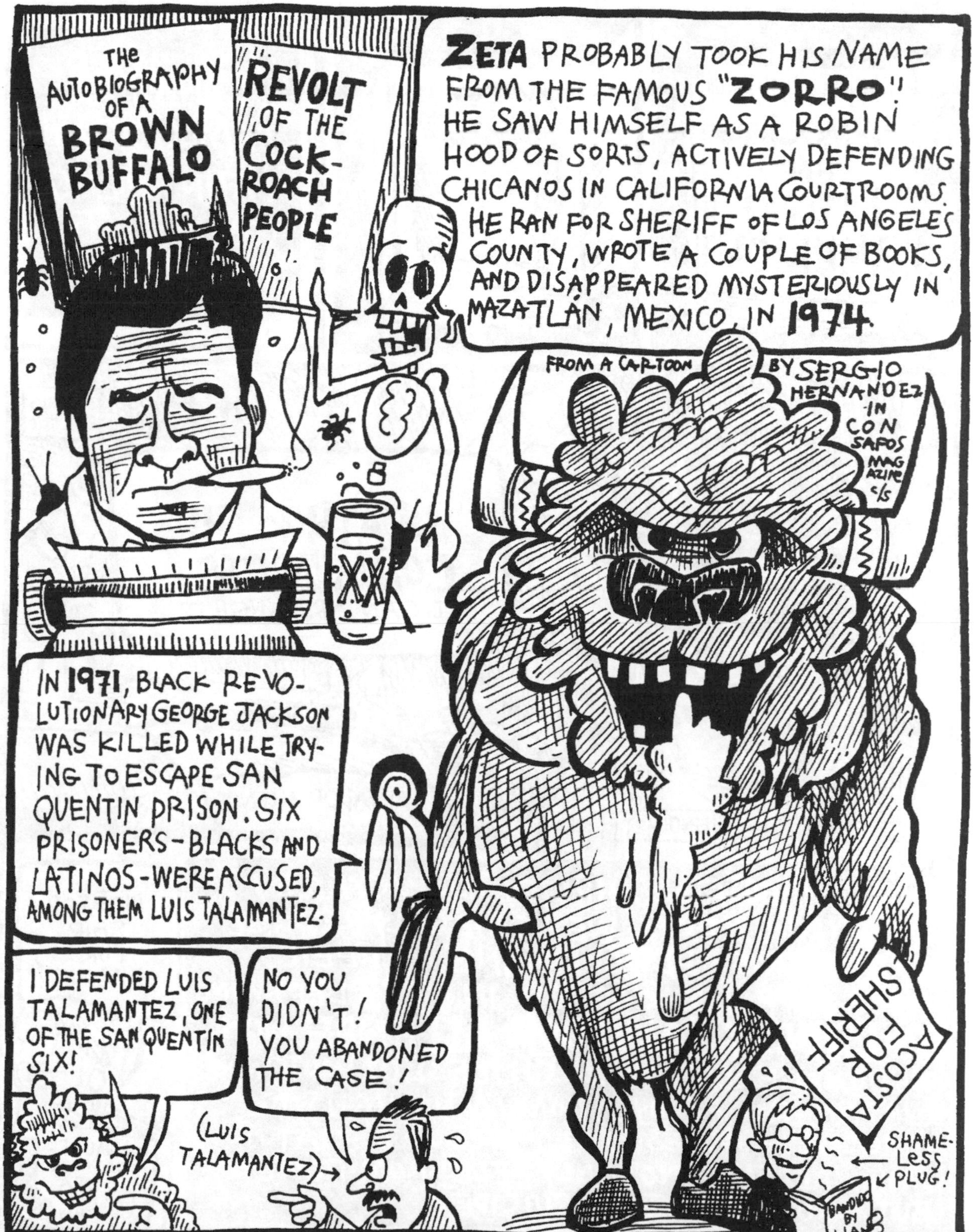

THE AUTOBIOGRAPHY OF A BROWN BUFFALO
REVOLT OF THE COCKROACH PEOPLE
ZETA PROBABLY TOOK HIS NAME FROM THE FAMOUS "ZORRO"! HE SAW HIMSELF AS A ROBIN HOOD OF SORTS, ACTIVELY DEFENDING CHICANOS IN CALIFORNIA COURTROOMS. HE RAN FOR SHERIFF OF LOS ANGELES COUNTY, WROTE A COUPLE OF BOOKS, AND DISAPPEARED MYSTERIOUSLY IN MAZATLÁN, MEXICO, IN 1974.
FROM A CARTOON BY SERGIO HERNANDEZ IN CON SAFOS MAGAZINE C/S
IN 1971, BLACK REVOLUTIONARY GEORGE JACKSON WAS KILLED WHILE TRYING TO ESCAPE SAN QUENTIN PRISON. SIX PRISONERS - BLACKS AND LATINOS - WERE ACCUSED, AMONG THEM LUIS TALAMANTEZ.
I DEFENDED LUIS TALAMANTEZ, ONE OF THE SAN QUENTIN SIX!
NO YOU DIDN'T! YOU ABANDONED THE CASE!
(LUIS TALAMANTEZ)
ACOSTA FOR SHERIFF
SHAME-LESS PLUG!
BANDIDO BY IAN

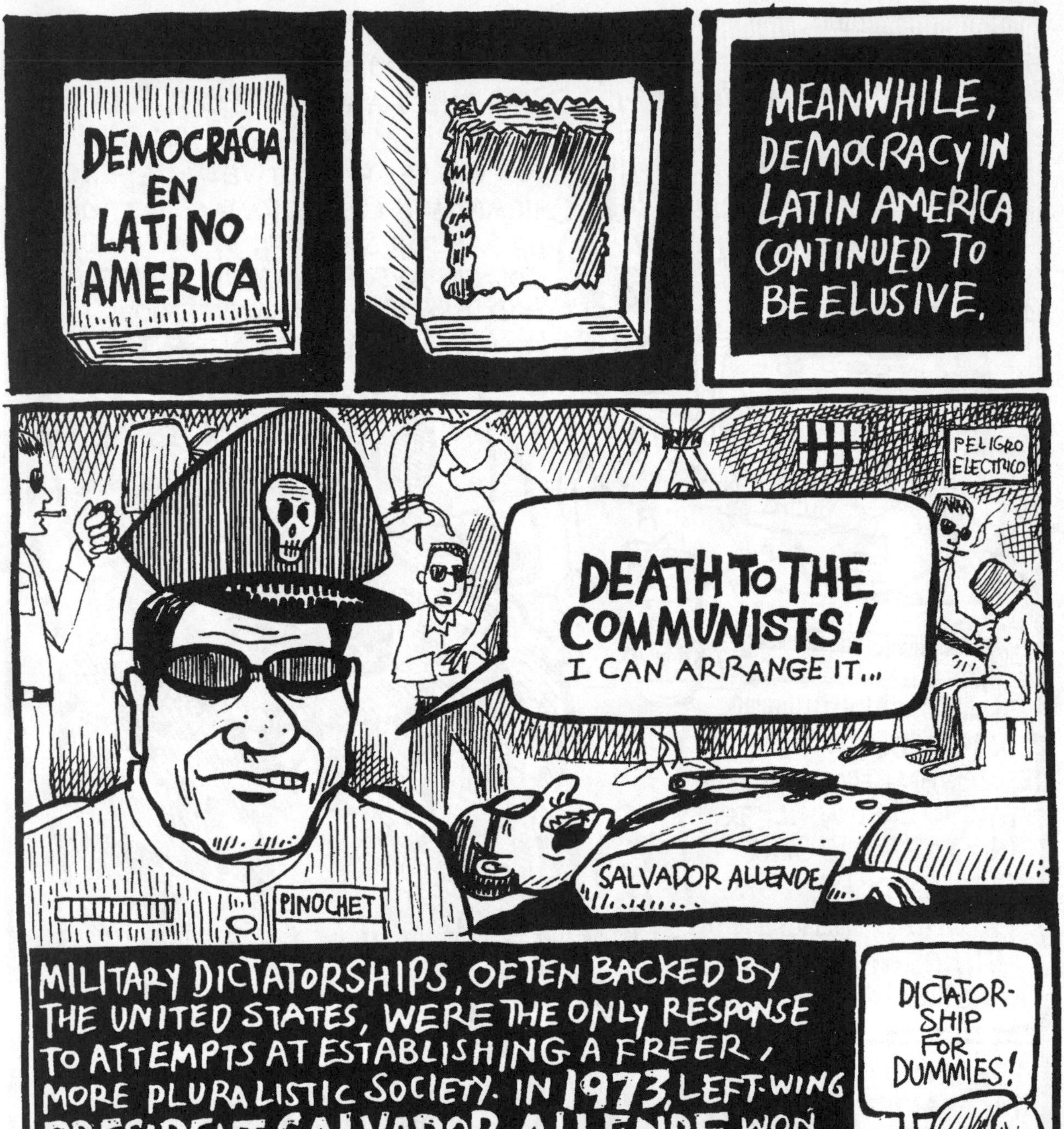
DEMOCRÁCIA EN LATINO AMERICA
MEANWHILE, DEMOCRACY IN LATIN AMERICA CONTINUED TO BE ELUSIVE.
PELIGRO ELECTRICO
DEATH TO THE COMMUNISTS! I CAN ARRANGE IT...
SALVADOR ALLENDE
PINOCHET
MILITARY DICTATORSHIPS, OFTEN BACKED BY THE UNITED STATES, WERE THE ONLY RESPONSE TO ATTEMPTS AT ESTABLISHING A FREER, MORE PLURALISTIC SOCIETY. IN 1973, LEFT-WING PRESIDENT SALVADOR ALLENDE WON NATIONAL ELECTIONS IN CHILE. BUT HIS TENURE WAS SHORT - ARMY STRONGMAN AUGUSTO PINOCHET ORCHESTRATED A COUP D'ETAT IN WHICH ALLENDE NOT ONLY FELL FROM POWER, BUT ALSO COMMITTED "SUICIDE."
DICTATOR-SHIP FOR DUMMIES!
MANUAL DEL PERFECTO IDIOTA LATINO-AMERICANO

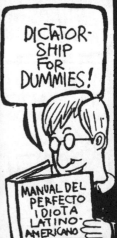

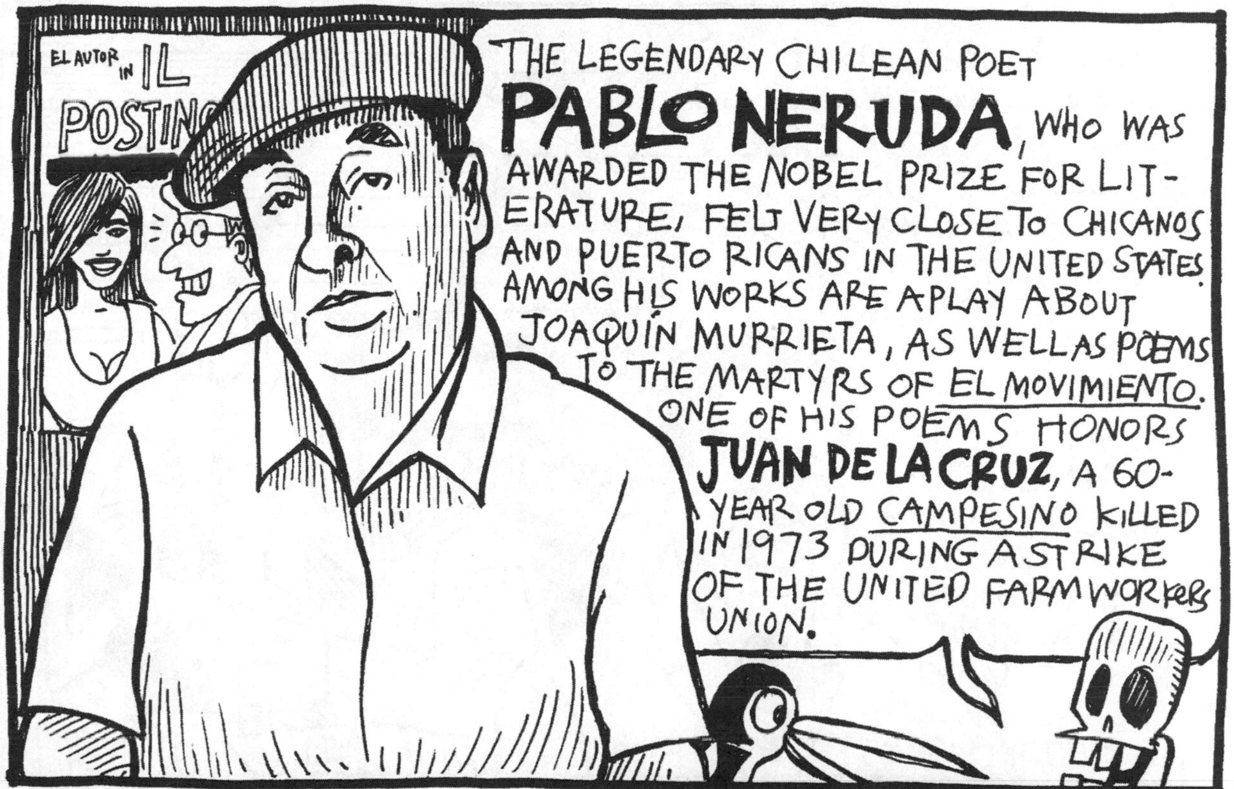
EL AUTOR IN IL POSTIN
THE LEGENDARY CHILEAN POET PABLO NERUDA, WHO WAS AWARDED THE NOBEL PRIZE FOR LITERATURE, FELT VERY CLOSE TO CHICANOS AND PUERTO RICANS IN THE UNITED STATES. AMONG HIS WORKS ARE A PLAY ABOUT JOAQUÍN MURRIETA, AS WELL AS POEMS TO THE MARTYRS OF EL MOVIMIENTO. ONE OF HIS POEMS HONORS JUAN DE LA CRUZ, A 60-YEAR OLD CAMPESINO KILLED IN 1973 DURING A STRIKE OF THE UNITED FARMWORKERS UNION.

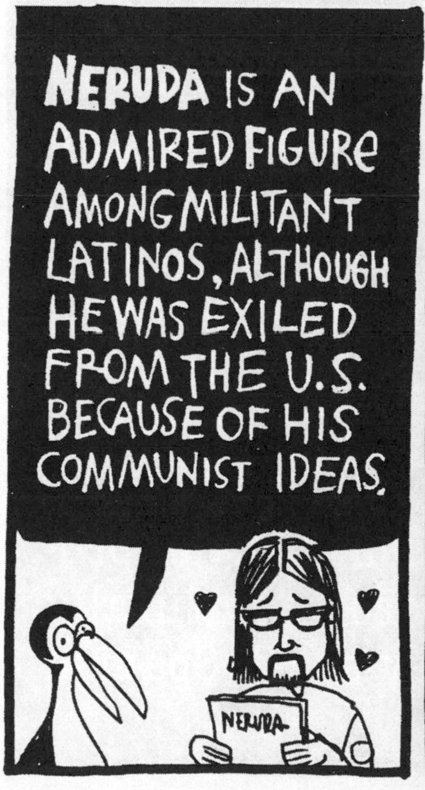
NERUDA IS AN ADMIRED FIGURE AMONG MILITANT LATINOS, ALTHOUGH HE WAS EXILED FROM THE U.S. BECAUSE OF HIS COMMUNIST IDEAS.
NERUDA

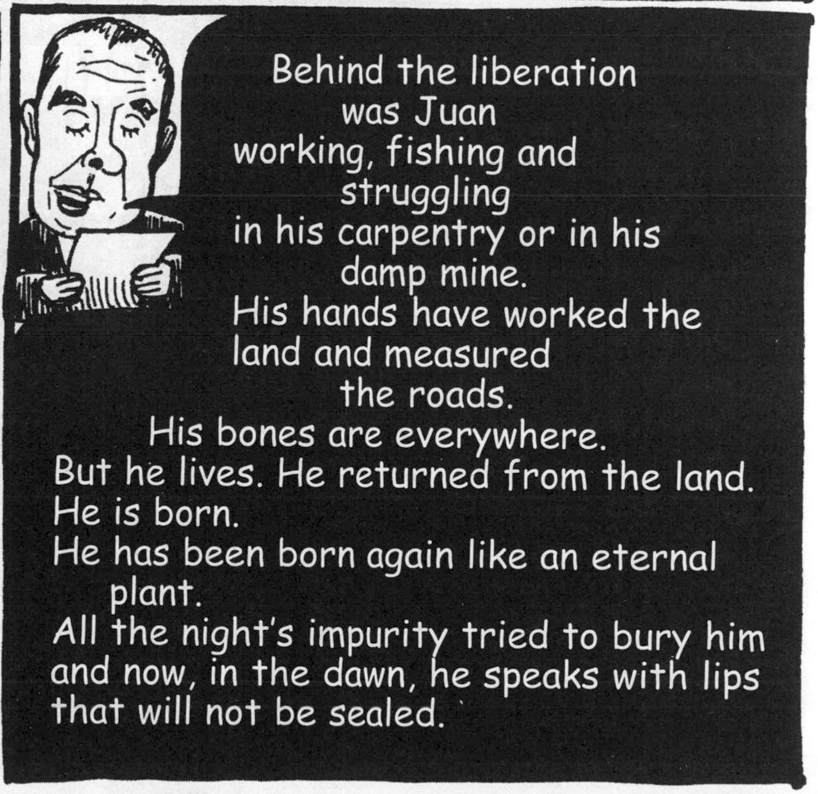
Behind the liberation
was Juan
working, fishing and
struggling
in his carpentry or in his
damp mine.
His hands have worked the
land and measured
the roads.
His bones are everywhere.
But he lives. He returned from the land.
He is born.
He has been born again like an eternal
plant.
All the night's impurity tried to bury him
and now, in the dawn, he speaks with lips
that will not be sealed.

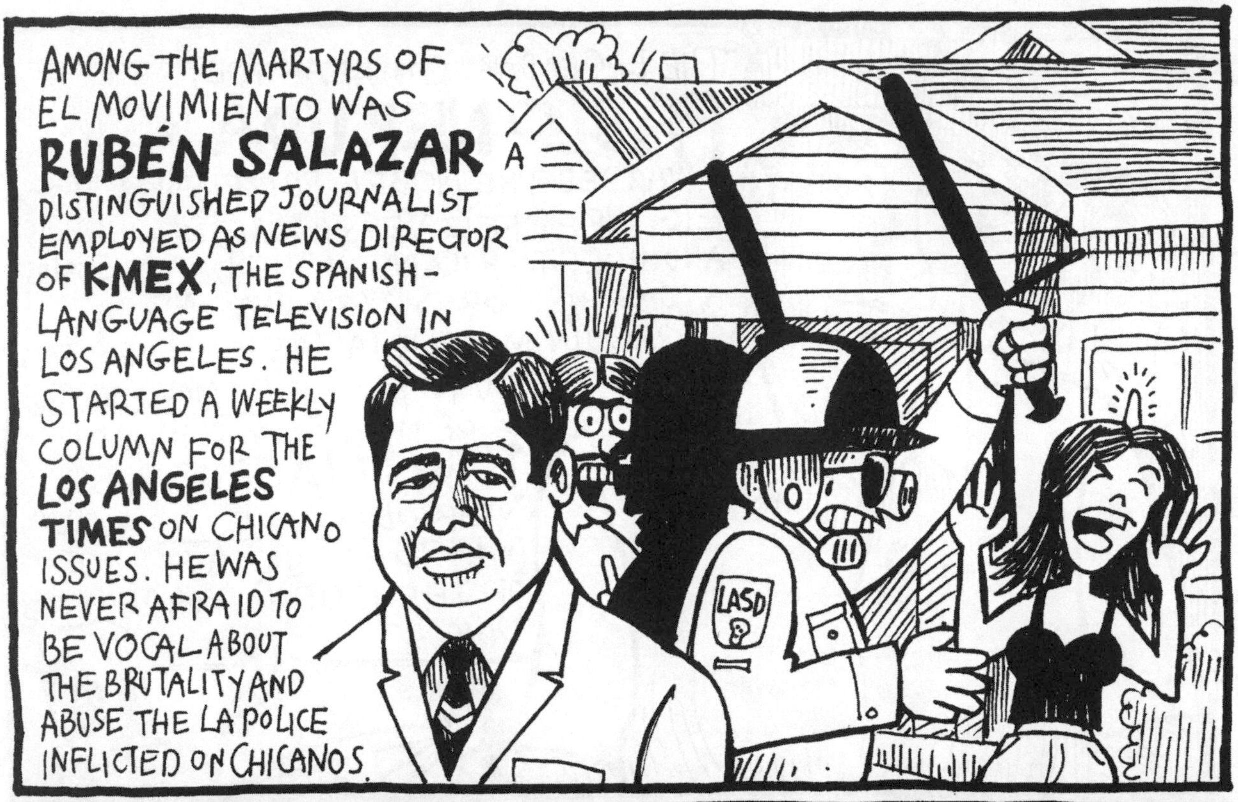
AMONG THE MARTYRS OF EL MOVIMIENTO WAS RUBÉN SALAZAR A DISTINGUISHED JOURNALIST EMPLOYED AS NEWS DIRECTOR OF KMEX, THE SPANISH-LANGUAGE TELEVISION IN LOS ANGELES. HE STARTED A WEEKLY COLUMN FOR THE LOS ANGELES TIMES ON CHICANO ISSUES. HE WAS NEVER AFRAID TO BE VOCAL ABOUT THE BRUTALITY AND ABUSE THE LA POLICE INFLICTED ON CHICANOS.
LASD

COMMENTARY by RUBÉN SALAZAR

"Who is a Chicano? And what is it the Chicanos want? A Chicano is a Mexican-American with a non-Anglo image of himself. He resents being told Columbus "discovered" America when the Chicano's ancestors, the Mayans and the Aztecs, founded highly sophisticated civilizations centuries before Spain financed the Italian explorer's trip to the "New World." Chicanos also resent Anglo pronouncements that Chicanos are "culturally deprived" or that the fact that they speak Spanish is a "problem."

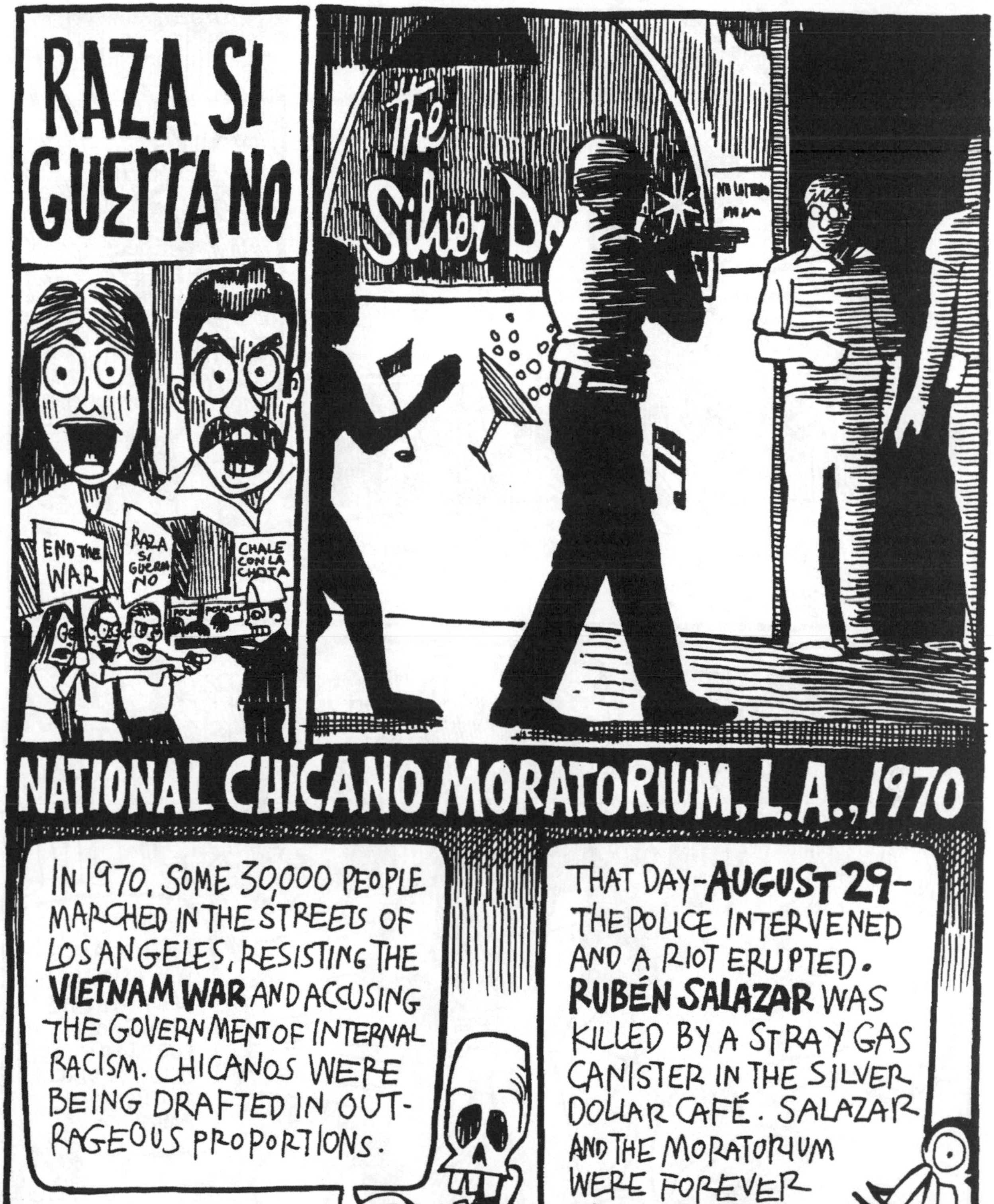
RAZA SI GUERRA NO
END THE WAR
RAZA SI GUERRA NO
CHALE CON LA CHOTA
the Silver Do
NATIONAL CHICANO MORATORIUM, L.A., 1970
IN 1970, SOME 30,000 PEOPLE MARCHED IN THE STREETS OF LOS ANGELES, RESISTING THE **VIETNAM WAR** AND ACCUSING THE GOVERNMENT OF INTERNAL RACISM. CHICANOS WERE BEING DRAFTED IN OUTRAGEOUS PROPORTIONS.
THAT DAY—**AUGUST 29**—THE POLICE INTERVENED AND A RIOT ERUPTED. **RUBÉN SALAZAR** WAS KILLED BY A STRAY GAS CANISTER IN THE SILVER DOLLAR CAFÉ. SALAZAR AND THE MORATORIUM WERE FOREVER MEMORIALIZED.

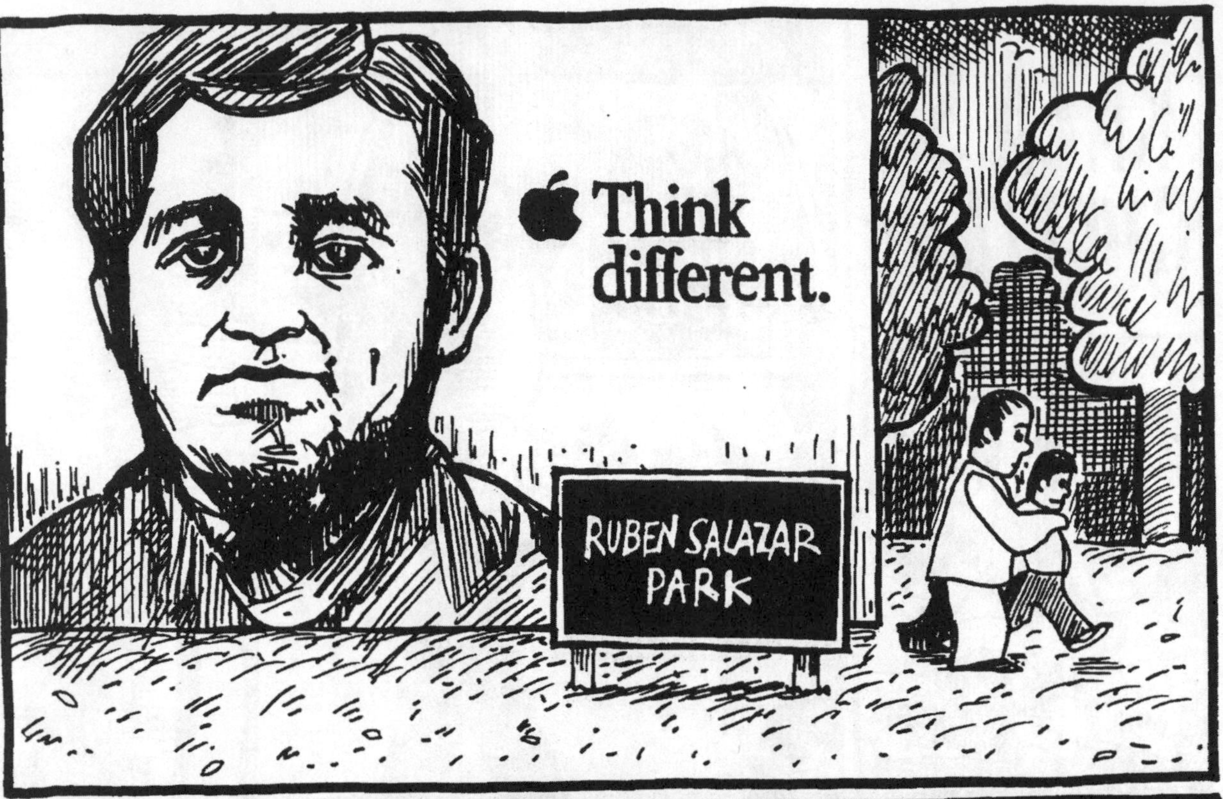
Think different.
RUBEN SALAZAR PARK

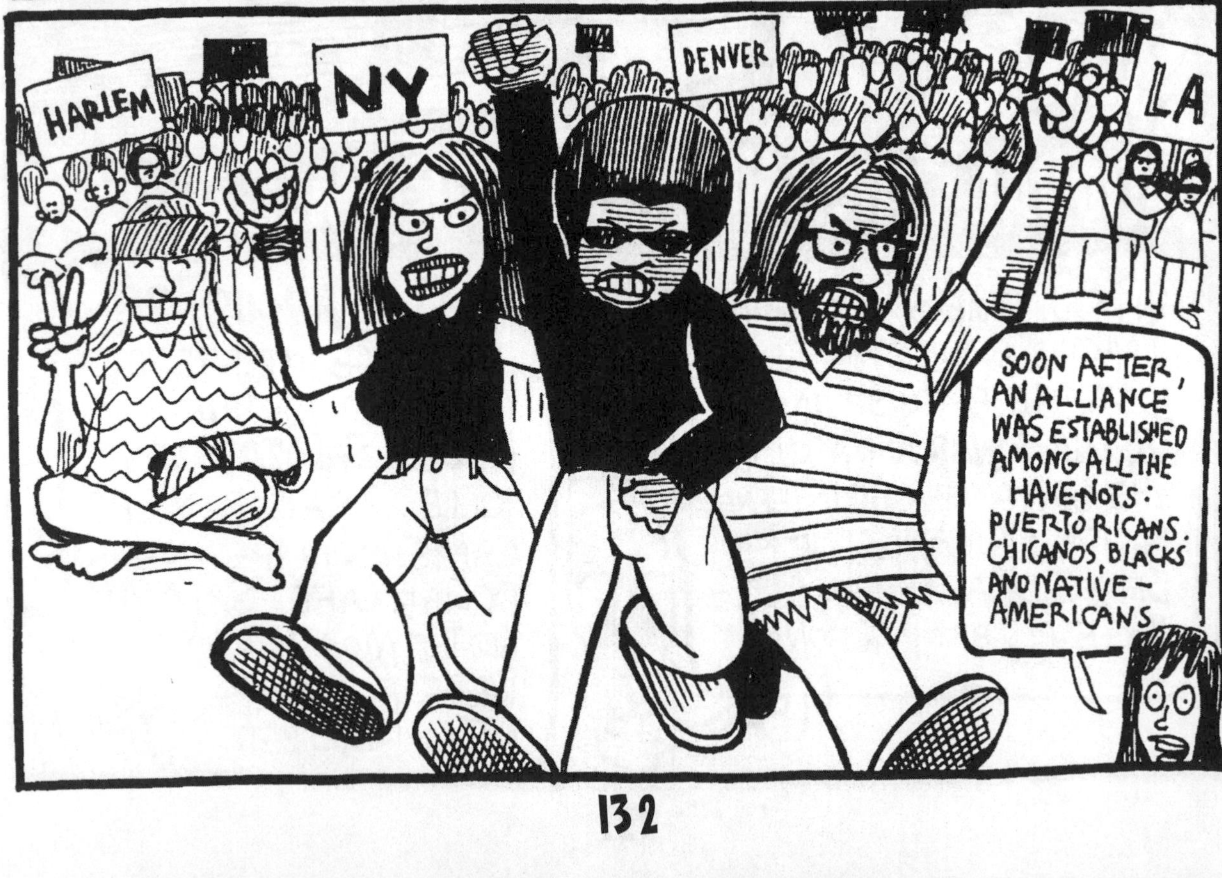
HARLEM
NY
DENVER
LA
SOON AFTER, AN ALLIANCE WAS ESTABLISHED AMONG ALL THE HAVE-NOTS: PUERTO RICANS, CHICANOS, BLACKS AND NATIVE-AMERICANS

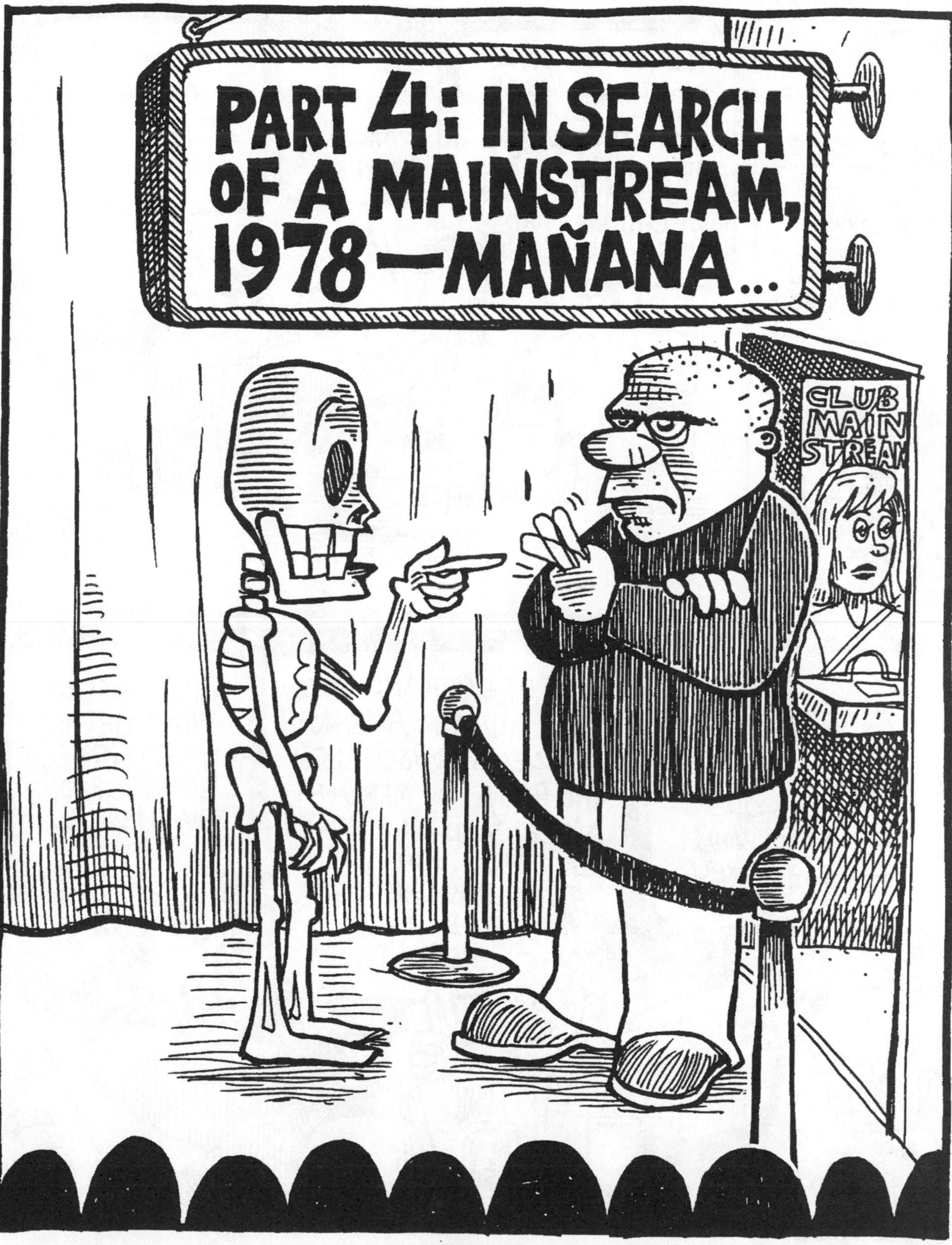
PART 4: IN SEARCH OF A MAINSTREAM, 1978—MAÑANA...
CLUB MAIN STREAM

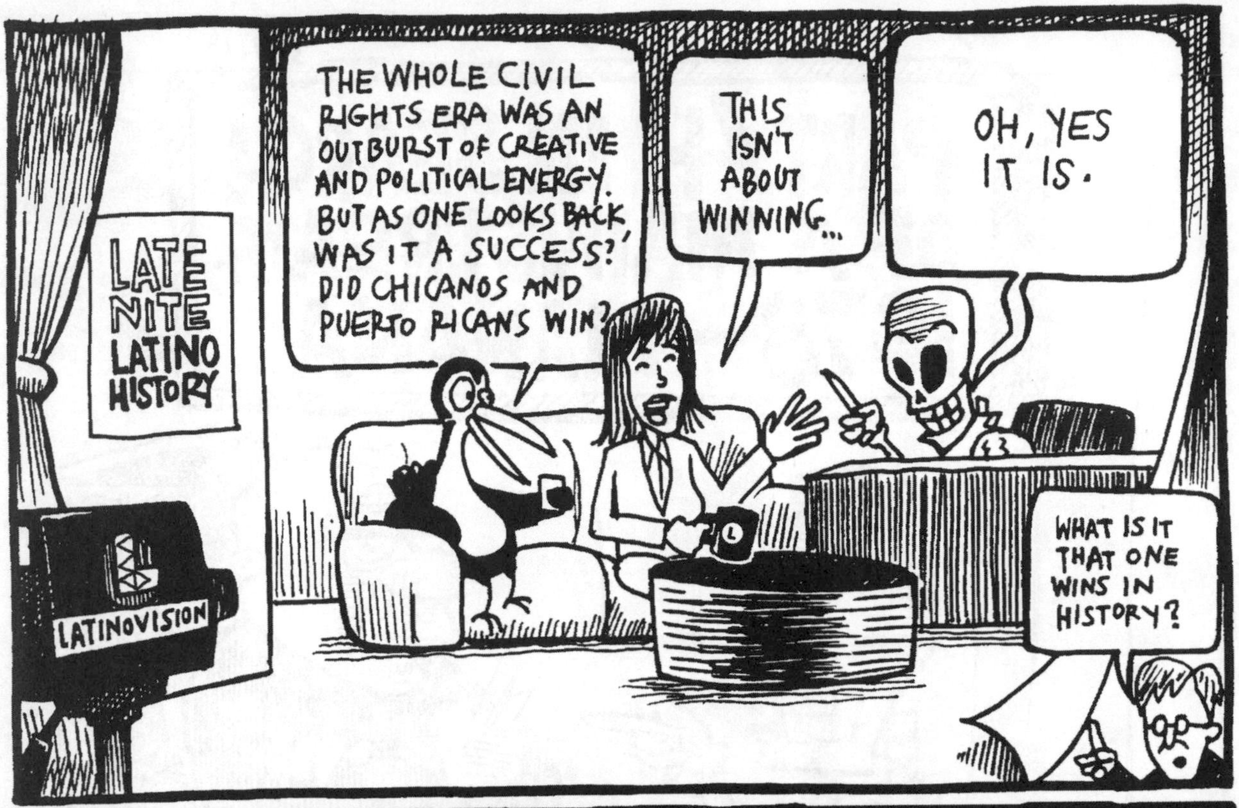
LATE NITE LATINO HISTORY
THE WHOLE CIVIL RIGHTS ERA WAS AN OUTBURST OF CREATIVE AND POLITICAL ENERGY. BUT AS ONE LOOKS BACK, WAS IT A SUCCESS? DID CHICANOS AND PUERTO RICANS WIN?
THIS ISN'T ABOUT WINNING...
OH, YES IT IS.
LATINOVISION
WHAT IS IT THAT ONE WINS IN HISTORY?

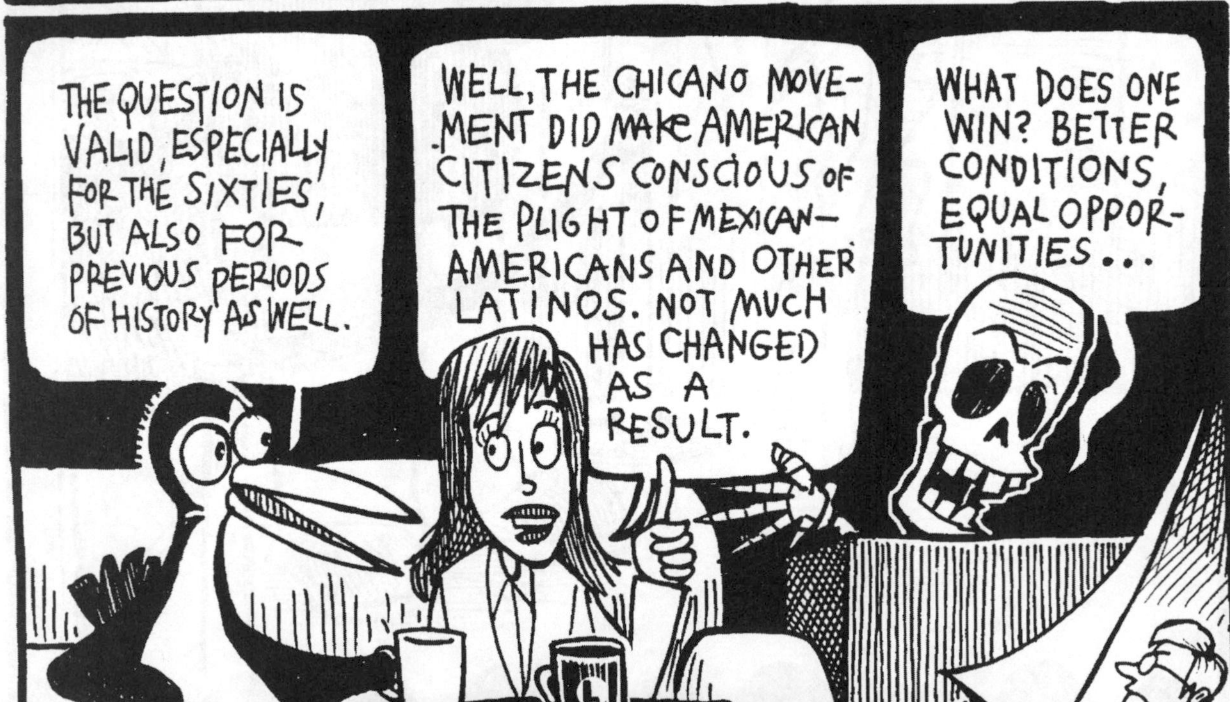
THE QUESTION IS VALID, ESPECIALLY FOR THE SIXTIES, BUT ALSO FOR PREVIOUS PERIODS OF HISTORY AS WELL.
WELL, THE CHICANO MOVEMENT DID MAKE AMERICAN CITIZENS CONSCIOUS OF THE PLIGHT OF MEXICAN-AMERICANS AND OTHER LATINOS. NOT MUCH HAS CHANGED AS A RESULT.
WHAT DOES ONE WIN? BETTER CONDITIONS, EQUAL OPPORTUNITIES...

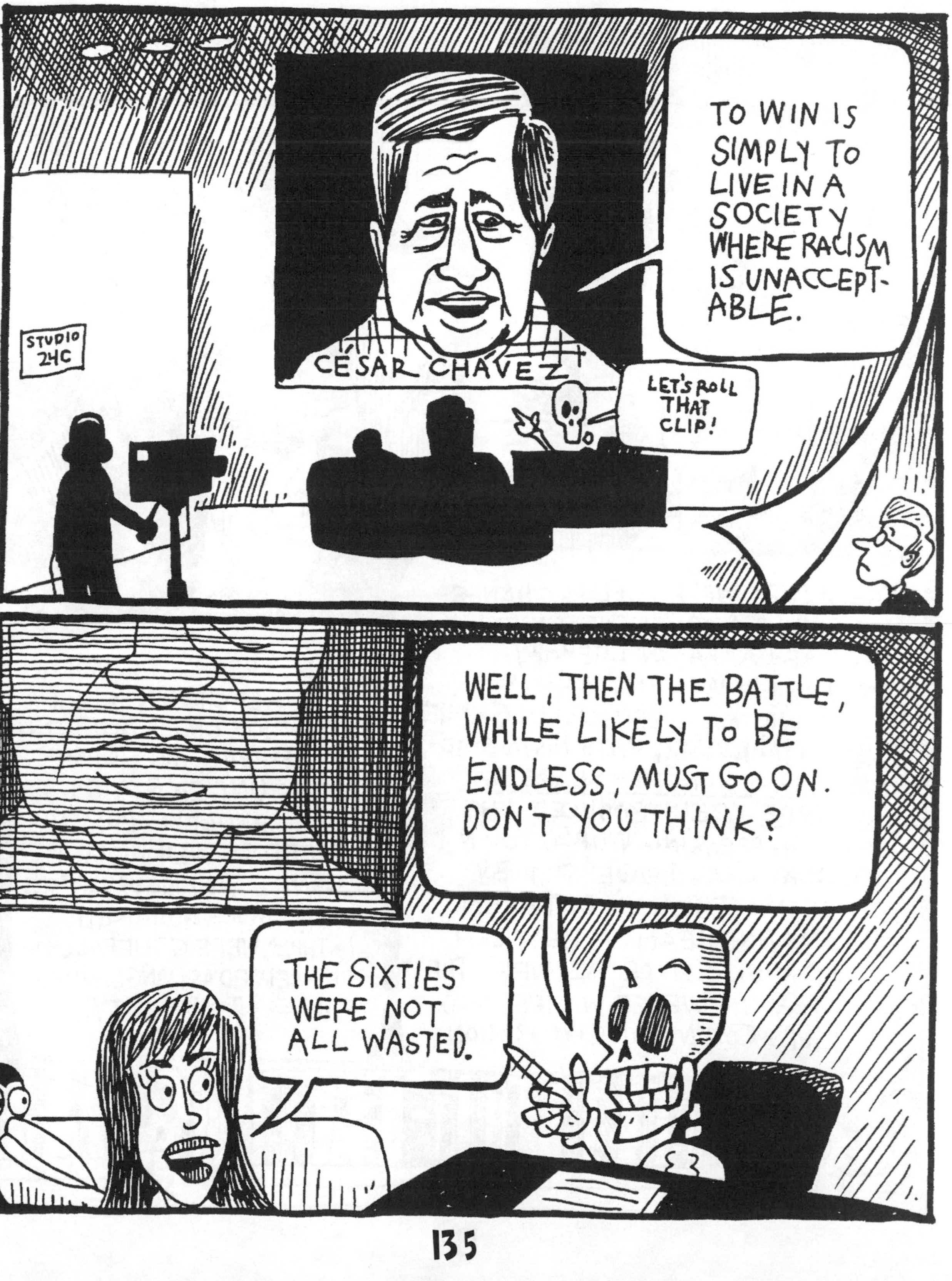
TO WIN IS SIMPLY TO LIVE IN A SOCIETY WHERE RACISM IS UNACCEPTABLE.
STUDIO 24C
CÉSAR CHÁVEZ
LET'S ROLL THAT CLIP!
WELL, THEN THE BATTLE, WHILE LIKELY TO BE ENDLESS, MUST GO ON. DON'T YOU THINK?
THE SIXTIES WERE NOT ALL WASTED.

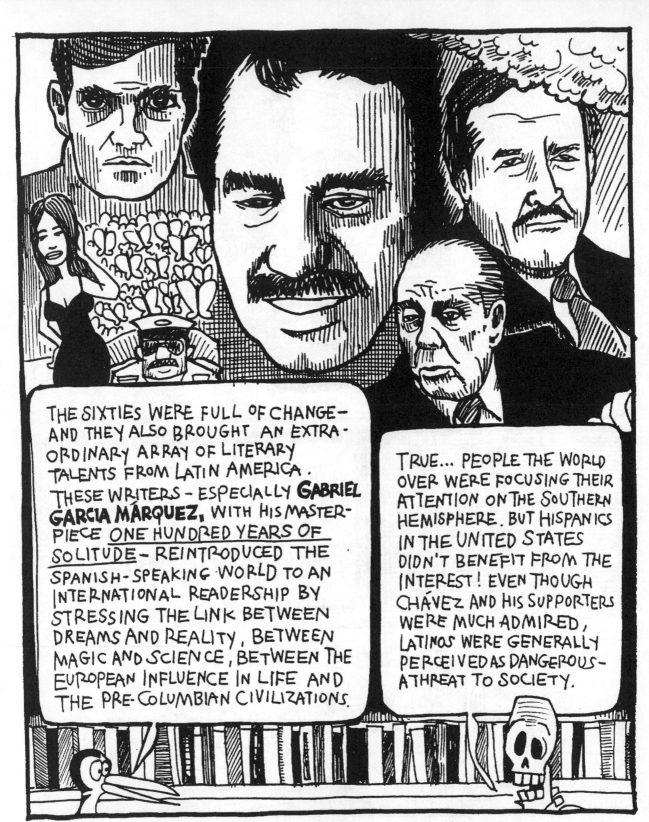

THE SIXTIES WERE FULL OF CHANGE—
AND THEY ALSO BROUGHT AN EXTRA-
ORDINARY ARRAY OF LITERARY
TALENTS FROM LATIN AMERICA.
THESE WRITERS - ESPECIALLY **GABRIEL
GARCÍA MÁRQUEZ,** WITH HIS MASTER-
PIECE <u>ONE HUNDRED YEARS OF
SOLITUDE</u> - REINTRODUCED THE
SPANISH - SPEAKING WORLD TO AN
INTERNATIONAL READERSHIP BY
STRESSING THE LINK BETWEEN
DREAMS AND REALITY, BETWEEN
MAGIC AND SCIENCE, BETWEEN THE
EUROPEAN INFLUENCE IN LIFE AND
THE PRE-COLUMBIAN CIVILIZATIONS.

TRUE... PEOPLE THE WORLD
OVER WERE FOCUSING THEIR
ATTENTION ON THE SOUTHERN
HEMISPHERE. BUT HISPANICS
IN THE UNITED STATES
DIDN'T BENEFIT FROM THE
INTEREST! EVEN THOUGH
CHÁVEZ AND HIS SUPPORTERS
WERE MUCH ADMIRED,
LATINOS WERE GENERALLY
PERCEIVED AS DANGEROUS-
A THREAT TO SOCIETY.

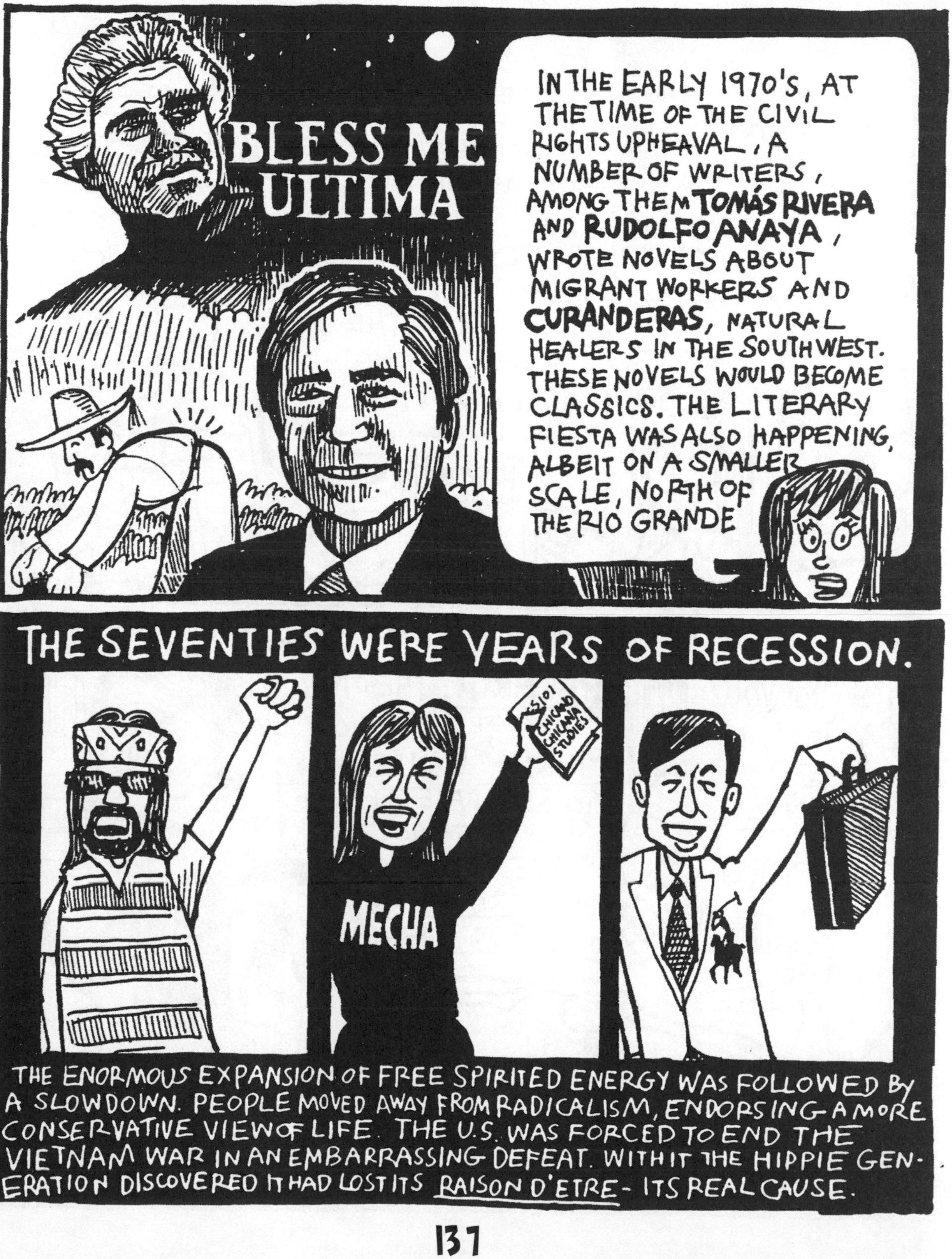
BLESS ME ULTIMA
IN THE EARLY 1970'S, AT THE TIME OF THE CIVIL RIGHTS UPHEAVAL, A NUMBER OF WRITERS, AMONG THEM TOMÁS RIVERA AND RUDOLFO ANAYA, WROTE NOVELS ABOUT MIGRANT WORKERS AND CURANDERAS, NATURAL HEALERS IN THE SOUTHWEST. THESE NOVELS WOULD BECOME CLASSICS. THE LITERARY FIESTA WAS ALSO HAPPENING, ALBEIT ON A SMALLER SCALE, NORTH OF THE RIO GRANDE
THE SEVENTIES WERE YEARS OF RECESSION.
CHICANO CHICANA STUDIES
MECHA
THE ENORMOUS EXPANSION OF FREE SPIRITED ENERGY WAS FOLLOWED BY A SLOWDOWN. PEOPLE MOVED AWAY FROM RADICALISM, ENDORSING A MORE CONSERVATIVE VIEW OF LIFE. THE U.S. WAS FORCED TO END THE VIETNAM WAR IN AN EMBARRASSING DEFEAT. WITH IT THE HIPPIE GENERATION DISCOVERED IT HAD LOST ITS RAISON D'ETRE - ITS REAL CAUSE.

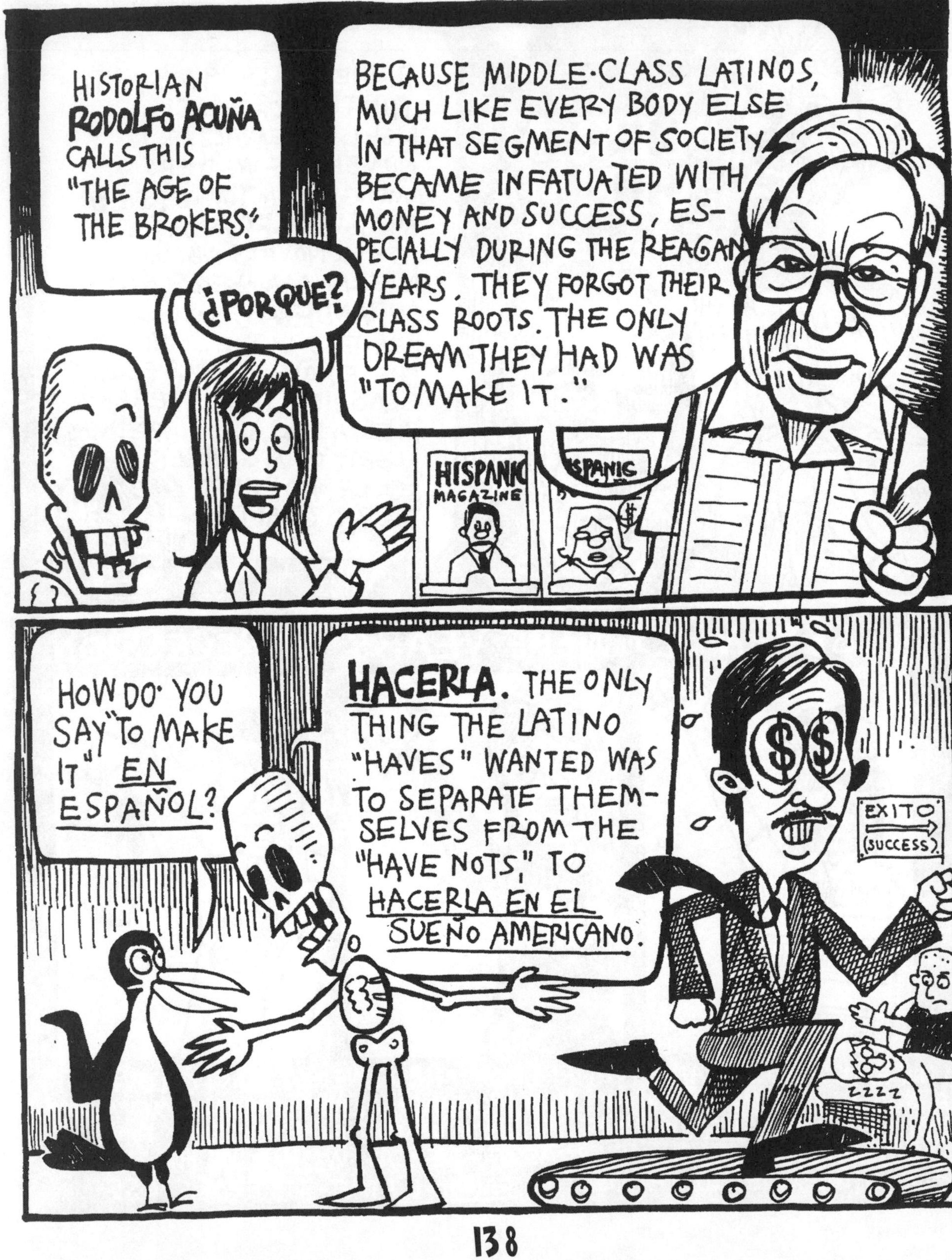
HISTORIAN RODOLFO ACUÑA CALLS THIS "THE AGE OF THE BROKERS."
¿PORQUE?
BECAUSE MIDDLE-CLASS LATINOS, MUCH LIKE EVERY BODY ELSE IN THAT SEGMENT OF SOCIETY, BECAME INFATUATED WITH MONEY AND SUCCESS, ESPECIALLY DURING THE REAGAN YEARS. THEY FORGOT THEIR CLASS ROOTS. THE ONLY DREAM THEY HAD WAS "TO MAKE IT."
HISPANIC MAGAZINE
HISPANIC
HOW DO YOU SAY "TO MAKE IT" EN ESPAÑOL?
HACERLA. THE ONLY THING THE LATINO "HAVES" WANTED WAS TO SEPARATE THEMSELVES FROM THE "HAVE NOTS," TO HACERLA EN EL SUEÑO AMERICANO.
EXITO (SUCCESS)
ZZZZ

IN 1978, WHEN PRESIDENT JIMMY CARTER WAS IN THE WHITE HOUSE, THE U.S. VOTED TO RETURN THE PANAMA CANAL TO THE PANAMANIANS IN 2000.

THIS MADE PEOPLE FEEL AS IF THE AGE OF UPHEAVAL WAS OVER, REPLACED BY ONE CHARACTERIZED BY RESTRAINT.

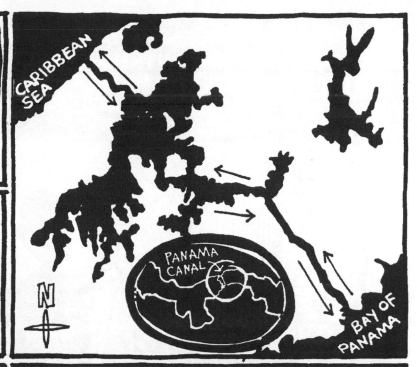

CARIBBEAN SEA

PANAMA CANAL

N

BAY OF PANAMA

THE PANAMA CANAL, AN ARTIFICIAL WATERWAY, IS STRATEGIC BECAUSE IT ALLOWS SHIPS TO GO FROM ONE OCEAN TO THE OTHER WITHOUT HAVING TO REACH TIERRA DEL FUEGO.

THE CANAL WAS BUILT IN 1914. FRANCE BEGAN THE PROJECT BUT THE U.S. COMPLETED IT UNDER PRESIDENT WOODROW WILSON. THE U.S. GAINED JURISDICTION IN 1903 WHEN THE HAY·BUNAU-VARILLA TREATY WAS SIGNED. JIMMY CARTER AND PANAMANIAN RULER OMAR TORRIJOS RENEGOTIATED IT.

CHICANO HISTORY + (LATIN AMERICAN HISTORY)

AS A RESULT OF THE UPHEAVAL, SEVERAL UNIVERSITIES IN THE SOUTHWEST OPENED CHICANO STUDIES PROGRAMS, AND TEXTBOOKS BEGAN INCLUDING SOME LATIN AMERICAN HISTORY.

NOT MUCH, THOUGH...

139

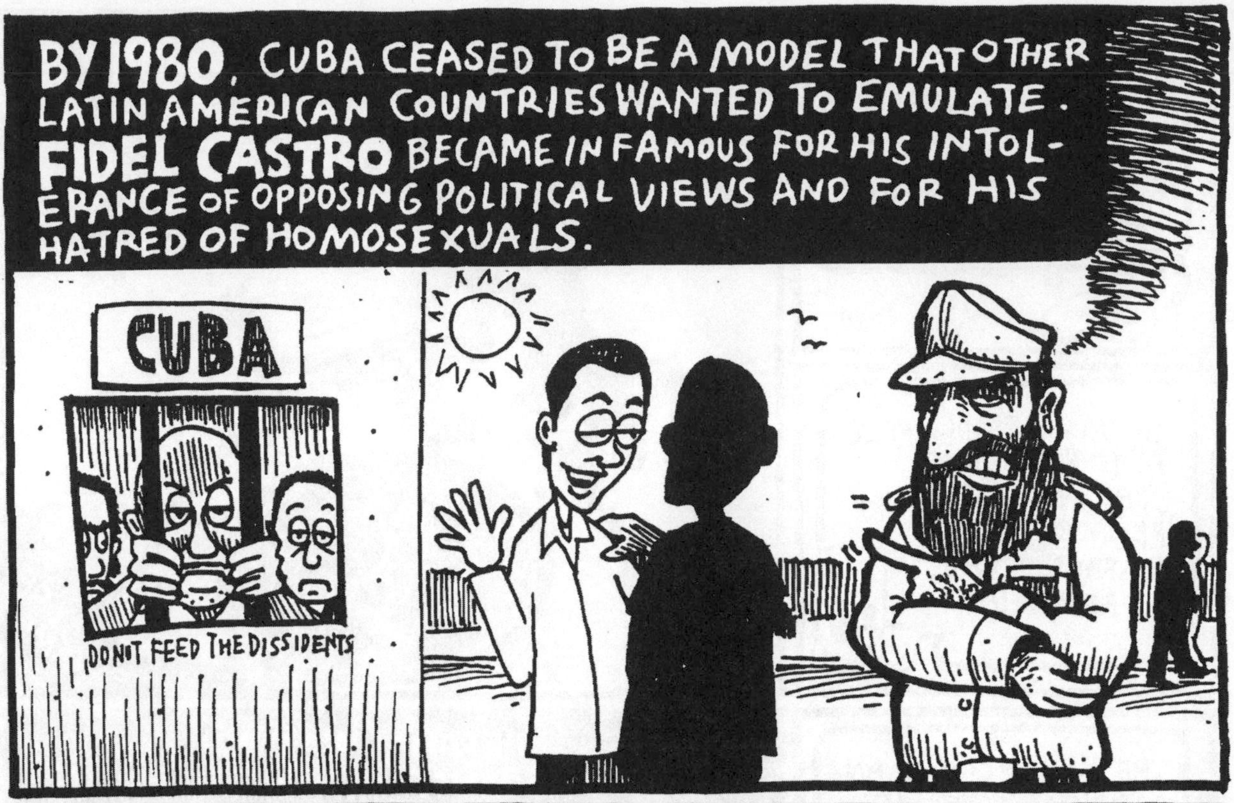
BY 1980, CUBA CEASED TO BE A MODEL THAT OTHER LATIN AMERICAN COUNTRIES WANTED TO EMULATE. FIDEL CASTRO BECAME INFAMOUS FOR HIS INTOLERANCE OF OPPOSING POLITICAL VIEWS AND FOR HIS HATRED OF HOMOSEXUALS.
CUBA
DO NOT FEED THE DISSIDENTS

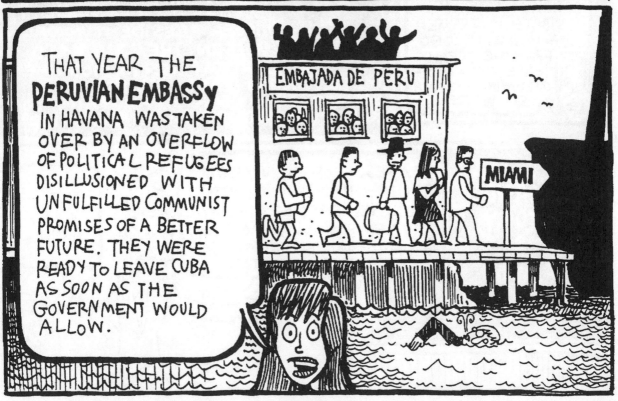

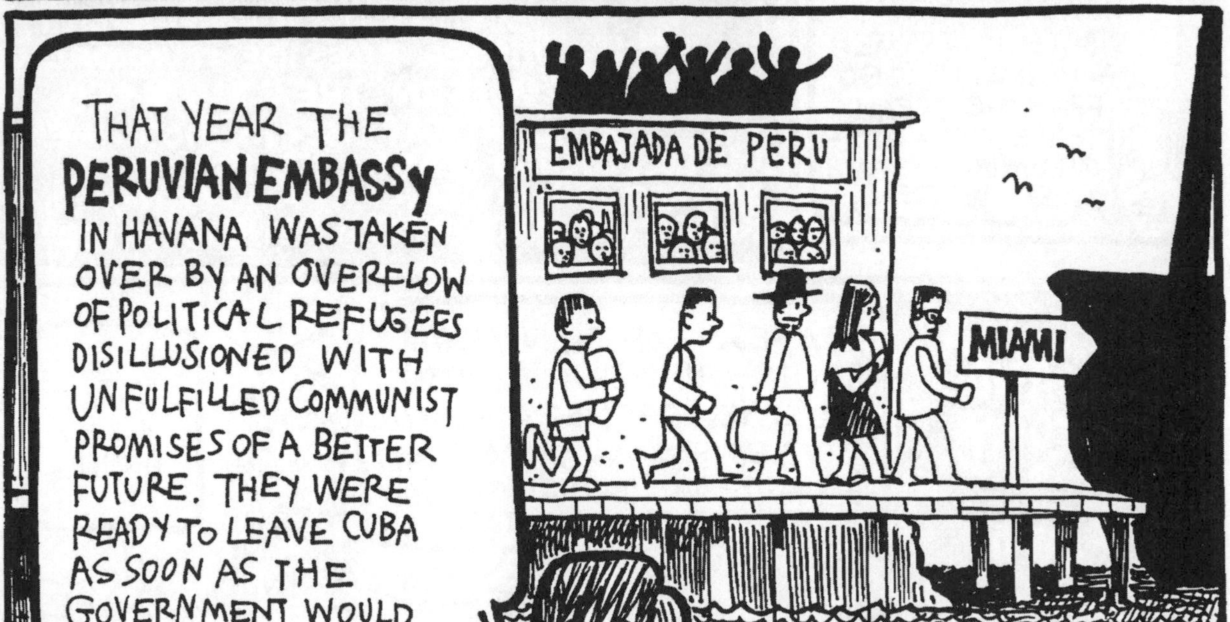
THAT YEAR THE PERUVIAN EMBASSY IN HAVANA WAS TAKEN OVER BY AN OVERFLOW OF POLITICAL REFUGEES DISILLUSIONED WITH UNFULFILLED COMMUNIST PROMISES OF A BETTER FUTURE. THEY WERE READY TO LEAVE CUBA AS SOON AS THE GOVERNMENT WOULD ALLOW.
EMBAJADA DE PERU
MIAMI

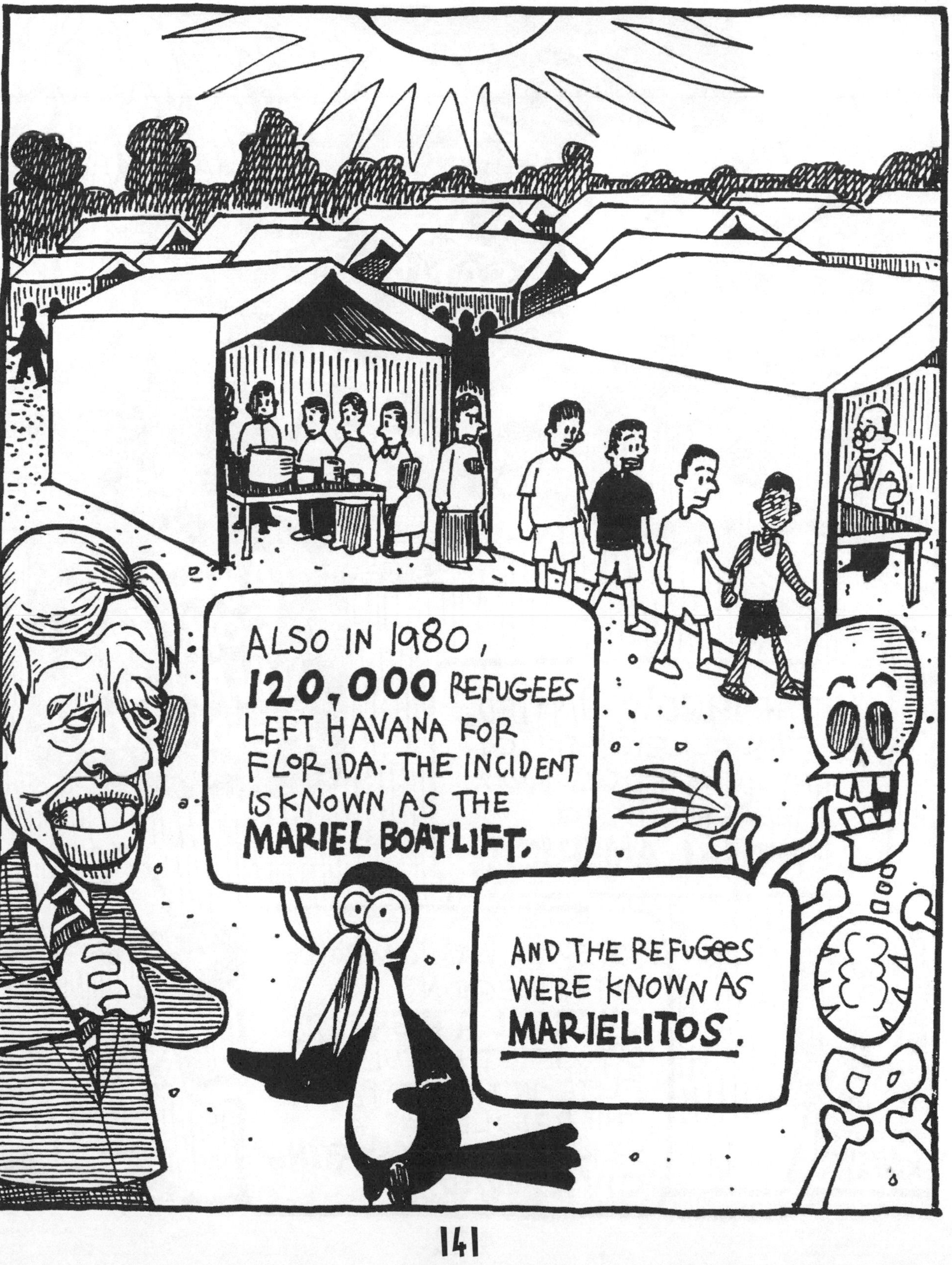
ALSO IN 1980, 120,000 REFUGEES LEFT HAVANA FOR FLORIDA. THE INCIDENT IS KNOWN AS THE MARIEL BOATLIFT.
AND THE REFUGEES WERE KNOWN AS MARIELITOS.

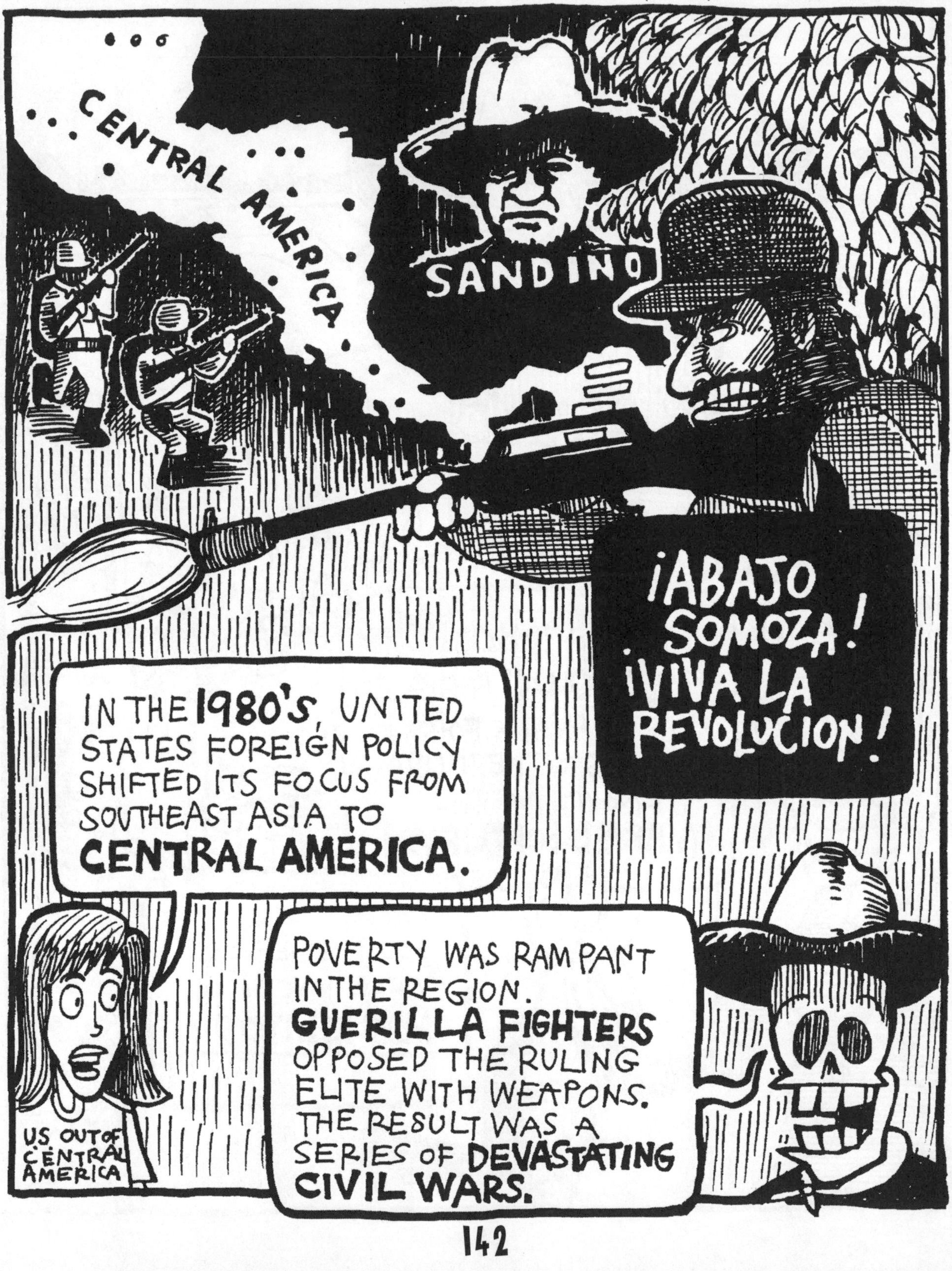
CENTRAL AMERICA
SANDINO
¡ABAJO SOMOZA! ¡VIVA LA REVOLUCION!
IN THE 1980'S, UNITED STATES FOREIGN POLICY SHIFTED ITS FOCUS FROM SOUTHEAST ASIA TO CENTRAL AMERICA.
POVERTY WAS RAMPANT IN THE REGION. GUERILLA FIGHTERS OPPOSED THE RULING ELITE WITH WEAPONS. THE RESULT WAS A SERIES OF DEVASTATING CIVIL WARS.
U.S. OUT OF CENTRAL AMERICA

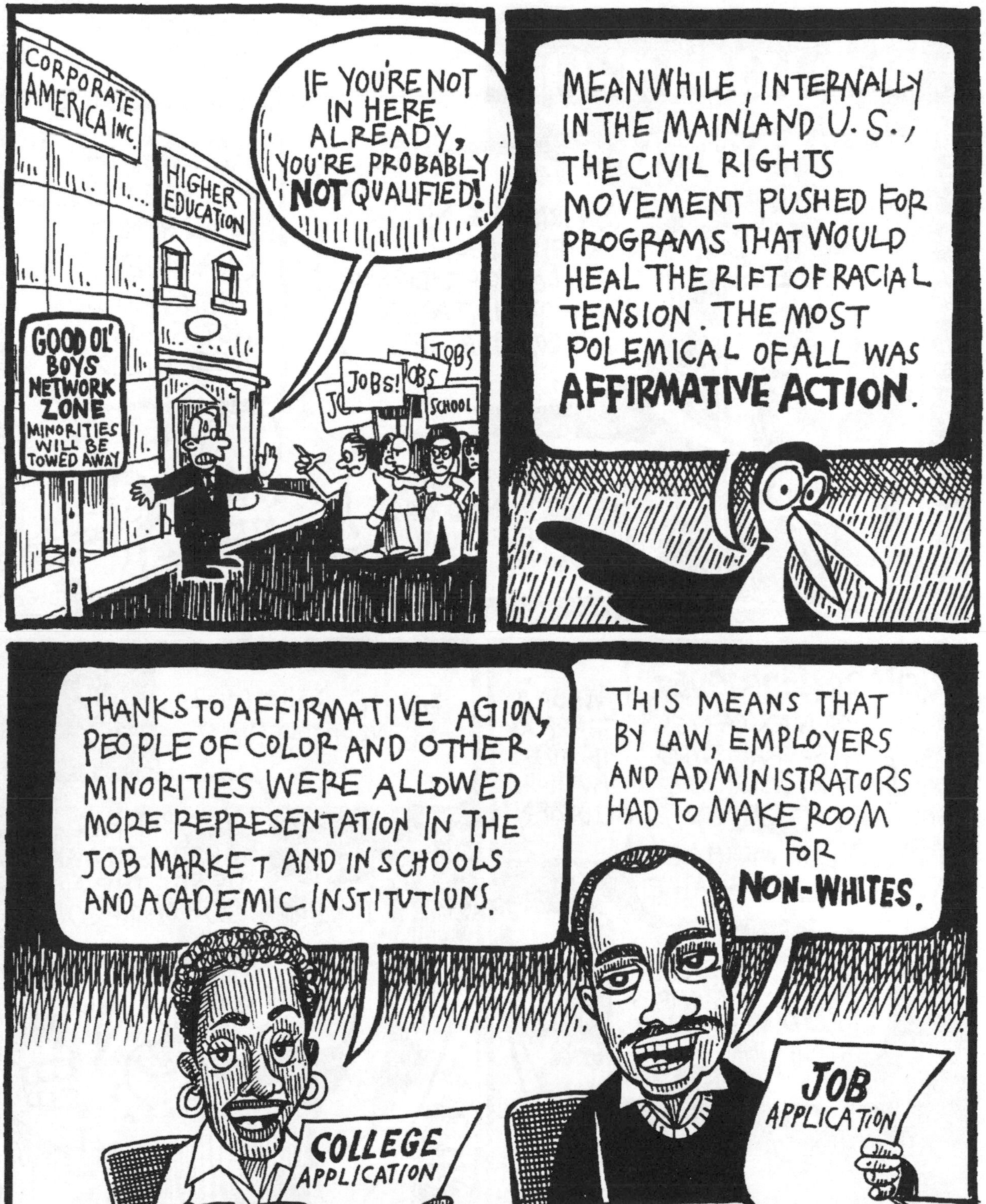
CORPORATE AMERICA INC.
HIGHER EDUCATION
GOOD OL' BOYS NETWORK ZONE MINORITIES WILL BE TOWED AWAY
IF YOU'RE NOT IN HERE ALREADY, YOU'RE PROBABLY **NOT** QUALIFIED!
JOBS!
JOBS
JOBS
SCHOOL
MEANWHILE, INTERNALLY IN THE MAINLAND U.S., THE CIVIL RIGHTS MOVEMENT PUSHED FOR PROGRAMS THAT WOULD HEAL THE RIFT OF RACIAL TENSION. THE MOST POLEMICAL OF ALL WAS **AFFIRMATIVE ACTION**.
THANKS TO AFFIRMATIVE ACTION, PEOPLE OF COLOR AND OTHER MINORITIES WERE ALLOWED MORE REPRESENTATION IN THE JOB MARKET AND IN SCHOOLS AND ACADEMIC INSTITUTIONS.
THIS MEANS THAT BY LAW, EMPLOYERS AND ADMINISTRATORS HAD TO MAKE ROOM FOR **NON-WHITES**.
COLLEGE APPLICATION
JOB APPLICATION

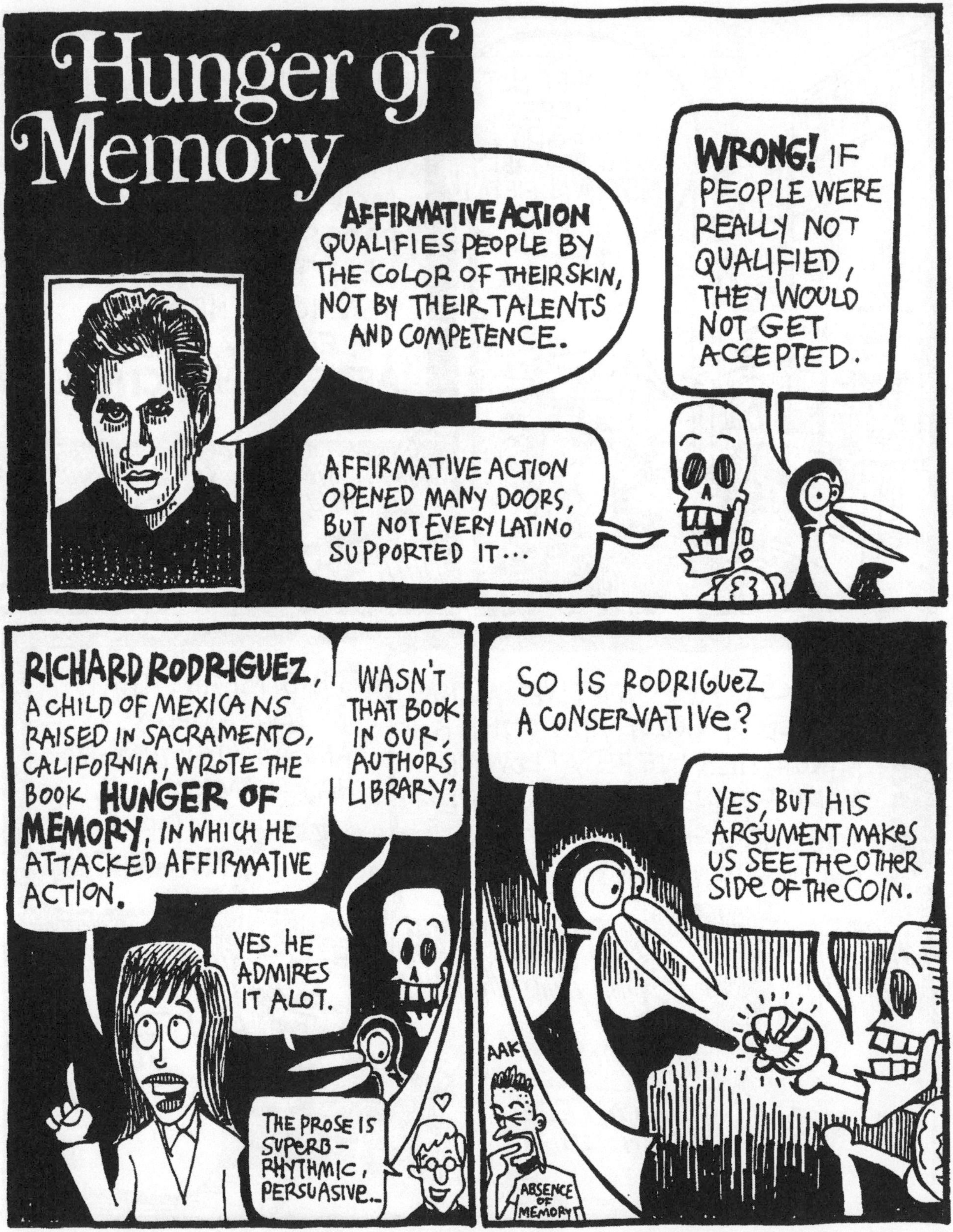
Hunger of Memory
AFFIRMATIVE ACTION QUALIFIES PEOPLE BY THE COLOR OF THEIR SKIN, NOT BY THEIR TALENTS AND COMPETENCE.
AFFIRMATIVE ACTION OPENED MANY DOORS, BUT NOT EVERY LATINO SUPPORTED IT...
WRONG! IF PEOPLE WERE REALLY NOT QUALIFIED, THEY WOULD NOT GET ACCEPTED.
RICHARD RODRIGUEZ, A CHILD OF MEXICANS RAISED IN SACRAMENTO, CALIFORNIA, WROTE THE BOOK HUNGER OF MEMORY, IN WHICH HE ATTACKED AFFIRMATIVE ACTION.
WASN'T THAT BOOK IN OUR AUTHORS LIBRARY?
YES. HE ADMIRES IT ALOT.
THE PROSE IS SUPERB—RHYTHMIC, PERSUASIVE...
SO IS RODRIGUEZ A CONSERVATIVE?
YES, BUT HIS ARGUMENT MAKES US SEE THE OTHER SIDE OF THE COIN.
AAK
ABSENCE OF MEMORY

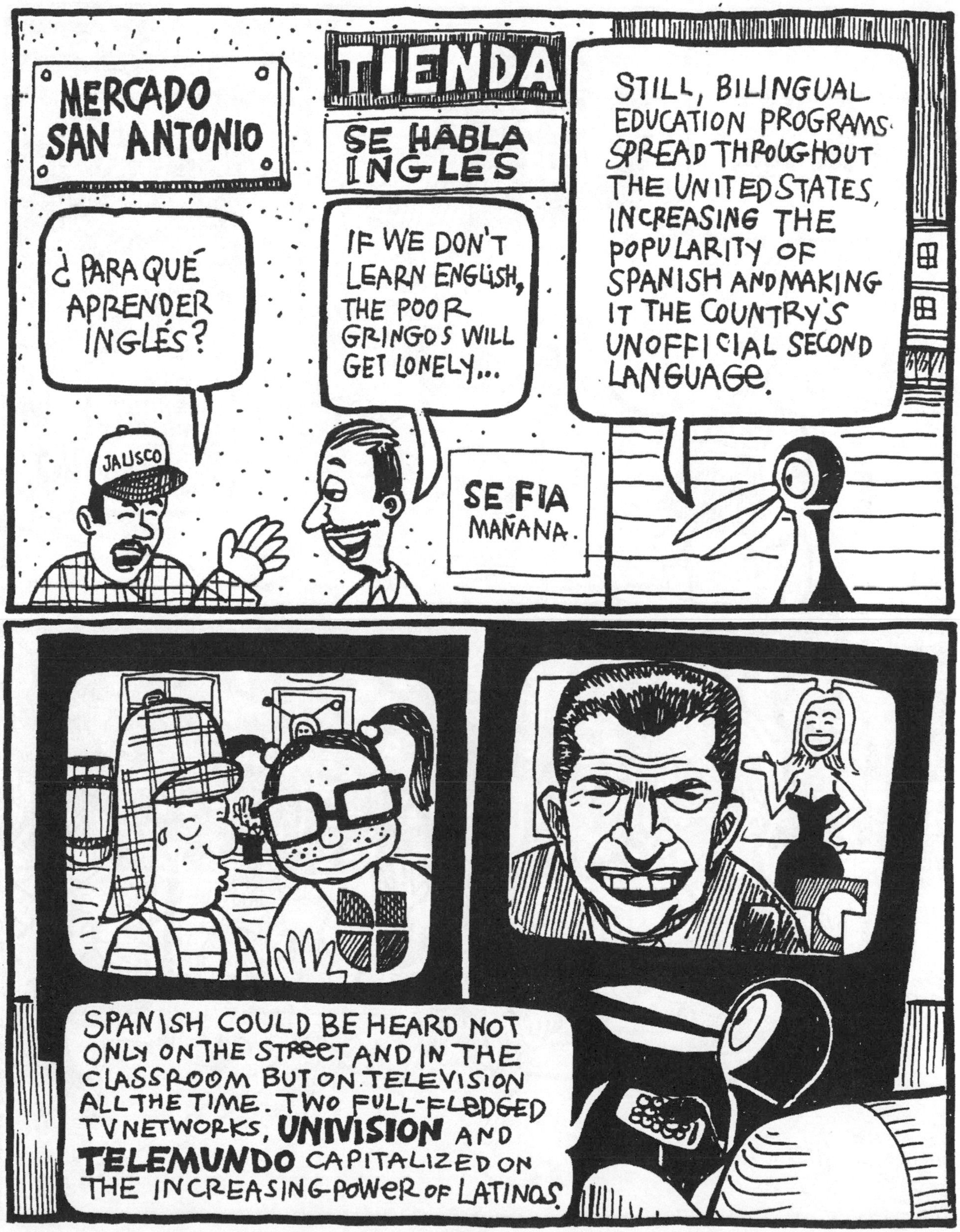
MERCADO SAN ANTONIO
TIENDA
SE HABLA INGLES
¿PARA QUÉ APRENDER INGLÉS?
JALISCO
IF WE DON'T LEARN ENGLISH, THE POOR GRINGOS WILL GET LONELY...
SE FIA MAÑANA.
STILL, BILINGUAL EDUCATION PROGRAMS SPREAD THROUGHOUT THE UNITED STATES, INCREASING THE POPULARITY OF SPANISH AND MAKING IT THE COUNTRY'S UNOFFICIAL SECOND LANGUAGE.
SPANISH COULD BE HEARD NOT ONLY ON THE STREET AND IN THE CLASSROOM BUT ON TELEVISION ALL THE TIME. TWO FULL-FLEDGED TV NETWORKS, UNIVISION AND TELEMUNDO CAPITALIZED ON THE INCREASING POWER OF LATINOS.

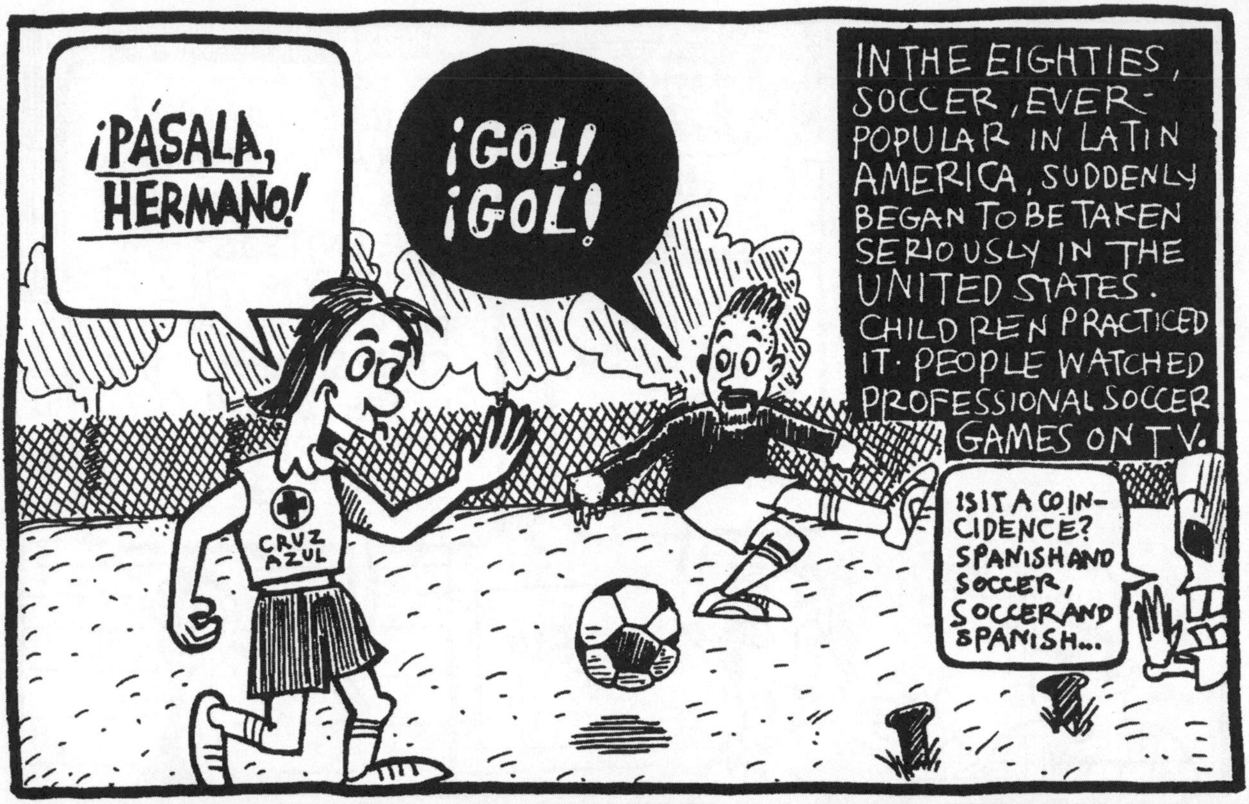
¡PÁSALA, HERMANO!
¡GOL! ¡GOL!
IN THE EIGHTIES, SOCCER, EVER-POPULAR IN LATIN AMERICA, SUDDENLY BEGAN TO BE TAKEN SERIOUSLY IN THE UNITED STATES. CHILDREN PRACTICED IT. PEOPLE WATCHED PROFESSIONAL SOCCER GAMES ON T.V.
CRUZ AZUL
IS IT A COINCIDENCE? SPANISH AND SOCCER, SOCCER AND SPANISH...

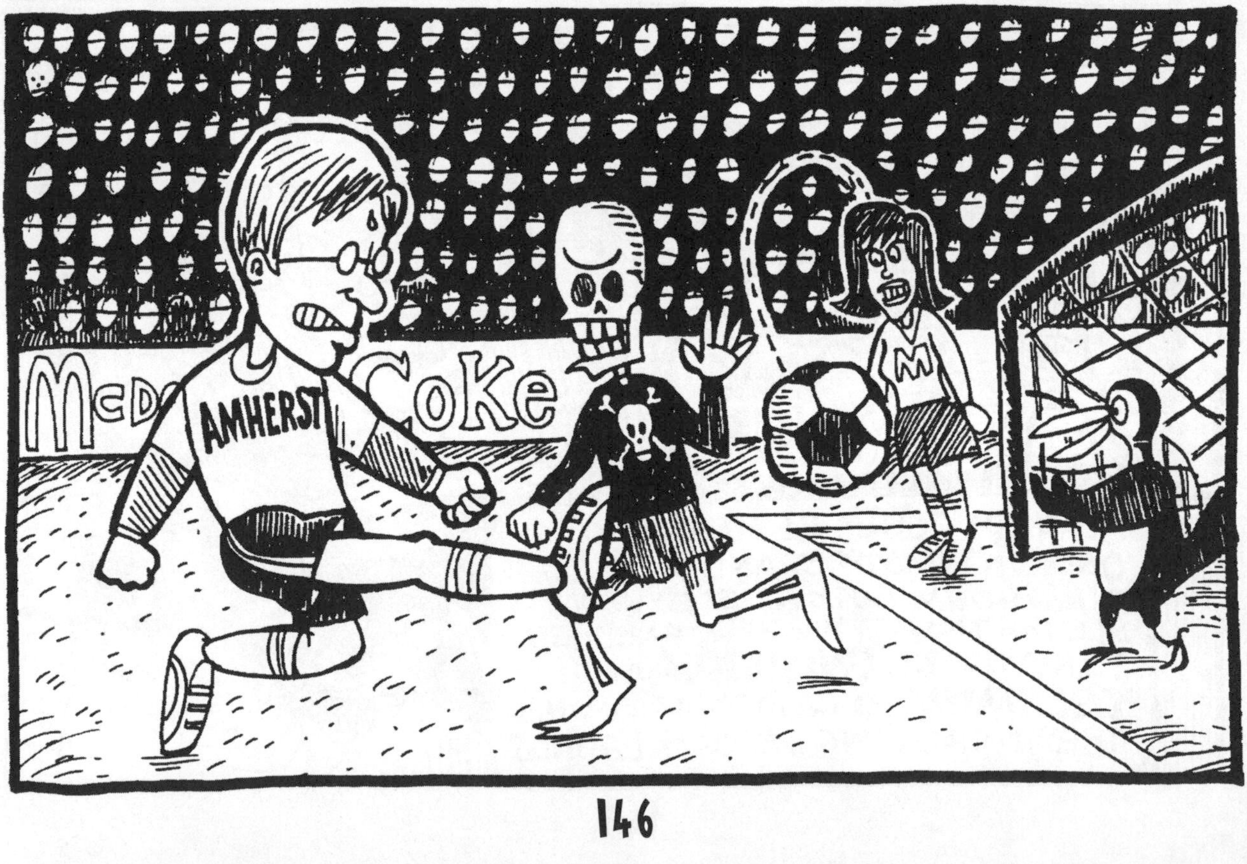
McD
AMHERST
CoKe
M

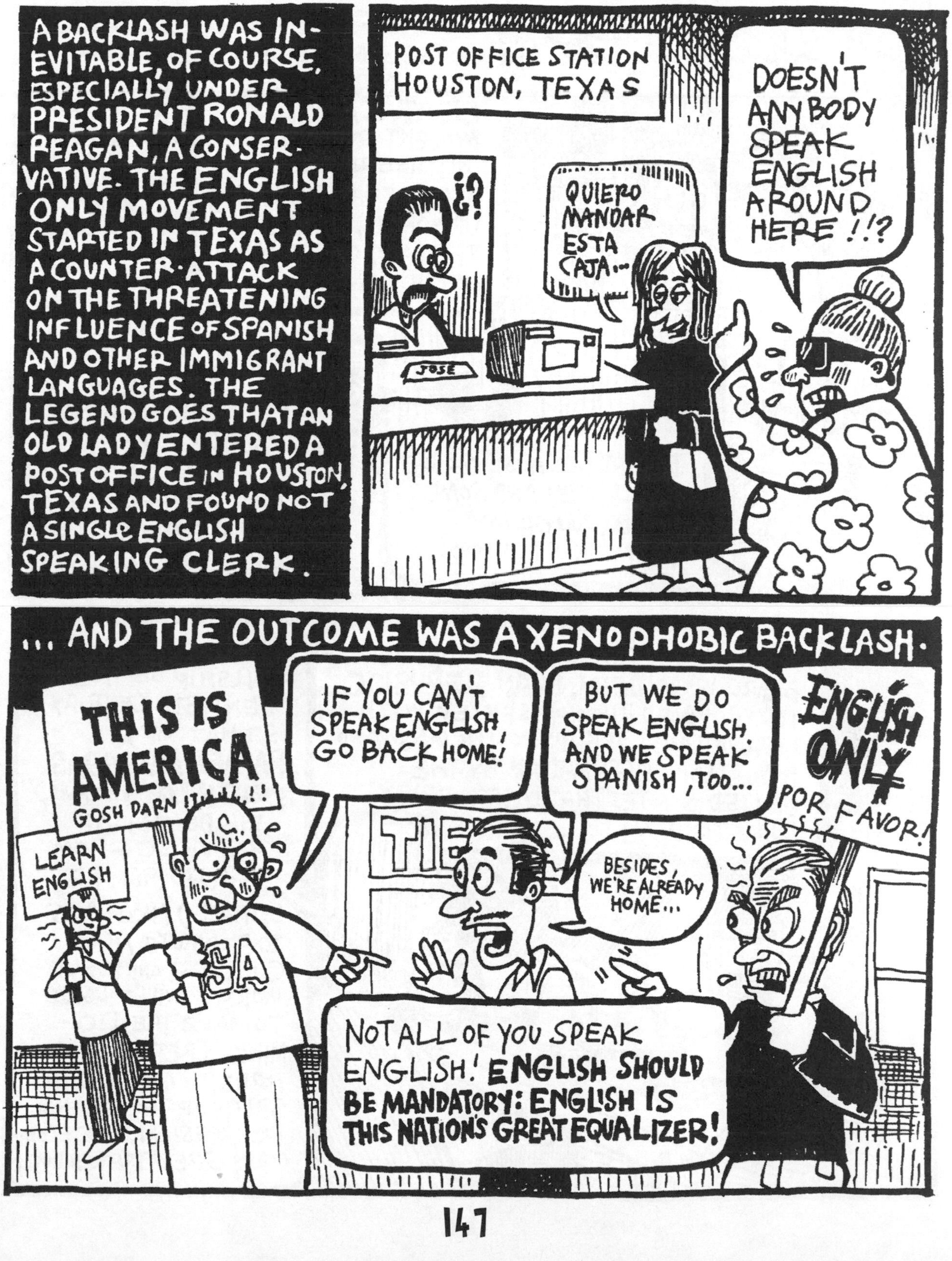
A BACKLASH WAS INEVITABLE, OF COURSE, ESPECIALLY UNDER PRESIDENT RONALD REAGAN, A CONSERVATIVE. THE ENGLISH ONLY MOVEMENT STARTED IN TEXAS AS A COUNTER-ATTACK ON THE THREATENING INFLUENCE OF SPANISH AND OTHER IMMIGRANT LANGUAGES. THE LEGEND GOES THAT AN OLD LADY ENTERED A POST OFFICE IN HOUSTON, TEXAS AND FOUND NOT A SINGLE ENGLISH SPEAKING CLERK.
POST OFFICE STATION HOUSTON, TEXAS
¿?
JOSÉ
QUIERO MANDAR ESTA CAJA...
DOESN'T ANYBODY SPEAK ENGLISH AROUND HERE!!?
... AND THE OUTCOME WAS A XENOPHOBIC BACKLASH.
THIS IS AMERICA GOSH DARN IT!!!
LEARN ENGLISH
IF YOU CAN'T SPEAK ENGLISH, GO BACK HOME!
USA
TIE
BUT WE DO SPEAK ENGLISH. AND WE SPEAK SPANISH, TOO...
BESIDES, WE'RE ALREADY HOME...
ENGLISH ONLY POR FAVOR!
NOT ALL OF YOU SPEAK ENGLISH! ENGLISH SHOULD BE MANDATORY: ENGLISH IS THIS NATION'S GREAT EQUALIZER!

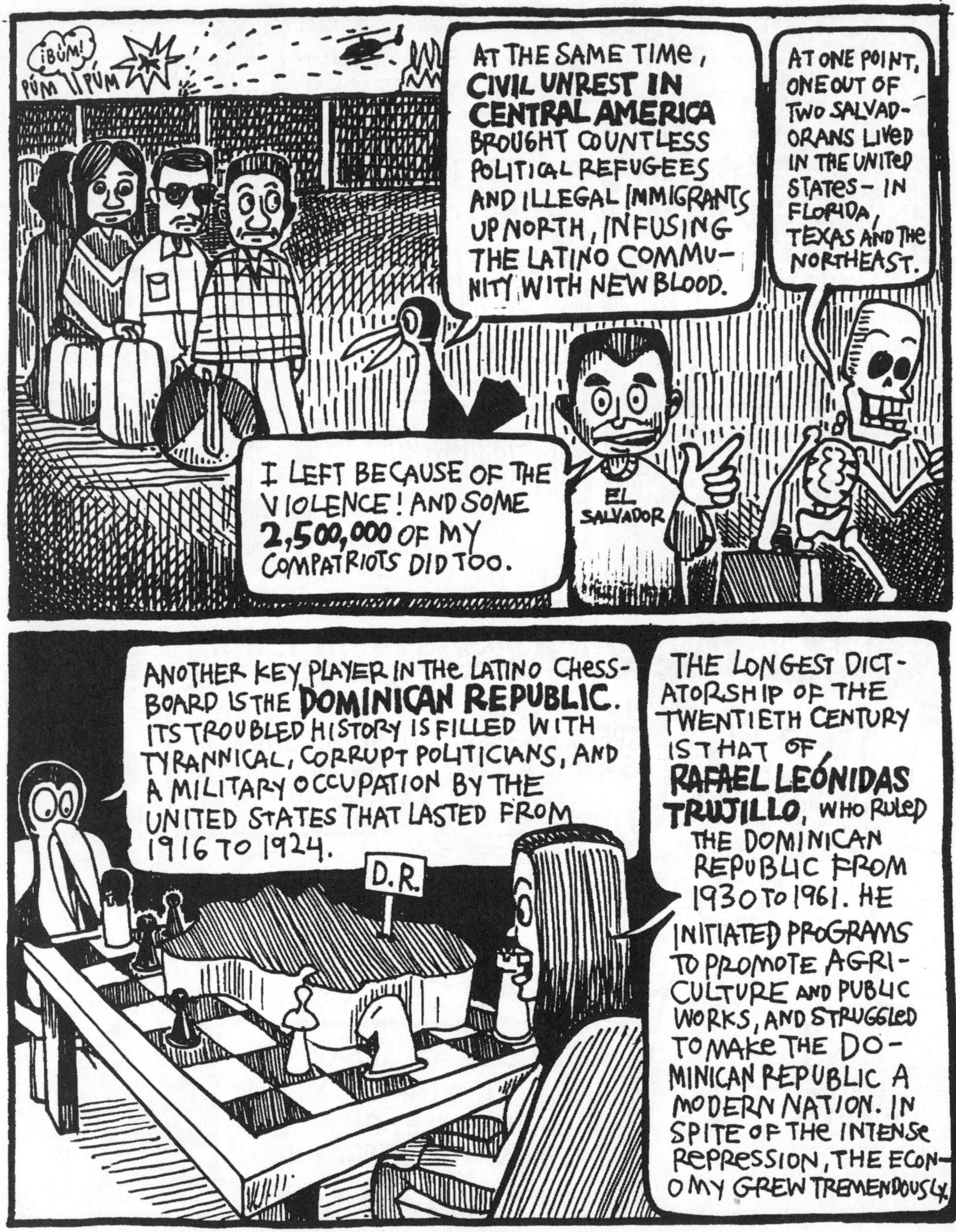
¡BÚM!
PÚM PÚM
AT THE SAME TIME, CIVIL UNREST IN CENTRAL AMERICA BROUGHT COUNTLESS POLITICAL REFUGEES AND ILLEGAL IMMIGRANTS UP NORTH, INFUSING THE LATINO COMMUNITY WITH NEW BLOOD.
AT ONE POINT, ONE OUT OF TWO SALVADORANS LIVED IN THE UNITED STATES—IN FLORIDA, TEXAS AND THE NORTHEAST.
I LEFT BECAUSE OF THE VIOLENCE! AND SOME 2,500,000 OF MY COMPATRIOTS DID TOO.
EL SALVADOR
ANOTHER KEY PLAYER IN THE LATINO CHESSBOARD IS THE DOMINICAN REPUBLIC. ITS TROUBLED HISTORY IS FILLED WITH TYRANNICAL, CORRUPT POLITICIANS, AND A MILITARY OCCUPATION BY THE UNITED STATES THAT LASTED FROM 1916 TO 1924.
D.R.
THE LONGEST DICTATORSHIP OF THE TWENTIETH CENTURY IS THAT OF RAFAEL LEÓNIDAS TRUJILLO, WHO RULED THE DOMINICAN REPUBLIC FROM 1930 TO 1961. HE INITIATED PROGRAMS TO PROMOTE AGRICULTURE AND PUBLIC WORKS, AND STRUGGLED TO MAKE THE DOMINICAN REPUBLIC A MODERN NATION. IN SPITE OF THE INTENSE REPRESSION, THE ECONOMY GREW TREMENDOUSLY.

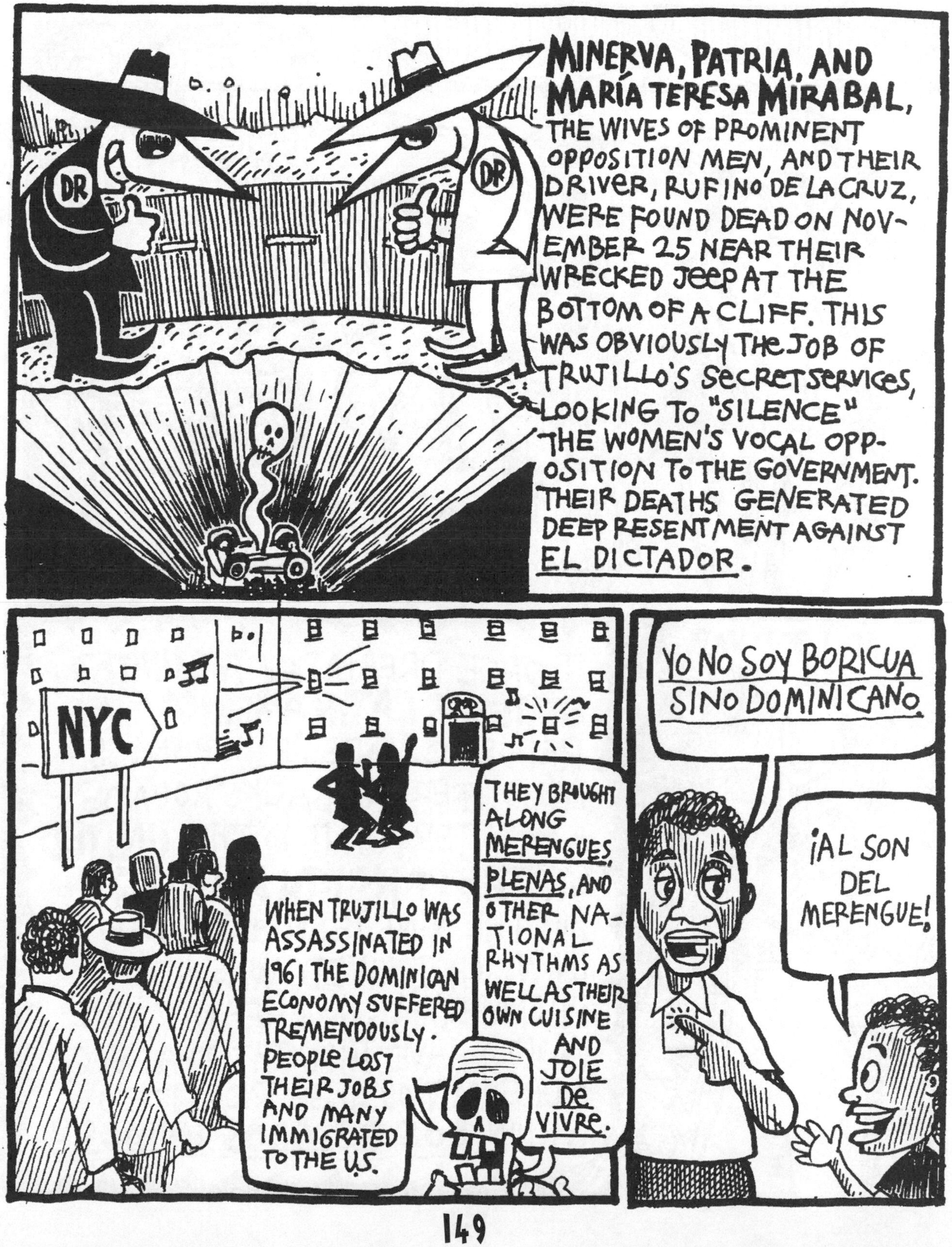
DR
DR
MINERVA, PATRIA, AND MARÍA TERESA MIRABAL, THE WIVES OF PROMINENT OPPOSITION MEN, AND THEIR DRIVER, RUFINO DE LA CRUZ, WERE FOUND DEAD ON NOVEMBER 25 NEAR THEIR WRECKED JEEP AT THE BOTTOM OF A CLIFF. THIS WAS OBVIOUSLY THE JOB OF TRUJILLO'S SECRET SERVICES, LOOKING TO "SILENCE" THE WOMEN'S VOCAL OPPOSITION TO THE GOVERNMENT. THEIR DEATHS GENERATED DEEP RESENTMENT AGAINST EL DICTADOR.
NYC
WHEN TRUJILLO WAS ASSASSINATED IN 1961 THE DOMINICAN ECONOMY SUFFERED TREMENDOUSLY. PEOPLE LOST THEIR JOBS AND MANY IMMIGRATED TO THE U.S.
THEY BROUGHT ALONG MERENGUES, PLENAS, AND OTHER NATIONAL RHYTHMS AS WELL AS THEIR OWN CUISINE AND JOIE DE VIVRE.
YO NO SOY BORICUA SINO DOMINICANO.
¡AL SON DEL MERENGUE!

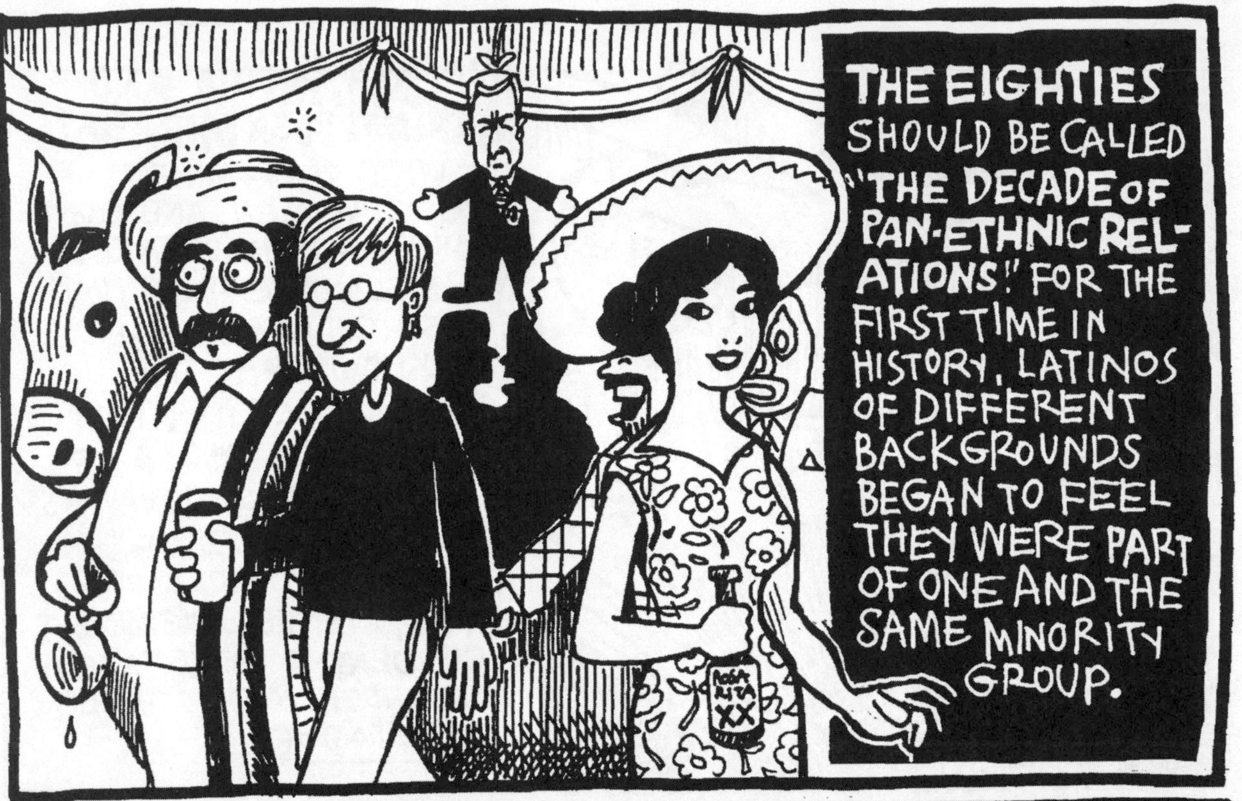
THE EIGHTIES SHOULD BE CALLED "THE DECADE OF PAN-ETHNIC RELATIONS!" FOR THE FIRST TIME IN HISTORY, LATINOS OF DIFFERENT BACKGROUNDS BEGAN TO FEEL THEY WERE PART OF ONE AND THE SAME MINORITY GROUP.
XX

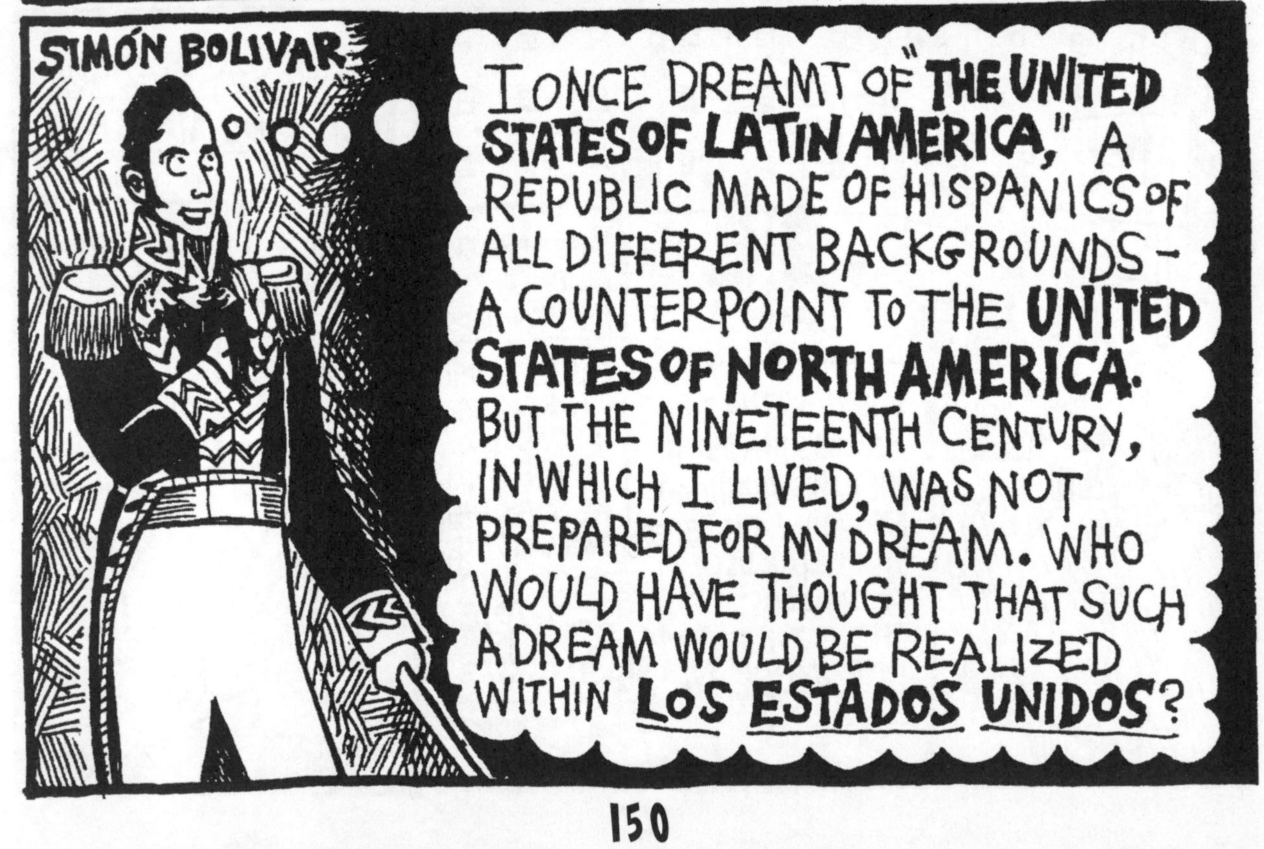
SIMÓN BOLIVAR
I ONCE DREAMT OF "THE UNITED STATES OF LATIN AMERICA," A REPUBLIC MADE OF HISPANICS OF ALL DIFFERENT BACKGROUNDS - A COUNTERPOINT TO THE UNITED STATES OF NORTH AMERICA. BUT THE NINETEENTH CENTURY, IN WHICH I LIVED, WAS NOT PREPARED FOR MY DREAM. WHO WOULD HAVE THOUGHT THAT SUCH A DREAM WOULD BE REALIZED WITHIN LOS ESTADOS UNIDOS?

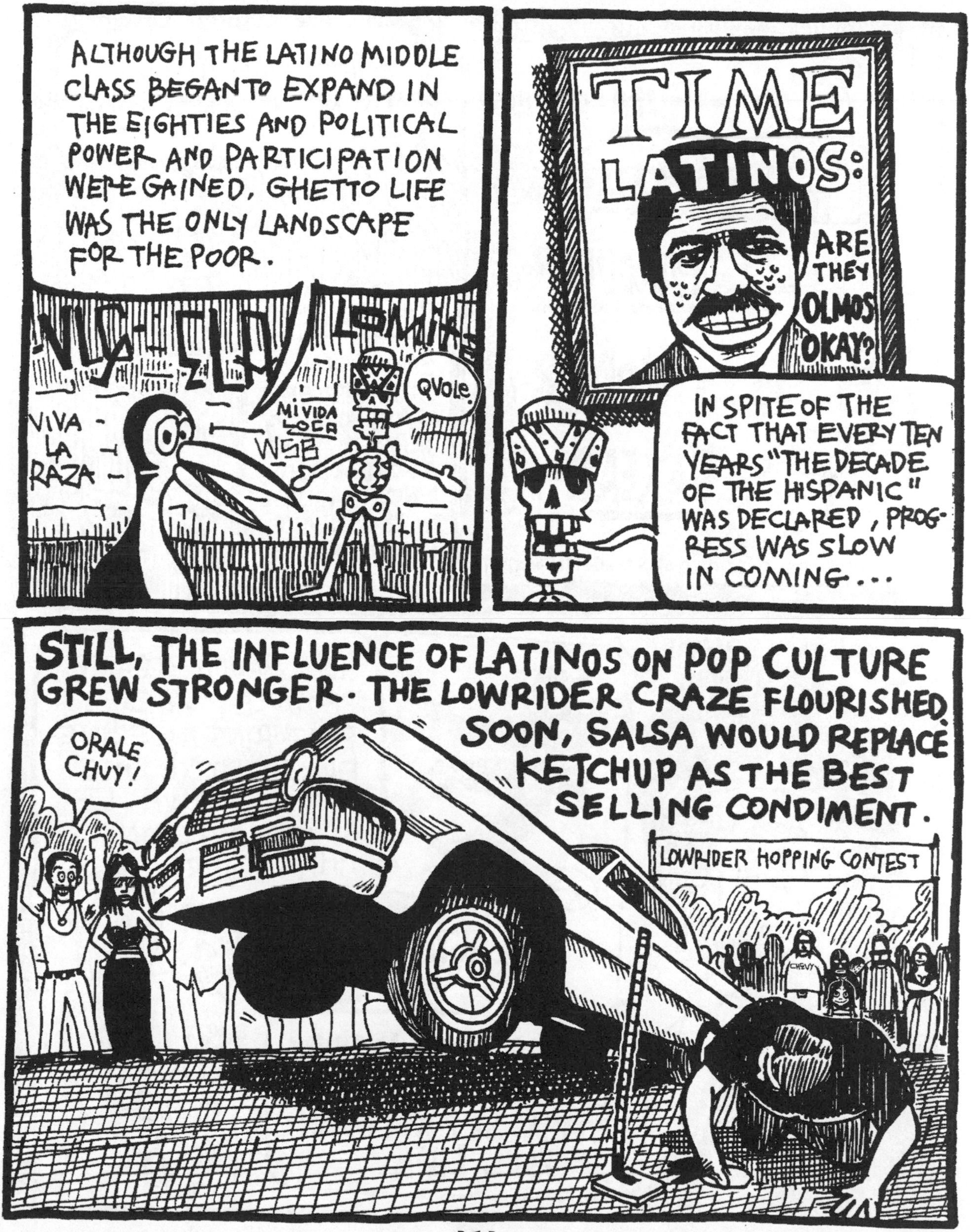
ALTHOUGH THE LATINO MIDDLE CLASS BEGAN TO EXPAND IN THE EIGHTIES AND POLITICAL POWER AND PARTICIPATION WERE GAINED, GHETTO LIFE WAS THE ONLY LANDSCAPE FOR THE POOR.
VIVA LA RAZA
MI VIDA LOCA
WSB
QVOLE.
TIME
LATINOS:
ARE THEY OLMOS OKAY?
IN SPITE OF THE FACT THAT EVERY TEN YEARS "THE DECADE OF THE HISPANIC" WAS DECLARED, PROGRESS WAS SLOW IN COMING...
STILL, THE INFLUENCE OF LATINOS ON POP CULTURE GREW STRONGER. THE LOWRIDER CRAZE FLOURISHED. SOON, SALSA WOULD REPLACE KETCHUP AS THE BEST SELLING CONDIMENT.
ORALE CHUY!
LOWRIDER HOPPING CONTEST
CHEVY

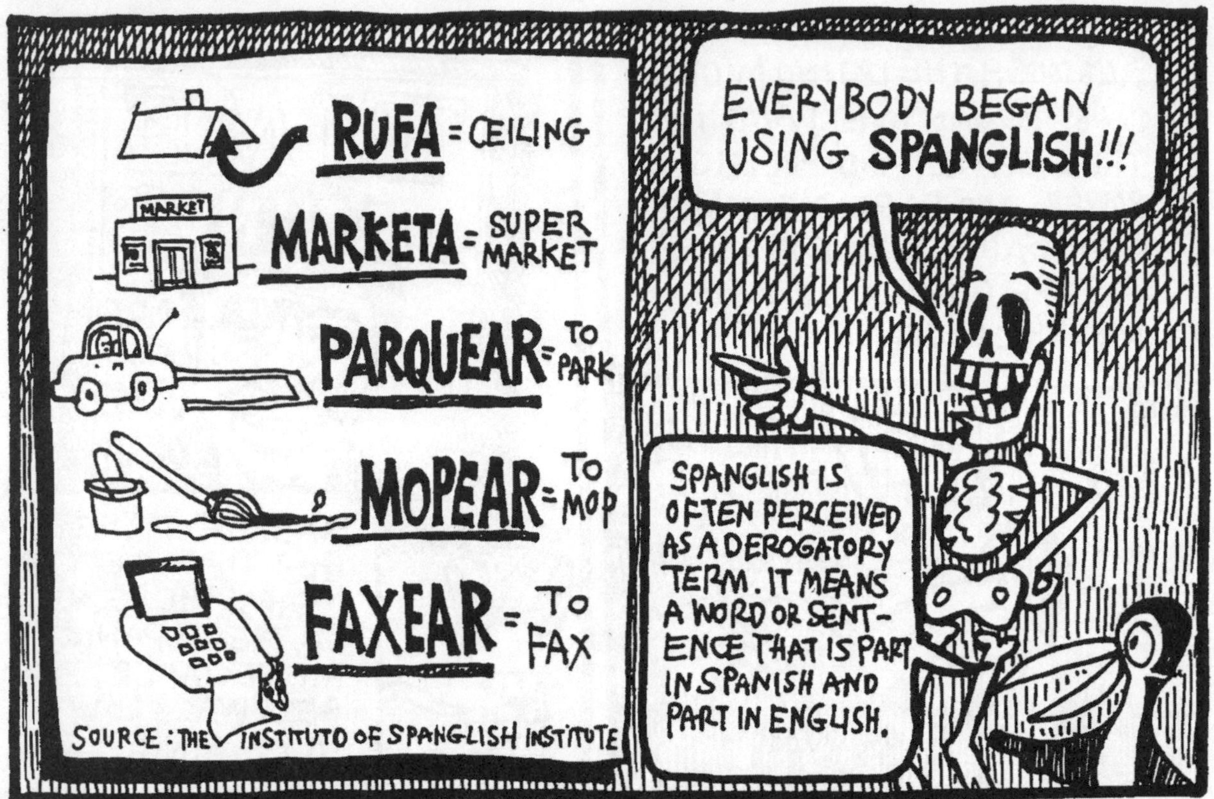
MARKET
RUFA = CEILING
MARKETA = SUPER MARKET
PARQUEAR = TO PARK
MOPEAR = TO MOP
FAXEAR = TO FAX
SOURCE: THE INSTITUTO OF SPANGLISH INSTITUTE
EVERYBODY BEGAN USING SPANGLISH!!!
SPANGLISH IS OFTEN PERCEIVED AS A DEROGATORY TERM. IT MEANS A WORD OR SENTENCE THAT IS PART IN SPANISH AND PART IN ENGLISH.

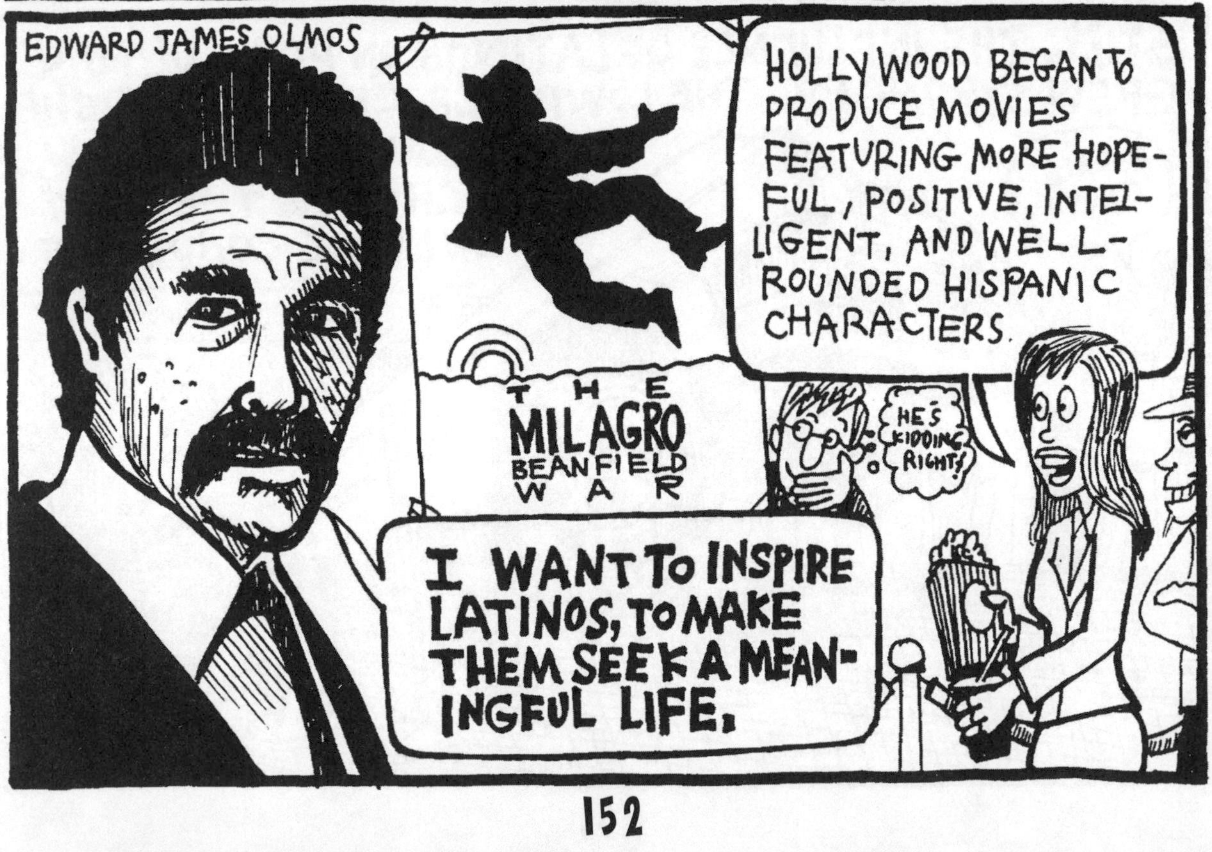
EDWARD JAMES OLMOS
THE MILAGRO BEANFIELD WAR
HOLLYWOOD BEGAN TO PRODUCE MOVIES FEATURING MORE HOPEFUL, POSITIVE, INTELLIGENT, AND WELL-ROUNDED HISPANIC CHARACTERS.
HE'S KIDDING, RIGHT?
I WANT TO INSPIRE LATINOS, TO MAKE THEM SEEK A MEANINGFUL LIFE.

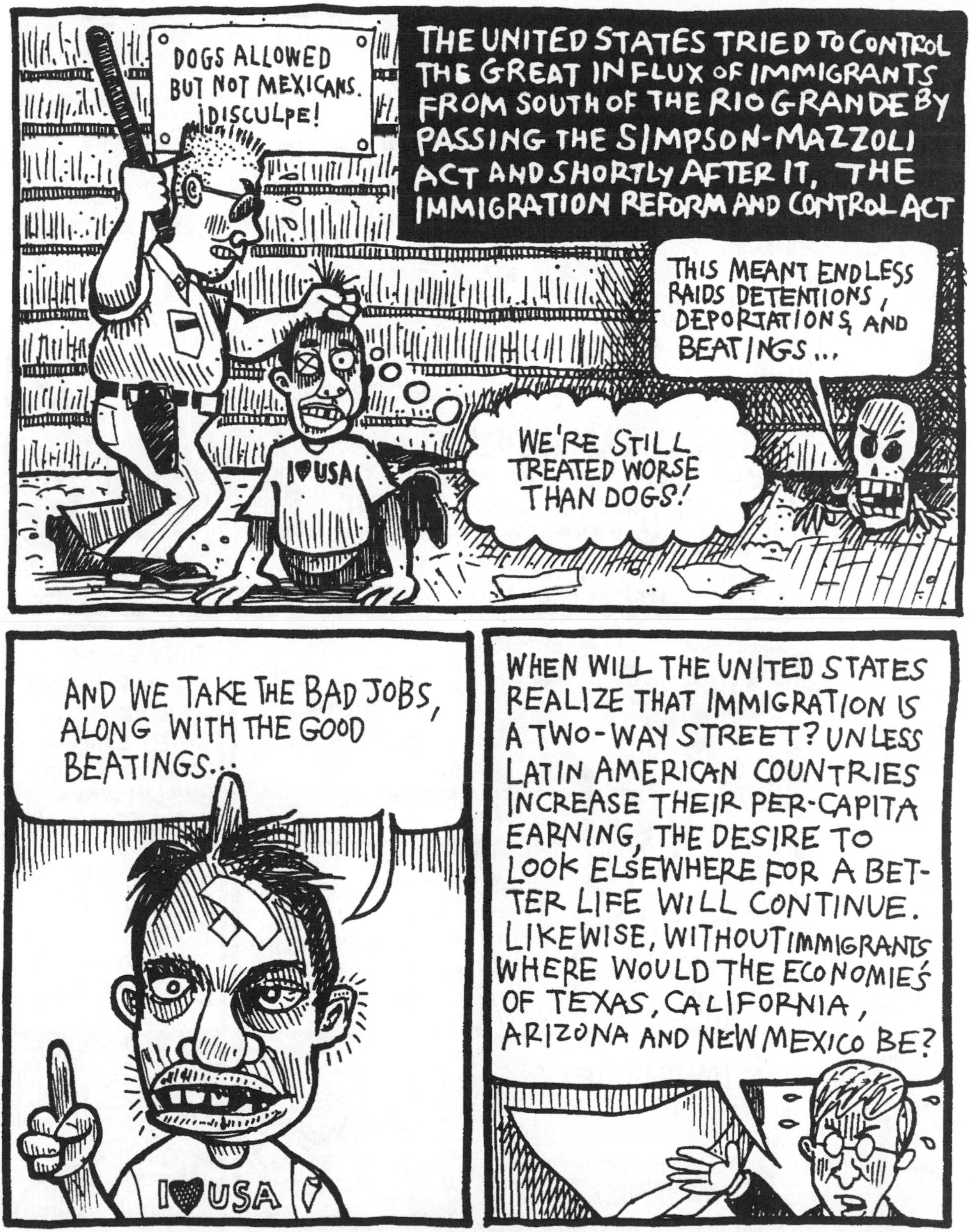
DOGS ALLOWED BUT NOT MEXICANS. ¡DISCULPE!
THE UNITED STATES TRIED TO CONTROL THE GREAT INFLUX OF IMMIGRANTS FROM SOUTH OF THE RIO GRANDE BY PASSING THE SIMPSON-MAZZOLI ACT AND SHORTLY AFTER IT, THE IMMIGRATION REFORM AND CONTROL ACT
THIS MEANT ENDLESS RAIDS DETENTIONS, DEPORTATIONS, AND BEATINGS...
I ♥ USA
WE'RE STILL TREATED WORSE THAN DOGS!
AND WE TAKE THE BAD JOBS, ALONG WITH THE GOOD BEATINGS...
I ♥ USA
WHEN WILL THE UNITED STATES REALIZE THAT IMMIGRATION IS A TWO-WAY STREET? UNLESS LATIN AMERICAN COUNTRIES INCREASE THEIR PER-CAPITA EARNING, THE DESIRE TO LOOK ELSEWHERE FOR A BETTER LIFE WILL CONTINUE. LIKEWISE, WITHOUT IMMIGRANTS WHERE WOULD THE ECONOMIE'S OF TEXAS, CALIFORNIA, ARIZONA AND NEW MEXICO BE?

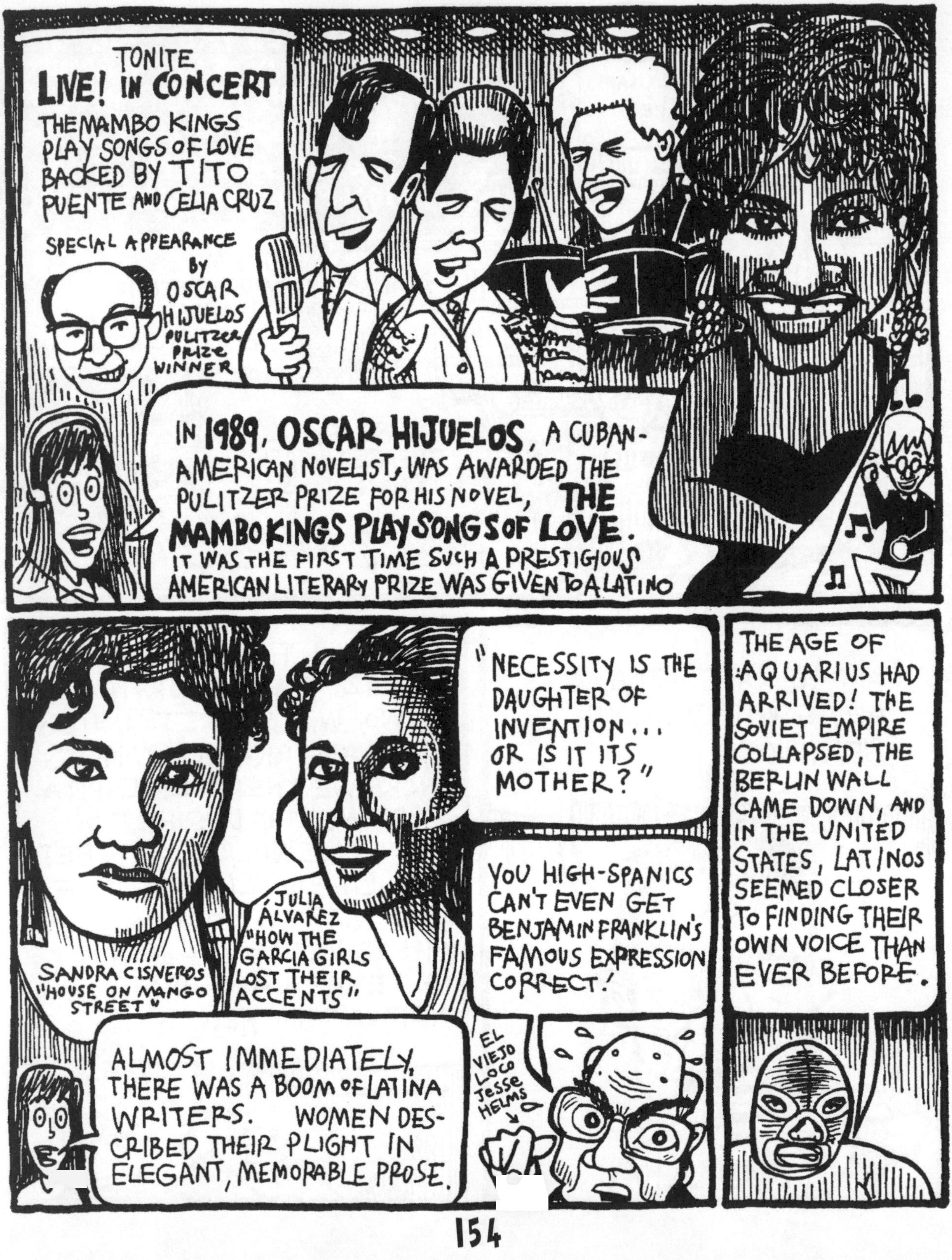
TONITE
LIVE! IN CONCERT
THE MAMBO KINGS PLAY SONGS OF LOVE BACKED BY TITO PUENTE AND CELIA CRUZ
SPECIAL APPEARANCE BY OSCAR HIJUELOS PULITZER PRIZE WINNER
IN 1989, OSCAR HIJUELOS, A CUBAN-AMERICAN NOVELIST, WAS AWARDED THE PULITZER PRIZE FOR HIS NOVEL, THE MAMBO KINGS PLAY SONGS OF LOVE. IT WAS THE FIRST TIME SUCH A PRESTIGIOUS AMERICAN LITERARY PRIZE WAS GIVEN TO A LATINO
SANDRA CISNEROS "HOUSE ON MANGO STREET"
JULIA ALVAREZ "HOW THE GARCIA GIRLS LOST THEIR ACCENTS"
"NECESSITY IS THE DAUGHTER OF INVENTION... OR IS IT ITS MOTHER?"
ALMOST IMMEDIATELY, THERE WAS A BOOM OF LATINA WRITERS. WOMEN DESCRIBED THEIR PLIGHT IN ELEGANT, MEMORABLE PROSE.
YOU HIGH-SPANICS CAN'T EVEN GET BENJAMIN FRANKLIN'S FAMOUS EXPRESSION CORRECT!
EL VIEJO LOCO JESSE HELMS
THE AGE OF AQUARIUS HAD ARRIVED! THE SOVIET EMPIRE COLLAPSED, THE BERLIN WALL CAME DOWN, AND IN THE UNITED STATES, LATINOS SEEMED CLOSER TO FINDING THEIR OWN VOICE THAN EVER BEFORE.

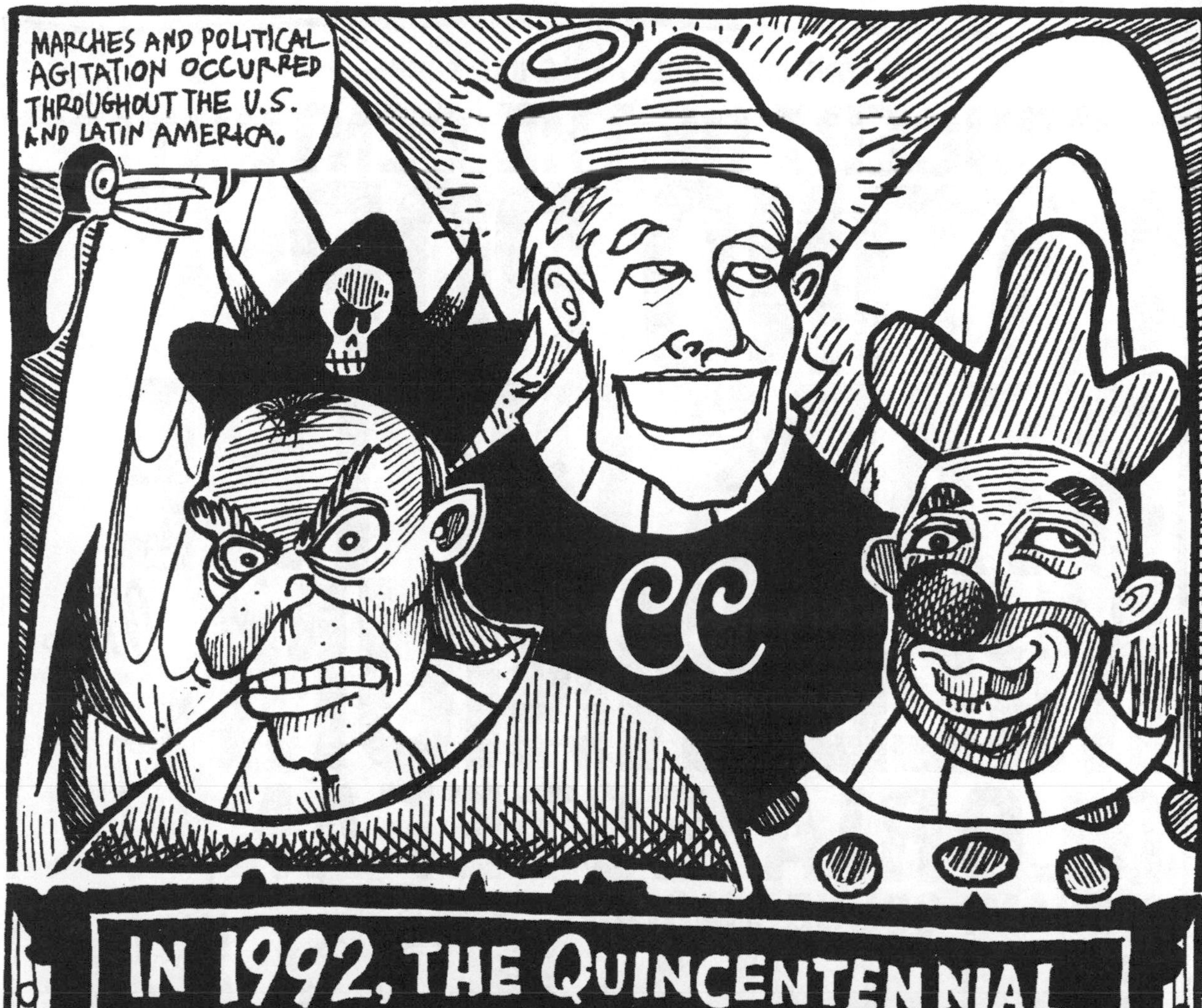
MARCHES AND POLITICAL AGITATION OCCURRED THROUGHOUT THE U.S. AND LATIN AMERICA.
CC
IN 1992, THE QUINCENTENNIAL OF COLUMBUS' VOYAGE TO THE NEW WORLD WAS CELEBRATED WORLDWIDE. A PUBLIC DEBATE ERUPTED: HAD THE SPANIARDS BEEN TOO VIOLENT IN THEIR ENTERPRISE ACROSS THE ATLANTIC? SHOULDN'T SUCH AN EVENT—THE ARRIVAL OF EUROPEANS TO THE AMERICAS—BE CONDEMNED?

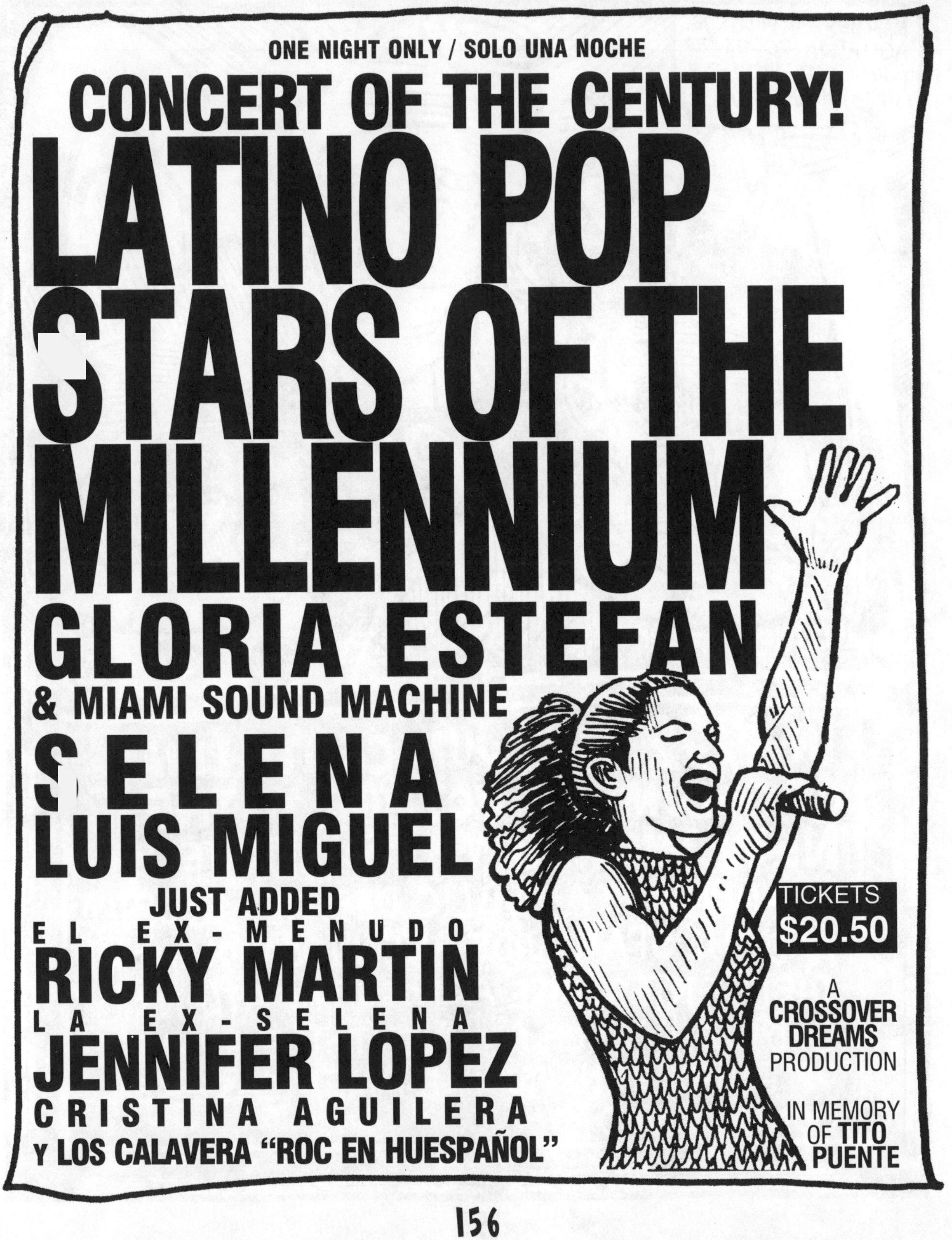
ONE NIGHT ONLY / SOLO UNA NOCHE
CONCERT OF THE CENTURY!
LATINO POP STARS OF THE MILLENNIUM
GLORIA ESTEFAN
& MIAMI SOUND MACHINE
SELENA
LUIS MIGUEL
JUST ADDED
EL EX-MENUDO
RICKY MARTIN
LA EX-SELENA
JENNIFER LOPEZ
CRISTINA AGUILERA
Y LOS CALAVERA "ROC EN HUESPAÑOL"
TICKETS $20.50
A CROSSOVER DREAMS PRODUCTION
IN MEMORY OF TITO PUENTE

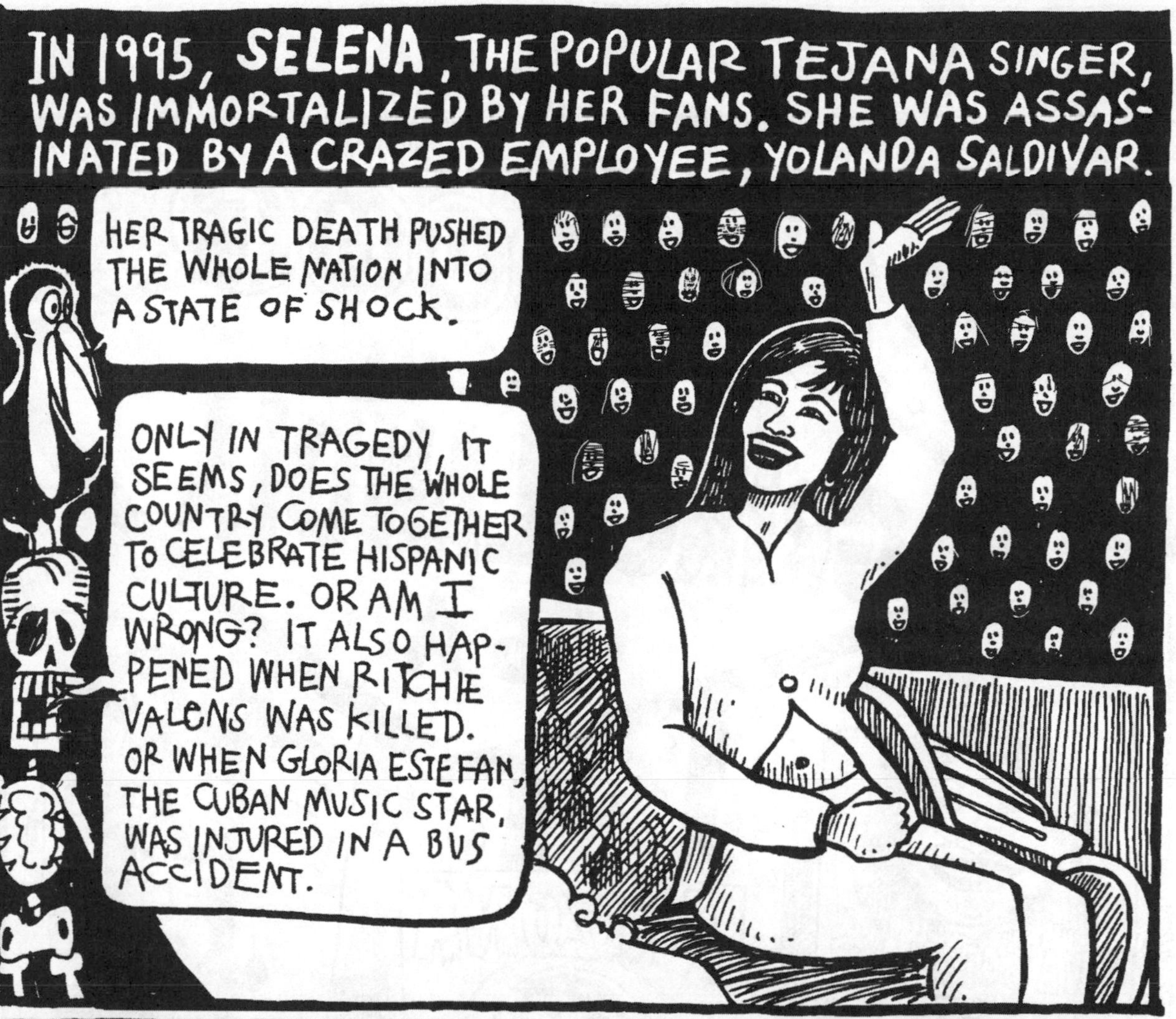
IN 1995, SELENA, THE POPULAR TEJANA SINGER, WAS IMMORTALIZED BY HER FANS. SHE WAS ASSASINATED BY A CRAZED EMPLOYEE, YOLANDA SALDIVAR.
HER TRAGIC DEATH PUSHED THE WHOLE NATION INTO A STATE OF SHOCK.
ONLY IN TRAGEDY, IT SEEMS, DOES THE WHOLE COUNTRY COME TOGETHER TO CELEBRATE HISPANIC CULTURE. OR AM I WRONG? IT ALSO HAPPENED WHEN RITCHIE VALENS WAS KILLED. OR WHEN GLORIA ESTEFAN, THE CUBAN MUSIC STAR, WAS INJURED IN A BUS ACCIDENT.
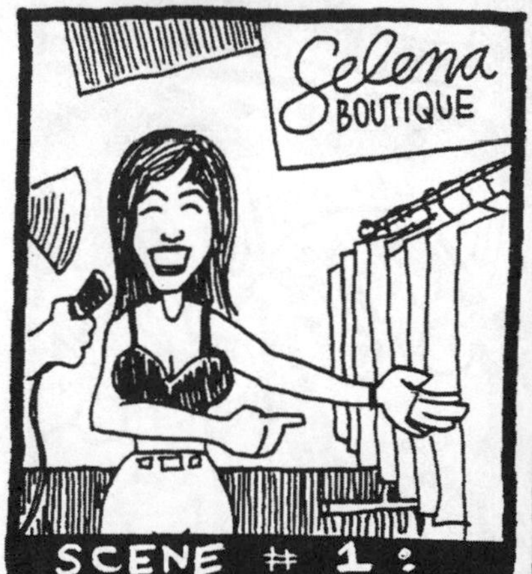
Selena BOUTIQUE
SCENE # 1: "NAME RECOGNITION"
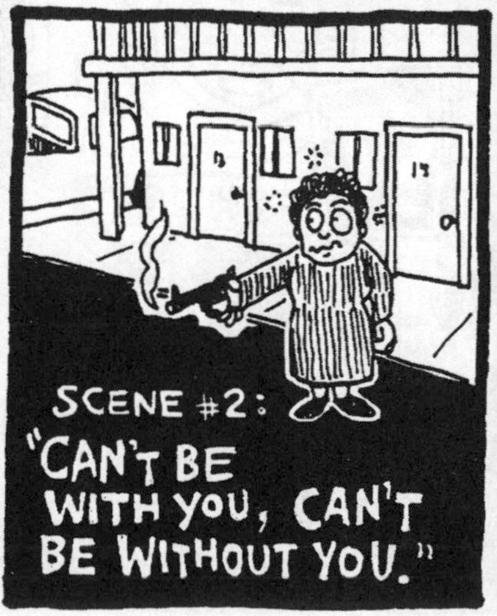
SCENE #2: "CAN'T BE WITH YOU, CAN'T BE WITHOUT YOU."
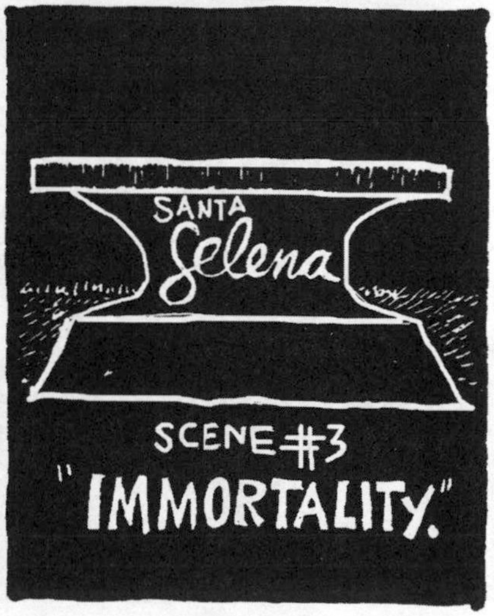
SANTA Selena
SCENE #3 "IMMORTALITY."

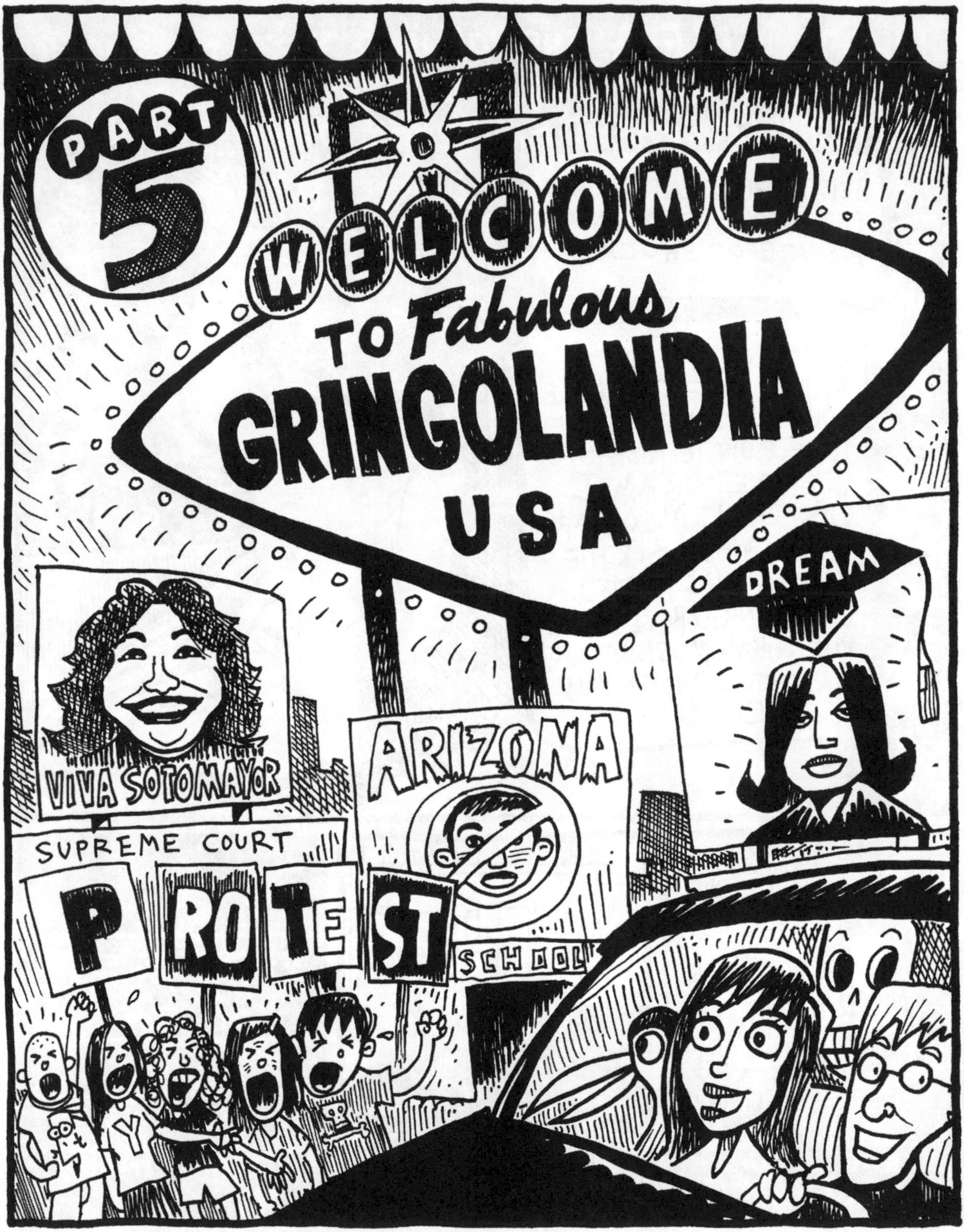
PART 5
WELCOME TO Fabulous GRINGOLANDIA USA
DREAM
VIVA SOTOMAYOR
ARIZONA
SUPREME COURT
PROTEST
SCHOOL

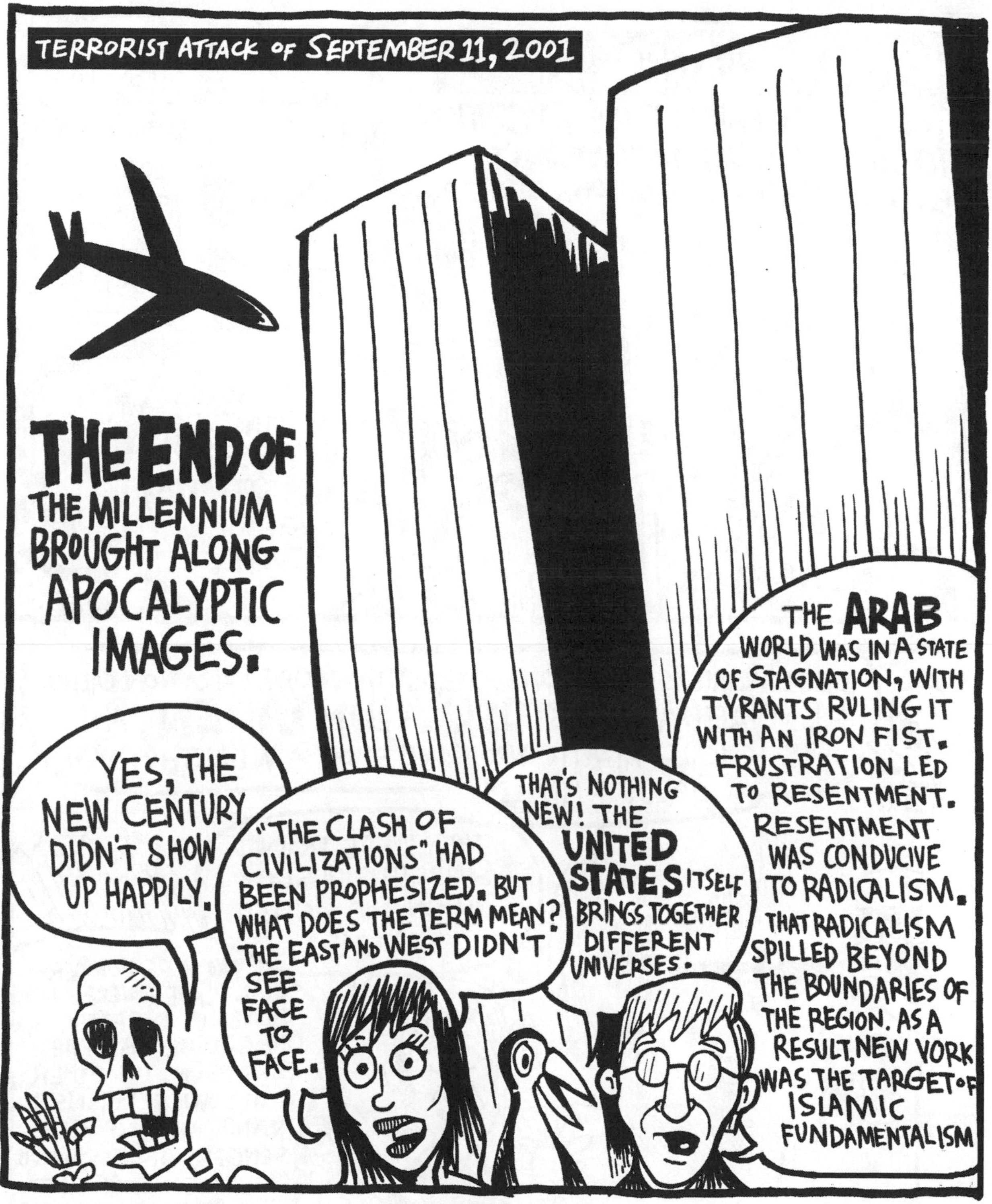
TERRORIST ATTACK OF SEPTEMBER 11, 2001
THE END OF THE MILLENNIUM BROUGHT ALONG APOCALYPTIC IMAGES.
YES, THE NEW CENTURY DIDN'T SHOW UP HAPPILY.
"THE CLASH OF CIVILIZATIONS" HAD BEEN PROPHESIZED. BUT WHAT DOES THE TERM MEAN? THE EAST AND WEST DIDN'T SEE FACE TO FACE.
THAT'S NOTHING NEW! THE UNITED STATES ITSELF BRINGS TOGETHER DIFFERENT UNIVERSES.
THE ARAB WORLD WAS IN A STATE OF STAGNATION, WITH TYRANTS RULING IT WITH AN IRON FIST. FRUSTRATION LED TO RESENTMENT. RESENTMENT WAS CONDUCIVE TO RADICALISM. THAT RADICALISM SPILLED BEYOND THE BOUNDARIES OF THE REGION. AS A RESULT, NEW YORK WAS THE TARGET OF ISLAMIC FUNDAMENTALISM

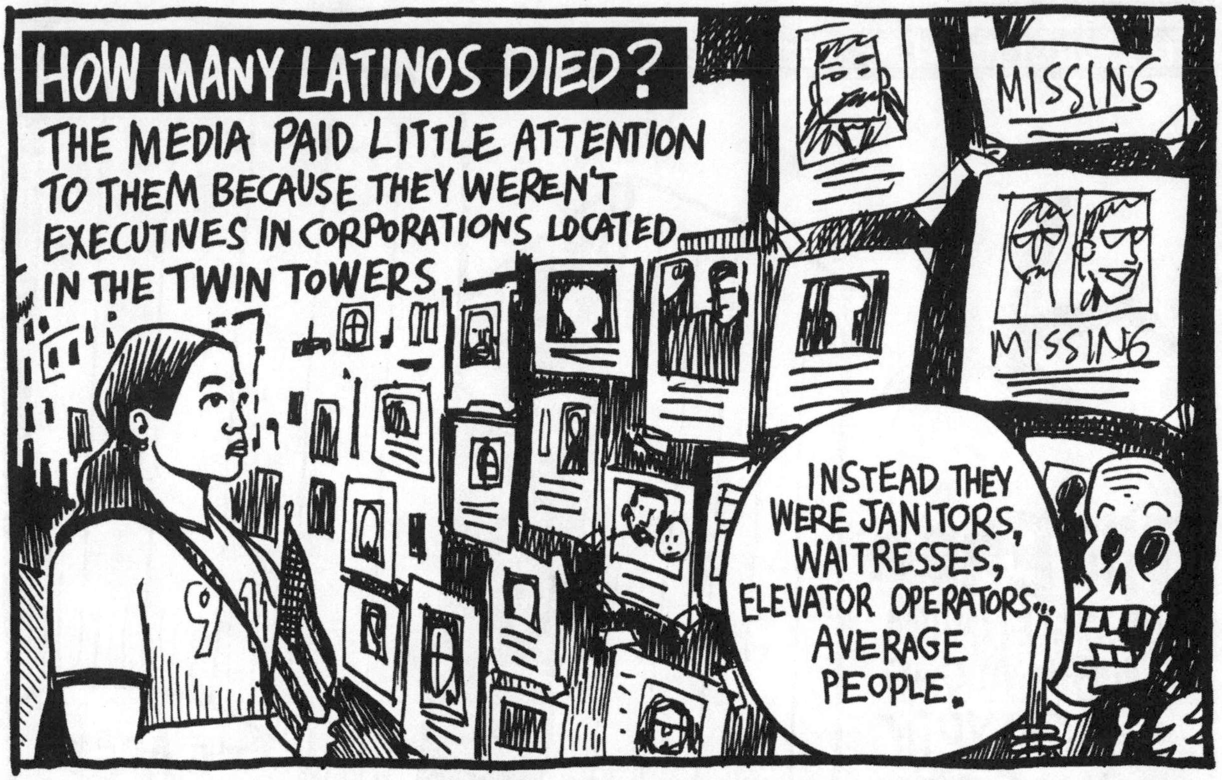
HOW MANY LATINOS DIED?
THE MEDIA PAID LITTLE ATTENTION TO THEM BECAUSE THEY WEREN'T EXECUTIVES IN CORPORATIONS LOCATED IN THE TWIN TOWERS
MISSING
MISSING
INSTEAD THEY WERE JANITORS, WAITRESSES, ELEVATOR OPERATORS... AVERAGE PEOPLE.

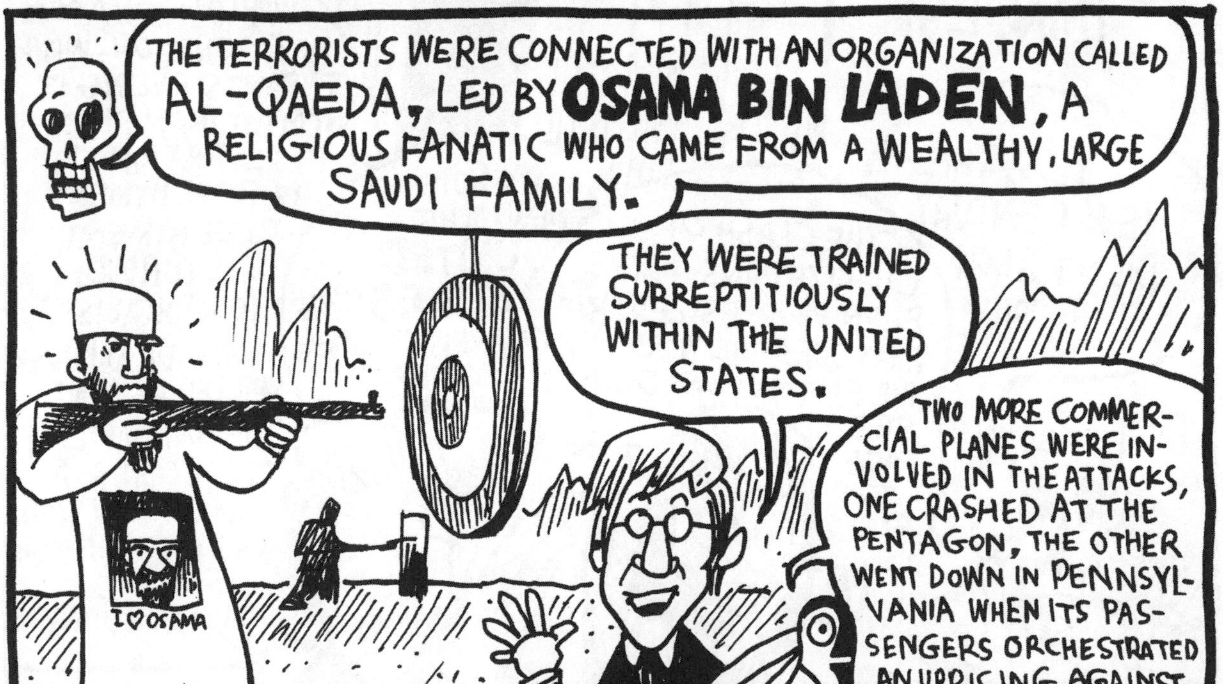
THE TERRORISTS WERE CONNECTED WITH AN ORGANIZATION CALLED AL-QAEDA, LED BY OSAMA BIN LADEN, A RELIGIOUS FANATIC WHO CAME FROM A WEALTHY, LARGE SAUDI FAMILY.
I ♡ OSAMA
THEY WERE TRAINED SURREPTITIOUSLY WITHIN THE UNITED STATES.
TWO MORE COMMERCIAL PLANES WERE INVOLVED IN THE ATTACKS, ONE CRASHED AT THE PENTAGON, THE OTHER WENT DOWN IN PENNSYLVANIA WHEN ITS PASSENGERS ORCHESTRATED AN UPRISING AGAINST THE AIRPLANES HIJACKERS

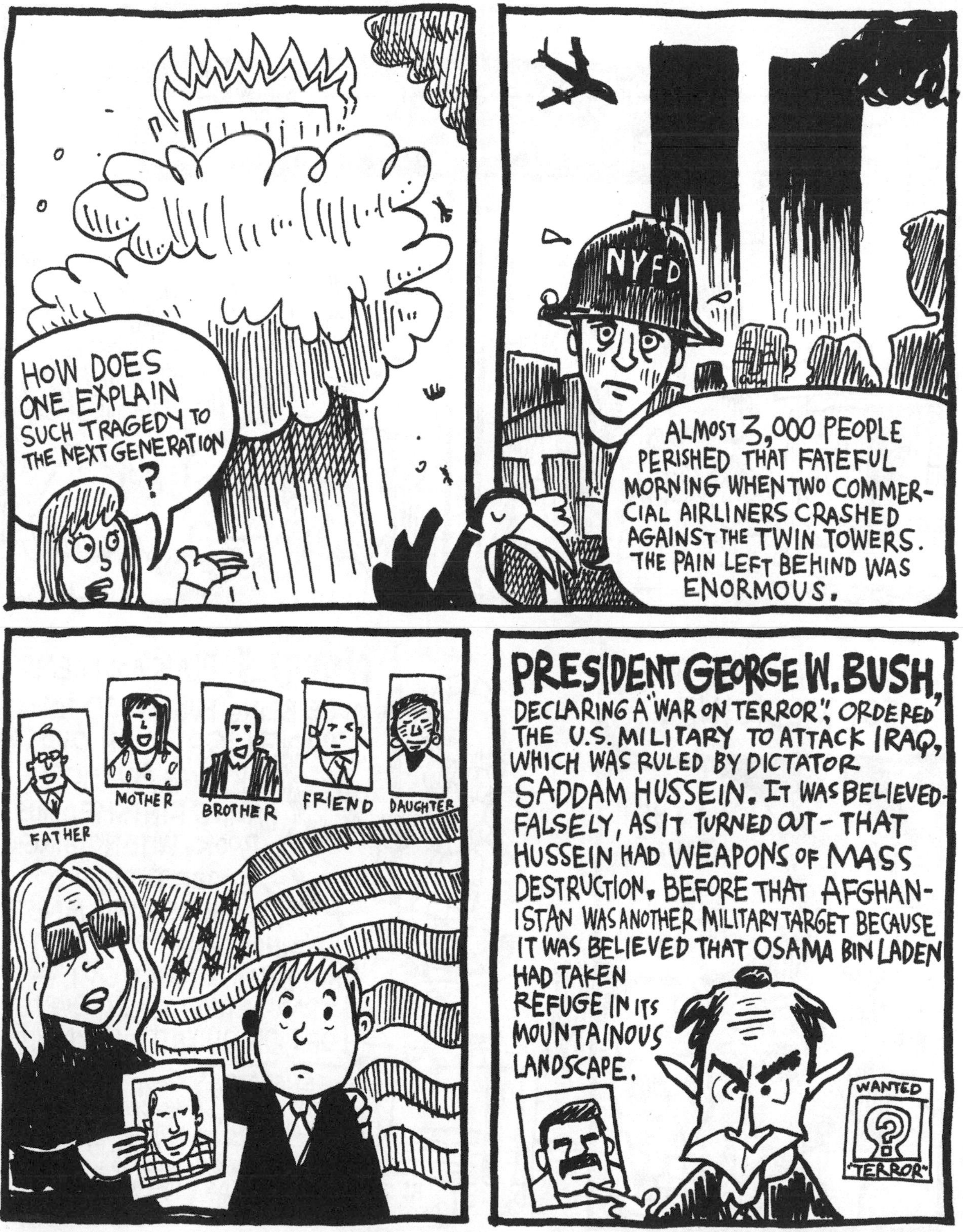
HOW DOES ONE EXPLAIN SUCH TRAGEDY TO THE NEXT GENERATION ?
NYFD
ALMOST 3,000 PEOPLE PERISHED THAT FATEFUL MORNING WHEN TWO COMMERCIAL AIRLINERS CRASHED AGAINST THE TWIN TOWERS. THE PAIN LEFT BEHIND WAS ENORMOUS.
FATHER
MOTHER
BROTHER
FRIEND
DAUGHTER
PRESIDENT GEORGE W. BUSH, DECLARING A "WAR ON TERROR", ORDERED THE U.S. MILITARY TO ATTACK IRAQ, WHICH WAS RULED BY DICTATOR SADDAM HUSSEIN. IT WAS BELIEVED- FALSELY, AS IT TURNED OUT - THAT HUSSEIN HAD WEAPONS OF MASS DESTRUCTION. BEFORE THAT AFGHANISTAN WAS ANOTHER MILITARY TARGET BECAUSE IT WAS BELIEVED THAT OSAMA BIN LADEN HAD TAKEN REFUGE IN ITS MOUNTAINOUS LANDSCAPE.
WANTED
"TERROR"

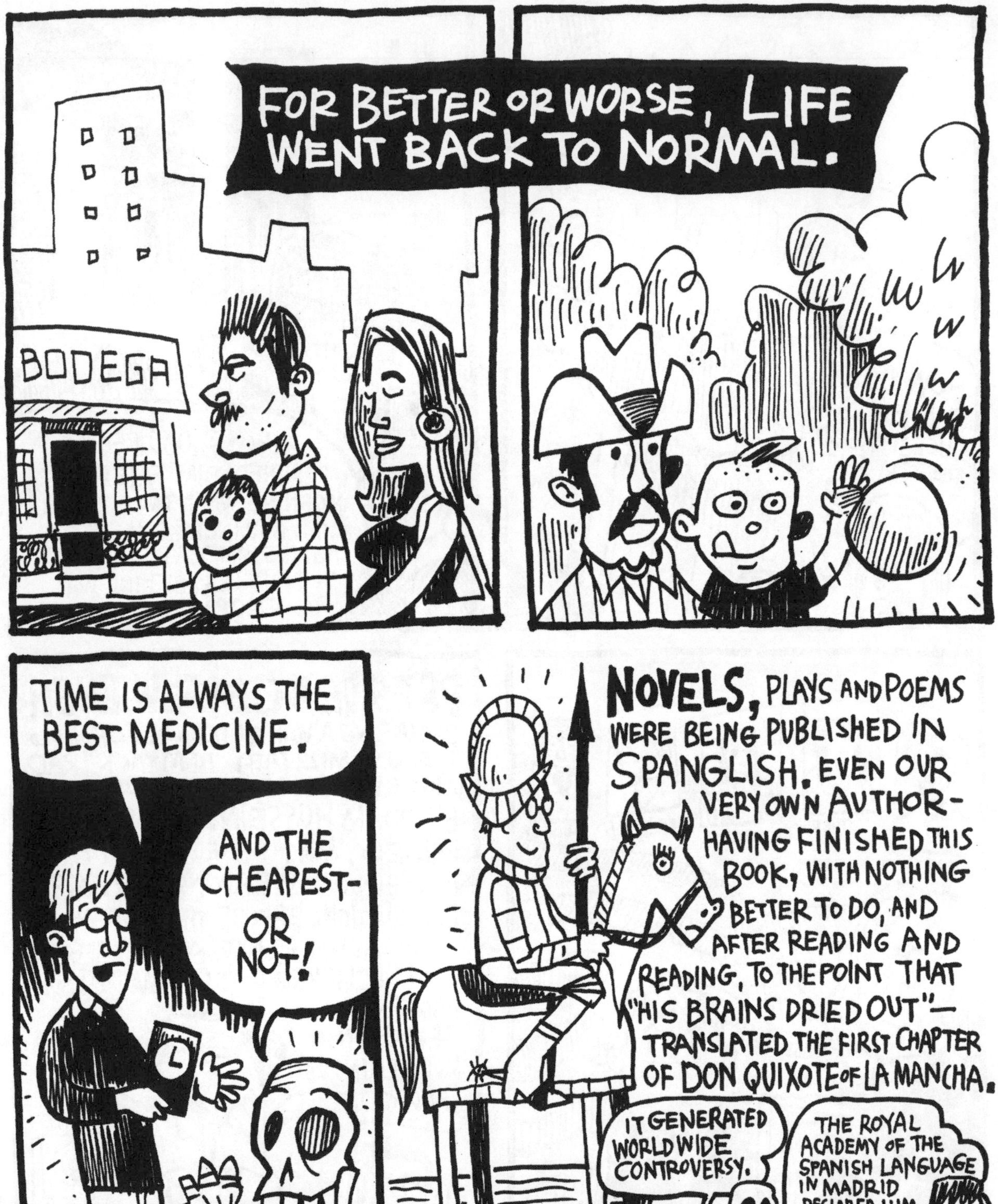
FOR BETTER OR WORSE, LIFE WENT BACK TO NORMAL.
BODEGA
TIME IS ALWAYS THE BEST MEDICINE.
AND THE CHEAPEST- OR NOT!
NOVELS, PLAYS AND POEMS WERE BEING PUBLISHED IN SPANGLISH. EVEN OUR VERY OWN AUTHOR- HAVING FINISHED THIS BOOK, WITH NOTHING BETTER TO DO, AND AFTER READING AND READING, TO THE POINT THAT "HIS BRAINS DRIED OUT"— TRANSLATED THE FIRST CHAPTER OF DON QUIXOTE OF LA MANCHA.
IT GENERATED WORLD WIDE CONTROVERSY.
HE GOT DEATH THREATS!
THE ROYAL ACADEMY OF THE SPANISH LANGUAGE IN MADRID DECLARED HIM PERSONA NON GRATA.

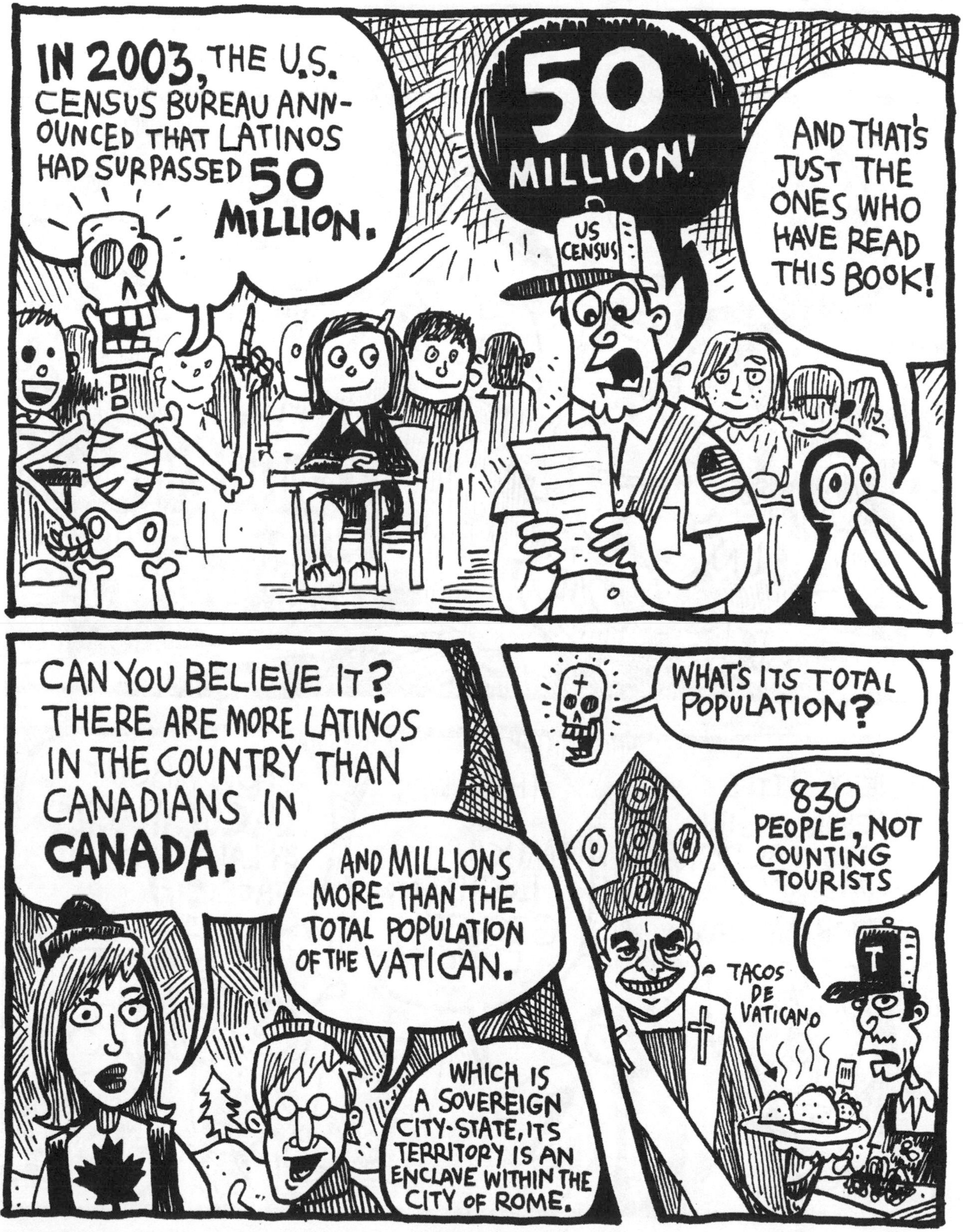
IN 2003, THE U.S. CENSUS BUREAU ANNOUNCED THAT LATINOS HAD SURPASSED 50 MILLION.
50 MILLION!
US CENSUS
AND THAT'S JUST THE ONES WHO HAVE READ THIS BOOK!
CAN YOU BELIEVE IT? THERE ARE MORE LATINOS IN THE COUNTRY THAN CANADIANS IN CANADA.
AND MILLIONS MORE THAN THE TOTAL POPULATION OF THE VATICAN.
WHICH IS A SOVEREIGN CITY-STATE, ITS TERRITORY IS AN ENCLAVE WITHIN THE CITY OF ROME.
WHAT'S ITS TOTAL POPULATION?
830 PEOPLE, NOT COUNTING TOURISTS
TACOS DE VATICANO
T

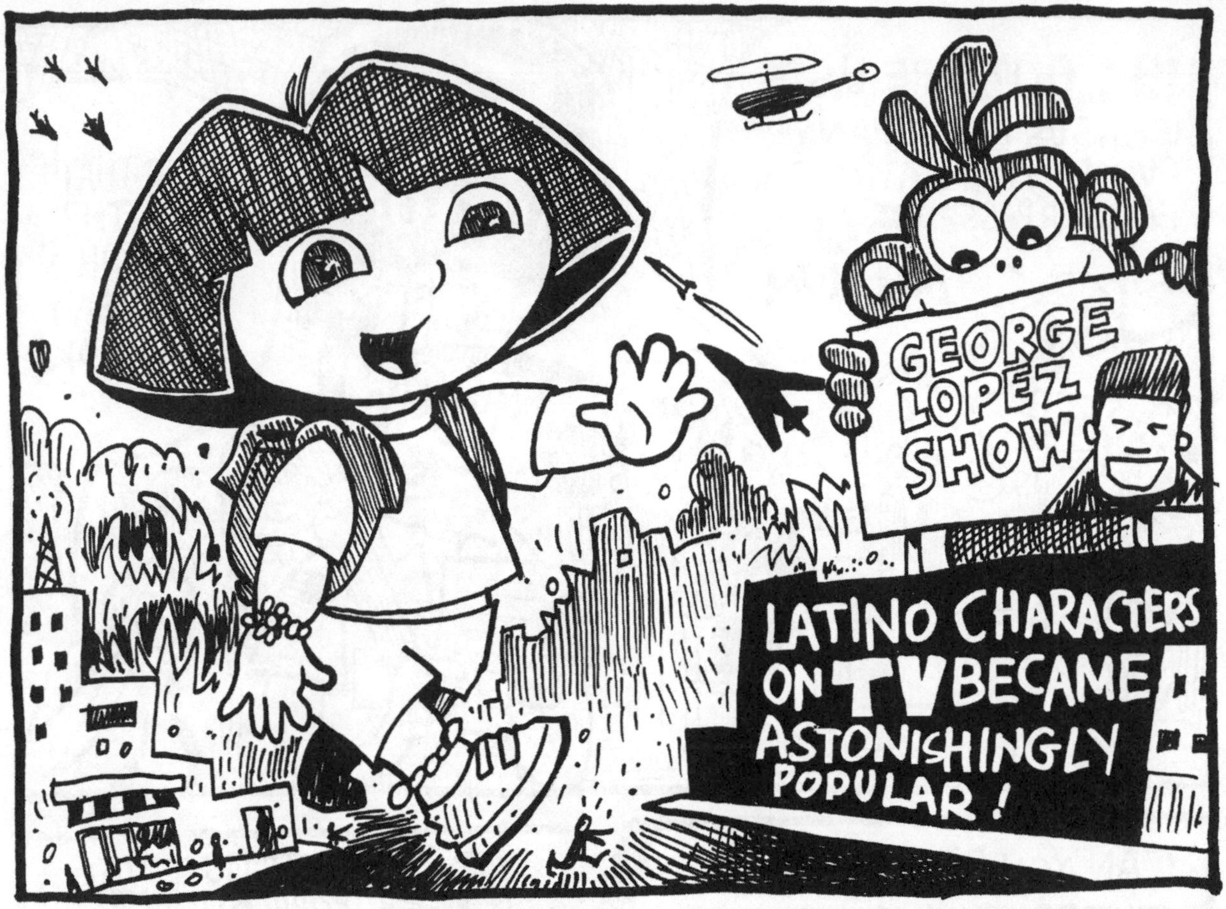
GEORGE LOPEZ SHOW
LATINO CHARACTERS ON TV BECAME ASTONISHINGLY POPULAR!

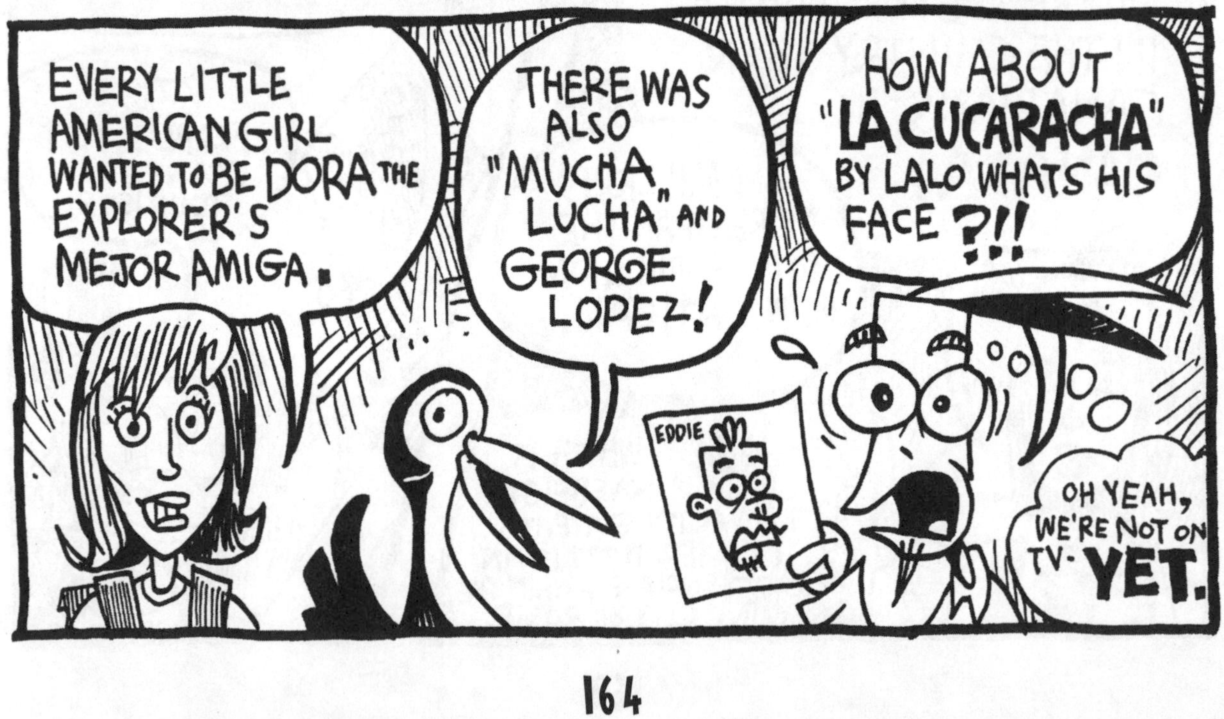
EVERY LITTLE AMERICAN GIRL WANTED TO BE DORA THE EXPLORER'S MEJOR AMIGA.
THERE WAS ALSO "MUCHA LUCHA" AND GEORGE LOPEZ!
HOW ABOUT "LA CUCARACHA" BY LALO WHATS HIS FACE ?!!
EDDIE
OH YEAH, WE'RE NOT ON TV- YET.

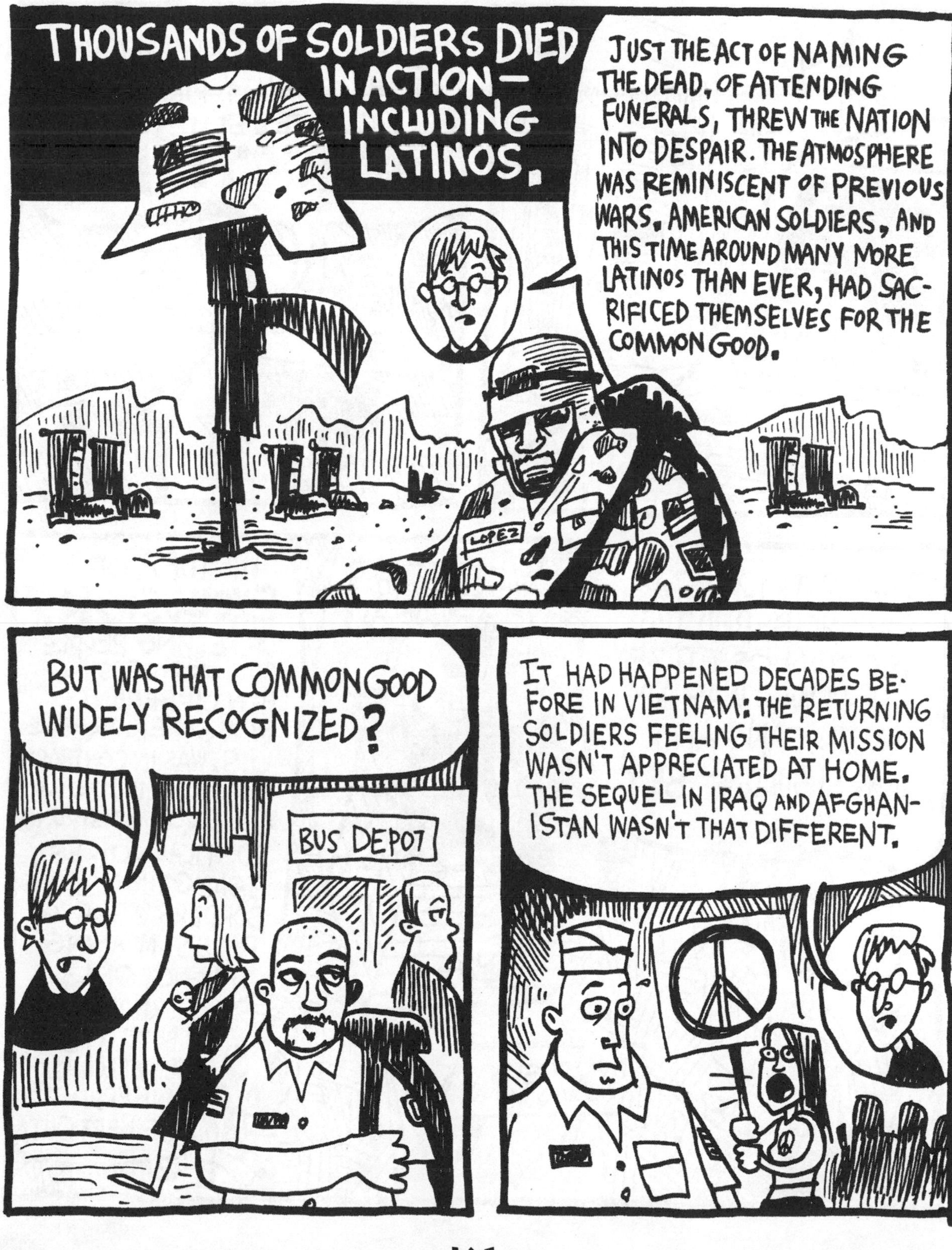
THOUSANDS OF SOLDIERS DIED IN ACTION— INCLUDING LATINOS.
JUST THE ACT OF NAMING THE DEAD, OF ATTENDING FUNERALS, THREW THE NATION INTO DESPAIR. THE ATMOSPHERE WAS REMINISCENT OF PREVIOUS WARS. AMERICAN SOLDIERS, AND THIS TIME AROUND MANY MORE LATINOS THAN EVER, HAD SACRIFICED THEMSELVES FOR THE COMMON GOOD.
LOPEZ
BUT WAS THAT COMMON GOOD WIDELY RECOGNIZED?
BUS DEPOT
IT HAD HAPPENED DECADES BEFORE IN VIETNAM: THE RETURNING SOLDIERS FEELING THEIR MISSION WASN'T APPRECIATED AT HOME. THE SEQUEL IN IRAQ AND AFGHANISTAN WASN'T THAT DIFFERENT.

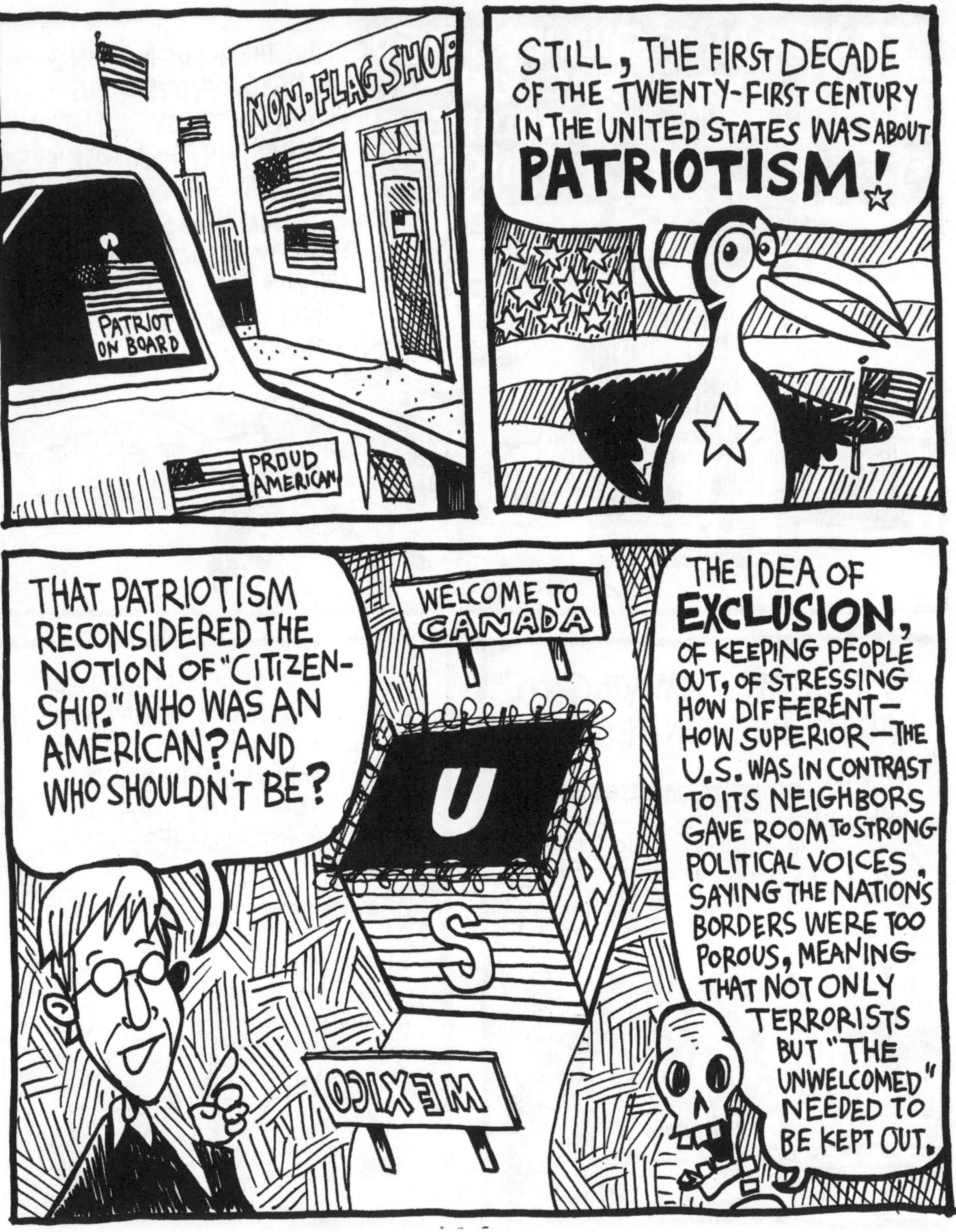

NON-FLAG SHOP
PATRIOT ON BOARD
PROUD AMERICAN
STILL, THE FIRST DECADE OF THE TWENTY-FIRST CENTURY IN THE UNITED STATES WAS ABOUT **PATRIOTISM!**
THAT PATRIOTISM RECONSIDERED THE NOTION OF "CITIZENSHIP." WHO WAS AN AMERICAN? AND WHO SHOULDN'T BE?
WELCOME TO CANADA
U
S
A
MEXICO
THE IDEA OF **EXCLUSION**, OF KEEPING PEOPLE OUT, OF STRESSING HOW DIFFERENT—HOW SUPERIOR—THE U.S. WAS IN CONTRAST TO ITS NEIGHBORS GAVE ROOM TO STRONG POLITICAL VOICES, SAYING THE NATION'S BORDERS WERE TOO POROUS, MEANING THAT NOT ONLY TERRORISTS BUT "THE UNWELCOMED" NEEDED TO BE KEPT OUT.

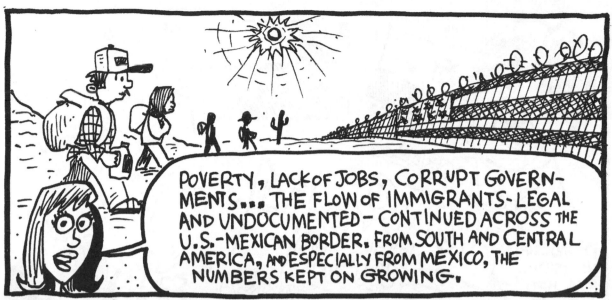

POVERTY, LACK OF JOBS, CORRUPT GOVERNMENTS... THE FLOW OF IMMIGRANTS - LEGAL AND UNDOCUMENTED - CONTINUED ACROSS THE U.S.-MEXICAN BORDER. FROM SOUTH AND CENTRAL AMERICA, AND ESPECIALLY FROM MEXICO, THE NUMBERS KEPT ON GROWING.

PRESIDENT BUSH WAS IN OFFICE. HE HAD BEEN CLOSE TO THE MEXICAN-AMERICAN COMMUNITY WHILE GOVERNOR OF TEXAS.

IN MEXICO, THE LONG-RULING PARTY **PRI** WAS PUSHED OUT OF OFFICE.

PAN

DEMOCRACY ARRIVED, ALTHOUGH IMPERFECTLY, AND PRESIDENTE VICENTE FOX WAS IN POWER. BUSH AND FOX WERE ABOUT TO OVERSEE A NEW ERA OF U.S.-MEXICAN RELATIONS. BUT BUSH GOT DISTRACTED BY...

THE WAR ON TERROR. HE GOT COLD FEET.

END IMMIG.

A CONSERVATIVE MOOD WAS ON THE RISE.

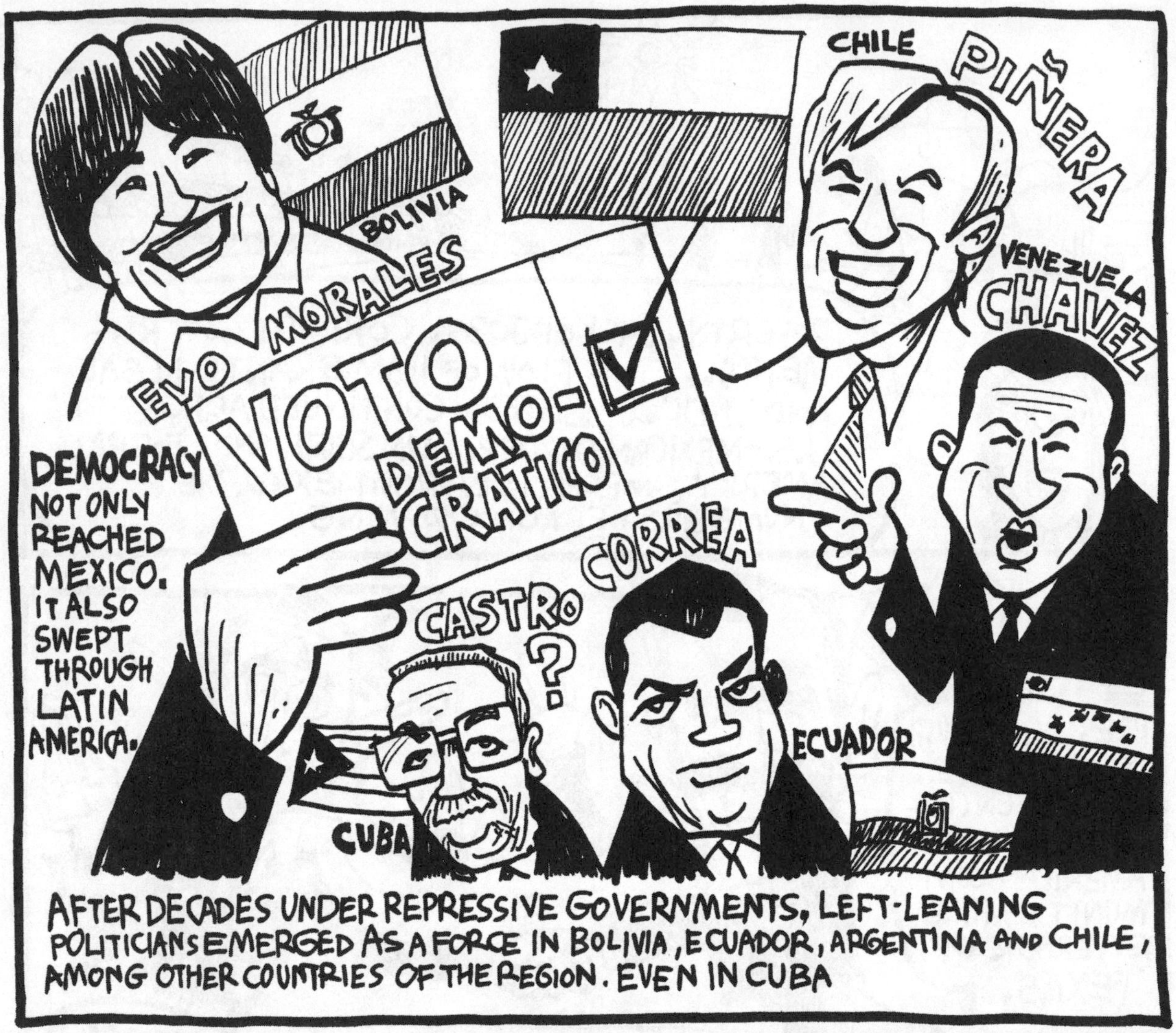
BOLIVIA
EVO MORALES
CHILE
PIÑERA
VENEZUELA
CHAVEZ
VOTO DEMO-CRATICO
DEMOCRACY NOT ONLY REACHED MEXICO. IT ALSO SWEPT THROUGH LATIN AMERICA.
CORREA
CASTRO ?
ECUADOR
CUBA
AFTER DECADES UNDER REPRESSIVE GOVERNMENTS, LEFT-LEANING POLITICIANS EMERGED AS A FORCE IN BOLIVIA, ECUADOR, ARGENTINA AND CHILE, AMONG OTHER COUNTRIES OF THE REGION. EVEN IN CUBA

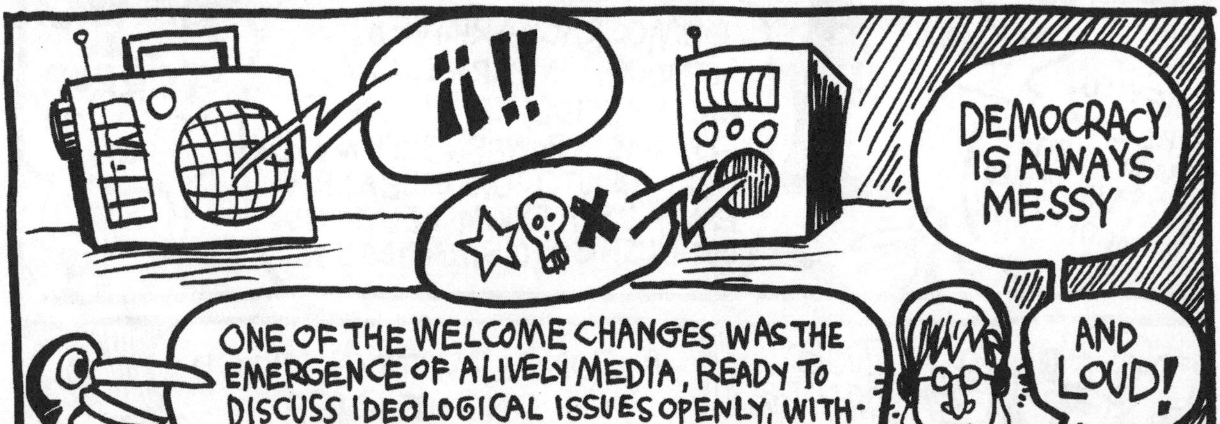
¡¡!!
DEMOCRACY IS ALWAYS MESSY
ONE OF THE WELCOME CHANGES WAS THE EMERGENCE OF A LIVELY MEDIA, READY TO DISCUSS IDEOLOGICAL ISSUES OPENLY, WITH-OUT RESERVATION.
AND LOUD!

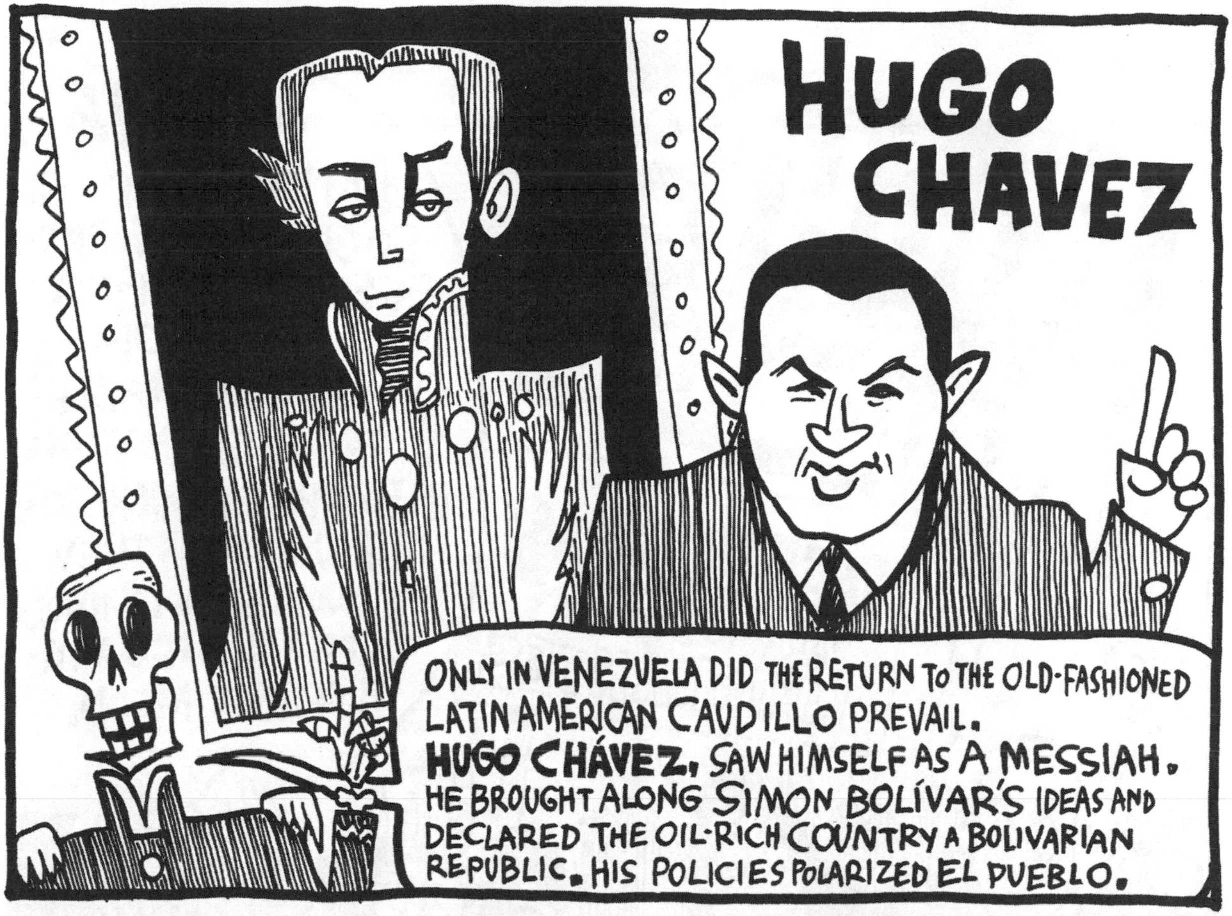
HUGO CHAVEZ
ONLY IN VENEZUELA DID THE RETURN TO THE OLD-FASHIONED LATIN AMERICAN CAUDILLO PREVAIL. HUGO CHÁVEZ, SAW HIMSELF AS A MESSIAH. HE BROUGHT ALONG SIMON BOLÍVAR'S IDEAS AND DECLARED THE OIL-RICH COUNTRY A BOLIVARIAN REPUBLIC. HIS POLICIES POLARIZED EL PUEBLO.

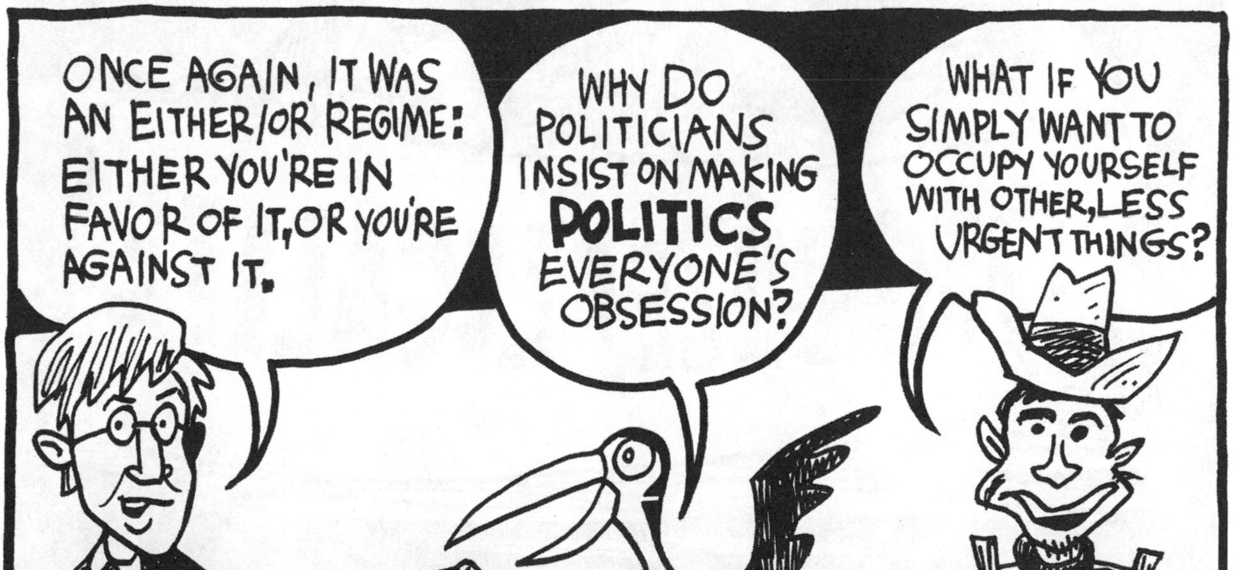
ONCE AGAIN, IT WAS AN EITHER/OR REGIME: EITHER YOU'RE IN FAVOR OF IT, OR YOU'RE AGAINST IT.
WHY DO POLITICIANS INSIST ON MAKING POLITICS EVERYONE'S OBSESSION?
WHAT IF YOU SIMPLY WANT TO OCCUPY YOURSELF WITH OTHER, LESS URGENT THINGS?

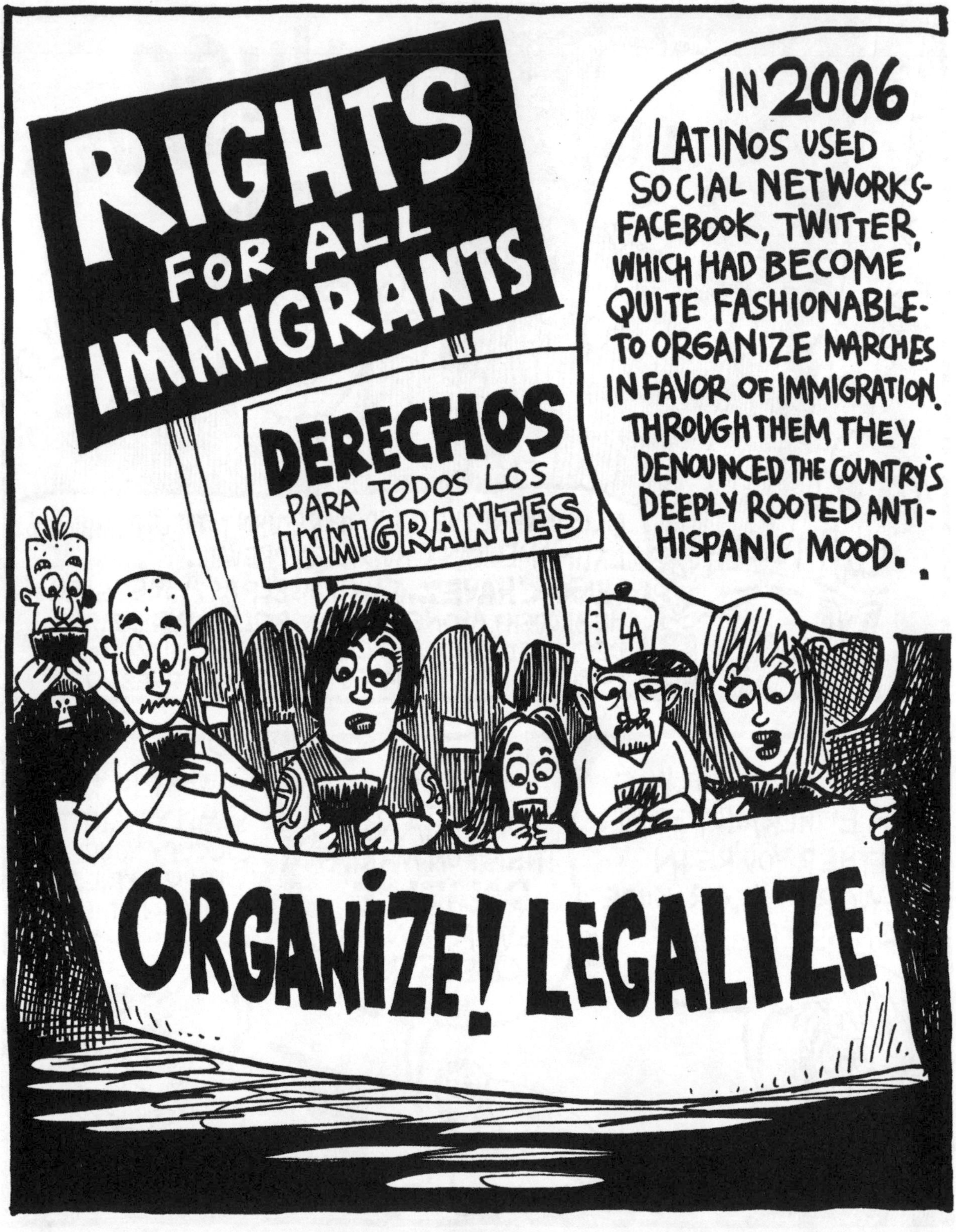
RIGHTS FOR ALL IMMIGRANTS
DERECHOS PARA TODOS LOS INMIGRANTES
IN 2006 LATINOS USED SOCIAL NETWORKS- FACEBOOK, TWITTER, WHICH HAD BECOME QUITE FASHIONABLE- TO ORGANIZE MARCHES IN FAVOR OF IMMIGRATION. THROUGH THEM THEY DENOUNCED THE COUNTRY'S DEEPLY ROOTED ANTI-HISPANIC MOOD..
LA
ORGANIZE! LEGALIZE

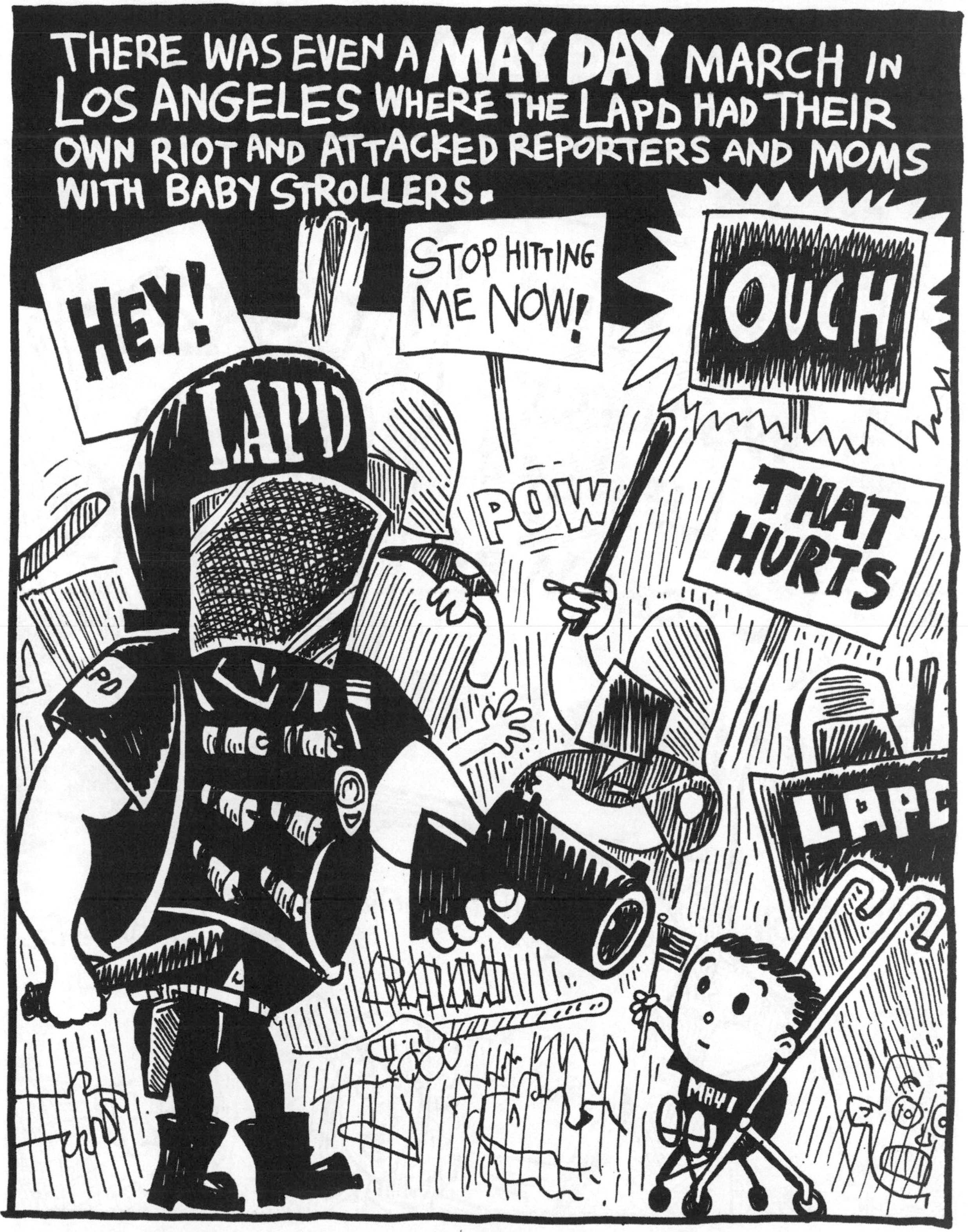
THERE WAS EVEN A MAY DAY MARCH IN LOS ANGELES WHERE THE LAPD HAD THEIR OWN RIOT AND ATTACKED REPORTERS AND MOMS WITH BABY STROLLERS.
HEY!
STOP HITTING ME NOW!
OUCH
LAPD
POW
THAT HURTS
PD
MAY 1

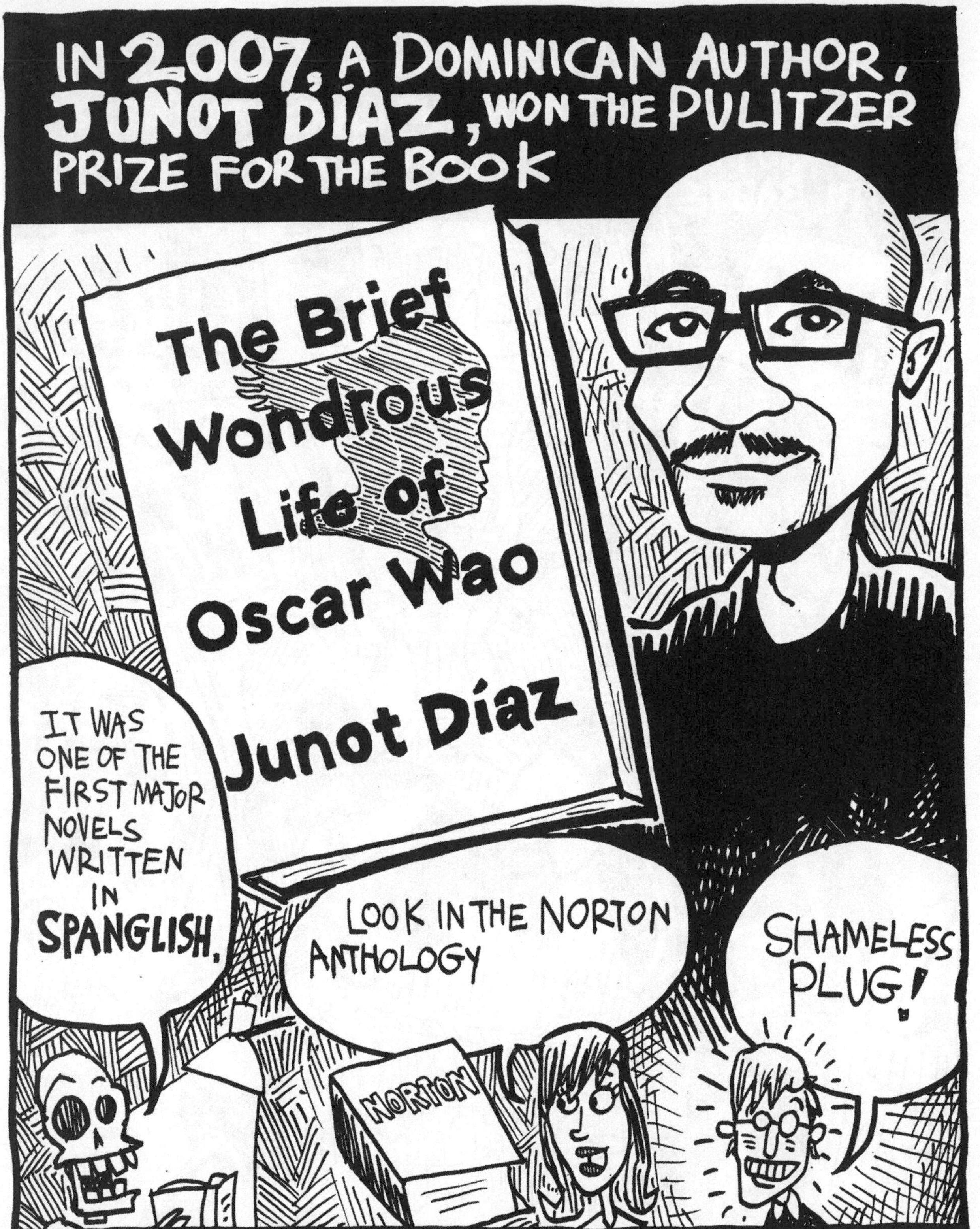
IN 2007, A DOMINICAN AUTHOR, JUNOT DÍAZ, WON THE PULITZER PRIZE FOR THE BOOK
The Brief Wondrous Life of Oscar Wao
Junot Díaz
IT WAS ONE OF THE FIRST MAJOR NOVELS WRITTEN IN SPANGLISH.
LOOK IN THE NORTON ANTHOLOGY
SHAMELESS PLUG!
NORTON

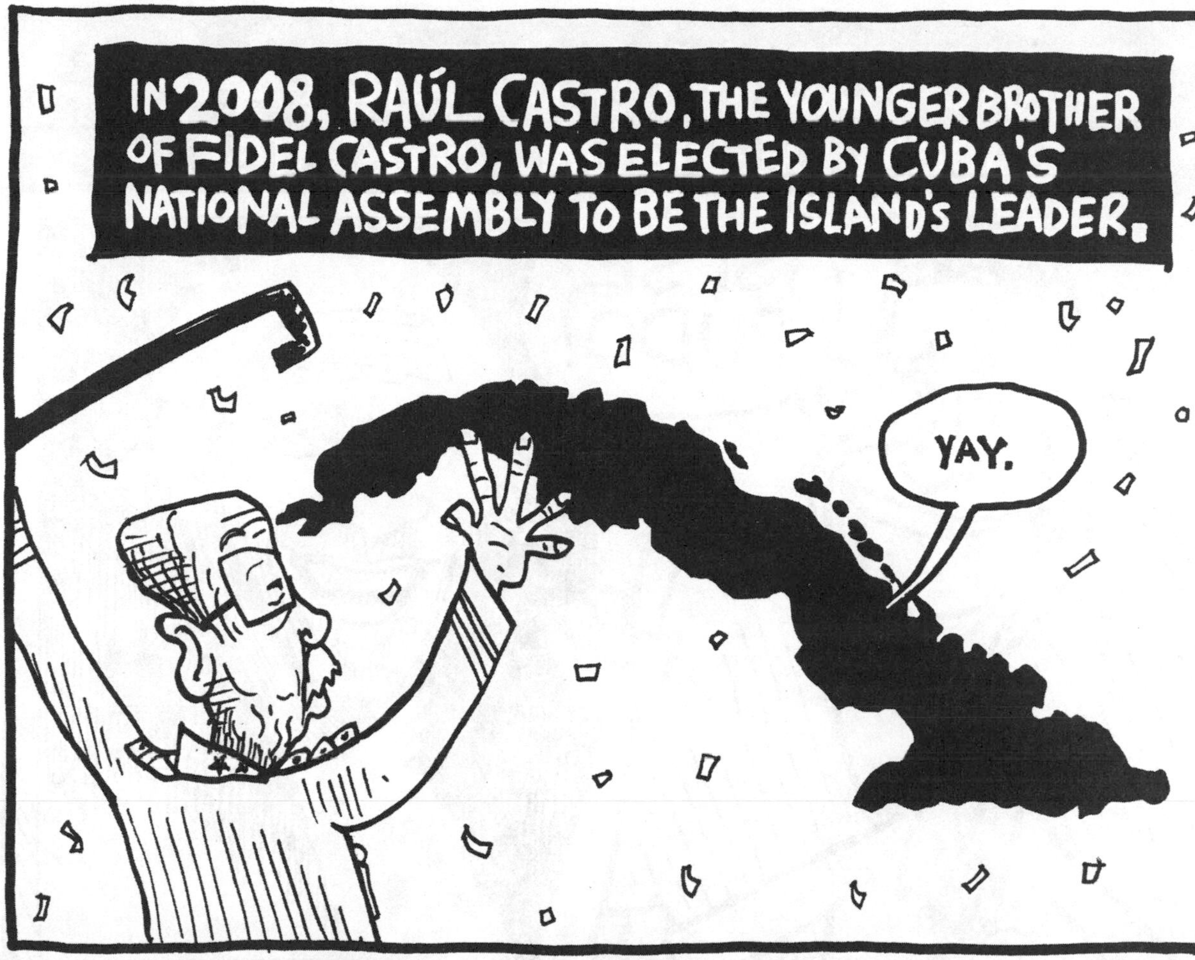
IN 2008, RAÚL CASTRO, THE YOUNGER BROTHER OF FIDEL CASTRO, WAS ELECTED BY CUBA'S NATIONAL ASSEMBLY TO BE THE ISLAND'S LEADER.
YAY.

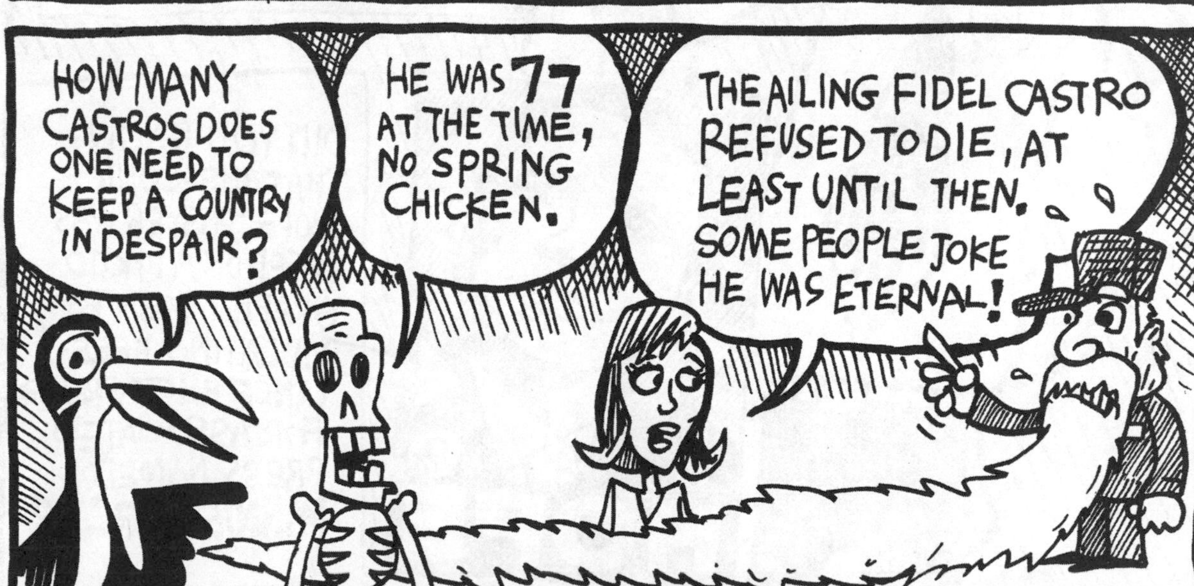
HOW MANY CASTROS DOES ONE NEED TO KEEP A COUNTRY IN DESPAIR?
HE WAS 77 AT THE TIME, NO SPRING CHICKEN.
THE AILING FIDEL CASTRO REFUSED TO DIE, AT LEAST UNTIL THEN. SOME PEOPLE JOKE HE WAS ETERNAL!

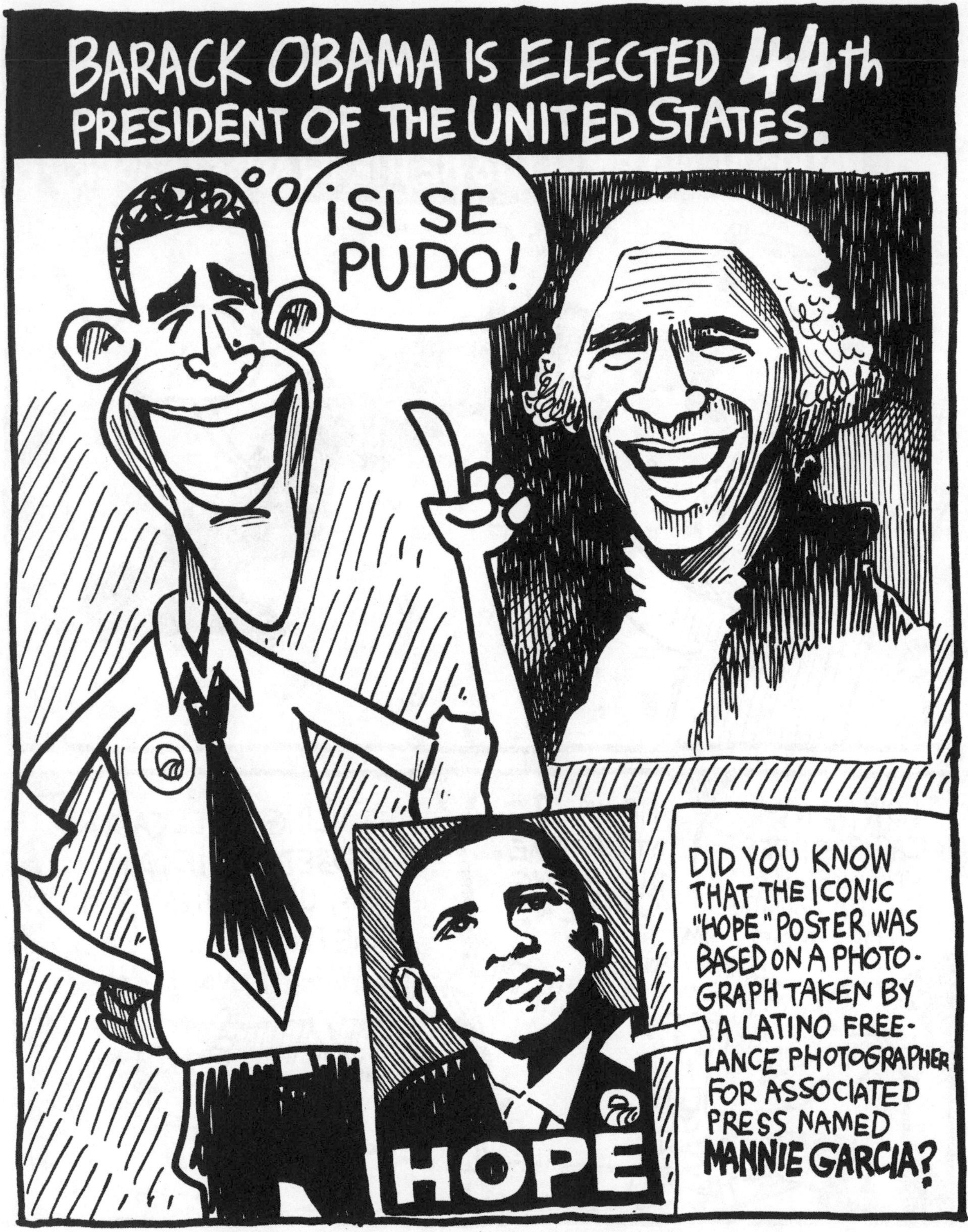
BARACK OBAMA IS ELECTED 44th PRESIDENT OF THE UNITED STATES.
¡SI SE PUDO!
HOPE
DID YOU KNOW THAT THE ICONIC "HOPE" POSTER WAS BASED ON A PHOTOGRAPH TAKEN BY A LATINO FREELANCE PHOTOGRAPHER FOR ASSOCIATED PRESS NAMED MANNIE GARCIA?

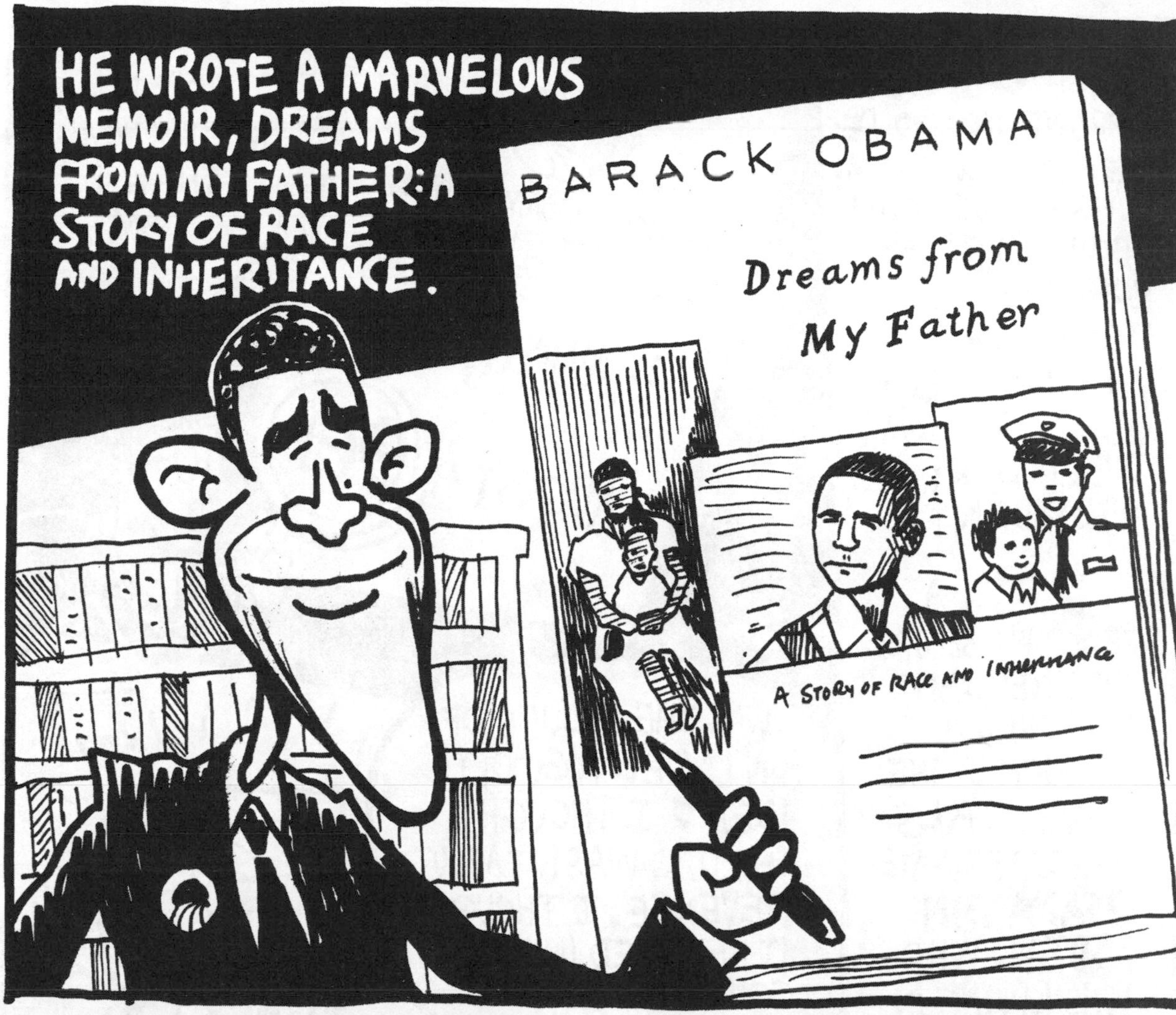
HE WROTE A MARVELOUS MEMOIR, DREAMS FROM MY FATHER: A STORY OF RACE AND INHERITANCE.
BARACK OBAMA
Dreams from My Father
A STORY OF RACE AND INHERITANCE

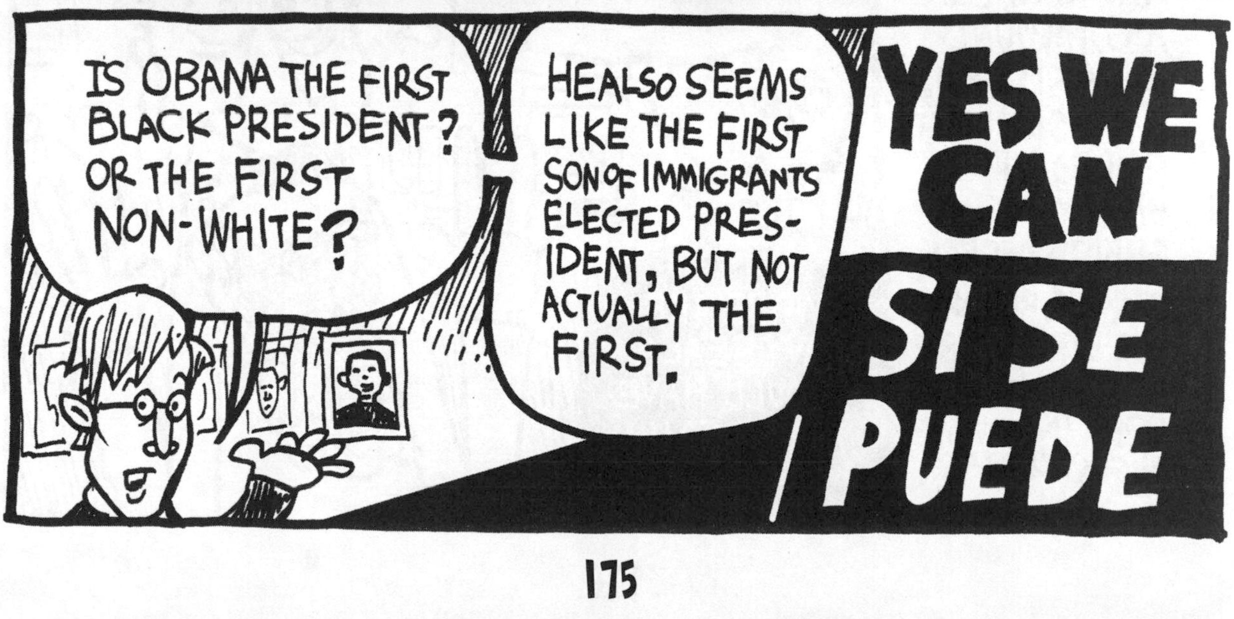
IS OBAMA THE FIRST BLACK PRESIDENT? OR THE FIRST NON-WHITE?
HE ALSO SEEMS LIKE THE FIRST SON OF IMMIGRANTS ELECTED PRESIDENT, BUT NOT ACTUALLY THE FIRST.
YES WE CAN
¡SI SE PUEDE

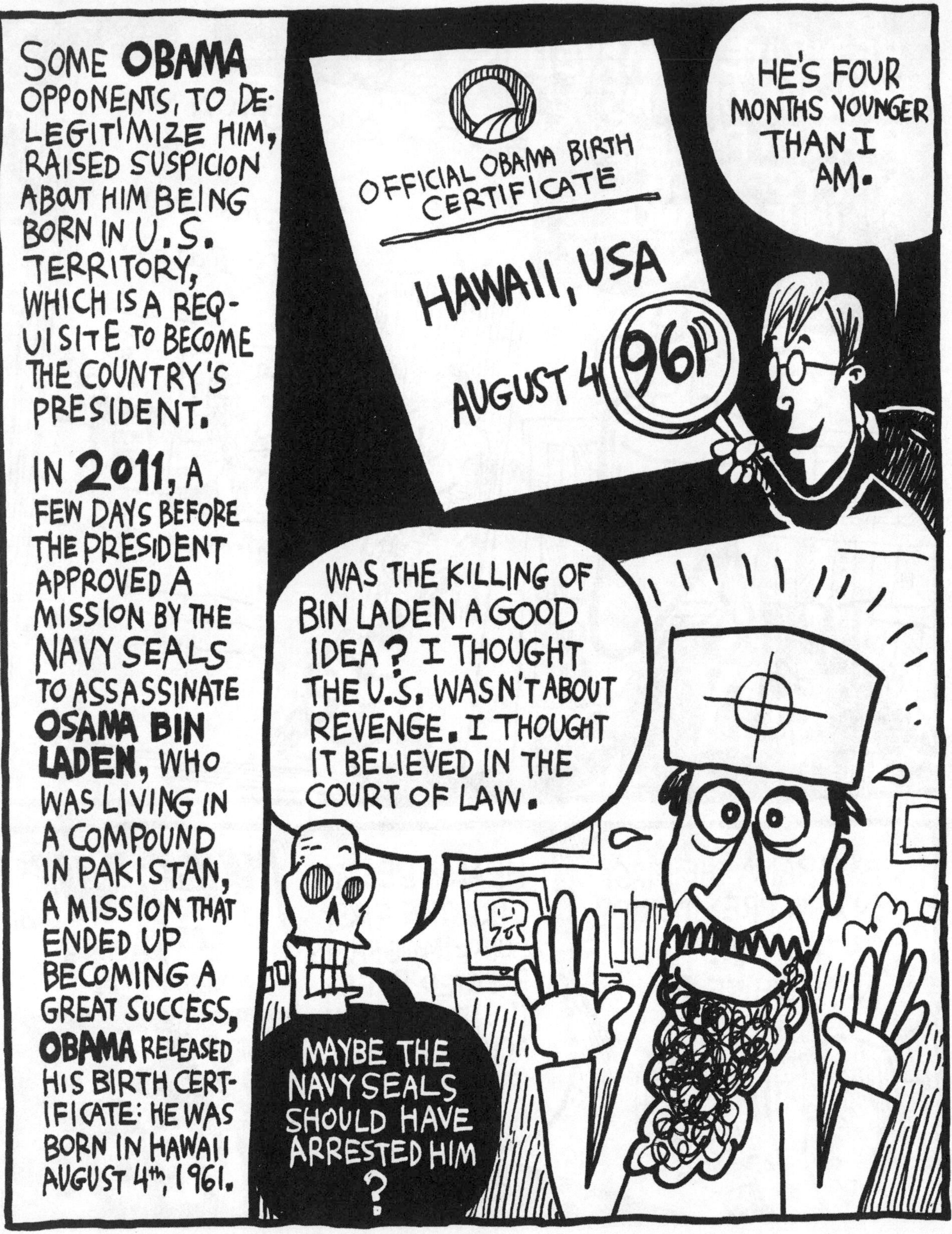
SOME OBAMA OPPONENTS, TO DE-LEGITIMIZE HIM, RAISED SUSPICION ABOUT HIM BEING BORN IN U.S. TERRITORY, WHICH IS A REQUISITE TO BECOME THE COUNTRY'S PRESIDENT.
IN 2011, A FEW DAYS BEFORE THE PRESIDENT APPROVED A MISSION BY THE NAVY SEALS TO ASSASSINATE OSAMA BIN LADEN, WHO WAS LIVING IN A COMPOUND IN PAKISTAN, A MISSION THAT ENDED UP BECOMING A GREAT SUCCESS, OBAMA RELEASED HIS BIRTH CERTIFICATE: HE WAS BORN IN HAWAII AUGUST 4th, 1961.
OFFICIAL OBAMA BIRTH CERTIFICATE
HAWAII, USA
AUGUST 4 961
HE'S FOUR MONTHS YOUNGER THAN I AM.
WAS THE KILLING OF BIN LADEN A GOOD IDEA? I THOUGHT THE U.S. WASN'T ABOUT REVENGE. I THOUGHT IT BELIEVED IN THE COURT OF LAW.
MAYBE THE NAVY SEALS SHOULD HAVE ARRESTED HIM?

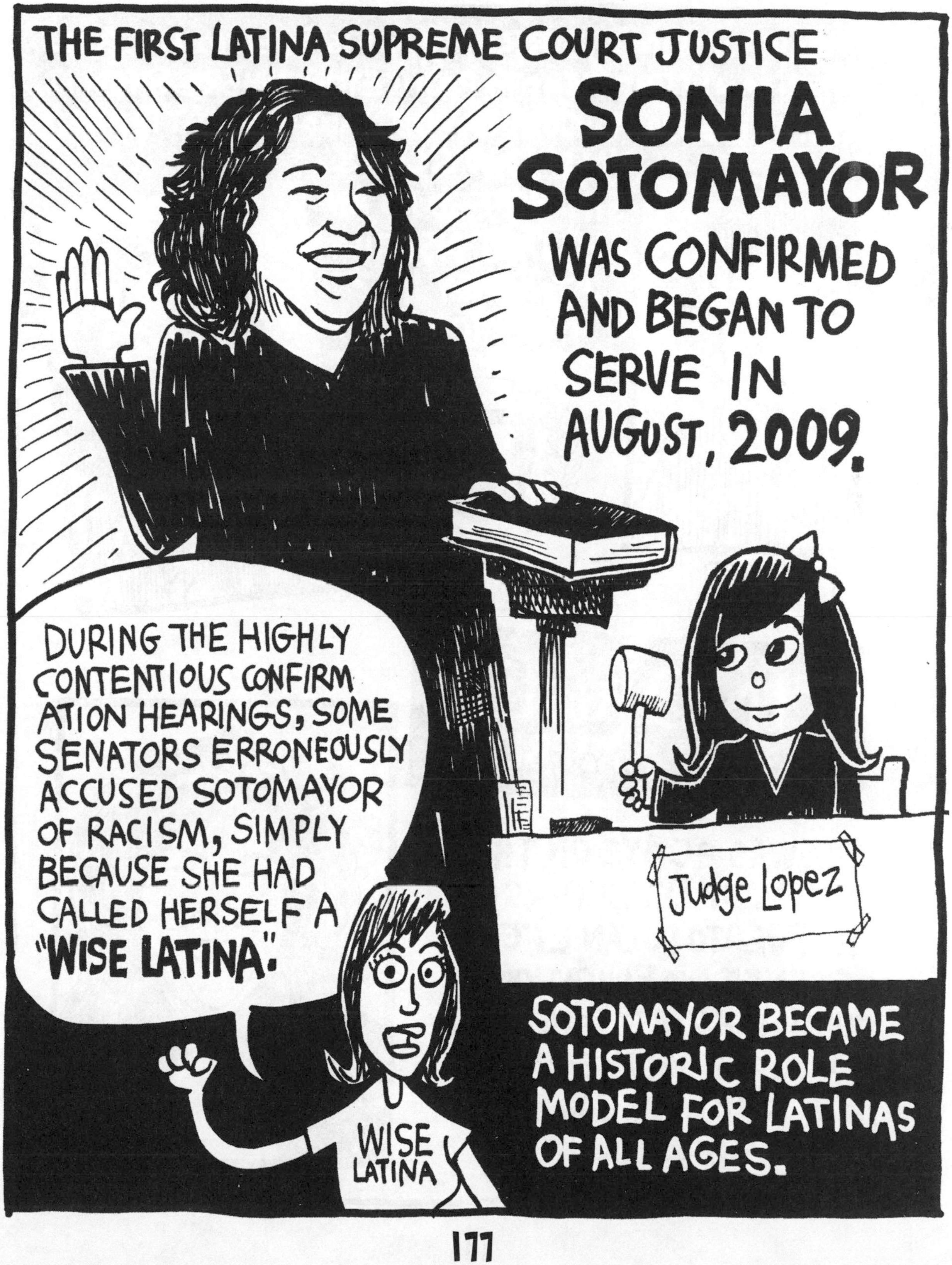
THE FIRST LATINA SUPREME COURT JUSTICE
SONIA SOTOMAYOR
WAS CONFIRMED AND BEGAN TO SERVE IN AUGUST, 2009.
DURING THE HIGHLY CONTENTIOUS CONFIRMATION HEARINGS, SOME SENATORS ERRONEOUSLY ACCUSED SOTOMAYOR OF RACISM, SIMPLY BECAUSE SHE HAD CALLED HERSELF A "WISE LATINA."
Judge Lopez
WISE LATINA
SOTOMAYOR BECAME A HISTORIC ROLE MODEL FOR LATINAS OF ALL AGES.

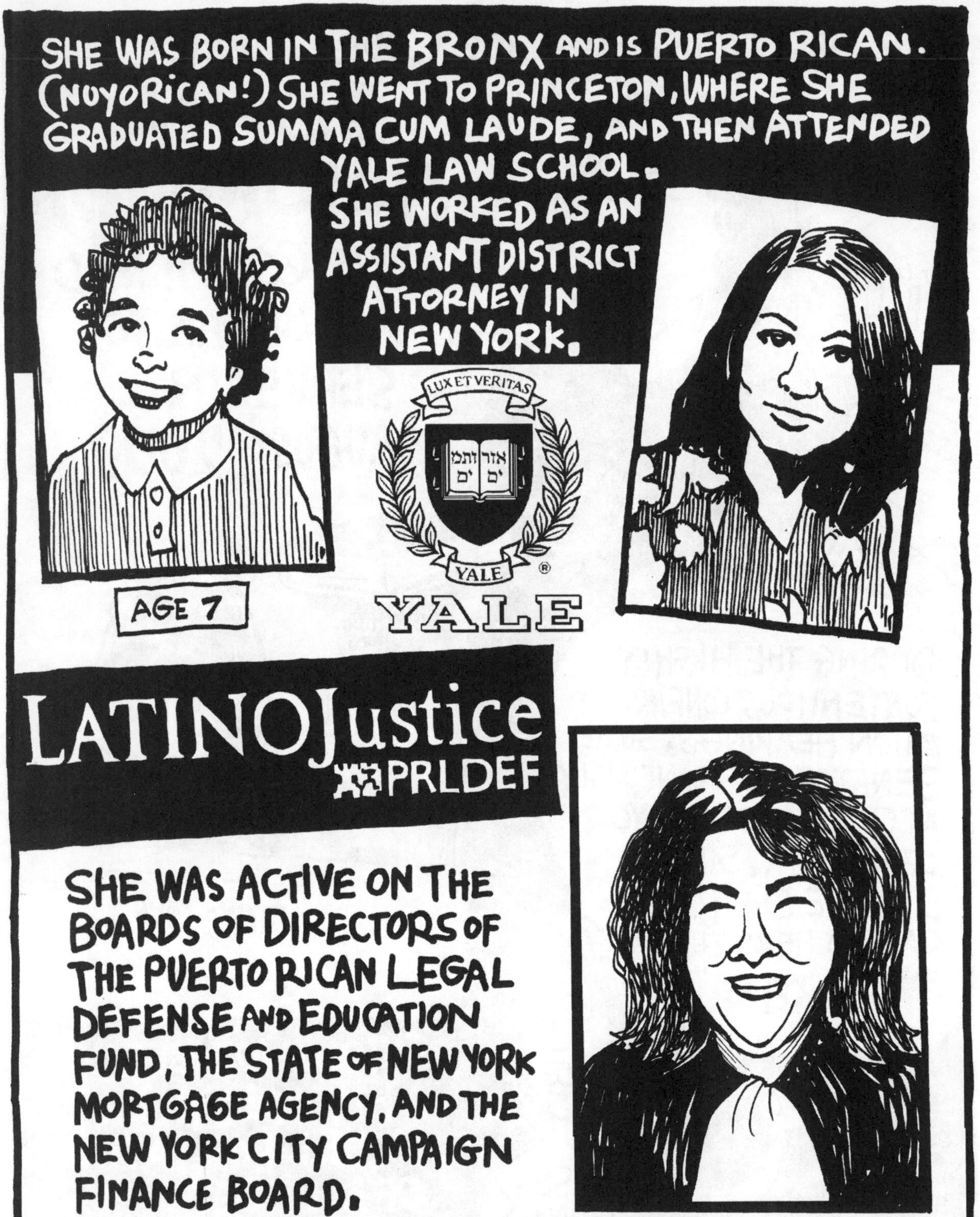
SHE WAS BORN IN THE BRONX AND IS PUERTO RICAN. (NUYORICAN!) SHE WENT TO PRINCETON, WHERE SHE GRADUATED SUMMA CUM LAUDE, AND THEN ATTENDED YALE LAW SCHOOL.
SHE WORKED AS AN ASSISTANT DISTRICT ATTORNEY IN NEW YORK.
AGE 7
LUX ET VERITAS
YALE
YALE
LATINOJustice
PRLDEF
SHE WAS ACTIVE ON THE BOARDS OF DIRECTORS OF THE PUERTO RICAN LEGAL DEFENSE AND EDUCATION FUND, THE STATE OF NEW YORK MORTGAGE AGENCY, AND THE NEW YORK CITY CAMPAIGN FINANCE BOARD.

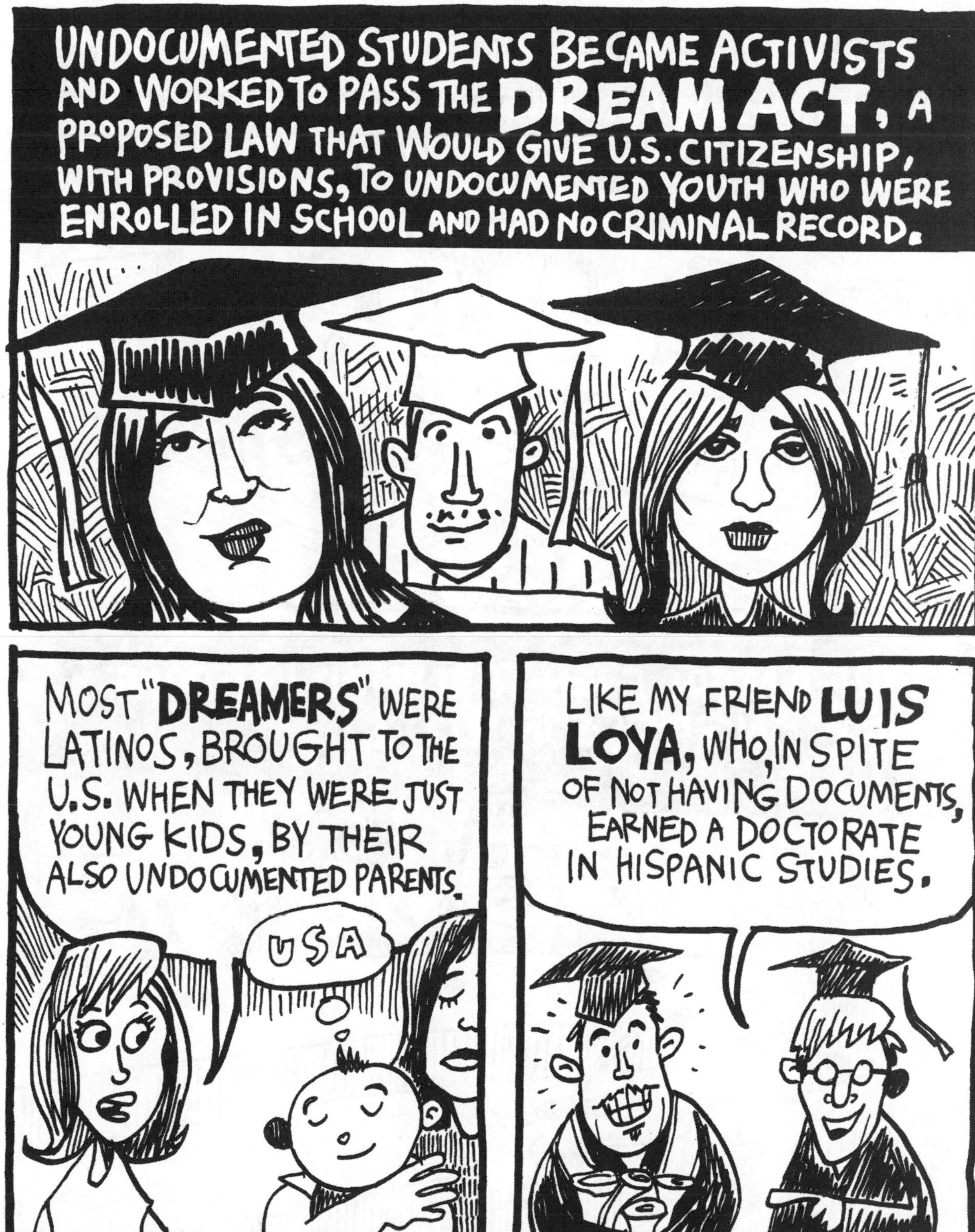
UNDOCUMENTED STUDENTS BECAME ACTIVISTS AND WORKED TO PASS THE DREAM ACT, A PROPOSED LAW THAT WOULD GIVE U.S. CITIZENSHIP, WITH PROVISIONS, TO UNDOCUMENTED YOUTH WHO WERE ENROLLED IN SCHOOL AND HAD NO CRIMINAL RECORD.
MOST "DREAMERS" WERE LATINOS, BROUGHT TO THE U.S. WHEN THEY WERE JUST YOUNG KIDS, BY THEIR ALSO UNDOCUMENTED PARENTS.
USA
LIKE MY FRIEND LUIS LOYA, WHO, IN SPITE OF NOT HAVING DOCUMENTS, EARNED A DOCTORATE IN HISPANIC STUDIES.

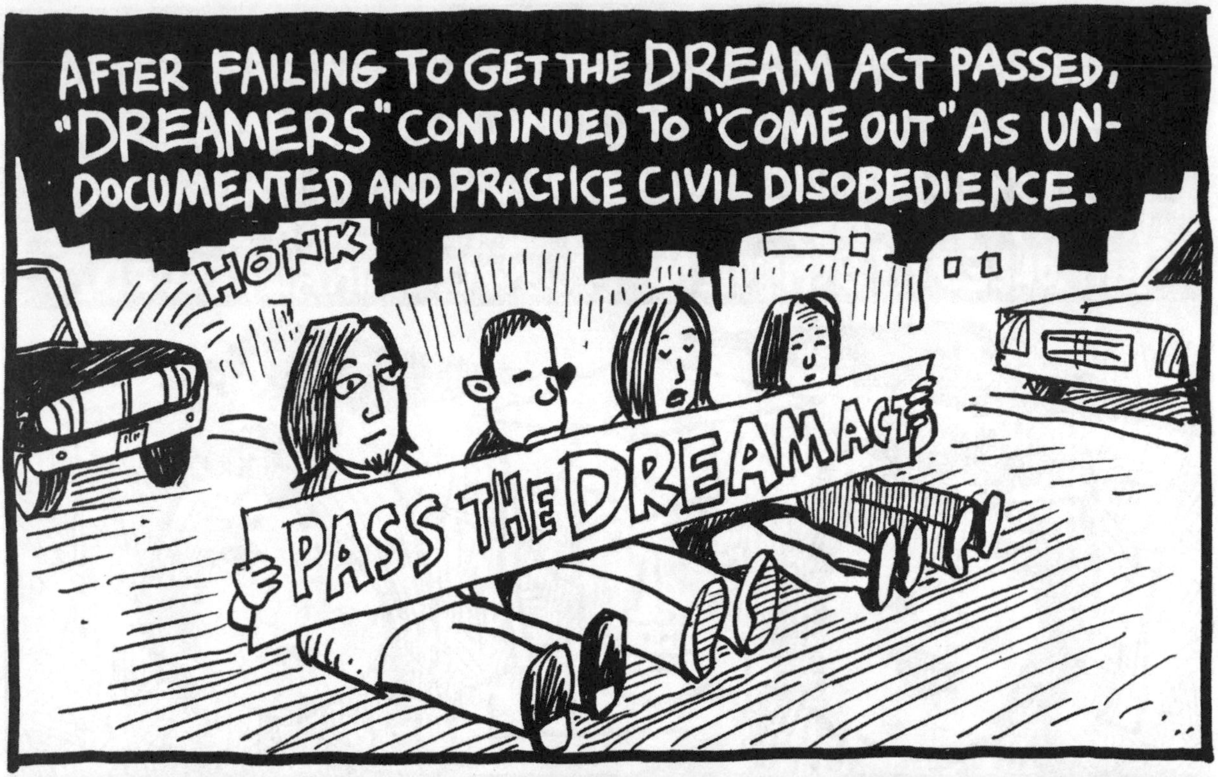
AFTER FAILING TO GET THE DREAM ACT PASSED, "DREAMERS" CONTINUED TO "COME OUT" AS UN-DOCUMENTED AND PRACTICE CIVIL DISOBEDIENCE.
HONK
PASS THE DREAM ACT

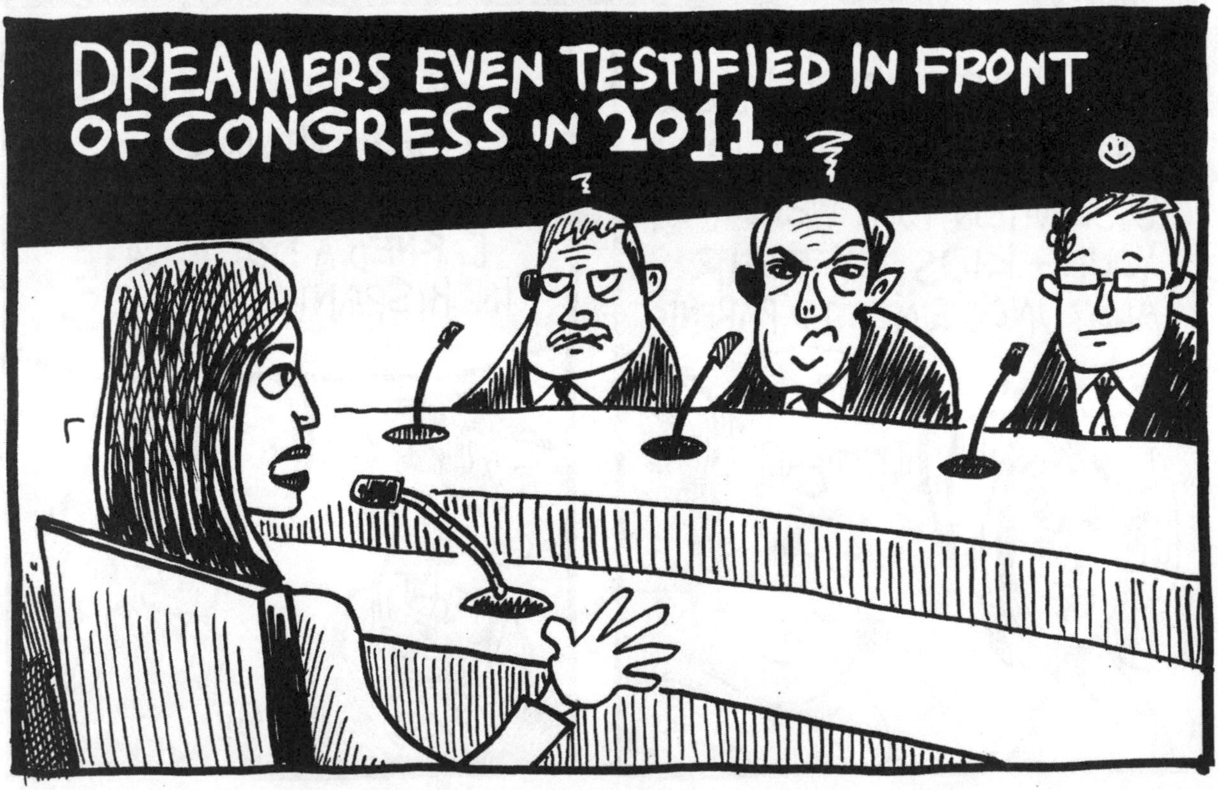
DREAMERS EVEN TESTIFIED IN FRONT OF CONGRESS IN 2011.

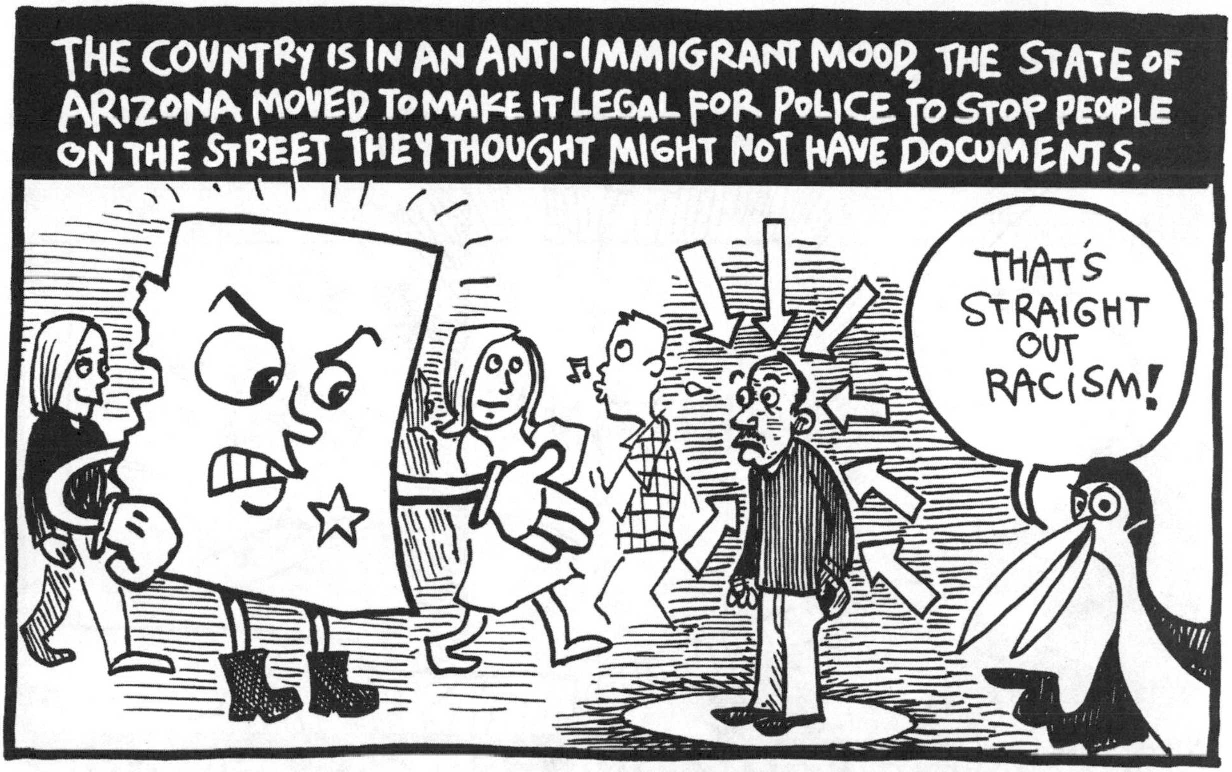
THE COUNTRY IS IN AN ANTI-IMMIGRANT MOOD, THE STATE OF ARIZONA MOVED TO MAKE IT LEGAL FOR POLICE TO STOP PEOPLE ON THE STREET THEY THOUGHT MIGHT NOT HAVE DOCUMENTS.
THAT'S STRAIGHT OUT RACISM!

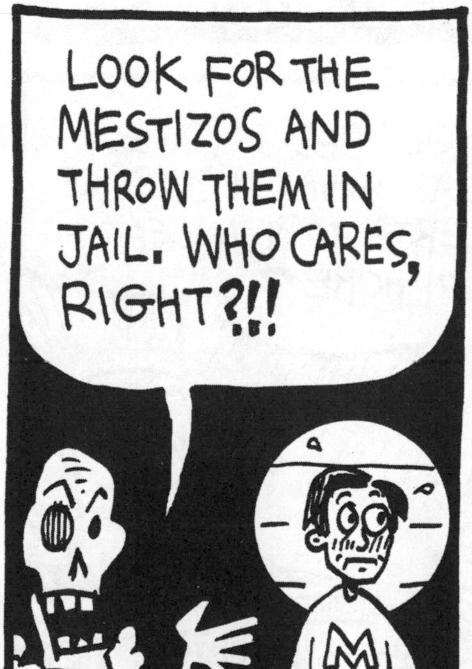
LOOK FOR THE MESTIZOS AND THROW THEM IN JAIL. WHO CARES, RIGHT?!!
M

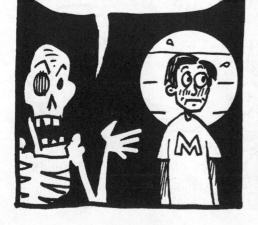

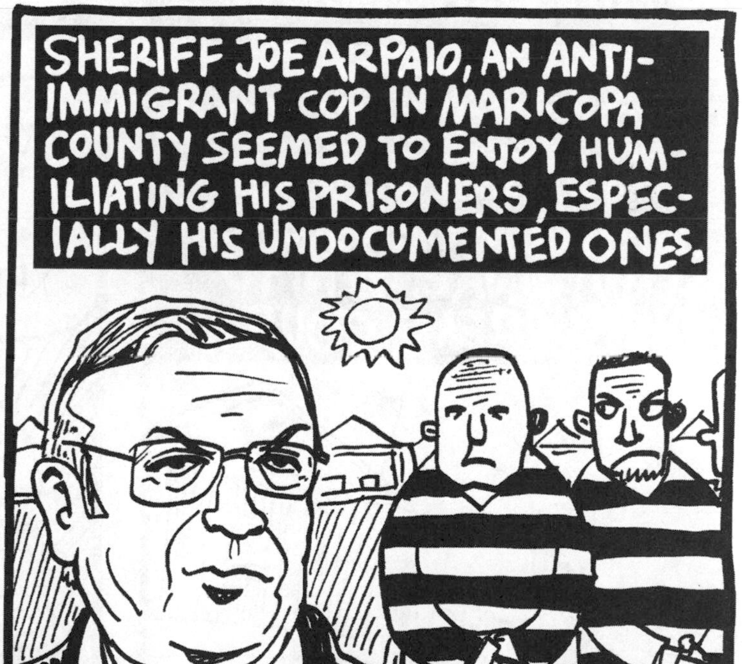
SHERIFF JOE ARPAIO, AN ANTI-IMMIGRANT COP IN MARICOPA COUNTY SEEMED TO ENJOY HUMILIATING HIS PRISONERS, ESPECIALLY HIS UNDOCUMENTED ONES.

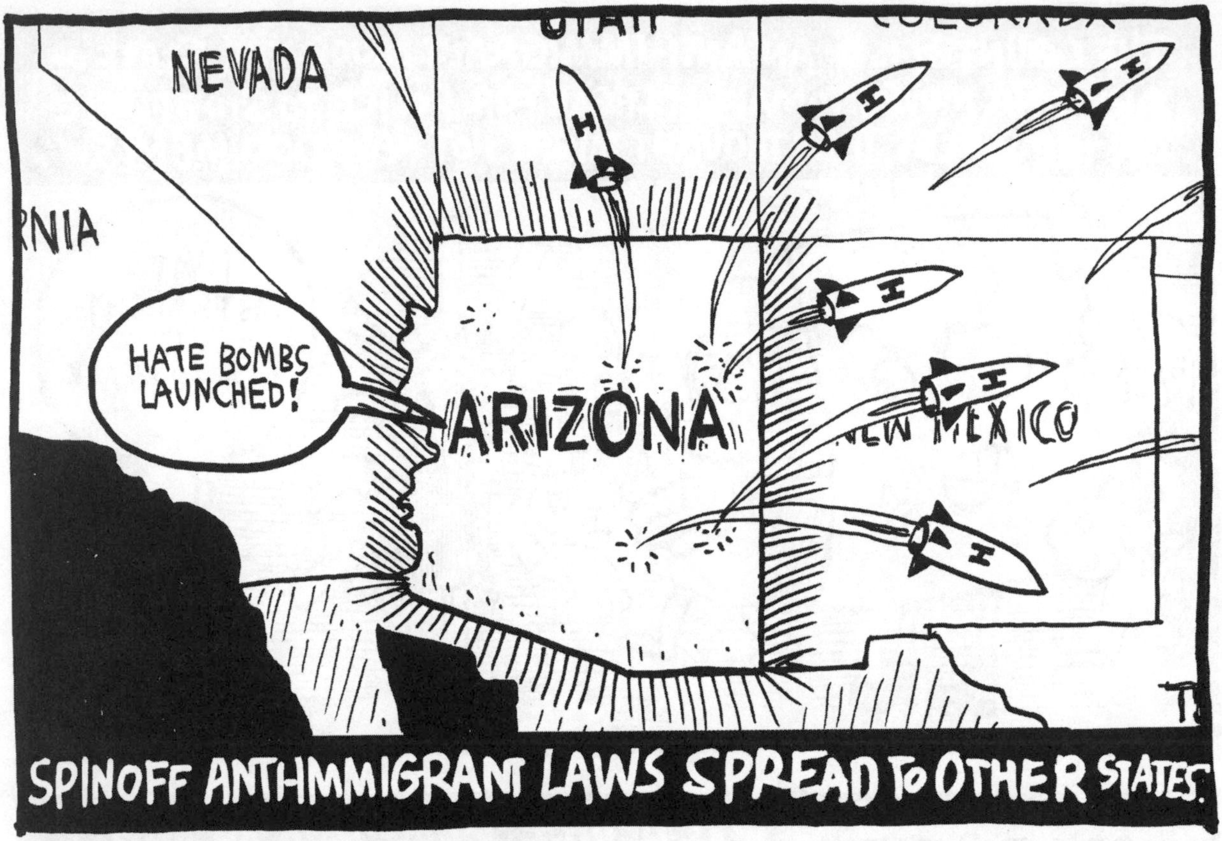
NEVADA
ARIZONA
NEW MEXICO
HATE BOMBS LAUNCHED!
SPINOFF ANTI-IMMIGRANT LAWS SPREAD TO OTHER STATES.

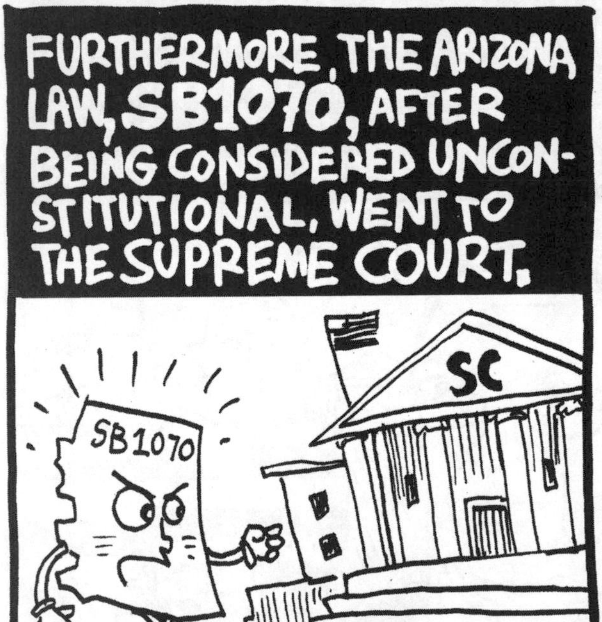
FURTHERMORE, THE ARIZONA LAW, SB1070, AFTER BEING CONSIDERED UNCONSTITUTIONAL, WENT TO THE SUPREME COURT.
SC
SB1070

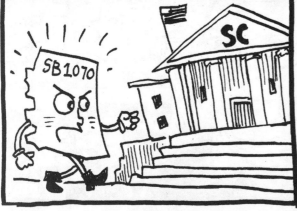

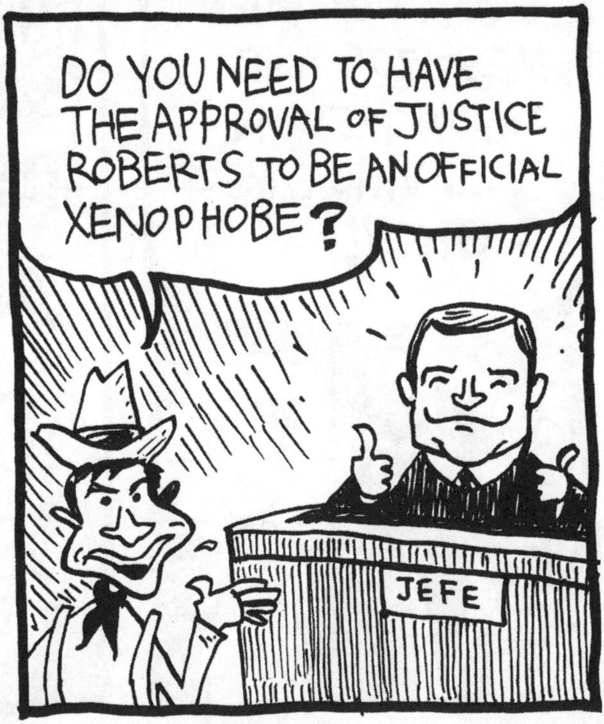
DO YOU NEED TO HAVE THE APPROVAL OF JUSTICE ROBERTS TO BE AN OFFICIAL XENOPHOBE?
JEFE

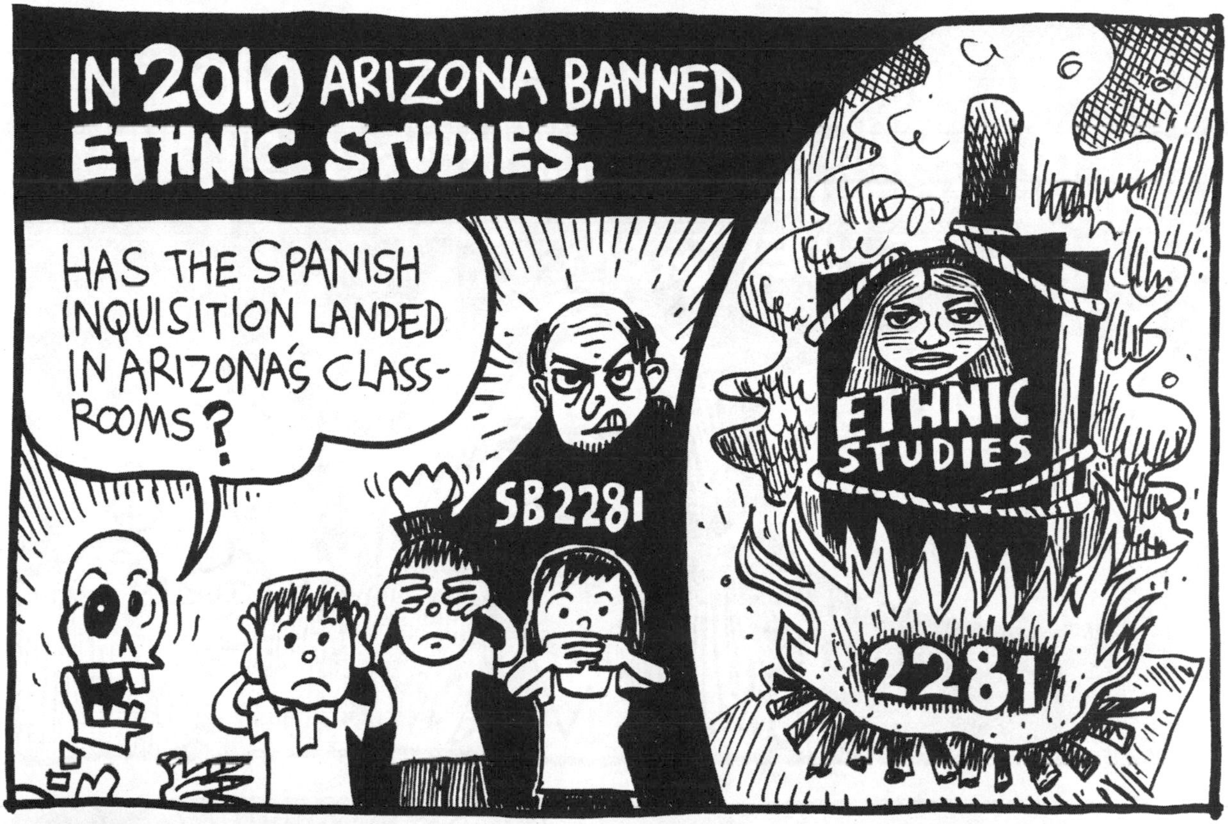
IN 2010 ARIZONA BANNED ETHNIC STUDIES.
HAS THE SPANISH INQUISITION LANDED IN ARIZONA'S CLASS-ROOMS?
SB 2281
ETHNIC STUDIES
2281

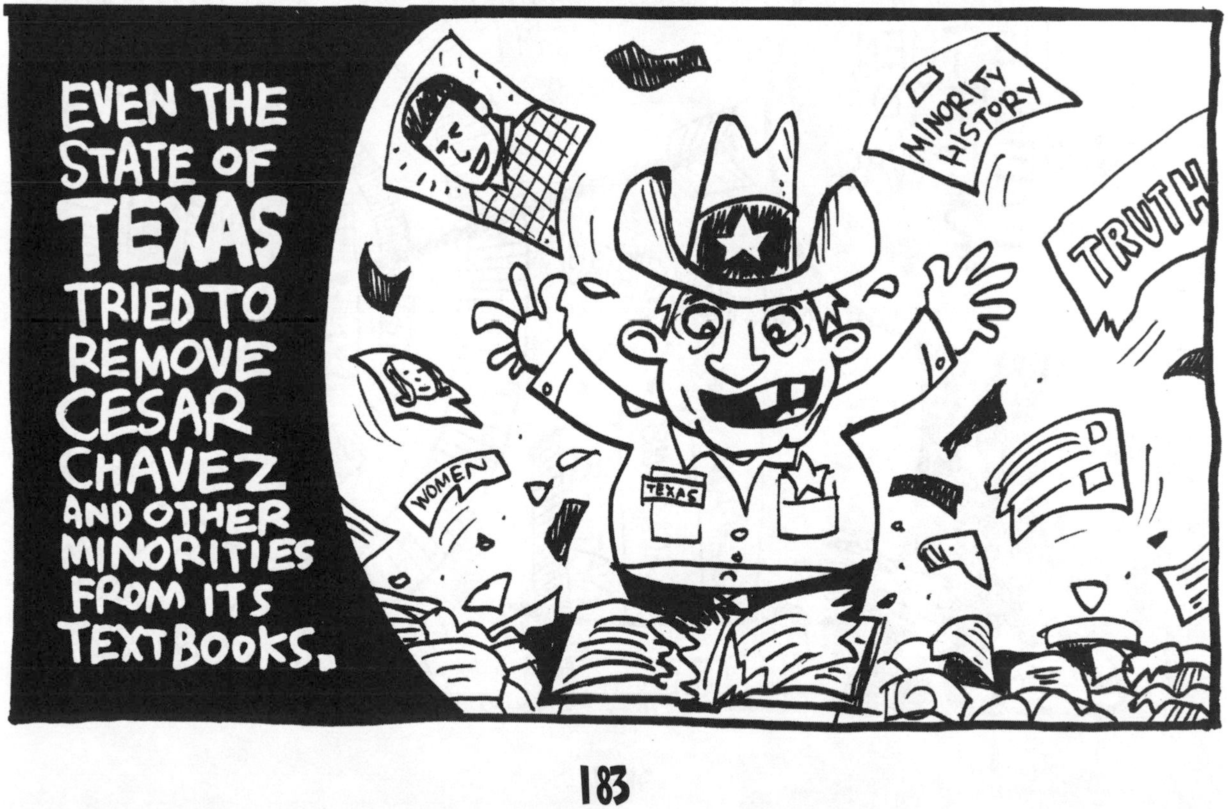
EVEN THE STATE OF TEXAS TRIED TO REMOVE CESAR CHAVEZ AND OTHER MINORITIES FROM ITS TEXTBOOKS.
MINORITY HISTORY
TRUTH
WOMEN
TEXAS

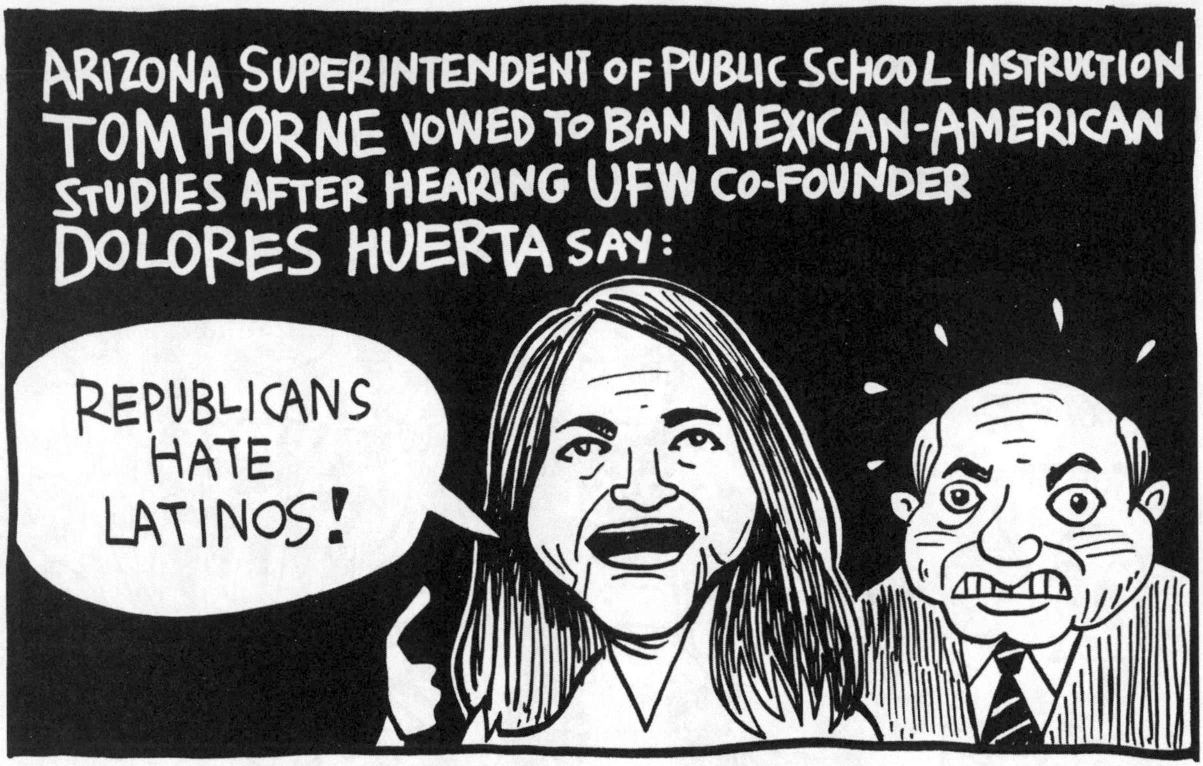
ARIZONA SUPERINTENDENT OF PUBLIC SCHOOL INSTRUCTION TOM HORNE VOWED TO BAN MEXICAN-AMERICAN STUDIES AFTER HEARING UFW CO-FOUNDER DOLORES HUERTA SAY:
REPUBLICANS HATE LATINOS!

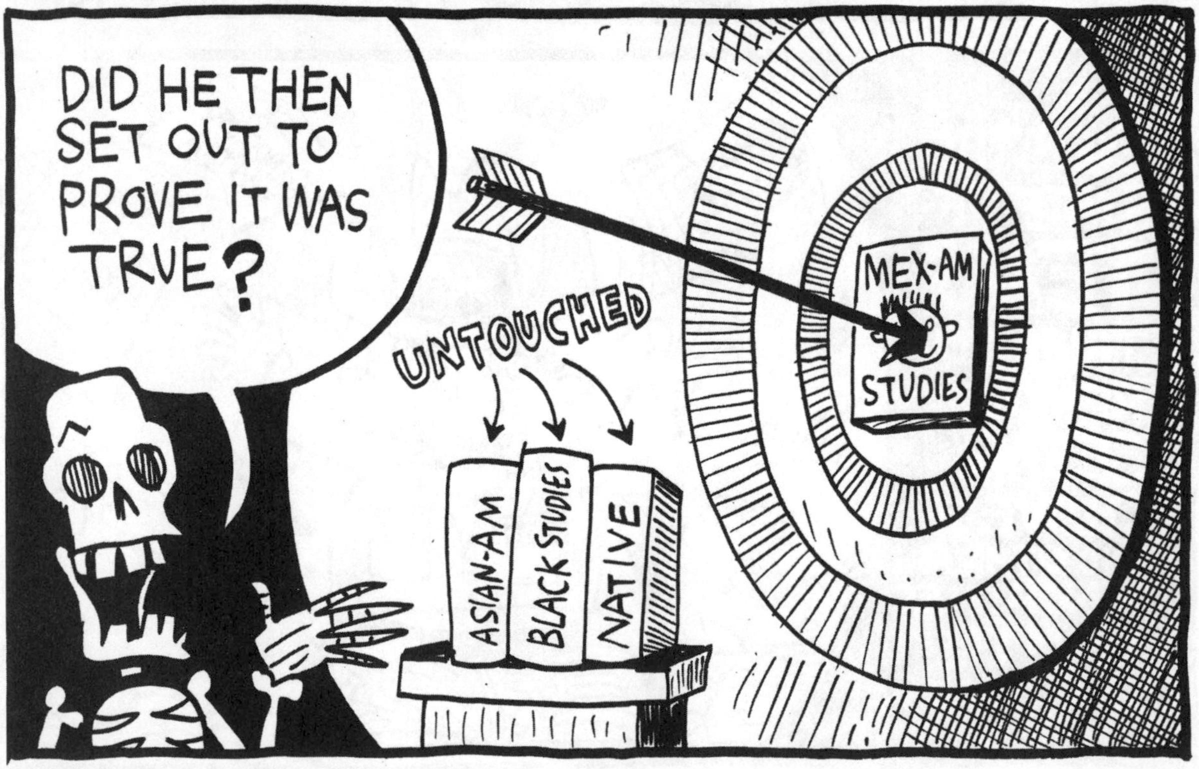
DID HE THEN SET OUT TO PROVE IT WAS TRUE?
UNTOUCHED
ASIAN-AM
BLACK STUDIES
NATIVE
MEX-AM STUDIES

AS BIG MANUFACTURING SITES WERE BUILT IN NORTHERN MEXICO - CALLED **MAQUILADORAS** - AND THE FEMALE WORK FORCE EXPANDED, HUNDREDS OF WOMEN WERE MURDERED IN **CIUDAD JUAREZ.**

CD. JUAREZ ZONA INDUSTRIAL Y DE LA MUERTE

WHY VIOLENCE AGAINST WOMEN? IS MACHISMO THE CAUSE?

SHAMEFUL.

PLENTY OF DEATH AND VIOLENCE TO GO AROUND! WHY DOESN'T MEXICO PACKAGE IT FOR EXPORT?

IMAGINE, MEXICO WOULD BE RICH!

THE CHILEAN NOVELIST ROBERTO BOLAÑO, WHO DIED IN 2003, WAS FASCINATED WITH MURDER. HIS MASTERPIECE, "2666," A MAMMOTH NARRATIVE, IS ABOUT SERIAL KILLER(S) LOOSE IN CIUDAD JUAREZ

2666 by Roberto

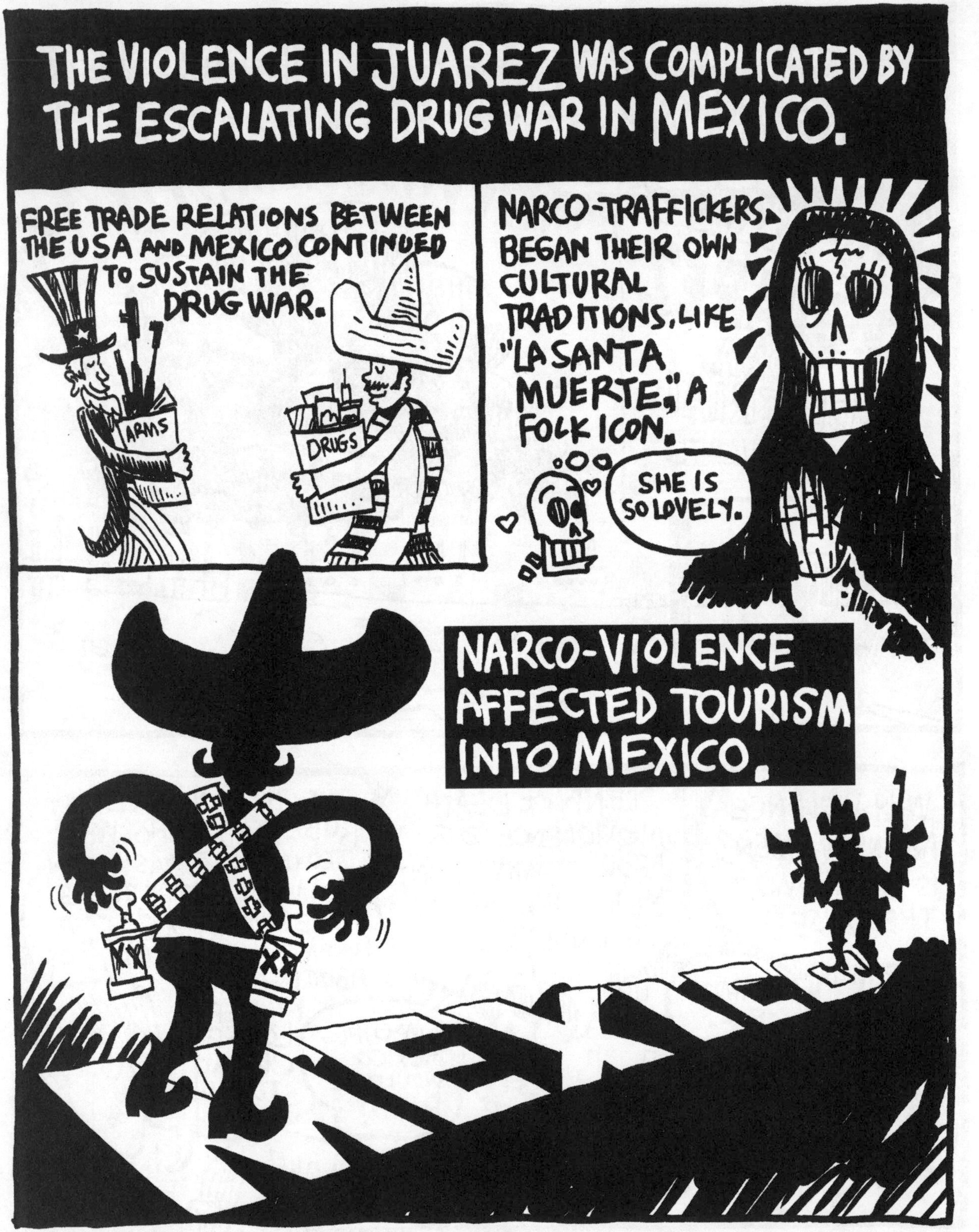
THE VIOLENCE IN JUAREZ WAS COMPLICATED BY THE ESCALATING DRUG WAR IN MEXICO.
FREE TRADE RELATIONS BETWEEN THE USA AND MEXICO CONTINUED TO SUSTAIN THE DRUG WAR.
ARMS
DRUGS
NARCO-TRAFFICKERS BEGAN THEIR OWN CULTURAL TRADITIONS, LIKE "LA SANTA MUERTE," A FOLK ICON.
SHE IS SO LOVELY.
NARCO-VIOLENCE AFFECTED TOURISM INTO MEXICO.

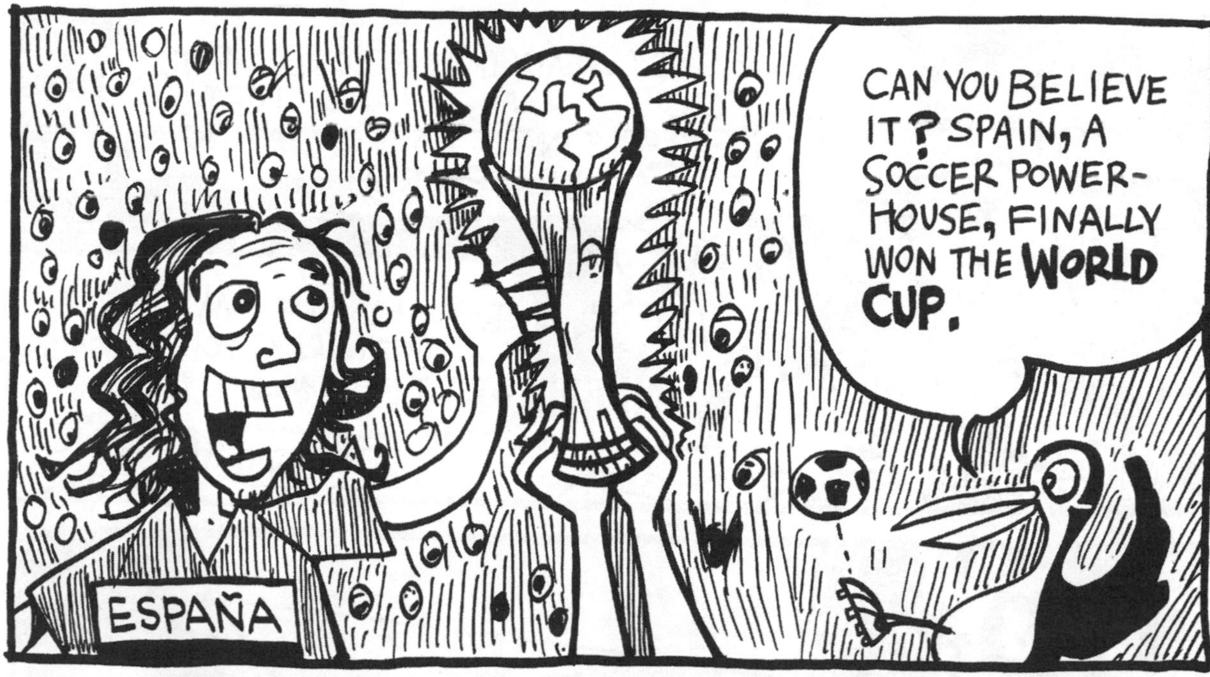
CAN YOU BELIEVE IT? SPAIN, A SOCCER POWER-HOUSE, FINALLY WON THE **WORLD CUP**.
ESPAÑA

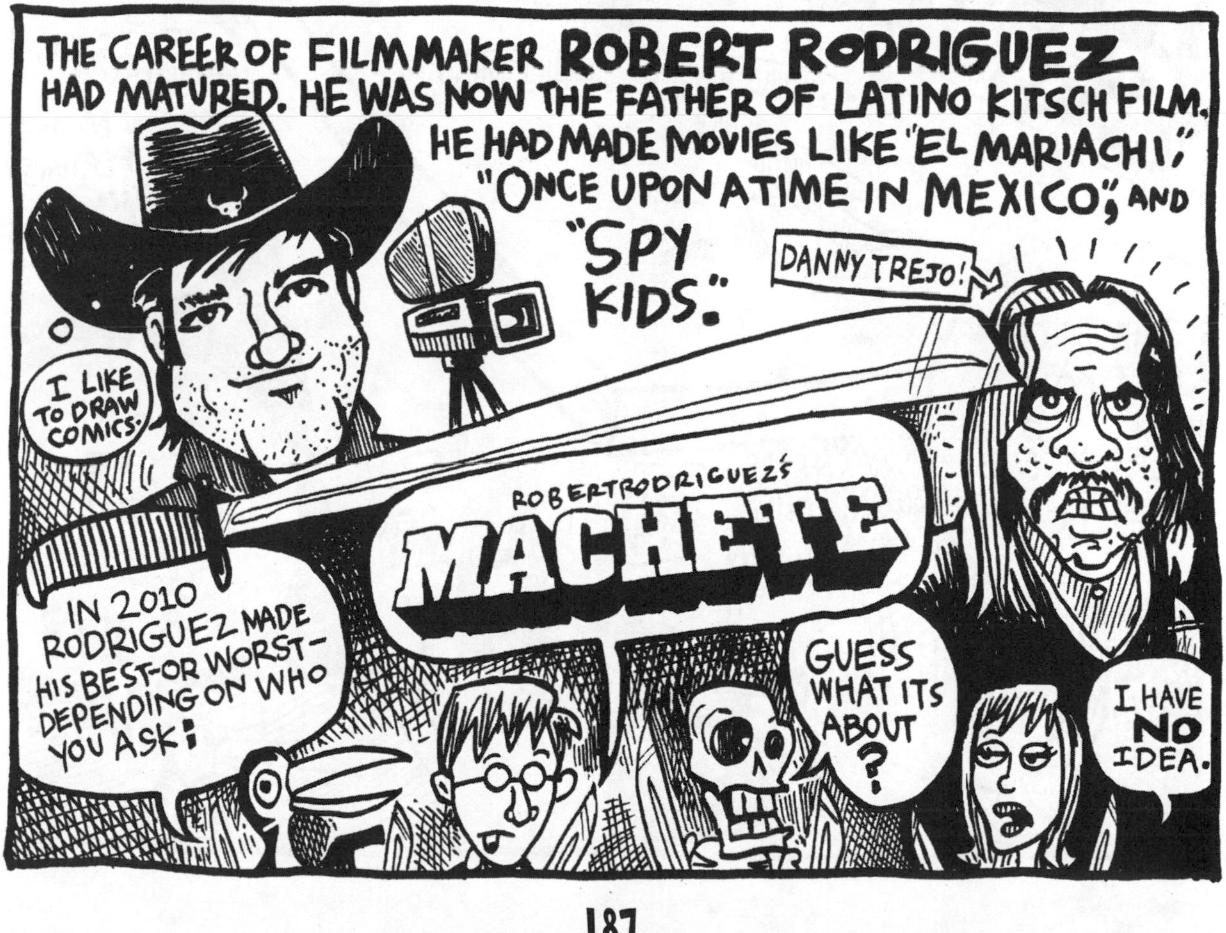
THE CAREER OF FILMMAKER **ROBERT RODRIGUEZ** HAD MATURED. HE WAS NOW THE FATHER OF LATINO KITSCH FILM. HE HAD MADE MOVIES LIKE "EL MARIACHI," "ONCE UPON A TIME IN MEXICO," AND "SPY KIDS."
I LIKE TO DRAW COMICS.
DANNY TREJO!
ROBERT RODRIGUEZ'S
MACHETE
IN 2010 RODRIGUEZ MADE HIS BEST-OR WORST-DEPENDING ON WHO YOU ASK:
GUESS WHAT ITS ABOUT?
I HAVE **NO** IDEA.

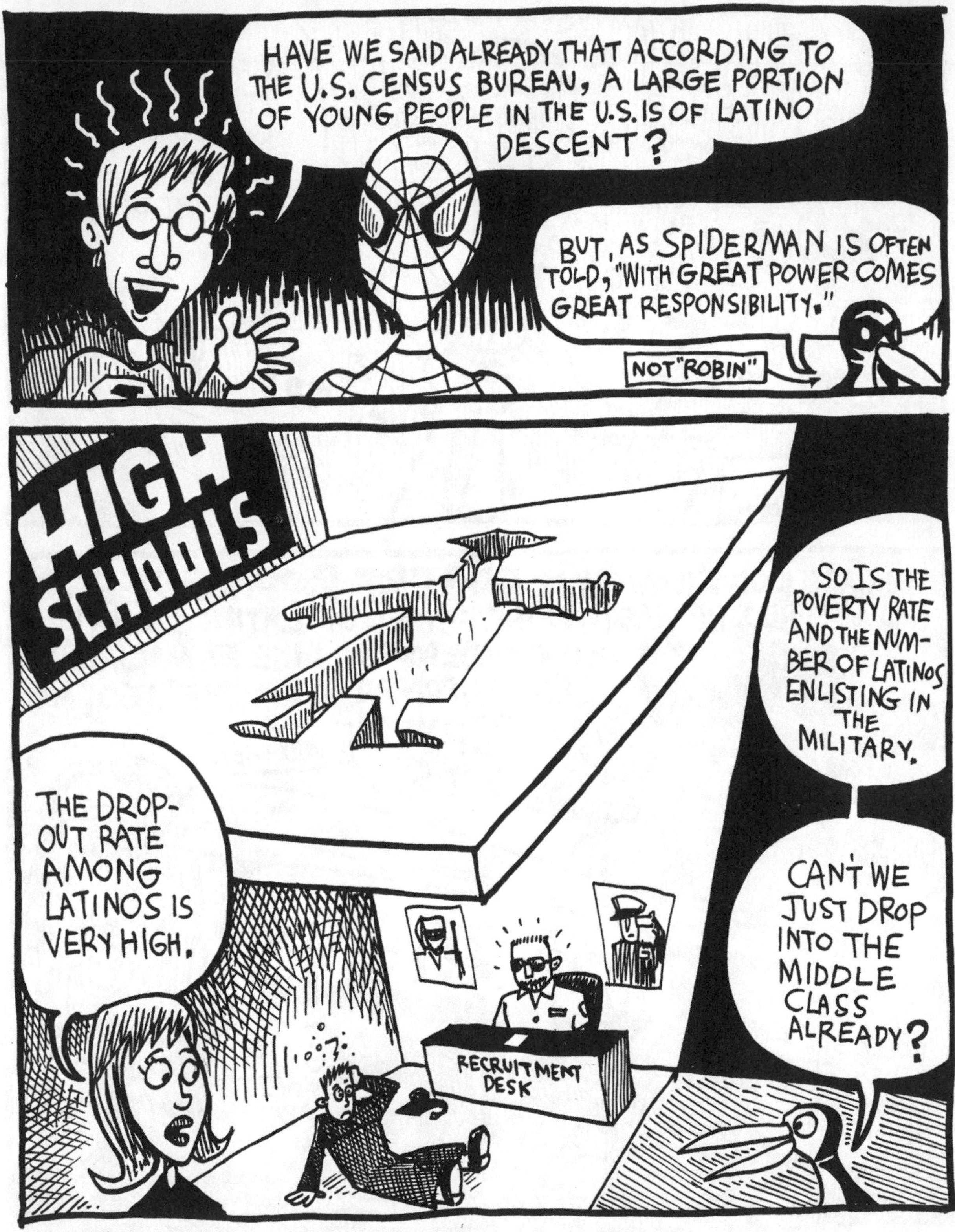
HAVE WE SAID ALREADY THAT ACCORDING TO THE U.S. CENSUS BUREAU, A LARGE PORTION OF YOUNG PEOPLE IN THE U.S. IS OF LATINO DESCENT?
BUT, AS SPIDERMAN IS OFTEN TOLD, "WITH GREAT POWER COMES GREAT RESPONSIBILITY."
NOT "ROBIN"
HIGH SCHOOLS
THE DROP-OUT RATE AMONG LATINOS IS VERY HIGH.
SO IS THE POVERTY RATE AND THE NUMBER OF LATINOS ENLISTING IN THE MILITARY.
CAN'T WE JUST DROP INTO THE MIDDLE CLASS ALREADY?
RECRUITMENT DESK

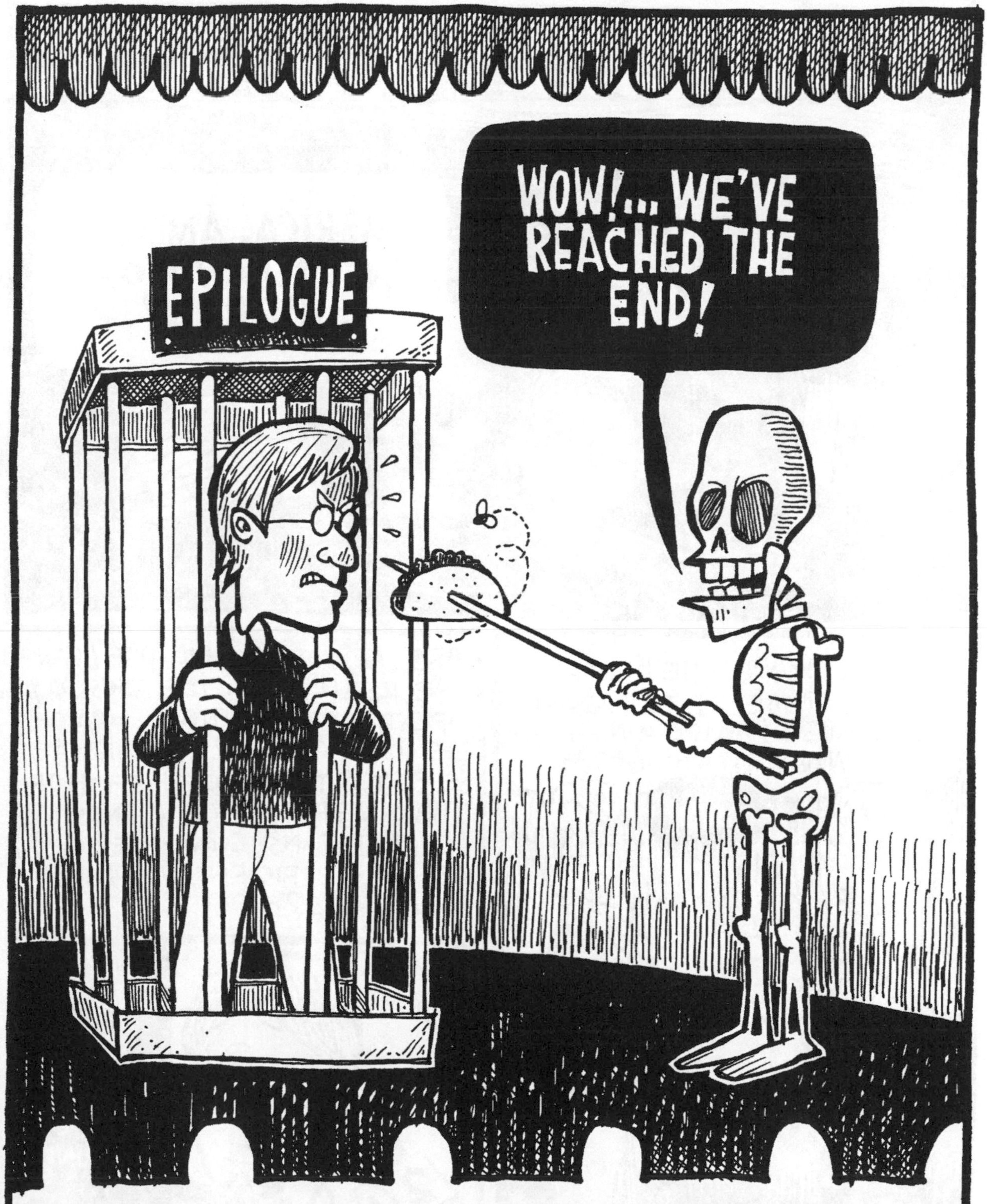
EPILOGUE
WOW!... WE'VE REACHED THE END!

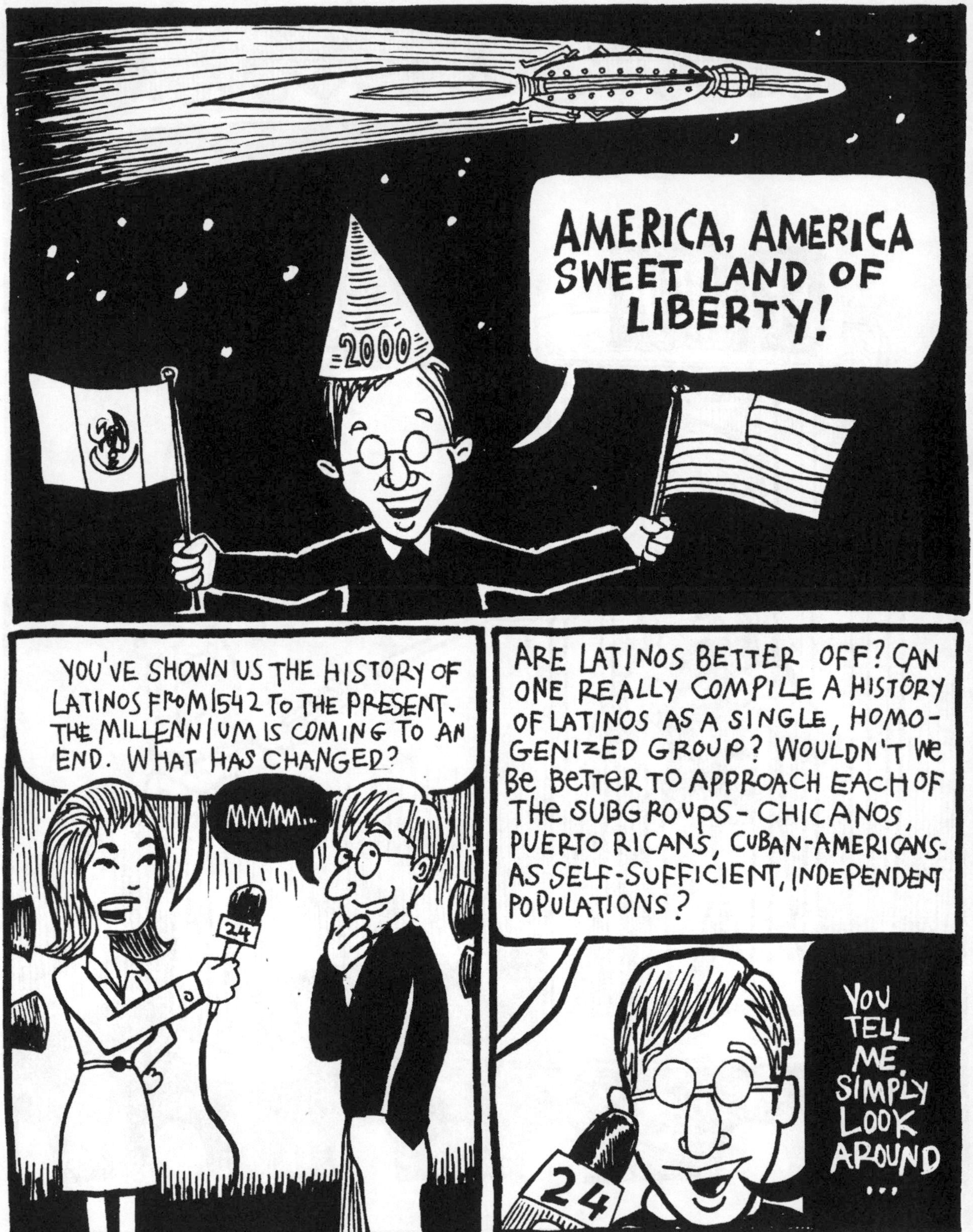
2000
AMERICA, AMERICA SWEET LAND OF LIBERTY!
YOU'VE SHOWN US THE HISTORY OF LATINOS FROM 1542 TO THE PRESENT. THE MILLENNIUM IS COMING TO AN END. WHAT HAS CHANGED?
MMMM...
24
ARE LATINOS BETTER OFF? CAN ONE REALLY COMPILE A HISTORY OF LATINOS AS A SINGLE, HOMO-GENIZED GROUP? WOULDN'T WE BE BETTER TO APPROACH EACH OF THE SUBGROUPS - CHICANOS, PUERTO RICANS, CUBAN-AMERICANS - AS SELF-SUFFICIENT, INDEPENDENT POPULATIONS?
YOU TELL ME. SIMPLY LOOK AROUND...
24

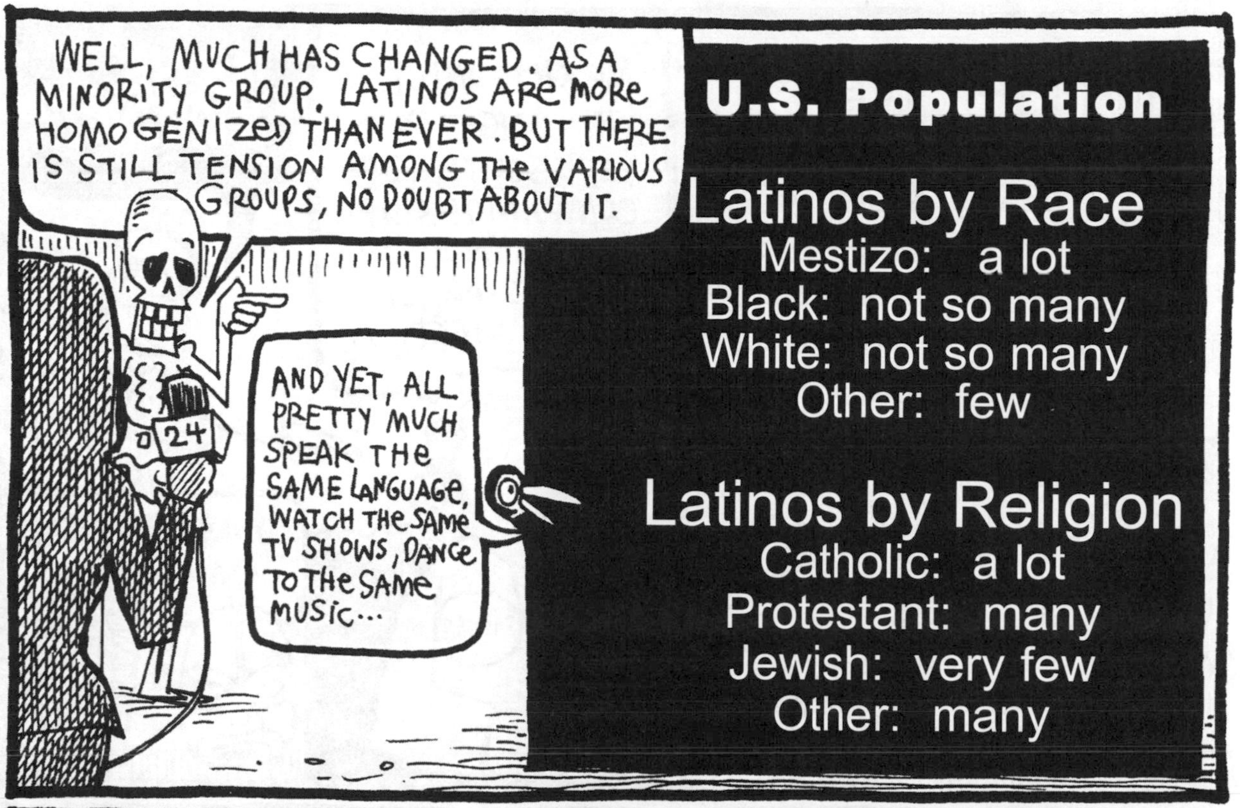
WELL, MUCH HAS CHANGED. AS A MINORITY GROUP, LATINOS ARE MORE HOMOGENIZED THAN EVER. BUT THERE IS STILL TENSION AMONG THE VARIOUS GROUPS, NO DOUBT ABOUT IT.
U.S. Population
Latinos by Race
Mestizo: a lot
Black: not so many
White: not so many
Other: few
AND YET, ALL PRETTY MUCH SPEAK THE SAME LANGUAGE, WATCH THE SAME TV SHOWS, DANCE TO THE SAME MUSIC...
Latinos by Religion
Catholic: a lot
Protestant: many
Jewish: very few
Other: many
24

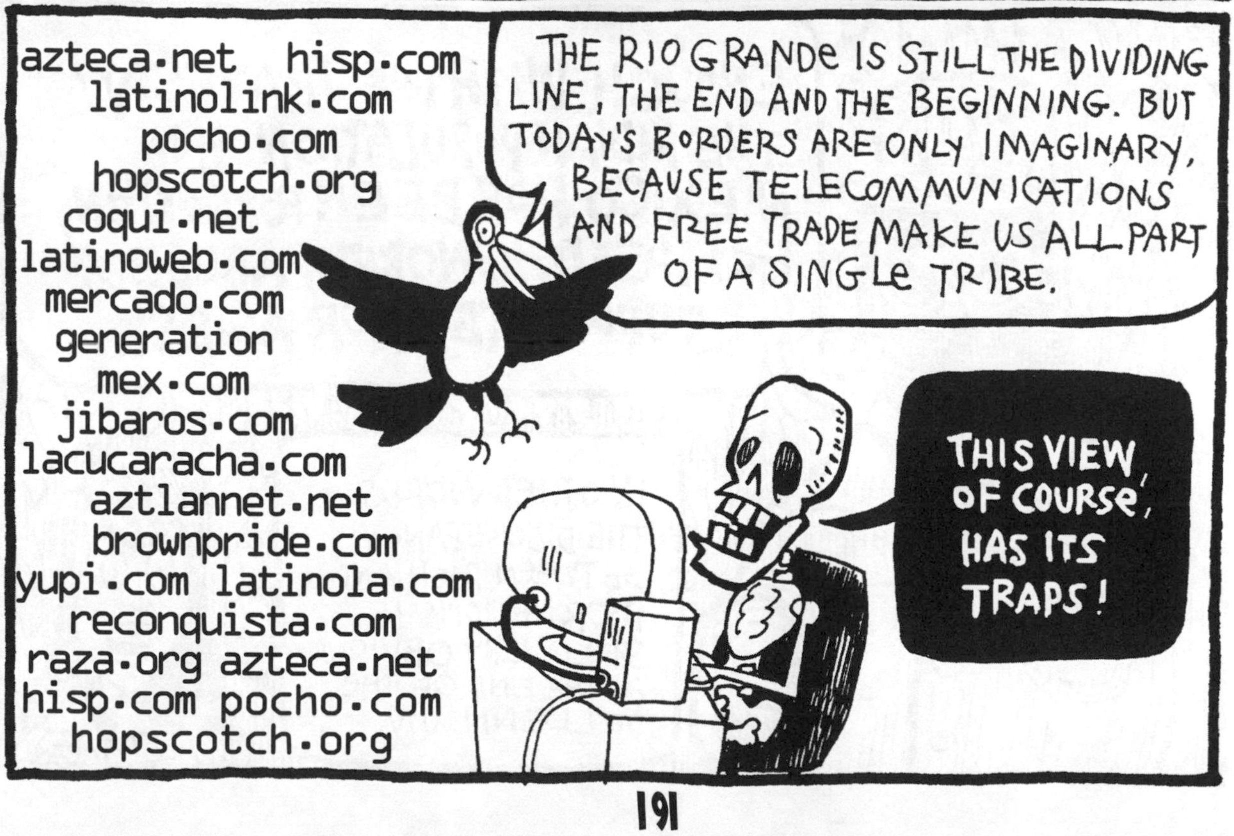
azteca.net hisp.com
latinolink.com
pocho.com
hopscotch.org
coqui.net
latinoweb.com
mercado.com
generation
mex.com
jibaros.com
lacucaracha.com
aztlannet.net
brownpride.com
yupi.com latinola.com
reconquista.com
raza.org azteca.net
hisp.com pocho.com
hopscotch.org
THE RIO GRANDE IS STILL THE DIVIDING LINE, THE END AND THE BEGINNING. BUT TODAY'S BORDERS ARE ONLY IMAGINARY, BECAUSE TELECOMMUNICATIONS AND FREE TRADE MAKE US ALL PART OF A SINGLE TRIBE.
THIS VIEW, OF COURSE, HAS ITS TRAPS!

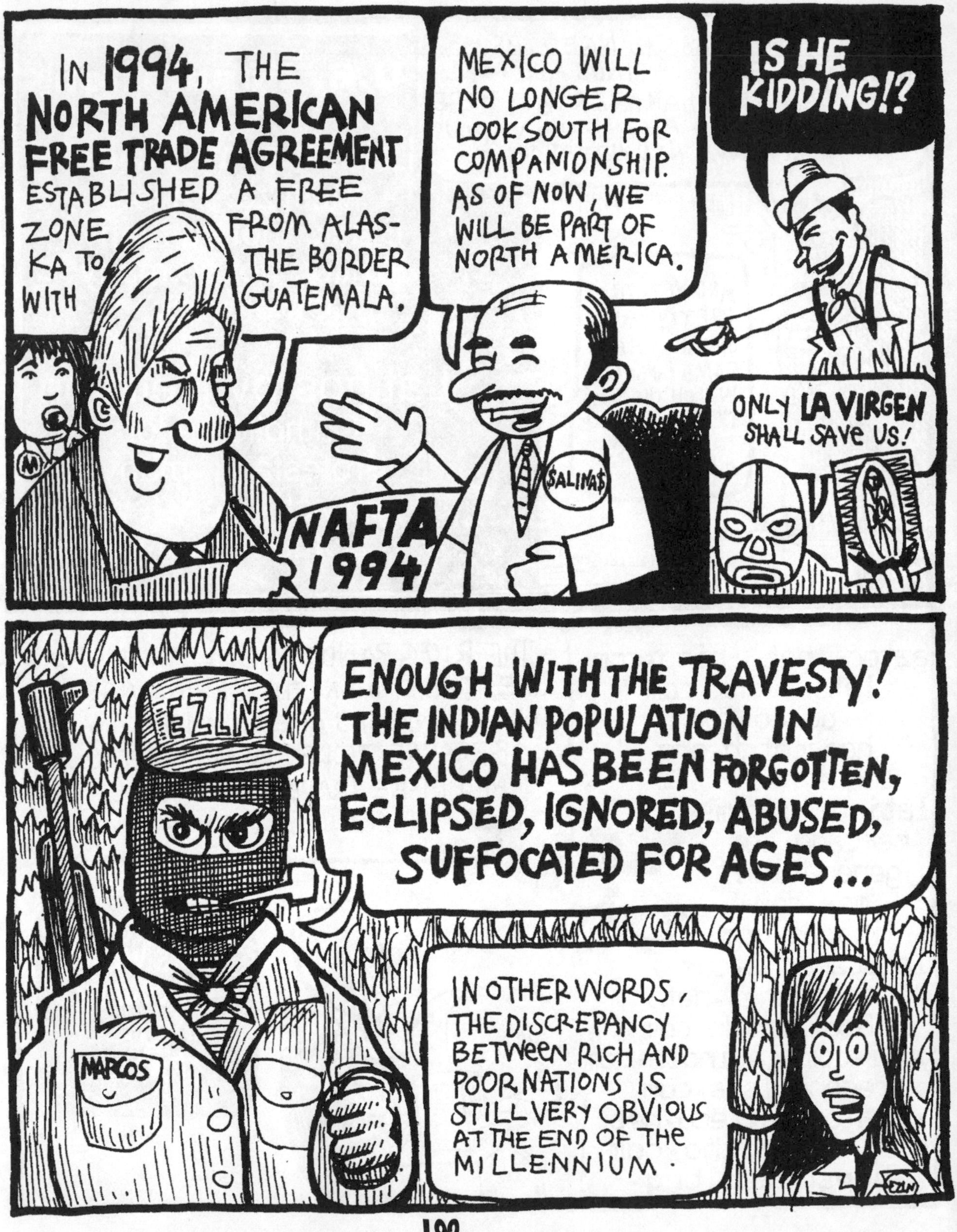
IN 1994, THE NORTH AMERICAN FREE TRADE AGREEMENT ESTABLISHED A FREE ZONE FROM ALASKA TO THE BORDER WITH GUATEMALA.
MEXICO WILL NO LONGER LOOK SOUTH FOR COMPANIONSHIP. AS OF NOW, WE WILL BE PART OF NORTH AMERICA.
IS HE KIDDING!?
ONLY LA VIRGEN SHALL SAVE US!
NAFTA 1994
SALINA$
EZLN
ENOUGH WITH THE TRAVESTY! THE INDIAN POPULATION IN MEXICO HAS BEEN FORGOTTEN, ECLIPSED, IGNORED, ABUSED, SUFFOCATED FOR AGES...
MARCOS
IN OTHER WORDS, THE DISCREPANCY BETWEEN RICH AND POOR NATIONS IS STILL VERY OBVIOUS AT THE END OF THE MILLENNIUM.
EZLN

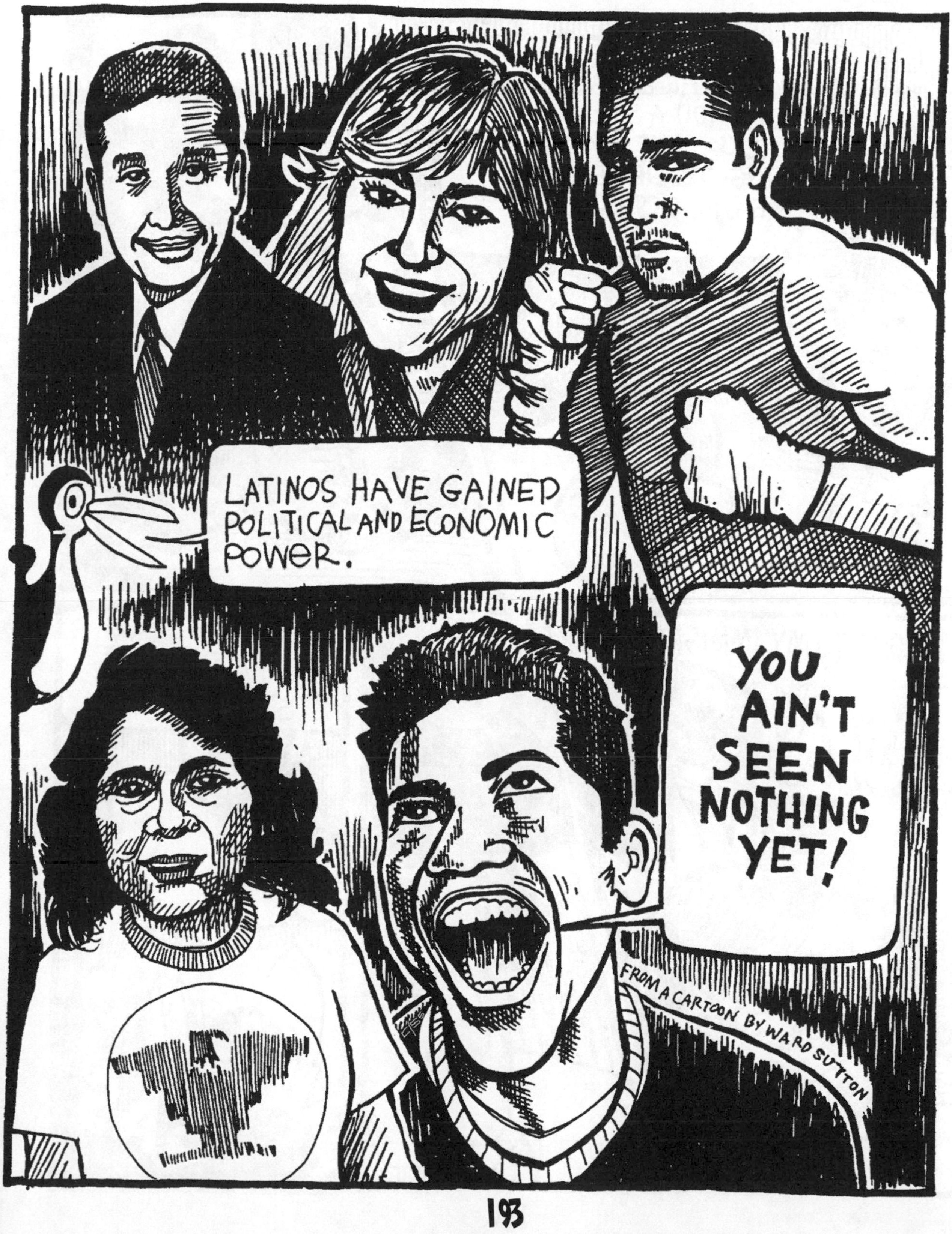
LATINOS HAVE GAINED POLITICAL AND ECONOMIC POWER.
YOU AIN'T SEEN NOTHING YET!
FROM A CARTOON BY WARD SUTTON

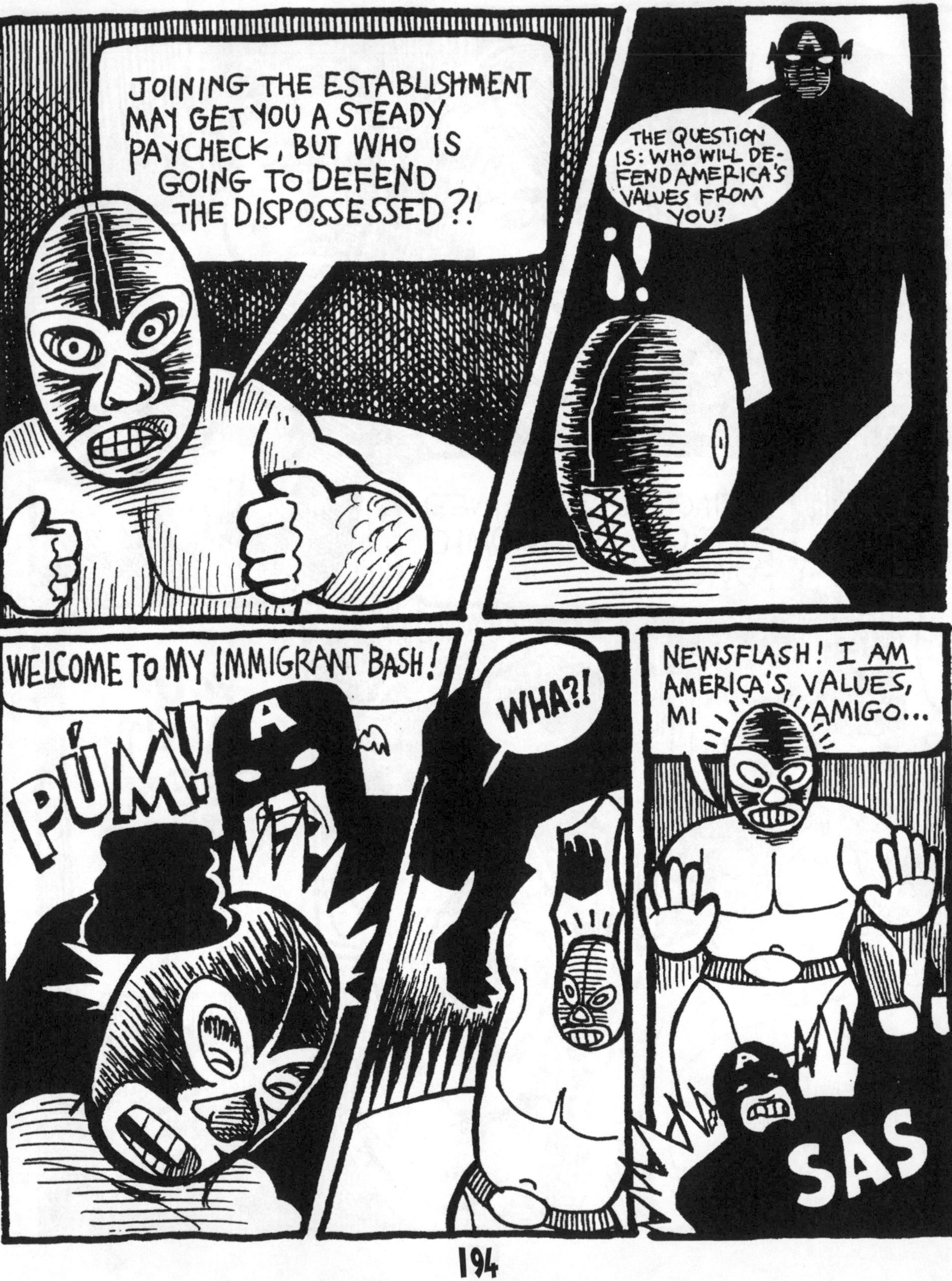
JOINING THE ESTABLISHMENT MAY GET YOU A STEADY PAYCHECK, BUT WHO IS GOING TO DEFEND THE DISPOSSESSED?!
THE QUESTION IS: WHO WILL DEFEND AMERICA'S VALUES FROM YOU?
¡!
WELCOME TO MY IMMIGRANT BASH!
¡PÚM!
WHA?!
NEWSFLASH! I AM AMERICA'S VALUES, MI AMIGO...
SAS

THERE IS A BACKLASH TO INCREASED LATINO POPULATION, MOSTLY FROM HIGHER BIRTHRATES, NOT IMMIGRATION, BY THE WAY.

ANTI-IMMIGRANT POLITICIANS ALSO ARGUED TO CHANGE THE 14th AMENDMENT IN A BACKLASH AGAINST SO-CALLED "ANCHOR BABIES", CHANGING WHO QUALIFIES TO BE U.S. CITIZENS.

I WAS BORN IN THE U.S. TO UNDOCUMENTED PARENTS SO I'M A U.S. CITIZEN.

I YAM WHAT I YAM...

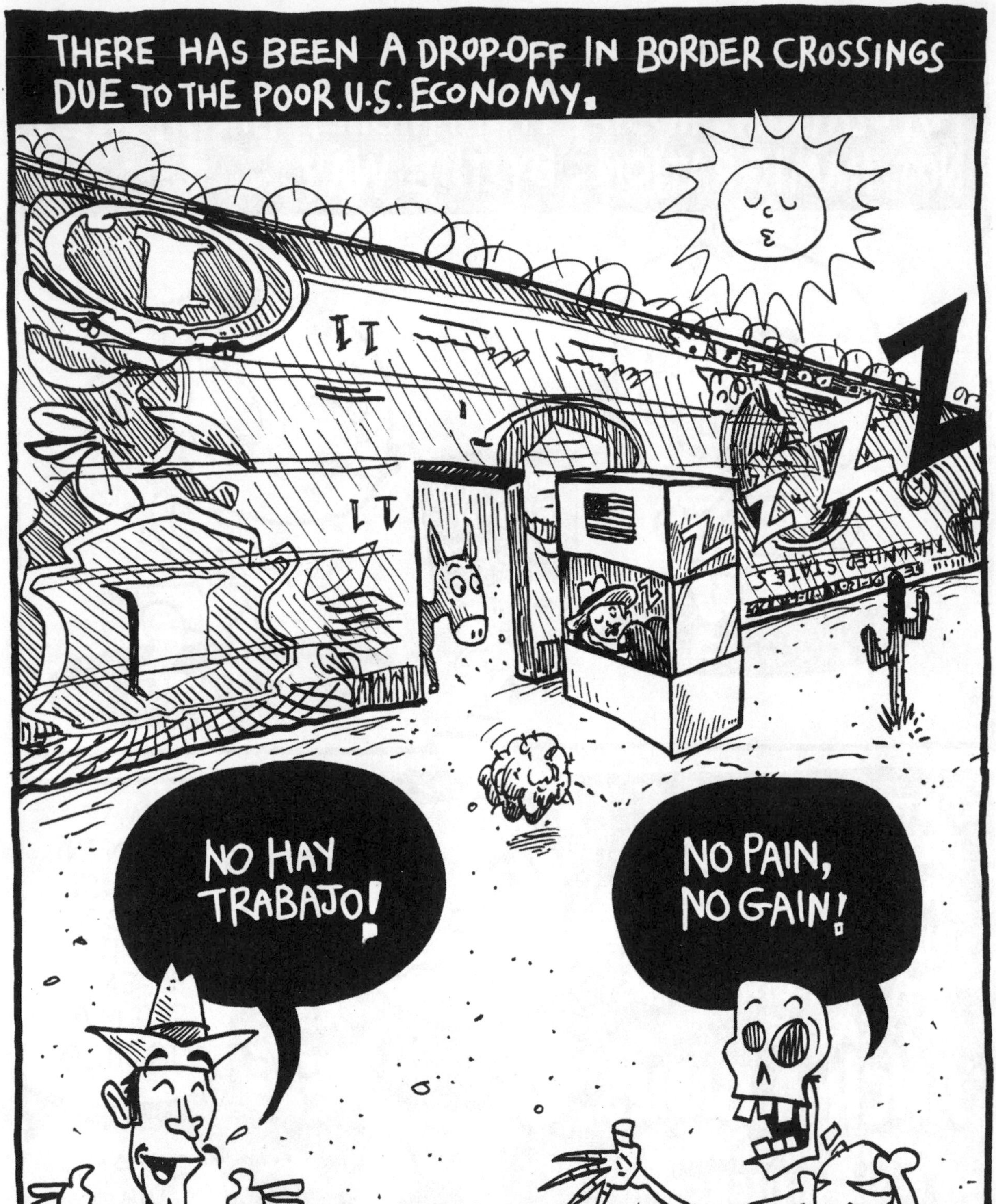
THERE HAS BEEN A DROP-OFF IN BORDER CROSSINGS DUE TO THE POOR U.S. ECONOMY.
NO HAY TRABAJO!
NO PAIN, NO GAIN!

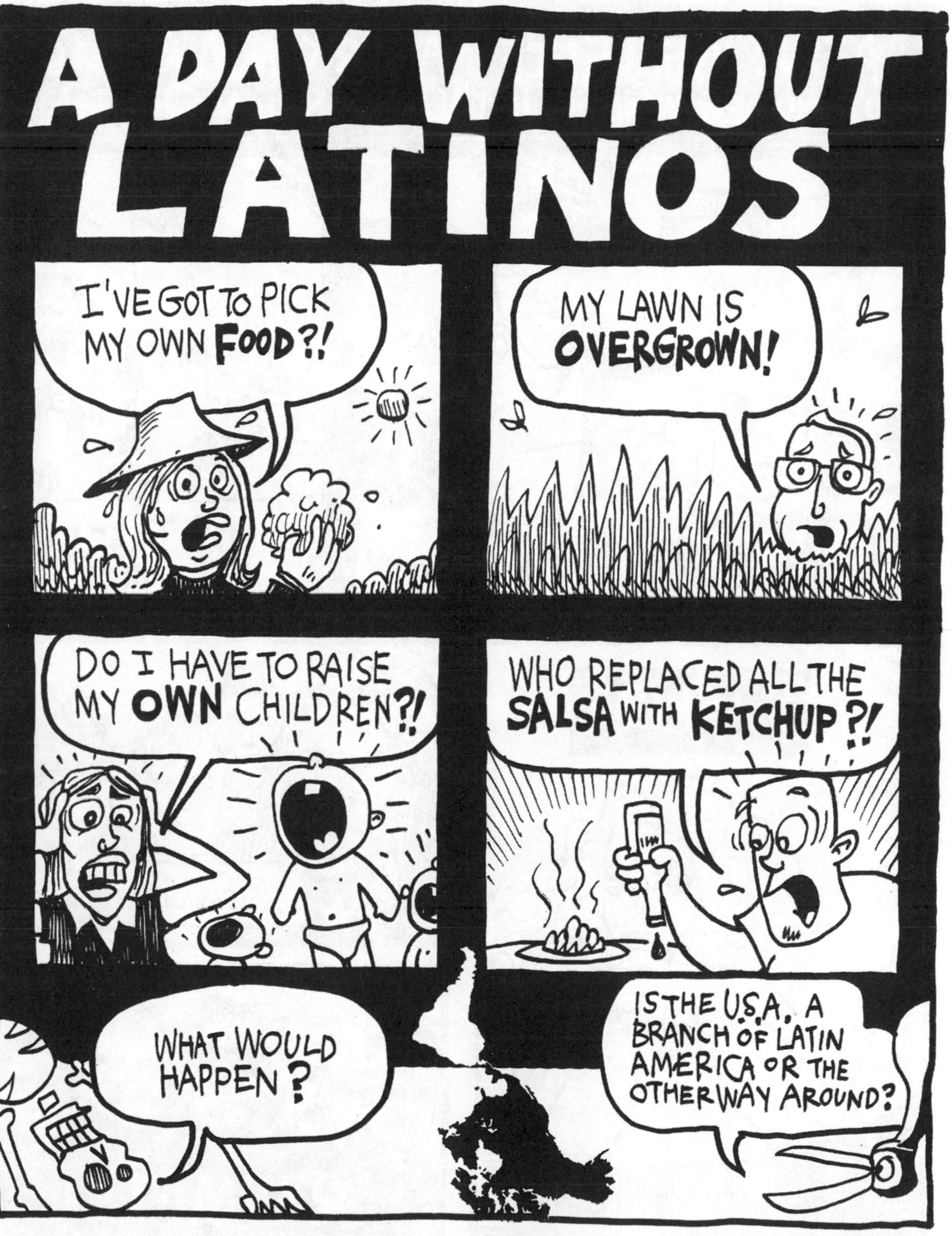
A DAY WITHOUT LATINOS
I'VE GOT TO PICK MY OWN FOOD?!
MY LAWN IS OVERGROWN!
DO I HAVE TO RAISE MY OWN CHILDREN?!
WHO REPLACED ALL THE SALSA WITH KETCHUP?!
WHAT WOULD HAPPEN?
IS THE U.S.A. A BRANCH OF LATIN AMERICA OR THE OTHER WAY AROUND?

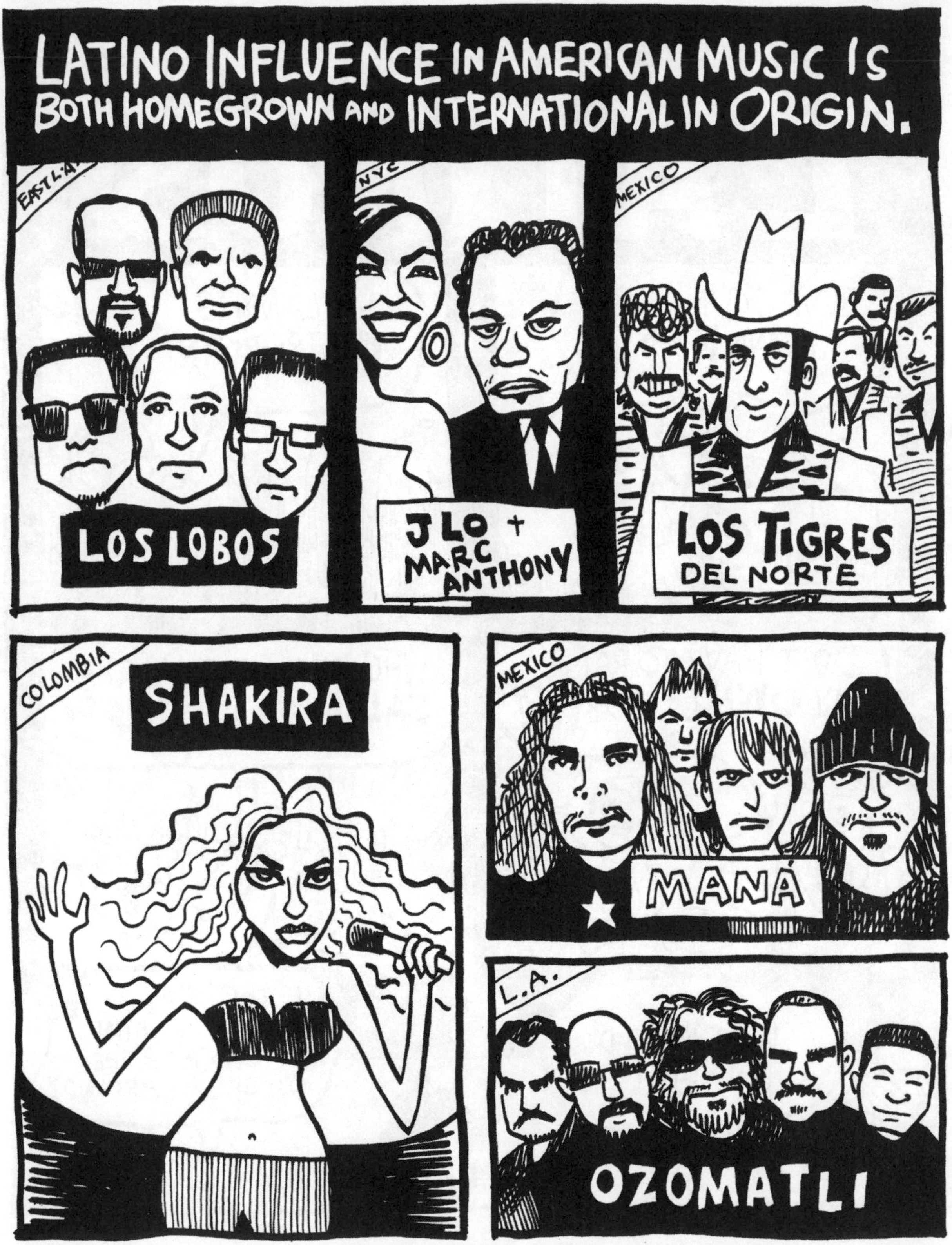
LATINO INFLUENCE IN AMERICAN MUSIC IS BOTH HOMEGROWN AND INTERNATIONAL IN ORIGIN.
EAST L.A.
LOS LOBOS
NYC
J LO + MARC ANTHONY
MEXICO
LOS TIGRES DEL NORTE
COLOMBIA
SHAKIRA
MEXICO
MANÁ
L.A.
OZOMATLI

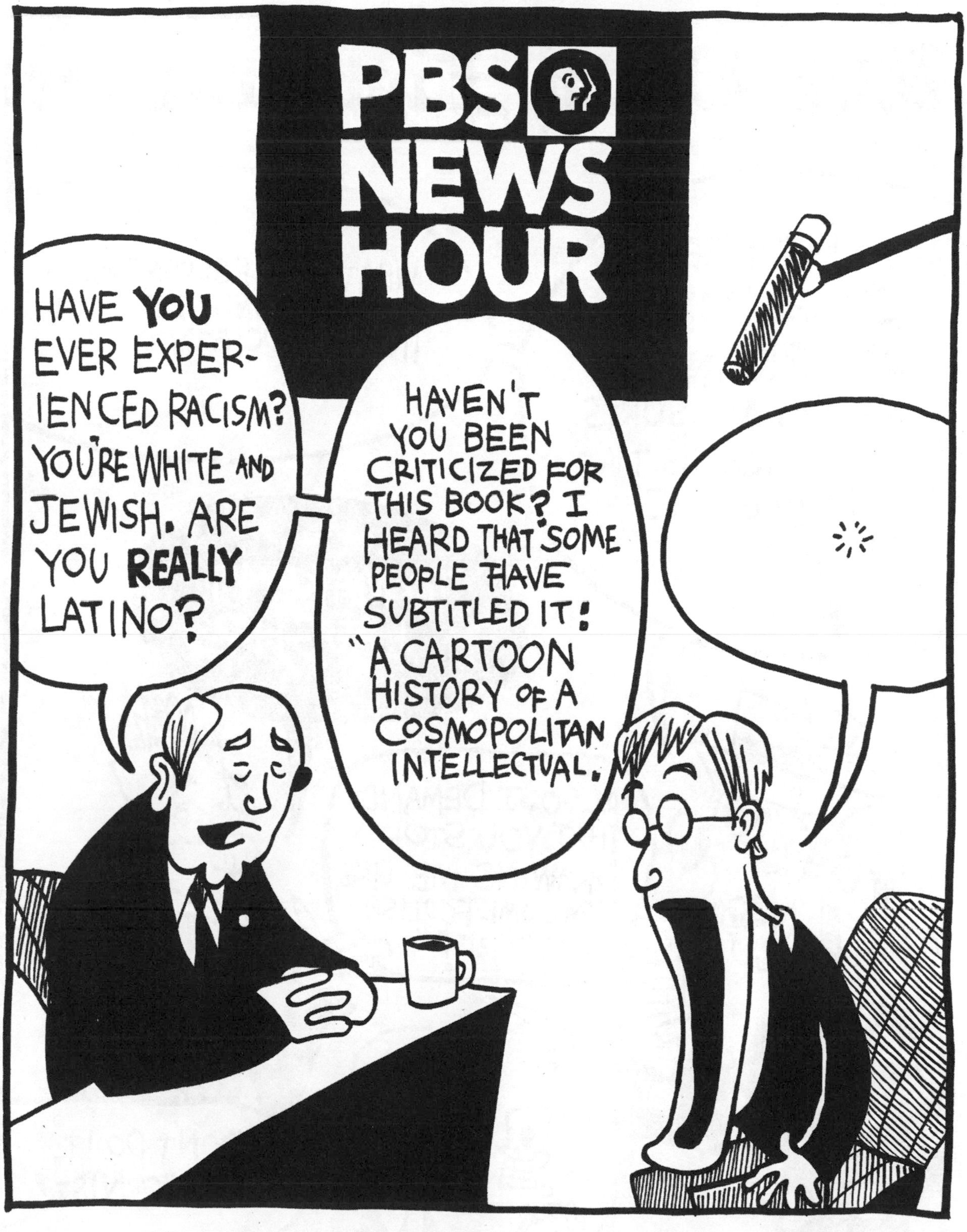
PBS NEWS HOUR
HAVE YOU EVER EXPERIENCED RACISM? YOU'RE WHITE AND JEWISH. ARE YOU REALLY LATINO?
HAVEN'T YOU BEEN CRITICIZED FOR THIS BOOK? I HEARD THAT SOME PEOPLE HAVE SUBTITLED IT: "A CARTOON HISTORY OF A COSMOPOLITAN INTELLECTUAL."

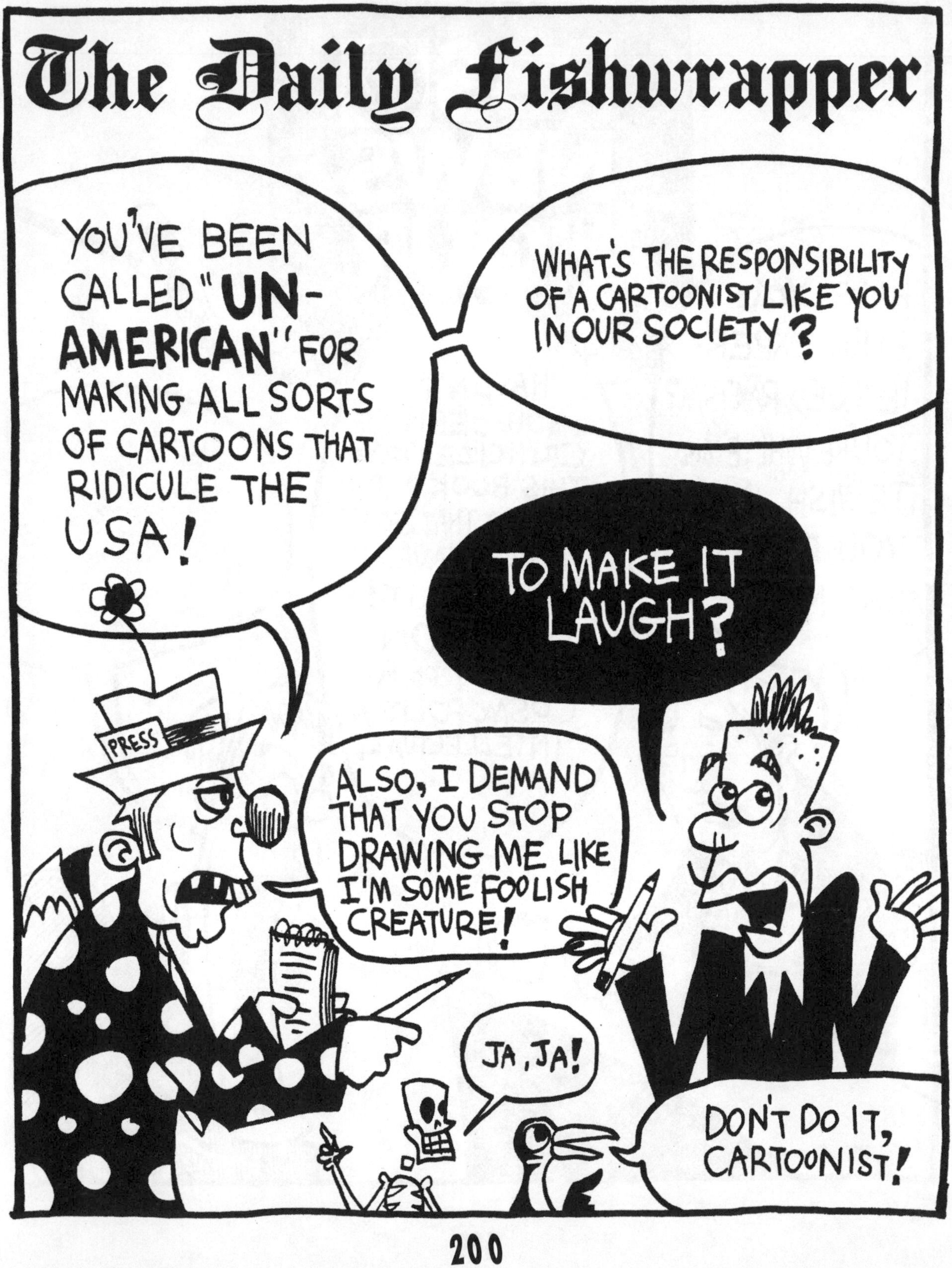
The Daily Fishwrapper
YOU'VE BEEN CALLED "UN-AMERICAN" FOR MAKING ALL SORTS OF CARTOONS THAT RIDICULE THE USA!
WHAT'S THE RESPONSIBILITY OF A CARTOONIST LIKE YOU IN OUR SOCIETY?
TO MAKE IT LAUGH?
PRESS
ALSO, I DEMAND THAT YOU STOP DRAWING ME LIKE I'M SOME FOOLISH CREATURE!
JA, JA!
DON'T DO IT, CARTOONIST!

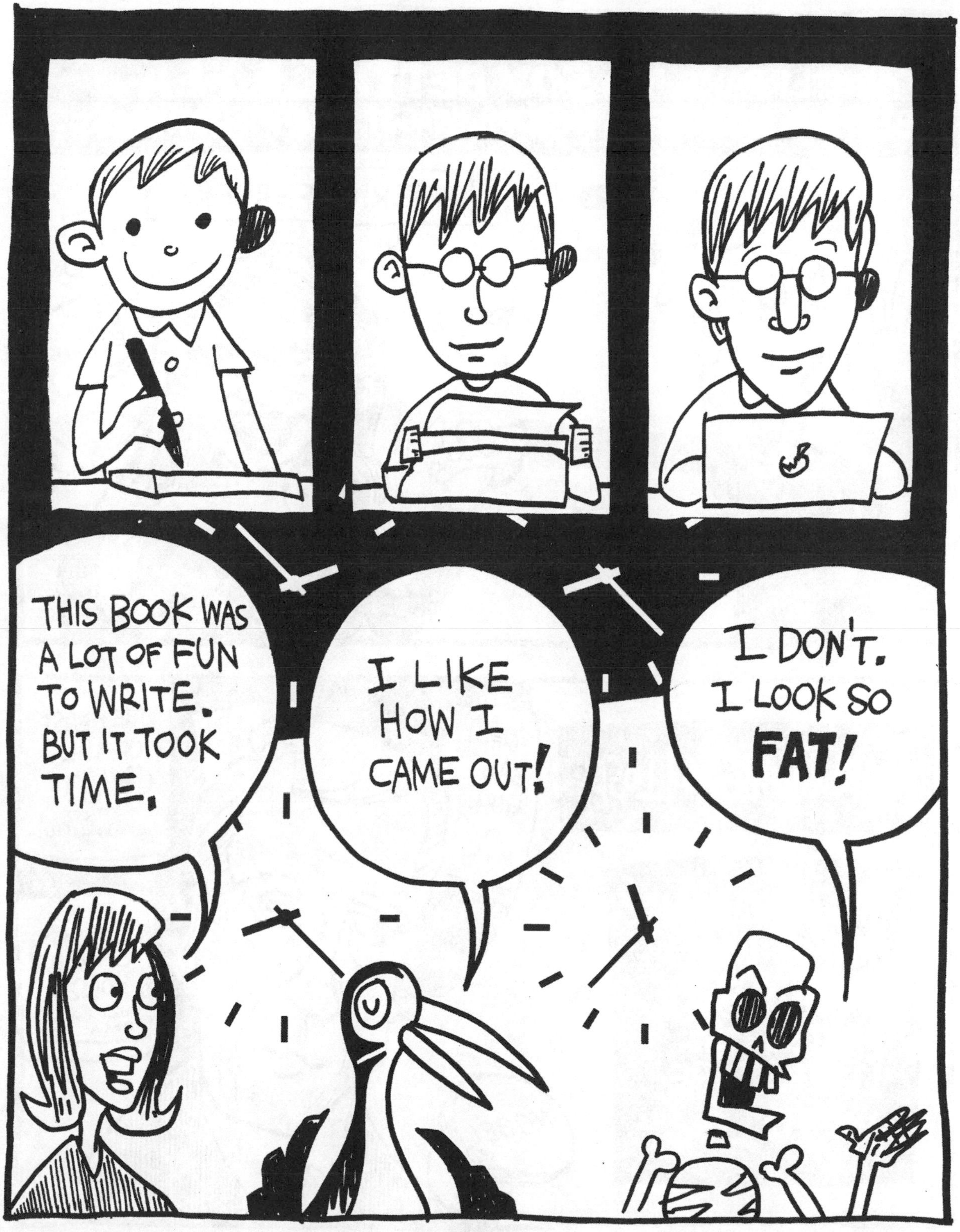
THIS BOOK WAS A LOT OF FUN TO WRITE. BUT IT TOOK TIME.
I LIKE HOW I CAME OUT!
I DON'T. I LOOK SO **FAT!**

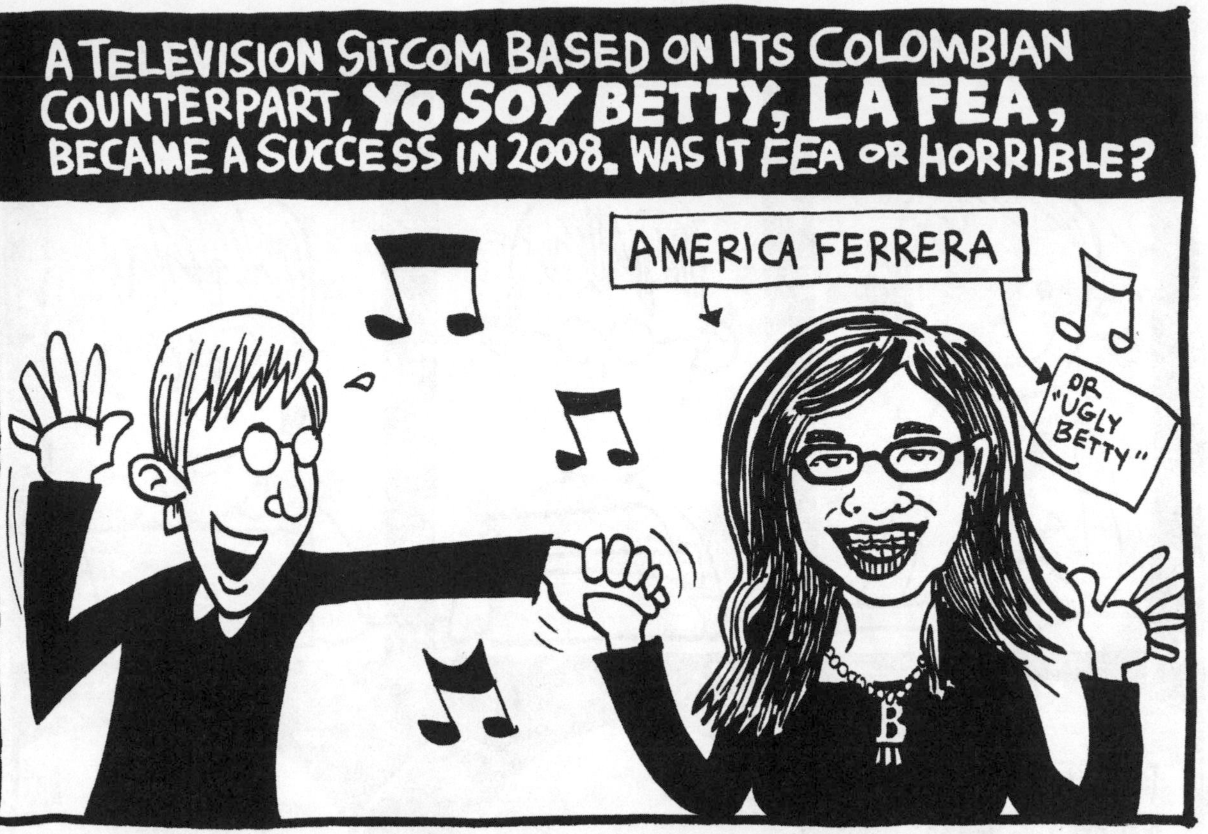
A TELEVISION SITCOM BASED ON ITS COLOMBIAN COUNTERPART, YO SOY BETTY, LA FEA, BECAME A SUCCESS IN 2008. WAS IT FEA OR HORRIBLE?
AMERICA FERRERA
OR "UGLY BETTY"
B

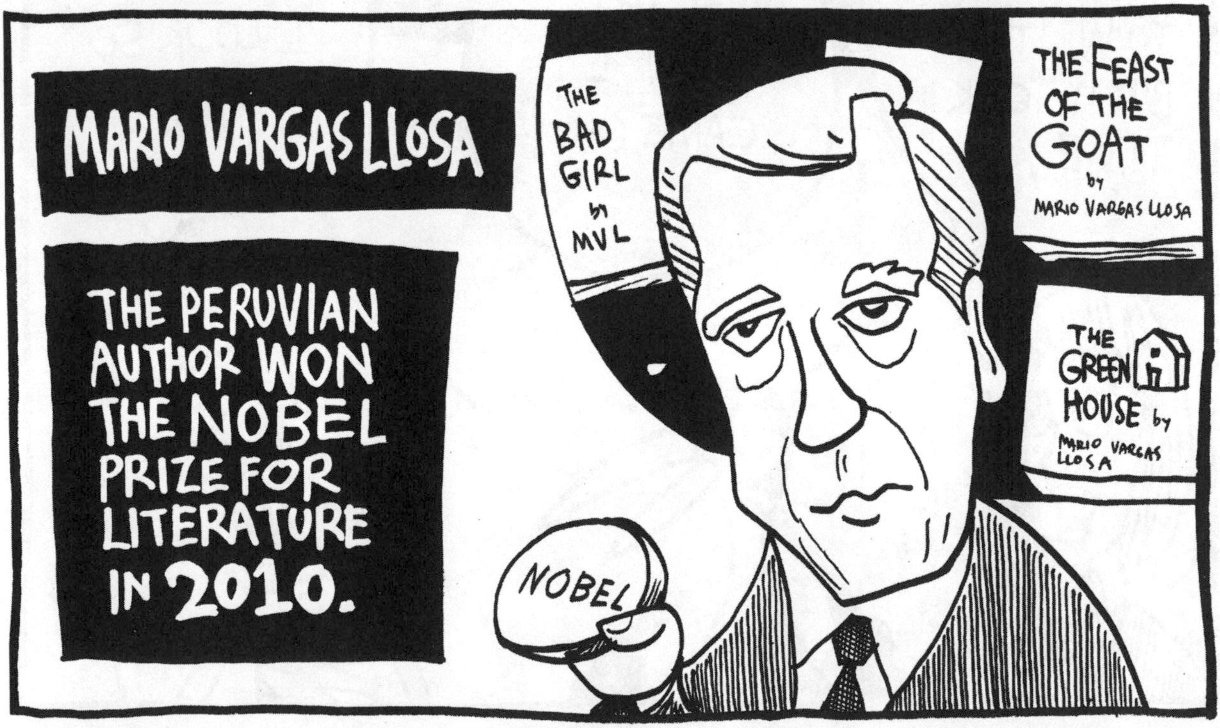
MARIO VARGAS LLOSA
THE PERUVIAN AUTHOR WON THE NOBEL PRIZE FOR LITERATURE IN 2010.
THE BAD GIRL by MVL
THE FEAST OF THE GOAT by MARIO VARGAS LLOSA
THE GREEN HOUSE by MARIO VARGAS LLOSA
NOBEL

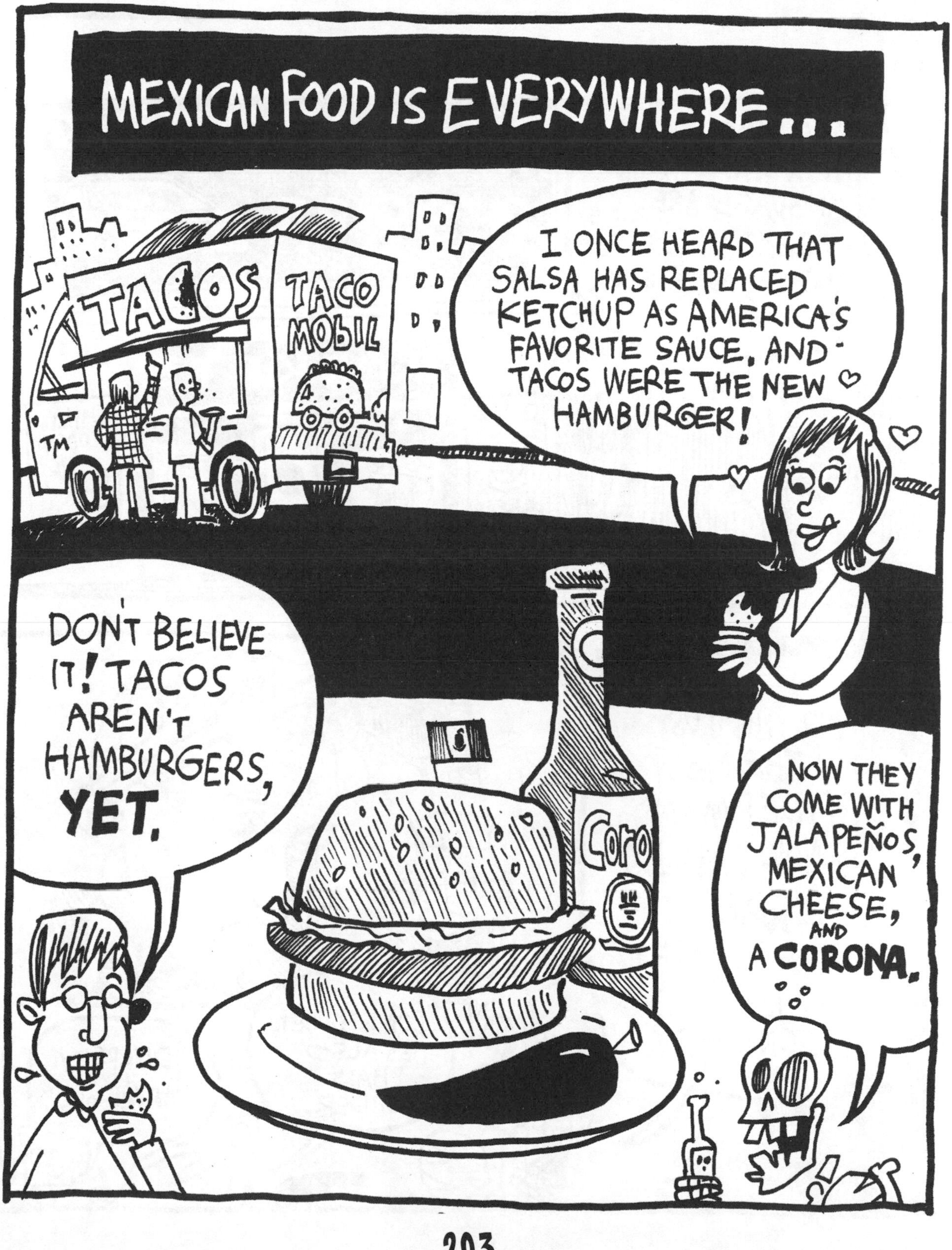
MEXICAN FOOD IS EVERYWHERE...
TACOS
TACO MOBIL
TM
I ONCE HEARD THAT SALSA HAS REPLACED KETCHUP AS AMERICA'S FAVORITE SAUCE, AND TACOS WERE THE NEW HAMBURGER!
DON'T BELIEVE IT! TACOS AREN'T HAMBURGERS, YET.
Coro
NOW THEY COME WITH JALAPEÑOS, MEXICAN CHEESE, AND A CORONA.

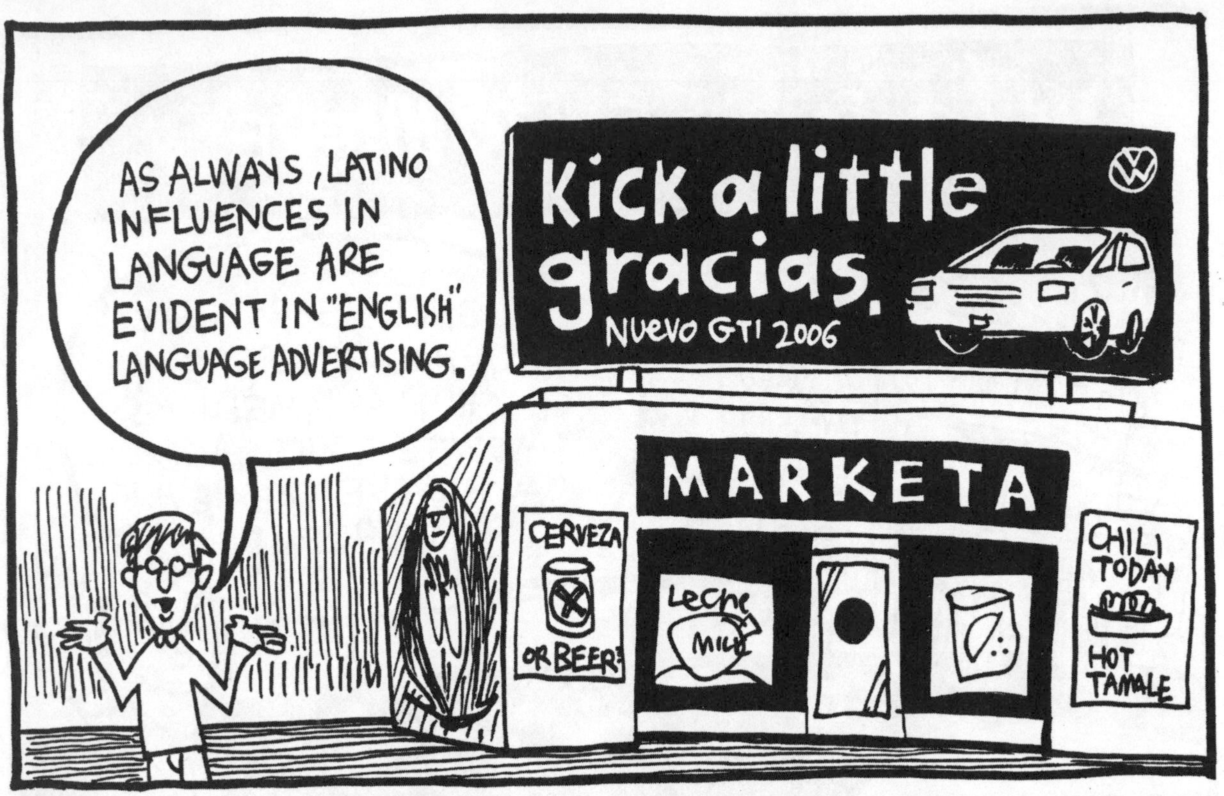
AS ALWAYS, LATINO INFLUENCES IN LANGUAGE ARE EVIDENT IN "ENGLISH" LANGUAGE ADVERTISING.
Kick a little gracias.
NUEVO GTI 2006
MARKETA
CERVEZA OR BEER!
Leche MILK
CHILI TODAY HOT TAMALE
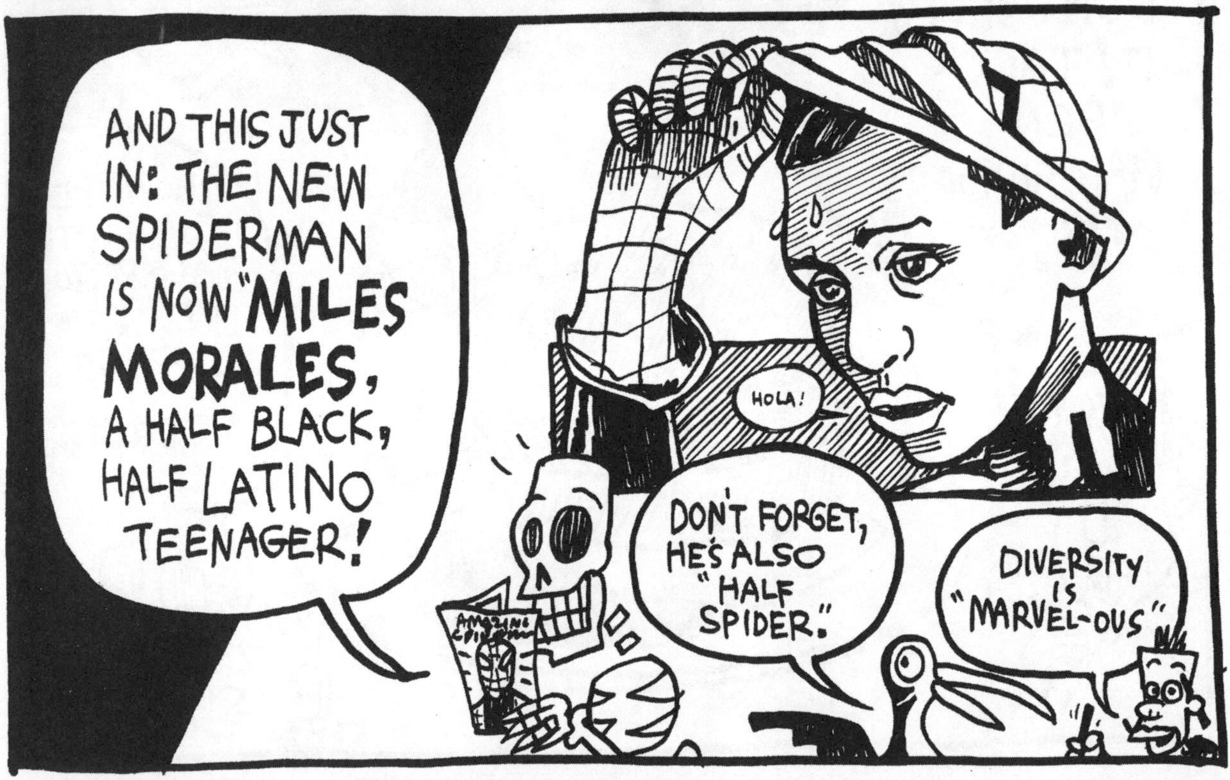
AND THIS JUST IN: THE NEW SPIDERMAN IS NOW "MILES MORALES, A HALF BLACK, HALF LATINO TEENAGER!
HOLA!
DON'T FORGET, HE'S ALSO "HALF SPIDER."
DIVERSITY IS "MARVEL-OUS"

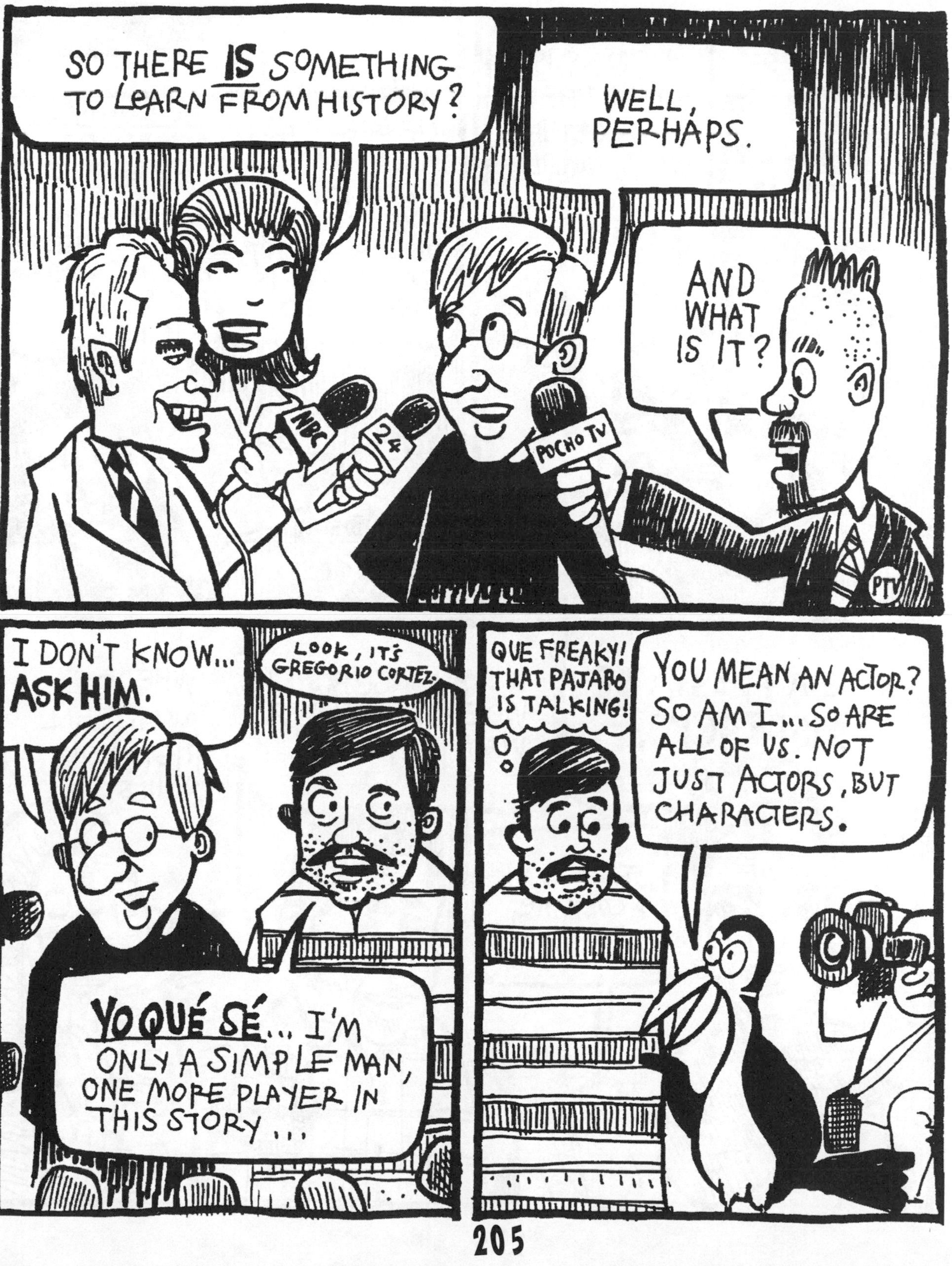
SO THERE **IS** SOMETHING TO LEARN FROM HISTORY?
WELL, PERHAPS.
AND WHAT IS IT?
NBC
24
POCHO TV
PTV
I DON'T KNOW... **ASK HIM.**
LOOK, IT'S GREGORIO CORTEZ.
YO QUÉ SÉ... I'M ONLY A SIMPLE MAN, ONE MORE PLAYER IN THIS STORY...
QUE FREAKY! THAT PAJARO IS TALKING!
YOU MEAN AN ACTOR? SO AM I... SO ARE ALL OF US. NOT JUST ACTORS, BUT CHARACTERS.

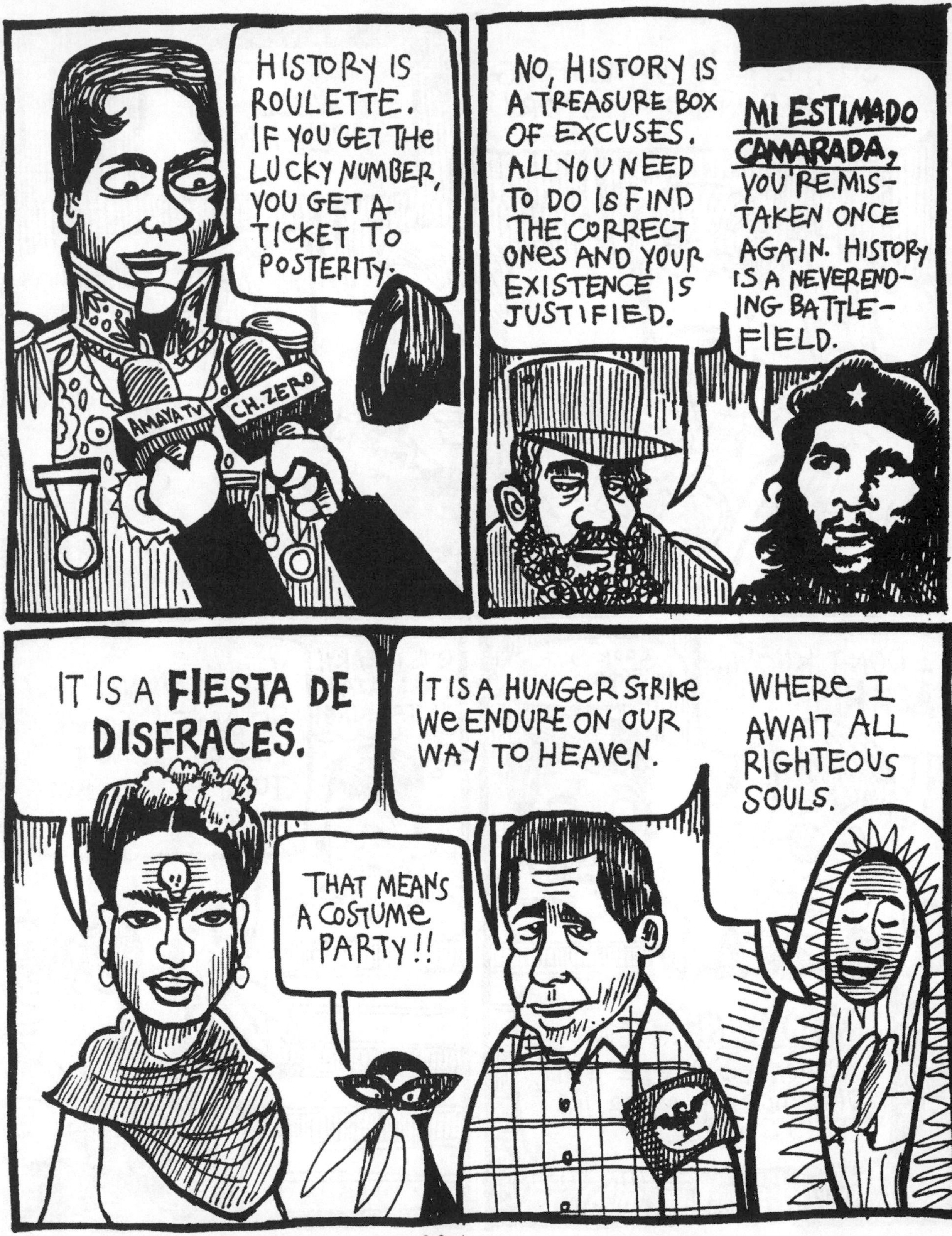
HISTORY IS ROULETTE. IF YOU GET THE LUCKY NUMBER, YOU GET A TICKET TO POSTERITY.
AMAYA TV
CH. ZERO
NO, HISTORY IS A TREASURE BOX OF EXCUSES. ALL YOU NEED TO DO IS FIND THE CORRECT ONES AND YOUR EXISTENCE IS JUSTIFIED.
MI ESTIMADO CAMARADA, YOU'RE MISTAKEN ONCE AGAIN. HISTORY IS A NEVERENDING BATTLEFIELD.
IT IS A FIESTA DE DISFRACES.
THAT MEANS A COSTUME PARTY!!
IT IS A HUNGER STRIKE WE ENDURE ON OUR WAY TO HEAVEN.
WHERE I AWAIT ALL RIGHTEOUS SOULS.

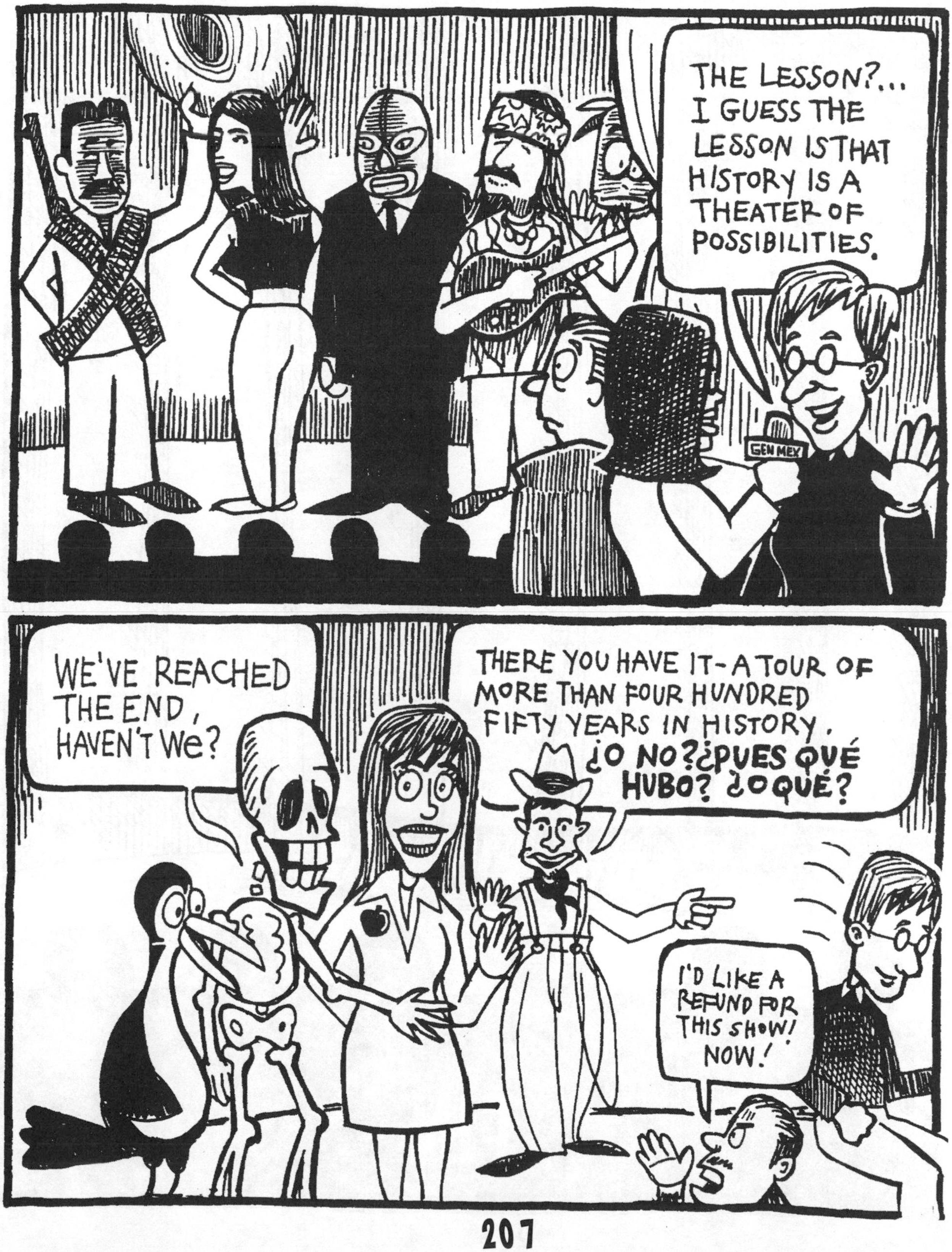
THE LESSON?... I GUESS THE LESSON IS THAT HISTORY IS A THEATER OF POSSIBILITIES.
GEN MEX
WE'VE REACHED THE END, HAVEN'T WE?
THERE YOU HAVE IT - A TOUR OF MORE THAN FOUR HUNDRED FIFTY YEARS IN HISTORY.
¿O NO? ¿PUES QUÉ HUBO? ¿O QUÉ?
I'D LIKE A REFUND FOR THIS SHOW! NOW!

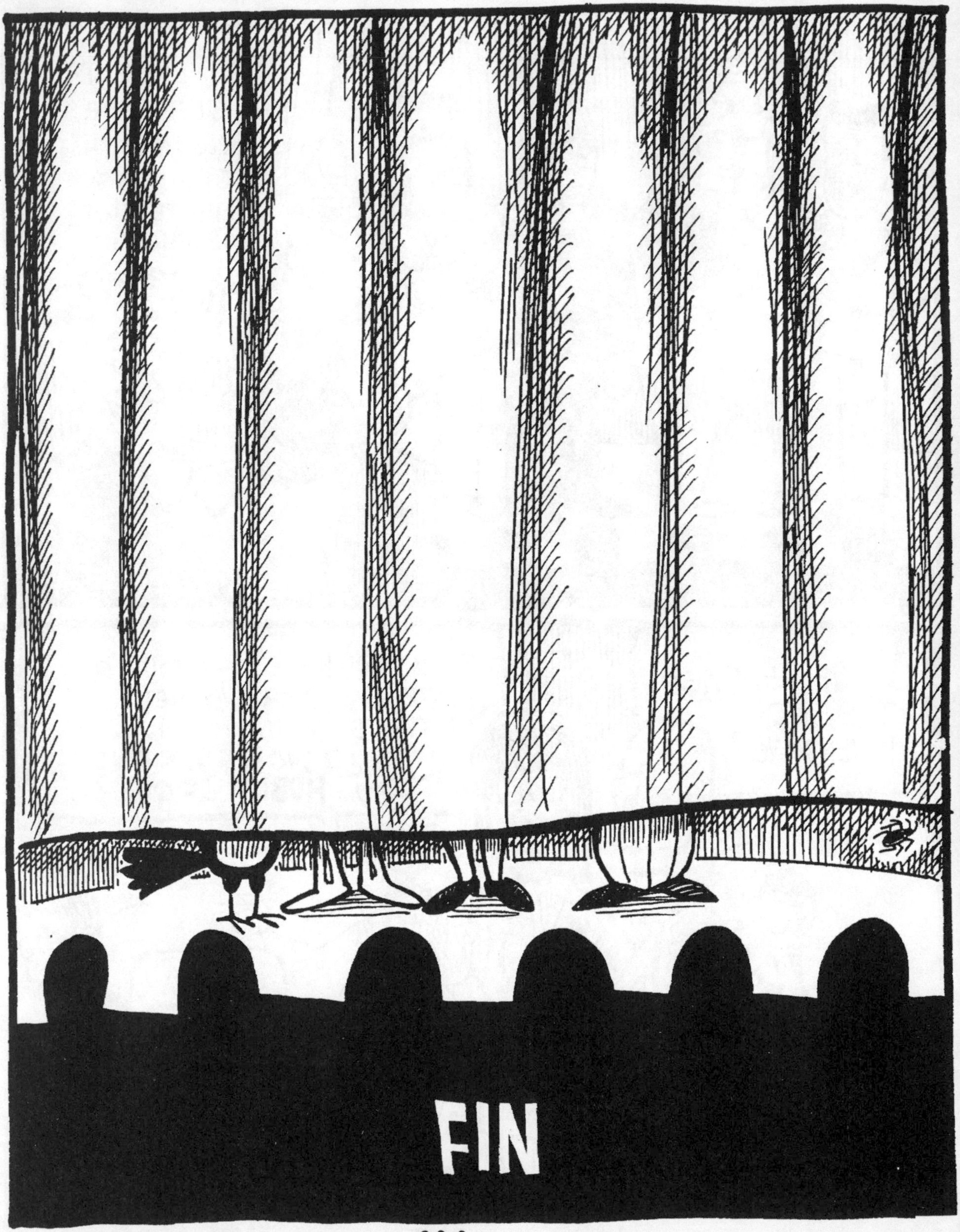
FIN

ACKNOWLEDGMENTS

My wholehearted gratitude to the many people who in one way or another helped while this book was taking shape. In naming them all I run the risk of inexcusable omission. But a handful stand out. Edna Acosta Belen, Harold Augenbraum, Antonio Benitez-Rojo, Ariel Dorfman, Don Fehr, Felipe Galindo, Maria Herrera Sobek, Rolando Hinojosa-Smith, Jill Kneerim, Himilce Novas, Gustavo Perez-Firmat, Abraham Stavans, Virgil Suarez, and Gerardo Villacres affected the content with their ideas and conversations. The people at the Institute of Latin American Studies at the University of London, where I was Visiting Research Fellow in 1998—99, as well as my British friend Anthony Rudolf, stood by undefeated while faxes and Fedexes went back and forth. And the staff of *Hopscotch: A Cultural Review*, at Amherst, Massachusetts, and Durham, North Carolina, especially Melissa Lorenzo, were invariably on the line wherever I found myself, if in Spain, London, New York, Berkeley, or Los Angeles. Sheila Friedling, formerly at Holmes and Meier and currently at The Jewish Museum of New York, thought of the idea first. Philip Lief nurtured it from the beginning and brought it to light. Linda Perrin guided me through a labyrinth of my own creation, Jamie Saxon brought light into the pages and orchestrated transatlantic communications, and Mercedes Anderson proofread it with a sharp eye. Don Fehr at Basic Books was a patient, encouraging in-house editor and an excellent friend, and John Kemmerer, his assistant, was *siempre listo*. My beloved Alison Sparks commented wisely at every stage of the creative and editorial process, and—in spite of their young ages—so did my children, Joshua and Isaiah. And of course, Lalo Lopez Alcaraz, who poured in his heart, time, and ink in equal measure. Lalo wishes to thank his lovely Chicana schoolteacher- wife, Victoria, for being the visual inspiration for Maestra, and their baby daughter Amaya for waking him up every morning at 730 a.m. without fail. He is also indebted to all the cartoonists, illustrators, and photographers whose visual material was the basis for many of the cartoons in this book.

The general sources I relied on directly or otherwise—historical, sociological, cultural, and literary—are countless. A complete list appears on pages 215—229 of my book *The Hispanic Condition: Reflections on Culture and Identity in America* (New York, 1996) and, in expanded, updated form, on pages 267—293 of the book's Spanish translation, *La condición hispánica* (Mexico, 1999).

The specific quotes and graphics I used come from, in order of appearance: *Castaways*, by Alvar Núñez Cabeza de Vaca, edited by Enrique Pupo-Walker (Los Angeles, 1993); Gaspar Pérez de Villagrá, *The History of New Mexico* (Albuquerque, 1992); the edict of May 26, 1570, *Historical Documents Relating to New Mexico, Nueva Viscaya, and Approaches Thereto, to 1773* (Washington, DC,

1923); Fray Bartolomé de Las Casas, *Very Brief Account of the Destruction of the Indies* (New York, 1909); Padre Junípero Serra, *Writings of Junípero Serra* (Washington, DC, 1955); General Scott's account of the *Battle of Puebla*, *Chronicles of the Gringos: The U.S. Army in the Mexican War, 1846—1848, Accounts of Eyewitnesses and Combatants,* edited by George Winston Smith and Charles Judah (Albuquerque, 1968); a Mexican account of the Alamo, "A Critical Study of the Siege of the Alamo and of the Personnel of Its Defenders," by Amelia Williams, *Southwestern Historical Quarterly* (July 1933); Daniel Cosmo Villegas, *American Extremes,* trans., Americo Paredes (Austin, TX, 1969); "The Ballad of Gregorio Cortez," from *With His Pistol in His Hand: A Border Ballad and Its Hero,* by Americo Paredes (Austin, TX, 1958); "Spain's Sense of Justice," by C. G. Bush, *Latin America in Caricature,* by John J. Johnson (Austin, TX, 1980); exchange between senior students and Charles Francis Adams at the University of Wisconsin, 1897, *The Mirror of War: American Society and the Spanish-American War,* by Gerald F. Linderman (Ann Arbor, MI, 1974); "The Cuban Melodrama," by C.J. Taylor, *Latin America in Caricature;* "Abandoned," by F.I. Richards, *Latin America in Caricature;* "The Cavalry at Santiago," *The Rough Riders,* by Theodore Roosevelt (New York, 1990); Miguel Antonio Otero's speech, *My Nine Years as Governor of the Territory of New Mexico* (Albuquerque, 1940); "To Columbus," by Rubén Darío, *Imagining Columbus: The Literary Voyage,* by Ilan Stavans (New York, 1993); "Two Cubas," by José Martí, *The Hispanic Condition* (New York, 1995); "La Guera," from *500 Años del Pueblo Chicano* (Albuquerque, 1991); Bernardo Vega, *Memoirs of Bernardo Vega* (New York, 1984); "To the Prosecuted," by José de Diego, trans. by Roberto Santiago, *Boricuas: Influential Puerto Rican Writings—An Anthology,* edited by Roberto Santiago (New York, 1995); Speech of 1936 by Pedro Albizu Campos, translated by Roberto Santiago; "On Recent Disturbances in Puerto Rico," by Luis Muñoz Marín, *Boricuas: Influential Puerto Rican Writing—An Anthology,* edited by Roberto Santiago; "To Elsie," by William Carlos Williams, *The Collected Poems of William Carlos Williams: vol. I: 1909—1939* (New York, 1987); *The Los Angeles Daily News,* from *Occupied America: A History of Chicanos,* by Rodolfo Acuña (3rd edition, New York, 1988); quote from Octavio Paz, *The Labyrinth of Solitude,* by Octavio Paz (New York, 1961); Rodolfo "Corky" Gonzáles, *Yo soy Joaquín/I Am Joaquín,* by Rodolfo "Corky" Gonzáles (New York, 1967); speech by The Raza Unida Party leader, *Youth, Identity, Power: The Chicano Movement,* by Carlos Muñoz, Jr. (London and New York, 1989); "La tierra se llama Juan," by Pablo Neruda, *Selected Poems of Pablo Neruda* (New York, 1983); Oscar "Zeta" Acosta, *The Autobiography of a Brown Buffalo,* (San Francisco, 1972); "Who Is a Chicano? And What Is It the Chicanos Want?," by Rubén Salazar, *Border Correspondent: Selected Writings, 1955—1970,* by Rubén Salazar, edited by Mario T. Garcia (Los Angeles, 1995).

INDEX

ILAN STAVANS, ONE OF TODAY'S PREEMINENT ESSAYISTS, CULTURAL CRITICS, AND TRANSLATORS IS LEWIS-SEBRING PROFESSOR IN LATIN AMERICAN AND LATINO CULTURE AND FIVE COLLEGE-FORTIETH ANNIVERSARY PROFESSOR AT AMHERST COLLEGE. THE RECIPIENT OF NUMEROUS AWARDS AND HONORS, HIS WORK HAS BEEN TRANSLATED INTO A DOZEN LANGUAGES.

LALO ALCARAZ IS THE PROLIFIC CREATOR OF THE NATIONALLY SYNDICATED COMIC STRIP "LA CUCARACHA" AS WELL AS AN AWARD-WINNING EDITORIAL CARTOONIST AND RADIO HOST. A SAN DIEGO STATE UNIVERSITY AND UC BERKELEY GRADUATE, HE IS A MEMBER OF THE FACULTY AT OTIS COLLEGE OF ART AND DESIGN. HIS ART AND ACTIVISM HAS BEEN RECOGNIZED ACROSS THE U.S.A.